MODERN MILITARY AIRCRAFT

MODERN MILITARY AIRCRAFT

THE AUTHORITATIVE ILLUSTRATED HISTORY

THOMAS NEWDICK & TOM COOPER

METRO BOOKS
New York

METRO BOOKS
New York

An Imprint of Sterling Publishing
387 Park Avenue South
New York, NY 10016

Editorial and design by
Amber Books Ltd
74–77 White Lion Street
London N1 9PF
www.amberbooks.co.uk

The material in this book has previously appeared in the books
The Essential Aircraft Identification Guide: Aircraft of the Cold War 1945–1991 and
The Essential Aircraft Identification Guide: Modern Military Airpower 1990–Present

ISBN: 978-1-4351-4850-5

For information about custom editions, special sales, and premium and corporate purchases,
please contact Sterling Special Sales at 800-805-5489 or specialsales@sterlingpublishing.com.

Manufactured in China

2 4 6 8 10 9 7 5 3 1

www.sterlingpublishing.com

PICTURE CREDITS
Air Team Images: 283
Art-Tech/Aerospace: 6, 18, 20, 62, 73, 109, 117, 159
Art-Tech/MARS: 58, 112
Australian Department of Defence: 367, 368
BAE Systems: 326
Canadian Air Force: 216
Cody Images: 6, 42, 51, 83, 84, 130, 134, 147, 174, 187 (both)
Corbis: 271 (Matko Biljac/Reuters)
Czech Ministry of Defence: 272 (Jan Kouba)
Bui Tuan Kheim: 343
Thomas Merkl: 305
Press Association Images: 341 (Chiang Ying-Ying)
U.S. Department of Defense: 78, 140, 188/189, 193, 198, 203, 204, 207, 208, 210, 213, 221, 225, 226, 238, 240, 241,
242, 246, 248, 253, 254, 256, 281, 291, 295, 297, 299, 307, 314, 321, 322, 325, 342, 369
Wikimedia Creative Commons License & GNU Free Documentation License: 285 (Boksi), 293 (Self Q),
322 (Retxham), 361 (Danie Van Der Werwe)

All artworks Amber Books and Art/Tech

Contents

Volume One:
Aircraft of the
Cold War

Chapter 1

Europe

'From Stettin in the Baltic to Trieste in the Adriatic
an iron curtain has descended across the Continent. Behind
that line lie all the capitals of the ancient states of Central
and Eastern Europe. Warsaw, Berlin, Prague, Vienna,
Budapest, Belgrade, Bucharest and Sofia; all these famous
cities and the populations around them lie in what I must
call the Soviet sphere, and all are subject, in one form or
another, not only to Soviet influence but to a very high and,
in some cases, increasing measure of control from Moscow.'

– Winston Churchill, Fulton, Missouri,
March 1946

◀ **Soviet Su-9 Interceptors**

In a shot redolent of the Cold War, Soviet airmen discuss their next mission while maintainers
ready a trio of Su-9 interceptors. The dawn of the nuclear age and increasing East–West tensions
meant that fighters such as these played a vital role in national defence in the post-war period.

The Iron Curtain Descends
1945–1955

Having fought together to bring about the defeat of Nazi Germany, the uneasy alliance between the communist Soviet Union and the Western powers broke down irrevocably after World War II.

SPEAKING AT FULTON in March 1946, British war leader Winston Churchill coined a phrase that has since come to be seen by some historians as signalling the starting point of the Cold War. Many of the realities of the postwar world had been defined previously – notably in successive conferences between the Allied powers at Yalta and Potsdam – but the terminology in Churchill's 'iron curtain' speech would define the tense years of East-West standoff that would follow.

After its surrender in May 1945, Germany lay in ruins. The liberation of nations from Nazi occupation in 1944-45 had established the battle lines of the Cold War in Europe, an ideological confrontation that would endure until the fall of the Berlin Wall in 1989 – an event that would in turn be followed by the collapse of the communist bloc and the USSR.

With Nazi resistance finally extinguished in 1945, much of Europe was now divided along lines drawn up at Yalta by the three major Allied powers: the Soviet Union, the U.S. and the UK. While the two victorious Western Allies (together with France) set about reinstating national governments, and ensuring a return to democracy in their respective occupation zones, the Soviets took a very different approach. Under Soviet leader Josef Stalin's guidance, the USSR established control zones and then created 'satellite' states within its zones of occupation. For Stalin, the territory in Eastern Europe that had been liberated by the Red Army represented legally agreed 'possessions', while the West viewed its occupation zones as more flexible 'spheres of influence'.

Soviet expansion

When Stalin prohibited Eastern European satellites from benefiting from Marshall Plan reconstruction aid in 1947, U.S. President Harry S. Truman announced that the U.S. would help defend Western Europe against communist aggression. In response, Soviet military strength was retained at 'wartime' levels, with a force of 5 million troops.

Differing attitudes came to a head when the three German zones occupied by the Western Allies were combined in September 1949. This development,

▲ **Republic P-47 Thunderbolt**

512th Fighter Squadron, 406th Fighter Group, USAAF / Nordholz, 1945

Typical of the USAAF fighters operating over Western Europe in the months immediately after VE-Day, this P-47D-30-RA was part of the occupation forces in Germany in summer 1945. Having helped the Allied air forces roll back the Germans, the brightly marked Thunderbolt flew with the 512th Fighter Squadron from Nordholz in northwest Germany.

Specifications

Crew: 1	Dimensions: span 12.42m (40ft 9in); length
Powerplant: 1 x 1891kW (2535hp) Pratt &	11.02m (36ft 2in); height 4.47m (14ft 8in)
Whitney R-2800-59W Double Wasp	Weight: 7938kg (17,500lb) loaded
Maximum speed: 697km/h (433mph)	Armament: 8 x 12.7mm (.5in) MGs in wings,
Range: 3060km (1900 miles)	plus provision for 1134kg (2500lb) external
Service ceiling: 12,495m (41,000ft)	bombs or rockets

together with Western plans to rebuild Germany's industry and economy, was a source of great concern to Stalin. The situation deteriorated further with the establishment of NATO in April 1949, and the acceptance of the now independent West Germany into the Alliance in May 1955.

As a direct result of West Germany's entry into NATO, the Soviets established the Warsaw Pact military alliance in May 1955. This created a buffer zone across Eastern Europe that would serve to protect the USSR from another invasion from the west. Based on earlier military agreements, the Warsaw Pact was inevitably viewed in the West as a

Moscow-led, expansionist initiative. For the Soviets, the Warsaw Pact was necessary to counter perceived Western imperialist aims.

In the event, the battles of the Cold War were fought almost exclusively outside Europe, between client states. Germany, however, was the front line. Here, NATO and Warsaw Pact aircraft were ranged on many of the same airfields that had been captured from the Nazis in 1944-45. Although the political landscape would change, and military strategies would be revised, these aircraft would remain at a high level of readiness until the final reunification of Germany in October 1990.

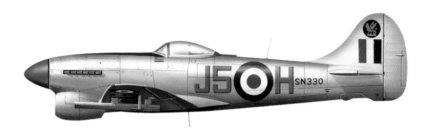

▲ Hawker Tempest Mk V

3 Sqn, RAF / Gütersloh, late 1940s

Represented by the commander's aircraft, 3 Sqn moved to Germany after the war, and retained its Tempests for another three years before transitioning to the Vampire in mid-1948, as the first RAF jet fighter unit in Germany. This particular aircraft wore a silver scheme combined with the squadron's green markings.

Specifications

Crew: 1	Dimensions: span 12.5m (41ft); length 10.26m
Powerplant: 1 x 1626kW (2180hp) Napier Sabre	(33ft 8in); height 4.9m (16ft 1in)
IIA H-type piston engine	Weight: 6142kg (13,540lb) loaded
Maximum speed: 686km/h (426mph)	Armament: 4 x 20mm (.78in) Hispano cannon in
Range: 2092km (1300 miles)	wings, plus up to 907kg (2000lb) of stores
Service ceiling: 10,975m (36,000ft)	consisting of either 2 bombs or 8 rockets

Specifications

Crew: 2	(36ft 6in); height 4.10m (13ft 5in)
Powerplant: 1 x 1320kW (1770hp) Mikulin	Weight: 6345kg (14,000lb) loaded
AM-42 liquid-cooled V-12 engine	Armament: 2 x 23mm (0.9in) Nudelman-
Maximum speed: 550km/h (342mph)	Suranov NS-23 cannons; 1 x 12.7mm (0.5in)
Range: 800km (550 miles)	UBST cannon in the BU-9 rear gunner station;
Service ceiling: 4000m (13,123ft)	up to 600kg (1320lb) bomb load
Dimensions: span 13.40m (44ft); length 11.12m	

▲ Ilyushin Il-10

Group of Soviet Forces in Germany / mid-1940s–early 1950s

With the end of the war, Soviet aviation units remained stationed in the eastern part of Germany, frequently occupying the airfields that had previously served the wartime German Luftwaffe. This specially marked Il-10 was typical of those aircraft that formed the initial equipment of the GSFG in the early 1950s.

Berlin Airlift
1948–1949

The first major confrontation of the Cold War occurred in Berlin, where Stalin hoped to force the Western Allies out of Germany's former capital, eventually subjecting the city to a blockade.

WHILE BRITAIN AND the U.S. intended that Germany would eventually be rehabilitated, Stalin feared a revival of German power and sought to strip its assets through reparations. British and U.S. occupation zones in the west saw the establishment of trade unions, a free press and a fledgling political framework. British and U.S. zones were then merged, later to be joined by the French zone, and a federal government was eventually established, together with currency reform – another bugbear for the Soviets.

The blockade begins

The major problem, however, was Berlin, isolated 160km (100 miles) within the Soviet zone and divided in turn between the four Allied powers. Stalin wanted the other three powers out and had begun to restrict access to the Western sectors. From 31 March 1948, road traffic to Berlin was subject to Soviet inspection. When the Western powers refused to comply, Stalin severed all links with the West, with the exception of food and freight trains.

Finally, at midnight on 18 June, all passenger traffic between Berlin and the Western zones was banned; 24 hours later, all food trains were stopped. The only option open to the Western powers was to maintain their garrisons and the local population by air. This mammoth task required an estimated 2000

USAF AND U.S. NAVY, BERLIN AIRLIFT		
Aircraft	Unit	Base
C-47, C-54, C-82	60th TCG	Rhein-Main, Wiesbaden
C-47, C-54	61st TCG	Rhein-Main
C-54	313rd TCG	Fassberg
C-54	513rd TCG	Rhein-Main
R5D	VR-6, VR-8	Rhein-Main
B-29A	2nd BG	Lakenheath
B-29A	28th BG	Scampton
B-29A	301st BG	Fürstenfeldbruck, Scampton
B-29A	307th BG	Marham, Waddington
F-80A/B	36th FG, 56th FG	Fürstenfeldbruck
WB-29A	18th WS	Rhein-Main

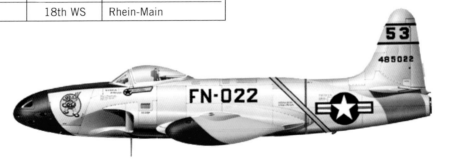

Specifications

Crew: 1

Powerplant: 1 x 17.1kN (3,850lb) J33-GE-11 or J33-A-9 turbojet engine

Maximum speed: 792km/h (492mph)

Range: 2317km (1440 miles)

Service ceiling: 13,716m (45,000ft)

Dimensions: span 11.81m (38ft 9in); length 10.49m (34ft 5in); height 3.43m (11ft 3in)

Weight: 6350kg (14,000lb) loaded

Armament: 6 x 12.7mm (0.5in) MGs, 10 x 127mm (5in) rockets or 907kg (2000lb) bombs

▲ **Lockheed F-80A Shooting Star**

62nd Fighter Squadron, 56th Fighter Group, USAF, Fürstenfeldbruck, 1948

Harassment by Soviet Yak-3s and La-9s in the Berlin air corridors during the airlift saw 42 dive-strafe incidents reported by U.S. aircrew, plus 14 more of gunfire close to transports, and 96 near-misses. The U.S. response was to deploy two groups of B-29 bombers to the UK, and a wing of F-80s to Fürstenfeldbruck airbase in Bavaria. This F-80A was one of those deployed to Fürstenfeldbruck.

tons of food and supplies per day, simply to prevent the city's 2.5 million Western inhabitants starving.

At the time, the RAF transport fleet was in poor shape, with just 153 aircraft available, primarily obsolescent Dakotas and Yorks. A full-scale airlift was nevertheless put into action, and by 29 June RAF Transport Command's entire Dakota fleet was in Germany, supported by Australian, New Zealand and South African personnel. From 1 July, Yorks and Sunderland flying boats became involved, together with the recently introduced Hastings, and the entire front-line RAF transport force was now dedicated to the operation, codenamed Plainfare by the British.

The RAF was supplemented by large numbers of civilian transports, including converted Haltons, Lancastrians and Liberators. Civil aircraft were active from August, but the major contribution was made by the USAF, which initially provided 102 C-47s and soon began to mobilize its more capable C-54 fleet. Eight C-54 squadrons were involved in the operation from 23 July, and at the same time Maj Gen William H. Tunner took command, with his reorganization maximizing the effect of the airlift. By mid-August, U.S. aircraft had begun operating from airfields in the British zone, Celle and Fassberg, which reduced the flying time to the beleaguered city.

RAF, BERLIN AIRLIFT		
Aircraft	**Unit**	**Base**
Dakota IV	30 Sqn, 46 Sqn, 18 Sqn, 240 OCU	Wunstorf, Fassberg, Lübeck
Dakota IV, Hastings C.Mk 1	53 Sqn	Wunstorf, Fassberg, Lübeck, Schleswigland
Dakota IV	77 Sqn	Fassberg, Lübeck
Dakota IV	238 Sqn, 10 Sqn	Wunstorf, Fassberg
Dakota IV	27 Sqn	Schleswigland, Wunstorf, Fassberg, Lübeck
Dakota IV	62 Sqn	Fassberg, Lübeck
Dakota IV, York C.Mk 1	24 Sqn	Lübeck, Bückeburg
York C.Mk 1	40 Sqn, 51 Sqn, 59 Sqn, 99 Sqn, 242 Sqn, 511 Sqn, 241 OCU, 206 Sqn	Wunstorf
Sunderland Mk V	201 Sqn, 230 Sqn	Finkenwerder
Hastings C.Mk 1	47 Sqn, 297 Sqn	Schleswigland
Tempest Mk II	135 Wing	Gütersloh

▲ **Tempest Mk II**

33 Sqn, RAF / Gütersloh, 1948

At the time of the Berlin Airlift, half of the 10 RAF fighter squadrons that equipped the British Air Force of the Occupation (BAFO) were equipped with Tempest day fighters. This Tempest Mk II served with 33 Sqn at Gütersloh, part of the Western effort to counter Soviet aggression during the months of the blockade.

Specifications

Crew: 1

Powerplant: 1 x 1931kW (2590hp) Bristol Centaurus V 17-cylinder radial engine

Maximum speed: 708km/h (440mph)

Range: 2736km (1700 miles)

Service ceiling: 11,430m (37,500ft)

Dimensions: span 12.49m (41ft); length 10.49m (34ft 5in); height 4.42m (14ft 6in)

Weight: 5352kg (11,800lb) loaded

Armament: 4 x 20mm (.0.78in) cannon, external bomb and rocket load of 907kg (2000lb)

Original estimates concerning required tonnage turned out to be far too low: at least 4000 tons was required each day, especially with winter approaching. In July over 2000 tons of supplies were flown in daily, before averages of 3839 and 4600 tons were achieved in September and October.

Tunner established the Combined Air Lift Task Force (Provisional) in mid-October, improving coordination, and 300 C-54s replaced the remaining USAF C-47s. The RAF contribution became less important, with Dakotas and Yorks departing Celle and Fassberg to make way for C-54s. The British effort thereafter focused on transport of awkward cargo, passengers and export of Berlin-made goods.

At the peak of operations, aircraft were taking off or landing at Berlin's Tempelhof and Gatow airports every 90 seconds, with a break in operations only for a brief period in November. Eventually, almost one ton of supplies was flown into the city for every Berliner, including 1,586,530 tons of coal, 92,282 tons of wet fuel and 538,016 tons of food, part of an overall total of over 2.3 million tons.

Soviet intimidation was countered by Western resolve, and Stalin lifted the blockade one minute after midnight on 12 May 1949, although the airlift continued until September. No longer in any doubt about the threat posed by the Soviets, the Western powers established NATO in August 1949.

Specifications

Crew: varied	Dimensions: span 31.60m (103ft 8in);
Powerplant: 4 x 1205kW (1615hp) Bristol	length 22.43m (73ft 7in); height 6.32m
Hercules XVI radial engines	(20ft 9in)
Maximum speed: 515km/h (320mph)	Weight: 30,844kg (68,000lb) loaded
Range: n/a	Armament: none
Service ceiling: 7620m (25,000ft)	

▲ Handley Page Halton

BOAC (later Bond Air Services) / late 1940s

One of 12 Halifax C.Mk 8 transports converted by Shorts for civilian use by BOAC, G-AHDN was later used in the Berlin Airlift, operated by Bond Air Services. The aircraft completed 139 sorties during the operation, carrying over 750 tons of cargo. The aircraft carried additional freight in its ventral pannier.

▲ Avro Lancaster Mk 3

Flight Refuelling Ltd / Wunstorf/Schleswigland, 1948

One of the more specialist aircraft employed by civilian operators during the Berlin Airlift was this Lancaster Mk 3. The aircraft was one of two that had been converted as an aerial tanker by Flight Refuelling, and undertook 40 sorties during the operation, transporting liquid fuels into Berlin.

Specifications

Crew: 7	Dimensions: span 31.09m (102ft);
Powerplant: 4 x 1088kW (1460hp) Rolls-Royce	length 21.18m (69ft 5in); height 5.97m
Merlin 28 or 38 piston engines	(19ft 7in)
Maximum speed: 452km/h (281mph)	Weight: 32,658kg (72,000lb) loaded
Range: 5567km (3459 miles)	Armament: none
Service ceiling: 7467m (24,500ft)	

Berlin Crisis
1961

With the superpowers still at loggerheads over Berlin, Soviet Premier Nikita Khrushchev saw an opportunity to push for a demilitarization plan in Germany, ending Western rights to Berlin.

WITH U.S. PRESIDENT John F. Kennedy only in office for a matter of months, Khrushchev hoped to force the Berlin issue. But West Germany was now a cornerstone of NATO, and the U.S. refused to give it up. Khrushchev issued an ultimatum: if the Berlin issue were not resolved by December 1961, the USSR would be forced to take action over the city.

The Vienna Summit to discuss the issue failed. In July 1961, the Soviet military budget was increased, so Kennedy built up conventional military forces and mobilized Reserve and National Guard units.

Kennedy saw a Soviet threat to take control of the city, and intimated nuclear war if West Berlin were lost. With the border between East and West Germany already secure, the USSR now set about building the Berlin Wall. Construction began in mid-August, and would conclusively separate the city and prevent further emigration from East to West.

As tensions increased, aircraft reserves were sent to Europe from the U.S. In October, 18,500 ANG personnel reported for duty, and 216 home-based USAF and ANG aircraft took up their war stations in Europe, together with an F-104A wing transported by air. Further reinforcements were provided by the RAF, which sent Lightning and Javelin fighter detachments from the UK. Eventually the Berlin Crisis subsided, but the city was now divided.

USAF AND ANG DEPLOYMENTS, BERLIN CRISIS		
Aircraft	Unit	Base
F-100D	55th TFS	Chaumont, France
F-104A	151st FIS	Ramstein AB, Germany
F-104A	157th FIS	Moron AFB, Spain
F-86H	102nd FW	Phalsbourg, France
F-84F	110th TFS	Toul-Rosières, France
F-84F	141st TFS	Chaumont, France
F-84F	163rd TFS	Chambley, France
F-84F	166th TFS	Etain, France
RF-84F	106th TRS	Dreux/Chaumont, France

Specifications

Crew: 1

Powerplant: 1 x 45kN (10,200lb) Pratt & Whitney J57-P-21/21A turbojet

Maximum speed: 1380km/h (864mph)

Range: 3210km (1995 miles)

Service ceiling: 15,000m (50,000ft)

Dimensions: span 11.8m (38ft 9in); length 15.2m (50ft); height 4.95m (16ft 3in)

Weight: 13,085kg (28.847lb) loaded

Armament: 4 x 20mm (0.79in) M39 cannon, 4 x AIM-9 Sidewinder missiles, provision for 3190kg (7040lb) nuclear bombs

▲ **North American F-100D Super Sabre**

20th TFW, USAFE / Wethersfield, 1961

This F-100D strike fighter was based at Wethersfield, England, during the Berlin Crisis. At the time, USAFE operated two tactical F-100D wings in the UK, plus a further two wings in West Germany. Additional fighter-bombers based in Europe comprised one wing each of F-105D Thunderchiefs and F-101C Voodoos.

NATO's Central Front
1949–1989

Had the Cold War ever turned hot, there is little doubt that Europe's Central Front theatre would have been the crucible in which NATO and Warsaw Pact forces went to war.

IN STARK CONTRAST to the postwar situation in the Soviet occupation zones, in Germany's Western zones demobilization was the order of the day. After the war, USAAF combat groups were reduced from 218 to just two, and troop numbers of the Western Allies were slashed from five million to one million in 12 months. What remained in occupied Germany's Western zones was essentially a 'policing' force. By way of example, at the end of 1947, the British Air

Force of Occupation (BAFO) had just 10 front-line squadrons in Germany, reduced from 34.

The situation changed in the wake of the Berlin Airlift, as superpower relations in Europe increasingly began to be defined by paranoia and mistrust, and opposing military alliances began a tense standoff. Air arms re-equipped and expanded, with jet aircraft coming on line in large numbers. After the Berlin Airlift, units were moved forward, towards the east, in

▲ **Canadair Sabre Mk 6**

Jagdgeschwader 71 'Richthofen', Luftwaffe / Wittmund, 1963

After Canada, West Germany was the major operator of the Sabre Mk 6, this example being flown by the Wittmund-based JG 71, an air defence wing, in 1963. Luftwaffe Sabre day fighters served with a total of three fighter wings (*Jagdgeschwader*), two of which were re-formed as fighter-bomber wings (*Jagdbombergeschwader*) in 1964.

Specifications

Crew: 1
Powerplant: 1 x 32.3kN (7275lb) Avro
  Orenda Mark 14 engine
Maximum speed: 975km/h (606mph)
Range: n/a
Service ceiling: 15,450m (50,700ft)
Dimensions: span 11.58m (38ft);
  length 11.58m (38ft); height 4.57m (15ft)
Weight: 6628kg (14.613lb) loaded
Armament: 6 x 12.7mm (0.50in) M2
  Browning machine guns; 2 x AIM-9
  missiles; 2400kg (5300lb) of payload

Specifications

Crew: 1
Powerplant: 1 x 32.3kN (7275lb) Avro
  Orenda Mark 14 engine
Maximum speed: 975km/h (606mph)
Range: n/a
Service ceiling: 15,450m (50,700ft)
Dimensions: span 11.58m (38ft);
  length 11.58m (38ft); height 4.57m (15ft)
Weight: 6628kg (14.613lb) loaded
Armament: 6 x 12.7mm (0.50in) M2
  Browning machine guns; 2 x AIM-9
  missiles; 2400kg (5300lb) of payload

▲ **Canadair Sabre Mk 6**

439 Sqn, Royal Canadian AF / Marville, late 1950s

Prior to the arrival of the CF-104, the RCAF maintained a wing of Canadian-built Sabre Mk 6s at bases in France (Gros Tenquin, Marville) and West Germany (Baden-Söllingen, Zweibrücken). 439 'Sabre-Toothed Tiger' Sqn flew this Sabre from Marville in the latter half of the 1950s. In the mid-1950s, each wing replaced a squadron of Sabres with CF-100s.

order to defend the air corridors to Berlin and to protect a 48-km (30-mile) deep air defence zone along the border with Soviet-controlled territory.

NATO establishment

NATO's predecessor was the Western Union, a military alliance created in March 1948 and comprising the UK, France, Belgium, Luxembourg and the Netherlands. The North Atlantic Treaty was signed in April 1949, with Denmark, Iceland, Italy, Norway and Portugal joining the U.S. and Canada plus the Western Union nations. Greece and Turkey would join the Alliance in 1952, followed by West Germany in 1955. With the creation of NATO, any aggression against its members was to be met by a coordinated military response.

With the Korean War, NATO's European forces were further bolstered, with the Western powers fearing Soviet expansionism. One expression of this was the 13 RAF Vampire FB.Mk 5 units stood up in Germany between 1950 and 1951, to counter the MiG-15 that had debuted over Korea. In April 1951,

Specifications

Crew: 1	Dimensions: span 10.62m (34ft 11in);
Powerplant: 2 x 72.7kN (16,360lb) Rolls-Royce	length 16.84m (55ft 3in); height 5.97m
Avon 301 engines	(19ft 7in)
Maximum speed: 2112km/h (1312mph)	Weight: 12,717kg (28,036lb) loaded
Range: 1290km (802 miles)	Armament: 2 x 30mm ADEN cannon; up to
Service ceiling: 16,770m (55,020ft)	2721kg (6000lb) of external ordnance

▲ **English Electric Lightning F.Mk 2A**

92 Sqn, RAF / Gütersloh, 1975

From the mid-1960s, RAF Germany provided two squadrons of Lightnings for air defence duties. This F.Mk 2A, armed with Firestreak air-to-air missiles, was based at Gütersloh in 1975. The other operator was 19 Sqn, also at Gütersloh. Both units re-equipped with the Phantom FGR.Mk 2 at Wildenrath in the mid-1970s.

Specifications

Crew: 1	Dimensions: span 13.05m (42ft 9in); length
Powerplant: 2 x 105kN (23,810lb) Pratt &	19.43m (63ft 9in); height 5.63m (18ft 5in)
Whitney F100-PW-100 turbofans	Weight: 25,424kg (56,000lb) loaded
Maximum speed: 2655km/h (1650mph)	Armament: 1 x 20mm M61A1 cannon, provision
Range: 1930km (1200 miles)	for up to 7620kg (16,800lb) of stores
Service ceiling: 30,500m (100,000ft)	

▲ **McDonnell Douglas F-15C Eagle**

32nd TFS, USAFE / Soesterberg, early 1980s

During the 1980s, USAFE maintained a single F-15 air superiority squadron operating from Soesterberg in the Netherlands. The Eagle introduced a powerful new beyond-visual-range engagement capability and also equipped three squadrons of the 36th TFW at Bitburg in West Germany.

▲ Fairchild A-10A Thunderbolt II

Northern Germany was 'tank country', and here USAFE's A-10s would have tackled Warsaw Pact armour, which included some 16,400 tanks by the mid-1980s.

Allied Command Europe became operational under Gen Dwight D. Eisenhower, while Allied Air Forces Central Europe stood up under Lt Gen Lauris Norstad. In September 1951 the former BAFO was subordinated to NATO's Supreme Allied Commander Europe (SACEUR) as the 2nd Tactical Air Force.

After the Mutual Defense Assistance Program (MDAP) had supplied many of the Alliance's European air arms with their initial equipment, NATO's posture on the Central Front was further strengthened starting in the late 1950s through the introduction of supersonic aircraft. By now, West Germany had been brought within the fold, with the Luftwaffe being re-established in September 1956. There followed an immense build-up programme, as

Specifications

Crew: 2	17.55m (57ft 7in); height 4.96m (16ft 3in)
Powerplant: 2 x 91.2kN (20,515lb) Rolls-Royce	Weight: 26,308kg (58,000lb) loaded
Spey 202 turbofans	Armament: 4 x AIM-7 Sparrow missiles; two
Maximum speed: 2230km/h (1386mph)	wing pylons for 2 x AIM-7, or 4 x AIM-9
Range: 2817km (1750 miles)	Sidewinders, provision for 20mm cannon;
Service ceiling: 18,300m (60,000ft)	pylons for stores to a maximum weight of
Dimensions: span 11.7m (38ft 5in); length	7257kg (16,000lb)

▲ McDonnell Douglas Phantom FGR.Mk 2

17 Sqn, RAF / Brüggen, 1970–75

Formerly a Canberra reconnaissance unit at Wahn, 17 Sqn reformed in September 1970 to operate the Phantom from Brüggen, home of a three-squadron strike wing. Phantoms were retained until December 1975, by which time the squadron had begun conversion to the Jaguar. In January 1985 the squadron began to convert to the Tornado GR.Mk 1.

▲ McDonnell Douglas F-4E Phantom II

32nd TFW, USAFE / Soesterberg, 1970s

For many years the backbone of USAFE, this F-4E was operated by the 32nd TFW based at Soesterberg (also known as Camp New Amsterdam). The 32nd TFW was part of the 17th Air Force, which was concentrated in West Germany, but this particular unit was unique in being stationed in the Netherlands.

Specifications

Crew: 2	length 17.76m (58ft 3in); height 4.96m
Powerplant: 2 x 79.6kN (17,900lb) General	(16ft 3in)
Electric J79-GE-17 turbojets	Weight: 26,308kg (58,000lb) loaded
Maximum speed: 2390km/h (1485mph)	Armament: 1 x 20mm M61A1 Vulcan cannon;
Range: 817km (1750 miles)	4 x AIM-7 Sparrow or other weapons up to
Service ceiling: 19,685m (60,000ft)	1370kg (3020lb); 2 x AIM-7, or 4 x AIM-9 air-
Dimensions: span 11.7m (38ft 5in);	to-air missiles

the Luftwaffe was reinstated, with 62,000 personnel enrolled within four years, including 1300 pilots.

Division of power

NATO's Central Front air power was ultimately divided more or less evenly between the 2nd Allied Tactical Air Force (2nd ATAF) in the north and the 4th Allied Tactical Air Force (4th ATAF) in the south. Ground forces were divided into Northern and Central Army Groups (NORTHAG and CENTAG), which were analogous to the 2nd and 4th ATAFs.

Both air forces were commanded by Allied Air Forces Central Europe (AAFCE) at Ramstein, West Germany. By the mid-1980s, around 45 squadrons of NATO combat aircraft were based on the Central Front.

Command positions were shared between nations. Supreme Allied Powers Europe (SHAPE) at Mons, Belgium, (formerly Paris) was under the command of SACEUR – always a U.S. officer. The chain of command included AAFCE, directing all air arms in theatre, while HQ Allied Forces Central Europe (AFCENT) at Brunssum in the Netherlands was coordinated land and air operations. In wartime, flying units would revert from national control to NATO, with the exception of the interceptor units, which were always under NATO control.

NATO's 2nd ATAF included Belgium, the UK, the U.S. and West Germany. The area of responsibility stretched from the East German border north to the Danish border and North Sea, from the

Specifications

Crew: 2	9.8m (32ft 2in) (swept); length 22.4m
Powerplant: 2 x 112kN (25,100lb) Pratt &	(73ft 6in); height 5.22m (17ft 1.6in)
Whitney TF30-P-100 afterburning turbofans	Weight: 37,577kg (82,843lb) loaded
Maximum speed: 2655km/h (1650mph)	Armament: 1 x 20mm (0.78in) M61 Vulcan
Range: 2140km (1330 miles)	Gatling cannon (optional) and 14,300kg
Service ceiling: 17,270m (56,650ft)	(31,500lb) bomb load
Dimensions: span 19.2m (63ft) (spread),	

▲ **General Dynamics F-111D**

20th TFW, USAFE / Upper Heyford, early 1980s

Arguably the most potent strike assets available to SACEUR, USAFE F-111s were based in England. The 2nd ATAF included F-111Es from three squadrons of the 20th TFW at Upper Heyford, while the more advanced F-111Fs of the 48th TFW at Lakenheath were assigned to the 4th ATAF. Both were supported by EF-111As.

Specifications

Crew: 1	Dimensions: span 9.45m (31ft); length 15.09m
Powerplant: 1 x 105.7kN (23,770lb) Pratt &	(49ft 6in); height 5.09m (16ft 8in)
Whitney F100-PW-200 turbofan	Weight: 16,057kg (35,400lb) loaded
Maximum speed: 2142km/h (1320mph)	Armament: 1 x General Electric M61A1 20mm
Range: operational radius 925km (525 miles)	multi-barrelled cannon; provision for up to
Service ceiling: above 15,240m (50,000ft)	9276kg (20,450lb) of stores

▲ **Lockheed Martin F-16A Fighting Falcon**

311 Sqn, Royal Netherlands AF / Volkel, mid-1980s

By 1984, the Netherlands had replaced its F-104s with the F-16. Lack of standardization was long an irritant for NATO's Central Front air arms, and the arrival of the F-16 helped address this issue. Armed with AGM-65 Maverick air-to-surface missiles, this F-16A served with a strike/fighter-bomber unit at Volkel.

Franco-German border to the northern end of Luxembourg, and across West Germany along an axis between Kassel and Göttingen. The wartime commander of the 2nd ATAF would have been the commander of RAF Germany (formerly the RAF's 2nd Tactical Air Force), with headquarters at Rheindahlen.

2nd ATAF numbers would have been boosted by deployments from the mainland U.S., while USAFE A-10As would leave the UK for West German soil in wartime, joining RAF Harriers at forward operating locations and dispersed sites, respectively.

▲ Harrier GR.Mk 3

Representing nothing less than a revolution in air warfare, the vertical take-off and landing Harrier provided RAF Germany with a uniquely survivable warplane.

Specifications

Crew: 1

Powerplant: 2 x 32.5kN (7305lb) Rolls-Royce/Turbomeca Adour Mk 102 turbofans

Maximum speed: 1593km/h (990mph)

Range: 557km (357 miles)

Service ceiling: 14,020m (45,997ft)

Dimensions: span 8.69m (28ft 6in); length 16.83m (55ft 2.5in); height 4.89m (16ft 0.5in)

Weight: 15,500kg (34,172lb) loaded

Armament: 2 x 30mm DEFA cannon; provision for 4536kg (10,000lb) of stores, including a nuclear weapon or conventional loads

▲ SEPECAT Jaguar GR.Mk 1

14 Sqn, RAF / Brüggen, 1975–85

The RAF's 14 Sqn flew Mosquitos from Wahn until these were replaced by Vampires in 1951, supplemented two years later by Venoms. In 1955, the unit received Hunters, before re-forming at Wildenrath with Canberras in the strike role. Phantoms arrived in 1970, and Jaguars replaced these in 1975.

▲ Fiat G.91R/3

Waffenschule der Luftwaffe 50, Luftwaffe / Erding, mid-1960s

Developed to meet a NATO requirement for a light tactical fighter, the G.91R served with two 'light' reconnaissance wings and four light combat wings (*Leichtes Kampfgeschwader*) from 1960 until 1980, when replaced by Alpha Jets. This aircraft served with a Luftwaffe training establishment based at Erding.

Specifications

Crew: 1

Powerplant: 1 x 22.2kN (5000lb) Bristol-Siddeley Orpheus 803 turbojet

Maximum speed: 1075km/h (668mph)

Range: 1150km (715 miles)

Service ceiling: 13,100m (43,000ft)

Dimensions: span 8.56m (28ft 1in); length 10.3m (33ft 9in); height 4m (13ft 1in)

Weight: 5440kg (11,990lb) loaded

Armament: 4 x 12.7mm (0.5in) M2 Browning MGs, provision to carry up to 1814kg (4000lb) bomb payload

The southern edge of the Central Front was covered by NATO's 4th ATAF, with an area of responsibility that comprised the lower half of West Germany, below a line running from Luxemburg northeast to Kassel. The 4th ATAF included air arms from Canada, Belgium, the Netherlands, the UK, the U.S. and West Germany, and was commanded by a U.S. officer, with his headquarters based in Heidelberg. The U.S. contribution included the 17th Air Force in the Netherlands and West Germany, and part of the UK-based U.S. 3rd Air Force.

Pending the arrival of British-built swept-wing fighters, the RAF acquired 430 Sabres from Canada, all but two squadrons of the type serving in Germany. The Sabre provided a three-year stopgap pending the delivery of Hunters to 13 squadrons. Meanwhile, night-fighters appeared in the form of Meteor NF.Mk 11s, replaced in turn by Javelins in 1957. By 1961, two squadrons of Javelin FAW.Mk 9s provided the RAF's forward defence in Germany. Later, RAF interceptors comprised Lightnings, and then Phantoms, the latter being switched from their previous strike role to undertake air defence

Specifications

Crew: 1

Powerplant: 2 x 15.56kW (3500lb) Rolls Royce
　Derwent 8 turbojets

Maximum speed: 925km/h (575mph)

Range: 2253km (1400 miles)

Service ceiling: n/a

Dimensions: span 13.11m (43ft 0in);
　length 13.49m (44ft 3in); height n/a

Weight: 6954kg (15,330lb) loaded

Armament: none

▲ Gloster Meteor PR.Mk 10

541 Sqn, RAF / Bückeburg, 1954

By the end of 1947, BAFO had just one Spitfire fighter-reconnaissance unit. In 1950-51, three squadrons of Meteors arrived for reconnaissance, with longer-range reconnaissance requirements met by Canberras from 1956. This photo-reconnaissance Meteor served with 541 Sqn at Bückeburg, Germany, in 1954.

▲ Gloster Meteor FR.Mk 9

79 Sqn, RAF / Bückeburg, 1951-56

79 Sqn reformed with Meteor FR.Mk 9s at Bückeburg in late 1951, and supported unarmed Meteor PR.Mk 10s and Canberras. The fighter-reconnaissance Meteor was replaced by the Swift FR.Mk 5 and the Hunter. Later, RAF Germany included one tactical reconnaissance Phantom unit, which subsequently received Jaguars.

Specifications

Crew: 1

Powerplant: 2 x 15.56kN (3500lb) Rolls Royce
　Derwent 8 turbojets

Maximum speed: 956km/h (595mph)

Range: 1110km (690 miles)

Service ceiling: n/a

Dimensions: span 11.33m (37ft 2in);
　length 13.26m (43ft 6in); height n/a

Weight: 7103kg (15,660lb) loaded

Armament: 4 x 20mm cannon

Specifications

Crew: 2

Powerplant: 2 x 79.4kN (17,845lbf) General
Electric J79-GE-17A turbojets

Maximum speed: 2370km/h (1472mph)

Range: 2600km (1615 miles)

Service ceiling: 18,300m (60,000ft)

Dimensions: span 11.7m (38ft 4.5in);
length 19.2m (63ft); height 5m (16ft 6in)

Weight: 18,825kg (41,500lb) loaded

Armament: Up to 8480kg (18,650lb) of
weapons on nine external hardpoints

▲ **McDonnell Douglas RF-4E Phantom II**

Aufklärungsgeschwader 52, Luftwaffe / Leck, late 1970s

Throughout most of the Cold War, the Luftwaffe provided NATO commanders with
two reconnaissance wings, initially equipped with 108 RF-84Fs. These were
replaced by RF-104Gs, before the arrival of the RF-4E. This RF-4E served with AG
52 at Leck, northern Germany, the wing being assigned to NATO's 2nd ATAF.

duties, and serving the 2nd ATAF with two units at
Wildenrath.

Royal Canadian AF units in Europe were initially
equipped with Sabres and CF-100s and were based in
France and Germany, until the former withdrew from
NATO. France itself had provided tactical fighters for
the 4the ATAF, as well as fulfilling obligations under
Berlin's four-power air traffic agreement. By 1962,
the French AF included Mirage III interceptors and
fighter-bombers, but France announced its intention
to leave NATO in March 1966.

The reborn Luftwaffe was mainly devoted to
offensive duties, but also included 225 Canadair
Sabres for air defence. The all-weather F-86K was
also supplied to the Luftwaffe, as well as the
Netherlands. Ultimately, the Luftwaffe air defence
capability was provided by two wings, one each
assigned to the 2nd and 4th ATAFs, and equipped
with F-104G interceptors, and later F-4Fs.

Belgium and the Netherlands both received Hunter
day fighters in the 1950s. A beneficiary of the U.S.
Offshore Procurement Act, which supported European
aircraft for European air arms, the Hunter was built in
Belgium and the Netherlands, and provided a
replacement for Dutch-built Meteor F.Mk 8s. The Act
also funded RAF Javelins and Canberras.

By 1961, the USAFE air defence contribution was
spearheaded by a wing of F-102As in West Germany
and a squadron of the same type in the Netherlands.
Significant change came in the first half of the 1980s,
with modernization through the introduction of the
F-15 and F-16. Eventually, USAFE declared one

F-15C unit at Soesterberg, the Netherlands, to the
2nd ATAF, while F-15Cs of the 36th TFW at Bitburg
were assigned to the 4th ATAF.

In 1978 the Alliance announced plans to establish
the NATO Airborne Early Warning Force, with the
acquisition of 18 E-3A Airborne Warning And
Control System (AWACS) aircraft starting in 1983.
Registered in Luxembourg, these were based in
Geilenkirchen, West Germany, and were operated by
multinational NATO crews.

Strike and close support

The development and subsequent fielding of tactical
nuclear weapons was the most critical factor in the
development of NATO strike formations on the
Central Front. Initially, the capability of the Western
powers to launch offensive air operations over
Germany was strictly limited. At the end of 1947, for
instance, the BAFO had just four squadrons of
Mosquito light bombers on strength.

Tactical nuclear weapons began to appear in the
mid-1950s, with the U.S.-produced Mk 5, Mk 7 and
Mk 12 lightweight bombs. By now, MDAP had
ensured that F-84Es (and by 1952) F-84Gs were
supplied in their hundreds to NATO air arms,
including Belgium and the Netherlands on the
Central Front. Swept-wing F-84Fs and RF-84Fs
arrived later, and these also served with West
Germany. France received F-100s, Thunderjets and
Thunderstreaks under MDAP, before withdrawing
from NATO, by which time indigenous jets had been
introduced to replace U.S.-supplied equipment. The

▲ Rockwell OV-10A Bronco

601st Tactical Control Wing, USAFE / Sembach, 1970s

Based at Sembach, West Germany, in the 1970s, this OV-10A forward air control aircraft was on strength with the 601st TCW, which also maintained a squadron of CH-53C helicopters. In the 1980s, the base was also a forward operating location for A-10A close support aircraft and was home to electronic warfare C-130s.

Specifications

Crew: 2

Powerplant: 2 x 533kW (715hp) Garrett T76-G-410/412 turboprop engines

Maximum speed: 452km/h (281mph)

Range: 358km (576 miles)

Service ceiling: 7315m (24,000ft)

Dimensions: span 12.19m (40ft); length 12.67m (41ft 7in); height 4.62m (15ft 2in)

Weight: 6552kg (14,444lb) loaded

Armament: 4 x 7.62mm M60C MGs; pods for 70mm (2.75in) or 125mm (5in) rockets; up to 226kg (500lb) of bombs

Specifications

Crew: 2

Powerplant: 2 x 634kW (850hp) Pratt & Whitney Canada PT6A-41 turboprop engines

Maximum speed: 491km/h (306mph)

Endurance: 5 hours

Service ceiling: 9449m (31,000ft)

Dimensions: span 16.92m (55ft 6in); length 13.34m (43ft 9in); height 4.57m (15ft)

Weight: 6412kg (14,136lb) loaded

Armament: none

▲ Beechcraft RC-12D

1st Military Intelligence Brigade, US Army, Wiesbaden, 1980s

An electronic intelligence (ELINT) platform, this RC-12D served with the U.S. Army at Wiesbaden in the 1980s. Charged with battlefield surveillance duties, the RC-12D served with the U.S. Army in both West Germany and Korea, and was equipped with an extensive antenna array for its Improved Guardrail ELINT suite.

'new' Luftwaffe emerged with a backbone provided initially by 375 F-84Fs in five wings, with a primary strike tasking.

Supersonic strike/attack equipment appeared in the form of the F-100, first deployed by the USAFE to Bitburg, West Germany, in March 1956. In 1960, France requested that nuclear-capable USAF aircraft be removed from its territory, so by 1961 there were two wings of USAFE F-100Ds in West Germany, together with a single wing of F-105Ds. At the same time, the UK hosted two wings of USAFE F-100Ds, one F-101 wing, and a bomb wing with the B-66. Offensive assets were supported by a smaller number of tactical reconnaissance units, with USAF RF-101s first deployed in France, and then in the UK. At the time of the Berlin Crisis, the 66th TRW was in France, with the RF-101, while the UK hosted a reconnaissance wing with RB-66s.

With an urgent need to procure more advanced equipment, West Germany ordered the 'multi-role'

Specifications

Crew: 2

Powerplant: 1 x 662kW (888shp) Rolls-Royce
BS 360-07-26 engine

Maximum speed: 296km/h (184mph)

Range: 1850km (999 miles)

Service ceiling: n/a

Dimensions: rotor diameter 12.8m (42ft);
length 12.34m (40ft 6in); height 3.4m
(11.25ft)

Weight: 3878kg (8551lb) loaded

Armament: 8 x BGM-71 TOW anti-tank missiles

▲ **Westland Lynx AH.Mk 1**

1 Wing (BAOR), British Army Air Corps / early 1980s

Helicopters were initially deployed on the Central Front in an observation, casualty evacuation or army cooperation capacity, before undertaking battlefield transport and ultimately anti-armour roles. The British Army Lynx AH.Mk 1 served in the latter, armed with eight TOW anti-tank guided missiles.

F-104G for the nuclear strike, fighter-bomber, air defence and reconnaissance roles, and 916 examples were eventually delivered. Benefiting from European assembly, the F-104G was also selected by Belgium, Canada and the Dutch for Central Front service.

No. 1 Canadian Air Group replaced its Sabres and CF-100s with CF-104s to equip a strike wing starting in 1962, before these began to give way to the CF-188 in the mid-1980s. Canada's eight squadrons were cut back to three in the first half of the 1980s, with the nuclear role now removed. The last three squadrons were assigned a conventional ground-attack role, operating from Baden-Söllingen, West Germany, under Commander, Canadian Forces Europe.

Before France withdrew from NATO, the French AF Mirage III fighter-bomber had been fielded, armed with indigenous tactical nuclear bombs.

British nuclear assets

After Korea, re-equipment of the British 2nd TAF was prioritized, and it grew to 25 squadrons, including Venom FB.Mk 1s for conventional ground attack. Four squadrons of Canberra B(I).Mk 6s and B(I).Mk 8s provided a tactical nuclear capability by 1958, each unit maintaining one aircraft on 15-minute readiness. Britain's 2nd TAF was reduced by half after the 1957 Defence White Paper, and the surviving 18 front-line squadrons were relocated to bases close to the Dutch border, offering improved protection against an initial Warsaw Pact thrust.

Valiants and Vulcans based in the UK supplemented RAF Germany Canberras in the low-level free-fall tactical role. Fatigue saw the Valiants withdrawn in 1964, while the Canberra interdictors continued into the early 1970s, armed with single Mk 28 tactical nuclear bombs. Replacing the Canberra in the offensive role was the Phantom, with three strike/attack squadrons equipped starting in 1970. When the Jaguar arrived as a replacement from 1975–76, the Phantoms were reassigned to air defence.

Towards the end of the Cold War, the USAFE strike force comprised two wings of F-111s at Lakenheath and Upper Heyford in England, divided between 2nd and 4th ATAFs and supported by EF-111As for defence suppression. Nuclear-capable F-4Es and F-16s were based in West Germany and, in addition, 100 or so more F-111s were available in the U.S. for deployment to Europe. At the time, the U.S. maintained around 1,850 free-fall nuclear bombs in Europe, including those provided to other NATO air arms under the 'dual-key' arrangement.

By the mid-1980s, the 2nd ATAF's strike/attack force included eight RAF Tornado squadrons at Brüggen and Laarbruch in West Germany (one for reconnaissance), and single Luftwaffe wings equipped with the Tornado and the F-4F fighter-bomber. Two squadrons of RAF Harriers would operate from dispersed sites near the front line, together with A-10As. Normally based with the 81st TFW at Bentwaters and Woodbridge in England, the A-10s were divided between 2nd and 4th ATAFs and

Specifications

Crew: 3

Powerplant: 2 x 1070kW (1435shp) Turbomeca
Turmo IIIC4 turbo-shafts

Maximum speed: 263km/h (163mph)

Range: 570km (360 miles)

Service ceiling: 4800m (15,750ft)

Dimensions: rotor diameter 15m (49ft 3in);
length 18.15m (59ft 6in); height 5.14m
(16ft 10in)

Weight: 7400kg (16,300lb) loaded

Armament: 20mm (0.8in) cannon and 7.62mm
(0.30in) MGs

▲ Aérospatiale Puma HC.Mk 1

230 Sqn, RAF / Gütersloh, early 1980s

RAF Germany support helicopter forces were technically assigned to 2nd ATAF but normally operated in support of the British Army of the Rhine (BAOR). This RAF Puma was based at Gütersloh, West Germany, and wears Tiger stripes associated with a NATO Tiger Meet. In the 1980s, Gütersloh also hosted two RAF Harrier squadrons and one Chinook squadron.

Specifications

Crew: 3

Powerplant: 2 x 2927kW (3925shp) General
Electric T64-GE-413 turboshaft

Maximum speed: 395km/h (196mph)

Range: 1000km (620 miles)

Service ceiling: 5106m (16,750ft)

Dimensions: rotor diameter 22.01m (72ft 3in);
length 26.97m(88ft 6in); height 7.6m
(24ft 11in)

Weight: 15,227kg (33,500lb) loaded

Armament: 2 x 7.62mm MG3 MGs

▲ Sikorsky CH-53G

Mittleres Transporthubscrauberregiment 35, Heeresflieger / Mendig, early 1980s

The German Army and Luftwaffe provided a significant transport force for NATO's battlefield commanders, eventually centered on a fleet of around 90 Transalls and 110 CH-53 transport helicopters. Heavy-lift CH-53Gs served with front-line *Heeresflieger* regiments at Rheine Bentlage, Lauphiem and Niedermendig.

Specifications

Crew: 1 or 2 (+ 4 passengers)

Powerplant: 2 x 313kW (420shp) Allison
250-C20B turboshaft engines

Maximum speed: 270km/h (168mph)

Range: 550km (342 miles)

Service ceiling: 5182m (17,000ft)

Dimensions: rotor diameter 9.84m
(32ft 3in); length 11.86m (38ft 10in);
height 3m (9ft 11.77in)

Weight: 2400kg (5291lb) loaded

Armament: none

▲ Messerschmitt Bo 105

300 Sqn, Royal Netherlands AF / Deelen, late 1970s

By the mid-1980s, the Netherlands provided army cooperation and liaison on the Central Front through a force of Alouette III helicopters (two units, at Soesterberg and Deelen) and Bo 105s (one unit, 300 Sqn based at Deelen from 1976). The Netherlands also maintained a single fixed-wing transport squadron, 334 Sqn, equipped with F.27 Troopships.

operated rotating detachments at four forward operating locations in West Germany. Conventional ground-attack assets included a wing of Luftwaffe Alpha Jets, three Belgian Mirage 5BA units and four squadrons of Dutch NF-5As. Tactical recce needs were addressed by one Dutch F-16 unit, one Belgian Mirage 5BR unit, USAFE RF-4Es of the 1st TRS at Alconbury, a wing of Luftwaffe RF-4Es, a squadron of RAF Jaguars and half a squadron of RAF Harriers.

The 4th ATAF offensive capability ultimately rested with three Luftwaffe Tornado wings, three Canadian CF-188 squadrons, F-16s of the USAFE's 50th TFW at Hahn and the 86th TFW at Ramstein, plus single wings of Luftwaffe Alpha Jets and F-4Fs. Electronic warfare and special operations support were provided by Spangdahlem-based Wild Weasel F-4Gs and F-4Es, EF-111As at Upper Heyford and MC-130Es at Ramstein. 4th ATAF recce missions were tasked to the 38th TRS RF-4Es at Zweibrücken, and a single Luftwaffe RF-4E wing.

The withdrawal of 35,000 U.S. personnel from Europe from 1967 increased the importance and

Specifications
Crew: 1/2
Powerplant: 1 x 236kW (317shp) Allison T63-A-700 turboshaft
Maximum speed: 222km/h (138mph)
Range: 481km (299 miles)
Service ceiling: 5800m (19,000ft)
Dimensions: span 10.77m (35ft 4in); length 9.8m (32ft 2in); height 2.92m (9ft 7in)
Weight: 1360kg (3000lb) loaded
Armament: 1 x 7.62mm (0.3in) M134 minigun or 1 x 40mm (1.57in) M129 grenade launcher

▲ **Douglas OH-58A Kiowa**
25th Aviation Company, U.S. Army / 1980s
In addition to the AH-1G and the TOW-equipped AH-1Q/S close support helicopters, U.S. Army formations in Europe were equipped with the OH-58A for observation and liaison. Additional U.S. Army helicopter types were dedicated to air mobility, and included the CH-47 Chinook and the UH-60A Black Hawk, 150 examples of which were in Germany by the mid-1980s.

Specifications
Crew: 6
Powerplant: 4 x 1834kW (3800hp) Pratt & Whitney R-4360 engines
Maximum speed: 520km/h (320mph)
Range: 3500km (2175 miles)
Service ceiling: 10,000m (34,000ft)
Dimensions: span 53.06m (174ft 1in); length 40m (130ft); height 14.7m (48ft 4in)
Weight: 98,000kg (216,000lb) loaded
Armament: none

▲ **Douglas C-124C Globemaster II**
63rd TCW, USAF / early 1960s
In times of tension, the sea lines of communication between the U.S. and Europe were reinforced by airlift. This C-124 was one of those involved in the deployment of troops, equipment and fighters to Europe during the 1961 Berlin Crisis. Also active were C-97s, both types flying into ex-13th Air Force bases in France.

urgency of upgrading the 'dual basing' concept and improving rapid reinforcement by home-based air and ground units. Deployments were regularly practised, with one of the first major exercises being Crested Cap I in 1969, when 96 F-4Ds and 3500 USAF personnel deployed to West Germany.

NATO standardization

After MDAP had paved the way in establishing postwar Western European air arms, NATO began issuing its own requirements, most notably resulting in the G.91 light attack aircraft, which served on the Central Front with West Germany.

Standardization of NATO air arms was never successfully addressed. For example, Belgium and the Netherlands selected different aircraft to replace the RF/F-84F in the late 1960s, opting for the Mirage 5 and NF-5 respectively. Things improved when both procured the licence-produced F-16 to replace the F-104. By 1982, Belgium and the Netherlands had placed orders for 116 and 124 respectively. Belgium's F-16s equipped four Cold War squadrons, though two wings of Mirage 5 fighter-bombers also survived into the 1980s. Assigned to NATO's 2nd ATAF, the Dutch Tactical Air Command eventually fielded five F-16 units, plus four squadrons of NF-5s.

▲ Lockheed C-5A Galaxy

436th Military Airlift Wing, USAF / Dover AFB, 1970s

Europe's NATO contingent would have been unable to sustain a robust defence in wartime without significant reinforcement from the U.S. Movement of U.S. troops and materiel to Europe was reliant on the USAF's Military Airlift Command, the backbone of which was eventually provided by C-5s and C-141s.

Specifications

Crew: 6

Powerplant: 4 x 191kN (43,000lb) General
Electric TF39-GE-1C turbofan engines

Maximum speed: 908km/h (564mph)

Range: 9560km (5940 miles)

Service ceiling: 10,895m (35,745ft)

Dimensions: span 67.88m (222ft 9in);
length 75.54m (247ft 10in); height 19.85m
(65ft 1in)

Weight: 379,657kg (837,000lb) loaded

Armament: None

Specifications

Crew: 5–6

Powerplant: 4 x 93.4kN (21,000lb) Pratt &
Whitney TF33-7 turbofans

Maximum speed: 912km/h (567mph)

Range: 4723km (2935 miles)

Service ceiling: 12,500m (41,000ft)

Dimensions: span 48.74m (159ft 11in); length
51.29m (168ft 3.5in); height 11.96m (39ft 3in)

Weight: 155,582kg (343,000lb) loaded

Armament: none

▲ Lockheed C-141B StarLifter

438th Military Airlift Wing, USAF / McGuire AFB, early 1980s

Deployments of U.S.-based units to the Central Front were practised through regular Reforger (Reinforcement of Forces in Germany) exercises. During one such exercise in 1976, the U.S. 101st Airborne Division deployed to West Germany, with 11,000 troops being ferried in the course of 125 C-141 sorties.

Greece and Turkey
1946–1974

While both Greece and Turkey became NATO members, the long-standing tensions between them more than once led to the outbreak of fighting, becoming a thorn in the side of the Alliance.

COMPARED TO NATO'S Central and Northern Fronts, the Southern Front was assigned much lower strategic importance. However, apathy between Greece and Turkey resulted in problematic relations with the U.S., numerous disputes and open conflict.

One of the earliest flashpoints of the Cold War, Greece saw a communist-inspired revolution gain a foothold immediately after the war. British air power was deployed, and Greece remained within the British sphere of influence. Aided by U.S. military deliveries, the Greek Monarchists eventually put down the communist rebellion.

War in Cyprus

After Cyprus was granted independence by the UK in 1960, Greek and Turkish troops remained on the island, watched by UN peacekeepers. Seeking amalgamation with Greece, Greek-Cypriot factions attacked villages near the Cypriot capital, Nicosia, in August 1963, triggering a response by Turkey, which sent F-84G and F-100C/D fighter-bombers to attack Greek-Cypriot positions.

TURKISH AF AND ARMY, 1974		
Aircraft	Unit	Base
F-100D/F	111 Filo, 132 Filo, 181 Filo	Adana
F-104G	141 Filo	Adana
C.160D	221 Filo	Erkilet
C-47	223 Filo	Etimesgut
UH-1, AB.204	Army	Antalya

In the wake of a Greek-Cypriot coup attempt in July 1974, Turkey invaded the island, with troops being delivered by AB.204 helicopters and C.160D and C-47 transports. An amphibious landing was accompanied by air strikes by F-100s and F-104s.

A Turkish destroyer was sunk in a 'friendly fire' incident by Turkish warplanes, while RAF transports and Royal Navy and U.S. Marine Corps helicopters mounted an evacuation for foreign nationals. After a renewed Turkish offensive in August – during which F-100s again attacked Greek-Cypriot targets – a ceasefire was declared, leaving the island divided.

Specifications

Crew: 1

Powerplant: 1 x 45kN (10,200lb) Pratt & Whitney J57-P-21/21A turbojet

Maximum speed: 1380km/h (864mph)

Range: 3210km (1995 miles)

Service ceiling: 15,000m (50,000ft)

Dimensions: span 11.8m (38ft 9in); length 15.2m (50ft); height 4.95m (16ft 3in)

Weight: 13,085kg (28,847lb) loaded

Armament: 4 x 20mm (0.79in) M39 cannon, 4 x AIM-9 Sidewinder missiles, provision for 3190kg (7040lb) nuclear bombs

▲ **North American F-100C Super Sabre**

111 Filo, Turkish AF / Eskisehir, mid-1960s

A former USAF aircraft, this F-100C normally served in the ground-attack role from Eskisehir. In 1964, the unit was based at Adana, and was among those involved in attacks against Greek targets in Cyprus. By the time of the 1974 fighting, the F-100C had been withdrawn, although F-100D/Fs remained in use.

Warsaw Pact on the Central Front
1955–1989

Forward-deployed U.S. and British air power rapidly contracted after VE-Day, but in the east, aircraft numbers were reduced only marginally and would form the backbone of the Warsaw Pact.

NINE DAYS AFTER West Germany joined NATO in May 1955, the Soviets organized the signing of the Treaty of Friendship, Mutual Assistance and Cooperation – better known as the Warsaw Pact. Under the terms of this treaty, the USSR was aligned militarily with Albania (which later withdrew from the Alliance), Bulgaria, Czechoslovakia, East

Germany, Hungary, Poland and Romania. Together, these nations were committed to the defence of the socialist states in Central and Eastern Europe, and their air arms formed a counter to those of NATO, arranged on the opposite side of the iron curtain. More importantly for Moscow, the new Alliance ensured that the Soviet satellite states in Eastern

▲ Ilyushin Il-10
Soviet Frontal Aviation / late 1940s–early 1950s

Soviet ground-attack regiments began to replace the Il-2 Shturmovik with the improved Il-10 from October 1944. The type remained an important asset for the Soviet air arms in the immediate postwar period, and examples were forward-deployed with the Group of Soviet Forces in Germany.

Specifications

Crew: 2	length 11.12m (36ft 6in); height 4.10m (13ft 5in)
Powerplant: 1 x 1320kW (1770hp) Mikulin	Weight: 6,345kg (14,000lb) loaded
AM-42 liquid-cooled V-12 engine	Armament: 2 x 23mm (0.9in) Nudelman-
Maximum speed: 550km/h (342mph)	Suranov NS-23 cannons; 1 x 12.7mm (0.5in)
Range: 800km (550 miles)	UBST cannon in the BU-9 rear gunner station;
Service ceiling: 4000m (13,123ft)	up to 600kg (1320lb) bomb load
Dimensions: span 13.40m (44ft);	

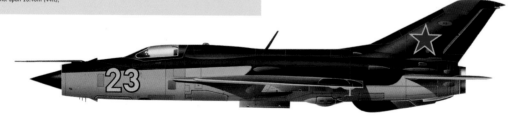

▲ Mikoyan-Gurevich MiG-21PF
Soviet Frontal Aviation / mid-1960s

In the days of 'massive retaliation', the focus of Soviet frontal air power was placed on air defence, with limited close support and ground-attack capabilities. In the 1970s, the MiG-21 was dominant among Soviet fighter units on the Central Front, this example being a MiG-21PF, which introduced a new R-11 engine.

Specifications

Crew: 1	(including probe) 15.76m (51ft 8.5in);
Powerplant: 1 x 60.8kN (13,668lb) thrust	height 4.1m (13ft 5.5in)
Tumanskii afterburning turbojet	Weight: 9400kg (20,723lb) loaded
Maximum speed: 2050km/h (1300mph)	Armament: 1 x 23mm cannon, provision for
Range: 1800km (1118 miles)	about 1500kg (3307lb) of stores, including air-
Service ceiling: 17,000m (57,750ft)	to-air missiles, rocket pods, napalm tanks or
Dimensions: span 7.15m (23ft 5.5in); length	drop tanks

Specifications

Crew: 1

Powerplant: 1 x 88.2kN (19,842lb) Lyulka AL-7F
turbojet

Maximum speed: 1700km/h (1056mph)

Range: 320km (199 miles)

Service ceiling: 15,150m (49,700ft)

Dimensions: span 8.93m (29ft 3.5in); length

17.37m (57ft); height 4.7m (15ft 5in)

Weight: 13,500kg (29,750lb) loaded

Armament: 2 x 30mm NR-30 cannon; four
external pylons for 2 x 750kg (1653lb) and
2 x 500kg (1102lb) bombs, but with two tanks
on fuselage pylons, total external weapon load
is reduced to 1000kg (2205lb)

▲ Sukhoi Su-7BMK
Soviet Frontal Aviation / early 1970s

The Su-7 was the first dedicated ground-attack jet to be deployed in significant numbers
by Soviet formations on the Central Front. This example is armed with unguided air-to-
ground rockets. The fixed-geometry Su-7 eventually gave way to the Su-17 series, which
featured a variable-geometry wing planform.

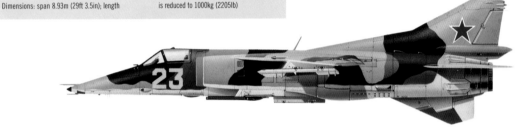

Specifications

Crew: 1

Powerplant: 1 x 103.4kN (23,353lb) Tumanskii
R-29B-300 turbojet

Maximum speed: 1885km/h (1170mph)

Range: 540km (335 miles)

Service ceiling: over 14,000m (45,900ft)

Dimensions: span 13.97m (45ft 10in) spread,
7.78m (25ft 6.25in) swept; length 17.07m
(56ft 0.75in); height 5m (16ft 5in)

Weight: 20,300kg (44,750lb) loaded

Armament: 1 x 23mm cannon, provision for up
to 4000kg (8818lb) of stores

▲ Mikoyan-Gurevich MiG-27
Soviet Frontal Aviation / mid-1980s

NATO's shift to the doctrine of 'flexible response' saw the increasing primacy of the fighter-
bomber with the Soviet air arms, and introduction of ever more capable strike/attack
assets. The MiG-27 was the backbone of the 16th Air Army strike force by the end of the
Cold War, with four regiments in East Germany.

▲ Mil Mi-8T
Soviet Army Aviation / late 1970s

Both the Mi-8 and Mi-24 were flexible, agile, well armed and could deliver troops
to the rear of the battlefield when needed. The example illustrated is of the Mi-8T
version, and is shown armed with external packs of 57mm rockets. Assault
regiments typically operated a mix of both Mi-8 and Mi-24 helicopters.

Specifications

Crew: 3

Powerplant: 2 x 1454kW (1950shp) Klimov
TV3-117Mt turboshafts

Maximum speed: 260km/h (162mph)

Range: 450km (280 miles)

Service ceiling: 4,500m (14,765ft)

Dimensions: rotor diameter 21.29m
(69ft 10in); length 18.17m (59ft 7in);
height 5.65m (18ft 6in)

Weight: 11,100kg (24,470lb)

Armament: up to 1500kg (3,300lb) of
disposable stores

▲ Mil Mi-24D

Soviet Army Aviation / early 1980s

The Mi-24 was especially feared in the West, carrying an eight-man infantry squad or armament that included anti-tank missiles and unguided rockets. This is an example of the Mi-24D, which introduced a re-profiled forward fuselage, with tandem seating under separate cockpit transparencies for the pilot and gunner.

Specifications

Crew: 2-3
Powerplant: 2 x 1600kW (2200hp) Isotov
  TV-3-117 turbines
Maximum speed: 335km/h (208mph)
Range: 450km (280 miles)
Service ceiling: 4500m (14,750ft)

Dimensions: rotor diameter 17.3m (56 ft 7in);
  length 17.5m (57ft 4in); height 6.5m (21ft 3in)
Weight: 12,000kg (26,500lb) loaded
Armament: 1 x 12.7mm Gatling type MG,
  57mm rockets, AT-2C/ SWATTER ATGMs; up to
  500kg (1,102lb) bomb load

Specifications

Crew: 2-3
Powerplant: 2 x 1600kW (2,200hp) Isotov
  TV-3-117 turbines
Maximum speed: 335km/h (208mph)
Range: 450km (280 miles)
Service ceiling: 4500m (14,750ft)

Dimensions: rotor diameter 17.3m (56 ft 7in);
  length 17.5m (57ft 4in); height 6.5m (21ft 3in)
Weight: 12,000kg (26,500lb) loaded
Armament: 1 x fixed 30mm twin gun on the
  right fuselage side, 57mm rockets, AT-6C/
  SPIRAL ATGMs

▲ Mil Mi-24P

Soviet Army Aviation / mid-1980s

The Mi-24P was a dedicated anti-armour version of the Mi-24, with a harder-hitting 30mm twin-barrel cannon replacing the previous 12.7mm four-barrel machine-gun. Known to NATO as 'Hind-F', the Mi-24P was developed on the basis of combat experience in Afghanistan.

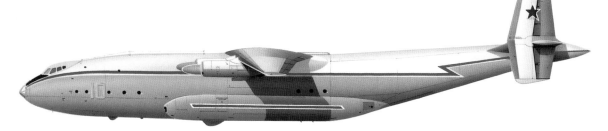

▲ Antonov An-22

Soviet Transport Aviation / 1970s

In the same way that USAFE and other European NATO forces relied upon strategic airlift capacity from the continental U.S., Soviet units forward-deployed in Eastern Europe were supplied by Soviet Transport Aviation. For much of the Cold War, the largest airlift asset available to the Soviets was the four-turboprop An-22.

Specifications

Crew: 5–6
Powerplant: 4 x 11,030kW (15,000hp)
  Kuznetsov NK-12MA turboprops
Maximum speed: 740km/h (460mph)
Range: 5000km (3100 miles)
Service ceiling: 8000m (26,240ft)

Dimensions: 64.4m (211ft 3in);
  length 57.9m (190ft 0in); height 12.53m
  (41ft 1in)
Weight: 250,000kg (551,000lb) loaded
Payload: 80,000kg (180,000lb)

SOVIET AF COMBAT UNITS IN GERMANY, 1990		
Aircraft	Unit	Base
MiG-29, MiG-23	33rd Fighter Regiment	Wittstock
MiG-29, MiG-23	733rd Fighter Regiment	Pütnitz
MiG-29, MiG-23	787th Fighter Regiment	Eberswalde
MiG-29, MiG-23	31st Fighter Regiment	Alt Lonnewitz
MiG-29, MiG-23	85th Fighter Regiment	Merseburg
MiG-29, MiG-23	968th Fighter Regiment	Nobitz
MiG-29, MiG-23	35th Fighter Regiment	Zerbst
MiG-29, MiG-23	73rd Fighter Regiment	Köthen
MiG-23	833rd Fighter Regiment	Altes Lager
MiG-27, MiG-23	559th Fighter-Bomber Regiment	Finsterwalde
MiG-27, MiG-23	296th Fighter-Bomber Regiment	Grossenhain
MiG-27, MiG-23	911th Fighter-Bomber Regiment	Brand
MiG-27, MiG-23	19th Fighter-Bomber Regiment	Mirow-Lärz
Su-17	20th Fighter-Bomber Regiment	Gross Dölln
Su-17	730th Fighter-Bomber Regiment	Neuruppin
Su-24	11th Reconnaissance Regiment	Welzow
Su-17	294th Reconnaissance Regiment	Allstedt
MiG-25	931st Reconnaissance Regiment	Werneuchen
Su-25	357th Combat Regiment	Brandis
Su-25	368th Combat Regiment	Tütow

Advantages of this included a robust command structure and the potential for a high degree of standardization, while the major disadvantage remained Soviet misgivings concerning the reliability of satellite states. The latter were manifest during the Soviet military response to uprisings in Hungary in 1956 and Prague in 1968.

In peacetime, the USSR was divided into 16 Military Districts (MDs), plus four land/air Groups of Soviet Forces forward-deployed in satellite countries: the Group of Soviet Forces in Germany; Northern Group of Soviet Forces (in Poland); Central Group of Soviet Forces (Czechoslovakia); and Southern Group of Soviet Forces (Hungary). It was these four groupings that were arranged against NATO's forces on the Central Front. Soviet air power in Poland eventually amounted to around 300 aircraft. The Poland-based Soviet inventory included the Su-24 strike aircraft (introduced there in 1982) and Su-27 interceptors that were expected to counter NATO's advanced low-level strike aircraft. A further 200 Soviet combat aircraft were based in Czechoslovakia, but the major contribution was provided by the 16th Air Army, part of the Group of Soviet Forces in Germany. Headquartered at Zossen-Wünsdorf in East Germany, by 1989 this comprised around 1500 aircraft, including three fighter divisions and two fighter-bomber divisions (each of three regiments), two Shturmovik regiments, plus three reconnaissance regiments and two transport regiments.

When the last Soviet combat aircraft (MiG-29s of the 733rd Fighter Regiment) left the former East Germany in April 1994, they ended a process of withdrawal that had seen the eastward movement of almost 700 fixed-wing aircraft, 600 helicopters, 4000 tanks, 8000 armoured vehicles and 3500 artillery pieces. These had been maintained and operated by a force of around 338,000 troops.

Qualitative improvements

Soviet air arms on the Central Front were prioritized when it came to the receipt of new equipment. Some of the first MiG-15 operators were in East Germany, and units here also received early batches of Il-28s, MiG-17s, MiG-19s and MiG-21s. In the 1960s, the Su-7 and Yak-28 were introduced, with the MiG-23/27 and Su-17 arriving in the 1970s. By the early 1980s significant progress was being made in terms of

Europe were integrated as a single defensive buffer zone, dissuading any future attack from the West.

By the mid-1980s, Warsaw Pact air power on the Central Front included around 2700 fixed-wing tactical aircraft, compared to 1300 in NATO's 2nd and 4th ATAFs. Total Warsaw Pact fixed-wing strength in Northern and Central Europe amounted to 4750 aircraft, against around 2000 for NATO. In the same way that home-based U.S. assets were available to reinforce NATO in wartime, additional Soviet air power could be provided by units normally based in the central and eastern USSR.

The Warsaw Pact was under Soviet control, with a Soviet commander-in-chief and chief-of-staff.

importance to NATO and the Warsaw Pact, because it could be used to assemble forces in order to launch a counter-attack or open a second front. If NATO could secure Denmark, it could then launch forces to sever any attempted Warsaw Pact drive across the North German Plain.

Allied Forces Northern Europe

NATO's defence of the north was the job of Allied Forces Northern Europe (AFNORTH), with headquarters at Kolsaas, Norway, and responsible for Denmark, Norway and the northern part of West Germany. Norway was divided along a north-south axis, with zones administered by Commander South Norway (COMSOR) and Commander North Norway (COMNON).

The task of sealing off access to the Baltic was handled by HQ Allied Forces Baltic Approaches (BALTAP), headquartered at Karup in Denmark, and under the command of AFNORTH. BALTAP was divided into four operational commands, which included Danish and West German land forces and navies, the West German naval air arm (Marineflieger), Danish air force and northern-based elements of the Luftwaffe, the latter ultimately including a light attack wing (Alpha Jets) and a reconnaissance wing (RF-4Es).

Additional support in the Baltic was also available from NATO Allied Command Europe Mobile Force (AMF). This was a multi-national, variable-content rapid reaction force that could be deployed to

Denmark or Norway as required, bolstering the two countries' relatively small, defensively configured air arms, both of which were eventually based around a nucleus of four squadrons of F-16s. Further assets could be provided by the UK Mobile Force (one Jaguar wing, and one Harrier squadron), the U.S. Marine Corps, the Netherlands-UK amphibious force, the U.S. Army and USAF. By the 1980s, a forward operating location for NATO E-3 AWACS aircraft had been established at Ørland, Norway.

Like Denmark, Norway was equally vital to NATO and the Warsaw Pact. For NATO, Norway offered a platform from which to attack the Soviet Northern Fleet, including its ballistic missile submarines. Control of Norway also aided closing down the Baltic approaches. Sharing a land border with the USSR, Norway was threatened by direct invasion, or an amphibious assault directed against the north. For the Soviets, control of Norway would have assisted in closing the Norwegian Sea to NATO reinforcements, with a submarine barrier extending between Norway and Iceland.

In time of war, Norway would have been rapidly reinforced by NATO units, including ground forces. U.S. carrier battle groups regularly deployed to the Norwegian Sea, and the UK's 3rd Commando Brigade and Dutch Marines were also active in the area. Air support was made available via AMF, as well as Canada's Air-Sea Transportable Brigade Group, including two squadrons of CF-5As normally based in Canada, but with wartime duties in Norway.

Specifications

Crew: 1	Dimensions: span 8.69m (28ft 6in); length
Powerplant: 2 x 32.5kN (7305lb) Rolls-	16.83m (55ft 2.5in); height 4.89m (16ft 0.5in)
Royce/Turbomeca Adour Mk 102 turbofans	Weight: 15,500kg (34,172lb) loaded
Maximum speed: 1593km/h (990mph)	Armament: 2 x 30mm DEFA cannon; provision
Range: 557km (357 miles)	for 4536kg (10,000lb) of stores, including a
Service ceiling: 14,020m (45,997ft)	nuclear weapon or conventional loads

▲ SEPECAT Jaguar GR.Mk 1
54 Sqn, RAF Coltishall / early 1980s

Based at Coltishall during peacetime, the RAF's three home-based Jaguar units could have been committed to the Northern Front during wartime as part of NATO's strategic reserve, and RAF Jaguars regularly undertook deployments to gain experience operating in the harsh conditions encountered in northern Norway.

Chapter 2

Air Power at Sea

Control of the sea became a vital facet of the Cold War, and aircraft were deployed for both offensive and defensive purposes. While carrier-based air power was one of the more visible indicators of naval prowess, equally important were shore-based patrol and strike aircraft. These, together with shipborne and land-based helicopters, were intended to complement navies in the protection of sea lanes and maritime resources, to protect the fleet and to challenge hostile surface vessels and submarine threats.

◀ **USS** *Carl Vinson*

Representing the unrivalled maritime might of the US Navy carrier force, the nuclear-powered USS Carl Vinson displays a 1980s air wing that includes F-14s, A-6s, A-7s, EA-6s, E-2s and an A-3. After World War II, air power ensured that the carrier assumed the role of capital ship in the US Navy.

U.S. Carrier Air Power
1945–1989

After its decisive showing during the war in the Pacific, the aircraft carrier took over from the battleship as the pre-eminent arbiter of naval warfare, with the U.S. Navy its leading exponent.

ALTHOUGH THE CARRIER had demonstrated its value during World War II, after VJ-Day the U.S. Navy carrier fleet was run down, and by 1950 only 15 carriers remained in commission. In addition, a projected new 'super-carrier' design, the USS *United States*, had been cancelled in 1948.

Completed too late to see service in World War II, later 'Essex'-class carriers served in a new 'power-projection' role in Korea, while the larger 'Midway' battle carriers were the first to support carrier-capable, nuclear-armed U.S. Navy bombers, the AJ-1 Savage being the first of this type to enter service.

Jet-age carriers

The arrival of the jet placed new demands on carriers, initially met though a modernization programme for 13 of the 'Essex' class, with reconfigured decks and elevators to better suit operations by jet aircraft. The revised 'Essex' design was available for deployment to Korea, by which time the U.S. Navy was increasingly concerned by the development of the Soviet submarine arm. In order to address the threat, new classes of light carrier (as well as converted escort

carriers) and aircraft configured for anti-submarine warfare (ASW) were fielded. At the same time, the U.S. was scheming a new type of carrier that could launch nuclear-armed bombers from their stations in the Atlantic against targets in the Soviet Union. Successor to the 'Midways' to prosecute this role was the first of a new class of 'super-carrier', the USS *Forrestal*, commissioned in 1955 as the first carrier purpose-built for jet operations. Most important of its revolutionary features were two British innovations: the angled deck and steam catapult.

A new 'super-carrier' was ordered each year between 1953–58, before the arrival of USS *Enterprise*, the first nuclear-powered aircraft carrier, commissioned in 1961. A nuclear powerplant allowed operations without refuelling, meaning that only the ship's stores and aviation fuel and ordnance needed to be replenished. *Enterprise*, the 'Forrestals' and surviving 'Essex'-class vessels (subject to a further upgrade, with angled decks and other improvements) were all active off the coast of Vietnam.

By now, the light carriers serving in the ASW role were proving too small, and it was the versatile 'Essex'

Specifications

Crew: 1

Powerplant: 1 x 156kW (2100hp) Pratt & Whitney R-2800-34W Double Wasp radial piston engine

Maximum speed: 678km/h (421mph)

Range: 1778km (1105 miles)

Service ceiling: 11,796m (38,700ft)

Dimensions: span 10.92m (35ft 10in); length 8.61m (28ft 3in); height 4.21m (13ft 9in)

Weight: 5873kg (12,947lb) loaded

Armament: 4 x 12.7mm (0.5in) M2 machine guns; up to 454kg (1000lb) of bombs or four 5in (127mm) rockets

▲ **Grumman F8F-1 Bearcat**

VF-72, U.S. Navy / USS Leyte, *1949–50*

Appearing too late to see combat in World War II, the F8F was regarded as one of the finest piston-engined fighters, but the arrival of the jet saw it serve principally with the U.S. Naval Reserve. This F8F-1, among the last of the 770 of this version built, was embarked aboard the carrier USS *Leyte* in 1949-50.

Specifications

Crew: 1

Powerplant: 2 x 7.1kN (1600lb thrust)
Westinghouse J30-WE-20 turbojets

Maximum speed: 771km/h (479mph)

Range: 1120km (695 miles)

Service ceiling: 12,525m (41,100ft)

Dimensions: span 12.42m (40ft 9in);
length 11.35m (37ft 3in); height 4.32m
(14ft 2in)

Weight: 4552kg (10,035lb) loaded

Armament: 4 x 12.7mm (0.50in) MGs

▲ McDonnell FH-1 Phantom

VF-171, U.S. Navy / Quonset Point, late 1940s

The first all-jet aircraft to be ordered into production by the U.S. Navy, the FH-1
entered squadron service July 1947. This aircraft served with VF-171 (the former
VF-17A), the only U.S. Navy unit to take the aircraft aboard carriers, before the
Phantom was demoted to Reserve and Marine Corps service.

Specifications

Crew: 1

Powerplant: 1 x 17.8kN (4000lb) Allison J35-
A-2 turbojet

Maximum speed: 880km/h (547mph)

Range: 2414km (1500 miles)

Service ceiling: 9754m (32,000ft)

Dimensions: span 9.8m (38ft 2in); length
10.5m (34ft 5in); height 4.5m (14ft 10in)

Weight: 7076kg (15,600lb) loaded

Armament: 6 x .5in machine guns

▲ North American FJ-1 Fury

VF-5A, U.S. Navy / San Diego, late 1940s

Only 30 production examples of the straight-wing FJ-1 were built, before North American switched to the swept-wing FJ-2 Fury
and its successors, which were based on the F-86 Sabre. The FJ-1 served with a single fleet unit, VF-5A, home-based at San
Diego, California. The unit was the first U.S. Navy jet squadron to go to sea under operational conditions, in March 1948.

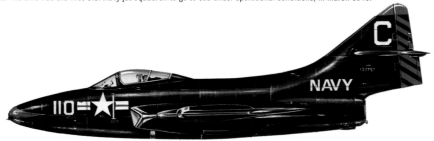

Specifications

Crew: 1

Powerplant: 1x 28.25kN (6354lb thrust)
Allison J33 engine

Maximum speed: 1041km/h (647mph)

Range: 2111km (1312 miles)

Service ceiling: 12,800m (42,000ft)

Dimensions: span 10.5m (34ft 6in); length
12.9m (42ft 2in); height 3.7m (12ft 3in)

Weight: 9116kg (20,098lb) loaded

Armament: 4 x 20mm (0.79in) M2 cannon; 6 x
127mm (5in) rockets; 4 x AIM-9 Sidewinder
air-to-air missiles; 2 x 454kg (1000lb) bombs

▲ Grumman F9F-7 Cougar

VF-21, U.S. Navy / Oceana, 1953

A swept-wing follow-on to the F9F Panther that saw combat over Korea, the
Cougar is seen here in the form of an Allison J33-powered F9F-7 serving at the
end of the Korean War in 1953. The Cougar did not see action in this conflict, but
became standard fleet fighter equipment in the mid-1950s.

class that was again modified for this role, deploying specialist aircraft in the form of the AF Guardian, and later the S2F Tracker. Known as CVS, these carriers operated within anti-submarine task groups, the first of which went to sea in 1958. Additional 'Essex'-class ships were converted to serve as helicopter carriers, these fulfilling an amphibious assault role.

After the 'Midway' class and the AJ-1 had proven the potential of carrier-based nuclear strike forces, the U.S. Navy introduced its first carrier-based nuclear-capable jet, the A3D Skywarrior, in the late 1950s.

The much smaller A4D Skyhawk was also nuclear-capable, but could operate from smaller carrier decks. The U.S. Navy's first Mach 2-capable fleet interceptors, the missile-armed F8U Crusader and F4H Phantom II, joined these attack aircraft.

Enter the 'Nimitz'

By the end of the Vietnam War, in which U.S. Navy carriers played a vital role, completing 71 cruises to the Western Pacific, the conventionally powered 'Kitty Hawk'-class carrier – effectively an improved

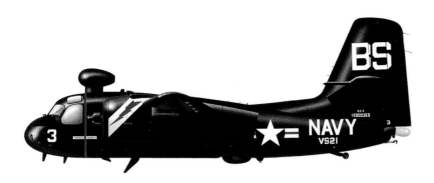

Specifications

Crew: 4	Dimensions: span 21m (69ft 8in); length 12.8m
Powerplant: 2 x 1135kW (1525hp) Wright	(42ft); height 4.9m (16ft 3in)
R-1820-82 radial piston engines	Weight: 11,069kg (24,408lb) loaded
Maximum speed: 438km/h (272mph)	Armament: torpedoes, rockets, depth charges or
Range: 1558km (968 miles)	1 x Mk 47 or Mk 101 nuclear depth bomb
Service ceiling: 6949m (22,800ft)	

▲ Grumman S2F-2 Tracker

VS-21, U.S. Navy / late 1950s

Backbone of the U.S. Navy's carrier-based anti-submarine fleet for much of the Cold War, the Tracker is seen here in the midnight-blue scheme in which it was originally delivered. The S2F-2 model featured an enlarged bomb bay and a wider span horizontal tail. The variant saw production between 1954-55.

Specifications

Crew: 2	(54ft 9in); height 4.93m (16ft 2in)
Powerplant: 2 x 41.4kN (9300lb) Pratt & Whitney	Weight: 26,581kg (58,600lb) loaded
J52-P-8A turbojets	Armament: five external hardpoints with
Maximum speed: 1043km/h (648mph)	provision for up to 8165kg (18,000lb)
Range: 1627km (1011 miles)	of stores, including nuclear weapons,
Service ceiling: 14,480m (47,500ft)	conventional and guided bombs, air-to-surface
Dimensions: span 16.15m (53ft); length 16.69m	missiles and drop tanks

▲ Grumman A-6E Intruder

VA-65, U.S. Navy / USS Independence, mid-1970s

A long-range all-weather strike aircraft, the A-6 entered operational service in 1964 and served until the end of the Cold War, seeing combat in Vietnam, Libya and elsewhere. This example of the definitive A-6E variant served with VA-65 'Tigers', part of Carrier Air Wing 7 (CVW-7) aboard USS Independence.

'Forrestal' design – was in service. The nuclear-powered 'Nimitz' class, the lead ship of which was commissioned in 1975, represented the next great technological advance. By now, the strategic nuclear tasking had passed over to the submarine force, and carriers were seen primarily as conventional tools for use in 'limited warfare' scenarios. The 'Nimitz' class, which began to be funded under the 1967 defence budget, remained the U.S. Navy's definitive carrier until the end of the Cold War, with five vessels in commission by 1989.

The 90,000-ton 'Nimitz' class were also the first of the truly multi-purpose carriers, combining attack and ASW functions in one hull. Each 'Nimitz' vessel could support an air wing of between 74–86 aircraft. By the time that offensive operations were launched against Libya in 1986, a typical U.S. Navy air wing included two squadrons of F-14A interceptors, a squadron of A-6E strike aircraft, two squadrons of A-7E attack aircraft and single squadrons each of EA-6B defence suppression aircraft, E-2C airborne early warning aircraft and SH-3H ASW helicopters.

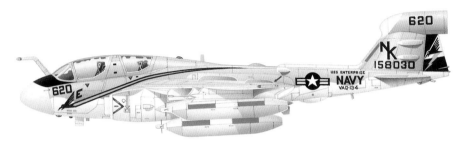

Specifications

Crew: 4	Dimensions: span 16.15m (53ft); length 18.24m
Powerplant: 2 x 49.8kN (11,200lb) Pratt &	(59ft 10in); height 4.95m (16ft 3in)
Whitney J52-P-408 turbojets	Weight: 29,484kg (65,000lb) loaded
Maximum speed: 982km/h (610mph)	Armament: none on early models, retrofitted
Range: 1769km (1099 miles)	with external hardpoints for four or six AGM-88
Service ceiling: 11,580m (38,000ft)	HARM air-to-surface anti-radar missiles

▲ Grumman EA-6B Prowler

VAQ-134, U.S. Navy / USS Enterprise, late 1970s

This EA-6B, which served aboard USS *Enterprise*, is depicted carrying the AN/ALQ-99 tactical jamming pods that formed the centrepiece of its electronic warfare suite. The EA-6B was developed from the EA-6A, itself an electronic warfare adaptation of the A-6A that was designed for the U.S. Marine Corps.

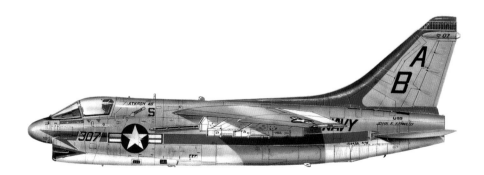

▲ Vought A-7B Corsair II

VA-46, U.S. Navy / USS John F. Kennedy, early 1970s

Operating from USS *John F. Kennedy*, this A-7B displays the vibrant markings prevalent in the earlier part of the Corsair II's fleet service. Developed as a successor to the A-4, the A-7 became standard equipment for U.S. Navy light-attack squadrons. This aircraft was part of CVW-1, assigned to the Atlantic Fleet.

Specifications

Crew: 1	Dimensions: span 11.8m (38ft 9in); length
Powerplant: 1 x 54.2kN (12,190lb) thrust Pratt &	14.06m (46ft 1.5in); height 4.9m (16ft 0.75in)
Whitney TF30-P-8 turbofan engine	Weight: 19,050kg (42,000lb) loaded
Maximum speed: 1123km/h (698mph)	Armament: 2 x 20mm Colt Mk 12 cannon; up to
Range: 1150km (4100 miles)	6804kg (15,000lb) of bombs, air-to-surface
Service ceiling: n/a	missiles or other stores

Specifications

Crew: 2

Powerplant: 2 x 92.9kN (20,900lb) Pratt &
   Whitney TF30-P-412A turbofans

Maximum speed: 2517km/h (1564mph)

Range: 3220km (2000 miles)

Service ceiling: 17,070m (56,000ft)

Dimensions: span 19.55m (64ft 1.5in) unswept;

11.65m (38ft 2.5in) swept; length 19.1m
(62ft 8in); height 4.88m (16ft)

Weight: 33,724kg (74,349lb) loaded

Armament: 1 x 20mm M61A1 Vulcan rotary
cannon; combination of AIM-7 Sparrow; AIM-9
medium range air-to-air missiles and AIM-54
Phoenix long range air-to-air missiles

▲ **Grumman F-14A Tomcat**

VF-14, U.S. Navy / USS John F. Kennedy, mid-1970s

The Tomcat was the definitive U.S. Navy interceptor fielded during the Cold War, based around the powerful AWG-9 radar system combined with AIM-54 Phoenix missiles. By the mid-1980s, a total of 22 front-line squadrons were equipped with the F-14, including VF-14, here serving CVW-1 aboard USS *John F. Kennedy.*

Specifications

Crew: 4

Powerplant: 2 x 41.26kN (9275lb) General
   Electric turbofans

Maximum speed: 828km/h (514mph)

Range: 5121km (2765 miles)

Service ceiling: 12,465m (40,900ft)

Dimensions: span (unfolded) 20.93m
(68ft 8in); (folded) 9m (29ft 6in); length
16.26m (53ft 4in); height 6.93m (22ft 9in)

Weight: 17,324kg (38,192lb) loaded

Armament: up to 2220kg (4900lb) bomb load

▲ **Lockheed S-3A Viking**

VS-24, U.S. Navy / USS Nimitz, early 1980s

In the latter half of the Cold War, U.S. Navy carrier-based anti-submarine capability was bolstered by the arrival of the S-3. Replacing the S-2, the Viking combined excellent range and a long loiter capability with advanced sensors and avionics. Operating from USS *Nimitz,* VS-24 was home-based at Oceana, Virginia.

British Carrier Air Power
1945–1989

Like the U.S. Navy, the Royal Navy had utilized the carrier with success in World War II, and carrier air power was to play an important role in British conflicts in the Cold War period.

THE END OF World War II saw a number of Royal Navy carriers either cancelled or transferred to foreign navies. In the early 1950s, the carrier fleet was based around surviving wartime vessels, joined in the middle of that decade by the new 'Colossus' class.

Although carrier power had been reduced after the war, events in Korea would see Royal Navy carriers return to combat, with a Commonwealth carrier always on station to provide air support to the UN effort. Development of jet-capable carriers was slower

Specifications

Crew: 1	(47ft 7in); height 3.71m (12ft 2in);
Powerplant: 1 x 95.6kN (21,500lb) Rolls-Royce	Weight: 11,884kg (26,200lb) loaded
Pegasus vectored thrust turbofan	Armament: 2 x 30mm cannon, provision for AIM-
Maximum speed: 1110km/h (690mph)	9 Sidewinder or Matra Magic air-to-air
Range: 740km (460 miles)	missiles, and two Harpoon or Sea Eagle anti-
Service ceiling: 15,545m (51,000ft)	shipping missiles, up to a total of 3629kg
Dimensions: span 7.7m (25ft 3in); length 14.5m	(8000lb) bombs

▲ **British Aerospace Sea Harrier FRS.Mk 1**

800 NAS, Royal Navy / HMS Invincible, *early 1980s*

Illustrated by an example operating from HMS *Invincible*, the Sea Harrier FRS.Mk 1 was essentially similar to the RAF's Harrier GR.Mk 3, but the redesigned nose housed a Blue Fox radar and a raised cockpit was fitted. Typical air-to-air armament comprised a pair of Sidewinder missiles and 30mm cannon pods.

than that in the U.S., however, and throughout the Korean War the Fleet Air Arm relied on piston-engined Seafire, Firefly and Sea Fury aircraft. Korea began a period of significant activity for the British carrier force, and was followed by actions in Malaya and in response to the coup in Iraq. Most significant, however, was the Suez action of 1956, by which time Royal Navy carriers were operating jet equipment.

The first of the Fleet Air Arm's carrier jets was the Attacker, introduced in 1951, and events in Korea also promoted the construction of new carriers, notably the 'Centaur' class and HMS *Eagle*. While the Fleet Air Arm's jets – joined by the turboprop Wyvern strike fighter and the U.S.-supplied Skyraider airborne early warning platform – went to war in Suez, a new focus was being put on anti-submarine operations, evidenced by the introduction of dedicated carrierborne ASW aircraft.

The jet age

HMS *Ark Royal* was completed in 1955 as the world's first angled-deck carrier, while the arrival of steam catapults allowed heavier aircraft to be operated. The Royal Navy was also quick to recognize the value of carrier-based helicopters, with early operations by Dragonfly search-and-rescue helicopters in Korea. The use of the Whirlwind in Malaya starting in 1953 helped pioneer carrier-based heliborne assault operations, and the same type would serve in Suez, launching the first large-scale heliborne assault.

By the beginning of the 1960s, the last of the 'Centaur'-class carriers were in service, two of which were soon adapted for heliborne assault duties. A new generation of carrier aviation was in service, including the Buccaneer, which entered service in 1963, optimized for the low-level nuclear strike role.

During the 1960s, Royal Navy carrier air power saw action over Kuwait, Borneo, Aden, East Africa and Rhodesia. At the same time, the Admiralty was planning a new class of 'super-carrier', the CVA-01. This promising design was cancelled in 1966, when the UK announced it would withdraw all forces from 'east of Suez'. This decision also marked the end of the conventional carrier in Royal Navy service. The Fleet Air Arm introduced the Phantom carrierborne fighter, but this would only serve operationally from one carrier, HMS *Ark Royal*. This vessel, the last of its type, was finally decommissioned in 1978.

With the focus of operations now on the ASW mission in the Atlantic, the Royal Navy introduced a new type of carrier. The 'Invincible' class was primarily equipped with Sea King ASW helicopters, with vertical/short take-off and landing (V/STOL) Sea Harriers for air defence. The latter fighters were provided with a 'ski-jump' launch ramp, rather than catapults and arrestor gear. The first of these new vessels, HMS *Invincible*, was joined by the reconfigured HMS *Hermes*, now also featuring a 'ski-jump' for Sea Harrier operations. Both carriers would play a vital role in the Falklands campaign of 1982.

Soviet Carrier Air Power
1968–1989

Although the Soviet Navy never commissioned a conventional aircraft carrier during the Cold War, its activities in the field of ASW carriers reflected the USSR's growing maritime ambitions.

AT THE END of World War II, U.S. naval power was unchallenged; by the end of the Cold War, and based on the primacy of sea-based nuclear weapons, the Soviet Navy had grown immeasurably, and now presented a very real threat to the U.S. and its allies.

'The flag of the Soviet Navy now proudly flies over the oceans of the world. Sooner or later, the United States will have to understand that it no longer has mastery of the seas'. The words of Sergey Gorshkov, Admiral of the Fleet of the Soviet Union, in 1973, reflected the importance of naval warfare and the establishment of a 'blue-water navy' to Soviet strategic thinking. Earlier carrier studies, pursued by Stalin, had come to nought.

ASW carriers

Once a primarily defensive organization, the development of sea-based strategic missiles saw the Soviet Navy establish a powerful naval nuclear capability, ultimately expressed through the deployment of nuclear-powered ballistic missile submarines. As a result of the significance of the nuclear-armed submarine, ASW became a critical Cold War mission for the Soviet Navy.

Not a true aircraft carrier in the Western sense, the 14,600-ton 'Moskva' class was described as an 'anti-submarine cruiser with aircraft armament'. Its air wing comprised Ka-25 ASW helicopters, and the first of two vessels put to sea in 1968, both serving with the Black Sea Fleet.

The altogether more capable 'Kiev' class, four of which were completed, followed the 'Moskva' design. A true aircraft carrier – although classed as a 'heavy aircraft-carrying cruiser' by the Soviets – the 'Kiev' air wing could include Yak-38 V/STOL fighters or Ka-25 (and later Ka-27) ASW helicopters. The lead ship of the class entered service in 1975, and the vessels were divided between the Northern and Pacific Fleets. As the Cold War drew to a close, the Soviets were working on a new design of conventional aircraft carrier, although this was destined never to see service under a Soviet flag.

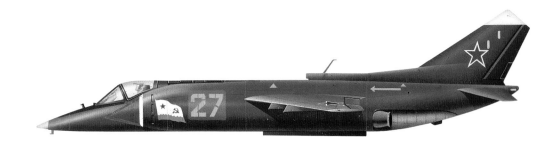

▲ **Yakovlev Yak-38**

AVMF / early 1980s

Although its capabilities were strictly limited, the Yak-38 provided the Soviet Navy with an entirely new ship-based, fixed-wing dimension. The aircraft's primary mission was light attack, but it could theoretically carry free-fall nuclear weapons. The Yak-38 made its first operational deployment aboard *Kiev* in 1975.

Specifications

Crew: 1

Powerplant: 2 x 29.9kN (6724lb) Rybinsk RD-36-35VFR lift turbojets; 1 x 6950kg (15,322lb) Tumanskii R-27V-300 vectored-thrust turbojet

Maximum speed: 1009km/h (627mph)

Range: 370km (230 miles)

Service ceiling: 12,000m (39,370ft)

Dimensions: span 7.32m (24ft); length 15.5m (50ft 10in); height 4.37m (14ft 4in)

Weight: 11,700kg (25,795lb) loaded

Armament: provision for 2000kg (4409lb) of stores

▲ **Kamov Ka-27**

AVMF / early 1980s

Developed as a successor to the Ka-25, the ship-based Ka-27, codenamed 'Helix' by NATO, initially appeared in anti-submarine warfare and utility/search and rescue variants. The basic design was later used as the basis for the Ka-29 assault transport, used from amphibious warships from the mid-1980s.

Specifications

Crew: 1-3

Powerplant: 2 x 1660kW (2225shp) Isotov turboshaft engines

Maximum speed: 270km/h (166mph)

Range: 980km (605miles)

Service ceiling: 5000m (16,400ft)

Dimensions: rotor diameter 15.80m (51ft 10in); length 11.30m (37ft1in); height 5.50m (18ft 1in)

Weight: 11,000kg (24,200lb) loaded

Armament: 1 x torpedoes or 36 RGB-NM & RGB-NM-1 sonobouys

Soviet Maritime Strike
1955–1989

The power of the U.S. Navy's carrier fleet dictated a response in kind by the USSR, which established the most powerful arm of maritime strike aircraft assembled during the Cold War.

THE SOVIET NAVY'S missile-armed strike aircraft were effectively in a class of their own during the Cold War. Based on land, these long-range aircraft were adaptations of air force strategic or theatre bombers, armed with dedicated anti-ship missiles.

The wartime targets of these aircraft, which included missile-carrying variants of the Tu-16, Tu-22 and Tu-22M bombers, included not only U.S. Navy carrier battle groups, but also the U.S. Navy fleet train that would have supplied Europe with vital supplies and reinforcements.

Anti-carrier doctrine

In the late 1960s, Marshal Vasily Sokolovsky noted the importance of 'attempting to destroy the attack carriers before they can launch their planes'. This was a mission that would have been carried out not only by missile-carrying naval aircraft but also by a series of submarines, surface warships and even ICBMs.

▲ **Tupolev Tu-16**

A mainstay of the Soviet Navy through most of the Cold War, the Tu-16 was deployed in a variety of roles, including missile-carrier, as illustrated.

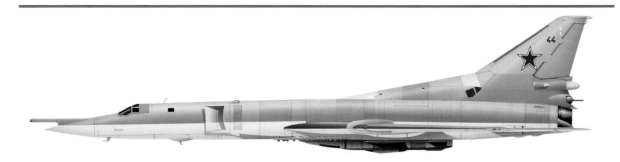

▲ **Tupolev Tu-22M-2**

AVMF / early 1980s

The Tu-22M served both with the Soviet AF and the Navy, the latter employing the
aircraft for long-range maritime strike, armed with Kh-22 anti-ship missiles.
Naval Tu-22s were operated by the Black Sea, Northern and Pacific Fleets, with
almost 150 examples in service by 1988. Eight regiments were equipped by 1991.

Specifications

Crew: 4	Dimensions: span (spread) 34.28m (112ft 6in),
Powerplant: 2 x 196kN (44,090lb thrust)	(swept) 23.3m (76ft 5in); length 41.46m
Kuznetsov NK-22 turbojet engines	(136ft); height 11.05m (36ft 3in)
Maximum speed: 1800km/h (1118mph)	Weight: 122,000kg (268,964lb) loaded
Range: 5100km (3169 miles)	Armament: 2 x 23mm (0.9in) GSH-23 guns; up
Service ceiling: 13,000m (42,651ft)	to 3 KH-22 air-to-surface missiles

Maritime Patrol
1946–1989

**The vital maritime patrol mission took on a new resonance in the Cold War era, as development
of the nuclear-powered submarine demanded the deployment of specialist air power.**

THE USE OF maritime patrol aircraft had effectively
countered the submarine menace by the end of
World War II, although the tables would be turned
by submarine developments in the 1950s. There now

began to appear faster and more agile submarines,
and ultimately nuclear-powered submarines of almost
unlimited endurance. The latter were soon armed
with nuclear missiles and became critical elements in

▲ **Beriev Be-6**

AVMF / early 1970s

The Soviet Navy was unusual in retaining flying boats for maritime patrol
operations until the end of the Cold War. Among the earliest equipment was the
Be-6, with a prominent MAD 'stinger' carried in a rear fuselage boom. The Be-6
(NATO codename 'Madge') was retained in Soviet service into the early 1970s.

Specifications

Crew: 7	Dimensions: span 33m (110ft); length 23.5m
Powerplant: 2 x 1800kW (2400hp) Shvetsov	(77ft 1in); height 7.64m (25ft 1in)
ASh-73TK radial engines	Weight: 23,456kg (51,711lb) loaded
Maximum speed: 414km/h (257mph)	Armament: 5 x 23mm (0.91in) Nudelman-
Range: 5000km (3100 miles)	Rikhter NR-23 cannon; 2 x 1000kg (2205lb)
Service ceiling: 6100m (20,013ft)	torpedoes or 8 mines

the strategic balance. A measure of the neglect to which maritime patrol forces had been subject is seen in the fact that, by 1946, RAF Coastal Command was in possession of just 50 front-line aircraft.

Demise of the flying boat

Anti-submarine warfare (ASW) therefore returned to prominence, with long-range shore-based aircraft initially being supported by flying boats. The increased endurance offered by newly developed maritime patrol aircraft saw the flying boat discarded relatively quickly by most countries, although the

USSR was a notable exception, retaining amphibious aircraft until the end of the Cold War.

After the Korean War, NATO was subject to naval expansion, amid fears surrounding the growth of the Soviet submarine arm. The first postwar U.S. Navy patrol aircraft to see widespread service had been the P2V (later P-2) Neptune, which served with many NATO allies for at least three decades, until the arrival of more capable equipment, such as the P-3 Orion, the Canadian CL-28 Argus and the RAF's Nimrod. The particular importance assigned to the maritime patrol mission by Canada was reflected in

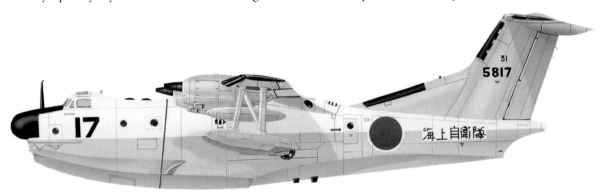

Specifications

Crew: 9

Powerplant: 4 x 2250kW (3017hp) General Electric T-64-IHI-10J turboprop engines

Maximum speed: 545km/h (339mph)

Range: 4700km (2921 miles)

Service ceiling: 9000m (29,550ft)

Dimensions: span 33.1m (108ft 7n); length 33.5m (109ft 11in); height 9.7m (31ft 10in)

Weight: 43,000kg (94,799lb) maximum

Armament: bombs, torpedoes or depth charges

▲ **Shin Meiwa PS-1**

31st Kokutai, Japanese Maritime Self-Defence Force / early 1980s

As a maritime nation with close proximity to the USSR, Japan's defensive Cold War posture put an emphasis on anti-submarine warfare operations. Until replaced by US-provided P-3s, the indigenous PS-1 flying boat operated on patrol duty, with an endurance of up to 15 hours and a payload of ASW sensors and weapons.

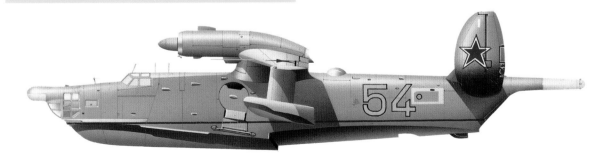

▲ **Beriev Be-12**

AVMF / late 1970s

The Be-12 was a dedicated maritime patrol and ASW amphibian, fitted with over-water sensors and equipment including a search radar and MAD boom. As the Be-12 began to be rendered obsolescent by submarine developments, examples were adapted for the transport and search-and-rescue roles.

Specifications

Crew: 4

Powerplant: 2 x 3864kW (5180hp) Ivchenko Progress AI-20D turboprop engines

Maximum speed: 530km/h (330mph)

Range: 3300km (2100 miles)

Service ceiling: 8000m (26,247ft)

Dimensions: span 29.84m (97ft 11in); length 30.11m (98ft 9in); height 7.94m (26ft 1in)

Weight: 36,000kg (79,200lb) loaded

Armament: 1500kg (3300lb) of bombs, depth-charges or torpedoes that country's development of the Argus, later replaced by the CP-140 Aurora, a local development of the P-3, in the early 1980s. CP-140s were deployed on Canada's east and west coasts, supplemented by shorter-range S-2 Trackers.

A NATO requirement for a Neptune replacement led to the development of the Atlantic maritime patrol aircraft, an entirely new design that was first flown in 1961 and which was acquired by West Germany, France, the Netherlands and Italy.

Typically, Cold War maritime patrol aircraft were powered by efficient turboprop engines and their airframes were large enough to accommodate comprehensive sensors and offensive weaponry. The British Nimrod was somewhat unusual in being powered by jet engines, although it was, in common with the turboprop P-3 and Soviet Il-38, based on an existing airliner design. Mission equipment included radar, sonobuoys, magnetic anomaly detection (MAD) gear and other systems

Specifications

Crew: 9–11	Dimensions: span 30.4m (100ft);
Powerplant: 2 x 1715kW (2300hp) Wright	length 22.9m (75ft 4in); height 8.6m
R-3350-8A engines	(28ft 6in)
Maximum speed: 487km/h (303mph)	Weight: 26,3030kg (58,000lb) loaded
Range: 6618km (4110 miles)	Armament: 6 x 12.7mm (0.5in) MGs and
Service ceiling: 8230m (27,000ft)	capacity for 16 underwing rockets

▲ Lockheed P2V-1 Neptune
VP-8, U.S. Navy / late 1940s

The West's dominant land-based maritime air patrol platform for the first three decades after World War II, the first of the Neptunes to enter service was the P2V-1, from March 1947. The aircraft carried a crew of seven, a weapons bay for two torpedoes or up to 12 depth charges, and six defensive machine-guns.

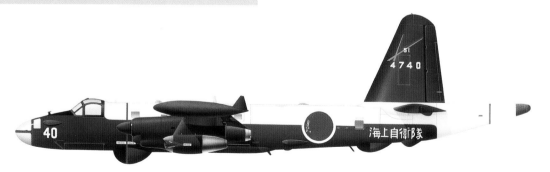

Specifications

Crew: 9	Dimensions: span 30.9m (101ft 4in); length
Powerplant: 2 x 2125kW (2850hp) General	27.9m (91ft 8in); height 8.9m (29ft 4in)
Electric T64-IHI-10 turboprop and 2 x 13.7kN	Weight: 34,020kg (75,000lb) maximum
(3081lb thrust) IHI-JE turbojet engines	Armament: up to 16 x 127mm (5in) rockets
Maximum speed: 650km/h (403mph)	and up to 3628kg (8000lb) of bombs, depth
Range: 5663km (3500 miles)	charges or torpedoes
Service ceiling: unknown	

▲ Lockheed P-2J Neptune
Japanese Maritime Self-Defence Force / mid-1970s

With increasing Soviet submarine activity in the seas surrounding its islands from the mid-1970s, Japan's ASW capacity rested with both fixed-wing and helicopter assets. Built by Kawasaki, the P-2J was an advanced local development of the Neptune, with a lengthened fuselage and a mixed turboprop/turbojet powerplant.

Specifications

Crew: 10

Powerplant: 4 x 1460kW (19600hp) Rolls-Royce
Griffon 57 liquid-cooled V12 engines

Maximum speed: 480km/h (300mph)

Range: 3620km (2250 miles)

Service ceiling: 6200m (20,200ft)

Dimensions: span 36.58m (120ft);
length 26.61m (87ft 4in); height 5.33m (17ft 6in)

Weight: 39,000kg (86,000lb) loaded

Armament: 2 x 20mm (0.8in) Hispano Mark V
cannon; 4536kg (10,000lb) bomb load

▲ **Avro Shackleton MR.Mk 1A**

120 Sqn, RAF / Aldergrove, 1959

Successor to the Neptune in RAF Coastal Command service was the Shackleton, which enjoyed a long career as a maritime patroller before being adapted to serve in the airborne early-warning role, which it fulfilled until the end of the Cold War. This example, from the third production batch of MR.Mk 1As, is seen in 1959.

Specifications

Crew: 4

Powerplant: 2 x 1137kW (1525hp) Wright R-
1820-82WA radial engines

Maximum speed: 450km/h (280mph)

Range: 2170km (1350 miles)

Service ceiling: 6700m (22,000ft)

Dimensions: span 22.12m (72ft 7in);
length 13.26m (43ft 6in); height 5.33m
(17ft 6in)

Weight: 11,860kg (26,147lb) loaded

Armament: 2 torpedoes

▲ **Grumman S-2A Tracker**

320 Sqn, Royal Netherlands Navy / Valkenburg, 1960s

Among Western Europe's NATO air arms, the Dutch Navy played an important Cold War maritime role over the North Sea. A total of 28 S2F-1s (S-2As) were delivered under MDAP in 1960-62, with a further 17 received from Canada in 1960-61. These served from land bases and from the Dutch carrier *Karel Doorman*.

Specifications

Crew: 11

Powerplant: 4 x 3356kW (4500hp) Allison T56-
A10W turboprop engines

Maximum speed: 766km/h (476mph)

Range: 4075km (2533 miles)

Service ceiling: 8625m (28,300ft)

Dimensions: span 30.37m (99ft 8in); length
35.61m (116ft 9in); height 10.27m (33ft 8in)

Weight: 60,780kg (134,000lb) loaded

Armament: up to 9070kg (20,000lb) of
ordnance, including bombs, mines and
torpedoes

▲ **Lockheed P-3A Orion**

VP-19, U.S. Navy / early 1960s

This Orion represents one of the very first examples to enter service with the U.S. Navy, and displays the midnight blue and white finish originally applied. The aircraft illustrated was part of the fourth production batch of P-3As, this variant entering service with VP-8 as a successor to the Neptune in mid-1962.

dedicated to the detection of surface and sub-surface threats. The search radar could detect surface contacts, or submarine periscopes, while MAD was also capable of uncovering a submerged target. Acoustic methods of detection employed were based on passive and active sonar, these being packaged as disposable sonobouys that could be dropped from the aircraft in patterns as it tracked its quarry, the onboard operators listening to the emitted signals via radio. As was the case with other maritime patrol aircraft in the latter half of the Cold War, data from the Nimrod's various mission sensors and navigation systems were brought together by a powerful data-processing computer that was designed to overcome potential electronic jamming and countermeasures. The resultant contacts were displayed on screens at the consoles of the radar operators, tactical navigators or plotters seated in the cabin and could also be transmitted to other air and surface assets using a secure radio link.

▲ Lockheed P-3B Orion

333 Sqn, Royal Norwegian AF / Andøya, early 1980s

Norway's extensive coastline and proximity to Soviet naval bases on the Kola Peninsula made the maritime patrol mission a vital component of the nation's defensive strategy. Based at Andøya in the north of the country, 333 Sqn was the first European operator of the Orion, the first five examples arriving in 1969.

Specifications

Crew: 11	Dimensions: span 30.37m (99ft 8in); length
Powerplant: 4 x 3700kW (4600hp) Allison T56-A-	35.61m (116ft 9in); height 10.27m (33ft 8in)
14 turboprop engines	Weight: 60,780kg (134,000lb) loaded
Maximum speed: 766km/h (476mph)	Armament: up to 9070kg (20,000lb) of
Range: 4075km (2533 miles)	ordnance, including bombs, mines and
Service ceiling: 8625m (28,300ft)	torpedoes

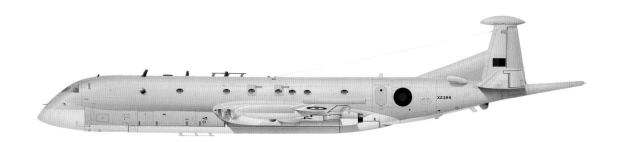

▲ British Aerospace Nimrod MR.Mk 2P

42 Sqn, RAF / Kinloss, early 1980s

The definitive RAF maritime patrol aircraft of the Cold War – and one of the most capable in its class – the Nimrod replaced the Shackleton MR variants. The MR.Mk 2P version of the Nimrod appeared during the Falklands campaign, and introduced an aerial refuelling capability, with a forward fuselage probe.

Specifications

Crew: 12	Dimensions: span 35m (114ft 10in); length
Powerplant: 4 x 53.98kN (12,140lb thrust)	38.65m (126ft 9in); height 9.14m (31ft)
Rolls-Royce Spey Mk 250 turbofans	Weight: 87,090kg (192,000lb) loaded
Maximum speed: 925km/h (575mph)	Armament: provision for 6123kg (13,500lb) of
Range: 9265km (5755 miles) (on internal fuel only)	dropped stores
Service ceiling: 12,800m (41,995ft)	

Naval Helicopters
1948–1989

One of the answers to the ASW challenge during the Cold War was the deployment of the helicopter as an adjunct to surface warships, or as a coastal defensive asset.

THE HELICOPTER SAW only limited use in World War II, but it was already apparent that its capabilities suited it particularly to operations from warships. The first naval rotorcraft were handicapped by their limited range and payload, but as improved designs became available, the importance of the helicopter as a naval tool increased exponentially. Indeed, by the end of the Cold War, almost all of the world's navies deployed helicopters, while operators of fixed-wing maritime aircraft remained limited.

In addition to the ASW role, Cold War naval helicopters routinely undertook search and rescue (SAR), plane guard (aboard aircraft carriers), amphibious assault, mine countermeasures and vertical replenishment (Vertrep) tasks, as well as more mundane liaison and communications work. Towards the end of this period, the helicopter was being increasingly used as a weapon deployed against surface targets, primarily through the introduction of anti-ship missiles. The USSR was unusual in deploying helicopters for targeting and mid-course guidance of land attack and anti-ship missiles launched from Soviet Navy warships.

Land-based designs
As well as the typically compact designs specifically intended for use from surface vessels, land-based maritime helicopters were also fielded, generally undertaking ASW and SAR missions in coastal areas.

In common with their fixed-wing counterparts, ASW helicopters relied upon sensors that included radar, MAD (normally a towed 'bird' sensor) and sonobuoys. A key advantage offered by the helicopter, however, was its ability to operate a dipping sonar in place of disposable sonobuoys. The number of sensor operators was clearly restricted by cabin dimensions, but the crew were provided with consoles similar to those found in fixed-wing maritime patrol aircraft.

Specifications

Crew: 4	Dimensions: rotor diameter 15.7m (51ft 8in);
Powerplant: 2 x 671kW (900shp) Glushnekov	length 9.8m (32ft 3in); height 5.4m (17ft 7in)
GTD-3 engines	Weight: 7100kg (16,100lb) loaded
Maximum speed: 220km/h (137mph)	Armament: none
Range: 400km (247 miles)	
Service ceiling: 3500m (11,483ft)	

▲ **Kamov Ka-25**
AVMF / mid-1970s

Serving both as a shipborne and land-based ASW helicopter, the Ka-25 featured a co-axial main rotor arrangement that made it notably compact. In addition to the ASW version depicted here, the Ka-25 was also fielded in utility/SAR and missile-targeting variants, the latter providing over-the-horizon guidance for missiles.

▲ Lynx HAS.Mk 2

The British-designed Lynx was representative of the lighter ASW helicopters
intended for operations from the flight decks of destroyers and frigates.

Weapons were similar too, but typically lighter, and chiefly comprised torpedoes and depth bombs.

For NATO, the 'standard' shipborne naval helicopters were successive Sikorsky designs, the maritime versions of the S-55 being followed by the S-58. The purpose-designed S-61 Sea King appeared in 1959, and was finally superseded by the S-70 Seahawk. The first three of these types were also built under licence in the UK and all were widely exported, with additional licence production undertaken elsewhere. The Lynx, a British design optimized for use from the decks of smaller warships, was also widely deployed towards the end of the Cold War.

▲ Mil Mi-14

AVMF / mid-1970s

The Mi-14 was the primary Soviet shore-based ASW helicopter, and carried a
useful load of ordnance that could include rocket-propelled torpedoes and nuclear
depth charges. Illustrated is the ASW version (with MAD 'bird' stowed behind the
rear fuselage), but mine countermeasures and SAR versions were also used.

Specifications

Crew: 4

Powerplant: 2 x 1400kW (1950shp) Klimov
TV3-117MT turboshaft engines

Maximum speed: 230km/h (143mph)

Range: 1135km (705 miles)

Service ceiling: 3500m (11,500ft)

Dimensions: rotor diameter 21.29m (69ft 10in);
length 18.38m (60ft 3in); height 6.93m (22ft 9in)

Weight: 14,000kg (30,865lb) loaded

Armament: 1 x E45-75A torpedo or B-1 nuclear
depth bomb

U.S. Marine Air Power
1950–1989

While other Cold War protagonists also maintained an amphibious warfare capability, none was as powerful as that of the U.S. Marine Corps, which also boasted organic fixed-wing air power.

AMPHIBIOUS WARFARE HAD been a decisive factor in World War II, and the U.S. Marine Corps (USMC) retained this capability in the postwar period, with a powerful force of amphibious assault ships supported by both shipborne helicopters and fixed-wing aviation. Ultimately, the latter would also include V/STOL AV-8 Harrier warplanes capable of operating from the decks of assault carriers.

Successive military actions in Korea and Suez during the 1950s reinforced the importance of amphibious assault, with the latter conflict also demonstrating the efficacy of the helicopter as an assault transport, replacing the landing craft employed in earlier conflicts. After Suez, the helicopter carrier came to prominence, able to deliver troops and equipment to the beachhead and beyond.

Marine Corps air assets

Typically, Cold War doctrine saw the USMC's amphibious capability expressed as a self-contained rapid-reaction force that could be deployed to trouble spots, from where they would stand just over the horizon, awaiting the call to action. Where U.S. Marines were fighting ground campaigns, as in both Korea and Vietnam, USMC air power was also on hand, operating from land bases alongside USAF warplanes. In a further measure of USMC air power versatility, its aircraft also routinely operated from carrier decks, components within mixed air wings that also included U.S. Navy squadrons.

A prime example of the use of USMC amphibious forces as a tool for rapidly intervening in a global crisis was presented in Lebanon in August 1983, when the U.S. took action in support of a multi-national stabilizing force in the country. The amphibious assault ship USS *Iwo Jima* and the embarked 24th Marine Expeditionary Unit were on station, standing off the coast, when two U.S. servicemen were killed in Beirut. The immediate response was conducted by AH-1T SeaCobra attack helicopters from the *Iwo Jima*, supported by a naval artillery bombardment.

By the mid-1980s, the USMC numbered almost 200,000 soldiers within three mobile divisions. Each

▲ McDonnell Douglas RF-4B Phantom II
VMFP-3, USMC / El Toro, early 1980s

Wearing the low-visibility markings typical of the 1980s, this RF-4B was flown by the U.S. Marine Corps photo-reconnaissance squadron VMFP-3, based at El Toro, California. The RF-4B variant was developed specifically for the USMC and also provided a tactical reconnaissance capability for U.S. Navy Carrier Air Wings.

Specifications

Crew: 2	Service ceiling: 18,898m (62,000ft)
Powerplant: 2 x 75.5kN (17,000lb) General	Dimensions: span 11.7m (38ft 5in);
Electric J79-GE-8 engines	length 17.77m (58ft 3in); height 4.95m (16ft 3in)
Maximum speed: 2390km/h (1485mph)	Weight: 20,231kg (44,600lb) loaded
Range: 3701km (2300 miles)	Armament: none

▲ Grumman A-6E Intruder
VMA(AW)-121, USMC / El Toro, early 1980s

The Intruder was the most capable strike asset deployed by the USMC during the Cold War, eventually equipping five squadrons. Key features of the A-6E model included a new multi-mode navigation radar and computerized nav/attack system. VMA(AW)-121 'Green Knights' was home-based at El Toro, California.

Specifications

Crew: 2	(54ft 9in); height 4.93m (16ft 2in)
Powerplant: 2 x 41.4kN (9300lb) Pratt & Whitney	Weight: 26,581kg (58,600lb) loaded
J52-P-8A turbojets	Armament: five external hardpoints with
Maximum speed: 1043km/h (648mph)	provision for up to 8165kg (18,000lb)
Range: 1627km (1011 miles)	of stores, including nuclear weapons,
Service ceiling: 14,480m (47,500ft)	conventional and guided bombs, air-to-surface
Dimensions: span 16.15m (53ft); length 16.69m	missiles and drop tanks

division was allocated a Marine Air Wing, operating around 315 aircraft. As well as the assault helicopters used to bring troops and stores ashore, the MAW also included fighters, strike/attack aircraft, close support aircraft and helicopters, reconnaissance and electronic warfare aircraft, plus forward air control and liaison assets. In total, around 60 amphibious warfare vessels were available to support USMC operations by 1987.

Combined, the three active force MAWs had a strength of around 35,600 personnel, 440 fixed-wing aircraft and 100 armed helicopters by the mid-1980s. In terms of air assets, 12 fighter squadrons were provided, most of these equipped with the F-4, although the F/A-18 began to enter service in the early 1980s. A total of 13 attack squadrons included three AV-8 units, while the remaining 10 were divided equally between the A-4M and the A-6E. Single squadrons operated the photo-reconnaissance RF-4B and the EA-6B electronic warfare platform. Both fighter and attack squadrons regularly embarked on carriers as part of the Carrier Air Wing.

In addition to the three active force Marine Air Wings, the U.S. Marine Air Reserve offered support in the shape of the 4th Marine Aircraft Wing, comprising four aviation groups. These maintained 11 squadrons, with F-4N/S, A-4E, A-4F/M, EA-6A, OV-10 and KC-130 aircraft on strength. The introduction of the KC-130 was spurred by the experience of Vietnam, when the USMC required an aerial refuelling capability to deploy aircraft over long distances at short notice.

Support and second-line fixed-wing USMC air assets included the OV-10D (two squadrons for observation and forward air control), three assault transport/tanker squadrons with KC-130s, while TA-4J and OA-4M aircraft served with headquarters and maintenance units. A further 10 reserve squadrons operated helicopters, including the AH-1J, UH-1E/N, CH-53A and CH-46.

Rotary-wing fleet

Towards the end of the Cold War, the USMC operated 25 helicopter squadrons, eight of these equipped with the heavy-lift CH-53D/E. A further 11 front-line squadrons flew the medium-lift CH-46E/F. The UH-1N utility helicopter and the AH-1T attack helicopter were each flown by three squadrons.

In a European Cold War context, the USMC was expected to be active in Norway, in support of NATO's Northern Front. For this purpose, combat equipment was pre-positioned in Norway, with enough materiel to support a full USMC brigade. Had the Warsaw Pact launched an attack against Norway, up to three Marine Amphibious Brigades would have been on hand to counter it, supported by Norwegian forces, the Netherlands-UK Amphibious Group and a Canadian brigade, backed by air power.

The USMC's original helicopter carriers (LPHs) were the 'Essex' (modified fleet carriers) and 'Iwo

▲ **McDonnell Douglas/BAe AV-8A Harrier**

VMA-231, USMC / Cherry Point, late 1970s

The USMC's surviving force of Harriers had been upgraded from AV-8A to improved AV-8C standard by the mid-1980s, including improved defensive countermeasures systems. Armed with underwing rocket pods and cannon pods under the fuselage, this example, from VMA-231 'Ace of Spades', served at Cherry Point, North Carolina.

Specifications

Crew: 1

Powerplant: 1x 91.2kN (20,500lb) thrust Rolls-Royce Pegasus 10 vectored-thrust turbofan engine

Maximum speed: 1186km/h (737mph)

Range: 5560km (3455 miles)

Service ceiling: 15,240m (50,000ft)

Dimensions: span 7.7m (25ft 3in); length 13.87m (45ft 6in); height 3.45m (11ft 4in)

Weight: 11,340kg (25,000lb) loaded

Armament: maximum of 2268kg (5000lb) of stores on underfuselage and underwing points; one 30mm Aden gun or similar gun, with 150 rounds, rockets and bombs

Jima' classes. These were followed by altogether more capable vessels, the 'Tarawa' class, the first of which was commissioned in 1976. The final LPH was decommissioned in 1988, leaving the 'Tarawa' LHA as the primary base for USMC amphibious assault aviation. Each 'Tarawa' had a well deck to accommodate landing craft, amphibious assault vehicles and an assault hovercraft. The large flight deck could support any USMC helicopter, as well as the AV-8 Harrier and, when required, the OV-10 Bronco forward air control aircraft. The adoption of the British-designed Harrier by the USMC marked a

significant milestone, because high-speed air power could now be called upon over the beachhead, without the need for a local airfield or conventional carrier. USMC Harriers operated from shore bases, highways, beaches and a variety of warships, their typical mission being close air support, armed with rockets, guns and napalm. Further U.S. development of the basic design saw the fielding of the AV-8B Harrier II, a much improved aircraft with an entirely new wing of increased span and carbon-fibre construction, for additional fuel capacity and an increased payload.

Specifications

Crew: 1	(excluding probe) 12.22m (40ft 1.5in);
Powerplant: 1 x 49.82kN (11,500lb) thrust Pratt	height 4.66m (15ft 3in)
& Whitney J52-P408 turbojet engine	Weight: 12,437kg (27,420lb) loaded
Maximum speed: 1083km/h (673mph)	Armament: 2 x 20mm Mk 12 cannon; provision
Range: 3310km (2200 miles)	for 3720kg (8200lb) of stores, including AIM-
Service ceiling: 14,935m (49,000ft)	9G Sidewinder AAMs, rocket-launcher pods and
Dimensions: span 8.38m (27ft 6in); length	ECM pods

▲ Douglas A-4M Skyhawk II

VMA-324, USMC / Beaufort, early 1970s

The ultimate new-build, single-seat Skyhawk version was the A-4M, with numerous updates that included a reprofiled fin and canopy, a braking parachute and an uprated J52 engine, allowing operations from shorter airstrips. VMA-324 flew this aircraft from Beaufort, South Carolina, home of Marine Air Group 31.

▲ AH-1J SeaCobra

USMC / early 1980s

Developed specifically to meet USMC close-support requirements, the AH-1J introduced a twin-turboshaft powerplant to the AH-1 airframe, and its chin turret mounted a three-barrel M197 20mm cannon. USMC SeaCobras operated from ships and were used to support ground operations, particularly beach assaults.

Specifications

Crew: 2	length 13.5m (44ft 3in); height 4.1m (13ft 5in)
Powerplant: 1 x 1342kW (1800shp) Pratt &	Weight: 4525kg (9979lb) loaded
Whitney Canada T400-CP-400 turboshaft	Armament: 1 x 20mm (0.8in) M197 cannon;
Maximum speed: 352km/h (218mph)	14 x 70mm (2.75in) Mk 40 rockets;
Range: 571km (355 miles)	8 x 127mm (5in) Zuni rockets; 2 AIM-9
Service ceiling: 3475m (11,398ft)	anti-aircraft missiles
Dimensions: rotor diameter 13.4m (43ft 11in);	

Chapter 3

Strategic Bombers and Air Defence

The dawn of the nuclear age and the destruction of the cities of Hiroshima and Nagasaki in August 1945 changed the face of aerial bombing immeasurably. Prior to the development of ICBMs, manned bombers remained the only nuclear-delivery platforms with intercontinental reach. Throughout the Cold War, nuclear-armed bombers would play a major role in the strategic balance, and the threat they posed demanded ever more advanced interceptors to be fielded for national defence.

◄ **Boeing B-52G Stratofortress**
One of the most potent symbols of the superpower standoff, the Stratofortress served with the USAF from 1955 until the end of the Cold War. Towards the end of this period, B-52Gs like this were armed with cruise missiles in order to strike from beyond the reach of hostile air defences.

U.S. Bombers
1946–1989

Created in 1946, Strategic Air Command (SAC) would eventually provide two elements of the U.S. strategic nuclear triad: intercontinental ballistic missiles (ICBMs) and manned bombers.

THROUGHOUT THE COLD War, SAC aircraft stood on alert at their bases in the U.S., and made frequent forward deployments to locations including the UK, Guam and Okinawa. Prior to the fielding of land-based ICBMs and submarine-launched ballistic missiles, SAC's bomber fleet was the most visible – and viable – expression of U.S. nuclear power.

SAC's original equipment was based around the wartime B-29 and its improved development, the B-50. The formidable B-36 arrived in service in 1948, providing intercontinental range for the first time. The arrival of the jet engine meant the B-36 would remain interim equipment, however, and SAC's first all-jet bomber, the B-47, entered service in 1950, and

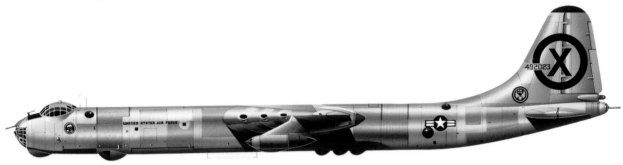

Specifications

Crew: 15

Powerplant: 6 x 2610kW (3500hp) Pratt & Whitney R-4360-41 engines

Maximum speed: 613km/h (381mph)

Range: 13,156km (8175 miles) (with bomb load)

Service ceiling: 12,954m (42,000ft)

Dimensions: span 70.10m (230ft); length 49.39m (162ft 1in); height 14.24m (46ft 8in)

Weight: 148,778kg (328,000lb) loaded

Armament: 16 x 20mm (0.8in) cannon; 32,659kg (72,000lb) bomb load

▲ Convair RB-36D Peacemaker

72nd Bomb Squadron (Heavy), SAC / Travis AFB, 1950s

A force of almost 400 B-36s formed the backbone of SAC between 1948-59. The type was the largest bomber to serve with USAF, the RB-36D illustrated being a strategic reconnaissance version, with a forward bomb bay adapted to carry 14 cameras. The aircraft's crew was increased from 15 to 22.

Specifications

Crew: 3

Powerplant: 6 x 26.54kW (5970lb thrust) General Electric J47-GE-23 turbojets

Maximum speed: 978km/h (608mph)

Combat radius: 3162km (1965 miles)

Service ceiling: 10,333m (33,900ft)

Dimensions: span 35.4m (116ft); length 32.56m (106ft 10in); height 8.51m (27ft 11in)

Weight: 83,873kg (184,908lb) loaded

Armament: 2 x 12.7mm (0.5in) MGs; up to 8165kg (18,000lb) bombs

▲ Boeing B-47B Stratojet

SAC / 1950s

The B-47B was the first true production version of the Stratojet and entered service in 1951, with 399 examples being built. This version introduced an in-flight refuelling capability, with uprated engines on later production machines. B-47 wings regularly deployed to bases in the Pacific, North Africa and UK.

equipped 28 bomb wings before the end of the decade. Using forward bases and aerial refuelling to extend its range, the B-47 was joined in 1955 by the B-52, which combined jet performance with intercontinental capability. Such was the value of the B-52 that it remained a front-line element of the U.S. nuclear deterrent until the end of the Cold War. In the mid-1980s, the B-52 was responsible for carrying 45 per cent of the total U.S. strategic megatonnage.

Advances in air defences threatened to render free-fall bombers obsolete by the early 1960s. Responses included a move to low-level operations and

introduction of the Short-Range Attack Missile in 1972. This was followed in the early 1980s by cruise missiles carried by B-52s, and a corresponding switch in targets from cities and industry to high-priority military installations and 'counter-force' targets.

By the end of the Cold War, SAC's B-52 force was complemented by supersonic FB-111As, while the advanced B-1B was active in SAC from the mid-1980s, carrying a payload of free-fall bombs. In terms of numbers, SAC in the 1980s was responsible for around one-fifth of U.S. strategic weapons, but wielded almost half of the total megatonnage.

▲ Boeing KC-97G

SAC, 1950s

The availability of aerial refuelling was a critical aspect of SAC's nuclear deterrent, which originally kept nuclear-armed aircraft airborne on 24-hour alert, ready to launch an attack at the shortest notice. The KC-97G version, of which 592 were built, was equipped for tanking, troop transport and cargo freighting duties.

Specifications

Crew: 5

Powerplant: 4 x 2610kW (3500hp) Pratt & Whitney R-4360-59B Wasp Major engines

Maximum speed: 604km/h (375mph)

Range: 6920km (4300 miles)

Service ceiling: 9205m (30,200ft)

Dimensions: span 43.05m (141ft 2in); length 35.79m (117ft 5in); height 11.68m (38ft 4in)

Weight: 69,400kg (153,000lb) loaded

Armament: none

Specifications

Crew: 6

Powerplant: 8 x 46.68kN (10,500lb) thrust Pratt & Whitney J57-P-29WA engines

Maximum speed: 1027km/h (638mph)

Range: 13,419km (8338 miles)

Service ceiling: 14,082m (46,200ft)

Dimensions: span 56.39m (185ft); length 47.73m (156ft 7in); height 14.73m (48ft 4in)

Weight: 204,116kg (450,000lb) loaded

Armament: 4 x 12.7mm (0.5in) M-3 MGs; up to 19,504kg (43,000lb) of bombs

▲ Boeing B-52C Stratofortress

7th Bomb Wing, SAC / Carswell AFB, 1971

Displaying the white undersides intended to reflect nuclear flash, the B-52C offered much improved performance and equipment compared to its B-52B predecessor, and 35 examples were completed. This particular aircraft served at Carswell AFB, Fort Worth, as part of the 2nd AF, and was one of the last C-model aircraft in service.

Specifications

Crew: 6

Powerplant: 8 x 61.1kN (13,750lb) Pratt & Whitney J57-P-43W turbojets

Maximum speed: 1014km/h (630mph)

Range: 13,680km (8500 miles)

Service ceiling: 16,765m (55,000ft)

Dimensions: span 56.4m (185ft); length 48m

(157ft 7in); height 12.4m (40ft 8in)

Weight: 221,500kg (448,000lb) loaded

Armament: remotely controlled tail mounting with 4 x .5in MGs; normal internal bomb capacity 12,247kg (27,000lb), including all SAC special weapons; external pylons for 2 x Hound Dog missiles

▲ Boeing B-52G Stratofortress

69th Bomb Squadron, 42nd Bomb Wing, SAC / Loring AFB, 1974

Penultimate model of the Stratofortress was the B-52G, this example being flown by the 69th BS during the 1974 Giant Voice bombing competition. The aircraft was home-based at Loring AFB, Maine. The B-52G introduced a remote-controlled tail gun turret, with all six crew now grouped together in a single forward compartment.

Specifications

Crew: 2

Powerplant: 2 x 56kN (12,500lbf) dry thrust Pratt & Whitney TF30-P-7 engines

Maximum speed: 2338km/h (1452mph)

Range: 7242km (4500 miles)

Service ceiling: 17,373m (57,000ft)

Dimensions: span 21.33m (70ft); length 22.4m (73ft 6in); height 5.18m (17ft)

Weight: 54,105kg (119,250lb) loaded

Armament: 6 x AGM-69A SRAMs or up to 16,100kg (35,500lb) bomb load

▲ General Dynamics FB-111A

380th Bomb Wing, SAC / Plattsburgh AFB, early 1980s

Just over 60 FB-111As were in use with SAC in the 1980s. The aircraft could be armed with Short-Range Attack Missiles (SRAMs) as well as free-fall (gravity) bombs. The FB-111A, a 'strategic' version of the basic F-111 strike aircraft, served with two wings, at Pease, New Hampshire, and Plattsburgh, New York.

Soviet Bombers
1946–1989

While the threat of Soviet bombers was taken extremely seriously in the West, the USSR ultimately regarded manned bombers as a lower priority than ICBMs and missile submarines.

IN THE EARLY 1950s, Soviet Long-Range Aviation (DA) relied on the piston-engined Tu-4 bomber, a copy of the American B-29. After a protracted development, the Tu-4 entered service in 1949. Theoretically nuclear capable, only a handful were ever equipped to carry operational atomic weapons, and the bomber's range was strictly limited.

The first modern Soviet bomber to enter service was the Tu-16, which began to be delivered in 1954, much to the consternation of Western defence officials. The DA had entirely replaced the Tu-4 by the early 1960s, by which time the Tu-16 was the standard bomber type. Versions were developed to undertake diverse roles including reconnaissance, aerial refuelling, electronic intelligence (ELINT) and electronic countermeasures (ECM) support.

Long-range equipment

With few bases available in the Soviet Arctic, the mid-1950s saw the experimental use of Tu-16s from temporary airstrips on tundra or Arctic ice. These proved unsuitable for use by heavy bombers, but DA's reach was improved through the introduction of the Tu-95 bomber in 1956. The turboprop-powered Tu-95 proved far more durable than the jet-powered M-4 bomber, which was also intended to offer intercontinental range. Although it entered service as a free-fall bomber in 1954, the M-4 (and its upgraded 3M derivative) was never satisfactory in this role and was eventually relegated to tanking duties.

The 1960s saw the increasing use of missile-carrying bombers. The supersonic Tu-22 superseded the Tu-16 with a number of units starting in 1962, but never entirely replaced its predecessor.

The intermediate-range Tu-16 would remain in large-scale service into the mid-1980s, by which time it had been supplanted by the Tu-22M theatre bomber, which was first deployed in 1972. In 1979, DA still retained almost 500 Tu-16s of various types. Starting in the mid-1970s the USSR was working on the long-range Tu-160, a supersonic bomber with cruise missile armament. The Tu-160 was beginning to enter service as the Cold War came to an end, by which time DA's long-range backbone was provided by the Tu-95MS variant armed with up to 16 air-launched cruise missiles with nuclear warheads.

Specifications

Crew: 4

Powerplant: 2 x 93.2kN (20,900lbf) Mikulin AM-3 M-500 turbojets

Maximum speed:1050km/h (656mph)

Range: 7200km (4500 miles)

Service ceiling: 12,800m (42,000ft)

Dimensions: span 33m (108ft 3in); length 34.8m (114ft 2in); height 10.36m (34ft)

Weight: 76,000kg (168,00lb) loaded

Armament: 6–7 x 23mm (0.9in) Nudelman-Rikhter NR-23 cannons; 9000kg (20,000lb) bomb load or 1 x Kh-10 anti-ship missile and 1 x Kh-26 anti-ship missile

▲ **Tupolev Tu-16**

Soviet Long-Range Aviation / mid-1950s

Soviet bombers were organized into Heavy Bomber Air Divisions (TBAD), each of which normally contained two Heavy Bomber Air Regiments (TBAP). In the early part of its service, a typical Tu-16 regiment had three squadrons: one of missile-carriers and two of free-fall bombers. The type was also used as an in-flight refuelling tanker.

Specifications

Crew: 7

Powerplant: 4 x 11,000kW (14,800shp) Kuznetsov NK-12MV turboprops

Maximum speed: 920km/h (575mph)

Range: 15,000km (9,400miles)

Service ceiling: 13,716m (45,000ft)

Dimensions: span 51.10m (167ft 8in); length 49.50m (162ft 5in); height 12.12m (39ft 9in)

Weight: 171,000kg (376,200lb) loaded

Armament: 1 or 2 x 23mm AM-23 cannon in tail turret and up to 15,000kg (33,000lb) of bombs

▲ **Tupolev Tu-95**

Soviet Long-Range Aviation / mid-1950s

The Tu-95 was the first Soviet bomber with genuine intercontinental range and served as the mainstay of DA until the end of the Cold War, ultimately being armed with cruise missiles. Illustrated is one of the very first Tu-95s to be built. Production of the Tu-95MS version was still under way when the Cold War ended.

British Bombers
1946–1970

Serving from 1955 until 1968, the RAF's V-Force provided Britain's strategic nuclear deterrent until superseded by the Royal Navy's Polaris submarine-launched missiles.

IN 1946 BRITISH chiefs-of-staff requested government approval for the development of a nuclear weapon, with the go-ahead given in January 1947. A new bomber would be required to carry the weapon, and to replace the ageing Lancasters, Lincolns and Mosquitoes with Bomber Command.

In the interim, ex-USAF B-29s were supplied for RAF use as Washingtons, while Canberras provided the RAF's initial jet bomber equipment, entering service in May 1951. In August 1952 the Vulcan and Victor were ordered as part of a three-tier bomber programme, these two advanced designs being complemented by the more conventional Valiant.

Until the V-Bombers became available, Bomber Command continued to rely on Lincolns and (from March 1950) Washingtons, the bomb bay of the

Specifications

Crew: 11

Powerplant: 4 x 1640kW (2,200hp) Wright R-3350-23 and 23A radial engines

Maximum speed: 574km/h (357mph)

Range: 9000km (5600 miles)

Service ceiling: 10,200m (33,600ft)

Dimensions: span 43.10m (141ft 3in);

length 30.20m (99ft); height 8.50m (29ft 7in)

Weight: 54,000kg (120,000lb) loaded

Armament: 10 x 12.7mm (.50in) caliber Browning M2/ANs, 2 x 12.7mm (.50in) and 1 x 20mm (.79in) M2 cannon in tail position plus bomb load of 9072kg (20,000lb)

▲ **Boeing Washington B.Mk 1**

90 Sqn, RAF / Marham, 1950–54

A total of 88 ex-USAAF Boeing B-29As were supplied to the RAF under MDAP as a stopgap between the Lincoln and the first jet bombers. The RAF's 90 Sqn operated the Washington (as the RAF's B-29 was known) from Marham and won trophies for visual bombing and gunnery excellence during 1952.

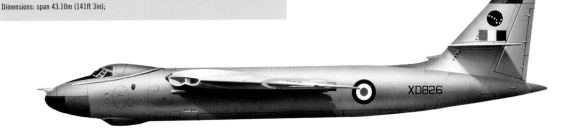

Specifications

Crew: 5

Powerplant: 4 x 44.7kN (10,054lb) Rolls-Royce Avon RA.28 turbojets

Maximum speed: 912km/h (576mph)

Range: 7242km (4500 miles)

Service ceiling: 16,460m (54,000ft)

Dimensions: span 34.85m (114ft 4in);

length 32.99m (108ft 3in); height 9.8m (32ft 2in)

Weight: 63,503kg (140,000lb) loaded

Armament: 1 x 4536kg (10,000lb) nuclear bomb or up to 9,525kg (21,000lb) conventional bombs

▲ **Vickers Valiant B.Mk 1**

7 Sqn, RAF / Honington, 1957–62

In October 1956 a Valiant dropped Britain's first air-launched nuclear weapon over southern Australia, and this was followed by a first British hydrogen bomb, dropped by another Valiant over Christmas Island in May 1957. Fatigue saw the Valiant prematurely withdrawn from service in 1964.

Canberra being too small for the carriage of early nuclear weapons. In October 1952 Britain's first nuclear device was detonated in western Australia and this weapon was adapted for service as the Blue Danube, the UK's first air-launched nuclear weapon, deployed from November 1953.

First of the V-bombers

By the end of 1957 the Washington had been almost completely replaced by seven Valiant bomber squadrons, and the following year the first hydrogen bombs were deployed, in the form of Yellow Sun.

The Vulcan B.Mk 1 entered operational service in February 1957 and would equip six front-line units. In April 1958, the first of four front-line Victor B.Mk 1 squadrons was stood up. However, the 1957

Defence White Paper effectively reduced the V-Force to the status of a stopgap nuclear deterrent pending the arrival of long-range missiles.

Improved Mk 2 versions of the Vulcan and Victor entered service in 1960 and 1962 respectively. Vulcan B.Mk 2s were flown by nine units, and Victor B.Mk 2s by two units, while Victor B.Mk 1s were converted for use as tankers. The loss of Gary Powers' U-2 in May 1960 pre-empted a switch to the low-level role. Valiants had already assumed a tactical nuclear strike role, while Vulcans and Victors begin to transition to the low-level mission in 1963, some being armed with Blue Steel missiles. The V-Force was finally relieved of its strategic role in July 1969. Victor B.Mk 2s were converted as tankers, while the Vulcan continued to serve in the low-level tactical role.

Specifications

Crew: 5	Dimensions: span 33.83m (111ft); length
Powerplant: 4 x 88.9kN (20,000lb) Olympus	30.45m (99ft 11in); height 8.28m (27ft 2in);
Mk.301 turbojets	Weight: 113,398kg (250,000lb) loaded
Maximum speed: 1038km/h (645mph)	Armament: internal weapon bay for up to
Range: 7403km/h (4600 miles)	21,454kg (47,198lb) bombs, or Blue Steel
Service ceiling: 19,810m (65,000ft)	nuclear missile

▲ **Avro Vulcan B.Mk 2**

617 Sqn, RAF / Scampton, early 1960s

The definitive B.Mk 2 version of the Vulcan arrived in 1960, with more powerful engines, in-flight refuelling capability, and a considerably modified wing of increased area. The Vulcan B.Mk 2 could be armed with the Blue Steel missile, as seen on this example, from 617 Sqn, which is painted in anti-flash white.

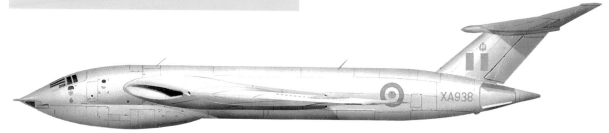

▲ **Handley Page Victor B.Mk 1**

10 Sqn, RAF / Cottesmore, early 1960s

Last of the three V-bombers to enter service, the crescent-winged Victor was first deployed by 10 Sqn at Cottesmore in April 1958. In common with many other B.Mk 1s, this aircraft, XA938, was later converted for use as an in-flight refuelling tanker. The first Victor tankers entered service with 55 Sqn in August 1965.

Specifications

Crew: 5	Dimensions: span 33.53m (110ft);
Powerplant: 4 x 49kN (11,050lbf) Armstrong	length 35.05m (114 ft 11in); height 8.15m
Siddeley Sapphire A.S.Sa.7 turbojets	(26ft 9in)
Maximum speed: 1,050km/h (650mph)	Weight: 75,000kg (165,000lb) loaded
Range: 4000km (2500 miles)	Armament: Up to 35 x 450kg (1,000lb) bombs
Service ceiling: 56,000ft (17,000m)	

U.S. Air Defence
1945–1989

Defence of the continental U.S. against a Soviet bomb or missile attack was entrusted starting in 1957 to North American Aerospace Defense Command (NORAD), covering the U.S. and Canada.

HEADQUARTERED AT CHEYENNE Mountain, Wyoming, NORAD consisted of both air and ground elements and provided early warning and defence against bombers and ICBMs. NORAD was in constant communication with SAC and the National Command Authorities, enabling the U.S. to launch a rapid nuclear counter-strike if required.

The limited reaction time in which to respond to a bomber attack from the USSR demanded the fielding of comprehensive interceptor defences. At the outset, the USAF's Air Defense Command (ADC) possessed over 50 interceptor squadrons, equipped with subsonic F-86D, F-89 and F-94 fighters, while Canada provided Sabres and CF-100s. After reaching a peak of around 1,000 interceptors, numbers were reduced in the 1960s as the true extent of the Soviet bomber threat was better understood.

By the mid-1970s ADC provided NORAD with just six F-106A squadrons, supported by Air National Guard (ANG) units operating F-101Bs, F-102s and F-106s, while Canada retained CF-101s. ADC was eventually disbanded, and its surviving units were passed on to SAC and Tactical Air Command (TAC), the latter being responsible for manned interceptors.

Early warning of bomber or missile attack was provided by a chain of radar stations including the Distant Early Warning Line, with important facilities in Alaska, Greenland and England in order to cover all lines of approach from the USSR and Asia.

Modernization

The 1980s saw improvements made to NORAD, in order to better counter the threat of low-level intruders and cruise missiles. F-15s began to replace F-106s in TAC, while ANG units received F-4s in order to allow F-101s and F-102s to be retired. As the Cold War came to an end, ANG F-106s had been withdrawn in favour of F-16s. Canada, meanwhile, introduced the CF-188 as a successor to its CF-101s in the early 1980s.

By the early 1980s, NORAD could also call upon TAC-operated E-3 AWACS, while the militarization of space saw the creation of Space Command specifically to defend against orbital threats.

Specifications	
Crew: 1	Dimensions: span 11.81m (38ft 9in); length
Powerplant: 1 x 17.1kN (3850lb) General	10.49m (34ft 5in); height 3.43m (11ft 3in)
Electric J33-GE-11 or Allison J33-A-9	Weight: 6,350kg (14,000lb) loaded
Maximum speed: 792km/h (492mph)	Armament: 6 x 12.7mm (0.5in) MGs,
Range: 2317km (1440 miles)	10 x 127mm (5in) rockets or 907kg
Service ceiling: 13,716m (45,000ft)	(2000lb) bombs

▲ **Lockheed F-80A Shooting Star**
61st Fighter Squadron, 56th Fighter Group, USAF / Selfridge Field, 1948
Operating from Selfridge Field, Michigan, this F-80A was on strength with the 61st Fighter Squadron in summer 1948. The F-80 (previously P-80) was the first jet fighter to enter service in the U.S., and around a dozen squadrons were equipped with the type for homeland defence by the late 1940s.

Specifications

Crew: 2

Powerplant: 1 x 26.7kN (6000lb) Allison J33-A-
33 turbojet

Maximum speed: 933km/h (580mph)

Range: 1850km/h (1150 miles)

Service ceiling: 14,630m (48,000ft)

Dimensions: span 11.85m (38ft 10.5in); length
12.2m (40ft 1in); height 3.89m (12ft 8in)

Weight: 7125kg (15,710lb) loaded

Armament: 4 x .5in machine guns

▲ Lockheed F-94B Starfire

334th Fighter Interceptor Squadron, USAF / mid-1950s

Carrying AN/APG-33 radar in the nose, the F-94B two-seat all-weather interceptor
carried an armament of four machine-guns, although the subsequent F-94C
Starfire version introduced rocket armament. Over two dozen ADC squadrons flew
F-94s, including units based in Alaska.

Specifications

Crew: 1

Powerplant: 1 x 76.5kN (17,200lb) Pratt &
Whitney J57-P-23 turbojet

Maximum speed: 1328km/h (825mph)

Range: 2172km (1350 miles)

Service ceiling: 16,460m (54,000ft)

Dimensions: span 11.62m (38ft 1.5in); length
20.84m (68ft 4.5in); height 6.46m (21ft 2.5in)

Weight: 14,288kg (31,500lb) loaded

Armament: Various combinations of AIM
missiles, some aircraft fitted with 12 x 70mm
(2.75in) folding-fin rockets

▲ Convair F-106A Delta Dart

87th Fighter Interceptor Squadron, USAF / K. I. Sawyer AFB, 1968–85

A successor to the F-102, the F-106 offered much improved performance and an
armament that included Falcon guided missiles and the Genie nuclear rocket.
Seen here in service with an active-duty ADC unit at K. I. Sawyer AFB, Michigan,
the type continued in service with ANG units into the mid-1980s.

Specifications

Crew: 2

Powerplant: 2 x 75.6kN (17,000lb) General
Electric J79-GE-15 turbojets

Maximum speed: 2414km/h (1500mph)

Range: 2817km (1750 miles)

Service ceiling: 18,300m (60,000ft)

Dimensions: span 11.7m (38ft 5in); length

17.76m (58ft 3in); height 4.96m (16ft 3in)

Weight: 26,308kg (58,000lb) loaded

Armament: 4 x AIM-7 Sparrow; two wing pylons
for 2 x AIM-7, or 4 x AIM-9 Sidewinder,
provision for 20mm M-61 cannon; provision
for stores to a maximum weight of 6219kg
(13,500lb)

▲ McDonnell Douglas F-4C Phantom II

*171st Fighter Interceptor Squadron / Selfridge ANGB, Michigan ANG,
1972–78*

The initial, minimum-change USAF version of the Phantom, the F-4C (originally
designated F-110) was passed on to ANG units once its active-duty days were
over. This example, which carries an infrared sensor under the nose, is seen in
service with an ANG squadron in 1980.

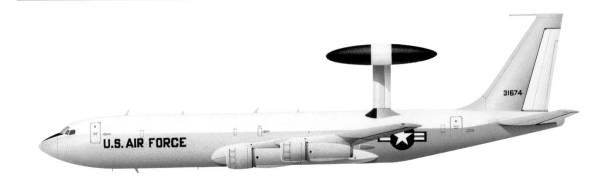

Specifications

Crew: 4

Powerplant: 4 x 93kN (21,000lb) Pratt & Whitney
TF33-PW-100A turbofan engines

Maximum speed: 855km/h (530mph)

Range: 7400km (4598 miles)

Service ceiling: 12,500m (41,000ft)

Dimensions: span 44.42m (145ft 9in); length
46.61m (152ft 11in); height 12.6m (41ft 4in)

Weight: 147,400kg (325,000lb) loaded

Armament: none

▲ **Boeing E-3A Sentry**

USAF, early 1980s

The first production E-3A Sentry was aircraft 73-1674, preceded by a pair of EC-137D
test aircraft. The E-3A AWACS (Airborne Warning And Control System) was based
around the AN/APY-1 radar, housed in a rotating radome. The radar could provide
surveillance of the entire airspace out to a range of around 400km (250 miles).

Soviet Air Defence
1946–1989

**The Air Defence Forces (PVO) existed as a separate branch of the Soviet military and was
equipped with a succession of dedicated interceptors with which to tackle Western bombers.**

TASKED WITH DEFENDING the USSR against
bombers, and later also against missile strikes, the
PVO was maintained on a high state of alert.
Ultimately, its functions included providing warning

of any attack and defeating bombers and missiles
through the use of manned interceptors and
successive layers of surface-to-air missiles (SAMs).
The PVO consisted of a number of commands,

Specifications

Crew: 2

Powerplant: 2 x 107.9kN (24,300lbf) Lyulka
AL-7F-2 turbojets

Maximum speed: 1740km/h (1089mph)

Range: 3200km (2000 miles)

Service ceiling: 18,000m (59,055ft)

Dimensions: span 18.10m (59ft 5in);
length 27.20m (89ft 4in); height 7m (23ft)

Weight: 40,000kg (88,185lb) loaded

Armament: 4 x Bisnovat R-4 air-to-air missiles

▲ **Tupolev Tu-128**

IA-PVO

The largest interceptor to enter service anywhere in the world, the Tu-128 was
tailored for long-range patrol missions in defence of the USSR's vast and
featureless northern and Arctic frontiers. The two-seat fighter was equipped with
four R-4 series air-to-air missiles and a powerful interception radar.

Specifications

Crew: 2

Powerplant: 2 x 66.8kN (13,669lb) Tumanskii
   R-11 turbojets

Maximum speed: 1180km/h (733mph)

Maximum combat radius 925km (575 miles)

Service ceiling: 16,000m (52,495ft)

Dimensions: span 12.95m (42ft 6in); length
   (long-nose late production) 23m (75ft 7.5in);
   height 3.95m (12ft 11.5in)

Weight: 19,000kg (41,890lb) loaded

Armament: 4 x underwing pylons for two AA-2,
   AA-2-2 or AA-3 air-to-air missiles

▲ Yakovlev Yak-28P

IA-PVO / mid-1960s

The Yak-28P was part of a family of twin-engined tactical jets that also included bomber and reconnaissance aircraft for Frontal Aviation use. The two-seat Yak-28P entered service with an IA-PVO unit defending the missile base at Semipalatinsk in November 1963. The last examples were finally retired in 1988.

▲ Sukhoi Su-15

IA-PVO / 1970s

The Su-15 gained notoriety for its role in the destruction of a Korean Airlines 747 airliner in September 1983. The twin-engined, all-weather interceptor was part of a new wave of equipment introduced by the IA-PVO in the 1970s, and could carry radar- and infrared-homing missiles as well as 23mm cannon pods.

Specifications

Crew: 1

Powerplant: 2 x 60.8kN (13,668lb) Tumanskii
   R-11F2S-300 turbojets

Maximum speed: 2230km/h (1386mph)

Combat radius: 725km (450 miles)

Service ceiling: 20,000m (65,615ft)

Dimensions: span 8.61m (28ft 3in); length

21.33m (70ft); height 5.1m (16ft 8in)

Weight: 18,000kg (39,680lb) loaded

Armament: 4 x external pylons for two R8M
   medium-range air-to-air missiles outboard and
   2 x AA-8 'Aphid' short-range AAMs inboard,
   plus 2 x pylons for 23mm UPK-23 cannon pods
   or drop tank

including the Radio-Technical Troops (responsible for surveillance and control), SAM Troops, Missile and Space Defence Forces (including early warning and missile defence) and Fighter Aviation (IA-PVO).

The first postwar equipment for the IA-PVO included modifications of the initial generation of jet fighters, such as the MiG-9, MiG-15 and MiG-17.

Second generation

The IA-PVO entered the supersonic era through the introduction of dedicated interceptors, rather than adaptations of Frontal Aviation types. Typical of these new aircraft were missile-armed and all-weather aircraft including the Su-9, Su-11, Yak-25P, Yak-28P and Tu-128. These were complemented by MiG-21 variants optimized for point defence.

Starting in the late 1960s, new equipment arrived in the form of the MiG-25, Su-15 and MiG-23, while a basic airborne early warning (AEW)

▲ Mikoyan-Gurevich MiG-31

The MiG-31 was the first IA-PVO interceptor capable of tracking and engaging multiple targets. Up to 10 targets could be tracked, and four of these engaged.

capability was introduced through the Tu-126. By the mid-1980s, IA-PVO regiments were beginning to re-equip with MiG-31 and Su-27 interceptors with improved capability against low-flying targets. These fighters operated with a new AEW aircraft, the A-50.

Specifications

Crew: 1

Powerplant: 1 x 98kN (22,046lb) Rumanskii
R-27F2M-300 turbojet

Maximum speed: 2445km/h (1520mph)

Range: 966km (600 miles)

Service ceiling: over 18,290m (60,000ft)

Dimensions: span 13.97m (45ft 10in) spread
and 7.78m (25ft 6.25in) swept; length 16.71m
(54ft 10in); height 4.82m (15ft 9.75in)

Weight: 18,145kg (40,000lb) loaded

Armament: 1 x 23mm GSh-23L cannon, AA-3,
AA-7 and/or AA-8 air-to-air missiles

▲ **Mikoyan-Gurevich MiG-23M**

IA-PVO

As well as equipping Frontal Aviation units in a tactical role, the MiG-23 was
supplied to the PVO for homeland defence. The MiG-23M was the first major
production version of the variable-geometry fighter and introduced a new radar
capable of illuminating targets for semi-active radar-homing R-23 missiles.

British Air Defence
1946–1989

**The experience of World War II meant the RAF was well aware of the importance of securing the
UK's airspace, and powerful air defences were maintained throughout the Cold War.**

BY 1946 THE RAF had reduced its fighter strength
to 24 squadrons with which to defend the UK,
these being equipped with Mosquito night-fighters,
Hornet day fighters, as well as Meteor and Vampire

jets. The burgeoning Soviet bomber threat and the
detonation of the USSR's first nuclear device in
September 1949 saw RAF Fighter Command re-
equipped and expanded, with 45 squadrons available

▲ **Gloster Meteor F.Mk 8**

500 Sqn, RAuxAF / West Malling, 1954

Flown by the commanding officer of 500 Sqn, this Meteor day fighter is typical of
the type in service with the Royal Auxiliary Air Force. This particular aircraft flew
from West Malling in 1954. The F.Mk 8 was the most numerous version of the
Meteor and featured a revised canopy and an additional belly fuel tank.

Specifications

Crew: 1

Powerplant: 2 x 16.0kN (3600lb) Rolls-Royce
Derwent 8 turbojets

Maximum speed: 962km/h (598mph)

Range: 1580km (980 miles)

Service ceiling: 13,106m (43,000ft)

Dimensions: span 11.32m (37ft 2in); length
13.58m (44ft 7in); height 3.96m (13ft)

Weight: 8664kg (19,100lb) loaded

Armament: 4 x 20mm Hispano cannon

by the end of 1951. Twenty Royal Auxiliary Air Force squadrons backed up regular Fighter Command units, this force having been re-formed in 1946, and organized on a regional basis. Initially equipped with piston-engined fighters, the RAuxAF later received Meteors and Vampires.

Fighter Command, which had been lagging behind in the fielding of swept-wing, transonic equipment, felt the lessons of the Korean War keenly. In late 1951 Fighter Command maintained 402 aircraft, mainly obsolescent Meteor and Vampire day fighters, supported by Meteor, Vampire and Mosquito night-fighters. Modern equipment finally arrived in the form of the Hunter, ordered as a 'super-

priority' programme in 1950, together with the disappointing Swift, which served with just one fighter unit. Beginning in October 1951, 29 squadrons eventually re-equipped with Hunters in the UK and Germany over a period of four years. The Hunter continued in use as day fighter until 1960, when it was replaced by the supersonic Lightning.

Force reduction

Having attained a 50-squadron peak in January 1957, the Defence White Paper of that year saw significant cuts to Fighter Command, and just 11 squadrons were available to defend the UK by 1962. As well as promising to entrust the future defence of

Specifications

Crew: 2	Service ceiling: 12,192m (40,000ft)
Powerplant: 2 x 16.0kN (3600lb) Rolls-Royce	Dimensions: wingspan 13.1m (43ft); length
Derwent 8 turbojets	14.78m (48ft 6in); height 4.22m (13ft 10in)
Maximum speed: 931km/h (579mph)	Weight: 9979kg (22,000lb) loaded
Range: 1580km (980 miles)	Armament: 4 x 20mm Hispano cannon

▲ Meteor NF.Mk 11

29 Sqn, RAF / Tangmere, 1951–58

The Meteor was also fielded in a series of two-seat night-fighter versions, the first of which was the NF.Mk 11, with AI radar in a lengthened nose, and an armament of four 20mm cannon carried in the wing. First flown in 1950, the NF.Mk 11 flew with 14 RAF squadrons, including 29 Sqn, based at Tangmere.

▲ Canadair Sabre F.Mk 4

92 Sqn, RAF / Linton on Ouse, 1954–56

Acquired as an interim measure pending the arrival of indigenous swept-wing fighter equipment, a total of 430 Canadian-built Sabres were received by the RAF via MDAP channels. This aircraft served with 92 Sqn at Linton on Ouse. The Sabre F.Mk 4 was similar to the USAF F-86E and most featured slatted wings.

Specifications

Crew: 1	Dimensions: span 11.29m (37ft 1in);
Powerplant: 1 x 32.35kW (7275lb) Avro Orenda	length 11.42m (37ft 6in); height 4.57m (15ft)
Mark 14 turbojet	Weight: 6628kg (14.613lb) loaded
Maximum speed: 1113km/h (692mph)	Armament: 6 x 12.7mm (0.50in) M2 Browning
Range: 1930km (1200 miles)	machine guns; up to 1360kg (3000lb) of
Service ceiling: 14,935m (49,000ft)	payload

the UK to guided missiles (most of which never materialized), the 1957 Defence White Paper cancelled all manned fighter development with the exception of the Lightning. At the same time, budget cuts saw the dissolution of the RAuxAF squadrons in spring 1957.

After 1957, priority was placed on the point defence of V-bomber and Thor missile bases, in keeping with NATO 'tripwire' strategy. This doctrine proposed meeting Soviet aggression with an all-out nuclear attack, but this strategy began to be replaced by 'flexible response' beginning in the late 1960s. With a return to limited nuclear warfare options and the use of conventional arms, the manned interceptor returned to the fore. Moreover, the UK's Cold War status as a 'rear depot' from where troops and materiel could be assembled in time of war, made it a prime target for Warsaw Pact air attack.

Starting in the mid-1970s, the RAF's interceptor arm was subject to improvement, with particular emphasis on countering low-level attack aircraft and cruise missiles. The two key aircraft projects for the

▲ Hawker Hunter F.Mk 5
1 Sqn, RAF / Tangmere, 1956-58

Powered by a Sapphire engine, the Hunter F.Mk 5 was otherwise similar to the F.Mk 4 (with an Avon engine) and was equipped with a pair of underwing pylons for drop tanks and also carried additional fuel in the wing leading edge. Based at Tangmere, 1 Sqn replaced its Meteor F.Mk 8s with Hunters in 1955.

Specifications

Crew: 1

Powerplant: 1 x 35.59kN (8000lb) Armstrong-
    Siddeley Sapphire turbojet engine

Maximum speed: 144km/h (710mph)

Range: 689km (490 miles)

Service ceiling: 15,240m (50,000ft)

Dimensions: span 10.26m (33ft 8in); length
    13.98m (45ft 10.5in); height 4.02m (13ft 2in)

Weight: 8501kg (18,742lb) loaded

Armament: 4 x 30mm Aden cannon; up to
    2722kg (6000lb) of bombs or rockets

▲ English Electric Lightning F.Mk 3
56 Sqn, RAF / Wattisham, 1965

Natural metal finish and striking markings were a feature of RAF Lightning units in the 1960s. Armed with a pair of Firestreak missiles, this F.Mk 3 was based at Wattisham in 1965. This variant introduced more powerful Avon engines, Red Top missile capability, an extended fin and improvements to the avionics suite.

Specifications

Crew: 1

Powerplant: 2 x 72.7kN (16,360lb) Rolls-Royce
    Avon 301R engines

Maximum speed: 2415km/h (1500mph)

Range: 1300km (800 miles)

Service ceiling: 18,000m (60,000ft)

Dimensions: span 10.62m (34ft 11in);
    length 16.84m (55ft 3in); height 5.97m
    (19ft 7in)

Weight: 18,900kg (41,700lb) loaded

Armament: 2 x 30mm ADEN cannon; up to
    2750kg (6000lb) of external ordnance

1980s were the Tornado F.Mk 2 interceptor and the Nimrod AEW.Mk 3 airborne early warning platform. The latter proved a failure, while the definitive Tornado F.Mk 3 was beginning to enter service towards the end of the Cold War, as a replacement for Lightning and Phantom interceptors.

Strike Command successor

Fighter Command was succeeded by No. 11 Group, part of RAF Strike Command, under permanent NATO control. Further upgrades saw the increased use of hardened aircraft shelters and command and control facilities, new surface-to-air missiles (SAMs),

mobile radars and armed Hawk trainers. In order to meet the Soviet bomber threat head on, most No. 11 Group airfields were located on the east coast, from where raiders could be met over the North Sea.

In the mid-1980s, the RAF maintained two interceptor quick reaction alert (QRA) facilities, each with two aircraft held on 10-minute readiness to cover northern (with a QRA based at Leuchars) and southern sectors (QRA shared by Wattisham, Coningsby and Binbrook). An interceptor force of mainly Lightnings and Phantoms was supported by a large tanker fleet of Victor, VC10 and Tristar aircraft, as well as Bloodhound and Rapier SAMs.

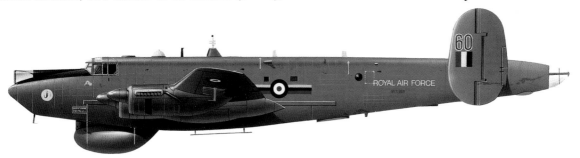

▲ Avro Shackleton AEW.Mk 2

8 Sqn, RAF / Lossiemouth, early 1980s

Until the end of the Cold War, the RAF's airborne early warning capability was entrusted to the veteran Shackleton AEW.Mk 2, based at Lossiemouth in Scotland. The U.S.-built AN/APS-20 surveillance radar was inherited from the Gannet AEW.Mk 3 aircraft that had once served aboard carriers of the Royal Navy.

Specifications

Crew: 8–10

Powerplant: 4 x 1831kW (2455hp) Rolls-Royce Griffon 57A V-12 piston engines

Maximum speed: 500km/h (311mph)

Range: 5440km (3380 miles)

Service ceiling: 6400m (21,000ft)

Dimensions: span 36.58m (120ft); length 26.59m (87ft 3in); height 5.1m (16ft 9in)

Weight: 39,010kg (86,000lb) loaded

Armament: none

Specifications

Crew: 2

Powerplant: 1 x 23.1kN (5200lb) Rolls-Royce/Turbomeca Adour Mk 151 turbofan

Maximum speed: 1038km/h (645mph)

Endurance: 4 hours

Service ceiling: 15,240m (50,000ft)

Dimensions: span 9.39m (30ft 9.75in); length

11.17m (36ft 7.75in); height 3.99m (13ft 1.75in)

Weight: 7750kg (17,085lb) loaded

Armament: underfuselage/wing hardpoints with provision for up to 2567kg (5660lb) of stores, wingtip mounted air-to-air missiles

▲ British Aerospace Hawk T.Mk 1A

151 Sqn, RAF / Chivenor, early 1980s

A total of 89 Hawk trainers were converted to T.Mk 1A standard from 1983, with Sidewinder missile interface, in order to provide a clear-weather point-defence capability. It was planned to use the T.Mk 1A as a wartime adjunct to the Tornado F.Mk 3, with the latter illuminating targets for the Hawk with its Foxhunter radar.

Chapter 4

Strategic Reconnaissance

Aircraft have long been used for the collection of intelligence, and great importance was attached to strategic aerial reconnaissance during the Cold War in order to keep track of military developments in 'areas of interest'. As well as intelligence gathering by optical or infrared means, the electromagnetic spectrum was exploited as a means of developing an electronic order of battle for opposition forces and potential enemies.

◀ **Lockheed SR-71 Blackbird**
Flying higher and faster than any other operational spyplane, the USAF's SR-71 was typical of Cold War strategic reconnaissance assets: developed in great secrecy, it was used to fly intelligence-gathering missions over some of the most hazardous areas on Earth.

Cold War Aerial Spies
1946–1989

Photo-reconnaissance, together with electronic intelligence (ELINT), were among the most important – and hazardous – missions flown during the Cold War.

THE PRACTICE OF undertaking reconnaissance from the air was not limited to manned platforms during the Cold War, with satellites, balloons and remotely piloted vehicles (RPVs) all being widely used for strategic intelligence gathering. Typically, Cold War strategic reconnaissance involved gathering information on military developments, classifying national-level command and communications networks, and monitoring bomber dispositions, ballistic missiles and other strategic capabilities.

In the early years of the Cold War, the hazardous nature of spyplane missions was reflected in a number of high-profile shoot-downs, culminating on 1 May 1960, when Soviet air defences downed a CIA-operated U-2C flown by Francis Gary Powers over Sverdlovsk. As well as highlighting the threat posed by SAMs, the loss of the U-2 effectively put an end to direct over-flights of Soviet and Warsaw Pact territory. This series of U-2 over-flights of the USSR had begun just a month earlier, and followed the earlier Soviet rejection of President Dwight D. Eisenhower's 'Open Skies' plan for arms-control over-

flights. U-2 units (operating under the guise of USAF Weather Reconnaissance Squadrons) had been deployed to bases in West Germany and Turkey since 1956, with photographic over-flights beginning in July that year. A third U-2 squadron was formed in Japan in 1957.

Early operations

While the exotic U-2 had been designed specifically for the high-altitude reconnaissance mission, other early Cold War intelligence-gatherers were based on existing airframes, typically bombers or patrol aircraft. The U.S. Navy operated modified P4M and P4Y aircraft, while key USAF assets included variants of the prolific B-47 and C-130, as well as the RB-45.

The first recorded Cold War spyplane shoot-down occurred in April 1950, when Soviet fighters attacked a U.S. Navy PB4Y over the Baltic Sea. Other shoot-downs involving USAF aircraft saw an RB-29 downed by MiGs in October 1952, an RB-50 shot down by MiGs over the Sea of Japan in July 1953, an C-130 shot down over Armenia in September 1958

▲ **Boeing B-29A Superfortress**

55th Strategic Reconnaissance Wing, USAF / early 1950s

The B-29 remained in widespread service for a variety of duties after World War II, this example being a reconnaissance-configured B-29A-70-BN that operated on clandestine missions over Manchuria in 1953. RB-29A models were among the early equipment of the 55th SRW, the USAF's premier strategic recce wing.

Specifications

Crew: 11	length 30.2m (99ft); height 8.5m (29ft 7in)
Powerplant: 4 x 1640kW (2200hp) Wright R-3350-23	Weight: 54,000kg (120,000lb) loaded
and 23A turbosupercharged radial engines	Armament: 10 x 12.7mm (.50in) caliber
Maximum speed: 574km/h (357mph)	Browning M2/ANs, 2 x 12.7mm (.50in) and
Range: 9000km (5600 miles)	1 x 20mm (.79in) M2 cannon in tail position
Service ceiling: 10,200m (33,600ft)	
Dimensions: span 43.1m (141ft 3in);	

Specifications

Crew: 9

Powerplant: 2 x 20kN (4,600lbf) Allison J33-A-
23 turbojets and 2 x 2420kW (3250hp) Pratt &
Whitney R-4360 Wasp Major radial engines

Maximum speed: 660km/h (410mph)

Range: 4570km (2840 miles)

Service ceiling: 10,500m (34,600ft)

Dimensions: span 34.7m (114ft);
length 26m (85ft 2in); height 8m (26ft 1in)

Weight: 40,088kg (88,378lb) loaded

Armament: 4 x 20mm (.79in) cannons in nose
and tail turrets, 2 x 12.7mm (.50in) machine
guns in dorsal turret and up to 5400kg
(12,000lb) of bombs, mines, depth charges
or torpedoes

▼ Martin P4M-1 Mercator

VP-21, U.S. Navy / early 1950s

VP-21 replaced its PB4Y-2s with P4M-1s in June 1950 and deployed with the type
to the Mediterranean in 1951-52. A P4M-1Q of VQ-1 was lost over eastern China
in August 1956, and another example from the same unit was forced down by
North Korean MiG-17s in June 1959, while
engaged on an intelligence-gathering
mission.

Specifications

Crew: 3

Powerplant: 6 x 32kN (7,200lb) General Electric
J47 GE-25 turbojets

Maximum speed: 982km/h (610mph)

Range: 6437km (4000 miles)

Service ceiling: 11,826m (38,800ft)

Dimensions: span 35.36m (116ft);
length 32.92m (108ft); height 8.53m (28ft)

Weight: 56,699kg (125,000lb) loaded

Armament: 2 x 20mm (.79in) cannons in the
tail plus 9,072kg (20,000lb) internal
ordanance

▲ Boeing RB-47H Stratojet

55th Strategic Reconnaissance Wing, USAF / mid-1950s

Configured for ELINT, the RB-47H housed equipment and three systems operators (known as 'Crows') in the former bomb
bay, with additional sensors in the nose, under-fuselage and wing radomes. Active around the borders of the Eastern Bloc,
the RB-47Hs were charged with gathering intelligence on ground radar installations.

▲ Lockheed U-2C

100th Strategic Reconnaissance Wing, USAF, 1975

Built as a U-2A, the aircraft illustrated was later modified for high-altitude
atmospheric sampling as a WU-2A. The same aircraft was later converted to
become a U-2C, and served with the 100th SRW. It is seen here in 1975, with a
two-tone grey camouflage intended for operations in Europe.

Specifications

Crew: 1

Powerplant: 1 x 75.62kN (17,000lb) Pratt &
Whitney J75-P-13 turbojet

Maximum speed: 850km/h (530mph)

Range: 4830km (2610 miles)

Service ceiling: 25,930m (85,000ft)

Dimensions: span 24.30m (80ft);
length 15.1m (49ft 7in); height 3.9m (13ft)

Weight: 9523kg (21,000lb) loaded

Armament: none

while flying from Turkey, and a 55th SRW RB-47 flying from Brize Norton, England, that was downed over the Barents Sea in July 1960.

In the wake of the U-2 incident, the USAF and CIA continued to develop more advanced strategic reconnaissance aircraft, and the U.S. ultimately fielded the SR-71, the fastest and highest-flying air-breathing vehicle of its era, as well as increasingly advanced derivatives of the U-2, and the RC-135, the latter capable of carrying a plethora of ELINT sensors, side-looking airborne radar and other intelligence-gathering

equipment capable of operating across a wide range of frequencies. Prolific development during the Cold War saw the USAF field 28 RC-135s in at least 12 different configurations, the ultimate versions being the RC-135V/W. The RC-135S version, operating from Shemya in the Aleutians, was tasked with intercepting telemetry intelligence (TELINT) from Soviet missile tests. The SR-71, U-2 and RC-135 were all active at the end of the Cold War, the information they gathered being of prime importance both to Strategic Air Command and the Pentagon. As well as

Specifications

Crew: 27

Powerplant: 4 x 80kN (18,000lb) Pratt & Whitney
TF33-P-9 turbojets

Maximum speed: 991km/h (616mph)

Range: 4305km (2675 miles)

Service ceiling: 12,375m (40,600ft)

Dimensions: span 39.88m (130ft 10in); length
41.53m (136ft 3in); height 12.7m (41ft 8in);

Weight: 124,965kg (275,500lb) loaded

Armament: 6 x 7.92mm (.3in) MGs; 1000kg
(2205lb) bomb load

▲ **Boeing RC-135V**

55th Strategic Reconnaissance Wing, USAF / Offutt AFB, early 1980s

During the Cold War, USAF RC-135s could be found operating patrols lasting up to 10 hours over the Baltic, Barents and Black Seas in the west, and over the Bering and Siberian seas to the east. The aircraft carried a crew of around 16 specialist ELINT operators. The 55th SRW was based at Offutt, Nebraska.

Specifications

Crew: 1

Powerplant: 2 x 144.5kN (32,500lb) Pratt &
Whitney JT11D-20B turbojets

Maximum speed: 3219km/h (2000mph)

Range: 4800km (2983 miles)

Service ceiling: 30,000m (100,000ft)

Dimensions: span 16.94m (55ft 7in);
length 32.74m (107ft 5in); height 5.64m
(18ft 6in)

Weight: 77,111kg (170,000lb) loaded

Armament: none

▲ **Lockheed SR-71A**

9th Strategic Reconnaissance Wing, USAF / early 1980s

Flying at speeds in excess of Mach 3 and at an altitude of almost 30,000m (100,000ft), the SR-71A, popularly known as 'Blackbird', was effectively immune to enemy air defences. The SR-71A operated along the borders of the USSR, China and the Eastern Bloc, as well as over Cuba, Nicaragua, North Korea and Vietnam.

monitoring Soviet activity, U.S. strategic reconnaissance assets were active over Korea, with aircraft including RC-135s and U-2s operating from Kadena to observe activity in the north.

The U.S. Navy also possessed a strategic reconnaissance capability, ultimately expressed through 12 examples of the EP-3E, an adaptation of the P-3 maritime patrol aircraft, outfitted with an Aries ELINT suite. Primary mission for the EP-3E involved gathering data on Soviet warships and their electronics and weapons systems. U.S. Navy EA-3Bs could undertake carrier-based ELINT missions. Both EP-3E and EA-3B aircraft were active over the Mediterranean, flying from Rota in Spain, with further EP-3Es stationed out of Guam.

Soviet capabilities

For the Soviets, the strategic aerial reconnaissance mission was assigned a lower priority, and focused on maritime intelligence-gathering, prosecuted by types based on the Tu-16 and Tu-95 bombers, as well as derivatives of the An-12 airlifter and the Il-20, an ELINT platform based on an airliner. These aircraft kept a close watch on NATO naval operations, and while the Tu-16 could frequently be found operating in the Baltic, North Sea and Mediterranean, the longer-range Tu-95 variants ventured as far as Angola, Cuba, South Yemen and Vietnam. Another important mission for adapted Soviet bombers was monitoring the reaction times and capabilities of

▲ **Tupolev Tu-16R**

A Soviet Navy Tu-16R 'Badger-F' reconnaissance aircraft swoops low over the North Sea while monitoring NATO maritime activity in the 1960s.

Western fighters, achieved by flying attack profiles against the coasts of the U.S. and UK.

The RAF maintained a strategic reconnaissance capability through the deployment of three Nimrod R.Mk 1s, supported by specially modified Canberras, and other nations also operated small fleets of strategic intelligence-gatherers, notably France, Israel and Sweden. These last three all operated dedicated reconnaissance adaptations of civilian airliners, comprising the DC-8, 707 and Caravelle, respectively. West Germany, meanwhile, fielded a small fleet of Atlantics adapted for signals intelligence (SIGINT) missions over the Baltic Sea.

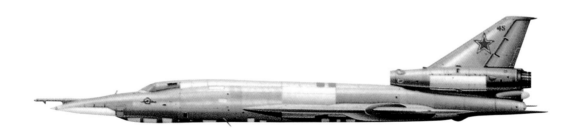

Specifications

Crew: 3	length 41.6m (136ft 5in); height 10.13m
Powerplant: 2 x 161.9kN (36,376lbf) Dobrynin	(33ft 3in)
RD-7M-2 turbojets	Weight: 85,000kg (187,390lb) loaded
Maximum speed: 1510km/h (938mph)	Armament: 1 x AM-23 23mm cannon in tail
Range: 4900km (3045 miles)	turret plus 9000kg (20,000lb) of bombs or
Service ceiling: 13,300m (40,540ft)	1 x Kh-22 cruise missile
Dimensions: span 23.17m (76ft);	

▲ **Tupolev Tu-22RD**

Soviet Long-Range Aviation, 1970s

Known to NATO as 'Blinder-C', the reconnaissance variant of the Tu-22 theatre bomber was flown by both Soviet AF and Navy units. For the DA Tu-22R units, areas of operation included tracking the U.S. Sixth Fleet in the Mediterranean, as well as wartime missions over central and southern Europe and the Baltic.

Chapter 5

The Middle East

Possessing wealth in the form of oil, commanding access to the Far East via the Suez Canal, and home to various opposing religious and political groups, the Eastern Mediterranean and Arabian Peninsula were long host to conflict and local rivalry. The escalation of the Cold War combined with the establishment of the state of Israel in 1948 to increase tensions. Now, the 'new' superpowers fought to fill the vacuum left in the wake of the departure of the former European powers, with the U.S. and Soviet Union battling for influence in this strategically vital region.

◀ **Sikorsky S-58**
The creation of Israel in 1948 precipitated a series of conflicts that would last the duration of the Cold War. Much of the battle lines of the Middle East were redrawn following the Six-Day War, illustrated here by a pair of Israeli Defence Force soldiers hunkering down in the desert as an Israeli S-58 passes overhead.

Britain in Arabia
1946–1967

Once the dominant power on the Arabian Peninsula, Britain's interests were based on the oilfields of Iraq and Persia, with Iraq, Transjordan and Palestine all governed by British mandate.

BRITAIN'S INFLUENCE OVER the Arabian Peninsula, Persia, Egypt and the Suez Canal Zone was expressed through a powerful military presence, including units of the RAF, which had been active since the start of the British mandates in the wake of World War I. The Arabian Peninsula saw a gradual reduction in British forces after World War II, in the midst of increasing Arab hostility towards the British.

Eventually the RAF withdrew entirely from its former stronghold in Iraq, as the focus increasingly shifted towards the Canal Zone. Nevertheless, Iraq remained home to a limited RAF presence, the primary role of which was to protect its vital oilfields. Into the mid-1950s, the British presence in Iraq included five squadrons variously equipped with Vampires, Beaufighters and Tempests, plus Valetta transports.

▲ **De Havilland Venom FB.Mk 4**

8 Sqn, RAF / Khormaksar, 1955–60

Operating from Khormaksar for over two decades starting in 1946, 8 Sqn flew the Venom FB.Mk 4 between 1955 and 1960. The FB.Mk 4 replaced the FB.Mk 1 in service with this unit, and the new version was in combat over South Arabia beginning in the summer of 1955, mostly launching strikes against dissident tribes.

Specifications

Crew: 1

Powerplant: 1 x 22.9kN (5150lb) de Havilland Ghost 105 turbojet

Maximum speed: 1030km/h (640mph)

Range: (with drop tanks) 1730km (1075 miles)

Service ceiling: 14,630m (48,000ft)

Dimensions: span (over tip tanks) 12.7m (41ft 8in);

length 9.71m (31ft 10in); height 1.88m (6ft 2in)

Weight: 6945kg (15,310lb) loaded

Armament: 4 x 20mm (.78in) Hispano cannon with 150 rounds, 2 x wing pylons capable of carrying either 2 x 454kg (1000lb) bombs or 2 x drop tanks; or 8 x 27.2kg (60lb) rocket projectiles carried on centre-section launchers

▲ **Hawker Hunter FGA.Mk 9**

8 Sqn, RAF / Khormaksar, 1955–60

Khormaksar-based 8 Sqn operated its Hunters on ground attack duties against Yemeni insurgents along the border with Aden during the final years of the British presence in South Arabia. The Hunter was therefore the final type to be employed by 8 Sqn in the colonial policing role that it undertook for almost 50 years.

Specifications

Crew: 1

Powerplant: 1 x 45.13kN (10,145lbf) Rolls-Royce Avon 207 turbojet

Maximum speed: 1,150km/h (715mph)

Range: 715km (445 miles)

Service ceiling: 15,240m (50,000ft)

Dimensions: span 10.26m (33ft 8in); length 14m (45ft 11in); height 4.01m (13ft 2in)

Weight: 8050kg (17,750lb) loaded

Armament: 4 x 30 mm (1.18 in) ADEN cannons, various rockets and missiles and up to 3357kg (7400lb) of payload

The most important focus for RAF operations in the Arabian Peninsula was Aden, and the major base at Khormaksar was home in the 1950s to Brigands, Vampires, Venoms and Meteors.

Maritime operations

Shackletons, tasked with protecting oil shipping between the Persian Gulf and the Red Sea, provided a maritime patrol presence out of Khormaksar. Lancasters, Valettas, Twin Pioneers and Pioneers provided transport capability.

Eventually the UK granted autonomy to the Aden states of Muscat and Oman, these following the examples of Jordan, Kuwait, Qatar and the United Arab Emirates. In 1967 the UK had announced its intention to withdraw forces from territories 'east of Suez', however, the precarious security situation in Yemen meant that the RAF still had a role to play in the region. Until the final British withdrawal in 1969, RAF squadrons at Khormaksar were involved in combat operations in the wake of the October 1962 revolution in Yemen, after which hostile dissident tribes, incursions from Yemen and terrorist activity confronted security forces in South Arabia.

Specifications

Crew: 10

Powerplant: 4 x 1831kW (2455hp) Rolls-Royce
Griffon 57A V-12 piston engines

Maximum speed: 500km/h (311mph)

Range: 5440km (3380 miles)

Service ceiling: 6400m (21,000ft)

Dimensions: span 36.58m (120ft);
length 26.59m (87ft 3in); height 5.1m (16ft 9in)

Weight: 39,010kg (86,000lb) loaded

Armament: 2 x Hispano No. 1 Mk 5 20mm
(.79in) cannon in nose turret and up to
4536kg (10,000lb) of bombs

▲ **Avro Shackleton MR.Mk 2**

37 Sqn, RAF / Khormaksar, 1957–67

As well as ensuring the safe passage of oil from the Persian Gulf to the entrance of the Red Sea, 37 Sqn's Shackleton maritime reconnaissance aircraft were active countering various hostile Arab groups operating around Aden and the Gulf states. Khormaksar was home to 37 Sqn between 1957 and 1967.

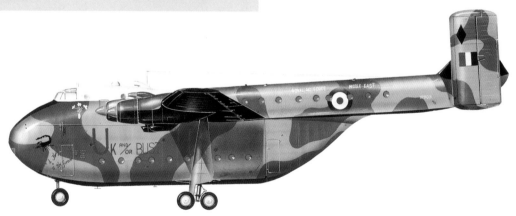

Specifications

Crew: 6

Powerplant: 4 x 2125kW (2850hp) Bristol
Centaurus 173 radial piston engines

Maximum speed: 383km/h (238mph)

Range: 5938km (3690 miles)

Service ceiling: 4875m (16,000ft)

Dimensions: span 49.38m (162ft); length 30.3m
(99ft 5in); height 11.81m (38ft 9in)

Weight: 64,864kg (143,000lb) loaded

Armament: none

▲ **Bristol Beverley C.Mk 1**

84 Sqn, RAF / Khormaksar, 1958–67

Bearing the legend 'UK and/or bust' on the fuselage, this Beverley was operated by 84 Sqn in the mid-1960s. Capable of operating from small desert strips, the Beverley provided vital tactical support for Army actions in the Middle East, including operations in the Aden Emergency, based out of Khormaksar.

Oman
1952–1976

Britain's departure from the Gulf did not put an end to the region's troubles, and Oman in particular was subject to inter-factional hostilities starting in the late 1960s.

POSSESSING BOTH OIL reserves and overseeing access to strategically important waterways, Oman was of long-term interest to the UK.

In the early 1950s, RAF Vampires were deployed from Iraq to conduct shows of force in response to Saudi Arabia's claims on Omani oilfields. With the Saudis refusing to back down, Vampires and Meteor FR.Mk 9s were deployed to Sharjah in 1953 in support of a blockade, before being replaced by Lancasters and Valettas, and later Ansons. Continued operations were staged from 1955 in response to further disputes and incursions by Saudi Arabia, with RAF Lincolns and Valettas engaged on reconnaissance missions, with support from Venom fighter-bombers and various transport types.

Confronting the OLA

Operations were stepped up in 1957 when Saudi-backed Omani Liberation Army (OLA) troops occupied villages in Oman. Venoms were soon in action, attacking ground targets, while Shackletons dropped leaflets, and Beverley and Valetta transports provided airlift support. Sorties were flown from Sharjah and Bahrain. Canberras and Meteors flew reconnaissance missions, before ground troops were deployed in force from August 1957. While the OLA was removed from Omani villages it was not extinguished, and began operating from the safety of more remote locations.

When the rebels threatened to regain the initiative and take more territory, the British established a blockade, launched in earnest in 1958 and undertaken in conjunction with the Sultan's Armed Forces. With the OLA continuing to receive arms, the RAF returned to offensive operations, with Shackletons being used for bombing raids in autumn 1958, supported by Fleet Air Arm Sea Hawk and Sea Venom fighter-bombers operating from the carrier HMS *Bulwark*. A final, successful, assault on OLA positions was launched by SAS troops in January 1959, and the vast majority of

RAF units began to be withdrawn from the region the following month.

Following the departure of UK forces from the region, the Sultan of Oman AF was established with British support, and began to receive combat aircraft in 1968. As well as equipment, the UK also provided personnel to fly and maintain Omani aircraft. Between 1968 and 1976 Soviet-supported Popular Front for the Liberation of Oman guerrillas were active on the border between Oman and South Yemen and in Dhofar, while Oman received military backing from the UK, India, Iran, Jordan, Pakistan and Saudi Arabia.

RAF IN OMAN, 1952–59		
Aircraft	**Unit**	**Base**
Lincoln B.Mk 2	7 Sqn (det)	Khormaksar
Lincoln B.Mk 2	1426 Flt (det)	Sharjah
Venom FB.Mk 4	249 Sqn (det)	Sharjah
Venom FB.Mk 4	8 Sqn (det)	Sharjah
Vampire FB.Mk 5, Venom FB.Mk 1	6 Sqn	Sharjah
Meteor FR.Mk 9	208 Sqn (det)	Sharjah
Canberra PR.Mk 7	58 Sqn (det)	Bahrain
Lancaster GR.Mk 3	37 Sqn	Sharjah
Lancaster GR.Mk 3	38 Sqn	Sharjah
Lancaster PR.Mk 1	683 Sqn (det)	Sharjah
Shackleton MR.Mk 2	37 Sqn (det)	Masirah
Shackleton MR.Mk 2	42 Sqn (det)	Masirah
Shackleton MR.Mk 2	224 Sqn (det)	Masirah
Shackleton MR.Mk 2	228 Sqn (det)	Masirah
Valetta C.Mk 1	ACF	Sharjah
Valetta C.Mk 1, Beverley C.Mk 1	84 Sqn	Sharjah, Bahrain
Anson C.Mk 19, Pembroke C.Mk 1	1417 Flt	Sharjah
Pembroke C.Mk 1, Twin Pioneer CC.Mk 1	152 Sqn	Sharjah
Sycamore HR.Mk 14	SAR Flt (det)	Sharjah

▲ Short Skyvan 3M

2 Sqn, Sultan of Oman AF / 1970s

Employed on light transport duties, the robust Skyvan was supplied by the UK between 1970 and 1975 and proved suitable for operations from rough desert airstrips. Major dissident groups had been contained by the early 1970s, and infiltration by guerrilla forces originating in South Yemen was also countered.

Specifications

Crew: 1-2

Powerplant: 2 x 533kW (715hp) Garrett
  AiResearch TPE-331-201 Turboprops

Maximum speed: 324km/h (202mph)

Range: 1200km (694 miles)

Service ceiling: 6858m (22,500ft)

Dimensions: span 19.79m (64ft 11in);
  length 12.21m (40ft 1in); height 4.6m (15ft 1in)

Weight: 5670kg (12,500lb) loaded

Armament: none

Iran–Iraq War
1980–1988

Widely misunderstood in the West, the prolonged 'Holy War' saw extensive and sophisticated use of air power, with Iran, once a staunch ally of the West, clashing with its neighbour Iraq.

PRO-WESTERN UNTIL THE Islamic revolution of 1979, Iran's air arms were previously primarily equipped by the U.S., which sought a strong ally in the Middle East and signed orders worth around $20 billion in the late 1970s, including advanced F-14A interceptors. The Iraqi AF, which was previously equipped with Western equipment, was turning increasingly towards the USSR for aircraft, but also fielded French equipment, such as Mirage F1s, outfitted as fighter-bombers or for reconnaissance.

The military potential of post-revolution Iran was underestimated both in the West and by Iraq, which chose to reignite a long-running border dispute after Iranian shelling of frontier positions in early September 1980. After a series of small-scale clashes, major fighting broke out on 22 September, and this included pre-emptive air strikes by the Iraqi AF against Iranian airfields. Other early targets for the

Iraqi AF included Tehran and air raids, some of which were prosecuted by Tu-22 bombers, were followed almost immediately by troops crossing the border into Iran. Both air arms also attacked oil installations, and the campaign to target opposition oil industry would continue throughout the conflict.

Iraqi forces crossed the border in several locations, with the primary drive focused on Abadan and the southern end of the vital Shatt al-Arab waterway.

Helicopter warfare

The initial Iraqi drive was soon blunted by Iranian ground forces, supported by air power that included armed helicopters – Iraqi Mi-8s and Gazelles and Iranian AH-1Js. The latter type primarily saw action in the north, and confronted Iraqi forces around Dezful. With the Iraqi advance on the ground stalled, the Islamic Republic of Iran AF (IRIAF) was able to

Specifications

Crew: 2

Powerplant: 2 x 92.9kN (20,900lb) Pratt & Whitney TF30-P-412A turbofans

Maximum speed: 2517km/h (1564mph)

Range: 3220km (2000 miles)

Service ceiling: 17,070m (56,000ft)

Dimensions: span 19.55m (64ft 1.5in) unswept; 11.65m (38ft 2.5in) swept; length 19.1m (62ft 8in); height 4.88m (16ft)

Weight: 33,724kg (74,349lb) loaded

Armament: 1 x 20mm M61A1 Vulcan rotary cannon; combination of AIM-7 Sparrow; AIM-9 medium range air-to-air missiles, and AIM-54 Phoenix long range air-to-air missiles

▲ Grumman F-14 Tomcat
Islamic Republic of Iran AF / 1980s

Among the huge numbers of aircraft acquired by Iran before the fall of the Shah, the F-14A proved highly successful during the war with Iraq, despite Western reports that serviceability was limited. A number of Iranian crews made 'ace' status on the F-14A, and the type scored aerial victories against MiG-25s.

Specifications

Crew: 11

Powerplant: 4 x 3356kW (4500hp) Allison T56-A10W turboprop engines

Maximum speed: 766km/h (476mph)

Range: 4075km (2533 miles)

Service ceiling: 8625m (28,300ft)

Dimensions: span 30.37m (99ft 8in); length 35.61m (116ft 9in); height 10.27m (33ft 8in)

Weight: 60,780kg (134,000lb) loaded

Armament: up to 9070kg (20,000lb) of ordnance, including bombs, mines and torpedoes

▲ Lockheed P-3F Orion
Islamic Republic of Iran AF / Bandar Abbas, 1980s

Iran acquired six examples of the P-3F variant of the Orion, which featured an in-flight refuelling capability. The first example was delivered in 1975. During the Iran-Iraq War, these maritime patrol aircraft flew from Bandar Abbas, and were active during the 'Tanker War' in the Persian Gulf.

Specifications

Crew: 2

Powerplant: 1 x 14.7kN (3308lbf) Ivchenko AI-25T turbofan

Maximum speed: 635km/h (395mph)

Range: 1260km (783 miles)

Service ceiling: 13000m (42,650ft)

Dimensions: span 9.50m (31ft 2in); length 12.30m (40ft 4in); height 4.70m (15ft 5in)

Weight: 2600kg (5732lb) loaded

Armament: 1 x 23mm cannon and up to 1100kg (2425lb) of weapons

▲ Aero L-39ZO
Iraqi AF / 1980s

Acquired by Iraq as an advanced trainer during the course of the 1980-88 conflict, the L-39 saw limited use in the light attack role during the Iran-Iraq War. Flying from bases at Mosul and Kirkuk, the primary role of the L-39 fleet was schooling prospective Iraqi AF combat aircrew, as well as weapons training.

make its mark, launching a series of reprisal strikes against the Iraqi capital, Baghdad. Aircraft involved included F-4s and F-5Es and the threat posed by IRIAF air strikes force Iraq to evacuate many of its aircraft to foreign bases. Periodic long-range attacks against the two countries' cities would remain a feature of the war, both sides incurring losses in the process, in air combat, and against increasingly sophisticated ground-based air defences.

Iraq had taken a risk in launching its offensive shortly before the onset of winter and the rainy season, with the aim of capturing territory that would then be denied to any Iranian counter-offensive by adverse weather. However, Iran was able to organize a response, which came in January 1981. The Iraqis contained the Iranian counter-thrust that came in the same month. Close support air power was utilized by both sides, Iraqi AF aircraft flying as many as 400-450 missions per day.

There followed a long period of stalemate, a war of attrition punctuated by limited, renewed ground offensives, while the opposing ground forces dug in across a front line of almost 1200 kilometres (750 miles). By September 1981, Iraqi gains were effectively limited to the town of Khorramshar. A return to strategic bombing missions came in September 1981, in the wake of abortive Iraqi attempts to capture the besieged town of Abadan. The renewed bombing campaign saw the Iraqi AF attack the oil pipeline at Gorreh at the end of September, this installation

being the last Iranian pipeline dedicated to export. The IRIAF response involved air strikes on a number of Iraqi power stations. For strikes against high-value targets, both sides used guided weaponry, typically employed by IRIAF F-4s and Iraqi AF Mirage F1s and Su-22s.

IRIAF F-14s, long thought by the West to have seen little in the way of combat, racked up an impressive tally of air-to-air victories, while the F-4 fleet undertook the bulk of IRIAF offensive missions. For air defence the Iraqi AF relied on MiG-25s and MiG-21s, the latter armed with Magic AAMs.

The 'Tanker War'

As the war expanded to the waters of the Persian Gulf, the Iraqi AF put to good use French-supplied Exocet anti-ship missiles against shipping and oil rigs. Exocets were launched by Super Frelon helicopters, Mirage F1EQ-5s and a handful of Super Etendards loaned from France in late 1983.

Early 1984 saw an Iranian attack against Majinoon Island in the Howizah marshes, aiming to sever the Iraqi front, and this was met by concerted Iraqi AF close air support. The 'Tanker War' escalated in 1984, with 51 sinkings, by both sides, Iran attacking tankers coming out of Iraq, Kuwaiti and Saudi ports.

In August 1990 the two nations agreed to a truce, which held despite some border incidents. By now, the Iraqi AF had received advanced new equipment – the MiG-29 fighter and Su-25 close support aircraft.

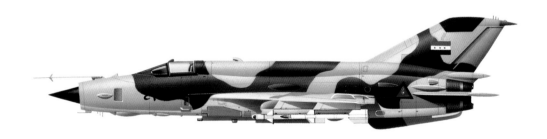

▲ **Mikoyan-Gurevich MiG-21MF**

Iraqi AF / 1980s

The most important air defence fighter of the Iraqi AF in the early part of the war, the MiG-21 was operated in a number of variants, ultimately supplemented by Chinese-built F-7 versions, used for training. The MiG-21MF variant was flown by two Iraqi AF units at the outbreak of fighting in September 1980.

Specifications

Crew: 1	length 15.76m (51ft 9in); height 4.1m (13ft 6in)
Powerplant: 1 x 60.8kN (14,550lb) thrust	Weight: 10,400kg (22,925lb) loaded
Tumanskii R-13-300 afterburning turbojet	Armament: 1 x 23mm (.91in) cannon, provision
Maximum speed: 2229km/h (1385mph)	for about 1500kg (3307lb) of stores,
Range: 1160km (721 miles)	including air-to-air missiles, rocket pods,
Service ceiling: 17,500m (57,400ft)	napalm tanks or drop tanks
Dimensions: span 7.15m (23ft 6in);	

Britain in Palestine
1945–1948

In British hands after World War I, Palestine was subject to increased attention after 1945, with local strife and Jewish resettlement combining with the struggle for control of the Suez Canal.

PALESTINE HAD BEEN host to a major RAF airfield-building programme in World War II as part of a general build-up of squadrons in the Middle East. Postwar, Britain decided to limit Jewish immigration into Palestine to 100,000, prompting additional settlers to enter Palestine illegally. At the same time, militant Jewish groups stepped up their campaign against the British occupiers, the assassination of a British Minister of State in Cairo in 1945 being followed by deployment of Hurricanes and Spitfires to Meggido and Ramat David. RAF Mustangs and Halifaxes carried out bombing sorties, and as the Jewish insurgents' campaign intensified, the RAF mounted standing fighter patrols.

In reaction to continued immigration, the Royal Navy began a blockade, which was supported from the air by RAF maritime reconnaissance and air-sea rescue units, flying from Ein Shemer and Aqir.

Israel established

In November 1946 the UN announced plans to partition Palestine west of Jordan. Britain's proposal to end land sales to the Jewish settlers led to a further decline in UK-Jewish relations before the British mandate finally ended, and the state of Israel was established on 15 May 1948. In the meantime, anti-immigration patrols continued, now prosecuted by RAF Lancasters.

Created in November 1947, the fledgling Israeli air arm was equipped with a handful of types, flown by both local Jewish pilots and former World War II servicemen from various Allied nations. The establishment of the Israeli AF prompted the RAF to deploy a squadron of Spitfires to Ein Shemer.

The RAF Spitfires were used against the Jewish settlement at Bat Yam in April 1948, part of an abortive British effort to prevent the Jewish militia from taking Arab Jaffa.

With the end of the British mandate, evacuation of British forces from the area was the responsibility of Halifax, Lancaster and Dakota transports. British military units redeployed from Palestine to the Canal Zone. From their bases in Egypt, the British would now set about defending the Suez Canal, in order to ensure the safe passage of shipping to the Far East.

RAF IN PALESTINE, 1945–48		
Aircraft	**Unit**	**Base**
Spitfire Mk VC/IX/FR.Mk 18	32 Sqn	Ramat David, Petah Tiqva, Aqir, Ein Shemer, Nicosia
Spitfire Mk VC/IXC	208 Sqn	Ramat David, Petah Tiqva, Aqir
Spitfire FR.Mk 18E	208 Sqn	Ein Shemer, Nicosia
Hurricane Mk IV	6 Sqn	Meggido, Petah Tiqva, Ramat David
Spitfire Mk IX, Tempest F.Mk VI	6 Sqn	Ein Shemer, Nicosia
Mustang Mk III/V, Tempest F.Mk VI	213 Sqn	Ramat David, Nicosia
Mosquito Mk XVI/PR.Mk 34	680 Sqn	Aqir, Ein Shemer
Mosquito Mk XVI/PR.Mk 34	13 Sqn	Ein Shemer, Kabrit, Fayid
Auster AOP.Mk 5	651 Sqn	Haifa
Warwick GR.Mk 5, Lancaster GR.Mk 3	621 Sqn	Aqir, Ein Shemer
Halifax Mk VII/IX	644 Sqn	Quastina
Halifax Mk VII	620 Sqn	Aqir
Halifax Mk VII, Dakota C.Mk 4	113 Sqn	Aqir
Lancaster GR.Mk 3	37 Sqn	Ein Shemer
Lancaster GR.Mk 3	203 Sqn	Ein Shemer
Dakota C.Mk 4	78 Sqn	Kabrit, Aqir
Dakota C.Mk 4	216 Sqn	Kabrit, Fayid
Dakota C.Mk 4	215 Sqn	Kabrit
Dakota C.Mk 4	204 Sqn	Kabrit
Dakota C.Mk 4	114 Sqn	Kabrit

▲ Hawker Tempest F.Mk 6

213 Sqn, RAF / Nicosia, 1946–47

This Tempest was delivered to an RAF Maintenance Unit at Shurbra, Egypt, in 1946 before being put into service by 213 Sqn, based at Shallufa as part of the Middle East fighter force. Beginning in 1946 the unit operated from Nicosia, Cyprus, and replaced its Tempests with Vampires in 1950.

Specifications

Crew: 1

Powerplant: 1 x 2340hp (1745kW) Napier Sabre VA H-24 piston engine

Maximum speed: 686km/h (426mph)

Range: 2092km (1300 miles)

Service ceiling: 10,975m (36,000ft)

Dimensions: span 12.5m (41ft); length 10.26m (33ft 8in); height 4.9m (16ft 1in)

Weight: 6142kg (13,540lb) loaded

Armament: 4 x 20mm (.8in) Hispano cannon in wings, up to 907kg (2000lb) stores of either 2 bombs or 8 rockets for ground attack role

Early Israeli Air Wars
1948–49

As soon as the state of Israel declared its independence, the Jewish state was under attack by its Arab neighbours. Soon, however, it had assembled an air arm with which it could fight back.

INITIALLY EQUIPPED WITH mainly light aircraft, including Taylorcraft and Auster types, the Israeli AF was active on reconnaissance, communications and transport work during early fighting against Palestinian Arabs and their villages soon after its establishment in late 1947. By May 1948, the Israeli AF was in possession of 54 aircraft, while air power assembled in support of the Egyptian Expeditionary

Specifications

Crew: 1

Powerplant: 1 x 1170kW (1565hp) 12-cylinder Rolls-Royce Merlin 61 engine

Maximum speed: 642km/h (410mph)

Range: 698km (435 miles)

Service ceiling: 12,650m (41,500ft)

Dimensions: span 11.23m (36ft 10in); length 9.47m (31ft 1in); height 3.86m (12ft 8in)

Weight: 3343kg (7370lb) loaded

Armament: 4 x 7.7mm (.303in) MGs and 2 x 20mm (.8in) cannons

▲ Supermarine Spitfire LF.Mk 9

2 Sqn, Royal Egyptian AF / El Arish, 1948–49

In the early days of Jewish-Arab fighting in Palestine, the REAF operated 15 Spitfire Mk 9s in support of the Egyptian Expeditionary Force. The aircraft were acquired in 1946 and a REAF detachment operated from El Arish. Both Israel and Egypt made use of surplus RAF equipment during their early confrontations.

▲ **Boeing B-17G Flying Fortress**

69 Sqn, Israeli AF / Ramat David, 1948-49

By the time the second truce ended in October 1948, the Israeli AF was able to field three B-17s, which bombed Cairo on their delivery flight. Israel's acquisition of a dedicated bomber forced Egypt to obtain Stirling transports, which were in turn used for a handful of daylight bombing raids later in the conflict.

Specifications

Crew: 10

Powerplant: 4 x 895kW (1200hp) Wright R Cyclone nine-cylinder radial engines

Maximum speed: 475km/h (295mph)

Range: 5085km (3160 miles)

Service ceiling: 10,850m (35,600ft)

Dimensions: span 31.62m (103ft 9in); length 22.8m (74ft 9in); height 5.85m (19ft 2in)

Weight: 29,710kg (65,500lb) loaded

Armament: 13 x 12.7mm (.5in) machine guns; up to 6169kg (13,600lb) bomb load

Force in Palestine was based around Royal Egyptian AF Spitfires and Lysanders plus C-47s adapted for bombing. Additional support for the Arabs was provided by the Royal Iraqi AF, which sent Austers and Harvards. Further ground attack Harvards were made available by the recently established Syrian AF.

REAF Spitfires, Dakotas and Lysanders supported Egyptian ground forces in the attempt to put the Israeli AF out of action. On 15 May 1948, one day after the declaration of the state of Israel, two Egyptian AF Spitfires attacked Sde Dov. Combined with strikes on other airfields, many of Israel's aircraft were temporarily put out of action. Ramat David was also attacked by the REAF, apparently unaware that it was still occupied by the RAF, whose Spitfires in turn shot down four of the Egyptian attackers.

Starting on 18 May the REAF turned against strategic objectives, C-47s bombing targets around Tel Aviv. The Arab forces enjoyed success in June, with Spitfires assisting in taking the town of Nitzanin and in the defence of Isdud and Suweidan, both of which were kept in Arab hands.

With the receipt of new equipment, including Czech-built S.199 fighters in May, the Israeli AF was able to put up a better defence. Although losses were heavy, the S.199s helped limit C-47 raids.

The Israeli AF was also able to undertake bombing missions, striking Amman and Damascus in June with its own C-47s, and also raiding towns on the

West Bank. The Israeli AF met with less success in the support of ground forces, which suffered a major reverse at Jenin in May-June, while air assets proved increasingly vulnerable to Arab ground fire.

The Iraqi and Syrian air forces in the north were also involved in the support of ground operations. The Royal Iraqi AF participated in the action at Jenin, while Syrian AF Harvards first went into action in support of ground forces attacking Israeli positions near Lake Tiberias.

Ceasefire and rearmament

On 11 June a UN-engineered ceasefire came into being. Although brief, this allowed both Egypt and Israel to acquire new equipment and for the latter to send reinforcements to El Arish. From 9 July, combat resumed, with Israel attempting to take control of western Jerusalem, capture Arab territory in the north, and to break the Egyptian blockade of the Negev. S.199s provided close support while the Israeli AF resumed its bombing campaign. The initial ground operation was a major success, but a day later Syrian AF Harvards proved their worth in attacking Israeli infantry. Israeli AF B-17s then bombed Cairo on 14 July, although the air arm's primary mission remained ground support. A second truce was in place before the end of the month, allowing the Israeli AF to comprehensively re-equip. Sporadic fighting was followed by a renewed Israeli offensive beginning on 15 October. At this time the Israeli AF possessed numerical superiority, which was now focused against the Egyptians. Dispersal of REAF assets rendered their destruction on the ground difficult, although Beaufighters and Spitfires struck El Arish and other airfields. The Israeli AF continued to sustain losses, but the Egyptian forces on the ground were by now on the back foot, and the REAF was suffering the heavier losses both in the air and on the ground. Israeli AF operations in Galilee effectively concluded the campaign in the north before the end of October. By the end of December, El Arish was in Israeli hands, with the REAF forced out onto airstrips in the Sinai. British pressure forced Israel to give up some captured territory before a definitive ceasefire was agreed in January 1949.

ISRAELI AF, 1948–49		
Aircraft	Unit	Base
B-17	69 Sqn	Ramat David
Avia S.199, Spitfire Mk V/IX, P-51D	101 Sqn	Herzliya, Ekron
Avia S.199, Spitfire Mk IX	105 Sqn	Herzliya
C-46, C-47, Norseman	13 Sqn	Ekron
C-47, Beaufighter Mk X	103 Sqn	Sde Dov, Ramat David
Auster	1 Sqn	Sde Dov
Auster AOP.Mk 5	Judean Flt	Yavneel
Taylorcraft J-2	Negev Flt	Beit Daras
Harvard	35 Flt	
Autocrat, RWD-8/13/15	Tel Aviv Flt	Sde Dov

Sinai and Suez
1956

Linking Britain with the Middle East, East Africa and the Far East, the Suez Canal was assigned great strategic importance, but UK prestige would be seriously damaged by the Suez Crisis.

BRITAIN WAS LONG the dominant power in the Canal Zone region, and the waterway itself was a vital trade route. During World War II, numerous RAF airfields had been built or commandeered along the Canal, most of these being handed over to the REAF after the war. By the mid-1950s, RAF air power in the Mediterranean was centred on Cyprus and Malta, and the last of the bases in Egypt had been evacuated in 1955, with Britain the beneficiary of an agreement that ensured access to the Canal. Then, in July 1956, President Nasser nationalized the Canal.

Anglo-French response
As soon as Nasser announced the nationalization of the Canal, British Prime Minister Anthony Eden called on chiefs of staff to plan a military intervention in order to regain control of the waterway. The plan, codenamed Musketeer, emerged as a joint French-British operation. Air strikes on Egyptian AF airfields would aim to disable the recently modernized air arm that included Soviet-supplied Il-28 jet bombers and MiG-17 and MiG-15 jet fighters. Raids on airfields

would be followed by an airborne assault that would capture the Canal Zone.

In order to justify the operation, the Canal had to appear to be under threat, and the plan therefore also involved Israel. The latter hoped to defeat Egypt's military and occupy territory, notably the Gaza Strip. The war plan envisaged an Israeli paratroop raid against the Mitla Pass, in Sinai, as supposed retaliation for Palestinian terrorist actions that were being launched by the Fedayeen group, and others, out of Gaza. The Israeli assault would in turn provide Britain and France with a valid reason to issue Nasser an ultimatum concerning the Canal.

In addition to the RAF and Fleet Air Arm assets available for Musketeer, the French AF deployed four fighter-bomber units, three transport units and an aircraft carrier; three squadrons of French Mystère IVAs would be stationed in Israel to defend Tel Aviv against raids by EAF Il-28 bombers. Since the Israeli AF was lacking in terms of numbers, French Noratlas transports and F-84F fighter-bombers were also soon in Israel in order to support the

▲ De Havilland Mosquito FB.Mk 6

110 Sqn, Israeli AF / Ramat David, 1956

At the time of the Suez Crisis, Israel could call on around 70 jet fighters and 45 piston-engined warplanes. The latter included Mosquitoes operating in the ground attack role. Other Israeli AF assets comprised B-17s, Meteor F.Mk 8s and NF.Mk 13s, Mystère IVAs, Ouragans, P-51Ds, Harvards and assorted transports.

Specifications

Crew: 2

Powerplant: 2 x 1103kW (1480hp) Rolls-Royce Merlin 23 V-12 piston engines

Maximum speed: 612km/h (380mph)

Range: 2655km (1650 miles)

Service ceiling: 11,430m (37,500ft)

Dimensions: span 16.5m (54ft 2in); length 12.47m (40ft 11in); height 4.65m (15ft 3in)

Weight: 10,569kg (22,300lb) loaded

Armament: 4 x .303in (7.7mm) Browning MGs and four 20mm Hispano MGs; up to 1361kg (3000lb) of bombs or eight rockets

▲ Dassault Ouragan

113 Sqn, Israeli AF / Hatzor, 1956

Operator of Israel's French-supplied Ouragan fighters during the Suez Crisis was 113 Sqn. While some Ouragans flew in bare metal, this example wears a pale sand/slate blue camouflage scheme. One unusual Ouragan action during the campaign was a successful attack against an Egyptian destroyer on 31 October.

Specifications

Crew: 1

Powerplant: 1 x 22.2kN (4990lbf) Rolls-Royce Nene 104B turbojet

Maximum speed: 940km/h (584mph)

Range: 920km (570 miles)

Service ceiling: 13,000m (42,650ft)

Dimensions: span 13.16m (43ft 2in); length 10.73m (35ft 2in); height 4.14m (13ft 7in)

Weight: 7404kg (16,323lb) loaded

Armament: 4 x 20mm (.787in) Hispano-Suiza HS.404 cannon, rockets and up to 2270kg (5000lb) of payload

forthcoming Israeli ground offensive in the Mitla Pass and Sinai. This began on 29 September, when the first Israeli paratroops landed on the Mitla Pass, the troop-carrying C-47s backed by close-support P-51s and escorted by Meteors and Ouragans. The French Noratlas force was used to deliver artillery, vehicles and ammunition. Despite the attentions of EAF MiG-15s, Meteors and Vampires near Mitla on 30 November, Israeli troops were soon in a strong position along the Canal, as protecting Mystères fought with MiGs in the skies overhead.

The expiry of the Anglo-French ultimatum (which called for Israeli and Egyptian forces to withdraw from a 16-kilometre (10-mile) zone either side of the Canal) on 31 October was the trigger for Musketeer to begin. Three waves of bombers, primarily RAF Valiants and Canberras flying from Malta and Cyprus, hit over a dozen Egyptian airfields the same evening, to destroy the EAF on the ground. The next day the RAF sent reconnaissance Canberra PR.Mk 7s over Egypt, one of these being damaged by an EAF MiG. The imagery obtained by the Canberras revealed the limited effects of the night's bombing,

▲ Republic F-84F Thunderstreak

EC 3/3, French AF / Akrotiri, 1956

Normally based at Rheims, this EC 3/3 F-84F fighter-bomber was one of those deployed to Akrotiri, Cyprus, for the Suez action. Also flying from Akrotiri were the French AF's EC 1/3 and EC 4/33, with the F-84F and the reconnaissance-configured RF-84F respectively. Further F-84Fs were based in Lydda, Israel.

Specifications

Crew: 1
Powerplant: 1 x 32kN (7220lb) Wright J65-W-3
   turbojet
Maximum speed: 1118km/h (695mph)
Combat radius (with drop tanks): 1304km (810 miles)
Service ceiling: 14,020kg (46,000ft)

Dimensions: span 10.24m (33ft 7.25in); length
   13.23m (43ft 4.75in); height 4.39m (14ft 4.75in)
Weight: 12,701kg (28,000lb) loaded
Armament: 6 x .5in Browning M3 machine-guns,
   external hardpoints with provision for up to
   2722kg (6000lb) of stores

▲ Gloster Meteor NF.Mk 13

10 Sqn, Egyptian AF / Almaza, 1956

The EAF's Meteor night-fighters were not provided with early warning of the Anglo-French air attacks on 31 October, and were therefore of little value in defending Egyptian airbases, although one example reportedly fired on an RAF Valiant during the first night of Anglo-French bombing raids.

Specifications

Crew: 2
Powerplant: 2 x 17.48kN (3933lbf)
   TJE Rolls-Royce Derwent RD.8
Maximum speed: 931km/h (578mph)
Range: 1580km (982 miles)
Service ceiling: 12200m (40,026ft)

Dimensions: span 13.11m (43ft); length
   14.47m (47ft 6in); height 4.24m (13ft 11in)
Weight: 9979kg (22,000lb) loaded
Armament: 4 x 20mm (.787in) British Hispano
   cannons

and tactics now switched to daylight raids launched from British and French carriers stationed in the Mediterranean, and by land-based fighter-bombers.

Therefore, 1 November saw attacks against all Egyptian airfields west of Sinai, offensive assets comprising RAF Canberras, Meteors and Venoms, FAA Sea Hawks, Sea Venoms and Wyverns, plus French AF F-84Fs and French Navy F4Us and F6Fs from the carrier *Arromanches*. Around 500 sorties were flown, without loss to the Allies. Despite the concerted attacks on airfields, the EAF Vampires in particular remained active, and were on hand to attack Israeli ground troops at Mitla on 1 November. As the EAF struggled to disperse its aircraft to safer

locations, the attacks continued on 2-3 November, and were now extended to include military barracks, repair facilities and, starting on 6 November, air defence sites and railways. By targeting airfields near the port city of Alexandria, it was hoped that maximum surprise would be gained for the invasion of Port Said and Port Fuad in the Canal Zone.

Air war over Sinai

With the Anglo-French air effort tying up the EAF, the Israelis were able to launch a major armoured assault that precipitated the Egyptian withdrawal from Sinai. Following a bombing raid by B-17s, the Israelis occupied the Gaza Strip, leaving the Egyptian forces in retreat towards the Canal, which they duly crossed on 2 November. Although not all Israeli actions on the ground proceeded without loss, the Egyptians were rapidly leaving their positions, troops typically moving out at night to avoid air attack. The EAF was meanwhile limited since quantities of aircraft had either been destroyed or damaged on their airfields, or had fled to Saudi Arabia or Syria for their protection. The feared Il-28s that evacuated to the relative safety of Luxor were eventually discovered and attacked on the ground by F-84Fs.

With the Israelis in control on the ground, the Israeli AF clashed with the EAF over Sinai, while Egyptian aircraft continued to disperse to safer airfields. EAF Meteors and MiG-15s fought against

French AF Mystères over Sinai. Sharm el Sheikh was the last major Egyptian garrison standing in Sinai and was backdrop to intense fighting on 2 November, when Israeli paratroops continued their advance. For Israel, capture of this garrison was important as it had a commanding position over the port of Eilat. Israeli AF P-51s and B-17s were available to support the ground offensive on 3 November. Finally, on 4 November, Israeli troops entered Sharm el Sheikh. Aided by P-51s and Ouragans flying attack sorties armed with napalm and rockets, Sharm el Sheikh eventually fell to the Israelis on 5 November.

The Anglo-French airborne assault, meanwhile, began at dawn on 5 November. After carrier aircraft had 'softened up' Egyptian positions, British

▲ **Gloster Meteor NF.Mk 13**

39 Sqn, RAF / Nicosia, 1956

The Meteor NF.Mk 13 was deployed by Egypt and Israel, as well as by the RAF, during the Suez campaign. This example wears the black and yellow 'Suez stripes' around the rear fuselage that served as identification during the operation. The semi-tropicalized Meteor NF.Mk 13 served with just two RAF units.

Specifications

Crew: 2	Dimensions: span 13.11m (43ft); length
Powerplant: 2 x 17.48kN (3933lbf)	14.47m (47ft 6in); height 4.24m (13ft 11in)
TJE Rolls-Royce Derwent RD.8	Weight: 9979kg (22,000lb) loaded
Maximum speed: 931km/h (578mph)	Armament: 4 x 20mm (.787in) British Hispano
Range: 1580km (982 miles)	cannons
Service ceiling: 12200m (40,026ft)	

▲ **Hawker Hunter F.Mk 5**

34 Sqn, RAF / Nicosia, 1956

Home-based at Tangmere for UK air defence, RAF Hunters from 1 and 34 Sqns were mainly used for providing defensive top cover for the daylight strikes against Egyptian targets. Since their external fuel tanks had been damaged, their time on station was limited to around 10 minutes only. Note the incomplete 'Suez stripes'.

Specifications

Crew: 1	Dimensions: span 10.26m (33ft 8in); length
Powerplant: 1 x 35.59kN (8000lb) Armstrong-	13.98m (45ft 10.5in);height 4.02m (13ft 2in)
Siddeley Sapphire turbojet engine	Weight: 8501kg (18,742lb) loaded
Maximum speed: 144km/h (710mph)	Armament: 4 x 30mm Aden cannon; up to
Range: 689km (490 miles)	2722kg (6000lb) of bombs or rockets
Service ceiling: 15,240m (50,000ft)	

paratroops landed at Gamil airfield, near Port Said, having being conveyed to their objective by Hastings and Valetta transports flying from Nicosia. Despite some resistance, the British landings were successful. Minutes after the first British paratroops had touched down, their French counterparts landed near Port Fuad, delivered by Noratlas and C-47s flying from Tymbou, Cyprus. Again, the French paratroopers faced resistance, but completed their objectives.

Heliborne assault

The British planned to launch a heliborne assault against bridges along the Canal, using Fleet Air Arm and RAF Whirlwinds and RAF Sycamores flying from the carriers *Ocean* and *Theseus*. The assault was the first of its kind to be successfully carried out using helicopters, the hard-working rotorcraft making 200 deck landings in the course of the day's operations, and bringing casualties back to the carriers on the return journeys. Further reinforcements for the Anglo-French effort arrived in the Canal Zone in the form of amphibious landings, these beginning on 6 November. The landings were also preceded by air attack by carrier-based fighter-bombers, combined with naval bombardment, and carrier fighters remained on hand in 'cab rank' patrols. By 7 November, Anglo-French invasion forces had reached El Kap, and were making good progress despite having to contend with street fighting.

Ultimately it was international pressure that put an end to Musketeer, and the British and French agreed to a ceasefire on 7 November. For the British in particular, the Suez Crisis was a serious blow to the country's credibility on the world stage.

RAF, SUEZ, 1956		
Aircraft	Unit	Base
Valiant B.Mk 1	138 Sqn	Luqa
Valiant B.Mk 1	148 Sqn	Luqa
Valiant B.Mk 1	207 Sqn	Luqa
Valiant B.Mk 1	214 Sqn	Luqa
Canberra B.Mk 6	9 Sqn	Luqa, Hal Far
Canberra B.Mk 6	12 Sqn	Luqa, Hal Far
Canberra B.Mk 6	101 Sqn	Luqa
Canberra B.Mk 6	109 Sqn	Luqa
Canberra B.Mk 6	139 Sqn	Luqa
Canberra B.Mk 2	21 Sqn	Malta
Canberra B.Mk 2	10 Sqn	Nicosia
Canberra B.Mk 2	15 Sqn	Nicosia
Canberra B.Mk 2	27 Sqn	Nicosia
Canberra B.Mk 2	44 Sqn	Nicosia
Canberra B.Mk 2	18 Sqn	Nicosia
Canberra B.Mk 2	61 Sqn	Nicosia
Canberra B.Mk 2	35 Sqn (det)	Nicosia
Hunter F.Mk 5	1 Sqn	Nicosia
Hunter F.Mk 5	34 Sqn	Nicosia
Venom FB.Mk 4	6 Sqn	Akrotiri
Venom FB.Mk 4	8 Sqn	Akrotiri
Venom FB.Mk 4	249 Sqn	Akrotiri
Meteor NF.Mk 13	39 Sqn	Nicosia
Meteor FR.Mk 9	208 Sqn	Ta Kali
Canberra PR.Mk 7	13 Sqn	Akrotiri
Canberra PR.Mk 7	58 Sqn	Akrotiri
Shackleton MR.Mk 2	37 Sqn	Luqa
Hastings C.Mk 1	70 Sqn	Nicosia
Hastings C.Mk 1	99 Sqn	Nicosia
Hastings C.Mk 1	511 Sqn	Nicosia
Valetta C.Mk 1	30 Sqn	Nicosia
Valetta C.Mk 1	84 Sqn	Nicosia
Valetta C.Mk 1	114 Sqn	Nicosia
Whirlwind HAR.Mk 2, Sycamore HC.Mk 14	JHU	HMS Ocean

FLEET AIR ARM, SUEZ, 1956		
Aircraft	Unit	Base
Sea Hawk FGA.Mk 4/6	800 NAS	HMS *Albion*
Sea Hawk FB.Mk 3	802 NAS	HMS *Albion*
Sea Hawk FGA.Mk 6	804 NAS	HMS *Bulwark*
Sea Hawk FGA.Mk 4	810 NAS	HMS *Bulwark*
Sea Hawk FB.Mk 3	895 NAS	HMS *Bulwark*
Sea Hawk FGA.Mk 6	897 NAS	HMS *Eagle*
Sea Hawk FGA.Mk 6	899 NAS	HMS *Eagle*
Sea Venom FAW.Mk 21	809 NAS	HMS *Albion*
Sea Venom FAW.Mk 21	892 NAS	HMS *Eagle*
Sea Venom FAW.Mk 21	893 NAS	HMS *Eagle*
Wyvern S.Mk 4	830 NAS	HMS *Eagle*
Skyraider AEW.Mk 1	849 NAS	HMS *Eagle* and *Albion*
Whirlwind HAS.Mk 22	845 NAS	HMS *Theseus*

Specifications

Crew: 2

Powerplant: 2 x 28.9kN (6500lb) Rolls-Royce
Avon Mk 101 turbojets

Maximum speed: 917km/h (570mph)

Range: 4274km (2656 miles)

Service ceiling: 14,630m (48,000ft)

Dimensions: span 29.49m (63ft 11in); length
19.96m (65ft 6in); height 4.78m (15ft 8in)

Weight: 24,925kg (54,950lb) loaded

Armament: bomb bay with provision for up to
2727kg (6000lb) of bombs, plus 909kg
(2000lb) of underwing pylons

▲ English Electric Canberra B.Mk 2

10 Sqn, RAF / Nicosia, 1956

The Canberra bombers of 10 Sqn were normally based at Honington, as evidenced
by the Honington Wing emblem on the fin. For the Suez operation, RAF Canberra
B.Mk 2s and B.Mk 6s were based at Hal Far, Luqa and Nicosia and took part in
the initial raids on Egyptian airfields, flown at high altitude.

Specifications

Crew: 1

Powerplant: 2 x 16.0kN (3600lb) Rolls-Royce
Derwent 8 turbojets

Maximum speed: 962km/h (598mph)

Range: 1580km (980 miles)

Service ceiling: 13,106m (43,000ft)

Dimensions: span 11.32m (37ft 2in);
length 13.58m (44ft 7in); height 3.96m (13ft)

Weight: 8664kg (19,100lb) loaded

Armament: 4 x 20mm (.787in) Hispano
cannon, 2 iron bombs or 8 rockets

▲ Gloster Meteor FR.Mk 9

208 Sqn, RAF / Ta Kali, 1956

The longest-serving RAF squadron in the Middle East, 208 Sqn operated from
Egypt and Malta during 1951-58. As such, the unit was the primary tactical
reconnaissance asset in the region. During the Suez Crisis, 208 Sqn operated the
fighter-reconnaissance Meteor FR.Mk 9 variant from Ta Kali, Malta.

Specifications

Crew: 1

Powerplant: 1 x 24kN (5400lb) Rolls-Royce
Nene 103 turbojet

Maximum speed: 969km/h (602mph)

Range: 370km (230 miles)

Service ceiling: 13,565m (44,500ft)

Dimensions: span 11.89m (39ft);

length 12.09m (39ft 8in); height 2.64m
(8ft 8in)

Weight: 7348kg (16,200lb) loaded

Armament: 4 x 20mm Hispano cannon;
provision for 4 x 227kg (500lb) bombs, or
2 x 227kg (500lb) bombs and 20 x three-inch
or 16 five-inch rockets

▲ Hawker Sea Hawk FB.Mk 3

802 NAS, Royal Navy / HMS Albion, 1956

The Sea Hawks of 802 NAS operated from the deck of HMS *Albion* for Operation
Musketeer. The unit lost one Sea Hawk that was providing support during the
Anglo-French landings on 5 November, with another example damaged by anti-
aircraft artillery on 2 November, although this aircraft recovered to the carrier.

Six-Day War
1967

The destruction wrought on Arab air power by Israel's pre-emptive strike on opposition airbases in June 1967 was such that Operation Moked would serve as a template for future campaigns.

THE BUILD-UP TO the Six-Day War had seen increasing tensions since April 1967, culminating in an air battle over the Golan Heights involving Israeli AF Mystères and Syrian AF MiG-21s, while Israeli jets targeted artillery in the Golan Heights. Meanwhile, cross-border raids into Israel by Arab insurgents had been escalating in the wake of the 1956 war, these mainly originating in Jordan and Syria. After having been established in the Sinai to prevent such raids, a UN peacekeeping force departed in May 1967. In the same month, Egypt, Syria and Jordan formulated a new defence pact, while air assets began to be redeployed.

Although troops were mobilized in May, Nasser apparently did not expect another conflict against Israel so soon, and moved aircraft from Sinai to the Canal Zone. Meanwhile, United Arab AF MiG-17s and MiG-19s were deployed to Dumeyr, near Damascus, with other UARAF combat aircraft in Yemen or at Hurghada on the Red Sea. Egypt's force of Tu-16 bombers were also no longer kept on alert by June, although Egyptian troops were now in control of all posts in the Sinai after the UN withdrawal, and the Gulf of Aqba had been closed off to Israeli shipping.

The first day of the campaign, codenamed Moked, saw almost the entire strength of the Israeli AF attack airfields in Egypt, Syria and Jordan. Beginning in 1967, the Israelis had conducted regular air patrols over the Mediterranean, often in large formations, and at low level to avoid detection by radar. Therefore, the Israeli strike package that assembled on the morning of 5 June 1967 was not met with an appropriate response.

The first waves

Departing after dawn, the first package of Israeli AF strike aircraft heading west included Mirage IIIs and Mystères, with around 120 aircraft in three waves. These flew below Egyptian radar cover, then turned south towards the Egyptian coast and raided at least 10 airfields, including El Arish, Bir Gifgafa, Cairo West (home to Egypt's force of Tu-16 bombers), Fayid, Jebel Libni, Bir Thamada, Abu Sueir, Kabrit, Beni Sueif and Inchas. While Mirages and Super Mystères flew across the Mediterranean before turning to attack from the west, striking airbases in the Canal Zone and along the Nile, Mystère IVAs and Ouragans approached on a direct course from bases in southern Israel to raid airfields in Sinai. In most cases, 10 flights of four aircraft made a bombing run, followed by strafing. The second and third waves then arrived at 10-minute intervals.

After the initial eight waves had attacked their targets, the Israeli AF aircraft recovered to their airfields, before a further wave of strike aircraft set off for Egyptian airfields along the Nile.

Although claims were certainly exaggerated, Israel reported the destruction of 308 aircraft in total by the end of the assault on 5 June, of which 240 were Egyptian. The Israeli AF admitted losses amounting to 20 combat aircraft. In addition to the aircraft destroyed on the ground, the Israeli AF shot down a number of Egyptian aircraft, and others fell while attempting to scramble from their airfields during the course of the raids. Those Egyptian aircraft that did manage to take off – notably at Abu Sueir, where as many as 20 MiG-21s made it into the air – were generally only able to put up limited resistance, and sustained heavy losses in the process.

In response to the attack on Egypt, Jordan began an artillery bombardment of Israel, targeting Ramat David airfield. Air raids were then prosecuted against Israel by the Royal Jordanian AF, whose Hunter fighter-bombers struck Kfar Sirkin and Natanya, causing some damage to parked aircraft. The Iraqi AF, meanwhile, announced that it had attacked Lydda airfield, although this was denied by Israel.

With the war now opened up on the eastern front, Israel turned upon Egypt's allies. Operating MiG-17s, the Syrian AF had raided the oil installation at Haifa, and strafed Mahanyim airfield,

Specifications

Crew: 1

Powerplant: 1 x 27.9kN (6280lb) Hispano Suiza
Tay 250A turbojet; or 1 x 3500kg
(7716lb) Hispano Suiza Verdon 350 turbojet

Maximum speed: 1120km/h (696mph)

Range: unknown

Service ceiling: 13,750m (45,000ft)

Dimensions: span 11.1m (36ft 5.75in); length
12.9m (42ft 2in); height 4.4m (14ft 5in)

Weight: 9500kg (20,950lb) loaded

Armament: internal bomb bay with provision for
up to 10 bombs, underwing pylons
for two bombs up to 450kg (992lb), or two drop
tanks

▲ **Dassault Mystère IVA**

116 Sqn, Israeli AF / Tel Nov, 1967

Just over 30 serviceable Mystère IVA jets were available to the Israeli AF at the beginning of the offensive. These were operated by 109 and 116 Sqns, In one of the more notorious incidents of the war, Israeli AF Mystère IVAs were involved in an attack on the U.S. intelligence vessel *Liberty*, sailing off El Arish.

Specifications

Crew: 1

Powerplant: 1 x 44.1kN (9920lbf) SNECMA Atar
101G-2 turbojet

Maximum speed: 1195km/h (743mph)

Range: 870km (540 miles)

Service ceiling: 17,000m (56,000ft)

Dimensions: span 10.51m (34ft 6in); length
14.13m (46ft 4in); height 4.60m (15ft 1in)

Weight: 9000kg (20,000lb) loaded

Armament: 2 x 30mm (1.18in) DEFA 552
cannons, rockets, missiles and up to
2680kg (5000lb) of payload

▲ **Dassault Super Mystère B2**

105 Sqn, Israeli AF / Hatzor, 1967

Israel possessed just under 40 Mystère B2s in June 1967, these being operated by 105 Sqn, the largest combat unit within the Israeli AF. Despite relatively heavy losses, the Mystère B2 fleet was instrumental in the initial strikes against Arab airfields, with all available aircraft being sent within the first wave.

and Israel responded with strikes against airbases at Damascus, Dumayr, Marj Rial and Seikal. Later in the afternoon the Israeli AF turned its attentions to the Syrian base at T4, and H3 in Iraq.

The eastern front

After attacking Syria, Jordan was next to receive the attentions of the Israeli AF on 5 June. In the afternoon, the Israeli AF attacked Mafraq and Amman airbases in Jordan, together with an early warning radar station, a command centre, as well as

troops moving westwards. The almost total destruction of the RJAF Hunter force meant that Jordanian pilots were now seconded to the Iraqi AF.

The afternoon of 5 June saw the Israeli AF return to Egypt, hitting Cairo International and airfields at Al Minya, Bilbeis, Helwan, Hurghada, Luxor and Ras Banas, as well as a number of radar installations. Cairo International was assigned particular importance, because a number of Egyptian Tu-16s had fled here and thereby avoided destruction on the ground at Cairo West. The attacking force now

Specifications

Crew: 1

Powerplant: 1 x 58.72kN (13,200lb) thrust
SNECMA Atar 09B-3 afterburning turbojet
engine and one 16.46kN (3700lb) thrust
auxiliary SEFR 841 rocket motor

Maximum speed: 2350km/h (1460mph)

Range: 2012km (1250 miles)

Service ceiling: 17,000m (55,755 ft)

Dimensions: span 8.26m (27ft 2in); length
14.91m (48ft 10in); height 4.6m (14ft 10in)

Weight: 11,676kg (25,740lb) loaded

Armament: 2 x 30mm DEFA cannon;
1 x Matra R.511 or R.530 AAM, up to
2295kg (5060lb) of bombs

▲ **Dassault Mirage IIICJ**

119 Sqn, Israeli AF / Tel Nov, 1967

From an Israeli perspective, one of the undoubted 'stars' of the 1967 war was the
Mirage III, with 70 Mirage IIICJ single-seat fighters having been received by 1964,
together with a pair of photo-reconnaissance versions. As well as assembling an
enviable record in aerial combat, Mirages were used for ground attack.

also included Vautour bombers flying from their bases at Hatzerim and Ramat David.

After the 'lightning' attacks on Arab airfields, which dominated the first day of operations, 6 June saw the Israeli AF used increasingly in support of the offensive on the ground. Helicopters began to be used on the night of 5/6 June, with a party of commandos being delivered behind Jordanian lines by S-58. With Israeli troops having made a break through the Egyptian lines near Rafah, under the support of artillery, Israeli aircraft were active in support of troops in Sinai and on the West Bank.

Helicopters once again played a vital role in Israel's capture of Abu Agheila, a key position near the Sinai border. In the face of Israeli AF ground support missions flown over Gaza and Bir Lahfan, the Egyptian Army was in retreat, and rapidly moving out of Sinai. Resistance by Arab air power was limited, although two MiG-21s did attack Israeli troops near Bir Lahfan on 6 June, both reportedly being shot down in the process. A pair of Egyptian Su-7s also made it as far as El Arish, while several attempts were made by Arab fighters to destroy Israeli helicopters. RJAF personnel were now at H3, where they were operating alongside the Iraqi AF. The latter force managed to bomb industry in Natanya with a single Tu-16 on 6 June. The lone raider was shot down by air defences, but it prompted an Israeli AF response, and fighter-bombers were duly sent against H3, where they clashed with both Iraqi and

Jordanian defenders. Further aerial battles were reported over H3 in the days that followed.

Israel on the offensive

While the Israeli AF kept up its attacks on Jordanian positions on the West Bank, in Sinai the Egyptians were apparently in disarray. Israel therefore took the opportunity to capture the Mitla and Giddi Passes. This had the effect of encircling Egyptian units east of the mountains in Sinai. Here, they were left to the mercy of the Israeli AF, which set about destroying Egyptian vehicles in the Mitla Pass. Magister trainers, equipped with rockets, proved especially useful in the close support role, and operated in concert with Israeli armoured formations. Indeed, the massed tank battles fought during the Six-Day War were the largest witnessed since World War II.

With the Mitla and Giddi Passes now in Israeli hands, the Arab air forces assembled their remaining equipment for an attempt to drive out the Israelis. Around 50 Arab aircraft were available for the attacks, which began at dawn on 7 June. In order for the attacks to be staged, airfields and aircraft had been repaired, and pilots had been redeployed where necessary to make good losses; before the war was over, Algerian pilots were also fighting alongside the Egyptians. Although the pace of the Israeli advance was slowed by the attentions of Arab air power, sporadic ground attack sorties were not enough to alter the course of the war in

Sinai. Arab aircraft also had to contend with standing air patrols mounted by the Israeli AF in defence of the troops below.

Bolstered by UARAF personnel, the Egyptians were able to mount more concerted air attacks against the Israeli ground forces by 8 June. Despite some success by Arab pilots, the outcome of the Sinai ground war had effectively been decided, and although an increasing number of Arab air force sorties were being made, it was the Israeli AF that was in a position to mount a more telling new campaign. This was to be directed against Syria.

After Egypt had agreed to the terms of a UN ceasefire early on 9 June, and with Jordan also defeated, Syria was left to face Israel alone. After Israeli AF raids on the Golan Heights, Syria had accepted ceasefire terms on 8 June, but the next day Israel launched a full-scale attack against Golan. Syrian forces quickly retreated to defensive positions around Damascus, while air combat saw Israeli AF jets clash with both UARAF and Syrian AF assets. Finally, a UN ceasefire came into force on 10 June, by which time Israel had captured the Golan Heights and the town of Qunaytra. Spearheaded by air power, Israel had achieved a decisive victory over its Arab neighbours.

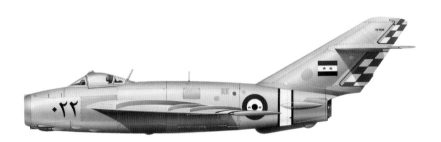

Specifications

Crew: 1	Dimensions: span 9.45m (31ft); length 11.05m
Powerplant: 1 x 33kN (7452lb) Klimov VK-1F	(36ft 3.75in); height 3.35m (11ft)
turbojet	Weight: 600kg (14,770lb) loaded
Maximum speed: 1145km/h (711mph)	Armament: 1 x 37mm N-37 cannon and
Range: 1470km (913 miles)	2 x 23mm NS-23 cannon, plus up to 500kg
Service ceiling: 16,600m (54,560ft)	(1102lb) of mixed stores on underwing pylons

▲ **Mikoyan-Gurevich MiG-17F**

20th Brigade, Egyptian AF, El Arish

The most numerous combat aircraft in the Arab inventory, the MiG-17 was used for both air defence and for ground attack duties in 1967. Towards the end of the fighting, surviving MiG-17s were active on offensive missions over the Mitla Pass and in southern Sinai, suffering a number of losses in the process.

▲ **Ilyushin Il-28**

61st Brigade, Egyptian AF

The efficiency of Israel's pre-emptive strikes meant that the Egyptian bomber force had little role to play in the subsequent fighting. Tu-16s and Il-28s suffered heavily on the ground at Cairo West, although at least one Il-28, escorted by MiGs, managed to launch a raid against Israeli aircraft at El Arish on 7 June.

Specifications

Crew: 3	17.65m (57ft 10.75in); height 6.70m (21ft
Powerplant: 2 x 26.3kN (5952lb) Klimov VK-1	11.8in)
turbojets	Weight: 21,200kg (46,738lb) loaded
Maximum speed: 902km/h (560mph)	Armament: 4 x 23mm cannon; internal bomb
Range: 2180km (1355 miles)	capacity 1000kg (2205lb), max bomb
Service ceiling: 12,300m (40,355ft)	capacity 3000kg (6614lb); torpedo version:
Dimensions: span 21.45m (70ft 4.5in); length	provision for two 400mm light torpedoes

▲ Sukhoi Su-7BMK

1st Brigade, Egyptian AF

Despite its limited range and payload, the Su-7 could have played a more significant role in the Six-Day War, but suffered heavily on the ground. By June 1967 the Egyptian AF had received 64 examples, but only a single unit, based at Fayid, had converted to the type, and just 15 examples were declared operational.

Specifications

Crew: 1

Powerplant: 1 x 88.2kN (19,842lb) Lyulka AL-7F turbojet

Maximum speed: 1700km/h (1056mph)

Range: 320km (199 miles)

Service ceiling: 15,150m (49,700ft)

Dimensions: span 8.93m (29ft 3.5in); length

17.37m (57ft); height 4.7m (15ft 5in)

Weight: 13,500kg (29,750lb) loaded

Armament: 2 x 30mm NR-30 cannon; four external pylons for 2 x 750kg (1653lb) and 2 x 500kg (1102lb) bombs, but with two tanks on fuselage pylons, total external weapon load is reduced to 1000kg (2205lb)

War of Attrition
1969–1970

Despite Israel's resounding victory in the Six-Day War, the fighting did not end with the UN-backed ceasefire. Instead there began a War of Attrition, in which air power played a key role.

THE CEASEFIRE OF June 1967 did not hold long, and on 1 July an Israeli patrol was ambushed by Egyptian troops on the eastern side of the Suez Canal. This was the catalyst for Israeli and Egyptian forces to begin a campaign of shelling across the Canal, which would in turn lead to the deployment of air power.

While the Israeli AF clashed with Arab MiGs over the Canal Zone, the Syrian AF launched longer-range raids into Israeli territory, losing a number of aircraft in the process. In October, for instance, Israeli air defences claimed the destruction of four Syrian AF MiG-19s. The same month saw the fighting escalate to include naval warfare, and the sinking of the Israeli destroyer *Eilat* by Egyptian gunboats.

Re-equipment programme

On the back of the losses sustained in the Six-Day War, Israel took the opportunity presented by the sporadic fighting that followed to re-equip its air arm. Most importantly, an order was placed in 1969 for 50 F-4E fighter-bombers and six RF-4E reconnaissance

aircraft, and the Israeli AF Phantom II fleet would go on to play a central role in the years to come. The Israelis also began to receive large numbers of A-4 attack aircraft, including examples delivered from U.S. Navy surplus, while renewal of the helicopter arm saw the S-58 progressively replaced by the S-65 and the Bell 205. At the same time Egypt was re-equipping its air force, with more advanced MiG-21PF/PFM variants delivered by the USSR.

The Egyptians deployed additional troops to the Canal Zone, and in September 1968 there began a major artillery battle fought across the waterway. From the following month, Israel stepped up its commando raids that ventured deep into Egyptian territory, often targeting air defence sites. The Israeli completion of the defensive Bar Lev Line along the Canal in March 1969 was the signal for Nasser to announce a war of attrition, which would be waged primarily by artillery and air power.

With the Egyptians possessing superior artillery, the Israeli AF was called into action, attacking

Egyptian troops along the West Bank starting in July 1969, knocking out radar sites in addition to artillery. In September the Israelis launched a large-scale raid against an Egyptian military complex at Ras Abu-Daraj, accompanied by air strikes. Meanwhile, the Israelis were also extracting a heavy toll on the EAF, through the use of both standing air patrols and surface-to-air missiles (SAMs).

With the Israeli AF able to operate over Egypt unscathed, Soviet advisors began to arrive in increasing numbers, manning air defence sites and flying MiGs on behalf of the Egyptians. After the Israeli AF hit targets around Cairo in early 1970, the Soviets sent additional air defence equipment, including squadrons of advanced MiG-21MFs.

Despite increasingly powerful Egyptian air defences organized along the Canal, the West Bank, and around major cities, the Israeli AF intensified its efforts, with numerous sorties flown over Egypt in the first quarter of 1970. The presence of Soviet 'advisors' was a concern, however, and Israel began to decrease its offensive operations as a result. This allowed the Egyptian AF to regain the initiative, with air strikes launched across the Canal. The Israeli bombing campaign was stepped up accordingly in May, with a considerable increase in air-to-air combat as a consequence. Although over-flights continued, both sides agreed to a ceasefire in August 1970.

Specifications

Crew: 1

Powerplant: 1 x 44.1kN (9920lbf) SNECMA Atar 101G-2 turbojet

Maximum speed: 1195km/h (743mph)

Range: 870km (540 miles)

Service ceiling: 17,000m (56,000ft)

Dimensions: span 10.51m (34ft 6in); length 14.13m (46ft 4in); height 4.6m (15ft 1in)

Weight: 9000kg (20,000lb) loaded

Armament: 2 x 30mm (1.18in) DEFA 552 cannons, rockets, missiles and up to 2680kg (5000lb) of payload

▲ **Dassault Super Mystère B2**

Israeli AF / 1969–70

Although by now relegated to ground attack and close support duties, the Super Mystère B2 remained a useful asset to the Israeli AF at the time of the War of Attrition. At around the same time, the survivors were re-engined with the same J52 as used in the U.S.-supplied A-4 Skyhawk.

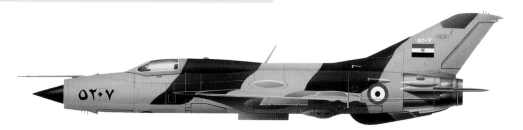

Specifications

Crew: 1

Powerplant: 1 x 60.8kN (13,668lb) thrust Tumanskii afterburning turbojet

Maximum speed: 2050km/h (1300mph)

Range: 1800km (1118 miles)

Service ceiling: 17,000m (57,750ft)

Dimensions: span 7.15m (23ft 5.5in);

length (including probe) 15.76m (51ft 8.5in); height 4.1m (13ft 5.5in)

Weight: 9400kg (20,723lb) loaded

Armament: 1 x 23mm cannon, provision for about 1500kg (3307lb) of stores, including air-to-air missiles, rocket pods, napalm tanks or drop tanks

▲ **Mikoyan-Gurevich MiG-21PF**

United Arab Republic AF/Egyptian AF / Mansourah, 1969

As part of its re-equipment programme in the wake of the Six-Day War, Egypt was the recipient of Soviet military materiel in the form of 70 MiG-21PFs and MiG-21PFMs, together with additional MiG-17Fs and Su-7s. Despite new aircraft, the Egyptian AF still suffered from shortages of trained aircrew, however.

Yom Kippur War
1973

Beginning on 6 October 1973, the Jewish Day of Atonement, the Yom Kippur War was launched by Israel's Arab neighbours in a bid to regain the territories that they had lost in 1967.

FOR THE ARAB forces, success relied on catching the Israelis off their guard. The objectives of a two-pronged attack included regaining the West Bank, Golan Heights and Sinai Peninsula, which had been lost so dramatically in 1967. In catching the Israelis by surprise, the Egyptian Army was successful. After artillery and air strikes against the Suez Canal, around 75,000 Egyptian troops and 400 tanks proved too strong for the Israeli defences on the eastern bank of the Canal. Using bridges to cross the Canal, the Egyptians pressed on into Sinai. At the same time, the Syrian Army began to attack

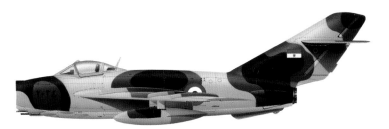

Specifications

Crew: 1

Powerplant: 1 x 33kN (7452lb) Klimov VK-1F turbojet

Maximum speed: 1145km/h (711mph)

Range: 1470km (913 miles)

Service ceiling: 16,600m (54,560ft)

Dimensions: span 9.45m (31ft); length 11.05m (36ft 3.75in); height 3.35m (11ft)

Weight: 6700kg (14,770lb) loaded

Armament: 1 x 37mm N-37 cannon and 2 x 23mm NS-23 cannon, plus up to 500kg (1102lb) of mixed stores on underwing pylons

▲ **Mikoyan-Gurevich MiG-17F**

Egyptian AF / 1970s

Approaching obsolescence by 1973, the MiG-17 remained in use with both Egypt and Syria, primarily for ground attack. However, MiG-21 losses meant that the MiG-17 was forced to undertake defensive missions, too. Together with Su-7s, MiG-17s played an important role during the Syrian advance on the Golan Heights.

▲ **Mil Mi-8**

Egyptian AF / 1970s

Helicopters played a vital role in the initial Egyptian assault across the Suez Canal, the Mi-8 being use to transport troops to their objectives both in Sinai and the Golan Heights. The Mi-8 was vulnerable to ground fire, however, and on 7 October alone Israel claimed no fewer than 10 Egyptian helicopters shot down.

Specifications

Crew: 3

Powerplant: 2 x 1454kW (1950shp) Klimov TV3-117Mt turboshafts

Maximum speed: 260km/h (162mph)

Range: 450km (280 miles)

Service ceiling: 4500m (14,765ft)

Dimensions: rotor diameter 21.29m (69ft 10in); length 18.17m (59ft 7in); height 5.65m (18ft 6in)

Weight: 11,100kg (24,470lb)

Armament: up to 1500kg (3300lb) of disposable stores

Israeli positions in the Golan Heights in the northeast, under the cover of air support provided by MiG-17 and Su-7 fighter-bombers.

Simultaneous with the land assault, Egyptian AF aircraft struck Israeli airfields, SAM sites, radar stations and other targets in Sinai. Targets deeper within Israel were attacked by Tu-16s launching standoff cruise missiles. Fighting a war on two fronts, the Israeli AF was required to launch air strikes against Egyptian and Syrian forward positions and rear areas, bringing to bear its F-4, A-4 and Mirage III and Nesher jets within 30 minutes of the invasion. In the first four days of the conflict, the Israeli AF launched 3555 sorties for the loss of 81 aircraft.

Having learned the lessons of 1967, the Arab forces were now much better protected against air attack. Egypt planned to occupy a narrow strip of Sinai desert, before a battle of attrition could begin. As well as defensive air patrols to defeat the Israeli AF in the air, the Arab forces were protected by Soviet-made SAMs and effective anti-aircraft artillery. Fixed SAM sites were deployed along the western bank of the Canal, while mobile and man-portable SAMs, together with self-propelled anti-aircraft artillery were deployed with the troops in the field.

The SAM threat

Operating in the face of modern ground-based air defences provided the Israeli AF with a steep learning curve, and initial electronic countermeasures (ECM) proved ineffective. From an estimated 120 Israeli aircraft lost during the conflict, around 90-100 of these were claimed by ground-based air defences.

Israel decided to focus on the northern front, and defeat the Syrians before becoming further involved in Sinai. After three days of fighting, including a tank battle, the Syrian Army was forced back, while the Israeli AF targeted the military HQ in Damascus and the Homs oil installation on 19 October.

Eventually, the Israeli loss rate was reduced to one aircraft for every 102 sorties, aided by the receipt of more advanced ECM equipment and guided weapons from the U.S., and through the use of revised tactics. In order to boost the Arab air forces' capabilities, Iraq provided a squadron of Hunters and one of MiG-21s, while Jordanian SAMs targeted any Israeli AF aircraft that were within range. The Syrians were pushed back in the north, with Israeli AF aircraft now ranging almost as far as the Turkish border. By mid-October the Arab air defences were in a state of disarray, and with the Syrian AF unable to defeat the Israelis in the air, the Israeli troops pressed on.

On the Sinai front, Egypt was in control of the eastern side of the Canal after two days. Numerous Israeli counter-attacks initially failed to make an impression, and Egypt was holding out for its planned war of attrition. Support for the Egyptian AF came in the form of Algerian Su-7s on 8 October, when both sides were engaged in attacking each other's airfields. From 14 October further back-up appeared in the form of Libyan AF Mirages. At the same time as the USSR was making good Arab aircraft losses, Israel was benefiting from huge

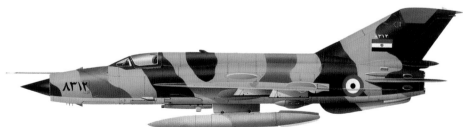

▲ Mikoyan-Gurevich MiG-21PFM
Egyptian AF / 1970s
The backbone of both the Egyptian and Syrian air arms in 1973 was provided by the MiG-21, in a number of different variants. In order to compensate for early losses to the Israeli AF the Soviets delivered additional MiG-21s later in the war, some of these being transferred from Warsaw Pact orders.

Specifications
Crew: 1	length (including probe) 15.76m (51ft 8.5in)
Powerplant: 1 x 60.8kN (13,668lb) thrust	height 4.1m (13ft 5.5in)
Tumanskii afterburning turbojet	Weight: 9400kg (20,723lb) loaded
Maximum speed: 2050km/h (1300mph)	Armament: 1 x 23mm cannon, provision for
Range: 1800km (1118 miles)	about 1500kg (3307lb) of stores, including
Service ceiling: 17,000m (57,750ft)	air-to-air missiles, rocket pods, napalm tanks
Dimensions: span 7.15m (23ft 5.5in);	or drop tanks

quantities of materiel delivered by air from the U.S., including additional A-4s and F-4s.

On 14 October Egyptian forces advanced without their air defence 'umbrella', playing into Israeli hands. After Israeli naval attacks on the Egyptian coast in the west, Israeli troops threatened the Egyptian flanks on both sides of the Canal. Israel established a bridgehead and began to take out Egyptian air defence sites, before Egypt requested a ceasefire on 20 October, although Israel continued to advance towards Suez. Ending with Israeli victory on 24 October, the war had been closely contested, and although the Arabs caught the Israelis off guard, their hopes of superpower intervention to force a ceasefire under favourable terms were not to be.

▲ **F-4E Phantom II**

A signature warplane of the Middle East wars, Israel began to receive the Phantom II in 1969. These 119 Sqn F-4Es are seen over Jerusalem.

Lebanon
1982

Having learned hard lessons during the October 1973 war, the Israeli AF was much better equipped when it took on the Syrian AF over Lebanon during the next major Middle East conflict.

AMID A BACKDROP of fighting between rival Palestinian and Christian factions, the Syrian Army intervened to bring a fragile peace to Lebanon. On the afternoon of 4 June, a day after an assassination attempt on the Israeli ambassador to the UK, Israel invaded Lebanon, sending seven waves of jets to attack Palestinian refugee camps and suspected terrorist strongholds located around the capital, Beirut. Also hit were the Palestine Liberation Organization (PLO) HQ and weapons dumps.

By now, the Israeli AF was better able to counter the SAM menace, using advanced ECM equipment

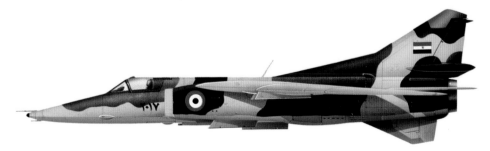

Specifications
Crew: 1

Powerplant: 1 x 98kN (22,046lb) Tumanskii R-27F2M-300 turbojet

Maximum speed: about 2445km/h (1520mph)

Range: 966km (600 miles)

Service ceiling: over 18,290m (60,000ft)

Dimensions: span 13.97m (45ft 10in), spread, 7.78m (25ft 6.25in) swept; length 16.71m (54ft 10in); height 4.82m (15ft 9.75in)

Weight: 18,145kg (40,000lb) loaded

Armament: 1 x 23mm GSh-23L cannon, provision for 3000kg (6614lb) of stores

▲ **Mikoyan-Gurevich MiG-23BN**
Syrian AF / early 1980s

The variable-geometry MiG-23BN was the most advanced offensive asset available to the Syrian AF at the time of the 1982 conflict. In fact, Syria had deployed its MiG-23BNs over Lebanon before the Israeli invasion, with two examples being claimed destroyed over Bekaa during an April 1982 raid.

and dedicated suppression of enemy air defence (SEAD) assets, including anti-radar missiles. The Israeli AF had been greatly improved through the induction of the F-15, widely used to provide defensive top cover over Lebanon, and the F-16. Between them, these two modern fighters were more than a match for the Syrian AF's fleet of MiGs, and Israel eventually posted claims for 85 aerial victories against the Syrian AF, 44 of these credited to F-16s.

Relentless campaign

After follow-up air raids on Palestinian targets in southern Lebanon, the Israeli AF carried out further air strikes on 5 June, these targeting Beirut, transport connections along the coast, and PLO positions. The

following day Israeli troops moved into Lebanon, a full-scale invasion being supported by helicopters, some of which were armed with anti-tank missiles to defeat Syrian armour. The Israelis' aim was to extinguish the fighting capability of the Palestinian militant groups in the south who had long been launching raids into Israeli-occupied territory, under the protection offered by the Syrian occupation.

In order to attempt to outflank PLO and Lebanese resistance, Israeli naval and airborne commando landings were conducted early in the campaign, supported by helicopters at Zahrani and Sidon. In the east, the ground campaign was fiercest in the Bekaa Valley, and here transport helicopters and helicopter gunships played a valuable role, under the cover of

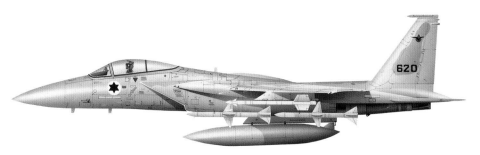

Specifications

Crew: 1	Dimensions: span 13.05m (42ft 9.75in); length
Powerplant: 2 x 106kN (23,810lb) Pratt &	19.43m (63ft 9in); height 5.63m (18ft 5in)
Whitney F100-PW-100 turbofans	Weight: 25,424kg (56,000lb) loaded
Maximum speed: 2655km/h (1650mph)	Armament: 1 x 20mm M61A1 cannon, pylons
Range: 1930km (1200 miles)	with provision for up to 7620kg (16,800lb)
Service ceiling: 30,500m (100,000ft)	of stores

▲ McDonnell Douglas F-15A Eagle

133 Sqn, Israeli AF / Tel Nov, early 1980s

Delivered to Israel under the Peace Fox programme, the F-15 played a vital role in establishing Israeli AF air supremacy over Lebanon, and claimed significant numbers of Syrian AF aircraft destroyed. Prior to the conflict, F-15s claimed five out of 12 MiG-21s that were attacking an Israeli strike package on 27 June 1978.

Specifications

Crew: 1	15.65m (51ft 4.25in); height 4.55m (14ft 4.25in)
Powerplant: 1x 79.6kN (17,900lb) General	Weight: 16,200kg (35,715lb) loaded
Electric J79-J1E turbojet	Armament: 1 x IAI (DEFA) 30mm cannon;
Maximum speed: 2445km/h (1520mph)	provision for up to 5775kg (12,732lb) of
Range: 346km (215 miles)	stores; for interception duties AIM-9
Service ceiling: 17,680m (58,000ft)	Sidewinder air-to-air missiles, or indigenously
Dimensions: span 8.22m (26ft 11.5in); length	produced AAMs such as the Shafrir or Python

▲ IAI Kfir

144 Sqn, Israeli AF / Hatzor, early 1980s

Developed on the basis of the Mirage 5, delivery of which had been embargoed, the Kfir was a further improvement on the indigenous Nesher, and first saw significant combat usage over Lebanon. The aircraft flew defensive missions, as well as prosecuting attacks against Syrian radar stations and other targets.

Israeli AF air supremacy. With the Israelis threatening to cut off the Syrian ground forces, the Syrian AF was called into action in a close support capacity.

The majority of the aerial fighting over Lebanon was recorded between 9-11 June, with F-16s frequently clashing with Syrian MiGs over Beirut. As well as the deployment of the advanced F-15 and F-16 fighters (the former armed with beyond-visual-range AAMs) the conflict was notable for the successful employment of remotely piloted vehicles (RPVs) for reconnaissance and targeting, and Israeli AF E-2Cs, which were operated in an airborne early warning and control capacity. Anti-armour helicopters would also prove their worth, Israel fielding the Hughes 500MD and AH-1G/S, while Syria deployed armed Gazelles, Mi-8s and Mi-25s.

Under the sheer weight of numbers, and bolstered by superior weaponry and tactics, the Israelis were able to overcome PLO forces, despite stiff resistance. A ceasefire came into force on 11 June, but the Israeli strikes against the PLO continued for another day until both sides agreed to put an end to the fighting. Although the Syrians had enjoyed some success on the ground, Israeli victory in the air was undisputed.

Specifications

Crew: 5	Dimensions: span 24.6m (80ft 7in); length
Powerplant: 2 x 3800kW (5100hp) Allison T56-	17.56m (57ft 7in); height 5.58m (18ft 4in)
A-427 turboprop engines	Weight: 24,655kg (60,000lb) loaded
Maximum speed: 604km/h (375mph)	Armament: none
Range: 2583km (1605 miles)	
Service ceiling: 10,210m (33,500ft)	

▲ Douglas A-4N Skyhawk II
Israeli AF / early 1980s

Israeli AF Skyhawks had first seen combat during the War of Attrition, and remained in service in 1982, examples including the improved A-4N version. The extended tailpipe was an Israeli modification that was designed to defeat heat-seeking SAMs. Nevertheless, at least two examples were lost over Lebanon.

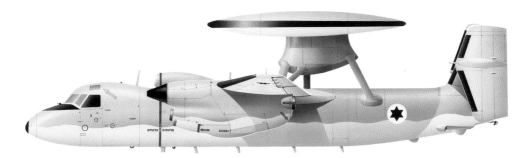

Specifications

Crew: 5	Dimensions: span 24.58m (80ft 7in);
Powerplant: 2 x 3800kW (5096hp) Allison T56-	length 17.56m (57ft 7in); height 5.58m
A-425 or -427 turboprop	(18ft 4in)
Maximum speed: 604km/h (375mph)	Weight: 23,391kg (55,000lb) loaded
Range: 2583km (1605 miles)	Armament: none
Service ceiling: 9300m (30,800ft)	

▲ Lockheed E-2C Hawkeye
Israeli AF / early 1980s

One of the decisive factors in the Israeli AF's aerial dominance over Lebanon was the presence of the E-2C. Carrying powerful surveillance radar, these were able to alert fighter assets of any incoming Syrian AF aircraft, and also coordinated defensive top cover (mainly F-15s and Kfirs) for Israeli offensive missions.

Chapter 6

Africa

In addition to a number of civil wars fought on the continent, the conflicts that afflicted Africa during the Cold War were typically colonial in origin. A result of the final break-up of empires after World War II, these conflicts frequently saw European powers attempt to extricate themselves from the continent in the face of local rebellion or insurgency. While well equipped Western powers clashed with rebel groups, the situation was made more complex by superpower rivalries, and attempts by eastern and western power blocs to influence politics on the African continent.

◀ **Aérospatiale SA 316B Alouette III**
Portuguese soldiers disembark from Alouette IIIs during operations in Mozambique. The 'Bush Wars' that afflicted Africa throughout the Cold War were typified by the use of helicopters to deliver troops across difficult terrain, and counter-insurgency tactics to put down guerrilla activity.

France in Algeria
1954–1962

In the early years of the Cold War France experienced the loss of its colonies in both Africa and Southeast Asia. In the former, Algeria's struggle for independence was most significant.

CONSIDERED PART OF metropolitan France, Algeria's Muslim community sought independence, while European settlers fought a civil war. In contrast to the former French colonies of Morocco and Tunisia, Algeria's road to independence would involve years of conflict, and French air power played an important role from the outset. Despite the involvement of over one million French troops, France failed to make a military breakthrough, and by 1958 a revolution was close. The fighting would continue until 1962, when Algerian independence was finally recognized.

The war broke out in 1954, with resistance from the Front de Libération Nationale (FLN) and its military Armée de Libération Nationale (ALN) wing. The French AF was initially unable to counter the guerrillas, with the only local combat aircraft being Mistral jets and F-47s. However, trainers were soon adapted for counter-insurgency (COIN) work.

France soon established a force of light COIN aircraft better able to tackle the insurrection. Closely integrated with the ground forces, three French AF tactical air groups (GATAC) were formed on a regional basis, conforming to Army deployment; the first light support squadrons became operational in 1955. Starting in 1956, squadrons (EALA) were reorganized within light aircraft groups (GALA), each assigned to a GATAC. A flexible, rapid-reaction force was created, with aircraft types including the M.S.500, M.S.733, the U.S.-supplied T-6, and SIPA S.111 and S.112. The major roles comprised ground support, reconnaissance and transport, and aircraft were also based in neighbouring Morocco and Tunisia. Light observation squadrons were fielded beginning in 1956, equipped with the Broussard, while French Army L-19s operated in a similar role.

In 1957-58 the French AF M.S.500 and M.S.733 were replaced by T-6s, while in 1959 the light aircraft groups were superseded by an *escadre/escadron* structure, and the light aircraft assets came under direct control of the GATAC, for increased flexibility. Improved COIN equipment then became available in the form of the T-28, which arrived in 1960, replacing the increasingly vulnerable T-6.

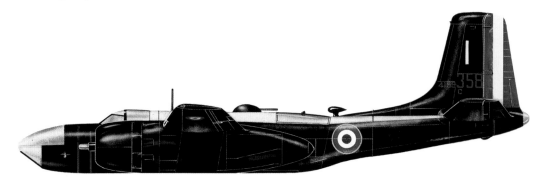

Specifications

Crew: 3	Dimensions: span 21.30m (70ft); length
Powerplant: 2 x 1491kW (2000hp)	16.60m (51ft 3in); height 5.6m (18ft 6in)
Pratt & Whitney R-2800-79	Weight: 15,876kg (35,000lb) loaded
Maximum speed: 571km/h (355mph)	Armament: Various 12.7mm (0.50in) M2
Range: 2255km (1400 miles)	Browning MGs and up to 2700kg (6000lb)
Service ceiling: 6735m (22,100ft)	bomb load

▲ **Douglas B-26C Invader**
EB 2/91, French AF / Oran, 1956–62

Among the 'heavy' offensive assets fielded by the French AF in Algeria was the B-26, deployed among bomber (B-26B/C/N) and reconnaissance units (RB-26P) based at Bone and Oran. EB 2/91 'Guyenne' was a bomber unit and served at Oran between 1956 and 1962.

Soon 26 light aircraft squadrons and three of liaison/observation aircraft were operational in Algeria, but arguably the most important development was France's use of military helicopters, deployed in their hundreds for assault transport and gunship missions. It was during the 250,000 (French AF) combat flying hours in Algeria that many of the initial tactics for rotary-winged warfare were developed. All three French armed forces deployed helicopters, primarily the Bell 47, H-21, S-55, S-58 and the Alouette II.

Helicopter war

Helicopters were active against the rebellion from the start, with a first French Army helicopter unit being established in 1954, and a first French AF unit following a year later. Capable of delivering commando raids or conducting casualty evacuation, observation and a range of other missions, the helicopters were ultimately used as an offensive tool against the ALN, armed with guns and rockets, as exemplified by the Pirate gunship conversion of the S-58. The arrival of this latter type in 1956 was critical in that it considerably increased troop-carrying capabilities and led to creation of French AF heavy helicopter *escadrons*. By late 1957 there were around 250 helicopters in Algeria, with all three services, including three active French AF escadres. Army strength included 32 flights by 1960, including 15 mixed units with helicopters and fixed-wing types.

After early French AF combat missions by the F-47, heavier fixed-wing assets appeared in the form of B-26s, deployed within two bomber groups. Almost certainly the most effective fixed-wing COIN type was, however, the AD-4, first joining EC 20 in early 1960. In many ways a template for later actions in Southeast Asia, the innovative use of air power in Algeria contained the rebels to an extent, but was not able to put an end to terrorist actions.

Morocco
1975–1989

After gaining independence from France in 1956, Morocco became involved in a long-running conflict fought against the Algerian-based guerrillas of the Polisario Front.

MOROCCO'S WAR AGAINST the Polisario Front began following the North African kingdom's annexation of the northern part of the former Spanish Sahara when the last Spanish colonial forces departed in early 1976. Mauritania occupied the southern part of the disputed area, and between them, the two nations took on the Polisario forces, which began attacking regular formations.

In July 1978 Mauritania signed a peace treaty and abandoned its claim to the territory, and Morocco was left to fight the guerrilla war alone, at this time with an air force that included F-5A jet fighters, RF-5As for reconnaissance, Magisters and C-130s. Early support was also provided by France, with French AF Jaguars involved in ground support missions, flown by EC 1/11 and EC 3/11 from Dakar in Senegal.

New combat aircraft equipment was soon ordered by Morocco, including Mirage F1s and Alpha Jets from France, and U.S.-supplied F-5Es and OV-10s.

Initially the U.S. was unwilling to allow its equipment to be used in the conflict zone, but attitudes changed when it became apparent to Washington that the Polisario Front was being supported by Algeria and Libya, two nations with pro-Soviet sympathies. The U.S. warplanes were delivered starting in 1981.

In its battle against the Polisario Front, the Royal Moroccan AF used its front-line aircraft for ground attack duties, with combat missions supported by CH-47 and AB.205 troop-transport helicopters. In a reflection of the improved weaponry available to the guerrillas, losses to man-portable SAMs began to be recorded in the early 1980s.

In late 1981 the conflict began to intensify, and Morocco increasingly struggled to finance its combat operations, despite funding from Saudi Arabia and military equipment received from both the U.S. and Israel. The construction of the Moroccan Wall in the mid-1980s finally led to a stalemate situation.

Specifications

Crew: 1-2

Powerplant: 1 x 1044kW (1400hp) Lycoming
T53-L-13B turboshaft

Maximum speed: 222km/h (138mph)

Range: 580km (360 miles)

Service ceiling: 4570m (15,000ft)

Dimensions: rotor diameter 14.63m (48ft);
length 12.69m (41ft 8in);
height 4.48m (14ft 8in)

Weight: 4309kg (9500lb) loaded

Armament: none

▲ **Agusta-Bell AB.205A**

Royal Moroccan AF / early 1980s

During the mid-1980s the Royal Moroccan AF operated 24 AB.205A helicopters, licence-built versions of the Bell 205 manufactured by Agusta in Italy. These were put to use in the campaign against the Polisario Front, conducting troop-transport missions in support of the larger CH-47s and fixed-wing C-130 airlifters.

Libya
1977–1986

Soon after assuming power in 1969, Libyan leader Muammar al-Gaddafi turned to the USSR for arms, and began to assume an increasingly belligerent stance on the world stage.

AFTER PROVIDING EGYPT with Mirage fighters during the Yom Kippur War, Libya turned on its former ally in July 1977, when a border dispute between Egypt and Libya escalated into a brief air war. After Libya began an artillery assault, Egyptian AF MiG-21s and Su-20s attacked Libyan radar sites, and ground-based air defences claimed a Libyan MiG and a Mirage. Fighting continued for some days, during which time the Egyptian AF bombed the Libyan airbase at El Adem and Libyan warplanes attacked Egyptian border settlements.

U.S. Navy involvement

After the action against Egypt, and intervention in regional conflicts in Uganda and Chad, Libya took on the might of the U.S. Navy. Behind this move was Libya's claim to the entire Gulf of Sidra as territorial waters. This was enforced through regular air patrols and harassment of U.S. Navy Sixth Fleet aircraft and

warships. Events came to a head in August 1981 when a pair of Libyan AF Su-22s were shot down by U.S. Navy F-14As from the carrier USS *Nimitz*.

Hostility between Libya and the U.S. increased, particularly because of Libya's sponsorship of terrorist acts by the PLO and other groups. Relations became especially strained in March 1986, when a number of Libyan SAMs were fired at U.S. Navy aircraft after a pair of F-14s turned away an intercepting Libyan AF MiG-25. In response, A-7Es from USS *Saratoga* launched anti-radar missiles against Libyan SAM sites. A-6Es from the USS *America* and *Saratoga* then sunk three Libyan patrol craft.

The April 1986 bombing of a discotheque in West Berlin was the trigger for the U.S. to launch a large-scale air offensive against Libya. This was spearheaded by USAF F-111s flying from bases in England, together with tanker support. Intelligence-gathering prior to the raids was conducted by USAF RC-135s

Specifications

Crew: 4

Powerplant: 2 x 2535kW (3400hp) General

  Electric T64-GE-P4D turboprops

Maximum speed: 540km/h (336mph)

Range: 1371km (852 miles)

Service ceiling: 7620m (25,000ft)

Dimensions: span 28.70m (94ft 2in);

  length 22.7m (74ft 6in); height 9.8m

  (32ft 2in)

Weight: 28,000kg (61,730lb) loaded

Armament: none

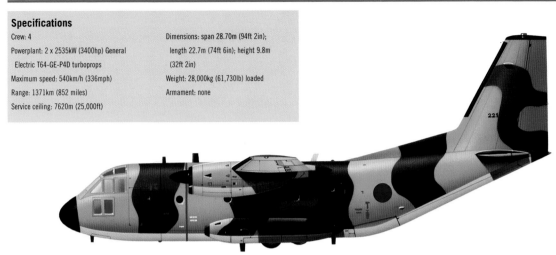

▲ **Aeritalia G.222**

Libyan AF / early 1980s

Although Libya was a major customer of Soviet aircraft during the 1970s and 1980s, the country's oil wealth enabled it to purchase equipment from France and Italy, too. Mk 82 227-kg (500-lb) conventional bombs dropped by USAF F-111Fs destroyed at least one Italian-supplied G222 transport on the ground at Tripoli.

and by U.S Navy EP-3Es and EA-3Bs, while targets were reconnoitred by SR-71As, U-2Rs and TR-1As.

The 18-strong force of F-111Fs (plus six support aircraft) left the UK on the evening of 15 April, supported by EF-111A jamming aircraft. The plan, codenamed El Dorado Canyon, involved a joint USAF/U.S. Navy strike on targets that included Tripoli airport, Benina airbase, plus various training facilities, military barracks and command centres. U.S. Navy strike aircraft were launched by the carriers USS *Coral Sea* and *America*, and offensive assets comprised F/A-18s, A-6Es and A-7Es, supported by EA-6B jamming aircraft. For the loss of one F-111, the U.S. air arms claimed the destruction or damage of numerous Libyan aircraft and helicopters on the ground, and the operation was judged a success.

USAF, LIBYA, 1986		
Aircraft	**Unit**	**Base**
F-111F	48 TFW	RAF Lakenheath
EF-111A	42 ECS	RAF Upper Heyford
U-2R, TR-1A	9 SRS (Det)	RAF Akrotiri
SR-71A	9 SRW (Det)	RAF Mildenhall
KC-10A	various units	RAF Mildenhall, RAF Fairford
KC-135A/E/Q	various units	RAF Mildenhall, RAF Fairford

▲ **F/A-18 Hornet**

The U.S. attacks on Libya in 1986 marked the combat debut of the U.S Navy's F/A-18 Hornet attack fighter, launched from the USS *Coral Sea*. Here, aviation ordnancemen load AGM-88 missiles on one of the carrier's VFA-131 Hornets.

Chad
1968–1987

Soon after it had gained independence from France in 1960, Chad began to be beset by internal strife, and the situation intensified when Libya intervened in the civil war in 1980.

AFTER ITS INDEPENDENCE, A French military presence remained in Chad in order to help the Christian administration counter Islamic anti-government rebels. Staring in 1968 French AF AD-4s were stationed N'Djamena, and within a year these COIN assets were supported by French military transports and helicopters. As the rebel offensive intensified, and threatened N'Djamena, additional French ground forces were deployed.

With the AD-4s flying numerous close support sorties, the French succeeded in pushing the rebels back to isolated pockets of resistance. In 1973 Libya intervened by taking control of the disputed Aouzou region in the north of Chad, and continued to provide support to the rebels. A French military presence remained in Chad in order to help preserve security until a military coup in 1975. After the last French troops left in October 1975, a handful of AD-4s were turned over for use by Chad for anti-guerrilla work in support of the now Muslim-led government.

The French military returned to Chad in April 1978, with Jaguars being deployed between April 1978 and January 1980 in support of a French Army presence. At least four Jaguars were lost during operations before the French departed again in mid-1980. By this stage it was apparent that the ceasefire between government and guerrilla forces could no longer be effectively enforced.

Libya strikes

Libya then intervened more directly in the civil war. In 1980, large numbers of Libyan troops were sent to Chad, and in October of that year Libyan AF Tu-22s bombed anti-government Forces Armées du Nord (FAN) rebel positions near N'Djamena. However, the most widely used Libyan AF type was the turboprop-powered SF.260W COIN aircraft.

International pressure prevented Libya from annexing Chad, and Libyan forces were encouraged to depart the country in late 1981. The presence of an African peacekeeping force thereafter was not enough to prevent FAN forces taking power in Chad. Libya then joined the ousted government forces, which had assembled in the north of the country, to wage a counter-attack. The Libyan AF employed MiG-23s, Su-22s and SF.260Ws in an operation

▲ **Dassault Mirage 5M**

21 Wing, Zairean AF / Kamina/N'Djamena, 1981–83

In addition to air power from Chad, France and Libya, the air force of Zaire was active during the fighting in Chad in the early 1980s. Initially deployed in support of the African peacekeeping force in Chad, Zairean AF Mirages and close-support M.B.326s were active against Libyan-backed rebels through much of the 1980s.

Specifications

Crew: 1

Powerplant: 1 x 58.72kN (13,200lb) thrust SNECMA Atar 09C afterburning turbojet engine

Maximum speed: 2350km/h (1460mph)

Range: 1307km (812 miles)

Service ceiling: 16,093m (52,800ft)

Dimensions: span 8.26m (27ft 2in); length 15.65m (51ft 4in); height 4.51m (14ft 10in)

Weight: 13,671kg (30,140lb) loaded

Armament: 2 x 30mm DEFA 552A cannon; various AAMs, up to 3991kg (8800lb) of bombs from June 1983, with aircraft forward deployed in Aouzou. The Libyan assault, which also involved the use of Mirage fighter-bombers and Mi-25 helicopter gunships, eventually forced the anti-government guerrillas to agree to a ceasefire and withdrawal.

A mutual treaty meant that France was compelled to intervene in support of Chad, and ground-attack Jaguars and air defence Mirage F1s went into action, again flying from N'Djamena, and supplemented by Puma and Gazelle helicopters. Additional support was provided by Zaire, with Mirage 5s and M.B.326s, while the U.S. delivered man-portable SAMs. Libyan AF attacks were halted as a result, but the Libyan-supported rebels remained in control of the north of the country, under an uneasy stalemate.

In autumn 1984 France and Libya agreed to withdraw from Chad, but hostilities resumed in 1986 with a new Libyan-backed rebel offensive and French air strikes against the Libyan base at Ouadi Doum. In response, Libyan air sorties were stepped up, with Tu-22 raids against N'Djamena. Finally in August 1987 government forces briefly held Aouzou before Chad attacked Libyan AF bases. A ceasefire was signed, and a stabilizing French AF presence remained in Chad.

FRENCH AF/FRENCH NAVAL AIR ARM/FRENCH ARMY, CHAD, 1968–88		
Aircraft	Unit	Base
AD-4 Skyraider	EAA 1/21	N'Djamena
AD-4 Skyraider	EAA 1/22	N'Djamena
Noratlas, Alouette II, Broussard	GMT 59	N'Djamena, Mongo
H-34	DPH 2/67	N'Djamena
Jaguar A/E	EC 11	N'Djamena, Bangui, Libreville
Jaguar A	EC 7	Bangui
Noratlas, Alouette II	ETOM 55	N'Djamena
Mirage F1C	EC 5	N'Djamena, Bangui
Mirage F1CR	ER 33	N'Djamena, Bangui
C.160NG Transall	ET 1/63	N'Djamena, Bangui
KC-135F	ERV 93	N'Djamena, Bangui
Atlantique	22F	N'Djamena, Bangui, Dakar
Gazelle	1 RHC	N'Djamena, Abeche
Gazelle	2 RHC	N'Djamena, Abeche
Puma	5 RHC	N'Djamena, Abeche

Portugal in Africa
1959–1975

Three Portuguese colonies in Africa – Angola, Mozambique and Portuguese Guinea – all waged campaigns for independence, during which major use was made of Portuguese air power.

FIRST OF PORTUGAL'S surviving African colonies to take up arms against its colonial occupier was Portuguese Guinea. In Portuguese Guinea, as in Angola and Mozambique, the Portuguese AF was widely used in the COIN role. The rebellion in Portuguese Guinea began in August 1959, at which time only a small number of Portuguese AF T-6s were available, although these were followed by F-84Gs from 1963. As rebel activity escalated, the Portuguese AF presence was strengthened from 1967, with the arrival of the first G.91s. The jungle and swamp typical of the country made operations especially difficult, although these problems were countered to an extent by the arrival of Alouette III helicopters

starting in 1968. The Portuguese military began to take a harder line from 1970, with extensive use of napalm and defoliants, with the rebels now receiving support from Nigerian AF MiG-17s based at Conakry, which were used for reconnaissance, as well as Soviet-supplied Mi-4 helicopters for transport. The rebels claimed 21 aircraft shot down in seven years, using man-portable SAMs and anti-aircraft artillery (AAA). Independence was declared by the rebels in 1973, before the Portuguese military coup in Lisbon saw independence granted in September 1974.

While Portugal became entrenched in a COIN campaign in Portuguese Guinea, trouble flared in Angola where the Movimento Popular de Libertação

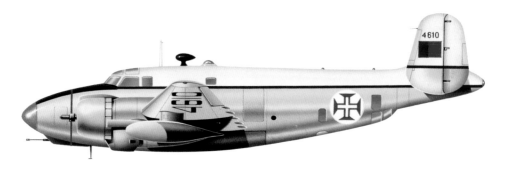

Specifications

Crew: 2-6

Powerplant: 2 x 1490kW (2000hp) Pratt & Whitney R-2800-31 air-cooled radial engines

Maximum speed: 454km/h (282mph)

Range: 2880km (1790 miles)

Service ceiling: 7285m (23,900ft)

Dimensions: span 22.86m (75ft 0in); length 15.87m (52ft 1in); height 4.04m (13ft 3in)

Weight: 15,271kg (33,668lb) loaded

Armament: three fixed 0.50-inch machine guns, Eight 127mm (5in) HVAR rockets, 1814kg (4000lb) bomb load

▲ Lockheed PV-2 Harpoon
Esq 91, Portuguese AF / BA9 (Luanda), 1962

The PV-2 played an important role early on in Angola's colonial conflicts in Africa, when dedicated COIN equipment was at a premium. This example of the veteran Lockheed design served at BA9 (Luanda) in Angola during 1962. Outfitted for bombing, the PV-2s were among the first combat aircraft available in Angola.

Specifications

Crew: 1

Powerplant: 1 x 24.7kN (5560lbf) Allison J35-A-29 turbojet

Maximum speed: 1000km/h (622mph)

Range: 1600km (1000 miles)

Service ceiling: 12,344m (40,500ft)

Dimensions: span 11.1m (36ft 5in); length 11.6m (38ft 1in); height 3.84m (12ft 7in)

Weight: 8,200kg (18,080lb) loaded

Armament: 6 x 12.7mm (.50in) M3 Browning MGs, and up to 2020kg (4450lb) of rockets and bombs

▲ Republic F-84G Thunderjet
Esq 93, Portuguese AF / BA9 (Luanda), early 1960s

The F-84G saw action in Angola in the ground support role, although a number of losses were sustained – primarily due to operational accidents, which claimed at least five examples during the first three years of operations in Angola. Typical weapons for the Thunderjet included fragmentation bombs and napalm.

Specifications

Crew: 2

Powerplant: 1 x 450kW (600hp) Pratt & Whitney R-1340-AN-1 Wasp radial engine

Maximum speed: 335km/h (208mph)

Range: 1175km (730 miles)

Service ceiling: 7400m (24,200ft)

Dimensions: span 12.81m (42ft); length 8.84m (29ft); height 3.57m (11ft 8in)

Weight: 2548kg (5617lb) loaded

Armament: up to 3 x 7.62mm (.30in) MG, plus light bombs and rockets

▲ North American T-6G Texan
Portuguese AF / Sintra, Portugal

A widely used COIN type, the T-6G served in numerous post-colonial conflicts during the Cold War. This example was operated from Sintra, Portugal, but Portuguese AF Texans saw action in Guinea, Angola and Mozambique. The type proved well suited to attacks on guerrilla forces, using light bombs and rockets.

▲ **Fiat G.91R/4**

Esq 121, Portuguese AF / BA12 (Bissalanca), 1967-74

The most potent ground attack aircraft deployed by Portugal in Africa was the Fiat G.91R/4, which served in Portuguese Guinea, Angola and Mozambique. Esq 121 flew from BA12 Bissalanca in Portuguese Guinea, and was equipped with G.91s supplied by West Germany. Three examples fell to SAMs in spring 1973.

Specifications

Crew: 1

Powerplant: 1 x 22.2kN (5000lbf) Bristol-
Siddeley Orpheus 803 turbojet

Maximum speed: 1075km/h (668mph)

Range: 1150km (715 miles)

Service ceiling: 13,100m (43,000ft)

Dimensions: span 8.56m (28ft 1in);
length 10.3m (33ft 9in); height 4m (13ft 1in)

Weight: 5440kg (11,990lb) loaded

Armament: 4 x 12.7mm (0.5in M2 Browning
MGs, provision to carry up to 1814kg (4000lb)
bomb payload

▲ **Aérospatiale Alouette III**

Esq 121, Portuguese AF / BA12 (Bissalanca), 1971

Workhorse of the Portuguese military in its African colonial campaigns was the Alouette III. This example was based at BA12 Bissalanca in 1971, and was used to transport troops during operations against insurgents in Guinea-Bissau. The first 12 examples of the helicopter arrived in Guinea in 1969.

Specifications

Crew: 2

Powerplant: 1 x 649kW (870hp) Turbomeca
Artouste IIIB turboshaft

Maximum speed: 220km/h (137mph)

Range: 604km (375 miles)

Service ceiling: 3200m (10,500ft)

Dimensions: rotor diameter 11.02m (36ft 2in);
length 10.03m (32ft 11in);
height 3m (9ft 10in)

Weight: 2200kg (4950lb) loaded

Armament: 20mm cannons, carried in the rear
cabin and fired over the side

de Angola (MPLA) became increasingly active, and the local Portuguese Army units struggled to contain the rebellion. The Portuguese AF deployed PV-2s and C-47s to Luanda. These were supported by impressed civilian aircraft types used as transports to resupply military outposts, with DC-3s and Beech 18s converted into makeshift bombers.

Jets over Angola

F-84Gs were available to the Portuguese AF in Angola starting in June 1961, although these suffered a number of losses, mainly through accidents. In order to relieve besieged towns, paratroops were

delivered by C-47, and later Noratlas. Despite a U.S. arms embargo, Portugal managed to obtain a number of B-26s, which were used to strike MPLA targets, supported by F-84Gs, T-6s and Do 27s.

As the USSR provided increasing support to the MPLA, from 1966 Portugal faced another insurgent group, União Nacional para a Independência Total de Angola (UNITA). Portuguese AF aircraft waged a constant COIN campaign. In both Angola and Guinea, as it had with the French in Algeria, the T-6 bore the brunt of anti-guerrilla operations.

With MPLA forces advancing towards the west, the Portuguese AF stationed G.91s in Angola from

▲ **Dornier Do 27A-4**

Portuguese AF

During the Portuguese operations in Angola, Do 27 liaison aircraft were operated from BA9 (Luanda), AB3 (Negage) and AB4 (Henriques de Carvalho), and were flown alongside Austers. Do 27s were also flown on COIN sorties, and an example was the first aircraft claimed shot down by the MPLA, in June 1967.

Specifications

Crew: 1-2

Powerplant: 1 x 201kW (270hp) Lycoming GO-480-B1A6 6-cylinder piston engine

Maximum speed: 232km/h (144mph)

Range: 1100km (684 miles)

Service ceiling: 3353m (11,000ft)

Dimensions: span 12m (39ft 4in); length 9.60m (31ft 5in); height 3.5m (11ft)

Weight: 1850kg (4079lb) loaded

Armament: none

PORTUGUESE AF, ANGOLA, 1961–75		
Aircraft	**Unit**	**Base**
G.91R/4	Esq 93	BA9
PV-2, B-26B/C	Esq 91	Luanda, BA9
T-6G	Esq 501	Luanda, Nacala
DC-6A/B, 707	Gr. Trans.	Lisbon
C-54, Noratlas	Esq 92	BA9, Maguela, BA4
C-47, Beech 18	Esq 801	Lorenco Marques
Auster, Do 27	n/a	BA9, AB3, AB4
Alouette II/III, Puma	Esq 94	BA9, Gago, Cuito and others

PORTUGUESE AF, MOZAMBIQUE, 1962–75		
Aircraft	**Unit**	**Base**
G.91R/4	Esq 502	Nacala
G.91R/4	Esq 702	Tete
PV-2, T-6G	Esq 101	Beira
T-6G, C-47, PV-2, Alouette III	BA10	Beira
T-6G, Auster, Do 27, Alouette III	AB5	Nacala, Mueda, Porto Amelia
T-6G, Auster, Do 27	AB6	Nova Freixo
T-6G, Auster, Do 27, Alouette III	AB7	Tete
Noratlas	Esq Trans	Beira
C-47	Esq 801	Lourenço Marques

1972, while helicopters began to be used increasingly for troop transport. Angola was finally granted independence in November 1975, bringing Portugal's African operations to a close.

In Mozambique the Portuguese faced resistance from Frente da Libertação de Moçambique (FRELIMO) starting in 1962. As in Angola, the Portuguese AF in Mozambique was initially equipped only with C-47s and T-6s when major fighting began in 1964. Before long, troop numbers increased to 16,000, backed by further T-6s, PV-2s, Do 27s and Alouette IIIs. FRELIMO was operating from bases in Tanzania and Zambia, and eventually the Portuguese AF commitment in Mozambique was larger than that in either Angola or Guinea. Major air operations took place beginning in 1968, with FRELIMO increasing

PORTUGUESE AF, PORTUGUESE GUINEA, 1963–74		
Aircraft	**Unit**	**Base**
G.91R/4	Esq 121	Bissalanca
T-6G	n/a	Bissalanca
Do 27	Esq 121	Bissalanca
Noratlas	Esq 123	Bissalanca
Alouette III	Esq 122	Bissalanca

the intensity of its own campaign from 1970. With Portuguese forces struggling to make an impact, the G.91s returned home in 1974, before Mozambique was granted independence in June 1975.

Nigeria
1967–1970

Granted independence in 1960, Nigeria remained relatively peaceful until 1966, when the federal government collapsed, and the country descended into bloodshed.

AFTER MASSACRES OF the Ibom people in the north of the country, the military authorities in the east – homeland of the Ibo tribe – declared independence in turn in 1961. The result was brutal civil war fought between the federal government and the newly created state of Biafra. Initial equipment for the Nigerian AF was primarily supplied by the Eastern Bloc, and use was made of contract aircrew. These maintained a bombing campaign of Biafran villages in which, between May and October 1968, around 3000 people were killed.

Rebel air wing

In contrast, the Biafran air arm maintained an assortment of impressed, generally obsolete civilian aircraft that were mainly flown by mercenary pilots. The most potent aircraft available in 1967 included a pair of B-26s that were used in a daring raid on a Nigerian destroyer at Port Harcourt. More effective equipment arrived in the form of MFI-9B Minicoin light aircraft equipped with rockets for COIN work, and flown against the federal forces by mercenaries

NIGERIAN AF, 1967–70	
Aircraft	**Base**
Il-28	Port Harcourt, Calabar, Benin City
MiG-17	Benin City, Lagos, Enugu, Kaduna, Port Harcourt
Jet Provost	Lagos, Benin City
L-29	Benin City, Kaduna
DC-3	Benin City
DC-4, Noratlas	Benin City, Lagos
Do 28	Benin City
Do 27	Benin City, Kaduna, Kano
Azec	Benin City
Whirlwind 2/3	Kaduna

including the Swedish Count Gustav von Rosen. The Minicoins were used primarily for attacks against the Nigerian oil industry, causing some damage.

The civil war ended in January 1970 with the collapse of the Biafran regime, and as a result its leader, Colonel Ojukwu, fled to Ivory Coast.

▲ **Ilyushin-28**

Nigerian AF / Port Harcourt/Calabar/Benin City, 1967-70

Nigeria received six Il-28 bombers from Algeria and Egypt for use during the Biafran War of 1967-69. These were flown by Egyptian, mercenary and Nigerian pilots and were used to bomb Biafran villages. At least three Il-28s were claimed damaged or destroyed on the ground by the fleet of Biafran Minicoins.

Specifications

Crew: 3

Powerplant: 2 x 26.3kN (5952lb) Klimov VK-1 turbojets

Maximum speed: 902km/h (560mph)

Range: 2180km (1355 miles)

Service ceiling: 12,300m (40,355ft)

Dimensions: span 21.45m (70ft 4in); length

17.65m (57ft 10.75in); height 6.7m (21ft 11.8in)

Weight: 21,200kg (46,738lb) loaded

Armament: 4 x 23mm cannon; internal bomb capacity 1000kg (2205lb), maximum bomb capacity 3000kg (6614lb); torpedo version: provision for two 400mm light torpedoes

Specifications

Crew: 4

Powerplant: 4 x 2610kW (3500hp) Pratt &
  Whitney R-4360B Wasp Major radial engines

Maximum speed: 603km/h (375mph)

Range: 6920km (4300 miles)

Service ceiling: 10,670m (35,000ft)

Dimensions: span 43.1m (41ft 3in);
  length 33.7m (110ft 4in); height 11.7m
  (38ft 3in)

Weight: 54,420kg (120,000lb) loaded

Armament: none

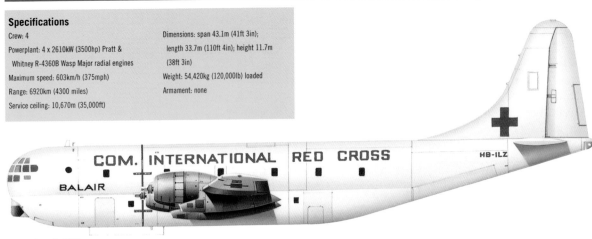

▲ Boeing C-97G

International Red Cross, Biafra, 1969–70

HB-ILZ, an ex-USAF C-97G, was one of three examples that were wet-leased to the International Red Cross in 1969-70 for relief missions to war-torn Biafra. Military equipment, including the aerial refuelling installation and underwing tank/jet pylons, was removed for humanitarian operations.

Congo
1960–1963

With little in the way of preparation, Belgium granted Congo independence in 1960 and the country was quickly sucked into a tribal civil war that would continue for seven years.

WHILE BELGIAN SETTLERS were subject to attack, a secessionist movement attempted to separate the Katanga region from the Congo Republic. The UN formulated a charter that established a peacekeeping force in the Congo, and air support was eventually provided by Canada, Ethiopia, India, Italy and Sweden. Among the most effective aircraft deployed by the Organization Nations-Unies au Congo

▲ English Electric Canberra B(I).Mk 58

Indian AF/ONUC / Luluabourg, 1961-62

Wearing ONUC titles, this Indian Canberra bomber-intruder was part of a small detachment of the type that was based at Luluabourg between 1961-62. While the Swedish AF Saab 29 excelled, the Canberra was found ill suited to low-level strike in the Congo, but still conducted a number of night raids against Elisabethville.

Specifications

Crew: 2

Powerplant: 2 x 28.9kN (6500lb) Rolls-Royce
  Avon Mk 101 turbojets

Maximum speed: 917km/h (570mph)

Range: 4274km (2656 miles)

Service ceiling: 14,630m (48,000ft)

Dimensions: span 29.49m (63ft 11in); length
  19.96m (65ft 6in); height 4.78m (15ft 8in)

Weight: 24,925kg (54,950lb) loaded

Armament: bomb bay with provision for up to
  2727kg (6000lb) of bombs, plus 909kg
  (2000lb) of underwing pylons

(ONUC) were volunteer-flown Swedish AF Saab 29 jets, armed with guns and rockets for ground attack against the Katangan separatists, but also used for reconnaissance (in the form of the S29C). These operated from 1961-63 and took part in surprise December 1962 and January 1963 raids on Kolwezi that succeeded in destroying most of the fledgling Katangan air arm on the ground.

The country, now known as Zaire, saw a further attempt at Katangan secession in 1977-78, leading to French and Moroccan military intervention, as well as the use of Zairean AF Mirage IIIs and M.B.326s.

ONUC, 1960–64		
Aircraft	**Unit**	**Base**
Canberra B(I). Mk 58	5 Sqn, Indian AF	Kamina
J29B, S29C	F22, Swedish AF	Luluabourg, Kamina
F-86F	Ethiopian AF	Luluabourg, Kamina
Sabre Mk 4	4 Aerobrigata, Italian AF	Leopoldville
C-119G	46 Aerobrigata, Italian AF	Leopoldville, Kamina

Rhodesia
1965–1979

When Ian Smith's white minority regime declared unilateral independence from Britain in 1965, an economic blockade was the result, involving the RAF and British aircraft carriers.

THE BLOCKADE AGAINST Rhodesia was imposed by the UN and involved RAF Shackletons based in Madagascar, as well as Royal Navy carriers. At the time, the Royal Rhodesian AF was spearheaded by Hunters and Canberras, but the measures against Rhodesia remained ecomomic rather than military.

After the blockade the Rhodesian AF was increasingly involved in fighting guerrillas both inside Rhodesia and outside its borders. Early tasks included air supply, patrol and reconnaissance, and a number of AL.60 transports were received by covert means in 1967. A republic was declared in 1969, and in 1972

▲ **Percival Provost T.Mk 52**
4 Sqn, Royal Rhodesian AF / Thornhill, mid-1960s
Operated in the mid-1960s, this Provost wears the insignia used before Rhodesia's declaration of unilateral independence. Among the first actions after the declaration of UDI saw Provosts relocate to form detachments at Wankie and Kariba, in order to defend against attacks by the insurgents.

Specifications
Crew: 2
Powerplant: 1 x 410kW (550hp) Alvis Leonides 126 9-cylinder radial engine
Maximum speed: 320km/h (200mph)
Range: 1020km (650 miles)
Service ceiling: 7620m (25,000ft)
Dimensions: span 10.7m (35ft 0in); length 8.73m (28ft 6in); height 3.70m (12ft 0in)
Weight: 1995kg (4399lb) loaded
Armament: no fixed armament

Rhodesia began to be infiltrated by groups based in Botswana, Mozambique and Zambia. Air power was used to counter the guerrillas, with airborne landings, commando raids and air strikes by Canberras and Hunters against terrorist bases. From 1976 new COIN types were deployed, including the Reims-Cessna 337 Lynx, Alouette III and SF.260W. Despite sanctions, Rhodesian kept up its COIN offensive until 1979, when an internal settlement was reached on majority rule and Rhodesia became Zimbabwe.

ROYAL RHODESIAN AF, 1965		
Aircraft	Unit	Base
Canberra B.Mk 2	5 Sqn	New Sarum
Hunter FGA.Mk 9	1 Sqn	Thornhill
Vampire FB.Mk 9	2 Sqn	Thornhill
Provost T.Mk 52	4 Sqn	Thornhill
C-47	3 Sqn	New Sarum
Alouette II	7 Sqn	New Sarum

▲ **English Electric Canberra B.Mk 2**

5 Sqn, Rhodesian AF / New Sarum, 1970

This Canberra was used for long-range bombing and reconnaissance missions against guerrilla groups, attacking targets within Rhodesia as well as in Angola, Botswana, Mozambique and Zambia. Two Rhodesian Canberras were lost during operations over Mozambique.

Specifications

Crew: 2

Powerplant: 2 x 28.9kN (6500lb) Rolls-Royce
  Avon Mk 101 turbojets

Maximum speed: 917km/h (570mph)

Range: 4274km (2656 miles)

Service ceiling: 14,630m (48,000ft)

Dimensions: span 29.49m (63ft 11in); length
  19.96m (65ft 6in); height 4.78m (15ft 8in)

Weight: 24,925kg (54,950lb) loaded

Armament: bomb bay with provision for up to
  2727kg (6000lb) of bombs, plus 909kg
  (2000lb) of underwing pylons

South Africa
1961–1988

Ostracized by the international community, apartheid South Africa faced cross-border attacks for over two decades, and air power was used widely in order to put down hostile guerrillas.

ULTIMATELY ABLE TO strike well beyond South Africa's borders from the air, and over land, the COIN forces of the South African military were the best equipped in Africa, their capabilities resting in a powerful indigenous arms industry and covert cooperation with foreign powers including Israel.

South Africa left the British Commonwealth in 1961 after which the UN imposed sanctions. These were counter-productive, hardening white South African resolve against Marxist-leaning neighbours and guerrillas. From the early 1960s, South Africa's armed forces were used to prevent infiltration from

across the northern borders with Angola, Botswana, Mozambique, Zambia and Zimbabwe. Prior to sanctions, South Africa had received warplanes from the UK, including Canberras and Buccaneers. These were later complemented by French Mirage IIIs and F1s, together with licence-built Impalas for COIN work, the latter based on the Italian M.B.326.

SWAPO standoff

From autumn 1965 the nationalist South West African People's Organization (SWAPO) group infiltrated Namibia, which was illegally administered by South Africa. SWAPO waged its war against South Africa from bases in Angola and Zambia, and these were targets for South African forces. A low-intensity COIN campaign was fought in Namibia throughout the 1960s and 1970s, before South Africa's cross-border campaign saw SWAPO forces pursued deep into neighbouring countries.

After 1975 Angola became the main base for anti-South African groups disputing control of Namibia. Within Angola the pro-western Frente Nacional da Libertação de Angola (FNLA) and UNITA (itself recipient of South African arms) fought the Marxist

MPLA in a civil war that commenced after Angolan independence. This ultimately pitched large numbers of Cuban troops against South African forces.

By spring 1976 most of Angola was controlled by the MPLA, and the South African AF responded by deploying aircraft to bases in northwestern South Africa. As the MPLA – supported by the Soviet-equipped Angolan AF – stepped up its campaign against the FNLA, fighting crossed over into South Africa. Between 1974 and 1987 South Africa mounted commando raids and air strikes against MPLA strongholds, and air combat pitched South

Specifications

Crew: 1	Dimensions: span 11.58m (38ft);
Powerplant: 1 x 32.35kW (7275lb) Avro Orenda	length 11.58m (38ft); height 4.57m (15ft)
Mark 14 engine	Weight: 6628kg (14.613lb) loaded
Maximum speed: 975km/h (606mph)	Armament: 6 x 12.7mm (0.50in) M2 Browning
Range: n/a	machine guns; 2 x AIM-9 missiles; 2400kg
Service ceiling: 15,450m (50,700ft)	(5300lb) of payload

▲ **Canadair Sabre Mk 6**

1 Sqn, South African AF / Pietersburg, 1970s

When the South African AF first became involved in the campaign against insurgents in neighbouring countries, the Sabre Mk 6 remained in use, primarily in the air defence role. 1 Sqn flew the fighter from Waterkloof between 1956 and 1967, before moving to Pietersburg, where the type was flown until 1975.

▲ **Aérospatial Alouette III**

South African AF / early 1980s

The Alouette III was used throughout South Africa's 'Bush War' beginning with the first attack against SWAPO camps in northern Namibia in August 1966, when the helicopters delivered South African security forces during a raid on a camp in Ovamboland. At least three squadrons operated the Alouette III.

Specifications

Crew: 2	Dimensions: rotor diameter 11.02m (36ft 2in);
Powerplant: 1 x 649kW (870hp) Turbomeca	length 10.03m (32ft 11in); height 3m
Artouste IIIB turboshaft	(9ft 10in)
Maximum speed: 220km/h (137mph)	Weight: 2200kg (4950lb) loaded
Range: 604km (375 miles)	Armament: 20mm cannons, carried in the rear
Service ceiling: 3200m (10,500ft)	cabin and fired over the side

AFRICA

SOUTH AFRICAN AF, FIGHTER/BOMBER UNITS, 1966–88		
Aircraft	Unit	Base
Buccaneer S.Mk 50	24 Sqn	Waterkloof
Canberra B(I).Mk 12	12 Sqn	Waterkloof
Sabre Mk 6, Impala I, Mirage F1AZ/CZ	1 Sqn	Waterkloof, Pietersburg, Hoedspruit
Mirage F1CZ	3 Sqn	Waterkloof
Mirage IIIAZ/BZ/CZ/DZ/RZ	2 Sqn	Waterkloof
Mirage IIIDZ/EZ, Impala II	85 AFS	Pietersburg

African AF jets against Angolan fighters and helicopters. Supply of Soviet SAMs and AAA to the SWAPO provided a particular hazard.

Major South African AF pre-emptive operations took place in the early 1980s, with deep penetrations into Angola involving Buccaneers, Canberras, Mirages and Impalas in combined arms offensives. After the departure of Cuban troops from Angola, South African forces left Namibia in 1988, and Namibia itself was in turn granted independence.

▲ Atlas AM.3C Bosbok

42 Sqn, South African AF / Potchefstroom, early 1980s

Locally built under Italian licence, the Atlas Bosbok (based on the Aermacchi AM.3C) and the closely related Kudu single-engined types were used for light transport and liaison tasks respectively. The South African AF also used the Bosbok for forward air control and casualty evacuation duties.

Specifications

Crew: 2
Powerplant: 1x 236kW (340hp) Lycoming GSO-480-B1B6 piston engine
Maximum speed: 278km/h (173mph)
Range: 990km (619 miles)
Service ceiling: 2440m (8000ft)
Dimensions: span 11.73m (38ft 6in); length 8.73m (28ft 8in); height 2.72m (8ft 11in)
Weight: 1500kg (3300lb) loaded
Armament: Up to 2 machine gun pods, up to 4 smoke-rocket pods and up to 170kg (375lb) bombs

▲ Atlas C4M Kudu

41 Sqn, South African AF / Swartkop/Lanseria, early 1980s

The robust Kudu short take-off and landing (STOL) transport was used widely from unprepared strips in support of ground forces through the provision of air-dropping, medical evacuation and the delivery of small teams of troops. The South African AF received 40 Kudus up to 1979, for use with two front-line squadrons.

Specifications

Crew: 1
Powerplant: 1 x 253kW (340hp) Avco Lycoming GSO-480-B1B3
Maximum speed: 260km/h (161mph)
Range: 1297km (806 miles)
Service ceiling: n/a
Dimensions: span 13.08m (42ft 9in); length 9.31m (30ft 5in); height 3.66m (12ft)
Weight: 2040kg (4498lb) loaded
Armament: None

Kenya
1952–1955

Kenya, a former British colony, saw a rebellion in the Kikuyu province, which was mercilessly suppressed by the UK, with 11,000 Mau Mau casualties recorded in a period between 1952-55.

THE REMOVAL OF the leader of the Kenya African Union in 1952 did not put an end to the Kikuyu uprising, and Britain declared an emergency. Suspected tribal leaders were arrested, together with Kikuyu radicals, and the rebels, known as the Mau Mau, began to be relentlessly pursued.

Starting in April 1953 air power was used in a large-scale COIN campaign, with an initial group of RAF Harvards being forward deployed from Rhodesia. Used for ground attack, the Harvards completed 2000 sorties in a year. In November 1953 heavy bombers arrived in the form of Lincolns, which operated from Eastleigh on three-month rotations. Normally based at Khormaksar, Aden, a small number of Vampire fighter-bombers were provided by the RAF's Middle East Air Force, together with photo-reconnaissance Meteors.

Rebellion suppressed
Aided by Austers, Pembrokes and Valettas – plus Sycamore helicopters – used in support of forces on the ground, the RAF helped to put an end to the rebellion by 1955. However, the true results of the military operations cannot be easily calculated, since there was very little means of effectively discriminating between Mau Mau rebel and innocent local, and certain British Army commanders were reported to offer bounty money for dead Mau Mau.

After becoming independent within the Commonwealth, Kenya became a republic in 1965.

RAF, KENYA, 1952–56		
Aircraft	Unit	Base
Lincoln B.Mk 2	21 Sqn	Eastleigh2
Lincoln B.Mk 2	49 Sqn	Eastleigh
Lincoln B.Mk 2	61 Sqn	Eastleigh
Lincoln B.Mk 2	100 Sqn	Eastleigh
Lincoln B.Mk 2	214 Sqn	Eastleigh
Vampire FB.Mk 9	8 Sqn (Det)	Eastleigh
Meteor PR.Mk 10	13 Sqn (Det)	Eastleigh
Lancaster PR.Mk 1, Dakota Mk 3	82 Sqn	Eastleigh
Harvard Mk 2B	1340 Flt	Eastleigh
Anson C.Mk 21, Proctor Mk 4, Valetta C.Mk 1, Dakota Mk 3, Auster AOP.Mk 6, Pembroke C.Mk 1, Sycamore HR.Mk 14	Comms Flt	Eastleigh

Specifications
Crew: 7

Powerplant: 4 x 1305kW (1750hp) Rolls Royce
Merlin 68, 68A or 300 piston engines

Maximum speed: 491km/h (305mph)

Range: 4506km (2800 miles)

Service ceiling: n/a

Dimensions: span 36.58m (120ft 0in);
length 23.85m (78ft 3in); height n/a

Weight: 37,195kg (82,000lb) loaded

Armament: 2 x 20mm cannon and 4 x 7mm
(0.5in) MGs; provision for up to 6350kg
(14,000lb) of bombs

▲ **Avro Lincoln B.Mk 2**
214 Sqn, RAF / Eastleigh, 1954
The first RAF Lincolns were from 49 Sqn and were detached to Eastleigh, Kenya, in November 1953. The following year aircraft drawn from 110 and 214 Sqns replaced these. The Lincolns were used to pattern-bomb suspected Mau Mau supply dumps and terrorist strongholds.

Chapter 7

Southern Asia

While the series of wars fought between India and Pakistan during the course of the Cold War did not involve direct participation by the superpowers, the two belligerents on the Indian subcontinent made considerable use of advanced aircraft supplied by the U.S. and China (in the case of Pakistan) and by the Soviets (in the case of India). Events to the north would subsequently shift the focus in the region towards Afghanistan, where the Soviet Union became entrenched in a costly war of attrition fought against U.S.-supported Islamic insurgents.

◀ **Shenyang F-6**

The series of wars fought between Indian and Pakistan during the years of the Cold War saw use made of some of the most advanced warplanes available from both Eastern and Western manufacturers. These Pakistan AF F-6s were licence-built versions of the MiG-19 supersonic interceptor.

Early India–Pakistan conflicts
1947–1948

Previously united under British rule, the Indian subcontinent was divided into three states, and political and religious differences saw three major wars fought between India and Pakistan.

THE BRITISH WITHDREW from India in August 1947, and the country was left divided into three independent states: mainly Muslim East and West Pakistan, and predominantly Hindu India. Chiefly Muslim, but ruled by a Hindu Maharajah, Kashmir was one of a number of border areas the boundaries of which were subject to dispute by the rival states.

After independence, the Indian AF and Pakistan AF set about equipping themselves, both receiving ex-RAF Tempest FB.Mk 2 fighters (89 for India in 1947, 24 for Pakistan in 1948). Initially, both air arms would receive considerable support from Britain in terms of equipment and training. Other early aircraft types included Liberators, Dakotas, Austers, Harvards and Tiger Moths for India, and Furies, Halifaxes, Dakotas, Austers, Devons and Harvards for Pakistan, most of the Pakistan AF units being located at airfields in West Pakistan.

In October 1947 Pakistan-backed Pathan tribesmen from the Northwest Frontier began to move on Srinagar, the Kashmiri capital, which was relieved by Indian airborne forces flown in by Dakotas and civilian aircraft. Further Kashmiri insurrection was carried out by Muslim 'Free

Kashmiri' groups, which were countered by Indian AF Tempest FB.Mk 2 and Spitfire Mk XIV fighters.

By early 1948 Pakistan had entered the conflict more overtly, providing artillery support and later airlift using its Halifaxes. The campaign had ended in stalemate by 31 December 1948, before the UN intervened to establish a ceasefire line that was recognized as the border between the two countries.

Northwest Frontier

At the same time as Pakistan and India were fighting over Kashmir, Pakistani air power was involved in policing the borders of the Northwest Frontier with Afghanistan, where tribes were also in open revolt.

In order to counter the insurrection, the Pakistan AF deployed Tempests to Peshawar, and these fighters were in action in a policing role over the Khyber Pass starting in December 1947. Transport of Pakistan Army formations in the area was the responsibility of Pakistan AF Dakotas, and Halifaxes were also available for bombing. Pakistan was still engaged on the Northwest Frontier between 1948-49, sending Tempest units to the front in rotation, before Furies superseded these fighters beginning in 1950.

▲ **Consolidated B-24J Liberator**

5 Sqn, Indian AF / Cawnpore/Poona, 1948-49

In addition to its ex-RAF Tempest fighters, India set about developing a strategic air arm, through the fielding of Liberator bombers. These were mainly assembled using wartime airframes that were retrieved from storage yards at Kanpur. Used for bombing and reconnaissance, 5 Sqn Liberators served at Cawnpore and Poona.

Specifications

Crew: 8

Powerplant: 4 x 895kW (1200hp) Pratt & Whitney R-1830-65 14-cylinder two-row radial piston engines

Maximum speed: 483km/h (300mph)

Range: 3380km (2100 miles)

Service ceiling: 8535m (28,000ft)

Dimensions: span 33.53m (110ft); length 20.47m (67ft 2in); height 5.49m (18ft)

Weight: 29,484kg (65,000lb) maximum takeoff

Armament: 2 x .5in MGs in each of nose, dorsal, ventral and tail turrets, one .5in MG in each of waist positions; internal bomb load of 3992kg (8800lb)

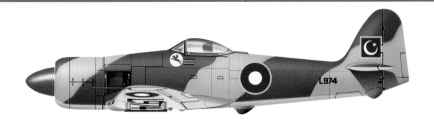

Specifications

Crew: 1

Powerplant: 1850kW (2480hp) Bristol
Centaurus XVIIC radial engine

Maximum speed: 740km/h (460mph)

Range: n/a

Service ceiling: 10,900m (35,800ft)

Dimensions: span 11.7m (38ft 5in);
length 10.6m (34ft 8in); height 4.9m
(16ft 1in)

Weight: 5670kg (12,500lb) loaded

Armament: 4 x 20mm (0.79in) Hispano Mk V
cannon; 12 x 76mm (3in) rockets or 908kg
(2000lb) of bombs

▲ **Hawker Fury FB.Mk 60**

9 Sqn, Pakistan AF / Peshawar, 1951

This Hawker Fury FB.Mk 60 was part of the second batch of deliveries that
Pakistan received in 1951. Pakistan was the most important operator of the land-
based Fury, taking 93 examples between 1949 and 1954. Subsequent British
deliveries provided Halifax bombers, Attacker fighters and Bristol 170 transports.

India–Pakistan

1965

**India and Pakistan went to war in 1965, once again over the issue of control of Kashmir. The
22-day war saw the outnumbered Pakistan AF perform well against Indian AF opposition.**

THE CONFLICT BEGAN when Pakistan began arming
and training irregulars to infiltrate Kashmir,
hopeful of sparking a revolution that would see the
territory fall into Pakistani hands. After supporting

the insurgency with artillery, Pakistan launched an
offensive against Indian military forces near Jammu.

During the conflict the Pakistan AF was able to
field 12 combat squadrons (including reserve units)

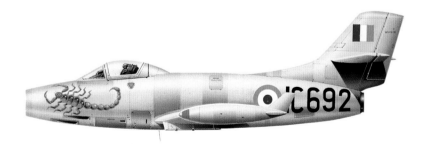

▲ **Dassault Ouragan**

29 Sqn, Indian AF / Gahauti, 1965

India was the recipient of 104 French-built Ouragan jet fighters between 1953
and 1954, the type receiving the local designation Toofani. Together with Indian
AF Vampires, Ouragans were relieved from front-line duties early in the 1965
campaign, after the former type proved vulnerable to Pakistan AF F-86s.

Specifications

Crew: 1

Powerplant: 1 x 22.2kN (4990lbf) Rolls-Royce
Nene 104B turbojet

Maximum speed: 940km/h (584mph)

Range: 920km (570 miles)

Service ceiling: 13,000m (42,650ft)

Dimensions: span 13.16m (43ft 2in); length
10.73m (35ft 2in); height 4.14m (13ft 7in)

Weight: 7404kg (16,323lb) loaded

Armament: 4 x 20mm (.787in) Hispano-Suiza
HS.404 cannon, rockets and up to 2270kg
(5000lb) of payload

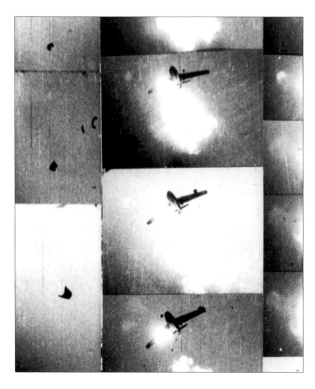

▲ F-86 Sabre

Gun camera footage reveals the final moments of a Pakistan AF F-86 as it falls to the guns of an Indian AF fighter. The backbone of the Pakistan AF in the 1965 war, additional ex-German Sabre Mk 6s were received in time for the 1971 conflict.

compared to the Indian AF's 14. However, Pakistan claimed a superior kill/loss rate in air combat, most victories being recorded by F-86s.

Most fighting took place along the northern Indo-Pakistan border, and the Indian AF held back much of its air power in the east, where fighting was limited. After 6 September both sides continued to launch raids into opposition territory, although these met little in the way of opposition. From now on, however, the Indian AF was able to generate a superior number of sorties, while the Pakistan AF regrouped and conserved its strength.

On the ground, an Indian Army counter-offensive pushed the Pakistani forces back across their own border in some areas, before the situation became one of stalemate, and a ceasefire was declared.

Inconclusive outcome

A subsequent treaty reinstated the pre-war borders of Kashmir. Outnumbered, the Pakistan AF had used skilful tactics to gain air superiority where it was needed. The Pakistan AF suffered losses of 25 aircraft during the war, compared to 60 for the Indian AF. However, Pakistan AF losses had removed around 17 per cent of its front-line strength. Equally damaging was the fact that as a result of the fighting Pakistan was denied military aid by the U.S., which would have a major impact on the course of the next conflict.

Specifications

Crew: 6–8

Powerplant: 2 x two 2610kW (3500hp) Wright R-3350-85 piston engines and one 22kN (4850lb) thrust Bristol Orpheus turbojet

Maximum speed: 470km/h (292mph)

Range: 3669km (2280 miles)

Service ceiling: 7300m (23,950ft)

Dimensions: span 33.3m (109ft 3in); length 26.37m (86ft 6in); height 8m (26ft 3in)

Weight: 33,747kg (74,700lb) loaded

Armament: none

▲ Fairchild C-119G Flying Boxcar

Indian AF

Three Indian AF squadrons were ultimately equipped with the C-119, these aircraft being fitted with an additional turbojet engine for improved performance under 'hot and high' conditions. At the time of the 1965 war, the Indian AF maintained two Flying Boxcar units, 12 and 19 Sqns.

▲ Martin B-57B

7 Sqn, Pakistan AF

A licence-built U.S. version of the British Canberra that was operated by the
Indian AF, the B-57 served the Pakistan AF in both reconnaissance and bomber
versions. The B-57B was widely used during the course of the 1965 campaign to
attack Indian airfields, flying from bases at Mauripur, Risalspur and Sargodha.

Specifications

Crew: 2

Powerplant: 2 x 32.1kN (7220lbf) Wright J65–
  W-5 turbojets

Maximum speed: 960km/h (598mph)

Range: 4380km (2720 miles)

Service ceiling: 13,745m (45,100ft)

Dimensions: span 19.5m (64ft 0in);

length 20m (65ft 6in); height 4.52m
  (14ft 10in)

Weight: 18,300kg (40,345lb) loaded

Armament: 4 x 20mm (0.787in) M39 cannon;
  2000kg (4500lb) in bomb bay; 1300kg
  (2800lb) on four external hardpoints,
  including unguided rockets

India–Pakistan
1971

In 1971 Pakistan and India went to war again, this time over mainly Bengali-populated East Pakistan, separated from West Pakistan by more than 1600km (1000 miles) of Indian territory.

IN EAST PAKISTAN Indian forces supported the
Mukti Bahani secessionist rebels and there was
widespread support for a Bengali breakaway from
West Pakistan.

Instigated by Pakistan, the 1971 war saw the
Pakistan AF severely hampered by the fact that fighting
took place a considerable distance from its primary
bases in the west. India had meanwhile prepared for

▲ Canadair Sabre Mk 6

17 Sqn, Pakistan AF / Rafiqui, 1971

Pakistan's fleet of Sabres played a major role during the fighting in 1971, as they
had in 1965. However, faced with numerical inferiority, the Pakistan AF suffered in
the air at the hands of Indian AF Hunters and Gnats, while aircraft were bombed
on their airfields by Indian Canberras, MiG-21s and Su-7s.

Specifications

Crew: 1

Powerplant: 1 x 32.35kN (7275lb) Avro Orenda
  Mark 14 engine

Maximum speed: 975km/h (606mph)

Range: n/a

Service ceiling: 15,450m (50,700ft)

Dimensions: span 11.58m (38ft);
  length 11.58m (38ft); height 4.57m (15ft)

Weight: 6628kg (14.613lb) loaded

Armament: 6 x 12.7mm (0.50in) M2 Browning
  machine guns; 2 x AIM-9 missiles; 2400kg
  (5300lb) of payload

the conflict, with a chain of heavily defended airfields along the borders with East and West Pakistan. The Indian AF planned two phases: an initial wave of airfield attacks followed by a campaign of interdiction against Pakistani forward areas and communications.

On 3 November, Indian interceptors scrambled in response to a Pakistan AF airspace infringement in the west. The first notable air combat came on 23 November, when four Pakistan AF Sabres on a strafing mission clashed with four Gnats northeast of Calcutta. Three Sabres were claimed shot down.

A full-scale assault was launched by Pakistan after it had accused India of launching attacks against East Bengal in support of the Mukti Bahani. Pre-emptive strikes were made against forward Indian AF airfields and radar sites in the west. The aim was to deny the Indian AF bases from which to launch attacks against

Pakistani ground formations in the north. The results of the first wave of airfield attacks were limited, however. Follow-on raids involved Pakistan AF B-57s launching nocturnal attacks against airfields and other Indian military targets in the west.

War on two fronts

War was officially declared on 4 December and the Indian AF launched its own wave of attacks against targets in the west and east, using Canberras and Su-7s. Sheer weight of numbers forced the Pakistan AF to operate on the defensive, and it was compelled to fight on both fronts. East Bengal hosted 10 Indian AF squadrons, while the carrier INS *Vikrant* also provided Sea Hawks and Alizés in the Bay of Bengal.

Hunters, MiG-21s and Su-7s targeted Pakistan AF bases at Tezgaon and Kurmitola beginning on

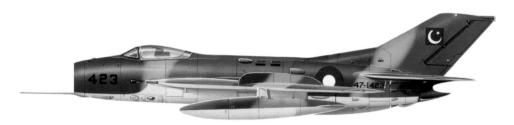

Specifications

Crew: 1	height 3.88m (12ft 8.75in)
Powerplant: 2 x 31.9kN (7165lb) Shenyang	Weight: 10,000kg (22,046lb) maximum
WP-6 turbojets	Armament: 3 x 30mm NR-30 cannon; four
Maximum speed: 1540km/h (957mph)	external hardpoints with provision for up to
Range: 1390km (864 miles)	500kg (1102lb) of stores, including air-to-air
Service ceiling: 17,900m (58,725ft)	missiles, 250kg (551lb) bombs, 55mm (2.1in)
Dimensions: span 9.2m (30ft 2.25in);	rocket-launcher pods, 212mm (8.34in)
length 14.9m (48ft 10.5in);	rockets or drop tanks

▲ **Shenyang F-6**

11 Sqn, Pakistan AF / Sargodha, 1971

In the absence of U.S. aircraft deliveries, Pakistan re-equipped with Chinese-supplied F-6 fighters (licence-built Chinese versions of the Soviet MiG-19), the first arriving in December 1965. This Pakistani F-6 was one of 135 delivered, and was reportedly one of the first to be received by the Pakistan AF, in 1966.

▲ **Dassault Mirage IIIEP**

5 Sqn, Pakistan AF / Sargodha, 1971

Additional new equipment in service with the Pakistan AF at the time of the 1971 war were French Mirage IIIs, a single squadron of which became operational in June 1969. As well as missile-armed Mirage IIIEP interceptor versions, the 1971 war saw Pakistan make use of the Mirage IIIRP version for reconnaissance.

Specifications

Crew: 1	Dimensions: span 8.22m (26ft 11.875in);
Powerplant: 1 x 60.8kN (13,668lb) SNECMA	length 16.5m (56ft); height 4.5m (14ft 9in);
Atar 9C turbojet	Weight: 13,500kg (29,760lb) loaded
Maximum speed: 1390km/h (883mph)	Armament: 2 x 30mm DEFA 552A cannon with
Range: 1200km (745 miles)	125rpg; three external pylons with provision
Service ceiling: 17,000m (55,755ft)	for up to 3000kg (6612lb) of stores

4 December. Outnumbered, Pakistani Sabres (some of which were missile-armed) put up stiff resistance.

On 6 December an Indian strike against Tezgaon and Kurmitola effectively put both bases out of action. Conversely, Pakistan only managed to launch five raids against India's major airfield in the west, Pathankot, which remained in operation.

Subsequent aerial activity focused on airfield denial, anti-radar and close support missions by both combatants, while Pakistan AF C-130s and B-57s and Indian AF Canberras and An-12s maintained nocturnal raids. The Indian AF Marut jet fighter-bomber made its debut, attacking Pakistani armour. Used for combat air patrols, Sidewinder-armed F-6s made claims against MiG-21s and Su-7s, and Mirages also proved their value in aerial combat, but

Pakistan was denied overall air superiority. On 7 December Indian infantry were lifted by Mi-4 and Mi-8 helicopters, in additionn to Alouette escorts, and helicopters also carried infantry to the western side of the Megha River on 10 December. A day later, Indian forces around Dacca launched an airborne assault, troops being delivered by An-12 and C-119G. The Indian AF kept up the pace of its raids in the following days, striking Pakistani forward bases, although the focus was now on interdicting lines of communication and close support.

After 14 days of fighting, the Indian AF had comprehensively bettered its Pakistani opposition, and contributed to Pakistan's military defeat. With the country's 'eastern wing' lost, East Pakistan now re-emerged as Bangladesh.

Specifications

Crew: 1

Powerplant: 1 x 60.8kN (13,668lb) thrust
Tumanskii afterburning turbojet

Maximum speed: 2050km/h (1300mph)

Range: 1800km (1118 miles)

Service ceiling: 17,000m (57,750ft)

Dimensions: span 7.15m (23ft 5.5in);

length (including probe) 15.76m (51ft 8.5in)

height 4.1m (13ft 5.5in)

Weight: 9400kg (20,723lb) loaded

Armament: 1 x 23mm cannon, provision for
about 1500kg (3307kg) of stores, including
air-to-air missiles, rocket pods, napalm tanks
or drop tanks

▲ MiG-21PF

1 Sqn, Indian AF / Adampur, 1971

As well as receiving MiG-21s from the USSR in the form of export deliveries, licence production of the fighter was undertaken by HAL in India. This MiG-21PF wears a hastily applied camouflage scheme for combat in the 1971 war, and is armed with a GSh-23 fuselage gun pack and R-13 air-to-air missiles.

▲ English Electric Canberra B.Mk 66

5 Sqn, Indian AF / Agra, 1971

While the B(I).Mk 58 bomber-interdictor served in the 1965 war, the 1971 conflict also saw the involvement of the B.Mk 66 version of the Canberra. The aircraft was active on both eastern and western fronts during 1971, and also saw service in a reconnaissance capacity, in the form of the Canberra PR.Mk 57 version.

Specifications

Crew: 3

Powerplant: 2 x 33.23kN (7490lb) thrust
turbojet engine Avon R.A.7 Mk.109 turbojet
engines

Maximum speed: 933km/h (580mph)

Range: 5440km (3380 miles)

Service ceiling: 15,000m (48,000ft)

Dimensions: span 19.51m (65ft 6in); length
19.96m (65ft 6in); height 4.77m (15ft 8in)

Weight: 24,948kg (55,000lb) loaded

Armament: 4 x 20mm cannon; two rocket pods
or up to 2772kg (6000lb) of bombs

Specifications

Crew: 1

Powerplant: 1 x 24kN (5400lb) Rolls-Royce
  Nene 103 turbojet

Maximum speed: 969km/h (602mph)

Range: 370km (230 miles)

Service ceiling: 13,565m (44,500ft)

Dimensions: span 11.89m (39ft);

length 12.09m (39ft 8in); height 2.64m
(8ft 8in)

Weight: 7348kg (16,200lb) loaded

Armament: 4 x 20mm Hispano cannon;
  provision for 4 x 227kg (500lb) bombs, or
  2 x 227kg (500lb) bombs and 20 x 76mm
  (3in) or 16 x 127mm (5in) rockets

▲ **Hawker Sea Hawk FGA.Mk 6**

300 Sqn, Indian Navy / INS Vikrant, *1971*

This Indian Navy Sea Hawk fighter-bomber operated from the carrier INS *Vikrant* during the 1971 conflict fought against Pakistan. Beginning operations on 4 December, the Sea Hawks claimed the destruction of seven ships and a submarine, and also mounted strikes against coastal installations and airfields.

Afghanistan
1979–1989

Sometimes dubbed 'Russia's Vietnam', the conflict waged by the USSR in Afghanistan saw air power deployed in force in a battle for supremacy against a resourceful guerrilla enemy.

THE ORIGINAL OBJECTIVE of the Soviet invasion of Afghanistan in December 1979 was the removal of President Hafizullah Amin, and restoration of order following the installation of a new regime. In the first instance the Soviets succeeded, aided by around 1000 Soviet 'advisors' already based in Afghanistan. However, they were unable to subjugate the country, which was soon gripped by a powerful Islamic insurgency and a rapidly escalating war.

Until withdrawal of the final Soviet troops in February 1989, the Red Army was bogged down in a guerrilla war, in which air power was put to use in various forms in an effort to extinguish resistance.

Guerrilla tactics

Although Soviet air power proved effective in certain instances, the mountainous terrain gave the insurgents the upper hand on the ground, and the Mujahideen guerrillas regularly exposed Soviet Army units to ambushes and hit-and-run attacks. In order to regain the initiative, the Soviet AF was employed not only to provide troops with direct support where required, but to maintain a bombing offensive,

deploying the Tu-16, Tu-22 and Tu-22M as free-fall bombers in order to weaken opposition resolve and deny it the resources needed to wage its campaign.

In direct support of troops on the ground, the Soviet AF used MiG-27, Su-17M, Su-24 and Su-25 aircraft in a close support role to target insurgents' positions. Meanwhile extensive use was made of rotorcraft to transport troops and also to provide organic fire support via the employment of helicopter gunships, such as the Mi-24 and heavily armed versions of the Mi-8. As well as increasing use of aircraft, the Soviet presence on the ground grew from 6000 troops in December 1979 to more than 130,000 troops by the mid-1980s. An-12, An-22 and Il-76 airlifters of Transport Aviation provided intra-theatre logistic support throughout. These transports came under increasing threat from the guerrillas as they complemented AAA with man-portable SAMs obtained via CIA channels.

In addition to Soviet AF assets, a more minor role was played by the Afghan AF itself, which was allied with the Soviets and equipped with similar types, including MiG-17s, MiG-21s, Mi-8s and Mi-24s.

Facing challenging weather conditions, the Soviets typically made use of the onset of spring to launch renewed offensives against the guerrillas, the first being initiated in 1980. By the end of 1980, it was reported that Soviet Mi-24 numbers had quadrupled to 240, with six airfields under construction.

Soviet tactics were increasingly reliant on helicopter gunships and heliborne assault, while a new facet to the air war was represented by the arrival of the Su-25 dedicated ground attack aircraft in spring 1981. In a similar timeframe, Soviet tactical jets began to make increasing use of precision-guided weapons. Other popular stores included thermobaric (fuel-air explosive) weapons, particularly for use against cave complexes and buildings.

After major operations that included the siege of Khost in 1983 and a combined-arms offensive against Najrab in the early months of 1984, a spring bombing offensive was launched against the Panjshir valley in 1984. The guerrillas waged a campaign of attrition for the next four years, prior to the beginning of the Soviet withdrawal in 1988. By the end of the Cold War the situation was stalemate, with the Mujahideen left to battle the Afghan military.

Specifications

Crew: 1

Powerplant: 2 x 44.1kN (9921lb) Tumanskii
  R-195 turbojets

Maximum speed: 975km/h (606mph)

Range: 750km (466 miles)

Service ceiling: 7000m (22,965ft)

Dimensions: span 14.36m (47ft 1.5in); length

15.53m (50ft 11.5in); height 4.8m (15ft 9in)

Weight: 17,600kg (38,800lb) loaded

Armament: 1 x 30mm GSh-30-2 cannon with
  250 rounds; 8 x external pylons with provision
  for up to 4400kg (9700lb) of stores, including
  AAMs, ASMs, ARMs, anti-tank missiles,
  guided bombs and cluster bombs

▲ **Sukhoi Su-25**

Soviet Frontal Aviation

The Su-25 ground attack aircraft received its combat debut in Afghanistan, where it was first observed by Western analysts. A successor to the wartime Il-2 Shturmovik, the Su-25 was tailored for survivability in a battlefield environment, and proved useful against the Mujahideen, on occasion working alongside Mi-24s.

Specifications

Crew: 5–6

Powerplant: 4 x 11,030kW (15,000hp)
  Kuznetsov NK-12MA turboprops

Maximum speed: 740km/h (460mph)

Range: 5000km (3100 miles)

Service ceiling: 8000m (26,240ft)

Dimensions: 64.4m (211ft 3in);
  length 57.9m (190ft); height 12.53m
  (41ft 1in)

Weight: 250,000kg (551,000lb) loaded

Payload: 80,000kg (180,000lb)

▲ **An-22**

Soviet Transport Aviation

Flying into Kabul and Shindand, the An-22 was the most capable strategic airlifter available to the Soviets at the time of the invasion of Afghanistan. The initial combat force of 6000 troops was sent to Afghanistan in around 300 sorties flown by transport aircraft between 24-26 December 1979.

Chapter 8

The Far East

During the years of the Cold War, Southeast Asia and the Far East saw the frequent application of air power in localized conflicts and post-colonial insurgencies. On the Korean peninsula, UN forces assembled to repulse a communist invasion of South Korea, while in Indo-China, the departure of the French colonizers left a power vacuum, and a guerrilla war in which the U.S. would rapidly become entrenched. Colonial history also led to British involvement in Malaya and Borneo, where air power was once again used to put down communist-inspired, nationalist insurrection.

◄ **Republic F-105 Thunderchief/Douglas B-66 Destroyer**
Four USAF F-105s formate on a B-66 pathfinder that guided the strike fighters to their targets using advanced navigation and attack electronics. The Vietnam air war was typified by America's deployment of increasingly advanced weapons and warplanes against a consistently elusive enemy.

Korean War
1950–1953

Divided in 1945 along the 38th Parallel, North and South Korea went to war in 1950 when the communist North invaded its neighbour, with support from both the USSR and China.

THE UN RESPONSE to the invasion of 25 June 1950 was to send a military coalition to attempt to drive the North Korean forces back across the 38th Parallel. The initial air power available to the UN forces comprised USAF Far East Air Force units based in

Japan, the Philippines and Okinawa, its fighter units equipped with three squadrons of F-82Gs and five wings of F-80Cs. The Republic of Korea AF in the south was not in possession of any combat types. As North Korean forces moved towards the South Korean

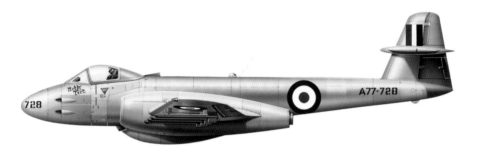

▲ **Gloster Meteor F.Mk 8**

77 Sqn, Royal Australian AF / K14 (Kimpo), 1951–53

Based at K14, the Royal Australian AF contingent supporting the UN forces in Korea flew the British-built Meteor F.Mk 8. Outclassed in air combat after the appearance of the MiG-15, the Meteor was switched from fighter sweeps and B-29 escort missions to ground attack, flying over 15,000 sorties in total.

Specifications

Crew: 1

Powerplant: 2 x 16kN (3600lb) Rolls-Royce Derwent 8 turbojets

Maximum speed: 962km/h (598mph)

Range: 1580km (980 miles)

Service ceiling: 13,106m (43,000ft)

Dimensions: span 11.32m (37ft 2in); length 13.58m (44ft 7in); height 3.96m (13ft)

Weight: 8664kg (19,100lb) loaded

Armament: 4 x 20mm Hispano cannon, foreign F.8s often modified to carry two iron bombs or eight rockets

Specifications

Crew: 1

Powerplant: 1 x 26.3kN (5952lb) Klimov VK-1 turbojet

Maximum speed: 1100km/h (684 mph)

Range: 1424km (885 miles)

Service ceiling: 15,545m (51,000ft)

Dimensions: span 10.08m (33ft .75in); length 11.05m (36ft 3.75in); height 3.4m (11ft 1.75in)

Weight: 5700kg (12,566lb) loaded

Armament: 1 x 37mm N-37 cannon and 2 x 23mm NS-23 cannon, plus up to 500kg (1102lb) of stores on underwing pylons

▲ **MiG-15**

People's Liberation Army AF

The first MiG-15s to be encountered by the UN forces in Korea were Chinese-flown examples, which began to cross the Yalu on 1 November 1950. The Soviet-built fighter quickly showed its superiority over the USAF's F-80 and as a result the first F-86As were hurried to Korea, the 4th FIW arriving on 11 November.

capital, Seoul, USAF fighters covered a civilian evacuation, F-82s and F-80s clashing with North Korean AF Yak-9s and Il-10s in the first aerial engagements of the war on 27 June.

With General Douglas MacArthur appointed head of the UN forces and Seoul fallen to the communists, the U.S. began to take a harder line. The F-80 formed the mainstay of UN fighter power, supported by F-51s flown by USAF, Australian and South African units. Such was UN air supremacy that the North Korean AF was restricted to only limited operations for several months starting in July.

The outbreak of the Korean War saw the USAF bomber force in the Far East equipped with a single B-29 wing on Guam, plus two squadrons of B-26s.

Early in the war the B-29s and Japan-based B-26s were directed against North Korean AF airfields in the north, where they succeeded in destroying many aircraft on the ground. North Korean AF opposition was limited, and the B-29s were able to raid North Korean industry almost unmolested.

Close support in Korea

On the ground, the UN air assets were struggling to blunt the advance by the North Koreans, with fighter-bombers targeting bridges and other transport infrastructure as well as columns of troops and armour. Although the UN air arms were dominant in the air, there was little they could do to prevent North Korean progress on the ground despite round-the-

Specifications

Crew: 1

Powerplant: 1 x 26.3kN (5952lb) Klimov VK-1 turbojet

Maximum speed: 1100km/h (684 mph)

Range: 1424km (885 miles)

Service ceiling: 15,545m (51,000ft)

Dimensions: span 10.08m (33ft .75in); length 11.05m (36ft 3.75in); height 3.4m (11ft 1.75in)

Weight: 5700kg (12,566lb) loaded

Armament: 1 x 37mm N-37 cannon and 2 x 23mm NS-23 cannon, plus up to 500kg (1102lb) of stores on underwing pylons

▲ MiG-15

North Korean AF

'2057' was a Korean-operated MiG-15, although UN forces would encounter examples of the fighter flown by Soviet, Chinese and North Korean pilots. Raids by the U.S. Fifth Air Force against North Korean airfields meant that the communists never dared to operate the MiGs from bases south of the Yalu River.

Specifications

Crew: 2

Powerplant: 1 x 26.7kN (6000lb) Allison J33-A-33 turbojet

Maximum speed: 933km/h (580mph)

Range: 1850km (1150 miles)

Service ceiling: 14,630m (48,000ft)

Dimensions: span not including tip tanks 11.85m (38ft 10.5in); length 12.2m (40ft 1in); height 3.89m (12ft 8in)

Weight: 7125kg (15,710lb) loaded

Armament: 4 x .5in machine guns

▲ Lockheed F-94B Starfire

319th Fighter Interceptor Squadron, USAF / K13 (Suwon), 1952–53

The first F-94 all-weather fighters arrived in Korea in March 1951 although the type's use was initially restricted, with the U.S. fearful that the E-1 fire control radar might fall into communist hands. Mounting B-29 losses then saw the two-seat F-94 fighters used as escorts for the USAF bombers.

Specifications

Crew: 1

Powerplant: 1 x 32.36kN (7275lb) thrust Avro
Orenda Mark 14 turbojet engine

Maximum speed: 965km/h (600mph)

Range: 530km (329 miles)

Service ceiling: 14,600m (48,000ft)

Dimensions: span 11.58m (39ft); length
11.4m (37ft 6in); height 4.4m (14ft 8in)

Weight: 6628kg (14,613lb) loaded

Armament: 6 x .5in (12.7mm) machine guns

▲ **North American F-86F Sabre**

2 Sqn, South African AF / K55 (Osan), 1952–53

In addition to the USAF, Sabres were operated over Korea by the South African AF, which replaced its F-51Ds with F-86Fs that were based at K55. The South African jets were primarily used in a fighter-bomber role, 2 Sqn being operated under the command of the USAF's 18th Fighter Bomber Group.

clock air attacks. By September, the UN forces were pinned back to a pocket around Pusan located in the far south of the Korean peninsula.

The UN regained the initiative on 15 September when, under the protection of air superiority, MacArthur launched an amphibious landing at Inchon further up the coast. With the North Korean forces overstretched on the ground, the UN started to make progress, the landings being followed by a counter-attack at Pusan, while air power continued to hit the North Korean forces on the ground. Carriers of the U.S. Navy and Royal Navy, operating F4U-4Bs, AD-4s, F9F-2s, Fireflies and Seafires provided air support at Inchon. These types were aided over the beachhead by OY-1 forward air control aircraft, F7F-3N night-fighters and HO3S-1 helicopters.

China intervenes

The audacious Inchon landings led to the recapture of the important airfield at Kimpo, and by the end of September most of the North Korean invasion force had been rolled back to positions just beyond the 38th Parallel. This was the signal for communist China to intervene on behalf of its ally, and Chinese troops were assembled north of the Yalu River. At the same time, MacArthur announced his objective of occupying the entire Korean peninsula, rather than a return to the 1945 border as originally envisaged by the UN. U.S.-led forces advanced deep into the

north, the North Korean capital, Pyongyang, being occupied by UN forces on 19 October.

On 1 November the UN forces encountered the MiG-15 fighter for the first time. Soviet-flown and operating out of Chinese bases north of the Yalu, which were immune to air attack, the swept-wing MiGs were superior to any UN fighter then in theatre. At the time of the MiG's combat debut, the USAF fighter arm in Korea comprised three wings of piston-engined F-51s, and two of F-80 jets. Further F-51s were operated by a single Royal Australian AF (RAAF) unit under the command of the USAF 35th Fighter Bomber Group.

Concurrent with the deployment of the MiG-15 was the arrival on the ground of Chinese troops, and

USAF FIGHTERS, KOREAN WAR		
Aircraft	**Unit**	**Base**
F-82G	4th F(AW)S	Naha
F-82G, F-94B	68th F(AW)S	Itazuke, K13 (det)
F-82G	339th F(AW)S	Yokota
F-51D, F-80C	8th FBW	Itazuke
F-51D	35th FIG	Johnson AB, K2
F-51D, F-80C	35th FIG	Johnson AB, K1, K3, K13
F-86A/E	4th FIG	K14, Japan, K2, K13
F-86E/F	51st FIG	K13, K14
F-94B	319th FIS	K13

UN aircraft stepped up their close support activity, land-based fighter-bombers being joined by carrier-based aircraft from Task Force 77 (including the British carrier HMS *Theseus*) at the mouth of the Yalu. Using B-29s to attack the Chinese assault over the Yalu was considered too high of a risk so it was left to the carrier-based fighter-bombers to attack bridges on the river. The raids were conducted by ADs and F4Us with top cover provided by F9Fs.

The first-ever confirmed jet-versus-jet combat pitched an F-80C against a MiG-15 over the Yalu on November 8, and in the following days, the

USAF FIGHTER-BOMBERS, KOREAN WAR, 1950		
Aircraft	**Unit**	**Base**
F-51D, F-80C	8th FBG	Itazuke, K2, K13
F-51D, F-80C	35th FIG	Johnson AB, K1, K2, K3
F-80C	44th FBS	Clark AB
F-51D, F-80C	18th FBG	K2, K24, K10
F-80C	49th FBG	K2, Misawa
F-80C	51st FIW	K14, K13
F-84E/G	27th FEG	Itazuke, K2

Specifications

Crew: 1

Powerplant: 1 x 24kN (5400lb) Allison
J33-A-35 turbojet

Maximum speed: 966km/h (594mph)

Range: 1930km (1200 miles)

Service ceiling: 14,000m (46,000ft)

Dimensions: span 11.81m (38ft 9in); length
10.49m (34ft 5in); height 3.43m (11ft 3in)

Weight: 5738kg (12,660lb) loaded

Armament: 6 x 0.50 in (12.7mm) M2 Browning
MGs; 2 x 1000lb (454kg) bombs;
8 x unguided rockets

▲ **F-80C Shooting Star**

36th Fighter Bomber Squadron, 8th Fighter Bomber Group, USAF / K13 (Suwon), 1951

At the outset of the Korean War the F-80 comprised the backbone of the USAF's fighter forces deployed in theatre. The appearance of the MiG-15 saw the F-80 outclassed in the air-to-air role, and it was thereafter used for fighter-bomber missions. This F-80C-5 flew with the 36th FBS, 8th FBG at K13.

Specifications

Crew: 1

Powerplant: 1 x 21.8kN (4900lb) thrust Allison
J35-A-17 turbojet engine

Maximum speed: 986km/h (613mph)

Range: 2390km (1485 miles)

Service ceiling: 13,180m (43,240ft)

Dimensions: span 11.1m (36ft 5in); length
11.41m (36ft 5in); height 3.91m (12ft)

Weight: 10,185kg (22,455lb) loaded

Armament: 6 x .5in (12.7mm) machine guns;
2 x 454kg (1000lb) bombs or 8 x 2.75in
rockets

▲ **F-84E Thunderjet**

9th Fighter Bomber Squadron, 49th Fighter Bomber Group, USAF / K2 (Taegu), 1951

Part of the 49th FBG, this F-84E fighter-bomber was based at K2 in late 1951. Visible beneath the cockpit canopy is a marking that commemorates the wing's first aerial victory against a MiG-15, achieved by Captain Kenneth L. Skeen on 19 September 1951. Note the bomb carried under the wing of this particular jet.

communist fighters exacted an increasing toll on B-29 bombers. By the end of the month the Chinese presence on the ground meant that the UN forces were matched in terms of numbers, while the introduction of the MiG-15 had threatened to conclusively turn the tables in terms of air superiority.

On 26 November the communists launched their new offensive, involving 250,000 Chinese troops as well as North Korean formations. The communist offensive caught the UN off guard, and its supply lines were now dangerously overstretched. The UN began to withdraw its troops from the north, using both transport aircraft and ships. By January 1951 the situation had

returned to a standoff just north of the 38th Parallel, while UN air power had been increased through the addition of further aircraft carriers and the deployment of the F-86A. A match for the MiG-15, the F-86A had first arrived in Korea with the 4th Fighter Interceptor Group at Kimpo in December 1950. Within a similar timeframe the USAF began to deploy F-84E fighter-bombers, while the RAAF unit re-equipped with Meteors. The Meteor was soon outclassed in aerial combat, and switched to ground attack, a role in which the F-84 would excel. F-84s would prove versatile, and its other missions included interdiction, armed reconnaissance and close support.

▲ **Ilyushin Il-10**

North Korean AF

At the outbreak of the war in June 1950 it was assumed that the North Korean AF included 70 single-seat piston-engined fighters (Yak-9s, La-7s and La-11s) plus around 65 Il-2 and Il-10 attack aircraft. An Il-10 is illustrated, examples of this type being among the first to be claimed by U.S. fighters on 27 June 1950.

Specifications

Crew: 2

Powerplant: 1 x 1320kW (1770hp) Mikulin
AM-42 liquid-cooled V-12 engine

Maximum speed: 550km/h (342mph)

Range: 800km (550 miles)

Service ceiling: 4000m (13,123ft)

Dimensions: span 13.40m (44ft); length

11.12m (36ft 6in); height 4.10m (13ft 5in)

Weight: 6345kg (14,000lb) loaded

Armament: 2 x 23mm (0.9in) Nudelman-
Suranov NS-23 cannons; 1 x 12.7mm (0.5in)
UBST cannon in the BU-9 rear gunner station;
up to 600kg (1320lb) bomb load

▲ **Yakovlev Yak-18**

North Korean AF

Designed as a trainer, the Yak-18 was used by North Korea for nocturnal harassment raids over UN airfields, with similar missions also being carried out by Po-2 utility biplanes. These nuisance raiders were dubbed 'Bedcheck Charlies' by the UN forces and proved to be challenging targets for Allied fighters.

Specifications

Crew: 2

Powerplant: 1 x 224kW (300hp) Ivchenko AI-
14RF radial piston engine

Maximum speed: 300km/h (187mph)

Range: 700km (436 miles)

Service ceiling: 5060m (16,596ft)

Dimensions: span 10.6m (34ft 9in);
length 8.35m (27ft 5in);
height 3.35m (11ft)

Weight: 1320kg (2904lb) maximum
takeoff

Armament: none

MiG-15 and F-86A first clashed in the air on 17 December, and successive marks of these fighters would contest air superiority until the end of the conflict, the principal area of combat being over the Yalu, a sector known as 'MiG Alley'.

A further communist advance forced the evacuation of the F-86s from Kimpo to Johnson AFB in Japan and temporarily out of the action. In the meantime it was left to the UN carriers to bring the air war to the North Korean forces, with close support missions being undertaken by ADs and F4Us, among others. At the same time the communists set about improving their airfields in North Korea, to extend the reach of air power beyond that offered by aircraft based in Manchuria, and further units were equipped with MiG-15 fighters. Meanwhile, USAF RB-26Cs were used for reconnaissance missions, flying from Japan, and latterly from Taegu and Kimpo in Korea.

Thunderjet offensive

Starting in January 1951 F-84Es of the 27th Fighter Escort Group were in action in an offensive role, interdicting communist supply routes, but also enjoying some success when tangling with MiGs in the air-to-air arena. Flying from Taegu in the south, the 27th FEG flew around 12,000 combat missions by the end of May 1951. The 27th FEG then returned to SAC command, and its place in Korea was taken by the 136th Fighter Bomber Wing, also with F-84Es. An additional Thunderjet group also arrived at around the same time, with the deployment of the 49th FBG, which had previously

been equipped with F-80Cs, and had been in Korea since the outbreak of the war.

By the time the communist spring offensive began in March 1951 the USAF still only had a single F-86 wing committed to the conflict. The F-86As returned to Korea from Japan in March, at which time B-29s were suffering losses to the MiGs. Because the communist MiG-15s were primarily held back at bases in the north and west, most air-to-air action was confined to the skies over the Yalu. However, some MiG-15s were closer to the front at Antung, and aerial fighting escalated in April, the MiG revealing itself to be superior to the F-84E, as well as being a lethal bomber-destroyer. In the latter role, MiGs were involved in the largest aerial battle of the war so far when they met B-29s, plus F-84E escorts and F-86A top cover over the Yalu on 12 April. Despite losses, the three B-29 wings – and to a lesser extent the two wings of B-26s – kept up their harassment of the communist forces, most missions being flown during the day, with fighter escorts provided.

As a result of the increasing intensity of the air war, a second F-86A squadron was moved forward to Suwon, and tactics were modified, ensuring that greater numbers of Sabres were in the air at any one time. The F-86s were soon showing their worth in the aerial fighting, posting claims for 22 MiGs destroyed by the end of May, in the course of over 3500 sorties.

With the spring offensive of 1951 stalled on the ground, the communists were forced into

USAF BOMBERS, KOREAN WAR		
Aircraft	**Unit**	**Base**
B-29A	19th BG(M)	Kadena
B-29A	22nd BG(M)	Kadena
B-29A	92nd BG(M)	Yokota
B-29A	98th BG(M)	Yokota
B-29A	307th BG(M)	Kadena
B-26B/C	3rd BG(L)	Iwakuni, K8, K16
B-26B/C	452nd BG(L)	Miho, K1
B-26B/C	17th BG(L)	K1

◀ **Douglas B-26 Invader**

First introduced to combat during the final stages of World War II, the B-26 remained the most important USAF light bomber during the conflict in Korea and was also used for reconnaissance missions and interdiction.

negotiation. In the meantime, both sides attempted to gain air superiority, and June and July saw pitched air battles in 'Mig Alley'. In the quest for air supremacy, the UN forces would eventually be able to call on an improved version of the Sabre, the F-86E model with a power-boosted 'flying tail', although they would have to wait until September 1951 for the fighter to become available in Korea.

The UN air forces staged a major air operation in June 1951 under the codename Strangle, with the aim of cutting off the communist forces from their supply lines and communications. To achieve this, the operation targeted road and rail targets, bridges and tunnels, and aircraft involved included USAF bombers, land-based U.S. Marine Corps aircraft and

U.S. Navy carrier aircraft from Task Force 77. An ambitious operation, Strangle failed to sever supply lines (although it did succeed in drawing MiG-15s into battle), but it continued to be pursued until September. The major drawback of Operation Strangle was the fact that the communists relied on roads rather than rail for transport of supplies, and there were simply too many targets for the U.S. air forces to address.

'Bedcheck Charlies'

With the F-86s operating from Suwon, the communists attempted to destroy the fighters on the ground, operating Po-2s and Yak-18s under the cover of darkness. Such raids began on 17 June, and the

Specifications

Crew: 1	Dimensions: span 11.6m (38ft); length 11.3m
Powerplant: 1 x 26.5kN (5950lb) thrust Pratt &	(37ft 5in); height 3.8m (11ft 4in)
Whitney J42-P-6/P-8 turbojet engine	Weight: 7462kg (16,450lb) loaded
Maximum speed: 925km/h (575mph)	Armament: 4 x 20mm M2 cannon; up to 910kg
Range: 2100km (1300 miles)	(2000lb) bombs, 6 x 5in (127mm) rockets
Service ceiling: 13,600m (44,600ft)	

▲ **Grumman F9F-2 Panther**

VF-781, US Navy / USS Bonne Homme Richard, *1951*

This F9F-2 served with VF-781 aboard the carrier USS *Bonne Homme Richard*, part of Carrier Air Group 102, on station in Korea between May and November 1951. Together with the F2H Banshee, the Panther was the major U.S. Navy carrier-based fighter deployed in Korea, and scored several aerial victories.

▲ **Supermarine Seafire FR.Mk 47**

800 NAS, Royal Navy / HMS Triumph, *1950*

The ultimate development of the Spitfire/Seafire line, the FR.Mk 47 was mainly used for ground attack work in Korea. This example flew from HMS *Triumph*, the first Royal Navy carrier to be deployed to Korea, arriving on station in July 1950 with an air wing comprising Seafires and the Firefly F.Mk 1s of 827 NAS.

Specifications

Crew: 1	Dimensions: span 11.25m (36ft 11in);
Powerplant: 1 x 1752kW (2350hp) Rolls-Royce	length 10.46m (34ft 4in); height 3.88m
Griffon 88 piston engine	(12ft 9in)
Maximum speed: 727km/h (452mph)	Weight: 4853kg (10,700lb) loaded
Range: 2374km (1375 miles)	Armament: 4 x 20mm Hispano V cannon; up to 8
Service ceiling: 13,135m (43,100ft)	x RP-3 rockets; up to 3 x 230kg (500lb) bombs

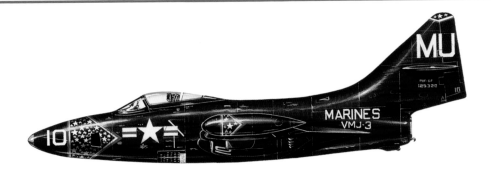

▲ Grumman F9F-5P Panther

VMJ-3, U.S. Marine Corps / Itami, 1953

The F9F-5P was a camera-equipped version of the Panther, and this example was operated by VMJ-3 of the U.S. Marine Corps over Korea, based at Itami, Japan. The 'VMJ' of the unit designation signified a Marine Photo-Reconnaissance Squadron. Carried-based U.S. Navy F9F-2Ps were also active over Korea in the same role.

Specifications

Crew: 1	Dimensions: span 11.6m (38ft); length 12.1m
Powerplant: 1 x 27.7kN (6250lb) thrust Pratt &	(40ft); height 3.7m (12ft 2in)
Whitney J48-P-6A turbojet engine	Weight: 8057kg (17,776lb) loaded
Maximum speed: 972km/h (604mph)	Armament: none
Range: 2093km (1300 miles)	
Service ceiling: 13,045m (42,800ft)	

UN air forces were unable to develop an effective counter to the slow-flying nuisance raiders. In the same month, the Yalu was scene to frenetic aerial combats, as F-86s again clashed with MiG-15s, and on 20 June communist Il-10s escorted by Yak-9s attacked a UN-held island off the Korean coast.

Chinese involvement meant that the UN could no longer hope to unify north and south as a single Korean entity. Stalemate on the ground led to both sides beginning peace talks in July 1951, MacArthur by now having been replaced by General Matthew B. Ridgway as the leader of the UN military contingent.

Summer 1951 saw continued B-29 raids against North Korean targets, the bombers now facing MiGs as well as increasingly accurate, radar-directed AAA. In June and July alone, 13 B-29s were damaged while, in August, a series of raids was staged by B-29s against the port and rail marshalling yard at Wojin,

▲ Grumman F7F-3N Tigercat

HEDRON 1, U.S. Marine Corps / K3 (Pohang), 1950–53

A specialist night-fighter, the F7F-3N was deployed to Korea in small numbers by the U.S. Marine Corps, serving exclusively from land bases. The aircraft carried air interception radar in the nose, and was armed with 30mm cannon in the wings. This Tigercat served with the headquarters squadron, HEDRON 1, at K3.

Specifications

Crew: 2	Dimensions: span 15.7m (51ft 6in); length
Powerplant: 2 x 1566kW (21000hp) Pratt &	13.8 (45ft 4in); height 4.6m (15ft 2in)
Whitney R-2800-34W radial piston engines	Weight: 11,880kg (26,190lb) loaded
Maximum speed: 700km/h (435mph)	Armament: 4 x 30mm cannon; up to 1814kg
Range: 1545km (960 miles)	(4000lb) of bombs
Service ceiling: 12,405m (40,700ft)	

ultimately with escort provided by U.S. Navy F2H-2 and F9F fighters. A further F-84 group was also available to the UN beginning in July, with the 116th Fighter Bomber Group arriving in the Far East.

August 1951 also saw the deployment of a new MiG-15 regiment at Antung, and in response F-86s

US MARINE CORPS, KOREAN WAR (MAG UNITS ONLY)		
Aircraft	Unit	Base
F9F-2B, F9F-4	VMF-115	K3, K6
F9F-2B	VMF-311	K3
F4U-4, AU-1	VMF-212	USS Badoeng Strait, K14, Wonsan, K3
F4U-4	VMF-312	K14, Wonsan, K27, K1, various carriers inc. USS Badoeng Strait
F4U-4	VMF-214	K9, Ashiya, USS Sicily, K1, K6
F4U-4, AU-1	VMF-323	K9, Ashiya, USS Sicily, USS Badoeng Strait, K1, K6
F4U-4N, F4U-5N, F7F-3N	VMF-542	K14, Wonsan, K27, K8
F7F-3N, F4U-5N, F3D-2N	VMF-513	Itazuke, Wonsan, K1, K6
AD-3	VMA-121	K3
F4U-4	VMA-332	USS Bairoko
AD-3	VMA-121	K3
HO3S-1, OY-2, OE-1	VMO-6	K9, USS Sicily, K14

were moved forward to Kimpo. The following month witnessed the arrival of the F-86E, with the 4th Fighter Interceptor Group, initially as attrition replacements for the F-86A. A first complete F-86E wing, the 51st FIG, was fully equipped before the end of the year. In the latter group the new F-86Es replaced the F-80C.

Improved MiGs arrive

Operation Strangle was superseded by a new UN air campaign that sought to destroy rail communications in the north, cutting off supplies before they began to be transported by road to the North Korean front line. In response to the new campaign, the communists deployed a further regiment of MiGs, by now equipped with the improved MiG-15bis variant. The new fighter was directed against the B-29s, and in October losses of the bomber again began to mount.

The largest air battle of the campaign took place on 22 October, and saw an estimated 100 MiGs clash with B-29s and F-84 and F-86 escorts. For the claimed destruction of six MiGs, the USAF lost three B-29s, with four more damaged, plus an F-84 destroyed. Eventually, the sheer numbers of MiGs now being put up by the communist air arms forced the USAF to abandon daylight raids by the B-29s. As an alternative, the UN began to rely increasingly on night-time attacks flown by carrier-based aircraft.

Specifications

Crew: 6–8

Powerplant: 2 x 2610kW (3500hp) Pratt & Whitney R-4360-20 piston engines

Maximum speed: 476km/h (296mph)

Range: 3669km (2280 miles)

Service ceiling: 7300m (23,950ft)

Dimensions: span 33.3m (109ft 3in); length 26.37m (86ft 6in); height 8m (26ft 3in)

Weight: 29,029kg (64,000lb) loaded

Payload: 4500kg (10,000lb) of cargo

▲ **Fairchild R4Q-1 Flying Boxcar**

VMR-253, U.S. Marine Corps / Itami, 1950–53

The U.S. Marine Corps version of the C-119 was the R4Q-1, and 41 examples of the type served in two squadrons, VMR-252 and VMR-253. Outfitted as an assault transport, the R4Q-1 was operated from Itami between 1950 and 1953. Other USMC transports in theatre were the R4D (C-47), R5D (C-54) and R5C (C-46).

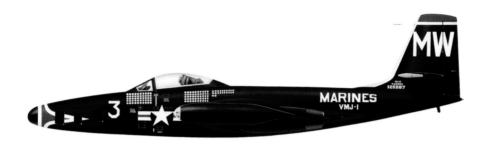

McDonnell F2H-2P Banshee

VMJ-1, U.S. Marine Corps / K3 (Pohang) and K14 (Kimpo), 1952–53

Displaying 122 mission markings on the fuselage, this photo-reconnaissance Banshee was operated by VMJ-1 over Korea from bases at K3 and K14. Operating under the command of the U.S. Fifth Air Force, VMJ-1 provided the USMC with an organic reconnaissance capability when it arrived in theatre in March 1952.

Specifications

Crew: 1

Powerplant: 2 x 1474kg (3250lb) Westinghouse J34-WE-34 turbojets

Maximum speed: 851km/h (529mph)

Range: 1930km (1200 miles)

Service ceiling: 14,785m (48,500ft)

Dimensions: span 13.6m (44ft 11in); length 12.9m (42ft 5in); height 4.4m (14ft 5in)

Weight: 9342kg (20,600lb) loaded

Armament: none

These involved night-capable U.S. Navy F4U-5N and AD-4N aircraft, while the U.S. Marine Corps provided land-based AD-3s for the first time, with an initial unit operating from K3 (Pohang).

Further offensive air power was made available by the basing of two B-26 groups at Kunsan and Pusan from May 1951. These units had previously been based in Japan and now began to undertake mainly nocturnal raids against communist convoys on their way to the front. At the same time, the B-29 force switched from primarily daylight missions to nocturnal raids, in an effort to reduce the losses at the hands of MiGs and AAA.

Night-fighter war

In the nocturnal realm, March 1951 saw the arrival in the Far East Air Force of the F-94A/B night-fighter as a successor to the ageing, propeller-driven F-82, which had been active within three Fighter (All Weather) Squadrons since the onset of hostilities, mainly flying out of Itazuke, Japan. Operational deficiencies kept the F-94 out of the fray until December 1951, however, when a pair of F-94Bs took up alert duties at Suwon with the 68th Fighter Interceptor Squadron.

In March 1952 the 319th Fighter Interceptor squadron arrived at Suwon, with F-94Bs, although these were prohibited from flying over enemy territory for fear that their sensitive radar equipment may end up in communist hands. B-29 losses to

MiGs continued at night, however, despite the presence of U.S. Marine Corps F7F-3N night-fighters of VMF(N)-513, and in December 1952 it was agreed that the F-94s could operate without restriction, the night-fighters forming patrols between the Chongchon and Yalu rivers in support of the night-bombing offensive.

Based at Misawa and Chitose, the primary mission of the 116th Fighter Bomber Group's F-84s was the air defence of Japan. However, it later undertook operations over Korea, aided by in-flight refuelling from KB-29P tankers. Project High Tide, as these missions were known, commenced in May 1952,

USAF RECONNAISSANCE, KOREAN WAR		
Aircraft	Unit	Base
RB-29A, RB-50A, RB-36A, WB-26, RB-45C, KB-29A	91st SRS	Yokota, Misawa
RB-29A	31st SRS	Yokota
RB-17G	6204th PMF	Yokota
RB-26C	162nd TRS	Itazuke, K2
RB-26C	12th TRS	K2
RF-80A	8th TRS	Yokota, Itazuke
RF-80A	15th TRS	K2
F-6D (RF-51D), RF-80C	45th TRS	Itazuke, K2
AT-6G, LT-6G	6148th TCS	K16, K47
AT-6G, LT-6G	6149th TCS	K47

Specifications

Crew: 1

Powerplant: 1 x 24kN (5400lb) Allison J33-A-35
turbojet

Maximum speed: 966km/h (594mph)

Range: 1328km (825 miles)

Service ceiling: 14,265m (46,800ft)

Dimensions: span 11.81m (38ft 9in); length
10.49m (34ft 5in); height 3.43m (11ft 3in)

Weight: 7646kg (16,856lb) loaded

Armament: none

▲ **Lockheed RF-80A Shooting Star**

67th Tactical Reconnaissance Wing, USAF / K13 (Suwon)

Wearing an experimental water-based drab olive paint scheme that was applied in
theatre, this USAF RF-80A was on strength with the 67th Tactical Reconnaissance
Wing at Suwon, Korea. The RF-80 proved itself capable of absorbing considerable
battle damage and was also used on long-range missions with tanker support.

with a raid against Sariwon in North Korea. The
same month also saw the first use of the USAF's F-
86E in the fighter-bomber role, when bomb-
equipped Sabres attacked Sinuiju airfield.

A significant large-scale UN raid on 23 June 1952,
involved over 200 ground attack aircraft from USAF
U.S. Navy, U.S. Marine Corps and Republic of Korea
AF units, escorted by over 100 F-86Es. Their objective
was the hydroelectric plant at Suiho. Surprisingly, the
North Korean AF put up no resistance, the MiGs
instead focusing on defending Manchuria's industries.
In general, MiG activity was decreasing, but the
arrival of the F-86E ensured that the USAF had a
qualitative edge over the communist air forces.

New Sabres

Peace talks continued into 1953, the final year of the
war, while the communists attempted to gain the
upper hand in the air war, while brokering an
agreement concerning the repatriation of prisoners of
war. In the air war, however, they were denied
superiority by the UN air forces, which were boosted
in particular by the arrival of an improved Sabre
variant, the F-86F, in June and July 1952. This model
introduced a more powerful engine for improved
performance, and could better the MiG in terms of
agility at all altitudes.

August 1952 saw an increase in MiG activity, met
by additional F-86 sorties, while the F-86F was

further improved through the introduction of a
modified wing, supplied in kit form from October.
As well as the new wing, which boosted
manoeuvrability, the Sabre began to be outfitted for
offensive missions, with the 8th and 18th Fighter
Bomber Groups receiving F-86Fs as replacement for
their F-80s and F-51s. After a lengthy period of crew
conversion, the 'fighter bomber' F-86F flew its first
combat missions in February 1953.

By the time the F-86F was in action as a fighter-
bomber, MiG activity had begun to increase once
again. However, the Chinese approach to the war
situation changed with the death of Stalin in March,
after which the People's Republic lost valuable
political support from the USSR. Fighting on the
ground continued, with air support for the UN
contingent now being supplied by the improved F-
84G model, based at Taegu and Kunsan starting in
the summer of 1952, as well as B-26s at Kunsan and
Pusan. Off the Korean coast, Task Force 77 kept at

US ARMY HELICOPTERS, KOREAN WAR		
Aircraft	**Unit**	**Base**
H-13, H-23A	MASH	various
H-19C	THC-6	various
H-5A/G, H-19	3rd ARS	Japan, K14, K96, Cho-do
H-19A	3rd ARS	Japan, Cho-do

▲ Sikorsky HO3S-1

MAMS-33, U.S. Marine Corps / Korea

Aircraft Maintenance Squadron (MAMS) 33 was equipped with a number of
different U.S. Marine Corps types, including the HO3S-1 and the fixed-wing F9F
and AD-2. Named *Southern Comfort*, this example of the former was used for ship
guard and rescue duties. The HO3S-1 was similar to the USAF's H-5F Dragonfly.

Specifications

Crew: 1

Powerplant: 1 x 335kW (450shp) Pratt &
Whitney R-985-AN-5 turboshaft

Maximum speed: 172km/h (107mph)

Range: 442km (275 miles)

Service ceiling: 4510m (14,800ft)

Dimensions: rotor diameter 14.9m (49ft);
length 17.6m (57ft 8in); height 3.9m
(12ft 11in)

Weight: 2495kg (5500lb) loaded

Armament: none

▲ Sikorsky HRS-1

HMR-161, U.S. Marine Corps / K18 (Kangnung), 1951–53

An assault transport with capacity for up to eight troops, 60 examples of the
HRS-1 served with nine U.S. Marine Corps transport helicopter squadrons before
the end of the war in Korea. The HRS-1 was also used for rescue missions, and
operations were based out of K18 from September 1951.

Specifications

Crew: 2

Powerplant: 1 x 450kW (600hp) Pratt &
Whitney R-1340-57 radial engine,

Maximum speed: 163km/h (101mph)

Range: 652km (405 miles)

Service ceiling: 3200m (10,500ft)

Dimensions: Rotor diameter: 16.16m (53ft);
length 62ft 7in (19.1m); height 4.07m
(13ft 4in)

Weight: 3266kg (7200lb) loaded

Armament: none

least three carriers on station, with the more advanced
F9F-5 fighter deployed beginning in October 1952.

June 1953, the final full month of fighting, saw the
F-86s maintain their superiority, with almost 8000
sorties flown. In July, the communists gave up on the
issue of repatriation at the peace talks, and fighting
came to an end on 27 June. The final claims made for
victories in aerial combat have long been disputed,
but it is clear that the UN air forces more than held

their own, and gained air superiority, despite being
heavily outnumbered by the end of the conflict.

The war also served as a compelling warning to
the U.S. military machine, which set about
modernizing its equipment and strengthening its
presence in key trouble spots, as well as granting
additional equipment and expertise to U.S. allies,
and to states seen to be at risk of communist invasion
or insurrection.

China and Taiwan
1946–1958

The end of World War II left power in China divided between the Soviet-backed communists, and the Nationalists of Chiang Kai-Shek, armed and supported by the U.S.

AFTER A PAUSE during the years of World War II, the Chinese Civil War resumed in 1946, following the departure of U.S. forces from China. Armed by the U.S., the Nationalists gained some early victories, but by 1949 Peking and Tienstsin had both fallen into communist hands. The People's Republic of China was established on 1 October 1949, and the nationalist force evacuated the

Specifications

Crew: 1

Powerplant: 1 x 1264kW (1695hp) Packard
   Merlin V-1650-7 V-12 piston engine

Maximum speed: 703km/h (437mph)

Range: 3347km (2080 miles)

Service ceiling: 12,770m (41,900ft)

Dimensions: span 11.28m (37ft); length 9.83m
   (32ft 3in); height 4.17m (13ft 8in)

Weight: 5488kg (12,100lb) loaded

Armament: 6 x 12.7mm (.5in) MGs in wings,
   plus up to 2 x 454kg (1000lb) bombs

▲ **North American P-51D Mustang**

People's Liberation Army AF

The P-51D was supplied in quantity to the Chinese AF during 1944-45. After the end of World War II, these aircraft were flown by the Chinese Nationalists as well as by the post-revolution People's Republic, as illustrated by this example. Prior to the arrival of MiG-15s, PLAAF fighters also included La-11s and Yak-9s.

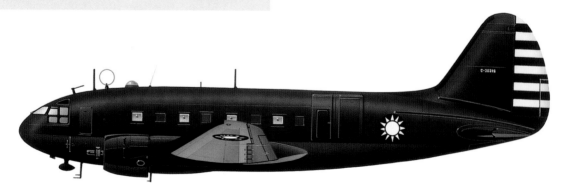

Specifications

Crew: 4

Powerplant: 2 x 1500kW (2000hp) Pratt &
   Whitney R-2800-51 radial piston engines

Maximum speed: 433km/h (269mph)

Range: 4750km (2950 miles)

Service ceiling: 8410m (27,600ft)

Dimensions: span 32.9m (108ft 1in);
   length 23.27m (76ft 4in);
   height 6.63m (21ft 9in)

Weight: 22,000kg (48,000lb) maximum

Armament: none

▲ **Curtiss C-46 Commando**

Transport Wing, Chinese Nationalist AF, Taipei

At the time of the Chinese Civil War in 1948, the Chinese Nationalist AF included two transport groups equipped with C-46s and C-47s. This ex-USAAF example was one of those that participated in the evacuation from mainland China to Taiwan in 1949. The Commando remained in CNAF service long into the 1950s.

mainland for the island of Formosa, to form the Republic of China (Taiwan). The People's Liberation Army AF played a significant role in the Korean War starting in 1950 and retained U.S.-built equipment at the outbreak of this conflict, before receiving new equipment from the USSR, beginning with MiG-15 jet fighters.

While the communists were recipients of military aid from the USSR, the U.S. supplied Taiwan with advanced weaponry as of 1951 in order to establish itself as a bulwark against the communist threat, while the U.S. 7th Fleet sailed in the Taiwan Straits.

Covert operations

Through the Taiwan-based Civil Air Transport (CAT), a CIA-operated front airline, the U.S. was able to maintain a covert military presence in Southeast Asia, supporting the French in Indo-China and inserting U.S. agents on the Chinese mainland.

Fighting between China and Taiwan broke out in 1958 over the issue of the islands of Quemoy and Matsu, which were claimed by the Nationalists. The PLA began an artillery bombardment against the island in September 1954, the nationalists responding with counter-bombardment and air raids. In August 1958 fighting erupted again, and China announced plans for a invasion of the islands, to be followed by an occupation of Taiwan.

The Chinese Nationalist AF mounted patrols over the disputed islands, and Sidewinder-armed F-86s

CHINESE NATIONAL AF, 1958		
Aircraft	Unit	Base
F-86F	1st FW	Taipeh
F-86F	2nd FW	Taipeh
F-86F	3rd FW	Tainan
F-84G	5th FBW	n/a
RF-84F	TRS	Taipeh
C-46D, C-47, SA-16A	TW	Taipeh

fought aerial engagements against Chinese MiG-15s and MiG-17s. On 24 September the CNAF claimed a number of MiGs destroyed, these victories marking the first successful combat usage of air-to-air missiles. In October the CNAF was recipient of more advanced U.S.-supplied equipment, including B-57s, F-100Ds, F-104As, F-101Cs and RF-101Cs.

The crisis surrounding Quemoy and Matsu passed, yet relations between the two Chinas remained tense. Further air-to-air confrontations were recorded in July 1959, when Sabres fought with MiG-17s. In 1967 CNAF F-104As battles against PLAAF MiG-19s, claiming two destroyed. As of 1959, the CNAF operated U-2 spyplanes over mainland China on behalf of the CIA, and at least eight were downed by Chinese air defences. Hostility would last until the end of the Cold War. The U.S. eventually withdrew overt support for Taiwan, but continued to supply the Nationalists with combat aircraft.

Specifications

Crew: 3

Powerplant: 2 x 26.3kN (5952lb) Klimov VK-1 turbojets

Maximum speed: 902km/h (560mph)

Range: 2180km (1355 miles)

Service ceiling: 12,300m (40,355ft)

Dimensions: span 21.45m (70ft 4in); length 17.65m (57ft 10.75in); height 6.7m (21ft 11.8in)

Weight: 21,200kg (46,738lb) loaded

Armament: 4 x 23mm cannon; internal bomb capacity 1000kg (2205lb), max bomb capacity 3000kg (6614lb)

▲ Ilyushin Il-28

People's Liberation Army AF

Received from the Soviets and locally built under licence as the H-5, the Il-28 was the first jet bomber to serve with the PLA. By far the largest export operator of the Il-28, China began to receive several hundred examples of the light bomber from the USSR in the late 1950s, with local manufacture beginning in 1967.

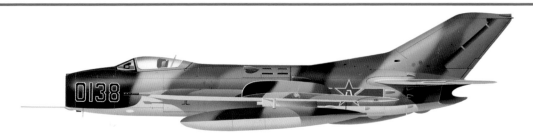

Specifications

Crew: 1

Powerplant: 2 x 31.9kN (7165lb) Shenyang
    WP-6 turbojets

Maximum speed: 1540km/h (957mph)

Range: 1390km (864 miles)

Service ceiling: 17,900m (58,725ft)

Dimensions: span 9.2m (30ft 2.25in); length
    14.9m (48ft 10.5in); height 3.88m (12ft 8.75in)

Weight: 10,000kg (22,046lb) maximum

Armament: 3 x 30mm NR-30 cannon; four
    external hardpoints with provision for up to
    500kg (1102lb) of stores, including air-to-air
    missiles, 250kg (551lb) bombs, 55mm (2.1in)
    rocket-launcher pods, 212mm (8.34in) rockets
    or drop tanks

▲ **Shenyang J-6**

People's Liberation Army AF

Entering service in the early 1960s, PLA J-6 fighters (licence-built versions of the
MiG-19) were involved in a number of Cold War skirmishes against Nationalist
Chinese and other air arms. In addition to clashes against the CNAF and USAF, the
J-6 was used in combat during China's border conflict with Vietnam as of 1979.

France in Indochina
1946–1954

**In the wake of World War II, tensions emerged between the French colony of Indo-China and its
European occupier and the Viet Minh forces that had fought previously against the Japanese.**

SERIOUS FIGHTING BROKE out between the French
and the communist Viet Minh in late 1946 when
the guerrillas tried to take control of Hanoi and other
cities. Among the first aircraft deployed to Indo-

China were French AF Spitfire Mk IXs, which arrived
at Saigon in 1946, joining a number of Ki-43s seized
from the Japanese. The Spitfires, serving with four
escadrilles, performed well in the anti-guerrilla role, in

▲ **Grumman F6F-5 Hellcat**

Escadrille 1F, French Navy / Arromanches, *1951-52*

Serving from the aircraft carrier *Arromanches*, this French Navy F6F saw action
over Indo-China in 1954. The carrier arrived on station off Indo-China in 1953 and
provided an air wing that included Flotilles 11F (F6Fs) and 3F (SB2Cs). These
were joined by the AU-1 Corsairs of 14F for the fighting at Dien Bien Phu.

Specifications

Crew: 1

Powerplant: 1 x 1491kW (2000hp) Pratt &
    Whitney R-2800-10W Double Wasp
    18-cylinder two-row radial engine

Maximum speed: 603km/h (375mph)

Range: 2559km (1590 miles)

Service ceiling: 11,705m (38,400ft)

Dimensions: span 13.06m (42ft 10in); length
    10.24m (33ft 7in); height 3.99m (13ft 1in)

Weight: 7025kg (15,487lb) maximum

Armament: 4 x 0.50in (12.7mm) Browning
    machine guns

contrast to the Mosquitoes. The latter arrived in 1947 but soon proved unsuitable for tropical operations. In addition to French AF types in theatre, the French Navy provided SBD-5 dive-bombers, PBY flying boats, Sea Otter amphibians and ex-Japanese E13A1 floatplanes.

The first wave of fighting ended in spring 1947 with French troops still in control of the cities. Later in 1947 the French began an offensive in order to defeat the guerrillas, who in turn began to establish strongholds in rural areas, led by Vo Nguyen Giap.

Throughout the campaign, French air power was used exclusively in support of the troops on the ground, and in 1949 the U.S. began to deliver war materiel, including P-63 fighters. As of June 1950, aircraft were organized into three autonomous tactical organizations (GATAC), one in the north, one in the south, and one in the central region. All answered directly to local commanders on the ground. The French Navy was also modernizing its force in the same period, now fielding carrier-based F6Fs and SB2Cs as well as land-based PB4Y-2 patrol aircraft.

Rural resistance

By 1950 the Viet Minh were influential across much of the rural north and central regions, while the French were in control in the south; the same year saw the arrival of the F6F as a replacement for the Spitfire and P-63. Also in 1950 the French began to deploy bombers to the war zone, in the form of the B-26B/C, which arrived in November, and eventually equipped four *groupes*. Other aircraft types on strength at this time included RB-26 and NC.701 reconnaissance types, assorted observation and communications types, and a number of helicopters, including the UH-12A, H-23A/B, S-51 and S-55.

Towards the end of 1950 the Viet Ming took Cao Bang and Lang Son, while French troops followed up with victories at Vinh Yen and Mao Khe in 1951.

In 1952-53 the fighting was focused on Tonkin and Laos, and the French began to establish garrisons in Viet Minh territory to encourage attacks in which the French would overcome the guerrillas with superior firepower. Initially successful, this concept would be defeated in humiliating circumstances at Dien Bien Phu, between Tonkin and Laos, in May 1954. In 1953 the French AF had re-equipped with the F8F as a replacement for the F6F that was phased out in January that year.

By the time of the siege of Dien Bien Phu the French had some 400 aircraft in Indo-China. Of particular importance from now on would be the French AF transport fleet, based around C-47s, plus smaller numbers of Ju 52/3ms. No fewer than 100 C-47s were involved in the final evacuation from Dien Bien Phu. The garrison fell on the evening of 7 May, after a bayonet charge by the last 600 French troops, facing encirclement by 40,000 Viet Minh. The loss of Dien Bien Phu sealed Viet Minh victory in Indo-China, and a ceasefire was agreed in July.

▲ **Grumman F8F-1 Bearcat**

GC II/21, French AF / Tan Son Nhut, 1953–54

Based at Tan Son Nhut, this French AF F8F was in action over Indo-China during 1953-54. First appearing with the French AF in Southeast Asia in 1951, the F8F was undoubtedly the most effective close support aircraft deployed by the French AF in Indo-China. Armament included rockets, bombs and napalm.

Specifications

Crew: 1

Powerplant: 1 x 156kW (2100hp) Pratt & Whitney R-2800-34W Double Wasp radial piston engine

Maximum speed: 678km/h (421mph)

Range: 1778km (1105 miles)

Service ceiling: 11,796m (38,700ft)

Dimensions: span 10.92m (35ft 10in); length 8.61m (28ft 3in); height 4.21m (13ft 9in)

Weight: 5873kg (12,947lb) loaded

Armament: 4 x .5in (12.7mm) M2 machine guns; up to 454kg (1000lb) of bombs or 4 x 127mm (5in) rockets

U.S. in Vietnam
1959–1975

After the French collapse, Indo-China was divided into four: North and South Vietnam, Cambodia and Laos. With North Vietnam 'lost' to communism, the U.S. expected the others to follow.

SOUTH VIETNAM WAS supported by the U.S., fearful it might go the way of the Viet Min-ruled North. U.S. military advisors remained in the South after the French withdrawal, providing support to the local regime, which maintained its own air power in the form of F8Fs, C-47s, H-19s, L-19s and others.

In 1959 the North Vietnamese leader, Ho Chi Minh, announced his intention to reunify the two Vietnams, and the North Vietnamese Army (NVA) began to support the communist Viet Cong (VC) guerrillas operating in South Vietnam. As the South descended into civil war, the U.S. sent more advisors, together with AD-6 (A-1) attack aircraft in September 1960, followed by H-34 helicopters. Before the end of the war rotorcraft would transform the concept of U.S. Army air-mobility, as well as

serving in other diverse roles including close support, re-supply, casualty evacuation and command.

The trigger for increased U.S. military involvement in Vietnam was the inauguration of President Kennedy in 1961. The first unit deployed was a USAF mobile command unit sent to Tan Son Nhut in October, followed by Project Farm Gate, under which jungle warfare specialists and COIN aircraft were sent to Bien Hoa. The first jet equipment were RF-101C photo-reconnaissance aircraft. The U.S. Army presence began with H-21 helicopters, together with heliborne troops. Further equipment for the VNAF included T-28s, with C-123s to boost local airlift capacity. As of 1962 the latter type was used to deliver defoliant under Project Ranch Hand, denying the VC jungle cover.

USAF IN VIETNAM, 1961–64			
Project	Aircraft	Unit	Base
Pipe Stem	RF-101C	15th TRS	Tan Son Nhut
Abel Mabel	RF-101C	45th TRS	Don Muang, Tan Son Nhut
Farm Gate	T-28D, SC-47, B-26B, RB-26C, U-10A, RB-26L	4400th CCTS	Bien Hoa
Farm Gate	T-28B, SC-47, B-26B, RB-26C/L, U-10A, A-1E	4410th CCTS	Bien Hoa, Pleiku
Farm Gate	O-1E	19th TASS	Bien Hoa, Can Tho
Mule Train	C-123B	346th TCS	Tan Son Nhut, Dan Nang
Mule Train	C-123B	776th TCS	Tan Son Nhut
Mule Train	C-123B	310th TCS	Tan Son Nhut
Mule Train	C-123B	309th TCS	Tan Son Nhut
Mule Train	C-123B	777th TCS	Dan Nang, Don Muang
Mule Train	C-123B	311th TCS	Dan Nang, Don Muang
Ranch Hand	UC-123B/K	SASF	Tan Son Nhut
Water Glass	TF/F-102A	509th FIS	Tan Son Nhut
Water Glass	AD-5Q	VAW-35	Tan Son Nhut
Patricia Lynn	RB-57E	33rd TG	Tan Son Nhut
Dragon Lady	U-2A/C	4080th SRW	Bien Hoa

Attacks on U.S. Navy destroyers by NVA torpedo boats in the Gulf of Tonkin in August 1964 were the catalyst for full-scale U.S. military intervention. In the first instance, F-8Es from USS *Ticonderoga* sank one torpedo boat, with attacks made by A-1s from the same carrier days later. Finally, U.S. Navy A-1s and A-4 attack aircraft from USS *Ticonderoga* and *Constellation* raided North Vietnamese naval bases and oil depots. Carrier air power would be an ever-present for the remaining eight years of the conflict.

Increasing presence

After the Gulf of Tonkin incident the Pentagon sent USAF B-57s to Bien Hoa in August, followed by F-100s and F-102s to Da Nang, while other aircraft were stationed in Thailand, using the Royal Thai AF bases at U-Tapao and Udorn. As airbases came under attack from VC, the U.S. planned Operation Flaming Dart, a series of retaliatory air strikes in February 1965. In response, U.S. Navy carrier aircraft hit NVA targets in the first of countless air attacks that would be launched by U.S. air power against communist positions in the coming years.

The F-100D bore the brunt of much of the early bombing sorties, as well as providing defensive low-level combat air patrols (CAPs). Less successful in the early days of the war was the F-104C, which was soon switched from its defensive mission to the role of low-level tactical bomber as of the autumn of 1965.

In Laos, meanwhile, the U.S. supplied T-28s for use against the North Vietnam-backed Pathet Lao guerrillas starting in 1965, supported from late 1964 by a U.S. air campaign codenamed Barrel Roll.

March 1965 saw the start of a new campaign of bombing against the NVA, known as Rolling Thunder. This aimed to break communist resolve, but was less than successful, merely hardening anti-U.S. feeling in the North, and failing to find enough targets of genuine military value. Furthermore, Hanoi and other cities were considered 'off bounds', together with North Vietnamese airfields and SAM sites – the U.S. unwilling to risk the loss of life of Chinese or Soviet advisors.

A final level of inefficiency in the Rolling Thunder campaign was ensured by the fact that targets had to be selected and approved in Washington, with little regard for local conditions. In terms of air combat, the hands of the U.S. pilots were further tied by a ruling that demanded that

▲ **Republic F-105 Thunderchief**
A line-up of bare-metal F-105 Thunderchiefs deployed to Southeast Asia

U.S. NAVY IN VIETNAM, 1964–65		
Aircraft	**Unit**	**Carrier**
F-8E	VF-191	USS *Bonne Homme Richard*
F-8C	VF-194	USS *Bonne Homme Richard*
A-4C	VA-192	USS *Bonne Homme Richard*
A-4C	VA-195	USS *Bonne Homme Richard*
A-1H/J	VA-196	USS *Bonne Homme Richard*
E-1B	VAW-11	USS *Bonne Homme Richard*
RF-8A	VFP-63	USS *Bonne Homme Richard*
A-3B	VAH-4	USS *Bonne Homme Richard*
UH-2A	HU-1	USS *Bonne Homme Richard*
F-4B	VF-142	USS *Constellation*
F-4B	VF-143	USS *Constellation*
A-4C	VA-144	USS *Constellation*
A-1H/J	VA-145	USS *Constellation*
A-4C	VA-146	USS *Constellation*
E-1B	VAW-11	USS *Constellation*
RF-8A	VFP-63	USS *Constellation*
A-3B	VAH-10	USS *Constellation*
UH-2A	HU-1	USS *Constellation*
F-8E	VF-51	USS *Ticonderoga*
F-8E	VF-53	USS *Ticonderoga*
A-1H/J	VA-52, VA-56	USS *Ticonderoga*
A-4B	VA-55	USS *Ticonderoga*
A-4E	VA-56	USS *Ticonderoga*
E-1B	VAW-11	USS *Ticonderoga*
RF-8A	VFP-63	USS *Ticonderoga*
A-3B	VAH-4	USS *Ticonderoga*

positive visual identification be acquired before an engagement could take place.

Another key event of March 1965 was the deployment of large numbers of ground troops, with 3500 U.S. Marines arriving at Da Nang to join the advisors already committed. Vital to the build-up and the subsequent support of the war effort was the USAF's fleet of airlifters, including the C-141 that entered service in 1965 and replaced the piston-engined C-124 and C-133. As well bringing troops and materiel from the U.S. to the war zone, the C-141 was responsible for flying casualties home. Once cargo and troops were brought to Southeast Asia it was the job of the C-130 and C-123 to bring these cargoes forward to airstrips near the front lines.

Throughout 1965 the air war escalated, and began to encompass aerial combat between the U.S. air arms and the North Vietnamese AF, and the use of SAMs and electronic countermeasures against them. The NVAF expanded starting in early 1965, and its MiG-15s and MiG-17s were increasingly sent into battle against U.S. aircraft, the first recorded instance being on 17 June when two F-4Bs from the USS *Midway* met four MiG-17s, claiming two shot down.

The first USAF fighter-bomber to be deployed to Vietnam in large numbers was the F-105, the basic F-105D being joined later by the Thunderstick II modification with enhanced mission avionics, and the two-seat F-105G for the defence suppression, or Wild Weasel role, analyzing and attacking North

Vietnamese air defence radars by active or passive means. Early bombing tactics saw the use of formations of aircraft flying at medium level, and typical scenarios involved a B-66 formation leader guiding a force of F-105s to the target. The EB-66C model was used to jam enemy air defence radars, in order to protect the attack formations. As an alternative to the formation leader, targets could be identified by forward air controllers (FACs), which would circle the combat area in slow-flying aircraft and call in strikes by tactical fighters.

Reconnaissance missions

Finding the targets in the first instance – and studying the results of the bombing raids – was the responsibility of reconnaissance aircraft, including the A-26A (a redesignated, COIN development of the B-26), the RF-101C and the U.S. Navy's carrier-based RA-5C and RF-8. More exotic reconnaissance assets were the Teledyne Ryan 147 series of remotely piloted vehicles (RPVs), equipped with a variety of sensors and used to fly hazardous, low-level missions over both Vietnam and China after launch from a specially equipped DC-130 drone carrier. After the mission, recovery was effected through the use of an HH-3E helicopter that snatched the drone after it had shut down its engine and deployed a parachute.

An almost insurmountable challenge for the U.S. was the Ho Chi Minh trail, a vast network of supply routes, which was crucial to the communist war

▲ **Douglas A-1H Skyraider**

83rd Special Operations Group, VNAF / Tan Son Nhut, 1966

Wearing an unusual low-visibility camouflage scheme, this A-1H was used for close support, attack and forward air control missions by the 83rd Special Operations Group, VNAF. Originally built for the U.S. Navy, this particular aircraft was based at Tan Son Nhut in 1966.

Specifications

Crew: 1	Dimensions: span 15.25m (50ft); length
Powerplant: 1 x 2013kW (2700hp) Pratt &	11.84m (38ft 10in); height 4.78m (15ft 8in)
Whitney R-3350-26WA radial piston engine	Weight: 11,340kg (25,000lb) maximum
Maximum speed: 520km/h (320mph)	Armament: 4 x 20mm cannon; up to 3600kg
Range: 2115km (1315 miles)	(8000lb) of bombs, rockets, or other stores
Service ceiling: 8660m (28,500ft)	

USAF FIGHTERS AND ATTACK, VIETNAM

Aircraft	Wing	Squadrons	Base
B-57B/C/E	405th TBW, 6252nd TFW	8th TBS, 13th TBS	Tan Son Nhut, Bien Hoa Da Nang, Phan Rang
F-102A	–	16th FIS	Tan Son Nhut
TF/F-102A	–	509th FIS	Tan Son Nhut, Bien Hoa
TF/F-102A	–	64th FIS	Bien Hoa
F-102A	–	82nd FIS	Da Nang
F-105D	4th TFW	36th TFS, 80th TFS	Takhli, Korat
F-104C	–	435th TFS, 476th TFS	Da Nang
F-105D	18th TFW	12th TFS, 44th TFS, 67th TFS	Korat
F-100D	405th TFW	511th TFS	Takhli
F-100D/F, B-57B/C/E	35th TFW	612th TFS, 614th TFS, 615th TFS, 352nd TFS, 8th TBS, 13th TBS, 120th TFS	Phan Rang, Da Nang, Tuy Hoa
F-105D	23rd TFW	562nd TFS, 563rd TFS	Da Nang
F-4C	12th TFW	45th TFS, 43rd TFS, 557th TFS, 558th TFS, 559th TFS, 389th TFS, 480th TFS	Ubon, Cam Ranh Bay, Phu Cat
F-100D	474th TFW	429th TFS, 481st TFS	Bien Hoa, Tan Son Nhut
F-100D/F, F-5A, A-37B	3rd TFW	307th TFS, 308th TFS, 510th TFS, 531st TFS, 90th TFS, 4503rd TFS, 8th AS, 90th AS	Bien Hoa
F-105D/F, F-111A	355th TFW	333rd TFS, 334th TFS, 335th TFS, 354th TFS, 357th TFS, 428th TFS, 44th TFS	Takhli
F-105D/F/G, F-4C/D/E, A-7D	388th TFW	421st TFS, 13th TFS, 469th TFS, 561st TFS, 561st TFS, 44th TFS, 12th TFS, 34th TFS, 6010th TFS, 17th TFS, 44th TFS, 354th TFS, 67th TFS, 25th TFS, 561st TFS, 3rd TFS	Korat
F-4C/D/E, B-57G	8th TFW	433rd TFS, 497th TFS, 25th TFS, 555th TFS, 435th TFS, 13th TBS, 35th TFS, 336th TFS, 334th TFS	Ubon, Korat
F-4C/D/E	366th TFW	389th TFS, 390th TFS, 480th TFS, 4th TFS, 421st TFS, 35th TFS, 7th TFS, 9th TFS, 417th TFS	Phan Rang, Da Nang, Takhli
F-104C	479th TFW	435th TFS, 476th TFS	Da Nang
F-100D/F	31st TFW	306th TFS, 308th TFS, 309th TFS, 355th TFS, 416th TFS, 136th, TFS, 188th TFS	Tuy Hoa
F-100D/F	37rd FTW	612 TFS, 355 TFS, 416 TFS, 174 TFS	Phu Cat
F-4C/D/E	432nd TRW	13th TFS, 555th TFS, 524th TFS, 8th TFS, 308th TFS, 307th TFS, 58th TFS, 523rd TFS, 4th TFS	Udorn
F-111A	347th TFW	429th TFS, 430th TFS	Takhli, Korat
A-7D	354th TFW	353rd TFS, 355th TFS, 356th TFS	Korat
F-5A, A-27A/B	3rd TFW	10th FCS, 604th ACS, 8th AS, 90th AS	Bien Hoa

Specifications

Crew: 1

Powerplant: 1 x 104.5kN (23,500lb) Pratt & Whitney J75 turbojet

Maximum speed: 2018km/h (1254mph)

Range: 370km (230 miles)

Service ceiling: 15,850m (52,000ft)

Dimensions: 10.65m (34ft 11.25in); length 19.58m (64ft 3in); height 5.99m (19ft 8in)

Weight: 18,144kg (40,000lb) maximum

Armament: 1 x 20mm M61 cannon; internal bay with provision for up to 3629kg (8000lb) of bombs; external load of 2722kg (6000lb)

▲ **North American F-100A Super Sabre**

208th TFS, 31st TFW / Tuy Hoa, 1970

This F-100A-61-NA, named *Jeanne Kay*, was typical of the type serving in Southeast Asia. The 'Hun' was in action over Vietnam almost from the outset and proved a robust ground attack platform, which bore the brunt of offensive operations in the early years of the conflict.

effort in South Vietnam. Arms and supplies were carried along the Trail to the front line, typically via Laos. Directing air power against the Trail was a difficult task, and the supply lines were never successfully broken. From 1965-67 U.S. air power focused on attacking particularly important targets along the Trail, raids being directed by FACs flying in aircraft such as the O-1 and its eventual replacement, the O-2. As well as running the gauntlet of AAA and SAMs, the FACs would have to approach close enough to the target to mark it with rockets.

One innovative method of interdicting supplies on the Trail was the Igloo White sensor that detected noise or vibration after having been dropped into the jungle by an OP-2E, or by a tactical jet. An EC-121R relay aircraft then picked up transmissions from these sensors, before they were transmitted to a ground station for analysis. Starting in 1971 a number of EC-121s were replaced by the smaller QU-22 under a programme known as Pave Eagle. Some QU-22s were also adapted to fly as pilotless RPVs. In addition to the data gathered by the Igloo White sensors, further inputs were delivered by AQM-34L (Ryan 147) RPVs, with their signals sent via the DC-130 drone controllers.

Even with the target identified, prosecuting an attack with a tactical jet was not easy, and most lacked the capacity for precision ordnance delivery. An exception was the A-6A, flown from U.S. Navy carriers and also operated from land bases by USMC units, which was equipped with sophisticated radar

U.S. MARINE CORPS FIGHTERS AND ATTACK, VIETNAM		
Aircraft	**Unit**	**Base**
MAG-11		
TF-9J, TA-4F	H&MS-11	Da Nang
F-8E	VMF-235	Da Nang
F-4B/J	VMFA-542	Da Nang
F-4B	VMFA-531	Da Nang
A-6A	VMA-242	Da Nang
OV-10A	VMO-2	Marble Mountain
A-6A	VMA-225	Da Nang
A-4E	VMA-311	Da Nang
MAG-12		
A-4C	VMA-224, VMA-225, VMA-214	Chu Lai
A-4E	VMA-311, VMA-223, VMA-211, VMA-121	Chu Lai, Bien Hoa
A-6A	VMA-533	Chu Lai
MAG-13		
F-4B	VMFA-323, VMFA-115, VMFA-122	Chu Lai
F-8E	VMF-232	Da Nang, Chu Lai
F-4J	VMFA-232	Chu Lai
MAG-15		
F-4B	VMFA-115	Da Nang, Nam Phong
F-4J	VMFA-232	Da Nang, Nam Phong
A-6A	VMA-533	Nam Phong

and attack navigation equipment. The A-6A's combat debut came in March 1965.

Precision bombing

In terms of USAF assets, the best-equipped aircraft in terms of navigation/attack avionics were a small number of considerably modified B-57Gs, and the sophisticated F-111A, which was first detached to Takhli with the 482nd Tactical Fighter Squadron in March 1968. After a dismal combat debut in which a number of losses were suffered, the all-weather-capable F-111 only completed a relatively small number of operational missions before two additional squadrons arrived at Takhli towards the end of 1972.

A less sophisticated method of interdicting the Trail was expressed by gunship conversions of

transport aircraft. The first of these to see combat was the AC-47, dubbed 'Puff the Magic Dragon', deployed to Tan Son Nhut in November 1965. The AC-47 was followed by the Shadow and Stinger, gun-toting modifications of the C-119. The ultimate gunship deployed in Vietnam was the AC-130, which carried an increasingly heavy armament of 7.62-mm rotary Miniguns, 40-mm cannon and 105-mm howitzers. As well as carrying their own sensors, the AC-130s worked on the basis of target coordinates established using the Igloo White sensors.

In addition to gunship versions, the venerable C-47 also served in Southeast Asia as the EC-47 electronic warfare platform, used for eavesdropping on communications along the Ho Chi Minh and Sihanouk supply lines. Others served in the

Specifications

Crew: 5	Dimensions: span 56.4m (185ft); length 48m
Powerplant: 8 x 44.5kN (10,000lb) Pratt &	(157ft 7in); height 14.75m (48ft 3in)
Whitney J57 turbojets	Weight: 204,120kg (450,000lb) loaded
Maximum speed: 1014km/h (630mph)	Armament: remotely controlled tail mounting
Range: 9978km (6200 miles)	with 4 x .5in MGs; internal bomb capacity
Service ceiling: 16,765m (55,000ft)	12,247kg (27,000lb) to 31,750kg (70,000lb)

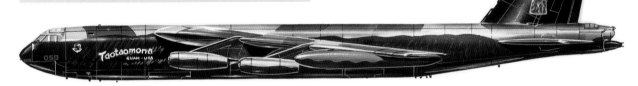

▲ **Boeing B-52D Stratofortress**

60th Bomb Squadron, 43rd Strategic Wing, USAF / Andersen AFB

B-52D 55-0069 is illustrated as it appeared at the height of the war in Vietnam. Operating out of Guam, the bomber received a coat of black paint to reduce its conspicuity for nocturnal missions over Southeast Asia. The aircraft's unit, the 60th Bomb Squadron, was part of the 43rd Strategic Wing, the final operator of the B-52D variant.

▲ **Boeing B-52G Stratofortress**

72nd Strategic Wing (Provisional), USAF / Andersen AFB, 1972–73

Operating out of Guam during the Linebacker offensive, this B-52G lacks the 'Big Belly' modification that was found on converted B-52Ds. As a result, its warload was decreased. The B-52G also lacked certain ECM equipment, so was assigned less heavily defended targets. However, the variant offered increased range.

Specifications

Crew: 5	Dimensions: span 56.4m (185ft); length 48m
Powerplant: 8 x 61.1kN (13,750lb) Pratt &	(157ft 7in); height 12.4m (40ft 8in)
Whitney J57-P-43W turbojets	Weight: 221,500kg (448,000lb) loaded
Maximum speed: 1014km/h (630mph)	Armament: 4 x .5in MGs; normal internal bomb
Range: 13,680km (8500 miles)	capacity 12,247kg (27,000lb); external pylons
Service ceiling: 16,765m (55,000ft)	for 2 x Hound Dog missiles

psychological warfare role, fitted with loudspeakers or carrying propaganda leaflets. Additional 'psy-war' assets included the smaller O-2B, the AU-23A and the U-10. Based on the O-2A observation/FAC aircraft, the O-2B arrived in theatre in 1967, fitted with loudspeakers and a leaflet dispenser. The AU-23A, meanwhile, was able to carry stores including guns and rockets, as well as psy-war equipment, and was also operated by Thailand. Finally, the U-10 was a dedicated STOL type used for psy-war and other specialist missions including the insertion of agents and paradropping. A more powerful development of the U-10 was the AU-24A, a dedicated COIN aircraft with various weapons options available.

The 'heavies' at war

U.S. air power was deployed over Vietnam in an almost exclusively tactical role, and the B-52 was no exception. The strategic bombers were soon adapted for the carriage of vast loads of conventional bombs, and were attacking targets across Southeast Asia under operations codenamed Arc Light, Linebacker and Linebacker II. As early as February 1965 two B-52F wings were forward-deployed to Andersen Air Base on Guam in the Marianas. Arc Light primarily involved the B-52F and began on 18 June 1965, the bombers using aerial refuelling to strike suspected VC bases in Binh Duong. Initial results of the bombing were less than satisfactory, but tactics were improved such that by November the B-52s were effectively

USAF HEAVY BOMBERS, VIETNAM		
Aircraft	Unit	Base
B-52D	3960th SW	Andersen AFB
B-52D/F	4133rd BW(P)	Andersen AFB
B-52D	43rd SW	Andersen AFB
B-52G	72nd SW(P)	Andersen AFB
B-52D	4252nd SW	Kadena AB
B-52D	376th SW	Kadena AB
B-52D	4258th SW	U-Tapao
B-52D	307th SW	U-Tapao
B-52D	310th SW(P)	U-Tapao

undertaking close support missions to relieve U.S. troops under fire from the NVA at Ia Drang.

In April 1966 the B-52D arrived at Guam, aircraft receiving the 'Big Belly' modification to carry even more bombs. The B-52 presence continued to grow, until there were 200 examples of the bomber on the island airbase by 1972. As of September 1967, however, the B-52s were under increasing threat from SAMs, and began to carry additional electronic warfare equipment. At the same time the focus of the bombers shifted from 'carpet bombing' to close support, necessitating the use of Combat Skyspot, a radar-directed bombing aid. In April 1967 B-52 missions were expanded through the addition of U-Tapao as an operating facility for the B-52D, which reduced the duration of the sorties.

▲ **Douglas A-1H Skyraider**

VA-145, US Navy, USS Constellation, 1964–65

Built for the U.S. Navy as an AD-6, this aircraft was redesignated as an A-1H in 1962. During the early years of the Vietnam War this aircraft served with VA-145 'Swordsmen' aboard USS *Constellation*. Despite its antiquated appearance, the A-1 offered a very useful endurance and carried a heavy warload.

Specifications

Crew: 1

Powerplant: 1 x 2013kW (2700hp) Pratt & Whitney R-3350-26WA radial piston engine

Maximum speed: 520km/h (320mph)

Range: 2115km (1315 miles)

Service ceiling: 8660m (28,500ft)

Dimensions: span 15.25m (50ft); length 11.84m (38ft 10in); height 4.78m (15ft 8in)

Weight: 11,340kg (25,000lb) maximum

Armament: 4 x 20mm cannon; up to 3600kg (8000lb) of bombs, rockets or other stores

In order to prevent the entry of war equipment to the North Vietnamese port of Haiphong, the U.S. launched a campaign to mine its entrances. Mining the port itself was prohibited, however, so instead the mines were deposited around the mouths of waterways. The first mines were delivered by A-6As from the USS *Enterprise* in February 1967.

In 1968 the OV-10A joined the ranks of the USMC in Vietnam, this purpose-designed COIN aircraft proving its value in both offensive and reconnaissance missions, for which it was able to operate from semi-prepared airstrips. In addition to USMC service, the OV-10 saw action with the USAF, with the most advanced versions being equipped with improved night vision and targeting equipment under the Pave Nail programme.

Vietnam is popularly remembered as a 'helicopter war', and the UH-1 'Huey' became an icon of the conflict, employed by the U.S. Army, U.S. Navy and USMC in all arenas of the war. The original UH-1B was joined in 1963 by the UH-1D with provision for 14 rather than seven troops. In 1967 the further improved UH-1H became available. Air Cavalry missions involved UH-1s (including at least one outfitted for command duties), aided by USAF close support assets, such as the A-37B. UH-1s were also backed by observation helicopters, such as the OH-6A, which would provide support around the landing

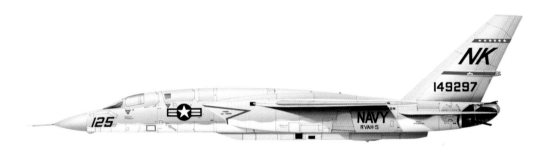

Specifications

Crew: 2

Powerplant: 2 x 79.4kN (17,860lb) General
Electric J79-GE-10 turbojets

Maximum speed: 2230km/h (1385mph)

Range (with drop tanks): 5150km (3200 miles)

Service ceiling: 20,400m (67,000ft)

Dimensions: span 16.15m (53ft); length
23.11m (75ft 10in); height 5.92m (19ft 5in)

Weight: 36,285kg (80,000lb) loaded

Armament: none

▲ **North American RA-5C Vigilante**

RVAH-5, US Navy, USS Constellation, 1968–69

Providing the carrier air wing with a useful reconnaissance-gathering capability was the RA-5C, this example serving aboard USS *Constellation* in the Gulf of Tonkin in 1968–69. The RA-5C's mission equipment included a large sideways-looking airborne radar (SLAR) and an infrared line-scanner.

▲ **Grumman EA-6A Intruder**

VMCJ-2, US Marine Corps / Da Nang, 1972–73

Part of a composite reconnaissance squadron, this EA-6A was deployed to Vietnam in 1966 to operate from Da Nang. An electronic warfare adaptation of the A-6A Intruder, the EA-6A was used for jamming enemy radio transmissions and for intelligence-gathering, replacing the EF-10 Skyknight in USMC service.

Specifications

Crew: 4

Powerplant: 2 x 37.8kN (8500lb) Pratt &
Whitney J52-P-6 turbojets

Maximum speed: 1016km/h (631mph)

Range: 3254km (2021 miles)

Service ceiling: 11,580m (38,000ft)

Dimensions: span 16.15m (53ft); length
16.90m (55ft 6in); height 4.7m (15ft 6in)

Weight: 18,918kg (41,715lb) loaded

Armament: none

zone, carrying both its own weaponry and delivering small numbers of troops to extinguish resistance on the ground and to serve as observers.

From September 1969 the OH-6A was complemented by a new light observation type, the OH-58A, widely used thereafter for reconnaissance and liaison duties. Protecting the UH-1 and OH-6 was the AH-1 HueyCobra gunship, which was first employed in Vietnam in autumn 1967. Carrying a wide array of offensive weaponry, the AH-1 provided airmobile companies with organic firepower. In addition to the lighter helicopters, the U.S. Army made good use of the CH-47 for movement of up to 44 fully equipped troops or equipment including light vehicles or artillery. One noteworthy development of the CH-47 was the ACH-47, a powerfully armed gunship with both fixed and

trainable armament. Only a handful was completed, and the concept did not prove successful. In addition, both the CH-47, and the CH-54 flying crane were put to use in the recovery of downed aircraft. If a landing zone was not available, the helicopters could put down in a clearing made in the jungle by a 'Daisy

USAF RECONNAISSANCE, VIETNAM		
Aircraft	Unit	Base
U-2A/C/F	4028th SRS	Bien Hoa
U-2C/F/R	349th SRS	Bien Hoa, U-Tapao
SR-71A	1st SRS	Kadena
RB-47H, KC-135R, RC-135C	55th SRW	Kadena
RC-135M/U	82nd SRS	Kadena
RC-135D	6th SW	Kadena
EC-121R	553rd RW	Nakhon Phanom
RB-57D, C-130A-II	6091st RS	Don Muang
EB-57E, C-130B-II	556th RS	Yokota, Don Muang
RB-57E	33rd TG	Tan Son Nhut
RF-101C	45th TRS	Tan Son Nhut
RF-4C	16th TRS	Tan Son Nhut
RF-101C	20th TRS	Tan Son Nhut, Udorn
RF-101C, RF-4C	12th TRS	Tan Son Nhut
RF-101C, RF-4C	15th TRS	Udorn
RF-4C	6461st TRS	Udorn
RF-4C	11th TRS	Udorn
RF-4C	14th TRS	Udorn
F-4D	25th TFS	Ubon
QU-22B	554th RS	Nakhon Phanom
DC-130A, CH-3E, AQM-34	4025th SRS	Bien Hoa
DC-130A/E, CH-53A, AQM-34	350th SRS	Bien Hoa, U-Tapao

U.S. ELECTRONIC WARFARE, VIETNAM		
Aircraft	Unit	Base
Early warning		
EC-121D/M	522 AEWCW, USAF	Tainan, Tan Son Nhut, Ubon, Udorn, Korat
C-130E-II	7 ACCS, USAF	Udorn
EC-121K	VW-1, U.S. Navy	Da Nang
USAF electronic warfare		
KC-135A, EC-135L	n/a	Kadena, Taiwan
EC-135L	70 ARS	U-Tapao
EC-121J	n/a	Cam Ranh Bay
RB-66B/C	41 TRS	Tan Son Nhut
EB-66C/E	41 TEWS	Takhli
RB-66B	6460 TRS	Takhli
EB-66B/E	42 TEWS	Takhli, Korat
EB-66E	39 TEWS	Korat
F-105F	44 TFS	Korat
EC-47N/P	360 TEWS	Pleiku, Tan Son Nhut
EC-47N/P	361 TEWS	Nha Trang, TSN, Phu Cat
EC-47N/P	362 TEWS	Pleiku, Da Nang
USAF defence suppression		
F-100F, F-105F/G	561 TFS	Korat
F-105F	357 TFS	Takhli
F-105F/G	6010 TFS	Korat
F-105G	17 TFS	Korat
F-4C	67 TFS	Korat
USMC		
EF-10B, EA-6A, RF-8A, RF-4B	VMCJ-1	Da Nang
EA-6A	VMCJ-2	Da Nang
EA-6B	VAQ-132	Cam Ranh Bay
TF-9J, TA-4F	H&MS-11	Da Nang
TF-9J	H&MS-13	Chu Lai
TF-9J	H&MS-17	Da Nang
U.S. Navy		
AP-2H	VAH-21	Cam Ranh Bay

Cutter' bomb – the most powerful weapon deployed during the conflict. Rolled from the rear ramp of a C-130, the bomb weighed 6800kg (15,000lb), and was triggered before impacting the ground.

'Jolly Green Giants'

One helicopter mission pioneered during the Vietnam War was combat search and rescue (CSAR), in which the USAF picked up downed airmen. The first helicopter dedicated to the role was the HH-3E 'Jolly Green Giant', outfitted with armour, external fuel tanks, a refuelling probe and a hoist. The type entered service in 1968 and the helicopter was armed in recognition of the hazardous nature of the missions it was called upon to undertake. Flying deep into enemy territory the HH-3Es were often escorted by slow-flying A-1H/J close support aircraft, known by

their call sign 'Sandy'. Refuelling was conducted using HC-130P or KC-130 tankers. The successor to the HH-3E was the HH-53B/C 'Super Jolly', offering increased range and a greater payload. Also used for rescue was the HU-16 amphibian, operated in coastal areas, and also used for general transport duties. Another flying boat operated in Vietnam was the U.S. Navy's SP-5, which undertook offshore patrols during Operation Market Time, a blockade of South Vietnam designed to prevent infiltration from the sea. The SP-5 was eventually replaced by the land-based P-2 and P-3.

In addition to an assortment of light types, such as the C-12, U-8 and U-12 that were used for liaison, and the OV-10 used for battlefield surveillance, fixed-wing U.S. Army types in Vietnam included the CV-2 (DHC-4 Caribou), a transport that offered good

▲ Bell AH-1G HueyCobra

1st Air Cavalry Division, U.S. Army / Vietnam

The AH-1G was the first HueyCobra model to see action in Vietnam. Powered by a single engine, the AH-1G was outfitted to carry the M28 armament subsystem, comprising a chin turret that could carry either a pair of 40-mm grenade launchers, a pair of 7.62-mm Miniguns, or a combination of both weapons.

Specifications

Crew: 2

Powerplant: 1 x 820kW (1100shp) Lycoming
T53-L-13 turboshaft

Maximum speed: 352km/h (219mph)

Range: 574km (357 miles)

Service ceiling: 3475m (11,400ft)

Dimensions: rotor diameter: 13.4m (44ft);
length 13.4m (44ft 5in); height 4.1m
(13ft 6in)

Weight: 4500kg (10,000lb) loaded

Armament: 2 x 7.62mm MGs; 70mm (2.75in)
rockets; M18 7.62mm Minigun pod

▲ Bell UH-1B Iroquois

'A' Company, 1st Aviation Battalion, 1st Infantry Division, US Army / Vietnam, 1960s

An iconic participant in the US war in Southeast Asia, the 'Huey' is illustrated here in the form of a 'slick' (unarmed) UH-1B model. Configured for transport duties, the helicopter wears the 'Big One' insignia of the 1st Infantry Division on its tail. 'Slicks' were typically escorted to more hazardous landing zones by gun- and rocket-armed UH-1 'hogs'.

Specifications

Crew: 2

Powerplant: 1 x 820kW (1100shp)
Lycoming T53-L-11 turboshaft engine

Maximum speed: 236km/h (147mph)

Range: 418km (260 miles)

Dimensions: main rotor diameter 13.4m
(44ft); length 12m (39ft 7in); height 4.4m
(14ft 7in)

Weight: 3854kg (8500lb) loaded

Armament: none

STOL performance, permitting use from rough or semi-prepared airstrips. Later transferred to USAF service as the C-7, the Caribou was particularly useful for supporting outlying villages or isolated pockets of troops. The Caribou was also operated in Vietnam by the Royal Australian AF, alongside Canberra B.Mk 20 bombers used for ground attack and bombing.

With much of neighbouring Cambodia used as safe areas by the VC, the U.S. turned its offensive against this neutral country, President Richard Nixon ordering a B-52 bombing campaign after his election victory in November 1969. The raids against Cambodia were undertaken clandestinely and were followed by tactical air strikes and an invasion by ground troops. The Sihanouk regime collapsed as a result of the offensive, precipitating the regime of terror by Pol Pot's Khmer Rouge.

The huge C-5A airlifter was available for participation as of 1969, and in the first half of 1972 almost the entire fleet was engaged in supporting the war effort. The transport was also to play a key role in the final evacuation of the U.S. forces.

In March 1972 the NVA launched a major new offensive, and the U.S. responded by sending B-52Gs to Guam. These offered longer range and could reach most targets without refuelling. The Linebacker missions of 1972 saw the B-52 used to hit targets north of the Demilitarized Zone, although these missions were curtailed in October while peace talks took place in Paris. When the North Vietnamese left

the talks Linebacker II began. This operation was the largest mounted by B-52s during the war, with groups of around 100 aircraft flying 729 sorties between 18-29 December, in the course of which over 15,000 tons of bombs were dropped on key targets, including the port of Haiphong. The attentions of MiG-21s and SAMs combined to claim 15 B-52s destroyed.

Laser-guided bombs

Towards the end of their involvement, the U.S. armed forces began to call upon increasingly sophisticated weaponry to aid their cause. Among the weapons making its debut was the laser-guided bomb (LGB), the first operational examples of which were used by USAF F-4Es on 27 April 1972. The raid in question targeted the Thanh Hoa railway bridge that had survived numerous previous bombing raids. The Paveway LGBs succeeded in destroying it.

In May 1972 the U.S. changed its policy towards mining Haiphong, and mines were now sown in the harbour itself. This had the effect of bringing the North Vietnamese to the negotiating table, but it also meant that the U.S. had to remove the mines in turn once they had done their job, for which it deployed RH-53D mine countermeasures helicopters, equipped with mine sleds to drag the harbour.

With the tide of public opinion at home turning against the U.S. involvement in Southeast Asia, the forces in theatre were gradually drawn down. The war against the NVA and VC was left to the South

▲ **Douglas A-1H Skyraider**

56th Special Operations Wing, USAF / Nakhon Phanom, 1968

This A-1H was flown by the 56th Special Operations Wing from Nakhon Phanom in 1968. The most prominent missions undertaken by the wing's Skyraiders involved 'Sandy' air support for aircrew rescue missions. The aircraft depicted was originally built for the U.S. Navy as an AD-6.

Specifications

Crew: 1	Dimensions: span 15.25m (50ft); length
Powerplant: 1 x 2013kW (2700hp) Pratt &	11.84m (38ft 10in); height 4.78m (15ft 8in)
Whitney R-3350-26WA radial piston engine	Weight: 11,340kg (25,000lb) maximum
Maximum speed: 520km/h (320mph)	Armament: 4 x 20mm cannon; up to 3600kg
Range: 2115km (1315 miles)	(8000lb) of bombs, rockets or other stores
Service ceiling: 8660m (28,500ft)	

Vietnamese. Nixon's process of 'Vietnamization' planned to withdraw U.S. troops and leave the South Vietnamese to tackle the communist forces. In order to fulfil this remit, the South Vietnamese military, trained by U.S. advisors, would be equipped with primarily U.S.-supplied equipment.

By 1970 the South Vietnamese AF had been expanded to include around 700 aircraft, including T-28 and A-37B COIN/light attack types, A-1s, AC-47s, C-47, C-119s and O-1s. Another type flown by the South Vietnamese was the F-5 light attack jet, which was also operated in small numbers by the USAF under a project codenamed Skoshi Tiger.

The fielding of an effective South Vietnamese AF foundered, however, and the U.S. was forced to continue providing air power, together with 40,000 troops. However, there was no turning back from the drawdown, and after a final wave of B-52 raids, a ceasefire was finally signed on 27 January 1973.

The U.S. continued to provide South Vietnam with financial support, although aid packages were much reduced from 1974. North Vietnam was now free to fulfil its objective of reunifying the two countries. Beginning in March 1975, the North launched a series of attacks into the South, overwhelming the defenders. The South Vietnamese military and the administration rapidly crumbled,

U.S. FORWARD AIR CONTROL, VIETNAM		
Aircraft	Unit	Base
USAF		
O-1E/G, O-2A, OV-10A	19th TASS	Bien Hoa
O-1E/F, O-2A	20th TASS	Da Nang
O-1E/F, O-2A	21st TASS	Phu Cat, Tan Son Nhut
O-1E/F, O-2A	22nd TASS	n/a
O-2A, OV-10A	23rd TASS	Nakhon Phnom
U.S. Marine Corps		
OV-10A	VMO-6	Quang Tri, Chu Lai
OV-10A/D	VMO-2	Marble Mountain

and by the end of April the last of the U.S. presence in Saigon was being evacuated. A huge airlift evacuated refugees and U.S. civilians, and after the last airports had fallen to the communists, Operation Frequent Wind provided UH-1, H-53 and CH-46 helicopters to carry the evacuees out of Tan Son Nhut and to ships offshore.

At dawn on 30 April the last helicopter out of South Vietnam left the roof of the U.S. embassy in Saigon. One day later Saigon was renamed Ho Chi Minh City. Despite the overwhelming military superiority of the U.S. and its air arms, the communist insurgents and NVA had succeeded in their aims.

▲ Grumman HU-16B Albatross

3rd Air Rescue and Recovery Group, USAF / Vietnam

One of the more unusual USAF types to see service in Vietnam was the HU-16B amphibian. This particular aircraft was used for command post duties, and wears a low visibility paint scheme. The insignia on the tail of this aircraft is that of Pan Am, reflecting the fact that it was operated by Air Force Reserve crews.

Specifications

Crew: 2

Powerplant: 2 x 1063kW (1425hp) Wright R-1820-76 Cyclone 9 radial engines; 2 or 4 x 4.4kN (1000lb) 15KS1000 rocket motors

Maximum speed: 380km/h (236mph)

Range: 4587km (2850 miles)

Service ceiling: 6553m (21,500ft)

Dimensions: span 24.4m (80ft); length 19.16m (62ft 10in); height 7.8m (25ft 10in)

Weight: 14,968kg (33,000lb) maximum

Armament: none

▲ Sikorsky HH-53C

3rd Air Rescue and Recovery Group, USAF / Vietnam

Known as the 'Super Jolly Green Giant', the HH-53C was equipped for flying long-range aircrew rescue missions in Southeast Asia, carrying additional armour, defensive armament and fitted with an in-flight refuelling probe. The HH-53C could also recover downed aircraft, using its external cargo hook.

Specifications

Crew: 6

Powerplant: 2 x 2927kW (3925shp) General
Electric T64-GE-7 turboshafts

Maximum speed: 315km/h (196mph)

Range: 869km (540 miles)

Service ceiling: 6220m (20,400ft)

Dimensions: main rotor diameter 22.02m
(72ft 3in); fuselage length 20.47m (67ft 2in);
height overall 7.6m (24ft 11in)

Weight: 19,050kg (42,000lb) loaded

Armament: 3 x 7.62mm Miniguns or .50 BMG
(12.7mm) machine guns

USAF RESCUE, VIETNAM

Aircraft	Unit	Base
HH-43B/F, HU-16B, CH-3C	33rd ARRS	Bien Hoa, Nakhon Phanom, Korat, Takhli, Udorn, Da Nang, Pleiku
HH-43B/F, HU-16B, HH-3E, HH-53B/C	37th ARRS	Udorn, Da Nang
HH-43B/F, HC-54, HC-130H, HH-3E	38th ARRS	Tan Son Nhut, Bien Hoa, Korat, Da Nang
HC-130P	39th ARRS	Tuy Hoa
HH-43B, HH-3E, HH-53C	40th ARRS	Nakhon Phanom, Udorn
HC-130P	56th ARRS	Korat
HC-54, HC-130H	31st ARRS	Clark AB
HH-43B, HC-54, HC-130H	36th ARRS	Tachikawa AB
HC-54, HC-130H	79th ARRS	Andersen AFB

USAF SPECIAL OPERATIONS, VIETNAM

Aircraft	Unit	Base
T-28D, A-1E/G	1st SOS	Bien Hoa, Pleiku
A-1E/H	6th SOS	Pleiku
A-37B	8th SOS	Bien Hoa
A-37A/B	604th SOS	Bien Hoa
AC-47D	4th SOS	Bien Hoa, Nha Trang, Tan Son Nhut, Da Nang
AC-47D	14th ACS	Nha Trang
AC-47D	3rd SOS	Pleiku
AC-130A, NC-123K	16th SOS	Ubon, Nha Trang
AC-119G	71st SOS	Nha Trang
AC-119G	17th SOS	Phu Cat
AC-119G/K	18th SOS	Phan Rang
AC-47D, U-10A	5th SOS	Nha Trang
AC-47D, O-2B	9th SOS	Tan Son Nhut
UH-1B/F/P, CH-3C	20th SOS	Tuy Ha, Nha Trang, Cam Ranh Bay, Nakhon Phanom
C-130E-I	15th SOS	Nha Trang
A-1E/G/H/J	602nd SOS	Bien Hoa, Nakhon Phanom
A-1E/G/H/J	1st SOS	Nakhon Phanom
A-1E/G/H/J	22nd SOS	Nakhon Phanom
T-28D, C-123K, A-26A	606th SOS	Nakhon Phanom
T-28D, A-26A	609th SOS	Nakhon Phanom
CH-3C/E	21st SOS	Nakhon Phanom
AC-119K	18th SOS	Nakhon Phanom
AC-130A/E/H	16th SOS	Ubon, Korat
MC-130E	318th SOS	Nha Trang, Korat
AC-47D	4th SOS	Udorn
UC-123B/K	12th SOS	Bien Hoa
UC-123K	310th TAS	Tan Son Nhut

Malaya
1948–1960

The Malayan Emergency pitted the British in a campaign of jungle warfare against primarily Chinese communist rebels who sought to gain independence from the colonial administration.

THE BRITISH BEGAN their campaign against the rebels in 1948, suppressing trade unions before the guerrillas adopted jungle warfare tactics. When the Emergency began the RAF maintained eight squadrons in Singapore and at Kuala Lumpur, spearheaded by Spitfire Mk 18s and Beaufighter Mk 10s. The terrorists' locations were uncovered using Mosquito PR.Mk 34s and in 1949 the RAF launched Operation Firedog to defeat the terrorists.

Dakotas delivered troops into the jungle, the same aircraft then dropping supplies. Brigands replaced the Beaufighters in 1949 and the Brigand was employed widely as an anti-terrorist weapon; in the same year the Tempest fighter-bomber began to arrive. By 1950 the RAF had 160 aircraft in theatre, while the terrorists strengthened their presence in the rural areas, operating out of village strongholds. Guerrilla movements off the coast were tracked by RAF Sunderland flying boats.

Hornet fighter-bombers were in action as of early 1951 as successors to the Tempest, while the first jets in theatre were Vampires, replacing the Spitfires

starting in December 1950. Beginning in 1952 the British and Commonwealth forces assumed the upper hand, aided by a refinement of tactics. Valettas meanwhile replaced Dakotas while helicopters appeared in the form of the Dragonfly from early 1953, rotorcraft being used to insert small units rapidly into the jungle. Reconnaissance work was passed from the Mosquito to the Meteor PR.Mk 10 in late 1953, and Pioneer STOL transports began to work the jungle airstrips from early 1954, by which time the RAF had committed 242 front-line aircraft. Further air support was provided by Australia, with Lincolns and Dakotas, and New Zealand, with Vampires, Venoms and Bristol 170s.

While British and Malay forces held on to the towns, the rebels were limited to a terror campaign against British interests. Eventually, a British programme of resettling Chinese populations left the guerrillas isolated. By the conclusion of the campaign in 1960, deployed assets included RAF and RAAF Canberras, Hastings and Twin Pioneer transports, Meteor night-fighters and Whirlwind helicopters.

▲ **De Havilland Hornet F.Mk 3**

33 Sqn, RAF / Tengah/Butterworth, 1951–55

Normally stationed at Tengah, this de Havilland Hornet single-seat fighter was deployed to Butterworth during the Malayan Emergency. The aircraft is armed with underwing rockets, typical weapons used in the campaign waged against the terrorists, who exploited the dense jungle of Malaya to their advantage.

Specifications

Crew: 1

Powerplant: 2 x 1551kW (2080hp) Rolls-Royce Merlin 130/131 12-cylinder engines

Maximum speed: 760km/h (472mph)

Range: 4828km (3000 miles)

Service ceiling: 10,668m (35,000ft)

Dimensions: span 13.72m (45ft 0in); length 11.18m (36ft 8in); height 4.3m (14ft 2in)

Weight: 9480kg (20,900lb) loaded

Armament: 4 x 20mm Hispano Mk. V cannons; 2 x 454kg (1000lb) bombs; 8 x rockets

Borneo
1962–1966

Coming in the wake of the Malayan Emergency, the Indonesian Confrontation was sparked by a border dispute between Britain and Indonesia, which began in December 1962.

AFTER OUTBREAKS OF violence in British-protected Brunei in northern Borneo, and in the British colony of Sarawak, the British faced hostility from Indonesia, with which it shared long borders on the island of Borneo.

Britain hoped to create a Greater Malaysia that would include its colonies of Sarawak and Sabah in the north of Borneo. Indonesia opposed the plan and hoped to gain control of these two territories, plus independent Brunei. Each territory supported anti-Malaysian, pro-communist factions, and Indonesia decided to foment rebellion by infiltrating these groups and providing support and training in Kalimantan, Indonesian territory in southern Borneo.

As well as dealing with the anti-colonialist groups in the northern territories, the UK had to guard the borders with Indonesia to prevent infiltration. At the time of the Emergency, the RAF's Far East Air Force was based around Hunter and Javelin fighters, Canberra bombers and reconnaissance aircraft,

RAF IN BORNEO, 1962–66		
Aircraft	**Unit**	**Base**
Canberra B.Mk 15	45 Sqn	Tengah, Labuan, Kuching
Canberra B.Mk 15	32 Sqn	Tengah, Kuantan
Hunter FGA.Mk 9	20 Sqn	Labuan, Kuching, Tengah
Javelin FAW.Mk 9	60 Sqn, 64 Sqn	Labuan, Kuching, Tengah
Meteor F.Mk 8	1574 Flt	Changi
Shackleton MR.Mk 2	205 Sqn	Labuan, Changi
Canberra PR.Mk 7	81 Sqn	Labuan, Tengah
Pioneer C.Mk 1, Twin Pioneer CC.Mk 1	209 Sqn	Labuan, Kuching, Brunei
Belvedere HC.Mk 1	66 Sqn	Labuan, Kuching, Seletar
Belvedere HC.Mk 1	26 Sqn	Seletar

▲ **Scottish Aviation Pioneer CC.Mk 1**

209 Sqn, RAF / Seletar/Bayan Lepas, late 1950s

Normally based at Seletar in Singapore, this Pioneer was flown operationally in Borneo during the confrontation with Indonesia. The aircraft's excellent STOL capability allowed it to operate from rough airstrips in support of ground troops fighting in the dense jungle of Borneo. The type also saw action in Malaya.

Specifications

Crew: 1

Powerplant: 1 x 388kW (520hp) Alvis Leonides 502/4 radial engine

Maximum speed: 261km/h (162mph)

Range: 676km (420 miles)

Service ceiling: 7010m (23,000ft)

Dimensions: span 15.17m (49ft 9in); length 10.47m (34ft 4in); height 3.13m (10ft 3in)

Weight: 2636kg (5800lb) loaded

Capacity: 4 passengers

Specifications

Crew: 2

Powerplant: 2 x 1092kW (1465hp) Napier
Gazelle N.Ga.2 turboshaft engines

Maximum speed: 231km/h (145mph)

Range: 740km (460 miles)

Service ceiling: 5275m (17,302ft)

Dimensions: rotor diameter, each 14.91m
(49ft); length rotors turning 27.36m
(90ft); height 5.26m (17ft)

Weight: 9072kg (19,958lb) maximum

Armament: none

▲ Bristol Belvedere HC.Mk 1

66 Sqn, RAF / Labuan/Kuching/Seletar, 1962-67

The RAF refined its helicopter tactics during the campaign in Malaya and rotorcraft played a major role in the Borneo campaign. 66 Sqn flew the Belvedere in Borneo from 1962 until 1969, transporting both troops and equipment and operating from forward bases in the jungle.

Specifications

Crew: 2

Powerplant: 2 x 48.94kN (11,007lb-thrust)
Armstrong Siddeley Sapphire 203 turbojets

Maximum speed: 1130km/h (702mph)

Range: 1600km (994 miles)

Service ceiling: 16,000m (52,493ft)

Dimensions: span 15.85m (52ft);
length 17.15m (56ft 3in); 4.88m (16ft)

Weight: 19,578kg (43,162lb) loaded

Armament: 2 x 30mm (1.18in) ADEN cannon
in each wing; 4 x de Havilland Firestreak
heat-seeking air-to-air missiles

▲ Gloster Javelin FAW.Mk 9

64 Sqn, RAF / Tengah/Kuching/Labuan, 1963-66

In order to counter the threat posed by Indonesian AF Il-28 and Tu-16 bombers, and MiG-17 and MiG-19 fighters, the RAF sent Javelin all-weather fighters to operate from Kuching and Labuan. The units involved were 60 and 64 Sqns, this 64 Sqn aircraft being armed with Firestreak air-to-air missiles.

Shackletons for maritime patrol, as well as a transport fleet. The main operating base was Tengah in Singapore. Support was provided by the RAAF, with Sabres and Canberras at Butterworth, and the RNZAF with Canberras and Bristol Freighters.

COIN campaign

From December 1962 UK forces entered Borneo to put down the insurgencies in the north. Order was soon restored in Sarawak, before attentions turned to Brunei. Using transport aircraft to deliver troops where they were most needed, Brunei was steadily returned to government control, with Hunters flying mock attacks over the rebels. Canberras, meanwhile, kept a check on infiltration across the land border from Kalimantan, and bases were set up along the border and supplied by air, with extensive use of helicopters. In the air, Hunters and Javelins policed the borders. Indonesian forces staged a series of naval landings and paradrops through 1964-65, but by 1966 the Confrontation had run its course, and a peace treaty was signed in August.

Chapter 9

Latin America

To some extent on the periphery of the Cold War, Central and South America nonetheless played host to some critical air battles during the postwar years, with Cuba more than once a major flashpoint in the superpower standoff of the 1960s, and the Falklands campaign in 1982 seeing modern air power deployed in action in a wide variety of roles. Meanwhile, the U.S. took a particular interest in the region as it sought to extinguish a number of regimes and guerrilla organizations it regarded as being dangerously pro-Soviet.

◀ **British Aerospace Sea Harrier FRS.Mk 1**
Although the Falklands conflict was little more than a sideshow in terms of the overall Cold War confrontation, it was notable for the deployment of a number of advanced warplanes and weapons, with undoubtedly the most successful being the Royal Navy Sea Harrier, seen here on the carrier HMS *Hermes*.

Cuba
1959–1962

Fidel Castro's revolution in Cuba brought the threat of communism to 'America's backyard', and tensions surrounding the Caribbean island brought the world to the brink of nuclear war.

WITH THE CORRUPT, pro-American regime of President Batista overthrown in 1958, Castro's Marxist Cuba increasingly became a Soviet outpost in the Caribbean. Located less than 160 kilometres (100 miles) from the coast of Florida, events in Cuba prompted a predictable reaction in Washington.

CIA air assets were used to wage a clandestine war in Cuba. In November 1959 U.S. aircraft dropped propaganda leaflets over Havana and C-46 transports began to drop weapons in support of counter-revolutionary forces on the island. Starting in 1960 the Agency meanwhile built up an armed force of around 1400 Cuban exiles who received training in Guatemala, for a planned invasion of Cuba.

Bay of Pigs invasion

The CIA-backed invasion was carefully staged in order to be 'plausibly deniable'. Various CIA front organizations operated C-46s and C-54s from Florida in support of the exile army, while B-26s that were to be used during the invasion proper received Cuban markings to give the impression that they had defected from Cuba. A Panamanian-registered PBY-5A flying boat was to serve as an aerial command post

for the invasion, which would take place at the Bay of Pigs, on Cuba's southern coast.

President Kennedy approved invasion plans in March 1961, and on 15 April eight ex-USAF B-26Bs left Nicaragua, armed with guns, bombs and rockets. Forming three flights, the aircraft struck Cuban airfields at San Antonio de los Banos, Campo Libertad and Antonio Maceo. At the first base a T-33 and a number of B-26s were destroyed on the ground, with a Sea Fury and a civilian DC-3 hit at Antonio Maceo. One B-26 raider crashed into the sea, and two more were forced down by engine trouble and fuel shortage respectively.

At the same time an amphibious landing force of Cuban exiles was sailing from Puerto Cabezas, Nicaragua, with air support provided by 24 more B-26s, six C-46s and six C-54s. On April 16 B-26s struck ground targets in preparation for the invasion, two from a force of 11 bombers being lost in combat, one crash-landing, and two being lost on the return flight to Nicaragua. The amphibious landing took place on 17 April, while B-26s kept up their attacks on Cuban airfields and troops. The Cuban AF sunk two invasion vessels, although the invaders took the

▲ **Hawker Sea Fury FB.Mk 11**

Escuadron Persecucion y Combate, Fuerza Aérea Revolucionaria (Cuban AF)
The small force of British-supplied Sea Furies inherited from the Batista regime saw some action in the hands of the Fuerza Aérea Revolucionaria (FAR) during the abortive Bay of Pigs invasion. Cuba operated up to 12 Sea Furies, and these claimed at least two B-26Bs destroyed during the Bay of Pigs invasion.

Specifications

Crew: 1	Dimensions: span 11.7m (38ft 4in);
Powerplant: 1 x 1850kW (2480hp) Bristol	length 10.6m (34ft 8in); height 4.9m
Centaurus XVIIC 18-cylinder twin-row radial	(16ft 1in)
engine	Weight: 5670kg (12,500lb) loaded
Maximum speed: 740km/h (460mph)	Armament: 4 x 20mm (.79 in) Hispano Mk V
Range: 1127km (700 miles)	cannon; 12 x 76.2mm (3in) rockets or
Service ceiling: 10,900m (35,800ft)	907kg (2000lb) of bombs

beachhead and established a landing strip to receive C-46s carrying supplies. B-26 raids continued during 18–19 April, but there was no sign of a popular uprising that might threaten the leadership in Havana. The last B-26 attack was covered by unmarked U.S. Navy A4D-2s from USS *Essex*, but two Invaders were still destroyed, one falling to a Cuban AF T-33 and the other to AAA. Out of the invaders' force of 24 aircraft, half had been lost, and the amphibious assault ended in disaster, with 120 exiles killed and another 1200 captured.

Cuban Missile Crisis

Soviet premier Khrushchev upped the stakes in the Cold War standoff with the decision to place medium-range nuclear missiles on Cuba in 1962. With Cuba concerned by the threat posed by the U.S., Castro's regime received major arms shipments from the USSR, ultimately including nuclear-armed Il-28 jet bombers, SS-4 and SS-5 medium-range ballistic missiles, and surface-launched cruise missiles.

Aware of the military build-up on Cuba, the U.S. increased CIA-operated U-2 spyplane overflights, which detected the missiles in August 1962. At the same time, U.S. Navy and USAF patrol and reconnaissance aircraft carefully monitored shipping headed towards Cuba. On 29 August U-2s detected SA-2 SAM sites similar to those used to defend

strategic missile bases in the USSR, and on 4 September Kennedy informed Moscow that the U.S. would not tolerate the presence of Soviet strategic weapons on Cuba. Khrushchev told Washington that there were no such weapons on the island, but photo imagery gathered by U.S. Navy P-2s and CIA U-2s painted an altogether different picture.

With further missiles having arrived in mid-September, 10 October saw U-2 flights become the responsibility of the USAF rather than the CIA. These identified additional construction work associated with missile sites, and confirmation of the presence of SS-4s was provided to Kennedy on 16 October, after a U-2E flight from Patrick Air Force Base (AFB), Florida. In response, USAF RF-101Cs began low-level reconnaissance flights over Cuba from Shaw AFB, Arkansas.

The Soviets continued to insist that only defensive arms were deployed on Cuba, while the U.S. weighed up its options: invasion of Cuba, air attack, political ultimatum or blockade. A naval blockade duly began on 22 October, while SAC B-52 bombers were placed on alert. Task Force 138 was responsible for the blockade, enforced with the aid of the carrier USS *Essex*, with two squadrons of S2F-1s (S-2As) onboard. The 'quarantine' zone was established as a zone 800 kilometres (500 miles) off the Cuban coast, while additional photo-reconnaissance support

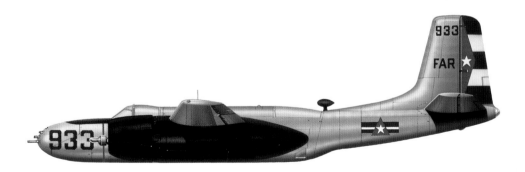

▲ **Douglas B-26B Invader**

'Cuban AF/CIA / Miami, April 1961

This 'Cuban' B-26 landed at Miami International after the attack on Cuban airfields on 15 April. The pilot claimed to be a defector, and that the raid had been planned by other defectors in collaboration with U.S.-based exiles. In fact, the ex-USAF Invader was part of a CIA operation, and the B-26B version was absent from the Cuban AF, which operated the B-26C model.

Specifications	
Crew: 3	Dimensions: span 21.71m (71ft 3in); length
Powerplant: 2 x 1431kW (1920hp)	16.60m (51ft 3in); height 5.6m (18ft 6in)
Pratt & Whitney R-2800-43 radial engines	Weight: 16,782kg (37,000lb) loaded
Maximum speed: 453km/h (282mph)	Armament: 11 x 12.7mm (0.50in) M2 Browning
Range: 1850km (1150 miles)	MGs and up to 3628kg (8000lb) bomb load
Service ceiling: 6614m (21,700ft)	

arrived in the form of further USAF RF-101Cs, and U.S. Navy and Marine Corps RF-8As.

Khrushchev offered to remove the Soviet-manned strategic weapons on 26 October, in exchange for the removal of U.S. missiles from Turkey, but a day later tensions were increased after a SAM shot down a U-2 over Cuba, and the situation worsened when another U-2 overflew Siberia in error.

Finally, on the morning of 28 October the Soviets stepped down, and agreed to remove their offensive missiles from Cuba, together with Il-28 bombers, which were in the process of being assembled. The missiles were dismantled and were returned to the USSR in the course of November, and the naval blockade was lifted before the end of the month. The U.S. in turn agreed to remove its obsolescent Jupiter missiles from Europe, and pledged not to interfere in Cuban issues. A year later a 'hotline' telephone link was established between Moscow and Washington, with the aim of improving superpower relations.

▲ **Lockheed U-2A**

4080th Strategic Reconnaissance Wing, USAF / Laughlin AFB, 1961

The U-2 played a critical role during the Cuban Missile Crisis, with 102 USAF sorties being flown by the type in the period between 14 October and 6 December. Painted light grey overall, this USAF U-2A was operated by the 4080th SRW from Laughlin AFB, Texas, at the time of the crisis.

Specifications

Crew: 1

Powerplant: 1 x 48.93kN (11,000lb) thrust Pratt & Whitney J75-P-37A turbojet engine

Maximum speed: 795km/h (494mph)

Range: 3542km (2200 miles)

Service ceiling: 16,763m (55,000ft)

Dimensions: span 24.3m (80ft); length 15.1m (49ft 7in); height 3.9m (13ft)

Weight: 9523kg (21,000lb) loaded

Armament: none

Falklands
1982

When Argentina invaded the British overseas territory of the Falkland Islands almost unopposed on 2 April 1982, the Argentine administration did not expect a military response.

THE INITIAL ARGENTINE landings on the Falklands were achieved without air support, but on the same day there arrived at Port Stanley Argentine AF Pucára COIN aircraft, followed by an Army Puma, Air Force Bell 212 and CH-47C helicopters, Navy Skyvans and a Coast Guard Puma. The bases on the Falklands – Stanley, Goose Green and Pebble Island – were too small for Argentine AF fighter-bombers that instead had to operate at extreme range from the mainland. Three Pumas, two A.109s and a UH-1 that arrived by ship from 7–9 April later boosted army strength on the islands.

The Argentine carrier ARA *25 de Mayo* had set sail on 28 March, with A-4Qs embarked, but the loss of the cruiser ARA *General Belgrano* to a British submarine saw the carrier return to port before Navy

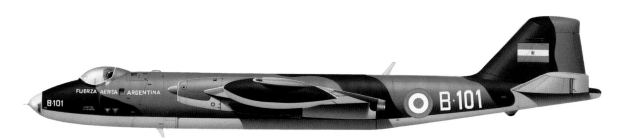

Specifications

Crew: 2

Powerplant: 2 x 28.9kN (6500lb) Rolls-Royce
Avon Mk 101 turbojets

Maximum speed: 917km/h (570mph)

Range: 4274km (2656 miles)

Service ceiling: 14,630m (48,000ft)

Dimensions: span 29.49m (63ft 11in); length
19.96m (65ft 6in); height 4.78m (15ft 8in)

Weight: 24,925kg (54,950lb) loaded

Armament: bomb bay with provision for up to
2727kg (6000lb) of bombs, plus 909kg
(2000lb) of underwing pylons

▲ English Electric Canberra B.Mk 62

Grupo 2 de Bombardeo (GB2), Argentine AF / Comodoro Rivadavia AB

The Argentine AF received 12 Canberras from BAC in 1970-71. On 1 May the type
was involved in a combined attack against the Task Force, also involving A-4s, with
Mirages and Daggers as top cover. In the ensuing air combats, a Canberra was
shot down by an 801 NAS Sea Harrier, 240km (150 miles) northwest of Stanley.

A-4s could make an impact. On 11 April, GC4 A-4Cs were detached to San Julian, with GC5 moving to Rio Gallegos from 14 April, both airfields being around 1125 kilometres (700 miles) from Stanley.

With the British Maritime Exclusion Zone (MEZ) in force by 12 April, the Argentine garrison had to be supported by air, using C-130s, Air Force and Navy F.27s, Navy Electras and civil types, and further UH-1s were delivered. As the British Task Force approached, Argentine air power in the Falklands included two CH-47s, five Pumas, nine UH-1s and three A.109s, with 12 Pucáras at Goose Green joining the 12 at Stanley. By 24 April the Navy had deployed six M.B.339s and four T-34Cs, tasked with harassing shipping and defending against the landings.

Black Buck raids

Fourteen Victor tankers were based at Ascension Island by the end of April. Most took part in the Black Buck 1 raid, in which Vulcan bombers targeted Port Stanley airfield after 18 aerial refuellings. Leaving Ascension on 30 April, the two Black Buck 1 Vulcans were armed with 21 450-kilogram (1000-lb) bombs, with one primary attack aircraft and one back-up. After the successful first raid hit Stanley on 1 May, five more Black Bucks were flown, plus another mission abandoned after a refuelling unit broke. At the time, the 12,390-kilometre (7700-mile) Vulcan missions were the longest-ever point-to-point bombing sorties.

The first of May saw the Sea Harrier enter the fray. During a dawn raid on Stanley airfield an

inconclusive air action followed, involving two 801 NAS Sea Harriers and three T-34Cs that were carrying out a strafing attack on British warships. On the ground, 800 NAS Sea Harriers destroyed a Pucara at Goose Green, and put two more out of action. The afternoon of 1 May saw around 20 Argentine aircraft sent against the Task Force. A pair of Mirages tangled

ARGENTINE AF, 1982		
Aircraft	**Unit**	**Base**
Canberra B.Mk 62	GB2	Trelew, Rio Gallegos
Mirage IIIEA	GC8	Comodoro Rivadavia, Rio Gallegos
Dagger	Esc.2 GC6	San Julian
Dagger	Esc.3 GC6	Rio Grande
A-4C	GC4	San Julian
A-4B	GC5	Rio Gallegos
Pucará	GA3	Santa Cruz, Port Stanley, Goose Green, Pebble Island
B707	Esc.2 GTA1	Comodoro Rivadavia, El Palomar, Ezeiza
Learjet	GAF 1	Comodoro Rivadavia, Trelew, Rio Gallegos, Rio Grande
C-130E/H, KC-130H	Esc.1 GTA1	Comodoro Rivadavia
F.27, F.28, Twin Otter, BAC 1-11, B737	GTA9	Comodoro Rivadavia
CH-47C, Bell 212	GC17	Port Stanley

with Sea Harriers, one falling to a Sidewinder. The surviving Mirage was severely damaged before being finished off by friendly AAA. Minutes later, an 800 NAS Sea Harrier pair was bounced by Daggers, avoiding an Argentine missile, before destroying a Dagger. From now on the Dagger would be demoted to the air-to-ground role. A pair of 801 NAS Sea Harriers intercepted three Canberras on their way to attack British warships, one being destroyed.

1 May also saw a Pucará lost in a heavy landing and another destroyed by Sea Harrier on the ground. Two more Pucarás were damaged, and the survivors moved to Pebble Island. The same day also marked the first A-4 mission, four GC5 aircraft being escorted by Mirage IIIEA escorts. Another mission by GC4 and 5, plus escorts, similarly failed to find its targets before bombs from a GC5 aircraft missed a (friendly) ship off Stanley. The loss of two escorting Mirages to Sea Harriers combined with the Black Buck raid of 1 May saw Mirages held back from further action over the Falklands.

Naval gunfire forced the dispersal of the Argentine helicopters, whose subsequent use was limited, and between 3–4 May naval artillery put a Skyvan and a Puma out of action, while a Sea Harrier fell to AAA during a raid on Goose Green. The most significant action of 4 May was the sinking of HMS *Sheffield* by a combination of Super Etendard and Exocet anti-

Specifications

Crew: 1

Powerplant: 1 x 49.8kN (11,200lb) Pratt & Whitney J52-P-408 turbojet engine

Maximum speed: 1110km/h (690mph)

Range: 4345km (2700 miles)

Service ceiling: 10,515m (34,500ft)

Dimensions: span 8.47m (27ft 6in); length 12.58m (41ft 4in); height 4.57m (15ft)

Weight: 11,113kg (24,500lb) loaded

Armament: 2 x 20mm cannon; 2721kg (6000lb) external bomb load

▲ **Douglas A-4B Skyhawk**

Grupo 5 de Caza (GC5), Argentine AF / Rio Grande AB

Two Air Force and one Navy A-4 unit led the effort against the Task Force, destroying four ships and a landing craft and damaging four more. In return, they suffered 22 losses (three of which were Navy aircraft) in 289 sorties: 106 by Grupo 4, 149 by Grupo 5 and 34 by the Navy. Nineteen Skyhawks fell to British action.

▲ **Dassault Super Etendard**

2 Escuadrilla de Caza y Ataque (2ECA), Argentine Navy / Rio Grande AB, 1982

Argentina had received just five from a total order of 14 Super Etendards at the time of the conflict, the possibility of further deliveries being ended by a French arms embargo. The aircraft (and their five Etendard anti-ship missiles) were operated by 2 Escuadrilla, 3 Escuadra Aéronaval, which moved to Rio Grande.

Specifications

Crew: 1

Powerplant: 1 x 49kW (11,023lb) SNECMA Atar 8K-50 turbojet

Maximum speed: 1180km/h (733mph)

Range: 850km (528 miles)

Service ceiling: 13,700m (44,950ft)

Dimensions: span 9.6m (31ft 6in);

length 14.31m (46ft 11.2in); height 3.86m (12ft 8in)

Weight: 12,000kg (26,455lb) loaded

Armament: 2 x 30mm cannon, provision for up to 2100kg (4630lb) of stores, including nuclear weapons and Exocet air-to-surface missiles ship missile. Two more Sea Harriers were destroyed in a mid-air collision after running into bad weather on 6 May. After the loss of an M.B.339 on an anti-ship patrol, a Sea Dart missile from HMS *Coventry* claimed another Puma on 9 May.

Poor weather limited further A-4 attacks until 12 May, following two operational losses (one aircraft flying into a cliff, another lost over the sea). On 12 May GC5 sent eight aircraft against British warships at Port Stanley. Despite flying at low level, Seawolf missiles from HMS *Brilliant* claimed two Skyhawks, and another crashed into the sea as it took evasive action. One bomb hit HMS *Glasgow*, forcing it to leave the battle, but friendly AAA then shot down the same A-4. This action was enough to dissuade the Royal Navy from continuing daylight bombardment.

SAS raid

The Pebble Island raid of 14–15 May saw two Sea King HC.Mk 4s deliver 45 British Special Air Service (SAS) troops and naval forward observers who would later direct shore bombardment. The SAS party also attacked Argentine aircraft at the airfield, destroying 11. Further SAS raiders were inserted by Sea King on 20–21 May, after which these helicopters remained on station to airlift equipment and stores during the invasion, including airlift of Rapier SAMs.

Originally configured for air defence, RAF Harriers had deployed to make up for possible Sea Harrier attrition. Joining the Task Force on 18 May, they transferred to HMS *Hermes* before assuming

ARGENTINE NAVY, FALKLANDS, 1982		
Aircraft	**Unit**	**Base**
Super Etendard	2 ECA	Bahia Blanca, Rio Grande
A-4Q	3 ECA	*25 de Mayo*, Bahia Blanca
MB.326GB, MB.339A	1 EA	Trelew, Bahia Blanca, Rio Grande, Port Stanley
T-34C-1	4 EA	PuntaIndio, Rio Grande, Port Stanley, Pebble Island
SP-2H	EE	Bahia Blanca, Rio Grande
Electra	1 ESLM	Rio Grande
F.28	2 ESLM	Rio Grande
S-2A	EAS	*25 de Mayo*, Bahia Blanca, Port Stanley, Rio Gallegos
S-61D-4	2 EH	Bahia Blanca, Almirante Irizar, *25 de Mayo*, Rio Grande
Lynx HAS.Mk 23, Alouette III	1 EH	various warships
Skyvan, Puma	PN	Port Stanley, Pebble Island

ground-attack duties on 20 May with a three-ship attack on an Argentine fuel dump on West Falkland.

21 May was the day of the Task Force's invasion, and landings began before dawn in Falkland Sound and San Carlos Water. Nimrods conducted surveillance, while Sea Kings monitored possible submarine activity. Other Sea Kings were used to deliver SAS teams from HMS *Hermes*, and the SAS also carried out a diversionary attack on Goose Green.

Specifications

Crew: 2

Powerplant: 1 x 17.8kN (4000lb thrust) Rolls-
Royce Viper Mk. 632 turbojet

Maximum speed: 898km/h (558mph)

Range: 1760km (1093 miles)

Service ceiling: 14,630m (48,000ft)

Dimensions: span 10.86m (35ft 7in);
length 10.97m (36ft); height 3.60m
(11ft 9in)

Weight: 4400kg (9700lb) loaded

Armament: up to 1800kg (3968lb) of weapons

▲ **Aermacchi M.B.339A**

1 Escuadrilla de Ataque (1EA), Argentine Navy / Port Stanley, 1982

Argentine Navy M.B.339s were among the more capable combat aircraft stationed on the Falklands, with six examples from 1 Escuadrilla de Ataque (1 EA) based at Stanley by late April. An advanced trainer, the M.B.339 was also capable of undertaking ground attack and reconnaissance missions.

Specifications

Crew: 2

Powerplant: 2 x 729kW (978hp) Turbomeca
  Astazou XVIG turboprop engines

Maximum speed: 500km/h (310mph)

Range: 3710km (2305 miles)

Service ceiling: 10,000m (31,800ft)

Dimensions: span 14.5m (47ft 6in); length
  14.25m (46ft 9in); height 5.36m (17ft 7in);

Weight: 6800kg (14,991lb) loaded

Armament: 2 x 20mm Hispano-Suiza HS.804
  cannon and four 7.62mm FM M2-20 MGs; up
  to 1500kg (3300lb) of bombs or rockets

▲ FMA Pucará

Grupo 3 de Ataque (GA3), Argentine AF / Port Stanley, 1982

The first Pucára COIN aircraft arrived in the Falklands on 2 April, the day of the
Argentine invasion. By late April 24 Pucáras were operating from Stanley and
Goose Green, which were known by the Argentines as Base Aérea Militar (BAM)
Malvinas and BAM Condor respectively.

▲ Lockheed SP-2H Neptune

Escuadrilla Exploracion (EE), Argentine Navy / Bahia Blanca AB/Rio Grande AB

Argentina operated both SP-2H models on support missions during the Falklands
campaign, and an example was responsible for locating the destroyer HMS
Sheffield, which was sunk by an Exocet missile. After this successful outing,
however, maintenance problems effectively kept the Neptunes grounded.

Specifications

Crew: 9–11

Powerplant: 2 x 2759kW (3700hp) Wright R-
  3350-32W Cyclone radial and 2 x 13.7kN
  (3085kg) thrust Westinghouse J-34-WE-36
  turbojet engines

Maximum speed: 586km/h (364mph)

Range: 3540km (2200 miles)

Service ceiling: 6827m (22,400ft)

Dimensions: span 31.65m (103ft 10in); length
  27.9m (91ft 8in); height 8.9m (29ft 4in)

Weight: 79,895lb (35,240kg) loaded

Armament: up to 4540kg (10,000lb) of bombs,
  mines or torpedoes

While RAF Harriers were to pin down Falklands-
based air assets, Sea Harriers would claim air
superiority. Although a Pucará fell to an SAS Stinger
SAM, it was an aircraft of this type that confirmed
that the Task Force had arrived.

Following an attack by eight Daggers, six A-4s
disabled HMS *Argonaut* and damaged HMS *Antrim*,
putting the warship temporarily out of action, for the
loss of one Dagger to a Seawolf missile. Two Goose
Green-based Pucárs then attacked *Ardent*, without
success, and one was shot down by Sea Harrier. The
next wave of Argentine attackers was a package of

eight A-4s. Two aircraft dropped out and another two
were shot down by Sea Harriers, with just one
abortive attack prosecuted against an Argentine ship.
Five Daggers were next on scene, one being lost to a
Sea Harrier, although *Ardent* was further damaged. A
second wave of three Daggers strafed *Brilliant*, but all
three fell to a combination of Sea Harriers and
Sidewinder AAMs soon after.

Three Navy A-4s left HMS *Ardent* sunk (the
warship had earlier been slightly damaged by a single
M.B.339), but at a cost of two of their own to Sea
Harriers, and one abandoned after sustaining

▲ Handley Page Victor K.Mk 2

55 Sqn, RAF / Marham

The RAF Victor K.Mk 2 tanker fleet comprised 23 aircraft at Marham, 22 of which were available for the Falklands campaign. As well as vital refuelling missions, four specially adapted Victors undertook maritime radar reconnaissance, and aided in the recapture of South Georgia, Operation Paraquat.

Specifications

Crew: 4

Powerplant: 4 x 91.6kN (20,600lb) Rolls-Royce
Conway Mk 201 turbofans

Maximum speed: 1030km/h (640mph)

Range: 7400km (4600 miles)

Service ceiling: 18,290m (60,000ft)

Dimensions: span 36.58m (120ft); length
35.05m (114ft 11in); height 9.2m
(30ft 1.5in)

Weight: 105,687kg (233,000lb) loaded

Armament: none

damage. RAF Harriers supported British troops landing at Port San Carlos, and also attacked Argentine helicopters near Mount Kent, destroying a Chinook and damaging a Puma and a UH-1, although one fell to a Blowpipe SAM. Despite the Argentine air attack, the transport vessels were generally unscathed, and a beachhead was established. Meanwhile, D-Day had seen Sea Harriers claim nine Argentine aircraft destroyed.

Also playing a key role during the landings were the helicopters of the Army Air Corps (AAC) and No. 3 Commando Brigade Air Squadron (CBAS) of the Royal Marines. Indeed, Gazelles from the landing ship Sir Tristram flew the first missions of the invasion, launching the SAS diversionary attack. Two more Gazelles from Sir Galahad helped secure sites for Rapier SAMs, and provided gunship escort for Sea Kings unloading stores from ships. One escort Gazelle was hit by small arms fire, becoming the first casualty of the day; a second Gazelle was also a victim of small arms fire near San Carlos.

Task Force under fire

In the wake of the British invasion, three Pumas and an A.109 were jumped by two Sea Harriers on 21 May, all but one Puma being destroyed. An RAF Harrier was also lost to AAA fire near Port Howard. Two days later a combined A-4 force hit HMS *Antelope* in San Carlos Water, and the vessel was later destroyed when an unexploded bomb detonated. However, two Skyhawks were lost, and a third limped home, while a Dagger was shot down by a Sea Harrier.

After three Daggers and an A-4 were destroyed on 24 May, A-4s attacked shipping off Pebble Island the next day, damaging HMS *Broadsword* and destroying HMS *Coventry*, which had been acting as a radar picket, but losing two aircraft in return. On the same day the container ship *Atlantic Conveyor* was destroyed by an Exocet anti-ship missile launched by Super Etendard, taking with it six Wessex, three Chinooks and a Puma helicopter, as well as other important stores, and Sea Harrier spares.

The A-4s switched to attacking British forces on the islands as of 27 May. On 28 May the Argentines attempted to reinforce Goose Green garrison (the first British objective after the breakout) with seven UH-1s, two A.109s, a Puma and a CH-47. On the same day Pucarás flew from Stanley to attack British troops, one claiming an Army Scout helicopter before being lost in bad weather. Scouts were the first British helicopters ashore, and were followed the next day by Gazelles, providing troop support from dispersed sites. An MB.339 was then lost to a Blowpipe SAM, with a Pucará downed by small arms fire.

After an attack on Argentine artillery near Goose Green on 28 May, the Argentine commander of the battery surrendered but losses to ground fire on 27 May and 30 May reduced the RAF Harrier fleet to three aircraft. Refuelled by Victor tankers, two reinforcements arrived on Hermes from Ascension on 1 June, and two more followed a week later.

By 30 May, the last airworthy M.B.339 had been withdrawn, with surviving Pucarás dispersed around Stanley town for protection. The final Exocet sortie

RAF, FALKLANDS, 1982		
Aircraft	**Unit**	**Base**
Vulcan B.Mk 2	44 Sqn 50 Sqn 101 Sqn	Ascension
Harrier GR.Mk 3	1 Sqn	Ascension, HMS *Hermes*, Stanley
Phantom FGR.Mk 2	29 Sqn	Ascension
Nimrod R.Mk 1	51 Sqn	Ascension, Chile
Canberra PR.Mk 9	39 Sqn	Punta Arenas
Hercules C.Mk 1/3	24 Sqn 30 Sqn 47 Sqn 70 Sqn	Ascension, Stanley
VC10 C.Mk 1	10 Sqn	Ascension, Stanley
Chinook HC.Mk 1	18 Sqn	Ascension, Port San Carlos
Nimrod MR.Mk 1	42 Sqn	Ascension
Nimrod MR.Mk 2	120 Sqn 201 Sqn 206 Sqn	Ascension
Victor K.Mk 2	55 Sqn 57 Sqn	Ascension
Sea King HAR.Mk 3	202 Sqn	Ascension

of the campaign, on 30 May, involved four A-4s accompanying two Super Etendards on an abortive attack against HMS *Invincible*. Two Skyhawks were shot down by SAMs, and the bombs missed the target (which was actually HMS *Avenger*).

With a beachhead established at Port San Carlos, an operating strip could be built, allowing Harriers and Sea Harriers to operate from dry land as of 5 June. RAF Harriers supported the British troops' advance on Stanley, their sorties including the first operational RAF use of laser-guided bombs.

On 8 June A-4s targeted the landing ships *Sir Tristram* (severely damaged) and *Sir Galahad* (destroyed) at Port Pleasant. Five A-4s caused much destruction; four more then attempted a follow-up raid, but three fell to Sea Harriers after sinking a landing craft – these were the Sea Harrier's final victories of the campaign. Meanwhile A-4s attacked troops at Port Pleasant. In the rescue that followed the attacks on the two troopships, Sea Kings were heavily involved in airlifting survivors.

Last Skyhawk raid

On 13 June eight Skyhawks attacked British positions at Mount Kent and Mount Longdon, in the final A-4 air raid of the war, and succeeded in damaging a number of helicopters.

Between 28–31 May the Argentines had evacuated Pebble Island, using a Twin Otter and two Sea Kings. In the same period the final Puma was shot down by 'friendly fire'. UH-1s continued casualty evacuation work from Stanley town, while CH-47s withdrew on 9 June. Night-time C-130 flights were conducted until 13 June, supported by Navy Electras and F.27s.

Helicopters again proved their value during the British advance on Port Stanley, with troop patrols supported by Scouts. The assault on Port Stanley also

▲ **Avro Vulcan B.Mk 2**

44 Sqn, RAF / Ascension Island, 1982

XM607 was the aircraft responsible for prosecuting the first Black Buck raid. Following two Black Buck sorties flown against the airfield at Port Stanley, to deny its access to the Argentines, two further Black Buck missions on 31 May and 3 June used Shrike anti-radar missiles to target long-range radars near the airfield.

Specifications

Crew: 5

Powerplant: 4 x 88.9kN (20,000lb) Olympus
Mk.301 turbojets

Maximum speed: 1038km/h (645mph)

Range: about 7403km/h (4600 miles)

Service ceiling: 19,810m (65,000ft)

Dimensions: span 33.83m (111ft); length
30.45m (99ft 11in); height 8.28m (27ft 2in)

Weight: 113,398kg (250,000lb) loaded

Armament: internal weapons bay for up to
21,454kg (47,198lb) of bombs

involved Sea Kings and Wessex, ferrying ammunition to Mount Kent. Only one Chinook was available throughout the campaign after the loss of the *Atlantic Conveyor*, and this was put to good use transferring supplies from ship to shore, ferrying ammunition and, on occasions, as many as 81 troops, which was twice its normal load. After a Gazelle spotted Argentine forces, Gurkhas were called in and transported by Sea Kings, while Scouts attacked

Argentine positions with AS.11 missiles and captured prisoners during vicious fighting that took place between 12–13 June. Scouts were heavily involved in the final hours of fighting, knocking out Argentine artillery, as well as conducting casualty evacuation from Tumbledown Mountain. A number of Pucára raids were staged between 10–13 June before the final collapse of the Argentine garrison and the Argentine surrender on 14 June.

FLEET AIR ARM, FALKLANDS, 1982		
Aircraft	**Unit**	**Base**
Sea Harrier FRS.Mk 1	800 NAS	HMS *Hermes*, Port San Carlos, Stanley
Sea Harrier FRS.Mk 1	801 NAS	HMS *Invincible*, Port San Carlos, Stanley
Sea Harrier FRS.Mk 1	809 NAS	HMS *Hermes*, HMS *Invincible*, HMS *Illustrious*
Sea King HAS.Mk 5	820 NAS	HMS *Invincible*, Ascension, Stanley
Sea King HAS.Mk 2	824 NAS	*Olmeda*, Port San Carlos, *Fort Grange*
Sea King HAS.Mk 2	825 NAS	*Queen Elizabeth 2*, *Atlantic Causeway*, Port San Carlos
Sea King HAS.Mk 5	826 NAS	HMS *Hermes*, Port San Carlos
Sea King HC.Mk 4	846 NAS	HMS *Hermes*, HMS *Fearless*, HMS *Intrepid*, *Canberra*, *Elk*, *Norland*, various island bases
Wessex HAS.Mk 3	737 NAS	HMS *Antrim*, HMS *Glamorgan*
Wessex HU.Mk 5	845 NAS	*Resource*, Stanley, *Fort Austin*, Port San Carlos, *Tidespring*, Ascension, *Tidepool*, various island bases
Wessex HU.Mk 5	847 NAS	*Engadine*, *Atlantic Causeway*, Port San Carlos, various island bases
Wessex HU.Mk 5	848 NAS	*Endurance*, *Regent*, *Olna*, *Fort Austin*, *Olwen*, *Atlantic Conveyor*, *Astronomer*, Port San Carlos
Lynx HAS.Mk 2	815 NAS	various warships
Wasp HAS.Mk 1	829 NAS	various warships

Specifications

Crew: 1

Powerplant: 1 x 95.6kN (21,500lb) Rolls-Royce Pegasus vectored thrust turbofan

Maximum speed: 1110km/h (690mph)

Range: 740km (460 miles)

Service ceiling: 15,545m (51,000ft)

Dimensions: span 7.7m (25ft 3in); length 14.5m (47ft 7in); height 3.71m (12ft 2in)

Weight: 11,884kg (26,200lb) loaded

Armament: 2 x 30mm cannon, provision for AIM-9 Sidewinder or Matra Magic air-to-air missiles, and two Harpoon or Sea Eagle anti-shipping missiles, up to a total of 3629kg (8000lb) bombs

▲ Hawker Siddeley (BAe) Sea Harrier FRS.Mk 1

809 NAS, Royal Navy / Falklands, 1982

Taking aircraft from storage and training units, 809 NAS was formed in April 1982 to reinforce 800 and 801 NAS. In total, 28 Sea Harriers flew over 2370 sorties in which they claimed 21 aircraft in aerial combat, as well as three helicopters and three Pucárs destroyed on the ground. This aircraft, ZA177, claimed two Mirages.

American Policing Actions
1954–1989

Whether working overtly or by clandestine means, during the Cold War the U.S. took a hard line against regimes in Latin America that it considered at risk from communism.

PUTTING INTO PRACTICE the 'domino theory', which proposed that the loss of one state to communism would lead to the spread of Marxism throughout a particular region, the U.S. participated in military action in Guatemala, overthrowing a left-wing government in 1954. Although U.S. air power was not deployed overtly in Guatemala, the CIA provided a B-26 bomber, which was operated from Nicaragua against government forces. A CIA-trained rebel army then invaded Guatemala from Honduras, supported by U.S.-supplied (and in some cases U.S.-flown) B-26, F-47, F-51 and C-47 aircraft operating out of Nicaragua. The operation was a success from a U.S. perspective, with Guatemala's left-wing government removed from power. The U.S. continued to take a military interest in Guatemala, supporting anti-guerrilla operations into the 1980s, and providing equipment including UH-1s and, later, gunship-equipped Bell 212 and 214 helicopters.

In 1961, U.S. forces put down a counter-revolution in Nicaragua. Next up was the Dominican Republic, where the U.S. intervened in 1965 in order to prevent a communist takeover. The U.S. deployed an invasion force to the Caribbean. This included the USS *Boxer*, carrying U.S. Marine Corps H-34, and UH-1 helicopters, which were used to effect a USMC landing on the island and to evacuate U.S. civilians.

Intervention in Grenada

As relations between the superpowers worsened in the early 1980s, the U.S. found itself once again embarking on military operations in Latin America, with an invasion of Grenada in 1983 to restore order after a coup. In particular, the presence of Cuban advisors on the island was a source of concern to the U.S., and SR-71A spyflights were followed by Operation Urgent Fury in October 1983, with the aim of evacuating U.S. citizens, neutralizing local military forces, and restoring order. The invasion force included C-130E/H transports for paradropping and C-141Bs and C-5As to bring follow-on supplies, while Marines were landed by CH-46E and CH-53D helicopters from USS *Guam*, escorted by AH-1Ts. Air support was provided by

▲ **Bell AH-1T SeaCobra**

U.S. Marine Corps

Four AH-1Ts were used in Grenada in support of the U.S. Marine Corps transport helicopters that delivered U.S. troops from the assault ship USS *Guam*. Two SeaCobras were shot down during the battle for Fort Frederick. The USMC helicopter component also included UH-1Ns for command and control duties.

Specifications

Crew: 2

Powerplant: 1 x 820kW (1100shp) Lycoming
  T53-L-13 turboshaft

Maximum speed: 352km/h (219mph)

Range: 574km (357 miles)

Service ceiling: 3475m (11,400ft)

Dimensions: rotor diameter: 13.4m (44ft);
  length 13.4m (44ft 5in); height 4.1m
  (13ft 6in)

Weight: 4500kg (10,000lb) loaded

Armament: 2 x 7.62mm MGs; 70mm (2.75in)
  rockets; M18 7.62mm Minigun pod

▲ **Sikorsky CH-53D Sea Stallion**
A US Marine Corps CH-53D is seen during the Grenada invasion, framed by a
Soviet-built, Cuban-operated ZSU-23 anti-aircraft gun. CH-53s operated from the
amphibious assault vessel USS *Guam* during the campaign.

▲ **Lockheed C-130E Hercules**
A C-130E of the USAF's 934th Airlift Wing over Panama in the wake of the 1989
military intervention, codenamed Operation Just Cause, during which USAF
C-130s, C-5s and C-141s had been used to deliver the first waves of US troops.

AC-130H gunships and air power from the USS
Independence, and U.S. Army UH-60A helicopters
made their combat debut. After eight days of
fighting, the U.S. forces realized their objectives.

The U.S. operated more covertly during the civil
wars fought in Nicaragua and El Salvador during the
early 1980s. With military assistance provided
through CIA channels, the U.S. backed the exiled
right-wing Contra rebels operating against the left-
wing Sandinista regime in Nicaragua, while propping
up the government during El Salvador's civil war.

El Salvador was victorious in a brief war fought
against Honduras in 1969, the air warfare having
witnessed the last dogfights between piston-engined
aircraft, but by 1980 El Salvador was suffering civil
war, with military 'death squads' used to maintain
internal security. U.S. military assistance resumed
from 1981, including UH-1Hs, American military
advisors and training for COIN teams. While the
Salvadorean AF flew ground support missions against
guerrillas, C-47s and helicopters were used to
transport troops. A guerrilla raid destroyed many
Salvadorean AF aircraft on the ground at Liopango in
January 1982, and the U.S. supplied more
helicopters, C-123s, O-2As and A-37Bs in response.
UH-1s played perhaps the most significant role, not

only transporting troops in pursuit of the guerrillas,
but also serving as gunships. C-47 gunship
conversions were also active as operations gathered
pace by the mid-1980s. The election of a new
president in El Salvador 1984 saw action reduced to
skirmishes that would endure until the end of the
Cold War.

In Nicaragua, the U.S. strove to topple the
Sandinista regime as of 1981, with CIA-based Contra
exile and mercenaries facing off against Nicaraguan
military power, which included Soviet-supplied Mi-8
and Mi-24 helicopters. Salvadorean AF A-37Bs were
used to stop infiltration by Nicaraguan guerrillas, with
El Salvador also serving as a base for O-2As, and other
types flown on clandestine missions by Nicaraguan
exile crews. The Honduran AF was also active in
support of the Contras. The civil war continued until
1990, when the Sandinistas were defeated in elections.

As the Cold War drew to a close, the U.S. was
involved in yet another military action in Latin
America, launching an operation against Panama in
1989. Again, USAF AC-130H, C-141B, C-5 and
C-130 aircraft were involved in a successful campaign
to oust General Manuel Noriega, and the December
1989 operation was notable for the first combat use
of the USAF's F-117A stealth attack aircraft.

Volume Two:
Military Airpower
1990–Present

CANADA

PACIFIC
OCEAN

USA

MEXICO

ATLANTIC
OCEAN

Chapter 10

North America

Comprising elements from Canada, Mexico and the United States, North American airpower is dominated by the air arms of the U.S. While the U.S. Air Force is the world's most powerful air arm, the aviation components of the U.S. Navy, Marine Corps and U.S. Army are each, in turn, far larger and more capable than the air forces of most other nations. As well as these formations, the U.S. can also call upon additional airpower and personnel held by the Air Force Reserve Command, Air National Guard and other reserve organizations. Both Canada and the U.S. deploy air power in support of the North Atlantic Treaty Organization (NATO) and its various overseas missions, and the two countries also combine to provide air defence of the North American continent through North American Aerospace Defence Command (NORAD).

United States

UNITED STATES AIR FORCE

The world's largest air arm, the United States Air Force (USAF) is also the most potent, capable of executing a diverse range of missions anywhere in the world, at a moment's notice.

ANY GIVEN DAY, around 40 per cent of the USAF fleet can be expected to be involved in operations. Currently, the focus is on the Global War on Terror, involving 25,000 USAF personnel deployed to U.S. Central Command. Outside of this, combat operations involve around 213,000 airmen, including 30,000 from the Air National Guard (ANG) and Air Force Reserve Command (AFRC). Deployed units are organized within 10 Air and Space Expeditionary Forces (AEF), which complete 120-day tours in rotation. Two AEFs are deployed at a time, each with around 175 aircraft and 17,500 personnel.

One of five Joint Chiefs of Staff, the Air Force Chief of Staff is responsible for 10 Major Commands (MAJCOM): Air Force Global Strike Command (AFGSC); Air Combat Command (ACC); Air Education and Training Command (AETC); Air Force Material Command (AFMC); Air Force Space Command (AFSPC); Air Force Special Operations Command (AFSOC); Air Mobility Command (AMC); Pacific Air Forces (PACAF); United States Air Force in Europe (USAFE); and Air Force Reserve Command (AFRC). The major commands are divided into one or more numbered air forces, six of

BOMBER UNITS

USAF Warfare Center / Nellis AFB, Nevada

53rd Wing / Eglin AFB, Florida

53rd TEG Nellis AFB, Nevada

31st TES	B-1B, B-2A, B-52H	Edwards AFB, California
72nd TES	B-2A	Whiteman AFB, Missouri
49th TES	B-52H	Barksdale AFB, Louisiana
337th TES	B-1B	Dyess AFB, Texas

57th Wing / Nellis AFB, Nevada

USAFWS / Nellis AFB, Nevada

77th WPS 'War Eagles'	B-1B	Dyess AFB, Texas
325th WPS	B-2A	Whiteman AFB, Missouri
340th WPS	B-52H	Barksdale AFB, Louisiana

Eighth Air Force / Air Force Global Strike Command / Barksdale AFB, Louisiana

2nd BW / Barksdale AFB, Louisiana

11th BS 'Mr. Jiggs'	B-52H
20th BS 'Buccaneers'	B-52H
96th BS 'Red Devils'	B-52H

5th BW / Minot AFB, North Dakota

23rd BS 'Bomber Barons'	B-52H

509th BW / Whiteman AFB, Missouri

13th BS 'Devil's Own Grim Reapers'	B-2A
393rd BS 'Tigers'	B-2A

Twelfth Air Forces / Air Forces Southern Davis-Monthan AFB, Arizona

7th BW / Dyess AFB, Texas

9th BS 'Bats'	B-1B
28th BS 'Grim Reapers'	B-1B

28th BW / Ellsworth AFB, South Dakota

34th BS 'Thunderbirds'	B-1B
37th BS 'Tigers'	B-1B

ARFC Tenth Air Force / NAS JRB Forth Worth / Carswell Field Texas

917th Wing / Barksdale AFB, Louisiana

93rd BS 'Indian Outlaws'	B-52H

Air Force Material Command

412th TW / Edwards AFB, California

419th FLTS 'Silent Sting'	B-1B, B-2A, B-52H

these being organized on a geographical basis, and four with functional duties. In addition to MAJCOMs and numbered air forces, the USAF includes smaller agencies reporting to headquarters in Washington DC. These agencies include the Air Force Flight Standards Agency, responsible for air traffic control and flight inspection; the Air Force District of Washington, which undertakes homeland and ceremonial duties around the capital; the USAF Academy, providing cadet training; and the USAF Auxiliary, with 52 mainly volunteer wings that undertake non-combat support missions in the U.S.

Air Force Global Strike Command

As its contribution to the U.S. nuclear deterrent, AFGSC possesses a fleet of 74 B-52Hs and 19 B-2As. Eventually, a new bomber is to be fielded, but this will be some time after the originally slated date of 2018. AFGSC commands the Eighth Air Force and the Twentieth Air Force, the latter operating ICBMs, and includes three bomber and four intelligence, surveillance and reconnaissance (ISR) wings.

As the largest MAJCOM, ACC maintains three numbered air forces and over 60 flying wings, including active, ANG and AFRC assignments, and the Air Warfare Center, responsible for tests and evaluation, and the USAF Weapons School. ACC equipment includes non-nuclear bombers, and all U.S.-based fighters, ISR and C2 assets. Numbered air forces are the First Air Force, with 10 ANG fighter wings that mainly support NORAD; the Ninth Air Force, responsible for the eastern U.S. and with five fighter wings; and the Twelfth Air Force, responsible for Central and Southern America, with seven active-duty wings, including the 65-strong fleet of B-1Bs.

With the F-22A in service and the F-35A waiting in the wings, the fighter arm is in an era of transition. By October 2012 the USAF intends to field 187 F-22s, with the first of 1763 F-35As coming on line.

▲ Rockwell B-1B Lancer
A formation of four B-1B bombers operated by the now-defunct 116th Bomb Wing from Robins AFB, Georgia. The Lancer force has now been streamlined, with two operational wings assigned to the Twelfth Air Force, and based at Dyess AFB, Texas, and Ellsworth AFB, South Dakota.

STRATEGIC RECONNAISSANCE UNITS		
USAF Warfare Center / Nellis AFB, Nevada		
53rd Wing / Eglin AFB, Florida		
53rd TEG / Nellis AFB, Nevada		
Det 2	RQ-4A/B, U-2S	Beale AFB, California
31st TES	RQ-4A/B	Edwards AFB, California
Eighth Air Force / Air Force Global Strike Command / Barksdale AFB, Louisiana, 9th RW / Beale AFB, California		
Det 1	U-2S	RAF Akrotiri, Cyprus
1st RS	U-2S, TU-2S, T-38A, RQ-4A	Beale AFB, California
5th RS 'Black Cats'	U-2S	Osan AB, Korea
12th RS 'Blackbirds'	RQ-4A/B	Beale AFB, California
99th RS	U-2S, T-38A	Beale AFB, California
55th Wing / Offutt AFB, Nebraska		
1st ACCS 'First Axe'	E-4B	Offutt AFB, Nebraska
38th RS 'Fighting Hellcats'	RC-135V/W, TC-135W	Offutt AFB, Nebraska
45th RS 'Sylvester'	WC-135W, OC-135B, RC-135S/U, TC-135S	
Det 1	RC-135S	Eielson AFB, Alaska
82nd RS 'Hog Heaven'	RC-135V/W	Kadena AB, Okinawa
95th RS 'Kickin' Ass'	RC-135V/W	RAF Mildenhall, England
Det 1	RC-135V/W	Souda Bay, Crete
343rd RS 'Ravens'	RC-135V/W, TC-135W	Offut AFB, Nebraska
41st ECS AFB, 'Scorpions'	EC-130H	Davis-Monthan AFB, Arizona
42nd ECS	TC-130H	Davis-Monthan AFB, Arizona

F-22 FIGHTER SQUADRONS

NINTH AIR FORCE / AIR FORCES CENTRAL / SHAW AFB, SOUTH CAROLINA

1st FW / Langley AFB, Virginia

27th FS 'Fightin' Eagles'	F-22A	Langley AFB, Virginia
94th FS 'Hat in the Ring'	F-22A	Langley AFB, Virginia

192nd FW / Langley, Virginia

149th FS 'Rebel Riders'	F-22A	Langley, Virginia

Twelfth Air Forces / Air Forces Southern Davis-Monthan AFB, Arizona

49th FW / Holloman AFB, New Mexico

7th FS 'Screamin' Demons'	F-22A	Holloman AFB, New Mexico

ARFC Tenth Air Force NAS JRB Forth Worth Carswell Field Texas

477th FG

302nd FS 'Sun Devils'	F-22A	Elmendorf AFB, Alaska

926th Group / Nellis AFB, Nevada

706th FS	F-22A	Nellis AFB, Nevada

Air Education and Training Command

325th FW / Tyndall AFB, Florida

43rd FS 'American Hornets'	F-22A	

PACIFIC AIR FORCES

Eleventh Air Force Elmendorf AFB, Alaska

3rd Wing / Elmendorf AFB, Alaska

90th FS 'Pair O'Dice'	F-22A	
525th FS 'Bulldogs'	F-22A	

The F-35 will eventually replace the F-16, numbers of which will drop from 1245 to 1086 in the year 2012. The 2012 fighter fleet will be completed by 178 F-15C/Ds and 217 F-15Es. Another type to be replaced by the F-35 is the A-10, of which 368 will remain in use in October 2012.

The USAF has moved with haste to field UAVs, and their operators are now permitted to graduate straight from undergraduate pilot training rather than first having to gain experience in a manned aircraft. The USAF's most numerically important UAVs are the MQ-1 and MQ-9, the latter with an attack capability.

AETC, headquartered at Randolph AFB, Texas, provides all aspects of flight and military training for USAF, via two numbered air forces, the Second (four wings and one group, but no flying units) and Nineteenth (five active component wings, five ANG wings and one AFRC wing). Headquartered at Peterson AFB, Colorado, AFSPC controls the Fourteenth Air Force, responsible for other space-based missions, and the Twenty-Fourth Air Force, the

Specifications

Crew: 1

Powerplant: 2 x 160kN (35,000lb) thrust Pratt & Whitney F119-PW-100 thrust-vectoring afterburning turbofan engines

Maximum speed: 2410km/h (1500mph)

Range: 2977km (1850 miles)

Service ceiling: 15,524m (50,000ft)

Dimensions: span 13.6m (44ft 6in); length 18.9m (62ft 1in); height 5.1m (16ft 8in)

Weight: 38,000kg (83,500lb) loaded

Armament: 1 x 20mm (0.78in) M61A2 Vulcan cannon; internal weapons bays for two AIM-9 Sidewinder and six AIM-120 ASRAAM air-to-air missiles

▼ **Lockheed Martin F-22A Raptor, 7th Fighter Squadron, 49th Fighter Wing, Holloman AFB**

Although orders for the stealthy, fifth-generation F-22A have been slashed, in the Raptor the USAF possesses the world's premier air defence fighter.

F-15 FIGHTER SQUADRONS

AIR COMBAT COMMAND / LANGLEY AFB, VIRGINIA

65th AGRS	F-15C/D	Nellis AFB, Nevada

First Air Force / Air Forces Northern / Tyndall AFB, Florida

120th FW / Great Falls International Airport, Montana

186th FS 'Vigilantes'	F-15C/D	

125th FW / Jacksonville International Airport, Florida

159th FS 'Jaguars'	F-15A/B/C/D	
Det 1	F-15A/C	Homestead ARB, Florida

142nd FW / Portland International Airport/ANGB, Oregon

123rd FS 'Red Hawks'	F-15A/B/C/D	

Ninth Air Force / Air Forces Central / Shaw AFB, S. Carolina

1st FW / Langley AFB, Virginia

71st FS 'Ironmen'	F-15C/D	

4th FW / Seymour Johnson AFB, North Carolina

333rd 'Lancers'	F-15E	
334th FS 'Eagles'	F-15E	
335th FS 'Chiefs'	F-15E	
336th FS 'Rocketeers'	F-15E	

33rd FW / Eglin AFB, Florida

58th FS 'Gorillas'	F-15C/D	

104th FW / Westfield Barnes Airport/ANGB, Massachusetts

131st FS 'Death Vipers'	F-15C/D	

Twelfth Air Forces / Air Forces Southern Davis-Monthan AFB, Arizona

366th FW / Mountain Home AFB, Idaho

389th FS 'Thunderbolts'	F-15E	
390th FS 'Wild Boars'	F-15C/D	
391st FS 'Bold Tigers'	F-15E	

131st FW / Lambert-St Louis International Airport, Missouri

110th FS 'Lindbergh's Own'	F-15C/D	

159th FW / NAS JRB New Orleans, Louisiana

122nd FS 'Cajuns'	F-15C/D	

ARFC Tenth Air Force / NAS JRB Forth Worth/Carswell Field Texas

307th FS 'Stingers'		Langley AFB, Virginia
Det 4	F-15C/D	Eglin AFB, Utah

926th Group / Nellis AFB, Nevada

706th FS	F-15C/D/E	

Air Education and Training Command

325th FW / Tyndall AFB, Florida

2nd FS 'American Beagles'	F-15C/D	
95th FS 'Boneheads'	F-15C/D	

173rd FW / Klamath Falls International Airport/Kingsley Field, Oregon

114th FS 'Eager Beavers'	F-15B/C/D	

PACIFIC AIR FORCES

Fifth Air Force / Yokota AB, Japan

18th Wing / Kadena AB, Japan

44th FS 'Vampires'	F-15C/D	
67th FS 'Fighting Cocks'	F-15C/D	

Eleventh Air Force Elmendorf AFB, Alaska

3rd Wing / Elmendorf AFB, Alaska

12th FS 'Dirty Dozen'	F-15C/D	
19th FS 'Gamecocks'	F-15C/D	

Thirteenth Air Force

154th Wing / Hickam AFB, Hawaii

199th FS	F-15A/BC/D	

UNITED STATES AIR FORCE IN EUROPE

Third Air Force / Air Forces Europe / Ramstein AB, Germany

48th FW / RAF Lakenheath, England

492nd FW 'Madhatters'	F-15E	
493rd FS 'Grim Reapers'	F-15C/D	
494th FS 'Panthers'	F-15E	

F-16 FIGHTER SQUADRONS

Air Combat Command Langley AFB, Virginia

USAF Warfare Center / Nellis AFB, Nevada

57th Wing / Nellis AFB, Nevada

USAF ADS 'Thunderbirds'	F-16C/D	Nellis AFB, Nevada
64th AGRS	F-16C/D	Nellis AFB, Nevada

First Air Force / Air Forces Northern / Tyndall AFB, Florida

601st AOC / Tyndall AFB, Florida

125th FS Det 1	F-16C/D	Ellington Field/ANGB, Texas
112th FS Det 1	F-16C/D	Selfridge Field ANGB, Michigan

144th FW / Fresno-Yosemite International Airport/ANGB, California

194th FS 'Griffins'	F-16C	
Det 1	F-16C	March ARB, California

148th FW / Duluth International Airport/ANGB, Minnesota

179th FS 'Bulldogs'	F-16C	
Det 1	F-16C	Tyndall AFB, Florida

158th FW / Burlington IAP/Ethan Allen ANGB, Vermont

134th FS 'Green Mountain Boys'	F-16C	
Det 1	F-16C	Langley AFB, Virginia

177th FW / Atlantic City International Airport/ANGB, New Jersey

119th FS 'Jersey Devils'	F-16C

Ninth Air Force / Air Forces Central / Shaw AFB, S. Carolina

20th FW / Shaw AFB, South Carolina

55th FS 'Lancers'	F-16C/D
77th FS 'Gamblers'	F-16C/D
79th FS 'Tigers'	F-16C/D

113th Wing / Andrews AFB, Maryland

121st 'Capital Guardians'	F-16C/D

122nd FW / Fort Wayne International Airport, Louisiana

163rd FS 'Marksmen'	F-16C

127th Wing / Selfridge ANGB, Michigan

107th FS 'Red Devils'	F-16C/D

169th FW / McEntire JNGS, South Carolina

157th FS 'Swamp Fox'	F-16C/D

174th FW / Syracuse Hancock International Airport, New York

138th FS 'Cobras' F-16C	

180th FW / Toledo Express Airport, Ohio

112th FS 'Stingers'	F-16C/D

187th FW / Montgomery Regional Airport/Dannelly Field, Alabama

100th FS 'Panthers'	F-16C/D

Twelfth Air Forces / Air Forces Southern Davis-Monthan AFB, Arizona

388th FW / Hill AFB, Utah

4th FS 'Fightin' Fujins'	F-16C/D
34th FS 'Rude Rams'	F-16C/D
421st FS 'Black Widows'	F-16C/D

114th FW / Sioux Falls Regional Airport/Joe Foss Field, South Dakota

175th FS 'Lobos'	F-16C/D

115th FW / Dane County Regional Airport/Truax Field, Wisconsin

176th FS 'Badgers'	F-16C

132nd FW / Des Moines International Airport, Iowa

124th FS 'Hawkeyes'	F-16C/D

138th FW / Tulsa International Airport, Oklahoma

125th FS 'Tulsa Vipers'	F-16C/D

140th Wing / Buckley AFB, Colorado

120th FS 'Cougars'	F-16C

150th FW / Kirtland AFB, New Mexico

188th FS 'Tacos'	F-16C/D

F-16 FIGHTER SQUADRONS

ARFC Tenth Air Force / NAS JRB Forth Worth/Carswell Field Texas

307th FS 'Stingers' / Langley AFB, Virginia

Det 1	F-16C/D	Shaw AFB, South Carolina
Det 2	F-16C/D	Hill AFB, Utah
Det 4	F-15C/D	Eglin AFB, Utah

926th Group / Nellis AFB, Nevada

706th FS	F-16C/D	Nellis AFB, Nevada

301st FW / NAS JRB Forth Worth/Carswell Field, Texas

457th FS 'Spads'	F-16C/D	

419th FW / Hill AFB, Utah

466th FS 'Diamondbacks'	F-16C/D	

482nd FW / Homestead ARB, Florida

93rd FS 'Makos'	F-16C/D	

Air Education and Training Command

56th FW Luke AFB, Arizona

21st FS 'Gamblers'	F-16A/B	
61st FS 'Top Dogs'	F-16C/D	
62nd FS 'Spikes'	F-16C/D	
63rd FS 'Panthers'	F-16C/D	
308th FS 'Emerald Kings'	F-16C/D	
309th FS 'Wild Ducks'	F-16C/D	
310th FS 'Top Hats'	F-16C/D	
425th FS 'Black Widows'	F-16C/D	

149th FW / Kelly Field, Lackland AFB, Texas

182nd FS 'Lone Star Gunfighters'	F-16C/D	

162nd FW / Tucson International Airport, Arizona

148th FS 'Kickin' Ass'	F-16E/F	
152nd FS 'Tigers'	F-16C/D	
195th FS 'Warhawks'	F-16C/D	

178th FW / Springfield-Beckley Municipal Airport, Ohio

162nd FS 'Sabres'	F-16C/D, F-16AM/BM

944th FW / Luke AFB, Arizona

301st FS 'Red Tail Devils'	F-16C/D

PACIFIC AIR FORCES

Fifth Air Force / Yokota AB, Japan

35th FW / Misawa AB, Japan

13th FS 'Panthers'	F-16C/D
14th FS 'Samurais'	F-16C/D

Seventh Air Force Osan AB, Korea

8th FW / Kunsan AB, Korea

35th FS 'Pantons'	F-16C/D
80th FS 'Juvats'	F-16C/D

51st FW / Osan AB, Korea

36th FS 'Flying Fiends'	F-16C/D

Eleventh Air Force Elmendorf AFB, Alaska

354th FW / Eielson AFB, Alaska

18th AGRS 'Blue Foxes'	F-16C/D

UNITED STATES AIR FORCE IN EUROPE

Third Air Force / Air Forces Europe / Ramstein AB, Germany

31st FW / Aviano AB, Italy

510th FS 'Buzzards'	F-16C/D
555th FS 'Triple Nickel'	F-16C/D

52nd FW / Spangdahlem, Germany

22nd FS 'Stingers'	F-16C/D
23rd FS 'Fighting Hawks'	F-16C/D

cyberspace combat component. Development, test and evaluation is the work of AFMC, its diverse test fleet headquartered at Wright-Patterson AFB, Ohio.

Special operations

Tasked with supporting unconventional warfare through the two wings of its Twenty-Third Air Force, AFSOC is headquartered at Hurlburt Field, Florida. Two special operations groups are additionally forward-deployed at bases in Japan and the UK.

AMC's 12 major air bases support its Eighteenth Air Force, providing airlift, tanker and aeromedical support. 18AF includes two Expeditionary Mobility Task Forces plus 13 active duty wings and one group, and 45 ANG and 24 AFRC wings.

Organic air support for overseas commands is handled by PACAF, headquartered at Hickam AFB,

▲ **Fairchild A-10 Thunderbolt II**
An A-10 takes off from Bagram Airfield, Afghanistan. The USAF maintains two Air Expeditionary Wings in Afghanistan: the 445th AEW at Bagram and the 451st AEW at Kandahar Airfield, with most assigned units deploying for four-month periods.

Hawaii, with four numbered air forces, and USAFE, headquartered at Ramstein AB, Germany, with two numbered air forces, one responsible for Africa.

Finally, ANG provides 87 flying wings across the U.S., units being assigned to ACC, AETC, AFSOC, AMC and PACAF, and also being committed to global operations. ANG aircraft represent around one-third of total strength, and cover a range of missions. AFRC, headquartered at Robins AFB, Georgia, controls three numbered air forces and 39 flying wings. It includes 'associate' units that operate aircraft in the possession of active duty units.

Specifications

Crew: 1	Dimensions: span 13.05m (42ft 9.75in); length
Powerplant: 2 x 106kN (23,810lb) thrust Pratt	19.43m (63ft 9in); height 5.63m (18ft 5in)
& Whitney F100-PW-100 turbofans	Weight: 25,424kg (56,000lb) loaded
Maximum speed: 2655km/h (1650mph)	Armament: 1 x 20mm (0.79in) M61A1 cannon,
Range: 1930km (1200 miles)	pylons with provision for up to 7620kg
Service ceiling: 30,500m (100,000ft)	(16,800lb) of stores

▼ **McDonnell Douglas F-15A Eagle, 199th Fighter Squadron, 154th Fighter Wing, Hickam AFB**
F-15A 77-083 wears the colours of the Hawaii ANG's 199th FS, and was upgraded to near-F-15C standard under the Multi-Stage Improvement Program (MSIP-II), which adds AIM-120 AMRAAM, among other upgrades.

serving with 10 squadrons. In order to avoid a 'fighter gap', the U.S. Navy is upgrading 'legacy' Hornets in order to extend aircraft service life. Designated successor to the F/A-18A/C is the F-35C, which is planned to attain initial operational capability in 2015, eventually equipping 18 squadrons.

Further new equipment is represented by the E-2D, which will replace E-2Cs in VAWs beginning in 2011.

Rotary fleet rationalization
As the U.S. Navy's latest helicopters, the MH-60R and MH-60S began to be assigned directly to CVWs in 2009, and 10 squadrons of each deployed type are

▲ **Grumman E-2C Hawkeye**
The U.S. Navy's 'eye in the sky', the E-2 serves with 10 front-line Airborne Command and Control Squadrons, including the 'Screwtops' of VAW-123, seen here embarked on board the aircraft carrier USS *Theodore Roosevelt.*

to be distributed among the CVWs by 2013. A further six 12-helicopter squadrons will be assigned to expeditionary duties and support of amphibious operations. These will operate from the new fleet of Littoral Combat Ships. Current Helicopter Anti-submarine Squadrons (HS) will become HSCs by 2012, adopting the MH-60S. Meanwhile, Helicopter Anti-submarine Light Squadrons (HSL) are becoming HSMs as they adopt the MH-60R.

AIRBORNE COMMAND AND CONTROL SQUADRONS

Airborne Command, Control, Logistics Wing – Naval Base Ventura County/NAS Point Mugu, California		
VAW-112 'Golden Hawks'	NAS Point Mugu, California	E-2C
VAW-113 'Black Hawks'	NAS Point Mugu, California	E-2C
VAW-115 'Liberty Bells'	NAF Atsugi, Japan	E-2C
VAW-116 'Sun Kings'	NAS Point Mugu, California	E-2C
VAW-117 'Wallbangers'	NAS Point Mugu, California	E-2C
VAW-120 (FRS) 'Greyhawks'	Chambers Field, NS Norfolk, Virginia	E-2C
VAW-121 'Bluetails'	Chambers Field, NS Norfolk, Virginia	E-2C
VAW-123 'Screwtops'	Chambers Field, NS Norfolk, Virginia	E-2C
VAW-124 'Bear Aces'	Chambers Field, NS Norfolk, Virginia	E-2C
VAW-125 'Tigertails'	Chambers Field, NS Norfolk, Virginia	E-2C
VAW-126 'Seahawks'	Chambers Field, NS Norfolk, Virginia	E-2C

The backbone of the land-based U.S. Navy is a fleet of 17 squadrons that between them field around 150 P-3C maritime patrol aircraft, 16 EP-3E ISR aircraft and 16 E-6B strategic communications aircraft. The P-8A will replace P-3Cs, with 84 on order for use by 12 active duty Patrol Squadrons (VP) from 2013.

Naval Reserve airlift

The U.S. Navy keeps a fleet of transport aircraft for logistical support, comprising C-9s, C-40s, C-130s (with KC-130Js replacing older models), C-20s and C-37s. Flown by Naval Reserve squadrons, these types routinely support overseas operations.

Instruction training is handled by the five Training Air Wings of Naval Air Training Command, with its HQ at NAS Corpus Christi, Texas, while conversion and tactics training takes place within Fleet Readiness Squadrons (FRS) assigned to the Atlantic and Pacific Fleets. The training community is undergoing modernization, with upgrades and new types coming on line. The planned fleet of 221 T-45s will be attained by 2012. The T-6B entered service in 2009 and will replace the T-34C by 2014. The rotary-wing training fleet is being rationalized, with TH-57B/Cs to be upgraded to a common TH-57D by 2014.

▲ **Sikorsky MH-60S Seahawk**

A rescue diver jumps out of an MH-60S while conducting SAR training in the Persian Gulf. The helicopter was operated by HSC-28 'Dragon Whales', which was embarked in the amphibious assault ship USS *Kearsarge* in support of the 'global war on terror'.

Commander, U.S. Naval Forces Southern Command maintains aircraft detachments at bases located in Central and South America, while Commander, U.S. Naval Forces Europe operates from European bases in support of the Sixth Fleet. Commander, U.S. Naval Forces Central Command is responsible for aircraft detachments in the Middle East (Fifth Fleet).

HELICOPTER MARITIME STRIKE SQUADRONS

Helicopter Maritime Strike Wing, Pacific – NAS North Island, California

HSL-37 'Easyriders'	MCAF Kaneohe Bay, Hawaii	SH-60B
HSL-43 'Battle Cats'	NAS North Island, California	SH-60B
HSL-45 'Wolfpack'	NAS North Island, California	SH-60B
HSL-49 'Scorpions'	NAS North Island, California	SH-60B
HSL-51 'Warlords'	NAF Atsugi, Japan	SH-60B/F
HSM-41 (FRS) 'Seahawks'	NAS North Island, California	MH-60R
HSM-47 'Sabrehawks'	NAS North Island, California	MH-60R
HSM-71 'Raptors'	NAS North Island, California	MH-60R

Helicopter Maritime Strike Wing, Atlantic – Naval Station Mayport, Florida

HSL-40 (FRS) 'Airwolves'	NS Mayport, Florida	SH-60B
HSL-42 'Proud Warriors'	NS Mayport, Florida	SH-60B
HSL-44 'Swamp Fox'	NS Mayport, Florida	SH-60B
HSL-46 'Grandmasters'	NS Mayport, Florida	SH-60B
HSL-48 'Vipers'	NS Mayport. Florida	SH-60B
HSL-60 'Jaguars'	NS Mayport, Florida	SH-60B
HSM-70 'Spartans'	NAS Jacksonville, Florida	MH-60R

HELICOPTER SEA COMBAT SQUADRONS

Helicopter Sea Combat Wing, Pacific – NAS North Island, California

HS-4 'Black Knights'	NAS North Island, California	SH-60F, HH-60H
HS-6 'Indians'	NAS North Island, California	SH-60F, HH-60H
HS-8 'Eightballers'	NAS North Island, California	SH-60F, HH-60H
HS-10 (FRS) 'Warhawks'	NAS North Island, California	SH-60F, HH-60H
HS-14 'Chargers'	NAF Atsugi, Japan	SH-60F, HH-60H
HSC-3 (FRS) 'Merlins'	NAS North Island, California	MH-60S
HSC-12 'Golden Falcons'	NAS North Island, California	MH-60S
HSC-21 'Blackjacks'	NAS North Island, California	MH-60S
HSC-23 'Wildcards'	NAS North Island, California	MH-60S
HSC-25 'Island Knights'	Andersen AFB, Guam	MH-60S
HSC-25 Det. 6	MCAS Iwakuni, Japan	MH-60S
HSC-85 'Golden Gators'	NAS North Island, California	MH-60S

Helicopter Sea Combat Wing, Atlantic – Chambers Field, Naval Station Norfolk, Virginia

HM-14 'Vanguard'	Chambers Field, NS Norfolk, Virginia	MH-53E
HM-14 Det. 1	Pohang AB, Republic of Korea	MH-53E
HM-15 'Black Hawks'	NAS Corpus Christi, Texas	MH-53E
HS-3 'Tridents'	NAS Jacksonville, Florida	SH-60F, HH-60H
HS-5 'Night Dippers'	NAS Jacksonville, Florida	SH-60F, HH-60H
HS-7 'Shamrocks'	NAS Jacksonville, Florida	SH-60F, HH-60H
HS-11 'Dragonslayers'	NAS Jacksonville, Florida	SH-60F, HH-60H
HS-15 'Red Lions'	NAS Jacksonville, Florida	SH-60F, HH-60H
HSC-2 (FRS) 'Fleet Angels'	Chambers Field, NS Norfolk, Virginia	MH-60S
HSC-22 'Sea Knights'	Chambers Field, NS Norfolk, Virginia	MH-60S
HSC-26 'Chargers'	Chambers Field, NS Norfolk, Virginia	MH-60S
HSC-28 'Dragon Whales'	Chambers Field, NS Norfolk, Virginia	MH-60S
HSC-84 'Red Wolves'	Chambers Field, NS Norfolk, Virginia	HH-60H

Specifications

Crew: 5–8

Powerplant: 2 x 64.5kN (14,500lb) thrust Pratt
& Whitney JT8D-9 turbofan engines

Maximum speed: 907km/h (562mph)

Range: 2388km (1480 miles)

Service ceiling: 11,000m (37,000ft)

Dimensions: span 28.47m (93ft 5in); length
36.37m (119ft 3in); height 8.38m (27ft 6in)

Weight: 50,000kg (114,000lb) loaded

Rate of climb: 900m per min. (3000ft per min)

▼ Douglas C-9B Skytrain II, VR-61 'Islanders', NAS Whidbey Island

Named City of Oak Harbor, C-9B BuNo. 164608 is assigned to Fleet Logistics Support Squadron 61 (VR-61), one of four such US Navy Reserve squadrons flying the Skytrain II.

Specifications

Crew: 3–4

Powerplant: 2 x 1210kW (1622hp) General
Electric T700-GE-700 turboshaft engines

Maximum speed: 296km/h (476mph)

Range: 964km (600 miles)

Service ceiling: 5790m (19,000ft)

Dimensions: rotor diameter 16.36m (53ft 8in);
length 17.38m (57ft); height 5.13m (16ft 9in)

Weight: 9979kg (22,000lb) loaded

Armament: MK-54 air-launched torpedoes,
Hellfire misssiles and usually 2 x 12.7mm
(0.5in) machine guns

▼ Sikorsky MH-60R Seahawk, HSM-71 'Raptors', USS *John C. Stennis*

MH-60R BuNo. 166520 is seen assigned to USS *John C. Stennis*, serving as part of CVW-9. The unit is shore-based at NAS North Island, San Diego. HMS-71 was the first fleet squadron to receive the MH-60R.

PATROL AND RECONNAISSANCE SQUADRONS

Patrol and Reconnaissance Wing Two – MCB Hawaii/MCAF Kaneohe Bay, Hawaii		
VPU-2 'Wizards'	MCAF Kaneohe Bay, Hawaii	P-3C
VP-4 'Skinny Dragons'	MCAF Kaneohe Bay, Hawaii	P-3C
VP-9 'Golden Eagles'	MCAF Kaneohe Bay, Hawaii	P-3C
VP-47 'Golden Swordsmen'	MCAF Kaneohe Bay, Hawaii	P-3C
Patrol and Reconnaissance Wing Ten – NAS Whidbey Island, Washington		
VP-1 'Screaming Eagles'	NAS Whidbey Island, Washington	P-3C
VP-40 'Marlins'	NAS Whidbey Island, Washington	P-3C
VP-46 'Gray Knights'	NAS Whidbey Island, Washington	P-3C
VP-69 (FRU) 'Totems'	NAS Whidbey Island, Washington	P-3C
VQ-1 'World Watchers'	NAS Whidbey Island, Washington	EP-3E, P-3C
VQ-2 'Batmen'	NAS Whidbey Island, Washington	EP-3E, P-3C
Patrol and Reconnaissance Group – Naval Station Norfolk, Virginia		
VP-30 (FRS) 'Pro's Nest'	NAS Jacksonville, Florida	P-3C
Patrol and Reconnaissance Wing Five – NAS Brunswick, Maine		
VP-8 'Tigers'	NAS Brunswick, Maine	P-3C
VP-10 'Red Lancers'	NAS Brunswick, Maine	P-3C
VP-26 'Tridents'	NAS Brunswick, Maine	P-3C
VPU-1 'Old Buzzards'	NAS Brunswick, Maine	P-3C
Patrol and Reconnaissance Wing Eleven – NAS Jacksonville, Florida		
VP-5 'Mad Foxes'	NAS Jacksonville, Florida	P-3C
VP-16 'War Eagles'	NAS Jacksonville, Florida	P-3C
VP-45 'Pelicans'	NAS Jacksonville, Florida	P-3C
VP-62 (FRU) 'Broadarrows'	NAS Jacksonville, Florida	P-3C

United States

UNITED STATES MARINE CORPS

With a long tradition of expeditionary warfare and integrated air, land and sea operations, the USMC maintains a fleet of more than 1200 fixed-wing aircraft and helicopters.

THE AIRCRAFT OF the USMC operate from both land bases and warships and are organized within four air wings as part of the U.S. Navy's operating forces and under the command of the Commandant of the Marine Corps. USMC air assets can be combined with Marine ground forces to create rapidly deployable Marine Air Ground Task Forces (MAGTF) for a variety of missions, with airpower the responsibility of the Aviation Combat Element (ACE).

The USMC is divided into Atlantic and Pacific Fleet Marine Forces, each headed by a Marine Forces Commander. Each MARFOR has three numbered Marine Expeditionary Forces (MEF) and component Marine Expeditionary Brigades (MEB). The MEF comprises one or more Marine Divisions, Marine Air Wings (MAW) and Marine Logistics Groups (MLG). The MEB is smaller, with a reinforced infantry regiment, Marine Air Group (MAG) and Combat Logistics Regiment (CLR). There is also a Marine Forces Reserve Commander, albeit without permanent MEFs or MEBs.

Reflecting the demands of overseas operations, the USMC is increasing in size, with the aim of

▲ **Sikorsky CH-53E Super Stallion**

A CH-53E from Marine Heavy Helicopter Squadron 464 (HMH-464) approaches a USAF HC-130P to refuel over Djibouti. In 2008 the USMC operated 152 CH-53Es, with plans to replace these with 200 CH-53Ks from 2015. The new CH-53K has double the lift capacity of the CH-53E.

I MARINE EXPEDITIONARY FORCE – MCB CAMP PENDLETON, CALIFORNIA

3rd Marine Aircraft Wing – MCAS Miramar, California

Marine Aircraft Group Eleven – MCAS Miramar, California

VMFAT-101 (FRS) 'Sharpshooters'	F/A-18A/B/C/D
VMFA(AW)-121 'Green Knights'	F/A-18D
VMFA(AW)-225 'Vikings'	F/A-18D
VMFA-232 'Red Devils'	F/A-18A+
VMFA-314 'Black Knights'	F/A-18C
VMFA-323 'Death Rattlers'	F/A-18C
VMGR-352 'Raiders'	KC-130J

Marine Aircraft Group Thirteen – MCAS Yuma, Arizona

VMA-211 'Avengers'	AV-8B/AV-8B+
VMA-214 'Black Sheep'	AV-8B/AV-8B+
VMA-311 'Tomcats'	AV-8B/AV-8B+
VMA-513 'Nightmares'	AV-8B/AV-8B+

Marine Aircraft Group Sixteen – MCAS Miramar, California

HMM-161 'Grey Hawks'	MV-22B
HMM-163 'Ridgerunners'	CH-46E
HMM-165 'White Knights'	CH-46E
HMM-166 'Sea Elks'	CH-46E
HMH-361 'Flying Tigers'	CH-53E
HMH-462 'Heavy Haulers'	CH-53E
HMH-465 'Warhorses'	CH-53E
HMH-466 'Wolfpack'	CH-53E

Marine Aircraft Group Three Nine – MCAS Camp Pendleton, California

HMM(T)-164 (FRS) 'Knightriders'	CH-46E
HMLA-169 'Vipers'	UH-1N, AH-1W
HMLA-267 'Stingers'	UH-1N/Y, AH-1W
HMM-268 'Red Dragons'	CH-46E
HMLA/T-303 (FRS) 'Atlas'	HH-1N, UH-1N/Y, AH-1W/Z
HMM-364 'Purple Foxes'	CH-46E
HMLA-367 'Scarface'	UH-1N/Y, AH-1W
HMLA-369 'Gunfighters'	UH-1N, AH-1W

▲ Bell-Boeing MV-22B Osprey

MV-22B Ospreys of Marine Medium Tilt-rotor Squadron 264 take part in a firepower demonstration. The Osprey first deployed to Iraq with VMM-263 in 2007. The latest Block C standard Osprey features weather radar, improved situational awareness and forward firing countermeasures.

establishing three Marine Expeditionary Forces (MEF) of a similar size by 2011.

Three active component MAWs are backed up by a reserve MAW. The MAW includes a Headquarters, various MAGs, a Marine Air Control Group and a Marine Wing Support Group (MWSG).

A MAW can deploy as an ACE for an MEF, or otherwise provide units to support the MAGTF. A MAW or MAG can be deployed alone, but is typically reinforced to provide balanced support to a MEB. Seven Marine Expeditionary Units (MEU) can deploy as Expeditionary Strike Groups (ESG) or Amphibious Ready Groups (ARG) and are assigned with an ACE based around a reinforced Marine Medium Tilt-rotor or Helicopter Squadron.

The USMC component of U.S. Joint Forces Command, Marine Corps Forces Command, headquartered at NS Norfolk, Virginia, incorporates the II MEF and the 2nd MAW. Marine Forces Pacific, with its headquarters at MCB H. M. Smith, Hawaii, includes the I MEF and III MEF and their respective 3rd MAW and 1st MAW. Headquartered at NAS New Orleans JRB, Louisiana, Marine Forces Reserve is responsible for the 4th MAW, with its four MAGs.

Tilt-rotor revolution

The most significant new aviation asset employed by the USMC is the MV-22B tilt-rotor, which has

II MARINE EXPEDITIONARY FORCE – MCB CAMP LEJEUNE, NORTH CAROLINA

2nd Marine Aircraft Wing – MCAS Cherry Point, North Carolina

Marine Aircraft Group Fourteen – MCAS Cherry Point, North Carolina		Marine Aircraft Group Two Nine – MCAS New River, North Carolina	
VMAQ-1 'Banshees'	EA-6B	VMM-162 'Golden Eagles'	MV-22B
VMAQ-2 'Death Jesters'	EA-6B	VMM-263 'Thunder Eagles'	MV-22B
VMAQ-3 'Moon Dogs'	EA-6B	VMM-365 'Blue Knights'	MV-22B
VMAQ-4 'Seahawks'	EA-6B	HMLA-269 'Gunrunners'	UH-1N, AH-1W
VMAT-203 (FRS) 'Hawks'	AV-8B, TAV-8B	HMLA-467 'Sabre Rattlers'	UH-1N, AH-1W
VMA-223 'Bulldogs'	AV-8B	HMT-302 (FRS) 'Phoenix'	CH-53E
VMA-231 'Ace of Spades'	AV-8B	HMH-366 'Hammerheads'	CH-53E
VMA-542 'Flying Tigers'	AV-8B	HMH-464 'Condors'	CH-53E
VMGR-252 'Otis'	KC-130J	**Marine Aircraft Group Three One – MCAS Beaufort, South Carolina**	
Marine Aircraft Group Two Six – MCAS New River, North Carolina		VMFA-115 'Silver Eagles'	F/A-18A+
HMLA-167 'Warriors	UH-1N, AH-1W	VMFA-122 'Werewolves'	F/A-18C
VMMT-204 (FRS) 'Raptors'	MV-22B	VMFA(AW)-224 'Bengals'	F/A-18D/C
VMM-261 'Raging Bulls'	MV-22B	VMFA-251 'Thunderbolts'	F/A-18C
HMM-264 'Black Knights'	MV-22B	VMFA-312 'Checkerboards'	F/A-18A+
VMM-266 'Fighting Griffins'	MV-22B	VMFA(AW)-533 'Hawks'	F/A-18D
HMH-461 'Ironhorse'	CH-53E		

Specifications

Crew: 2

Powerplant: 2 x 1300kW (1680hp) General
  Electric T700 turboshaft

Maximum speed: 352km/h (218mph)

Range: 587km (218 miles)

Service ceiling: 3720m (12,200ft)

Dimensions: rotor diameter 14.6m (46ft); length
  13.6m (44ft 7in); height 4.1m (13ft 5in)

Weight: 4953kg (14,750lb) loaded

Armament: 1 x 20mm (0.78in) M196 cannon;
  8 x 70mm (2.75in) Zuni rockets; 8 x TOW
  missiles; 2 x anti-aircraft missiles

▲ Bell AH-1W Super Cobra, U.S. Marine Corps

Armed with AGM-114 Hellfire missiles, this AH-1W is typical of the type in USMC service. While the older 'Whiskey' Cobras are being upgraded, the USMC is also due to receive the new AH-1Z, the first examples of which will serve with west coast squadrons at MCAS Camp Pendleton. Meanwhile, the USMC inventory includes just over 160 AH-1Ws, and the type has seen widespread combat use in Operations Iraqi Freedom and Enduring Freedom.

entirely replaced the CH-46E among east coast units. By 2017, the MV-22B will be in use with 19 active and four reserve squadrons, and the USMC hopes to acquire 360 examples. The USMC aims to introduce a new heavylift helicopter, the CH-53K, to replace the CH-53D/E in 10 active duty squadrons and one reserve squadron, with service entry planned for 2015.

The upgraded UH-1Y attained operational status in 2008. Developed alongside the UH-1Y, the AH-1Z is slated to enter operational service in 2011. The USMC hopes to field 226 AH-1Zs and 123 UH-1Ys in 10 active squadrons and one reserve squadron.

The arrival of the short take-off and vertical landing (STOVL) F-35B will see the USMC replace its fleet of F/A-18s, AV-8Bs and EA-6Bs. Of these 'legacy' types, the F/A-18 will remain in use until 2023, although of the fleet total of around 235 aircraft, the two-seat F/A-18D will be disposed of by

Specifications

Crew: 2–3

Powerplant: 2 x 1150kW (1546shp) GE T700-GE-
  401C turboshaft

Maximum speed: 304km/h (189mph)

Range: 241km (130 nautical miles)

Service ceiling 6100m (20,000ft)

Dimensions: rotor diameter 14.88m
  (48ft 10in); length 17.78m (58ft 4in);
  height 4.5m (14ft 7in)

Weight: 8390kg (18,500lb) loaded

Armament: 2 x 70mm (2.75in) Hydra 70 rockets,
  2 x mounts for 7.62mm (0.3in) M240D MGs

▲ Bell UH-1Y, HMLA/T-303 'Atlas', MCAS Camp Pendleton

UH-1Y Bu No. 167796 is operated by Marine Light Attack Helicopter Training Squadron 303, which prepares Marine aviators for the 'Huey' and Cobra communities. Part of the 3rd Marine Air Wing, the California-based unit is equipped with examples of the HH-1N, UH-1N/Y and AH-1W/Z.

III MARINE EXPEDITIONARY FORCE – MCB CAMP COURTNEY, OKINAWA, JAPAN

1st Marine Aircraft Wing – MCB Camp Foster, Okinawa, Japan

Marine Aircraft Group Twelve – MCAS Iwakuni, Honshu, Japan

VMA-211	AV-8B
VMFA(AW)-242 'Bats'	F/A-18D
VMFA(AW)-224	F/A-18D
VMFA(AW)-225	F/A-18D
VMAQ-*	EA-6B

Marine Aircraft Group Three Six – MCAS Futenma, Okinawa, Japan

HMM-262 'Flying Tigers'	CH-46E
HMM-265 'Dragons'	CH-46E
HMH-*	CH-53
HMLA-*	AH-1W, UH-1N
VMGR-152 'The Sumos'	KC-130J

* UDP unit

Marine Aircraft Group Two Four – MCB Hawaii/MCAF Kaneohe Bay, Hawaii

HMH-362 'Ugly Angels'	CH-53D
HMH-363 'Red Lions'	CH-53D
HMH-463 'Pegasus'	CH-53D

▲ **McDonnell Douglas F/A-18A+ Hornet**

A Hornet from Marine Fighter Attack Squadron 115 lands at Korat in Thailand. Pending the arrival of the F-35, the USMC is upgrading around 25 Hornets to F/A-18C+ standard, with helmet-mounted sights, AIM-9X missiles, modernized cockpit displays, and improved countermeasures.

2018. Under the Tactical Air Integration initiative, USMC F/A-18 units deploy aboard U.S. Navy carriers. Around 145 AV-8s remain in use and a programme of upgrades will keep the survivors in service until 2021, although retirements are to begin in 2013. The EA-6B will continue in use until 2019.

The first of three F-35B fleet readiness squadrons was scheduled to take its first aircraft in September 2010, with initial operational capability to follow in 2012. However, the programme has suffered from serious delays. By 2024 the fighter will be in service with 21 operational, three fleet readiness and one test squadron. The USMC plans to acquire a total of 420 F-35Bs, some of which will receive the Next Generation Jammer in order to supersede the EA-6B.

The USMC is responsible for Presidential airlift, for which it was waiting on a replacement for its VH-3Ds and VH-60Ns, operated by HMX-1. The planned new helicopter, the VH-71, was cancelled in 2009. Existing equipment will instead be upgraded.

Specifications

Crew: 1

Powerplant: 1 x 105.8kN (23,800lb) Rolls-Royce Pegasus vectored thrust turbofan

Maximum speed: 1065km/h (661mph)

Range: 277km (172 miles)

Service ceiling: 15,240m (50,000ft)

Dimensions: span 9.25m (30ft 4in); length

14.12m (46ft 4in); height 3.55m (11ft 7.75in)

Weight: 14,061kg (31,000lb) loaded

Armament: 1 x 25mm (0.98in) GAU-12U cannon, six external hardpoints with provision for up to 7711kg (17,000lb) (Short take-off) or 3175kg (7000lb) (Vertical take-off) of stores

▼ **Boeing AV-8B+ Harrier II, VMA-231 'Ace of Spades', MCAS Cherry Point**

Marine Attack Squadron 231 is one of three front-line Harrier II units within Marine Aircraft Group 14 (MAG-14), and the 2nd Marine Aircraft Wing (2nd MAW), the major USMC aviation unit on the east coast.

United States

UNITED STATES ARMY

Recent changes to the structure of the U.S. Army mean it is now better suited to expeditionary warfare, joint operations, 'plug and play' structuring, and long-term overseas deployments.

THE U.S. ARMY has been undergoing far-reaching changes since 2004, shifting from its previous divisional structure to one based on brigades.

U.S. Army Aviation consists of around 287,800 active and 26,900 reserve personnel. The basic force structure is the brigade, fielded either as a Combat Aviation Brigade (CAB) or a Theater Aviation Brigade (TAB), both of which can be tailored to meet particular operational demands. The CAB supports five battalions and can be used in support of up to four Brigade Combat Teams (BCT). The CAB is available in four configurations: heavy, medium, light and Aviation Expeditionary Brigade (AEB). The AEB is assigned to six of eight Army National Guard (ARNG) divisions.

The four different CAB configurations differ chiefly in their mix of reconnaissance and attack assets. Heavy division CABs have two attack/reconnaissance battalions (ARB), medium division CABs have one ARB and a cavalry squadron, the light variant has two cavalry squadrons, and the AEB maintains one ARB. Formations with only a single ARB are additionally equipped with a Security and Support Battalion (SSB), with a strength of three companies, although this is to be increased to four through the addition of an air ambulance company. Each CAB has a General Support Aviation Battalion (GSAB) attached, this including a command aviation

U.S. ARMY AVIATION FIXED-WING INVENTORY			
C-12C/D	14/12	C-31A	2
RC-12D	9	UC-35A	20
RC-12H	6	UC-35B	8
JRC-12G	1	C-37A	2
C-12J	2	C-37B	1
RC-12K	7	C-41A	2
RC-12N	14	O-2A	2
RC-12P	9	EO-5C	8
RC-12Q	3	TO-5C	1
C-12R/V	29	T-34C	4
C-12U	71	UV-18A	4
C-20E	1	Cessna 182	2
C-20F	1	Beech 1900D	1
C/JC-23A	3	DHC-7-102	1
C-23C	43	King Air 300	11
C-26B/E	13		

company, a heavy helicopter company and an air ambulance company.

Under the new brigade structure, two Theater Aviation Commands (TACs) are each responsible for a pair of TABs primarily equipped with CH-47 and UH-60 transport helicopters, as well as fixed-wing aircraft and medevac helicopters. TABs also have GSABs attached, although the latter are provided with two, rather than one, air ambulance company.

The 160th Aviation (Special Operations) (Airborne) provides air support for unconventional warfare. Essentially equivalent to a brigade, the 160th SOAR has approximately 2100 personnel and 190 aircraft within four battalions, three of which are dedicated to airlift (each with two heavy helicopter companies and one assault helicopter company, or with three heavy helicopter companies), plus one battalion with single light attack and light transport companies and two assault companies.

U.S. ARMY AVIATION HELICOPTER INVENTORY			
UH-1H/V	123	HH-60L	31
AH/MH-6M	51	UH-60L	664
CH-47D	309	HH-60M	11
CH-47F	65	UH-60M	31
MH-47E	6	AH-64A	155
MH-47G	50	AH-64D (Block I)	252
OH-58A/C	276	AH-64D (Block II)	280
OH-58D	339	TH-67A	181
UH-60A	954		

UNITED STATES

Specifications

Crew: 3

Powerplant: 2 x 3460kW (4640hp) Rolls-Royce
AE2100-D2A turboprop

Maximum speed: 602km/h (374mph)

Range: 1852km (1151 miles)

Service ceiling: 9144m (30,000ft)

Dimensions: span 28.7m (94ft 2in);
length 22.7m (74ft 6in); height 9.64m
(31ft 8in)

Weight: 30,500kg (67,241lb) loaded

Propellers: 6-bladed 4.15m (13ft 7in)

Dowty Propeller 391/6-132-F/10

▼ Alenia C-27J Spartan, Alaska ARNG, Redstone Arsenal, Alabama

Acquired as a replacement for the C-23C Sherpa among the U.S. Army's fleet of over 250 fixed-wing aircraft, the first C-27J was delivered in October 2008. The U.S. Army planned to purchase over 50 C-27Js, although the Department of Defense's 2010 budget request called for transfer of the C-27J to the USAF.

Specifications

Crew: 2

Powerplant: 1 x 1300kW (1800shp) Lycoming
T53-L-703 turboshaft

Maximum speed: 277km/h (172mph)

Range: 510km (315 miles)

Service ceiling: 3720m (12,200ft)

Dimensions: rotor diameter 13.6m (44ft)
length 16.1m (53ft); height 4.1m (13ft 5in)

Weight: 4500kg (10,000lb) loaded

Armament: 1 x 20mm (0.78in) M197 cannon;
7–19 x 70mm (2.75in) Hydra 70 rockets;
4 or 8 x TOW missiles

▼ Bell AH-1F Cobra, N Troop, 4th Squadron, 2nd Armored Cavalry Regiment, Iraq

Named Sand Shark, 67-15643 was a modernized Cobra that served during Operation Desert Storm in 1991. In 1999 the U.S. Army retired the AH-1F from the active duty inventory, final operator being the 25th Infantry Division (Light).

Specifications

Crew: 3–4

Powerplant: 2 x 1210kW (1622hp) General
Electric T700-GE-700 turboshaft engines

Maximum speed: 296km/h (476mph)

Range: 964km (600 miles)

Service ceiling: 5790m (19,000ft)

Dimensions: rotor diameter 16.36m (53ft 8in);
length 17.38m (57ft); height 5.13m (16ft 9in)

Weight: 9979kg (22,000lb) loaded

Armament: MK-54 air-launched torpedoes,
Hellfire misssiles and usually 2 x 12.7mm
(0.5in) machine guns

▼ Sikorsky EH-60A Quick Fix II, 1st Battalion, 212th Aviation Regiment 'Crusaders'

The EH-60A provided the U.S. Army with an organic electronic countermeasures (ECM) capability, the helicopter having an external antenna designed to intercept and jam enemy communications.

U.S. ARMY IN KOREA

Eighth U.S. Army, Korea – Yongsan Barracks, Seoul, Korea

2nd Infantry Division Camp Red Cloud, Uijeongbu, Korea

2nd Combat Aviation Brigade Desiderio AAF, Camp Humphreys, Pyeongtaek, Korea

1-2nd AVN	Butts AAF, Fort Carson, Colorado	AH-64D
2-2nd AVN	Seoul K-16 AB, Korea	UH-60A/L
3-2nd AVN	Desiderio AAF, Camp Humphreys, Pyongtaek, Korea	UH-60A, CH-47D, C-12J/U
4-2nd AVN	Desiderio AAF, Camp Humphreys, Pyongtaek, Korea	AH-64D

160TH AVIATION (SPECIAL OPERATIONS) (AIRBORNE), FORT CAMPBELL, KENTUCKY

1-160th AVN	Campbell AAF, Fort Campbell, Kentucky	AH/MH-6M, MH-60K/L
2-160th AVN	Campbell AAF, Fort Campbell, Kentucky	MH-47G
3-160th AVN	Hunter AAF, Savannah, Georgia	MH-47G, MH-60K/L
4-160th AVN	Gray AAF, Fort Lewis, Washington	MH-47G, MH-60K/L

There are three Regimental Aviation Squadrons (RAS), two of which are configured as air cavalry squadrons (ACS). The latest ACS consists of three reconnaissance/attack troops (OH-58Ds or AH-64Ds) and an assault helicopter troop (UH-60s). Of the five Military Intelligence Battalions (MIBN), three are based around one company of RC-12s, and one of RQ-5 UAVs. Of the other two MIBNs, one is based in Korea with two fixed-wing companies, while the other is stationed in the U.S., with one company.

New equipment

The U.S. Army is forging ahead with various re-equipment programmes. The Armed Reconnaissance Helicopter programme to replace the OH-58D scout/attack helicopter was axed in 2008, and as many as 368 Kiowa Warriors will now have to be upgraded. More successful is the UH-72A, which entered service in 2006 in the Light Utility Helicopter role, replacing UH-1s and OH-58A/Cs. Meanwhile the AH-64D continues to be built and produced via upgrade of AH-64As, with a target of 718 D-models to be fielded by 2013. Both the UH-60 and CH-47 also remain in production. The latest MH-47G upgrade entered service in 2005, followed by the newly built CH-47F two years later. Until 2019 the U.S. Army will receive 262 remanufactured CH-47Fs and 190 new-production models. The latest UH-60M variant was introduced in 2006, followed by the HH-60M air ambulance in 2008.

Plans call for 1235 M-models, including 303 HH-60Ms and 72 MH-60Ms to replace the MH-60K/L.

Over 250 fixed-wing aircraft serve in logistics support and electronic roles. Most numerous is the C-12 family, serving in a variety of roles. Eventually, both C-12 and C-26 will be replaced by 116 Future Utility Aircraft (FUA), while RC-12s and EO-5Cs will be replaced by an Aerial Common Sensor (ACS).

As a major operator of UAVs, the U.S. Army fields the RQ-7 and is replacing its RQ/MQ-5s with the MQ-1C. The U.S. Army also plans to operate MQ-8B vertical take-off and landing UAVs.

▲ **Beechcraft C-12 Huron**

The C-12 transport fleet includes around 100 aircraft, among them C-12U, C-12R and upgraded C-12V aircraft. Some C-12R/Vs and C-12C/Ds have been modified for Reconnaissance, Surveillance, Targeting and Acquisition (RSTA) missions.

Canada

CANADIAN ARMED FORCES

The world's second-largest country, with the world's longest coastline, the defence of Canada is entrusted to the Canadian Armed Forces, established as a unified formation in February 1968.

CANADA IS A member of both NATO and the North American Aerospace Defense Command (NORAD) and is a regular participant in UN peacekeeping missions.

The air component of the Canadian Armed Forces is led by the Commander of Air Command and the Chief of the Air Staff, with headquarters in Ottawa. Operational command and control of the Air Command in Canada and overseas is the responsibility of the Commander of 1 Canadian Air Division (1 Cdn Air Div) and Canadian NORAD Region, who maintains headquarters in Winnipeg.

Air Command fields a total of 13 wings across Canada, equipped with over 330 aircraft.

1 Wing is responsible for the CH-146 helicopter and includes six tactical helicopter and training squadrons located at bases throughout Canada. 3 Wing is a multi-role formation, while 4 Wing combines combat forces, a helicopter unit, and also provides training for fighter pilots. Canada maintains a SAR squadron at 5 Wing, Goose Bay, where NATO tactical flying training is conducted and the same base also hosts regular CF-188 detachments.

Air mobility and SAR are the tasks of 8 Wing, while 9 Wing provides SAR assets for Newfoundland and Labrador, flying the CH-149 helicopter.

Naval assignments

Naval aviation is embodied in 12 Wing, which provides detachments of CH-124s for Canadian warships. The maritime mission is also undertaken by 14 Wing, whose CP-140s conduct surveillance missions over the Atlantic, and support SAR taskings. Similar duties are conducted by 19 Wing, responsible for maritime patrol over the Pacific Ocean, as well as SAR and tactical training.

15 Wing is home to the NATO Flying Training in Canada (NFTC) programme, as well as Canada's Snowbirds aerobatic demonstration team. 16 Wing is the largest training wing, but does not have aircraft assigned to its various schools. Another training formation, 17 Wing, includes three squadrons plus ground schools and provides facilities for the Central Flying School. Finally, 22 Wing at North Bay is responsible for surveillance and early warning support of the aerospace defence of North America.

Specifications

Crew: 1	length 17.07m (56ft); height 4.66m
Powerplant: 2 x 71.1kN (16,000lb) General	(15ft 3.5in)
Electric F404-GE-400 turbofans	Weight: 25,401kg (56,000lb) loaded
Maximum speed: 1912km/h (1183mph)	Armament: 1 x 20mm (0.78in) M61A1 Vulcan
Combat radius: 740km (460 miles)	six-barrel rotary cannon with 570 rounds, nine
Service ceiling: 15,240m (50,000ft)	external hardpoints with provision for up to
Dimensions: span 11.43m (37ft 6in);	7711kg (17,000lb) of stores

▼ **McDonnell Douglas CF-188A Hornet, 425 Squadron, CFB Bagotville**

The backbone of Canada's combat fleet is the CF-188, of which an original 138 examples were acquired. The force has been greatly reduced, and now serves with just three squadrons, 80 survivors having received a mid-life upgrade.

CANADIAN ARMED FORCES FLYING SQUADRONS

1 Wing CFB Kingston, Ontario

Squadron	Aircraft	Base
400 Squadron	CH-146 Griffon	CFB Borden, Ontario
403 Squadron	CH-146 Griffon	CFB Gagetown, New Brunswick
408 Squadron	CH-146 Griffon	CFB Edmonton, Alberta
427 Squadron	CH-146 Griffon	CFB Petawawa, Ontario
430 Squadron	CH-146 Griffon	CFB Valcartier, Quebec
438 Squadron	CH-146 Griffon	St Hubert, Quebec

3 Wing CFB Bagotville, Quebec

Squadron	Aircraft	Base
425 Squadron	CF-188 Hornet	CFB Bagotville, Quebec
439 Squadron	CH-146 Griffon	CFB Bagotville, Quebec

4 Wing CFB Cold Lake, Alberta

Squadron	Aircraft	Base
409 Squadron	CF-188 Hornet	CFB Cold Lake, Alberta
410 Squadron	CF-188 Hornet	CFB Cold Lake, Alberta
417 Squadron	CH-146 Griffon	CFB Cold Lake, Alberta
419 Squadron	CT-155 Hawk	CFB Cold Lake, Alberta

5 Wing CFB Goose Bay, Newfoundland

Squadron	Aircraft	Base
444 Squadron	CH-146 Griffon	CFB Goose Bay, Newfoundland

8 Wing CFB Trenton, Ontario

Squadron	Aircraft	Base
412 Squadron	CC-144 Challenger	Ottawa, Ontario
424 Squadron	CH-149 Cormorant, CC-130 Hercules	CFB Trenton, Ontario
426 Squadron	CC-130 Hercules, CC-144 Challenger	CFB Trenton, Ontario
429 Squadron	CC-177 Globemaster III	CFB Trenton, Ontario
436 Squadron	CC-130 Hercules	CFB Trenton, Ontario
437 Squadron	CC-150 Polaris	CFB Trenton, Ontario

9 Wing CFB Gander, Newfoundland

Squadron	Aircraft	Base
103 Squadron	CH-149 Cormorant	CFB Gander, Newfoundland

12 Wing CFB Shearwater, Nova Scotia

Squadron	Aircraft	Base
406 Squadron	CH-124 Sea King	CFB Shearwater, Nova Scotia
423 Squadron	CH-124 Sea King	CFB Shearwater, Nova Scotia
443 Squadron	CH-124 Sea King	Victoria IAP, British Columbia

14 Wing CFB Greenwood, Nova Scotia

Squadron	Aircraft	Base
404 Squadron	CP-140 Aurora/Arcturus	CFB Greenwood, Nova Scotia
405 Squadron	CP-140 Aurora/Arcturus	CFB Greenwood, Nova Scotia
413 Squadron	CC-130 Hercules, CH-149 Cormorant	CFB Greenwood, Nova Scotia

15 Wing CFB Moose Jaw, Saskatchewan

Squadron	Aircraft	Base
431 Squadron 'Snowbirds'	CT-114 Tutor	CFB Moose Jaw, Saskatchewan

17 Wing CFB Winnipeg, Manitoba

Squadron	Aircraft	Base
402 Squadron	CC-142 Dash 8	CFB Winnipeg, Manitoba
435 Squadron	CC-130 Hercules	CFB Winnipeg, Manitoba
440 Squadron	CC-138 Twin Otter	Yellowknife, Northwest Territories

19 Wing CFB Comox, British Columbia

Squadron	Aircraft	Base
407 Squadron	CP-140 Aurora	CFB Comox, British Columbia
442 Squadron	CC-115 Buffalo, CH-149 Cormorant	CFB Comox, British Columbia

CANADA

Specifications

Crew: 3

Powerplant: 2 x 671 kW (900hp) Pratt & Whitney Canada PT6T-3D turboshafts

Maximum speed: 260km/h (160mph)

Range: 656km (405 miles)

Capacity: 10 troops or 6 stretchers

Dimensions: rotor diameter 14m (45ft 11in); length 17.1m (56ft 1in); height 4.6m (15ft 1in)

Weight: 5355kg (11,900lb)

Armament: 1 x 7.62mm (0.29in) C6 GPMG; 1 x 7.62mm (0.29in) Dillon Aero M134D 'Minigun'

▼ Bell CH-146 Griffon, 430 Squadron 'Silver Falcon', CFB Valcartier

A military version of the Bell 412CF, the CH-146 provides the backbone of the Canadian Armed Forces' tactical helicopter capability. Quebec-based 430 Squadron supports the 5e Groupe Brigade Mécanisé du Canada.

Specifications

Crew: 8–15

Powerplant: 4 x 3700kW (4600hp) Allison T-56-A-14-LFE turboprops

Maximum speed: 750km/h (462mph)

Range: 9300km (5737 miles)

Service ceiling: 10,700m (35,100ft)

Dimensions: span 30.38m (99ft 8in); length 35.61m (116ft 10in); height 10.49m (34ft 5in)

Weight: 27,892kg (61,362lb) loaded

Armament: Mk 46 Mod V torpedoes, signal chargers, smoke markers, illumination flares

▼ Lockheed CP-140 Aurora, 407 Squadron, CFB Comox

The CP-140 is essentially a P-3C built for Canada. Designed for anti-submarine warfare, the Aurora is also used to monitor illegal fishing, immigration, drug trafficking and pollution, as well as for search and rescue.

◄ Boeing CC-177 Globemaster III

Trenton-based 429 Squadron operates the Canadian Forces Globemaster III fleet. Received in 2007-08, the four airlifters have been used for humanitarian relief operations as well as in support of Joint Task Force Afghanistan under Operation Athena, which involves maintaining the air bridge between Canada and Afghanistan.

Mexico
MÉXICAN AIR FORCE AND MEXICAN NAVAL AVIATION

The smallest North American nation, Mexico's modest air arm is a reflection of limited external threats, although its aircraft are increasingly involved in internal and anti-narcotics operations.

THE ORGANIZATION OF the Fuerza Aérea Méxicana is based around two combat wings, subdivided into groups, which in turn maintain fixed- and rotary-wing squadrons located at 18 bases around the country, some of these installations not having aircraft permanently assigned. The overarching command structure is arranged on a geographical basis (divided between the Central Air Region, Western Air Region and Southeastern Air Region). Squadrons provide aircraft for fighter, close support, transport, training and various second-line duties.

The Armada de México includes both land-based and aircraft and helicopters that embark on Mexican warships, as well as an independent training element.

Specifications
Crew: 1

Powerplant: 1 x 1342kW (1800shp) Pratt & Whitney Canada PT6T-3 or -3B turboshaft

Maximum speed: 223km/h (138mph)

Range: 439km (237 nautical miles)

Service ceiling: 5305m (17,400ft)

Dimensions: rotor diameter 14.6m (48ft); length 17.43m (57ft 1.7in); height 3.8m (12ft 7in)

Weight: 5080kg (11,200lb) loaded

Armament: not known

▼ Bell 212, Escuadrón Aéreo 103, Oaxaca
Oaxaca-based Escuadrón Aéreo 103 of the Fuerza Aérea Mexicana is a mixed helicopter unit, also equipped with the Bell 206. Other rotary-wing types on strength with the Mexican Air Force include ex-Israeli CH-53s.

Specifications
Crew: 1

Powerplant: 2 x 22.2kN (5000lb) General Electric J85-GE-21B turbojets

Maximum speed: 1741km/h (1082mph)

Range: 306km (190 miles)

Service ceiling: 15,790m (51,800ft)

Dimensions: span 8.13m (26ft 8in); length 14.45m (47ft 4.75in);

height 4.07m (13ft 4.25in)

Weight: 11,214kg (24,722lb) loaded

Armament: 2 x 20mm (0.79in) cannon; two air-to-air missiles, five external pylons with provision for 3175kg (7000lb) of stores, including missiles, bombs, ECM pods, cluster bombs, rocket launcher pods and drop tanks

▼ Northrop F-5E Tiger II, Escuadrón Aéreo 401, Santa Lucia
Air Squadron 401 is responsible for Mexico's most potent fighter equipment, represented by the F-5E/F. Refitted in 2005 with AN/APQ-159 radar, and armed with AIM-9P air-to-air missiles, the Mexican Tiger IIs are based at Base Aérea Militar (BAM) No 1, at Santa Lucia, close to the capital, Mexico City.

CUBA

DOMINICAN
REPUBLIC

GUATEMALA   HONDURAS

EL SALVADOR   NICARAGUA

          COSTA RICA   VENEZUELA

               PANAMA

                    COLOMBIA

               ECUADOR

                              PERU   B R A Z I L

PACIFIC   BOLIVIA

OCEAN   PARAGUAY

                                                    URUGUAY

                              A R G E N T I N A

                    C H I L E   *ATLANTIC*

                                                                    OCEAN

Chapter 11

Central America and South America

Having emerged from years of conflict, the air forces of Central America today typically operate modest fleets of transport aircraft and helicopters, with only Honduras being equipped with high-performance jet fighters. In the Caribbean, a seriously depleted Cuban air arm remains that region's only significant player. With a few exceptions, recent economic woes have had an adverse effect on the composition and serviceability of the combat fleets of air arms in both Central and South America. In South America, where Argentina and Brazil have traditionally maintained the most capable air arms, Chile and Venezuela are now positioned to challenge them as among the best-equipped air forces on that continent.

Argentina

ARGENTINE AIR FORCE, ARMY AVIATION AND NAVAL AVIATION

Traditionally among the most powerful air arms in Latin America, Argentina's air force has suffered from a lack of funding in recent years and operates an ageing front-line fleet.

ARGENTINA'S THREE BRANCHES of the military each operate an independent aviation arm. There have been no major military actions since the Falklands War, but all three air arms participate in local crisis relief and counter-smuggling work.

Many Fuerza Aérea Argentina (FAA) aircraft are in need of replacement. Transport capability is provided by I Air Brigade, with various models of Hercules representing the main airlift assets, KC-130s also conducting aerial refuelling. Five 707s include one example equipped for electronic warfare – the others are outfitted for VIP and strategic transport. Lineas Aéreas del Estado (LADE), an FAA-operated airline, mainly uses five F28s.

II Air Brigade provides transport, liaison, photo-reconnaissance and other support missions. III Air Brigade is responsible for the fleet of around 40 Pucará counter-insurgency aircraft. Pucarás are widely used for countering drug-smuggling flights along the northern borders. As well as SAR helicopters and the Cruz del Sur aerobatic team (with Su-29s), IV Air Brigade operates 18 Pampas for training and light attack, with 12 more on order and older aircraft due to be upgraded.

V Air Brigade flies 33 OA/A-4AR Fightinghawk fighter-bombers, the FAA's most modern combat type, as well as the ageing Mirage interceptor fleet. Mirage survivors comprise nine Israeli-supplied Fingers and 10 Mirage IIIEAs, while a training unit operates seven Mirage 5A Mara, two Mirage IIIDAs and three two-seat Daggers.

FUERZA AÉREA ARGENTINA AIR BRIGADES

I Brigada Aérea	C-130B/H, KC-130H, L-100-30 Hercules, Fokker F28, Boeing 707	El Palomar
II Brigada Aérea	Learjet 31A, Fokker F27	Paraná
III Brigada Aérea	IA-58A/D Pucará	Reconquista
IV Brigada Aérea	IA-63 Pampa, SA315B Lama Su-29AR	Mendoza Morón
V Brigada Aérea	OA/A-4AR	Villa Reynolds
VI Brigada Aérea	Mirage IIIEA/DA, Mirage 5A Mara, Finger/Dagger	Tandil
VII Brigada Aérea	Chinook, Bell 212, UH-1N, Hughes 369/500	Moreno
IX Brigada Aérea	Saab 340, DHC-6	Comodoro Rivadavia

Specifications

Crew: 1

Powerplant: 1 x 41.97kN (9436lbf) (dry thrust) SNECMA Atar 09C turbojet

Maximum speed: Mach 2.2 (2350km/h; 1460mph)

Range: 4000km (2485 miles)

Service ceiling: 18,000m (59,055ft)

Dimensions: span 8.22m (26ft 11in); length 15.55m (51ft 0.25in); height 4.50m (14ft 9in)

Weight: 13,700kg (30,203lb) loaded

Armament: 2 x 30mm (1.18in) DEFA 552 cannons, bombload of 5774kg (12,730lb)

▼ **IAI Finger, I Escuadrón, VI Brigada Aérea, Tandil**

An Israeli-upgraded Dagger (itself an IAI-built Mirage 5), the Finger is in service with Escuadrón I, alongside the Mirage and Dagger fleet at Tandil. Aircraft C412 wears markings to confirm its role in the damage of two Royal Navy warships during the 1982 Falklands War.

FAA helicopter activity is focused on VII Air Brigade, although its Chinooks are non-operational. IX Air Brigade flies on behalf of LADE and supports Argentina's Antarctic mission. A Military Aviation School is equipped with T-34s and EMB-312s.

The Comando de Aviación de Ejército (Argentine Army Aviation Command) is dominated by the UH-1H, and is centred upon Agrupación Aviación de Ejército 601, at Campo de Mayo, with smaller Aviation Sections located across the country. Fixed-wing assets include OV-1D battlefield reconnaissance aircraft and G222 turboprop transports.

The Comando de Aviación Naval Argentina (Argentine Naval Aviation Command) is headed by S-2Ts for anti-submarine warfare, Super Etendard attack fighters, a large fleet of helicopters, and P-3Bs and Beech 200s for maritime patrol. Other units provide aerial photography, training and transport.

Specifications

Crew: 1

Powerplant: 1 x 49kN (11,023lb) SNECMA Atar 8K-50 turbojet

Maximum speed: 1180km/h (733mph)

Range: 850km (528 miles)

Service ceiling: 13,700m (44,950ft)

Dimensions: span 9.6m (31ft 6in); length 14.31m (46ft 11.2in); height 3.86m (12ft 8in)

Weight: 12,000kg (26,455lb) loaded

Armament: 2 x 30mm cannon, provision for up to 2100kg (4630lb) of stores, including nuclear weapons and Exocet air-to-surface missiles

▼ **Dassault Super Etendard, 2° Escuadrilla Aeronaval de Caza y Ataque, Base Aeronaval Comandante Espora**

Armed (as seen here) with Exocet anti-ship missiles, the Super Etendard is the Argentine Navy's most potent asset. The aircraft have also been deployed to Rio Grande in Tierra del Fuego.

▶ **Grumman S-2T Turbo Tracker**

The Argentine Navy's Fuerza Aeronaval No. 2, based at Comandante Espora (Bahía Blanca), incorporates the Escuadrilla Aeronaval Antisubmarina, equipped with five S-2T Turbo Trackers for anti-submarine warfare missions, and a single PC-6 Turbo Porter utility transport.

COMANDO DE AVIACIÓN NAVAL ARGENTINA NAVAL AIR SQUADRONS

Escuadrilla Aeronaval Antisubmarina	S-2T, PC-6	Base Aeronaval Comandante Espora
2° Escuadrilla Aeronaval de Caza y Ataque	Super Etendard	Base Aeronaval Comandante Espora
1° Escuadrilla Aeronaval de Helicópteros	SA316B Alouette III, AS555 Fennec	Base Aeronaval Comandante Espora
2° Escuadrilla Aeronaval de Helicópteros	SH-3D, ASH-3D	Base Aeronaval Comandante Espora
2° Escuadrilla Aeronaval de Sostén Logístico Móvil	Fokker F28	Base Aeronaval Ezeiza
Escuadrilla Aeronaval de Exploración	P-3B	Base Aeronaval Almirante Zar
Escuadrilla Aeronaval de Vigilancia Marítima	Beechcraft 200	Base Aeronaval Almirante Zar

Bolivia
BOLIVIAN AIR FORCE

With only limited combat equipment, the Fuerza Aérea Boliviana (FAB) focuses on transport and training, with squadrons divided between three geographical regions (I, II and III Air Brigades).

THE BOLIVIAN AIR Force maintains major bases at La Paz, Colcapiro and Santa Cruz. Each base is assigned an Air Brigade, responsible for Air Groups with particular assignments. Air Groups are in turn equipped with squadrons. Transporte Aéreo Militar is the FAB's military airline and is based at La Paz.

Specifications

Crew: 1–4

Powerplant: 1 x 1044kW (1400hp) Avco Lycoming T53-L-13 turboshaft engine

Maximum speed: 204km/h (127mph)

Range: 511km (317 miles)

Service ceiling: 3840m (12,600ft)

Dimensions: rotor diameter 14.63m (48ft); length 12.77m (41ft 11in); height 4.41m (14ft 5in)

Weight: 4309kg (9500lb) loaded

▲ **Bell UH-1H, Grupo Aéreo 51, Chapacura**
Primary rotary-wing unit in the FAB is Grupo Aéreo 51. This UH-1H serves with the 'Fuerza de Tarea' squadron at Chapacura air base.

Costa Rica
AIR SECTION

Part of the Civil Guard, Costa Rica's small Air Section operates from three bases (Liberia, San José and a naval station at Golfito), with the centre of operations at San José, the capital.

KNOWN AS THE Servicio de Vigilancia Aerea of the Fuerza Pública (Air Section of the Civil Guard), Costa Rica's air arm lacks armed aircraft, but is routinely engaged on counter-narcotics work and is also capable of staging rescue, medical evacuation and VIP transport missions. Piper and Cessna light aircraft are supported by MD500 helicopters.

Specifications

Crew: 1–2

Powerplant: 1 x 236kW (316hp) Allison 250-C18A turboshaft engine

Maximum speed: 244km/h (151mph)

Range: 606km (375 miles)

Initial climb rate: 518m/min (1700 fpm)

Dimensions: rotor diameter 8.03m (26ft 4in); length 9.24m (30ft 4in); height 2.48m (8ft 2in)

Weight: 1361kg (2994lb) loaded

▶ **McDonnell Douglas Helicopters MD500E, Servicio de Vigilancia Aérea, San José/Juan Santamaria**
San José is home to Costa Rica's Servicio de Vigilancia Aérea, within which the MD500 is the only helicopter asset, with two examples in use for surveillance duties. MSP018 also wears Police titles.

Brazil

BRAZILIAN AIR FORCE, ARMY AVIATION AND NAVAL AVIATION

Part of the largest armed forces in the region, the Força Aérea Brasileira (FAB) comprises five commands, while further air power is provided by air elements of the Brazilian army and navy.

THE BRAZILIAN AIR Force is eagerly awaiting a new fighter, which will be procured under the FX-2 programme as a replacement for existing Mirage 2000 and F-5 fighters, and eventually for the AMX.

Headquartered at Brasilia, the Terceira Força Aérea (3rd Air Force) includes the FAB's premier fighter unit, 1° Grupo de Defesa Aérea at Anápolis, with Mirage 2000B/Cs, plus EMB-326 Xavante jet trainers and EMB-312 Tucano turboprop trainers. 1° Grupo de Aviação de Caça at Santa Cruz has two squadrons, both with upgraded F-5 fighters and EMB-312s. 3° Grupo de Aviação (GAv) has three squadrons with mixed fleets of EMB-314 Super Tucanos, EMB-312s and Cessna 208s at Boa Vista, Porto Velho and Campo Grande. 5° GAv has an EMB-110 light transport squadron at Fortaleza. 6° GAv maintains a Learjet 35 and EMB-110 squadron at Recife, and a squadron with Cessna 208 and EMB-145SA/RS airborne early warning aircraft at Anápolis. 10° GAv at Santa Maria is a 3rd Air Force AMX wing, with two squadrons of the fighter-bombers. 14° GAv flies a unit of F-5s and EMB-312s from Canoas. Finally, 16° GAv operates a single AMX squadron at Santa Cruz.

The Quinta Força Aérea (5th Air Force), headquartered at Rio de Janeiro, is responsible for three transport groups, equipped primarily with C-130s, as well as the 9° GAv, with a squadron of C-295 transports at Manaus, and the 15° GAv, with a mixed EMB-110 and C-295 unit at Campo Grande.

The Segunda Força Aérea (2nd Air Force), also headquartered at Rio de Janeiro, comprises the 7° GAv with four EMB-111 squadrons at Salvador, Florianópolis, Belém and Santa Cruz. The last of these bases will receive P-3AM surveillance aircraft from 2010. The 2nd Air Force's helicopters are organized under the 8° GAv, with five squadrons operating a fleet of UH-1H, HB350 (locally manufactured AS350), AS332 and UH-60L (plus light fixed-wing types) from Belém, Recife, Afonsos, Santa Maria and Manaus. The 2nd Air Force also incorporates the 10° GAv, with a single UH-1H, EMB-110 and C-295 squadron at Campo Grande.

Training Command

The FAB's Comando Aéreo de Treinamento, with its HQ at Natal, includes 1°/4° GAv with EMB-326 jet trainers, 2°/5° GAv with EMB-314s, and 11° GAv with a squadron of HB350s. A separate Department of

Specifications

Crew: 1

Powerplant: 2 x 97kN (21,834lb) SNECMA M53-P2 turbofans

Maximum speed: 2338km/h (1453mph)

Range: 1480km (920 miles)

Service ceiling: 18,000m (59,055ft)

Dimensions: span 9.13m (29ft 11.5in); length 14.36m (47ft 1.25in);

height 5.2m (17ft 0.75in)

Weight: 17,000kg (37,480lb) loaded

Armament: 1 x DEFA 554 cannon; nine external pylons with provision for up to 6300kg (13,889lb) of stores, including air-to-air missiles, rocket launcher pods, and various attack loads, including 454kg (1000lb) bombs

▼ **Dassault Mirage 2000C, 1° Esq, 1° Grupo de Defesa Aérea, Anápolis**

Designated as the F-2000 in FAB service, the Mirage 2000 was acquired as a successor to the Mirage III. Flying from Anápolis, the Mirage fleet is chiefly tasked with the air defence of the capital, Brasilia.

Training handles initial flying training, with a varied fleet of light aircraft and gliders at Pirassununga. The public face of the FAB is the Esquadrão de Demonstração Aérea, or 'Esquadrilha da Fumaça' (Smoke Squadron), an aerobatic team equipped with EMB-312s and also based at Pirassununga.

With a vast territory, much of it yet to be opened up to land communications, the FAB maintains a considerable transport capability. The Comando Geral do Ar (General Air Command) is responsible for seven numbered Comandos Aéreos Regional, normally each with one Esquadrão de Transporte Aéreo equipped with EMB-110, EMB-120 and Cessna 208 aircraft. Bases are at Belém, Pernambuco, Galeão, São Paulo, Canoas and Santa Maria, Brasilia and Manaus (the latter bases houses the 7 Esquadrão de Transporte Aéreo, which also operates from additional bases at Boa Vista and Puerto Velho).

The Grupo de Transporte Especial consists of the 1°/1° GTE and 2°/1° GTE at Brasilia, with various VIP transport and governmental aircraft including the A319, ERJ-190, Boeing 737, AS332, EC635, HB355, Learjet 35/55, BAe 125 and Legacy 600.

The Comando Geral de Apoio (General Support Command) includes the Diretoria e Electrônica e Proteção, with its Grupo Especial de Inspeção em

Vôo flying the BAe 125 and EMB-110 on navaids inspection duties from Santos Dumont AP.

The Força Aeronaval da Marinha do Brazil is responsible for Latin America's only carrier air group, which embarks on the NAe *São Paolo*. Esquadrão de Aviões de Interceptação e Ataque 1 is the sole fixed-wing naval unit, responsible for TA/A-4KU fighters. Naval aircraft are primarily based on shore at São Pedro da Aldeia, and also include helicopter units, comprising a squadron of SH-3s (to be replaced by SH-60s), one of Lynx, a squadron of AS355s and HB350s, a squadron of AS332s (to be replaced by AS532s), two squadrons of HB350s at Manaus and Ilha do Terrapleno de Leste, and two squadrons of Bell 206s at Ladário and São Pedro da Aldeia.

Brazilian army aviation

The Aviação do Exército (AvEx), formed in 1986, consists of the 1° Grupo AvEx, with four component brigades. Of these, the 4° Brigada de Aviação de Exército is based at Manaus in the Amazon and does counter-narcotics work. Other AvEx units are at Taubaté. With the arrival of the AS532, a new base will be set up in Mato Grosso do Sul, in the south of the country. Other types in AvEx service comprise the AS550, HB350, AS565 and HB565 and the S-70A.

FORÇA AÉREA BRASILEIRA COMBAT AND TRANSPORT UNITS

Esquadrão de Demonstração Aérea			2° Comando Aéreo Regional Recife		
'Esquadrilha da Fumaça'	EMB-312	Pirassununga	2 Esquadrão de Transporte Aéreo	EMB-110, EMB-120	Recife
Grupo de Transporte Especial Brasilia			3° Comando Aéreo Regional		
1°/1° GTE	A319, ERJ-190, Boeing 737, AS332, EC635, HB355	Brasilia	3 Esquadrão de Transporte Aéreo	EMB-110, EMB-120	Galeão
2°/1° GTE	Learjet 35/55, BAe 125, Legacy 600	Brasilia	4° Comando Aéreo Regional		
Comando Geral de Apoio (General Support Command) Diretoria e Electrônica e Proteção			4 Esquadrão de Transporte Aéreo	EMB-110, EMB-120	São Paulo
			5° Comando Aéreo Regional		
Grupo Especial de Inspeção em Vôo	Santos BAe 125, EMB-110	Dumont AP	5 Esquadrão de Transporte Aéreo	EMB-110	Canoas*
Comando Geral do Ar (General Air Command)			6° Comando Aéreo Regional		
Comandos Aéreos Regional			6 Esquadrão de Transporte Aéreo	EMB-110, EMB-120, EMB-121	Brasilia
1° Comando Aéreo Regional			7° Comando Aéreo Regional Manaus		
1 Esquadrão de Transporte Aéreo	EMB-110, Cessna 208	Belém	7 Esquadrão de Transporte Aéreo	EMB-110, EMB-120, Cessna 208	Manaus

Chile

CHILEAN AIR FORCE, NAVAL AVIATION AND ARMY AVIATION

Acquisition of new fighters and upgrade programmes for older combat equipment mean that the Fuerza Aérea de Chile (FACH) is one of the most capable air forces in the region.

▲ **Lockheed Martin F-16D Fighting Falcon**
A Grupo 3 F-16D prepares to refuel from a USAF KC-135 over the Pacific. Chilean F-16C/Ds are equipped to a high standard, and are understood to use Israeli Python 4 and Derby missiles in addition to American weapons.

PREVIOUSLY A MUCH smaller and less capable force, the FACH is now perhaps the most powerful in Latin America. Modernization has seen the F-5E/F upgraded to Tigre III standard, and acquisition of the F-16C/D Block 50, 10 examples being delivered from March 2006. Mirage 5 Elkans have been replaced by 18 second-hand F-16AM/BMs acquired from the Netherlands in 2007, with a further 12 ex-Netherlands F-16s now arriving to replace the retired Mirage 50 Pantera. The EMB-314 Super Tucano has been acquired to begin replacement of the fleet of A/T-36 Halcón jet trainers. For initial pilot training, the T-35A/B remains in use with the Escuela de Aviación Militar (Military Aviation School).

The FACH transport fleet is based around three C-130Hs, as well as two Boeing 707s, one capable of aerial refuelling, the other electronic warfare. Ex-USAF KC-135E tankers supplement the latter. Other transports provide presidential transport, while light transport tasks are flown by the DHC-6 and C-212.

Five Beech 99A Petrels are equipped for maritime surveillance, although this role is now the preserve of Aviación Naval (Naval Aviation). Beech King Air and Learjet 35A aircraft are used for aerial photography. Other light aircraft in service include the Piper

FUERZA AÉREA DE CHILE	
I Brigada Aérea, Iquique	
Grupo de Aviación 1	A/T-36 Halcón, EMB-314
Grupo de Aviación 2	Beech 99A, C-212, SA315B Lama
Grupo de Aviación 3	F-16C/D
II Brigada Aérea, Santiago	
Escuela de Aviación Militar, El Bosque	T-35A/B Pillán
Grupo de Aviación 9	UH-1H, Bell 412, Bell 206, BK117, S-70A, PA-28 Dakota, O-2A
Grupo de Aviación 10	KC-135E, C-130H, Boeing 707, Boeing 737, Beechcraft 200, Gulfstream IV
Servicio Aerofotogramétrico	Learjet 35A, DHC-6, Beechcraft 100
Escuadrilla de Alta Acrobacia Halcones	Extra 300L
III Brigada Aérea, Puerto Montt	
Grupo de Aviación 5	DHC-6, C-212, Citation Jet
IV Brigada Aérea, Punta Arenas	
Grupo de Aviación 6	DHC-6, UH-1H
Grupo de Aviación 12	F-5E/F Tigre III
Grupo de Exploración Antártica 19, Eduardo Frei Base	UH-1H, BO105
Escuadrilla de Enlace	Bell 412
V Brigada Aérea, Antofagasta	
Grupo de Aviación 7	F-16AM/BM
Grupo de Aviación 8	F-16AM/BM
Escuadrilla de Enlace	Bell 412, C-212

Dakota, Cessna O-2A, Beech Super King Air and Cessna Citation. FACH helicopters include examples of the UH-1D/H, Bell 412 and SA315B Lama.

Aviación Naval

Responsible for over 5950 km (3,700 miles) of coastline, an Antarctic sector and various islands, Aviación Naval (Naval Aviation) is headed by Fuerza Aeronaval No. 1, heading most naval flying operations and including three operational squadrons (Vuelo de Patrulla 1/Patrol Flight 1, Escuadrón de Helicópteros de Ataque 1/1st Attack Helicopters Squadron, Helicópteros Utilitarios 1/Utility Helicopters 1, and Vuelo de Carga 1/Cargo Flight 1), as well as the Escuela de Aviación Naval (Naval Aviation School, VT-1) and Naval Aviation Maintenance Centre.

Fuerza Aeronaval No. 2 in the south of the country is headquartered at Punta Arenas, with smaller bases at Isla Dawson and Puerto Williams. Punta Arenas receives detachments from other squadrons, typically

SERVICIO DE AVIACIÓN DE LA ARMADA DE CHILE	
Fuerza Aeronaval 1, Base Aeronaval Viña del Mar	
VT-1	O-2, PC-7
VC-1	C-212
VP-1	EMB-111, P-3ACH, UP-3A
HU-1	Bell 206, BO105, SA365
Escuadrón Embarcadero, Base Aeronaval Viña del Mar	
HA-1	AS332, AS532, SA365
Fuerza Aeronaval 2, Punta Arenas	
Aircraft from various squadrons	EMB-111, C-212, BO105, SA365, P-3ACH Punta Arenas, Puerto Williams and Isla Dawson

hosting one or two P-3As and a single EMB-111 patrol aircraft, a single C-212 utility transport, plus various helicopters.

A smaller Aviación Naval presence is maintained in the north of the country, at Iquique, and this normally hosts an EMB-111 and a BO105.

The Brigada de Aviación del Ejército de Chile (BAVE, Chilean Army Aviation Brigade), headquartered at Rancagua, consists of Regimiento de Aviación No. 1 plus five aviation sections, the latter typically attached to an army division. Alongside C-212, Cessna 208 and lighter fixed-wing types, the BAVE operates Ecureuil, Esquilo, Lama, Puma (which the BAVE hopes to replace with Cougars), Super Puma and MD530F helicopters.

◀ Aérospatiale AS532SC Cougar
The Chilean Navy's Super Puma and Cougar helicopters carry the local designation SH-32 and are operated by the Escuadrón de Helicópteros de Ataque 1 (HA-1, 1st Attack Helicopters Squadron). Six Cougars (as seen here) were delivered in the 1990s, along with a single AS332B1. HA-1 embarks on Chilean Navy frigates.

▼ Lockheed Martin F-16D Fighting Falcon, Grupo de Aviación 3, Iquique
Assigned to I Brigada Aérea, the FACH's advanced F-16C/Ds are based at Iquique/Diego Aracena AB (also known as B.A. 'Los Condores').

Specifications

Crew: 1
Powerplant: 1 x 126.7kN (28,500lb) thrust Pratt & Whitney F100-PW-229 afterburning turbofan
Maximum speed: 2177km/h (1353mph)
Range: 3862km (2400 miles)
Service ceiling: 15,240m(49,000ft)

Dimensions: span 9.45m (31ft); length 15.09m (49ft 6in); height 5.09m (16ft 8in)
Weight: 19,187kg (42,300lb) loaded
Armament: 1 x GE M61A1 20mm (0.79in) multi-barrelled cannon, wingtip missile stations; seven external hardpoints with provision for up to 9276kg (20,450lb) of stores

Colombia

COLOMBIAN AIR FORCE

Subdivided into six major commands, the Fuerza Aérea Colombiana (FAC) is widely involved in the country's war on insurgents and is also active against narcotics production and trafficking.

THE SIX COMMANDS of the FAC are the Comando Aéreo de Combate (CACOM), Comando Aéreode Apoyo Táctico (CAATA), Comando Aéreo de Transporte Militar (CATAM), Escuela Militar de Aviación (EMAVI), Comando Aéreo de Mantenimiento (CAMAN) and the Servicio de Aeronavegación a Territorios Nacionales (SATENA).

Each command is responsible for a Grupo, and a number of constituent Escuadrones. Of the combat commands, CACOM 1 at Palanquero is responsible for air defence, with Kfir and Mirage 5 fighters and T-37 trainers, while CACOM 2 at Apiay flies counter-insurgency and anti-narcotics missions with Tucanos, Super Tucanos, AC-47s and AH-60Ls, among others. CACOM 2 also maintains an OV-10 squadron at Yopal, while most bases incorporate a COIN/anti-narcotics squadron with fixed- and rotary-wing types on strength. CACOM 3 at Barranquilla operates OA-37s and Super Tucanos, CACOM 4 at Melgar flies various helicopters, CACOM 5 at Rionegro flies AH-60L gunships, and CACOM 6 at Tres Esquinas has Tucanos. CATAM at Bogotá is the FAC transport command, primarily operating C-130s, CN235s and C-295s.

Specifications

Crew: 1

Powerplant: 1 x 79.41kN (17,860lb thrust) (with afterburner) IAI/General Electric license-built J79-JIE turbojet engine

Maximum speed: 2440km/h (1516mph)

Range: 548 miles (882km)

Service ceiling: 17,690m (58,038ft)

Dimensions: span 8.22m (26.97ft); length 15.65m (51.35ft); height 4.55m (14.93ft)

Weight: 16,500kg (36,376lb) loaded

Armament: 2 x 30mm Rafael DEFA 533 cannons plus cluster bombs and missiles

▼ **IAI Kfir C7, Escuadrón de Combate 111, Grupo de Combate 11, Palanquero**

As well as the Kfirs of Escuadrón de Combate 111, Palanquero air base hosts the Mirage 5s of Escuadrón de Combate 112 and the T-37B/C trainers of Escuadrón de Combate 116.

Specifications

Crew: 3

Powerplant: 2 x 1545kW (2225shp) Klimov TV3-117VM turboshafts

Maximum speed: 250km/h (156mph)

Range: 950km (594 miles)

Service ceiling: 6000m (19,690ft)

Dimensions: rotor diameter 21.35m

(69ft 10in); length 18.42m (60ft 5in); height 4.76m (15ft 7in)

Weight: 11,100kg (24,470lb) loaded

Armament: Capable of carrying up to 1500kg (3300lb) of bombs, rockets and gunpods on six hardpoints

▼ **Mil Mi-17MD, Batallón de Aviacion No. 3 Carga y Transporte, Comando Operativo 25 de Aviacion, Fuerte Tolemaida**

Batallón de Aviacion No. 3 utilizes a mixed fleet of Russian-supplied Mi-17MD, Mi-17-1V and Mi-17-5V helicopters, and the unit maintains numerous helicopter detachments around the country.

Cuba
CUBAN AIR FORCE

Once the most powerful air arm in Central America, the Defensa Anti-Aérea y Fuerza Aérea Revolucionaria (DAAFAR) is now in a parlous state, with limited funds and poor serviceability.

THE ORGANIZATION OF the DAAFAR is based around three air zones, each with squadrons that are operationally subordinated to Air Defence, Tactical Air, Logistic Support and Air Training Commands. In 2007, four major active bases supported an estimated 31 operational combat types.

Specifications

Crew: 1
Powerplant: 2 x 81.4kN (18,298lb) Sarkisov RD-33 turbofans
Maximum speed: 2443km/h (1518mph)
Range: 1500km (932 miles)
Service ceiling: 17,000m (55,775ft)

Dimensions: span 11.36m (37ft 3.75in); length (including probe) 17.32m (56ft 10in); height 7.78m (25ft 6.25in)
Weight: 18,500kg (40,785lb) loaded
Armament: 1 x 30mm (1.18in) GSh-30 cannon, provision for up to 4500kg (9921lb) of stores

▼ **Mikoyan MiG-29, 231° Escuadrón de Caza, 1779 Regimento, San Antonio de Los Baños**
The most potent combat aircraft available to the DAAFAR is the MiG-29, which equipped a single squadron. In 2007, Western estimates suggested that only three examples were still airworthy.

Dominican Republic
DOMINICAN AIR FORCE

The Fuerza Aérea Dominicana (FAD) divides the Dominican Republic into Southern and Northern Air Zones, with headquarters in San Isidro and Santiago de los Caballeros, respectively.

THE FLYING OPERATIONS of the FAD are handled by the Air Command, which supports air assets at eight bases, although most of the fleet is centred at San Isidro. Individual units include combat, transport, liaison, training and helicopter squadrons, with Super Tucanos being the most potent assets.

Specifications

Crew: 1–4
Powerplant: 1 x 1044kW (1400hp) Avco Lycoming T53-L-13 turboshaft engine
Maximum speed: 204km/h (127mph)
Range: 511km (317 miles)

Service ceiling: 3840m (12,600ft)
Dimensions: rotor diameter 14.63m (48ft); length 12.77m (41ft 11in); height 4.41m (14ft 5in)
Weight: 4309kg (9500lb) loaded

▶ **Bell UH-1H, FAD**
Approximately 11 UH-1Hs serve alongside the FAD's diverse fleet of OH-58, Bell 430, Dauphin, OH-6 and Schweizer 333 helicopters.

Panama
PANAMANIAN AIR FORCE

Previously the Fuerza Aérea Panameña, Panama's Servicio Nacional Aeronaval was resurrected in 1989 and today possesses a small force of fixed-wing aircraft and helicopters.

THE SERVICIO NACIONAL Aeronaval (SENAN) is a component of the Fuerzas Publicas Panameña. Tasked with coastal and border patrol, disaster relief and counter-narcotics, the SAN has three squadrons of aircraft at Tocumen, and a VIP flight at Balboa.

Specifications

Crew: 1–2

Powerplant: 1 x 1342kW (1800hp) Pratt & Whitney Canada PT6T-3B-1 Turbo Twin Pac turboshaft

Maximum speed: 259km/h (161mph)

Range: 695km (432 miles)

Service ceiling: 4970m (16,306ft)

Dimensions: rotor diameter 14.02m (46ft); length 12.92m (42ft 4in); height 4.32m (14ft 4in)

Weight: 5397kg (6470lb) loaded

▲ **Bell 412, 2nd Escuadrón de Helicópteros, Tocumen**
The 2nd Escuadrón flies Bell 205, 212, 407 and 412 types, among others.

Paraguay
PARAGUAYAN AIR FORCE

The Fuerza Aérea Paraguaya (FAP) is headed by the first brigade controlling seven Grupo Aereos each with a different tasking. FAP combat assets are controlled by the Grupo Aerotáctico (GAT).

RESPONSIBLE FOR COMBAT equipment, the GAT operates the EMB-312, with the EMB-326 now withdrawn. Other groups are responsible for transport (Brigada Aerotransportada), training (with T-35s) and rotary-wing (Grupo Aéreo de Helicópteros) equipment. Major FAP bases are Silvio Pettirossi, Asunción, Ñu-Guazú and Concepción.

Specifications

Crew: 2

Powerplant: 1 x 11.1kN (2500lbf) Bristol Siddeley Viper Mk. 11 turbojet

Maximum speed: 806km/h (501mph)

Range: 1665km (1035 miles)

Service ceiling: 12,500m (41,000ft)

Dimensions: span 10.56m (34ft 8in);

length 10.65m (34ft 11.25in); height 3.72m (12ft 2.5in)

Weight: 3765kg (8300lb) loaded

Armament: 2 x 12.7mm (0.5in) Browning MGs and up to 900kg (2000lb) of weapons on six hardpoints, including gun pods, bombs and rockets

▼ **Embraer EMB-326GB (AT-26) Xavante, 1 Escuadrón de Caza, Silvio Pettirossi IAP**
Operated from Silvio Pettirossi IAP, this Xavante (now retired) was flown by 1 Escuadrón de Caza 'Guarani', within which it was assigned to one of two flights: Escuadrilla Orion or Escuadrilla Centauro.

Peru
PERUVIAN AIR FORCE

The Fuerza Aérea del Peru (FAP) employs a wide variety of types, including Western and Russian designs, although current levels of serviceability and funding are poor.

STRUCTURE IS BASED on five numbered wings, most of which are responsible for up to three air groups with their own constituent squadrons. Types adopted by the FAP in the 1980s, and still in use, include Mirage 2000, MiG-29, MB339, Su-22M and Su-25 jets, and Bell 212, Mi-17 and Mi-25 helicopters.

Specifications

Crew: 1

Powerplant: 1 x 97.1kN (21,834lb) SNECMA M53-P2 turbofan

Maximum speed: 2338km/h (1453mph)

Range: 1480km (920 miles)

Service ceiling: 18,000m (59,055ft)

Dimensions: span 9.13m (29ft 11.5in);

length 14.36m (47ft 1.25in); height 5.2m (17ft 0.75in)

Weight: 17,000kg (37,480lb) loaded

Armament: 2 x DEFA 554 cannon with 125rpg; 9 external pylons with provision for up to 6300kg (13,230lb) of stores

▼ **Dassault Mirage 2000P, Escuadrón Caza-Bombardeo 412, Grupo Aéreo 4, La Doya-Mariano Melgar**

The Mirage 2000 remains Peru's most capable fighter, with 12 examples in use.

Uruguay
URUGUAYAN AIR FORCE

The current Fuerza Aérea Uruguaya fleet was primarily acquired in the 1980s, and comprises transports, trainers, utility aircraft, helicopters, as well as a light attack force.

CANELONES IS HOME to Brigada Aérea I, with single transport and helicopter squadrons. At Durazno, Brigada Aérea II provides OA/A-37s and Pucará unit, a liaison squadron, and an advanced training squadron. Brigada Aérea III consists of an observation/liaison squadron at Montevideo.

Specifications

Crew: 1–4

Powerplant: 1 x 1044kW (1400hp) Avco Lycoming T53-L-13 turboshaft engine

Maximum speed: 204km/h (127mph)

Range: 511km (317 miles)

Service ceiling: 3840m (12,600ft)

Dimensions: rotor diameter 14.63m (48ft); length 12.77m (41ft 11in); height 4.41m (14ft 5in)

Weight: 4309kg (9500lb) loaded

▲ **Bell UH-1H, Escuadón Aéreo No. 5 Helicópteros, Canelones**

Part of Brigada Aérea I, this 'Huey' serves with EA5H's AS365s and Bell 212s.

Venezuela
VENEZUELAN AIR FORCE

The Aviación Militar Venezolana (AMV) has emerged in recent years as one of the most powerful air arms in the region, pursuing an ambitious re-equipment programme.

COMBAT TYPES ACQUIRED in the 1970s and 1980s, including the F-16, VF-5, T-2, OV-10 and Tucano, remain in service, but are now being joined by new types, including the Su-30MKV multi-role fighter and K-8 Karakorum jet trainer. Much-needed transport and tanker capacity is due to arrive in the form of Il-76s and Il-78s. Primary fighter bases are Barcelona (home to the Su-30MKVs of Grupo 13), Maracay, home of Grupo 16 F-16s, and El Sombrero, where Su-30MKVs are replacing Grupo 11 Mirage fighters. Additional bases are at Boca del Rio (Grupo

14 training types), La Carlota (housing the presidential transport unit, Grupo 4, and transport units of Grupo 5), Barquisemeto (Grupo 12 VF-5s and K-8s), Maracaibo (Grupo 15 OV-10s and Tucanos) and Maracay (Grupo 6 transport operations and the helicopters of Grupo 10). Light transports are chiefly operated by Grupo 9 at Puerto Ayacucho. Both the army and navy also maintain air arms, as the Comando de la Aviación Naval and Aviación del Ejército. The army inventory includes A109, AS-61D, Mi-17, Mi-26 and Mi-35 helicopters.

Specifications

Crew: 2

Powerplant: 2 x 74.5kN (16,750lbf) AL-31FL low-bypass turbofans

Maximum speed: Mach 2.0 (2120km/h; 1320mph)

Range: 3000km (1864 miles)

Service ceiling: 17,300m (56,800ft)

Dimensions: span 14.7m (48ft 2.5in); length 21.94m (72in 11in); height 6.36m (20ft 9in)

Weight: 24,900kg (54,900lb) loaded

Armament: 1 x30mm (1.18in) GSh-3-1 gun, plus air-to-air and air-to-surface missiles

▼ **Sukhoi Su-30MKV, Escuadrón 131, Grupo Aéreo de Caza 13, Barcelona**

Grupo Aéreo de Caza 13 'Libertador Simon Bolivar' was the debut operator of the AMV's two-seat Su-30MKV fighter. One of 24, this example, carrying a Kh-29T air-to-surface missile, is flown by Escuadrón 131 'Ases'.

Specifications

Crew: 2

Powerplant: 1 x 16.01kN (3600lb) Garrett TFE731-2A-2A turbofans

Maximum speed: Mach 0.75 (800km/h; 498mph)

Range: 2250km (1398 miles)

Service ceiling: 13,000m (42,651ft)

Dimensions: span 9.63m (31ft 7in); length 11.6m (38ft); height 4.21m (13ft 9in)

Weight: 4330kg (9546lb) loaded

Armament: 1x 23mm (0.90in) cannon pod, 5 hardpoints with a capacity of 1000kg (2205lb)

▼ **Hongdu K-8, Escuadrón 35, Grupo Aéreo de Caza 12, Barquisemeto**

Deliveries of the K-8 to the Comando Aéreo de Instrucción (Training Command) began in 2010. The Chinese-built K-8 is replacing the T-2D Buckeye as primary jet trainer in service with the FAV.

ARCTIC

OCEAN

SWEDEN

FINLAND

NORWAY

DENMARK

UNITED
KINGDOM

IRELAND

NETHERLANDS

GERMANY

BELGIUM

LUXEMBOURG

FRANCE

AUSTRIA

SWITZERLAND

ITALY

SPAIN

PORTUGAL

GREECE

TURKEY

CYPRUS

Chapter 12

Western Europe

With the exception of those of neutral Austria, Finland, Sweden and Switzerland – and a handful of smaller non-aligned air arms – the composition of the major air forces of Western Europe is characterized to a significant degree by their position within the NATO Alliance. Previously poised to fight a large-scale campaign against the forces of the Warsaw Pact, the air arms of Western Europe have had to adapt to the post-Cold War world, and this has involved severly reduced defence budgets, large-scale force reductions and the shift towards more deployable units applicable for peacekeeping duties as well as asymmetric warfare. Western European air arms are also notable for their pursuit of multi-national aircraft projects, typified by the Eurofighter, the A400M airlifter and the NH90 multi-role helicopter.

Austria

ÖSTERREICHISCHE LUFTSTREITKRÄFTE

Entirely defensive in its posture, the Österreichische Luftstreitkräfte is a component of the Bundesheer, the armed forces of neutral Austria, and is primarily charged with air policing.

THE AIR ARM comes under the leadership of the Kommando Luftstreitkräfte, reporting to the defence ministry and responsible for a Surveillance Wing (equipped with EF2000s and Saab 105s), an Air Support Wing consisting of three squadrons, and a Helicopter Wing with various detachments. Eight bases are in regular use, with the most important at Zeltweg (fighters) and Langenlebarn (helicopters and light transports), while Schwaz/Tirol and Aigen/Ennstal both serve as helicopter bases. Alongside the EF2000 fighter, the types in use are three C-130K transports, armed Saab 105 jet and PC-7 turboprop trainers, AB212 and S-70A transport helicopters, PC-6 utility transports and Alouette III and OH-58 liaison/scout helicopters.

Specifications

Crew: 1

Powerplant: 2 x 90kN (20,250lbf) Eurojet EJ200 afterburning turbofans

Maximum speed: Mach 2 (2495km/h; 1550mph)

Range: 2900km (1840 miles)

Service ceiling: 19,810m (65,000ft)

Dimensions: span 10.95m (35ft 11in); length 15.96m (52ft 5in); height 5.28m (17ft 4in)

Weight: 16,000kg (35,300lb) loaded

Armament: 1 x 27mm (1.06in) Mauser BK-27 cannon; 13 hardpoints holding up to 7500kg (16,500lb) of payload

▼ **Eurofighter EF2000, 1. Staffel, Überwachungsgeschwader, Zeltweg**

Austria ordered 15 EF2000s, comprising nine new Tranche 1 Block 5 aircraft and six ex-Luftwaffe Tranche 1 Block 2 aircraft, the latter upgraded to Block 5 standard. Primary weapon is the IRIS-T air-to-air missile.

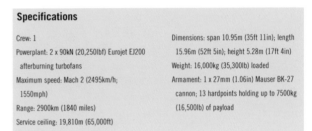

Belgium

BELGIUM AIR COMPONENT

A founder NATO member, Belgium's once-independent air arm has been rationalized with the end of the Cold War, and now operates as a branch of the unified Belgian Armed Forces.

BELGIAN AIR POWER is today represented by the Belgium Air Component (successor to the Belgische Luchtmacht/Force Aerienne Belge). As well as losing its independence in 2002, the force has experienced significant cutbacks since the early 1990s. The backbone of the combat fleet is the F-16,

▶ **Lockheed C-130H Hercules**

Belgium's fleet of 11 C-130H transports are operated by the Flight Tactical Transport Squadron, part of 15 Wing at Brussels-Melsbroek.

operated by 2 Wing at Florennes and 10 Wing at Kleine Brogel. From an original total of 160 F-16s, 90 have been upgraded, but some of these have since been disposed of, and a force of 60 jets is planned for 2015. Transport capability is provided by the C-130H (due to be replaced by A400Ms) and single examples of the A330 and A310, while VIP transport is handled by Dassault 20/900 and ERJ-135/145 jets. Basic training is conducted by 1 Wing at Beauvechain, equipped with SF260s. Fighter pilots continue on the Alpha Jet in France, including Belgian-owned Alpha Jet 1B+ aircraft operated by the Belgium-French Alpha Jet School on permanent detachment at Cazaux. Transport and helicopter pilots also complete their training in France.

▼ SABCA F-16B Fighting Falcon, 2 Wing, Florennes

Built locally by SABCA, this F-16B was originally delivered as a Block 15AA OCU aircraft in the late 1980s. FB-21 was one of 90 Belgian F-16s that were put through the Mid-Life Update programme, and re-entered service with 2 Wing in its new (Block 20 MLU) configuration in early 2001.

Naval helicopters

The Belgium Air Component is also responsible for maritime Sea King Mk48 helicopters and Alouette IIIs, the latter used for search and rescue. Both types operate from Koksijde and are to be replaced by 10 NH90 helicopters. Since 2004 the Belgium Air Component has also included former Army equipment, comprising the A109 attack/observation helicopter and Alouette II training/scout helicopter of the Heli Wing at Bierset.

Specifications

Crew: 2	Dimensions: span 9.45m (31ft); length 15.09m
Powerplant: 1 x 106kN (23,830lb) thrust Pratt	(49ft 6in); height 5.09m (16ft 8in)
& Whitney F100-PW-200 turbofan with	Weight: 17,010kg (37,500lb) loaded
afterburner	Armament: 1 x General Electric M61A1 20mm
Maximum speed: Mach 2	(0.78in) multi-barrelled cannon, wingtip
Range: 925km (525 miles)	missile stations; provision for up to 9276kg
Service ceiling: above 15,240m (50,000ft)	(20,450lb) of stores

Cyprus

CYPRUS NATIONAL GUARD AIR WING

Provided with a small air wing, the Cyprus National Guard was reformed as a Greek-Cypriot force in 1982, and in recent years has introduced a combat capacity with the Mi-35 helicopter.

ORIGINALLY ESTABLISHED IN 1960, the air wing of the Cyprus National Guard was disbanded following the Turkish invasion of Cyprus in 1974.

When re-established in 1982, the air wing was initially equipped with a single Islander utility transport, and this remains in use. Armed Gazelle utility helicopters were received in the late 1980s and all four examples remain active. More potent fixed-wing equipment then arrived in the form of the PC-9 turboprop trainer, which can also be used for light attack and counter insurgency. One example remains in use. A true combat capability is represented by 11 Mi-35P assault helicopters. Two Bell 206L utility helicopters are also in use, with three AW139 helicopters on order. The air wing operates from bases at Lakatamia and Paphos.

Cyprus also hosts an important RAF presence at Akrotiri, as well as a Turkish-Cypriot Security Force that has helicopters stationed in the northern (Turkish) part of the island.

Denmark

FLYVEVÅBEN

Responsible for a large area that also includes the Faeroe Islands and Greenland, the Danish air arm is part of a unified military, although it operates as an autonomous command.

THE DANISH AIR arm comprises two operational Commands: Tactical Air Command (Flyvertaktisk Kommando) with its headquarters at Karup, and Air Material Command (Flyvemateriel Kommando) with its HQ at Værløse. In addition, there is a Flying School (Flyveskolen), also at Karup.

The sharp end of the Flyvevåben is provided by two multi-role F-16 squadrons sharing a fleet of 62 aircraft: Esk 727 and Esk 730 at Skrydstrup. Esk 730 is assigned to NATO's Rapid Reaction Force, while Esk 727 is also responsible for conversion training.

Air Material Command includes Esk 721 at Værløse, which operates three examples of the C-130J-30 Hercules. In addition, three CL-604s are used for a range of support duties, including maritime surveillance, fishery protection and VIP transport.

Rotary-wing reorganization

The helicopter arm is in the middle of modernization, with 14 examples of the EH101 replacing the S-61A in the maritime search and rescue and heavylift transport roles. All helicopters are the responsibility of the Flyvevabnet Kommando (Air Force Command), headquartered at Karup. This base now supports the ex-Army Flying Service AS550 observation helicopters and the eight Lynx Mk90s formerly operated by the Danish navy, and which deploy aboard Danish warships.

Karup is also home to Flyvevåben basic flying training, with the Flying School (Flyveskolen) operating the Saab T-17. Future fighter pilots continue their training under the NATO Flying Training in Canada initiative, flying the CT-156 Harvard II and CT-115 Hawk from CFB Moose Jaw and CFB Cold Lake.

▲ **Westland Lynx Mk90B**
The Navy Helicopter Corps consists of eight Lynx Mk90B helicopters that are based at Karup and which deploy aboard Danish Navy warships. This example is armed with a door gun as used for counter-piracy and asymmetric maritime operations.

Specifications

Crew: 1

Powerplant: either 1 x 105.7kN (23,770lb) Pratt & Whitney F100-PW-200 or 1 x 128.9kN (28,984lb) General Electric F110-GE-100 turbofan

Maximum speed: 2142km/h (1320mph)

Range: 925km (525 miles)

Service ceiling: 15,240m (50,000ft)

Dimensions: span 9.45m (31ft); length 15.09m (49ft 6in); height 5.09m (16ft 8in)

Weight: 16,057kg (35,400lb) loaded

Armament: 1 x General Electric M61A1 20mm (0.78in) multi-barrelled cannon, wingtip missile stations; provision for up to 9276kg (20,450lb) of stores

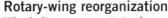

▼ **Fokker F-16A Fighting Falcon, Esk 730, Skrydstrup**
Built in the Netherlands by Fokker, this F-16A Block 15AA has undergone upgrade to Block 20 MLU standard. E-004 is seen armed with a wingtip AIM-120 AMRAAM missile and a GBU-12 laser-guided bomb underwing.

Finland

ILMAVOIMAT

Charged with the aerial defence of neutral Finland, the Ilmavoimat currently possesses exclusively defensive equipment, as well as its own transport, liaison and training facilities.

THE COMMAND STRUCTURE of the Finnish Air Force is based around three air defence commands, each responsible for a front-line wing at a single base. In addition, there are separate training, liaison and test squadrons. Main combat type is the F-18C/D Hornet, in three fighter squadrons. Also in use are C-295 transports, Hawk and Vinka trainers, while the Army operates the NH90 helicopter.

▶ **Boeing F-18C Hornet**

Finland is planning to introduce an air-to-ground capability to its Hornets, which are currently only equipped for defensive operations (hence the F-18 designation).

France

ARMÉE DE L'AIR, AVIATION NAVALE AND ALAT

Upgrade and restructuring have been the order of the day for the Armée de l'Air, with a major reorganization of the air force having been introduced in the late 1990s.

THE MOST SIGNIFICANT recent upgrade for the Armée de l'Air has been the induction of the Rafale omni-role fighter, introduced in 2004. The new fighter has replaced the Jaguar, and the Mirage F1 is to be similarly superseded, with the last two squadrons due to disband in 2010.

The current Armée de l'Air structure is headed by a high command, answering to the chief of the air staff, or Chef d'Etat-Major de l'AA (CEMAA). The latter is responsible for four major commands. Air Combat Command (Commandement de la Force

Specifications

Crew: 1

Powerplant: 1 x 83.36kN (18,839lb) thrust SNECMA M53-2 afterburning turbofan

Maximum speed: 2338km/h (1453mph)

Range: 1480km (920 miles)

Service ceiling: 18,000m (59,055ft)

Dimensions: span 9.13m (29ft 11.5in);

length 14.36m (47ft 1.25in); height 5.2m (17ft 0.75in)

Weight: 17,000kg (37,480lb) loaded

Armament: 2 x DEFA 554 cannon; 9 external pylons with provision for up to 6300kg of stores

▼ **Dassault Mirage 2000-5F, Escadron de Chasse 1/2 'Cigognes', BA102 Dijon**

Until the Rafale is fielded in greater numbers, the upgraded Mirage 2000-5F is the premier Armée de l'Air air defence fighter, with 36 examples in use. EC 1/2 maintains a permanent detachment at Al Dhafra, in Oman.

Aérienne de Combat, CFAC), is primarily tasked with defending French airspace, and controls all tactical combat jets. Air Mobility Command (Commandement de la Force Aérienne de Projection, CFAP), undertakes transport and aerial refuelling missions, using A310s, A340s, C-130s, C-135FRs, CN235s and Transalls, together with a large fleet of helicopters (Caracal, Ecureuil, Fennec, Puma, Super Puma) and assorted liaison, VIP transport (A310, A319, A330 and Falcon series) and light transport types. New transport types on order include the A330

tanker/transport and A400M airlifter. The only flying asset assigned to Air Surveillance, Information and Communication Systems Command (Commandement Air des Systèmes de Surveillance, d'Information et de Communication, CASSIC) is the E-3F AWACS. Air Force Education and Training Command (Commandement des Ecoles de l'AA, CEAA) is responsible for tri-service aircrew training, and its fleet includes Alpha Jet Es, Tucanos and Epsilons. There are also two organic commands: Strategic Air Command (Commandement des Forces

Specifications

Crew: 2

Powerplant: 2 x 73kN (16,424lb) SNECMA M88-
2 turbofans

Maximum speed: 2130km/h (1324mph)

Range: 1854km (1152 miles)

Service ceiling: classified

Dimensions: span 10.9m (35ft 9in); length 15.3m (50ft 2in); height 5.34m (17ft 6in)

Weight: 19,500kg (42,990lb) loaded

Armament: 1 x 30mm (1.18in) DEFA 791B cannon, up to 6000kg (13,228lb) of external stores

▼ **Dassault Rafale M, Flotille 12F,** *Charles de Gaulle*
This Rafale M carrier fighter displays a radar-guided Mica air-to-air missile on the wingtip and carries a GBU-12 laser-guided bomb underwing – the latter has been used in action by the Rafale M over Afghanistan.

ARMÉE DE L'AIR – COMMANDEMENT DE LA FORCE AÉRIENNE DE COMBAT (CFAC)

Escadron de Chasse 1/2 'Cigognes'	Mirage 2000-5F	BA102 Dijon	Escadron de Chasse 2/4 'La Fayette'	Mirage 2000N	BA116 Luxeuil
Escadron d'Entrainement 2/2 'Cote d'Or'	Alpha Jet E	BA102 Dijon*	Escadron de Chasse 2/5 'Ile de France'	Mirage 2000C/B	BA115 Orange
*EC 1/2 and EE 2/2 to move to Luxeuil in 2011. EC 1/2 maintains permanent detachment at Al; Dhafra AB, UAE.			Escadron de Chasse 3/4 'Limousin'	Mirage 2000N	BA125 Istres
Escadron de Chasse 1/3 'Navarre'	Mirage 2000D	BA133 Nancy	Escadron de Chasse 1/7 'Provence'	Rafale C/B	BA113 Saint-Dizier
Escadron de Chasse 2/3 'Champagne'	Mirage 2000D	BA133 Nancy	Escadron de Chasse 3/11 'Corse'	Mirage 2000C/D	BA188 Djibouti
Escadron de Chasse 3/3 'Ardennes'	Mirage 2000D	BA133 Nancy	Escadron de Chasse 1/12 'Cambresis'	Mirage 2000C	BA103 Cambrai*
Escadron de Chasse 1/4 'Dauphiné'	Mirage 2000N	BA116 Luxeuil*	* scheduled to disband in 2011		
* scheduled to disband in 2010			Escadron de Chasse 1/91 'Gascogne'	Rafale C/B	BA113 Saint-Dizier

ARMÉE DE L'AIR RECONNAISSANCE UNITS

Escadron de Reconnaissance 1/33 'Belfort'	Mirage F1CR	BA112 Reims
Escadron de Reconnaissance 2/33 'Savoie'	Mirage F1CR/CT/B	BA112 Reims

Note: both units scheduled to disband in 2010

OTHER ARMÉE DE L'AIR FIXED-WING UNITS

Escadron de Détection et de Commandement Aéroporté 0/36 'Berry'	E-3F	BA702 Avord
Groupe de Ravitaillement en Vol 2/91 'Bretagne'	C-135FR	BA125 Istres
Escadron de Transport, d'Entraînement et de Calibration 0/65	Falcon 50/7X, TBM 700, A319, AS332	BA107 Villacoublay-Velizy
Groupe Aérien Mixte 0/56 'Vaucluse'	DHC-6, AS532, Transall	IBA105 Evreux

AÉRONAUTIQUE NAVALE – FLOTILLES

Flotille 4F	E-2C	Lorient
Flotille 11F	Super Etendard	Landivisiau
Flotille 12F	Rafale M	Landivisiau
Flotille 17F	Super Etendard	Landivisiau
Flotille 21F	Atlantique NG	Nîmes-Garons
Flotille 23F	Atlantique NG	Lorient
Flotille 24F	Falcon 50, EMB-121	Lorient
Flotille 25F	Falcon 200 Guardian	Faaa, Tahiti*
* detachment at Tontouta, New Caledonia		
Flotille 28F	EMB-121	Nîmes-Garons
Flotille 31F	Lynx HAS2/2(FN)	Hyères
Flotille 32F	SA321G	Lanvéoc-Poulmic*
* Super Frelon scheduled to retire in 2010		
Flotille 34F	Lynx HAS2/2(FN)	Lanvéoc-Poulmic
Flotille 35F	SA365, Alouette III	Hyères*
* SA365 detachments at Cherbourg, La Rochelle and La Touquet.		
Flotille 36F	AS565	Hyères

Note: Nîmes-Garons is scheduled to close down in 2011

Aériennes, CFAS), and Air Defence and Air Operations Command (Commandement de la Défense Aérienne et des Opérations Aériennes, CDAOA). CFAS is responsible for nuclear-tasked assets (Mirage 2000N), while CDAOA is responsible for mission planning and deployment.

Aviation Navale
Part of the Marine Nationale, Aviation Navale includes the air wing for the carrier *Charles de Gaulle*, which comprises Rafale M and upgraded Super Etendard fighters, E-2C airborne early warning aircraft and a detachment of plane-guard helicopters. Land-based aircraft include Atlantique NG maritime patrol aircraft, Falcon 50 and Gardian surveillance aircraft, while Lynx and Panther helicopters detachments are provided for Navy warships.

Army aviation is the responsibility of the Aviation Légère de l'Armée de Terre (ALAT). Combat units are organized under the 4 Brigade Aéromobile, which

Specifications

Crew: 2

Powerplant: 1 x 134kW (180hp) Lycoming AEIO-360-B2F 4-cylinder air-cooled, horizontally opposed, fuel injected piston engine

Maximum speed: 270km/h (168mph)

Range: 1200km (745 miles)

Service ceiling: 5000m (16,400ft)

Dimensions: span 8.06m (26ft 5.25in); length 7.16m (23ft 6in); height 2.55m (8ft 5.4in)

Weight: 830kg (1829lb) loaded

▼ CAP 10B, Ecole de Pilotage Élémentaire de l'Armée de l'Air 05/315, Cognac BA709

The Armée de l'Air no longer operates the CAP 10B in the basic training role, although examples are still flown by the Aviation Navale and by the CEV, the French Air Force test unit. Cognac remains the centre of basic training and operates the Epsilon and Grob 120.

ARMÉE DE L'AIR TRANSPORT UNITS

Escadron de Transport 1/61 'Touraine'	Transall	BA123 Orléans
Escadron de Transport 1/62 'Vercors'	CN235	BA110 Creil
Escadron de Transport 1/64 'Béarn'	Transall	BA105 Evreux
Escadron de Transport 2/61 'Franche-Comte'	C-130H	BA123 Orléans
Escadron de Transport 2/64 'Anjou'	Transall	BA105 Evreux
Escadron de Transport 3/60 'Esterel'	A310, A340	Paris-Roissy
Escadron de Transport 3/61 'Poitou'	Transall	BA123 Orléans
Escadron de Transport 3/62 'Ventoux'	DHC-6, CN235	BA118 Mont-de-Marsan

▶ **Dassault Mirage 2000D**

A Mirage 2000D refuels from a USAF KC-135R over the Adriatic while conducting missions over the Balkans. The Mirage 2000D is a conventional strike specialist, with a range of precision weapons.

includes three combat helicopter regiments (1 Régiment d'Hélicoptères de Combat at Phalsbourg, 3 RHC at Etain and 5 RHC at Pau). ALAT regiments consist of flights, each of which undertakes a specific role. Main reconnaissance type is the Gazelle, while the Tigre is entering service to supplant Gazelles used in the attack, fire support and anti-helicopter roles. Transport types include the Puma, due to be replaced by the NH90, and the Cougar for combat search and rescue. ALAT also maintains training centres at Dax and Le Luc, and a special operations unit 4e Régiment d'Hélicoptères des Forces Spéciales at Pau.

Germany

LUFTWAFFE, MARINEFLIEGER AND HEERESFLIEGER

Vastly reduced in size since its Cold war heyday, the Luftwaffe is now making the transition to a leaner, more flexible force, with an increasing emphasis on overseas operations.

THE MODERN LUFTWAFFE is based on three divisional commands (Kommando Luftwaffendivision), respondible for combat assets, together with the Lufttransportkommado responsible for transport and liaison. Divisional commands have command units and surface-to-air missile wings. Aircraft are operated by wings (Geschwader) each with two squadrons (Staffeln), though aircraft are pooled across the wing, with only aircrew being assigned to different squadrons.

Kommando 1. Luftwaffendivision includes Jagdbombergeschwader 32 and Jagdgeschwader 74

and is also responsible for a tactical training detachment at Decimomannu in Italy, and contributes to the NATO E-3 AWACS force. Kommando 2. Luftwaffendivision includes two fighter-bomber wings, JBG 31 and 33, plus JG 73. Kommando 4. Luftwaffendivision includes JG 71, and Aufklärungsgeschwader 51.

The EF2000 will eventually take the place of the Tornado in all fighter-bomber wings with the exception of JBG 32, which is a specialist defence-suppression unit with the Tornado ECR version. The

LUFTWAFFE WINGS
Reconnaissance Wings

AG 51 'Immelmann'	Tornado Recce, Heron 1	Schleswig-Jagel

Fighter-Bomber Wings

JBG 31 'Boelcke'	EF2000, Tornado IDS	Nörvenich
JBG 32	Tornado ECR	Lechfeld
JBG 33	Tornado IDS	Büchel

Fighter Wings

JG 71 'Richthofen'	F-4F	Wittmund
JG 73 'Steinhoff'	EF2000	Laage
JG 74	EF2000	Neuburg an der Donau

Transport Wings

LTG 61	Transall, UH-1D	Penzing
LTG 62	Transall UH-1D	Wunsdorf Holzdorf
LTG 63	Transall	Hohn
Flugbereitschaft BMVg	A310, Challenger 601, AS532 Cougar	Köln/Bonn, Berlin-Tegel

EF2000 will also re-equip the final F-4F wing, with the Phantom II due to retire in 2013. Other new equipment includes the Heron 1 UAV, which is due to be joined within AG 51 by the Euro Hawk UAV, this carrying an electronic intelligence payload as a replacement for the Navy's last SIGINT-configured Atlantic. The Flugbereitschaft BMVg is receiving new equipment in the form of the A319, A340 and

Specifications
Crew: 1

Powerplant: 2 x 90kN (20,250lbf) Eurojet EJ200 afterburning turbofans

Maximum speed: Mach 2 (2495km/h; 1550mph)

Range: 2900km (1840 miles)

Service ceiling: 19,810m (65,000ft)

Dimensions: span 10.95m (35ft 11in); length 15.96m (52ft 5in); height 5.28m (17ft 4in)

Weight: 16,000kg (35,300lb) loaded

Armament: 1 x 27mm (1.06in) Mauser BK-27 cannon; 13 hardpoints holding up to 7500kg (16,500lb) of payload

▼ **Eurofighter EF2000, Jagdbombergeschwader 31 'Boelcke', Nörvenich**

JBG 31 became the first Luftwaffe fighter-bomber wing to receive the EF2000, with initial deliveries in 2009. Currently primarily operating the Tornado IDS, 'Boelcke' is the Luftwaffe's specialist precision-strike unit, for which it is equipped with laser-guided bombs.

Specifications
Crew: 2

Powerplant: 2 x 79.6kN (17,900lb) General Electric J79-GE-17 turbojets

Maximum speed: 2390km/h (1485mph)

Range: 817km (1750 miles)

Service ceiling: 19,685m (60,000ft)

Dimensions: span 11.7m (38ft 5in); length

17.76m (58ft 3in); height 4.96m (16ft 3in)

Weight: 26,308kg (58,000lb) loaded

Armament: 1 x 20mm (0.78in) M61A1 Vulcan cannon and four AIM-7 Sparrow recessed under fuselage or other weapons up to 1370kg (3020lb) on centreline pylon; four wing pylons for two AIM-7, or four AIM-9

▼ **McDonnell Douglas F-4F Phantom II, Jagdgeschwader 71 'Richthofen', Wittmund**

Germany's final Phantom operator is the 'Richthofen' wing, responsible for maintaining air defence commitments in the north of the country. JG 71 has also undertaken the NATO Baltic Air Policing mission.

Operated by a single Luftwaffe fighter-bomber wing, JBG 32 at Lechfeld, the Tornado ECR is a specialist defence-suppression aircraft, and saw active service over the Balkans during the 1990s. Key features of the ECR variant are an emitter-locator system (ELS) to locate enemy radar sites, which are then attacked with the AGM-88 High-speed Anti-Radiation Missile (HARM).

Global 5000 for VIP transport, while one Lufttransportgeschwader will be axed, and the remaining two will receive the A400M as replacements for the Transall. NH90s will supersede UH-1Ds used for combat search and rescue.

Marineflieger assets are divided between two bases, with Marinefliegergeschwader 3 operating the final Atlantic, plus Do 228s and Lynx from Nordholz, and MFG 5 operating Sea Kings from Kiel. The Heeresflieger is upgrading its CH-53 transport helicopters and introducing the Tiger attack helicopter, and NH90s will replace the UH-1D fleet. Heeresflieger helicopter regiments comprise two for medium transport (CH-53), two for transport (UH-1), and two for combat (BO105P and Tiger).

Specifications

Crew: 2	Dimensions: span 22.01m (72ft 2.7in); length
Powerplant: 2 x 2927kW (3925shp) General	26.97m (88ft 6in); height 7.6m (24ft 11in)
Electric T64-GE-413 turboshafts	Weight: 15,227kg (33,500lb) loaded
Maximum speed: 315km/h (196mph)	Armament: 2 x 7.62mm (0.3in) MG3 machine
Range: 1000km (540 nautical miles)	guns in the side doors
Service ceiling: 5106m (16,750ft)	

▼ Sikorsky CH-53GS, Einsatzgeschwader Termez

This is an example of the upgraded CH-53GS, with improved defensive equipment for operations in high-threat environments. The helicopter wears markings associated with its support of the ISAF mission in Afghanistan, for which it was based at Termez, Uzbekistan.

Specifications

Crew: 11	Dimensions: span 30.4m (99ft 8in);
Powerplant: 4 x 3700kW (4600shp) Allison	length 35.61m (116ft 10in);
T56-A-14	height 10.29m (33ft 9in)
Maximum speed: 750km/h (466mph)	Weight: 64,400kg (142,000lb) loaded
Range: 8944km (5557.5 miles)	Armament: Bombload of 9000kg (20,000lb),
Service ceiling: 10,400m (28,300ft)	missiles, torpedoes, mines and depth charges

▼ Lockheed P-3C Orion, Marinefliegergeschwader 3 'Graf Zeppelin', Nordholz

To replace its Atlantic maritime patrol aircraft, Germany acquired eight P-3Cs formerly operated by the Netherlands Naval Aviation Service. The aircraft have been deployed to Djibouti to support the anti-terror mission in the Horn of Africa.

Greece

HELLENIC AIR FORCE, ARMY AVIATION AND NAVAL AVIATION

The Hellenic Air Force (Elliniki Polemiki Aeroporia) operates a powerful and varied combat fleet, and also possesses transport, liaison, search and rescue, training and firefighting assets.

THE PRIMARY COMBAT types deployed by the Hellenic Air Force are the multi-role F-16C/D, the Mirage 2000 used for naval strike and air defence, upgraded F-4Es for air defence, A-7Es used for ground attack and maritime strike, and RF-4Es for reconnaissance. ERJ-145s are used for airborne early warning, while the primary transports are the C-27J and C-130. Major Hellenic Army types include the AB205 utility helicopter, AH-64A/DHA attack helicopter and CH-47DG/SD transport helicopter. The Hellenic Navy operates the AB212 and S-70B Aegean Hawk for anti-submarine warfare.

Specifications

Crew: 1

Powerplant: 1 x 97kN (21,834lb) SNECMA
    M53-P2 turbofan

Maximum speed: 2338km/h (1453mph)

Range: 1480km (920 miles)

Service ceiling: 18,000m (59,055ft)

Dimensions: span 9.13m (29ft 11.5in);
    length 14.36m (47ft 1.25in);

height 5.2m (17ft 0.75in)

Weight: 17,000kg (37,480lb) loaded

Armament: 2 x DEFA 554 cannon; nine external
pylons with provision for up to 6300kg
(13,889lb) of stores, including air-to-air
missiles, rocket launcher pods, and
various attack loads, including 454kg
(1000lb) bombs

▼ **Dassault Mirage 2000EGM, 114 PM, Tanagra**
Operated by 114 PM 'Antaios', from Tanagra, this Mirage apparently wears a 'kill' marking, representing a Turkish F-16D shot down in 1996. The aircraft is armed with a heat-seeking Magic 2 air-to-air missile.

HELLENIC AIR FORCE COMBAT WINGS

Hellenic Tactical Air Force			114 PM Tanagra		
110 PM Larissa*			331 Mira	Mirage 2000-5EG/BG	Tanagra
337 Mira	F-16C/D	Larissa	332 Mira	Mirage 2000EG/BG	Tanagra
346 Mira	F-16C/D	Larissa	**115 PM Souda**		
348 Mira	RF-4E	Larissa	340 Mira	F-16C/D	Souda
* maintains detachments at Limnos			343 Mira	F-16C/D	Souda
			116 PM Araxos		
111 PM Nea Anchialos*			335 Mira	F-16C/D	Araxos
330 Mira	F-16C/D	Nea Anchialos	336 Mira	A-7E, TA-7H	Araxos
341 Mira	F-16C/D	Nea Anchialos	**117 PM Andravida***		
347 Mira	F-16C/D	Nea Anchialos	338 Mira	F-4E	Andravida
* maintains F-16C/D detachments at Kasteli and Limnos			339 Mira	F-4E	Andravida
			* maintains F-4E detachment at Santorini		

AIR FORCE SUPPORT COMMAND

112 PM Elefsis		
352 Mira	ERJ-135, Gulfstream V	Elefsis
353 Mira	P-3B	Elefsis
354 Mira	C-27J	Elefsis
355 Mira	CL-215, Do 28D	Elefsis
356 Mira	C-130B/H	Elefsis
358 Mira	AB205A, Bell 212	Elefsis
380 Mira	EMB-145 AEW&C	Elefsis*
384 Mira	AS332	Elefsis
Medical Emergency Helicopter Squadron	A109E	Elefsis
independent unit, based at Elefsis		
113 PM		Thessaloniki
383 Mira	CL-415	Thessaloniki

▲ **F-4E Phantom II**

Surviving Hellenic Air Force Phantoms have undergone the Avionics Upgrade Programme and serve with two squadrons of 117 PM at Andravida. The same base also houses F-4Es assigned to the Tactical Weapons School, while 117 PM maintains a detachment on the island of Santorini.

Ireland

IRISH AIR CORPS

One of Western Europe's smallest air arms, the Irish Air Corps (Aer Chór na h-Éireann) operates a fleet of maritime patrol aircraft and VIP transports, as well as liaison and training assets.

OPERATING AS A component of the Irish Army, the Air Corps consists of two Operations Wings and an Air Corps College, with all units based at Baldonnel-Casement. 1 Operations Wing includes 101 (Maritime) Squadron with a pair of CN235 patrol aircraft, 102 (Ministerial Air Transport) Squadron with Beech 200, Gulfstream IV and Learjet 45 aircraft, and 104 (Army Co-operation) Squadron with five Cessna FR172s. 3 Operations Wing includes 301 (Search and Rescue) Squadron with six AW139s, 302 (Army Support) with EC135s. The Air Corps College flies eight PC-9 trainers.

Specifications

Crew: 1–2

Powerplant: 1 x Pratt & Whitney Canada PT6A-62 turboprop, 857kW (1149hp)

Maximum speed: 593km/h (368mph)

Range: 1593km (990 miles)

Service ceiling: 11,580m (37,992ft)

Dimensions: span 10.11m (33ft 2in); length 10.69m (35ft 1in); height 3.26m (10ft 8in)

Weight: 3200kg (7055lb) loaded

▼ **Pilatus PC-9M, Flying Training School, Baldonnel-Casement**

Irish Air Corps pilots are trained on the PC-9M fleet operated by the Flying Training School, part of the Air Corps College at Baldonnel-Casement. The PC-9M replaced SF260Ws previously in use with the unit.

Italy

AERONAUTICA MILITARE, MARINA MILITARE AND AVIAZIONE DELL' ESÈRCITO

The Italian Air Force is divided into three geographic regions, or Regioni Aeree, reporting directly to the head of the air force at AMI headquarters in Rome.

FLYING UNITS OF the AMI are based around the wing (Stormo), which in turn includes a number of air groups (Gruppi). There are also two larger formations organized as air brigades (Brigate Aeree), which include wings and/or groups.

Air defence is the responsibility of manned fighters and surface-to-air missiles, with the EF2000 now entering service to supplant the F-16. The primary offensive assets are the Tornado IDS strike aircraft, flown by a single wing, together with the AMX ground-attack aircraft, the latter equipping two wings. A single wing operates a Gruppo of Tornado IT-ECRs in the defence-suppression role. For reconnaissance, increasing use is being made of UAVs, with five examples of the RQ-1B in service.

Transport aircraft comprise the C-27J and C-130J, with four Boeing 767 tanker/transports due to be delivered in 2010. The last of the G222s are used in the radio calibration role. Initial training is undertaken using the SF260, with fighter pilots

Specifications

Crew: 1	Dimensions: span 10.95m (35ft 11in);
Powerplant: 2 x 90kN (20,250lbf) Eurojet EJ200	length 15.96m (52ft 5in);
afterburning turbofans	height 5.28m (17ft 4in)
Maximum speed: Mach 2 (2495km/h;	Weight: 16,000kg (35,300lb) loaded
1550mph)	Armament: 1 x 27mm (1.06in) Mauser BK-27
Range: 2900km (1840 miles)	cannon; 13 hardpoints holding up to 7500kg
Service ceiling: 19,810m (65,000ft)	(16,500lb) of payload

▼ Eurofighter EF2000, 12° Gruppo, 36° Stormo, Gioia del Colle

Seen in a typical air defence configuration with AIM-120 AMRAAM and IRIS-T air-to-air missiles, this single-seat EF2000 is one of an expected 96 likely to be ordered for the Italian Air Force.

Specifications

Crew: 1	13.23m (43ft 5in); height 4.55m (14ft 11in)
Powerplant: 1 x 49kN (11,000lbf) Rolls-Royce	Weight: 10,750kg (23,700lb) loaded
Spey 807 turbofan	Armament: 1 x 20mm (0.787in) M61 Vulcan
Maximum speed: 1160km/h (721mph)	rotary cannon; 2 x AIM-9 Sidewinder missiles
Range: 3330km (2070 miles)	or MAA-1 Piranha carried on wingtip rails;
Service ceiling: 13,000m (43,000ft)	3800kg (8380lb) bombload on 5 external
Dimensions: span 8.87m (29ft 1in); length	hardpoints

▼ AMX-International AMX, 14° Gruppo, 2° Stormo, Rivolto

Known as the Ghibli in Italian service, this AMX served with the now-disbanded 14° Gruppo during NATO's Allied Force campaign over Serbia in 1999, and is armed with laser-guided and retarded free-fall 'dumb' bombs and Sidewinder missile. This jet has since been transferred to 132° Gruppo at Istrana.

progressing to the MB339. The latter is also used by the Frecce Tricolori aerobatic team, the 313º Gruppo at Rivolto. An initial order has been placed for the M-346 advanced trainer, with further examples likely to supplant the MB339. SAR and CSAR are conducted by AB212 and HH-3H helicopters.

The Marine Militare Italiana jointly operates Atlantic maritime patrol aircraft with the AMI, and is otherwise responsible for providing aircraft for embarkation on Italian Navy ships. Key aircraft in use are the AV-8B+/TAV-8B strike fighter and AB212, AW101, NH90 and SH-3D helicopters.

The Aviazione dell' Esèrcito is spearheaded by A109, AB205, AB206, AB212 and AB412 utility helicopters, A129 Mangusta attack helicopters, and CH-47 heavy-lift transport helicopters.

AERONAUTICA MILITARE COMBAT AND TRANSPORT UNITS

Combat Forces Command

2° Stormo Rivolto

313° Gruppo Addestramento Acrobatico	MB339	Rivolto

4° Stormo Grosseto

| 9° Gruppo | EF2000 | Grosseto |
| 20° Gruppo | EF2000 | Grosseto |

5° Stormo Cervia

| 23° Gruppo | F-16A/B | Cervia |

6° Stormo — Ghedi

102° Gruppo	Tornado IDS	Ghedi
154° Gruppo	Tornado IDS	Ghedi
156° Gruppo	Tornado IDS	Ghedi

32° Stormo — Amendola

13° Gruppo	AMX	Amendola
28° Gruppo	RQ-1B	Amendola
101° Gruppo	AMX	Amendola

36° Stormo — Gioia del Colle

| 12° Gruppo | EF2000 | Gioia del Colle |

37° Stormo — Trapani

| 10° Gruppo | F-16A/B | Trapani |
| 18° Gruppo | F-16A/B | Trapani |

50° Stormo — Piacenza

| 155° Gruppo | Tornado IT-ECR | Piacenza |

51° Stormo — Istrana

| 103° Gruppo | AMX | Istrana |
| 132° Gruppo | AMX | Istrana |

1a Brigata Aerea Operazioni Speciali — Padua

9° Stormo — Grazzanise

| 21° Gruppo | AB212 | Grazzanise |

46a Brigata Aerea — Pisa

2° Gruppo	C-130J	Pisa
50° Gruppo	C-130J	Pisa
98° Gruppo	C-27J	Pisa

14° Stormo — Pratica di Mare

| 8° Gruppo | Boeing 767TCA, G222RM/VS | Pratica di Mare |
| 71° Gruppo | P-180 Avanti, P-166, MB339 | Pratica di Mare |

15° Stormo — Practica di Mare

81° Centro SAR	AB212	Practica di Mare
82° Centro CSAR	HH-3F	Trapani
83° Centro CSAR	HH-3F	Rimini
84° Centro CSAR	HH-3F	Brindisi
85° Centro CSAR	HH-3F	Practica di Mare

31° Stormo — Ciampino

| 93° Gruppo | Falcon 900, SH-3D | Ciampino |
| 306° Gruppo | A319CJ, Falcon 50 | Ciampino |

41° Stormo — Sigonella

| 88° Gruppo | Atlantic | Sigonella |

Note: Most Stormi (wings) within the AM also maintain a Squadriglia Collegamenti (liaison flight), normally with S-208M aircraft, MB339s in fast-jet units, and AB212AM SAR helicopters. 15° Stormo communication flight operates NH500s.

Specifications

Crew: 1

Powerplant: 1 x 105.8kN (23,800lb) Rolls-
   Royce Pegasus vectored thrust turbofan

Maximum speed: 1065km/h (661mph)

Combat radius: 277km (172 miles)

Service ceiling: more than 15,240m (50,000ft)

Dimensions: span 9.25m (30ft 4in);

length 14.12m (46ft 4in);

height 3.55m (11ft 7.75in)

Weight: 14,061kg (31,000lb) loaded

Armament: 1 x 25mm (1in) GAU-12U cannon,
   six external hardpoints with provision for up
   to 7711kg (17,000lb) (Short take-off) or
   3175kg (7000lb) (Vertical take-off) of stores

▼ Boeing (McDonnell Douglas) AV-8B+ Harrier II, 6° Reparto Aeromobili, 1° GRUPAER, Marine Militare Italiana, *Giuseppe Garibaldi*

Carrying a mixed load of laser-guided bombs and Sidewinder missiles, when not flying from the carriers *Cavour* or *Giuseppe Garibaldi*, this AV-8B+ is one of 15 examples (plus two two-seat TAV-8Bs) that are otherwise home-based at Grottaglie-Taranto.

Specifications

Crew: 1–2

Powerplant: 2 x 634kW (850shp) thrust Pratt &
   Whitney Canada PT6A-66B turboprop

Maximum speed: 732km/h (455mph)

Service ceiling: 12,500m (41,010ft)

Range: 2592km (1612 miles)

Dimensions: span 14.03m (46ft 0.5in);
   length 14.41m (47ft 31/2in);
   height 3.98m (13ft 0.75in)

Weight: 5239kg (11,550lb) loaded

▼ Piaggio P-180AM Avanti, 636a Squadriglia Collegamento, 36° Stormo, Gioia del Colle

This Avanti twin-turboprop executive transport was most recently operated by 71° Gruppo. Versions of the P-180 are also in service with the Air Section of the Marina Militare, the AMI's Aerial Weapons Training Establishment, and with the Army.

Luxembourg
NATO AIRBORNE EARLY WARNING & CONTROL FORCE

Although Luxembourg has a single A400M airlifter on order, its primary military air assets are the locally registered E-3 AWACS of the NATO Airborne Early Warning & Control Force.

CREATION OF THE NAEW&CF was authorized in 1978 by the NATO Defence Planning Committee. In terms of budget, the multi-national NAEW&CF is the single most important NATO project, and serves to provide Alliance members with air surveillance, airborne early warning and command and control capabilities.

The NATO-owned E-3A Sentry fleet has its main operating base at Geilenkirchen, in Germany, but its aircraft are registered in Luxembourg. Forward Operating Bases (FOB) are at Aktion in Greece, Trapani in Italy, Konya in Turkey, and Ørland in Norway. The fleet comprises 17 E-3A aircraft, one having been lost in an accident. Aircrew training and transport missions are conducted using three examples of the CT-49A Trainer Cargo Aircraft (TCA), these being based on modified Boeing 707-320C airframes.

Netherlands

ROYAL NETHERLANDS AIR FORCE AND MARINE LUCHTVAARTDIENST

The Royal Netherlands Air Force (Koninklijke Luchtmacht) is an active participant in NATO missions, with a force based around upgraded F-16 fighters, transports and helicopters.

THE STRUCTURE OF the RNLAF has changed following the end of the Cold War, with a reduced number of front-line F-16 units and a greater emphasis on airlift and overseas operations. Units come under the authority of the Commando Luchtstrijdkrachten (Air Force Command). The combat fleet comprises six squadrons of F-16s based at Leeuwarden, Volkel and Springfield, Ohio.

Main helicopter base is Gilze-Rijen, home of the Defensie Helikopter Commando (Defence Helicopter Commando), with CH-47Ds (with CH-47Fs on order), Cougars and AH-64Ds. Transport aircraft are based at Eindhoven in two squadrons, operating C-130Hs, one DC-10-30, two KDC-10s, Fokker 50s and a Gulfstream IV.

The Marine Luchtvaartdienst is due to receive 20 NH90s, replacing the SH-14D Lynx helicopters in service with two squadrons at De Kooy, as well as the AB412s currently used by a single reduced-size squadron for SAR duties from Leeuwarden.

Specifications

Crew: 2	Hovering ceiling: 3500m (3500ft)
Powerplant: 2 x 1599.5kW (2145hp)	Dimensions: rotor diameter 16.3m (53ft 5in);
Rolls-Royce/Turbomeca/MTU RTM	length 16.81m (55ft 2in);
322-01/9 turboshaft engines	height 5.42m (17ft 9in)
Maximum speed: 295km/h (183mph)	Weight: 9100kg (20,020lb) loaded
Combat radius: 1110km (688 miles)	

▼ **NH Industries NH90 NFH, Marine Luchtvaartdienst**

The Netherlands ordered 20 examples of the NH90 NATO Frigate Helicopter in order to replace the Lynx and AB412 in the anti-submarine warfare and search and rescue roles. NH90s will be stationed at Gilze-Rijen and De Kooy.

Specifications

Crew: 1	length 15.09m (49ft 6in);
Powerplant: either 1 x 105.7kN (23,770lb)	height 5.09m (16ft 8in)
Pratt & Whitney F100-PW-200	Weight: 16,057kg (35,400lb) loaded
Maximum speed: 2142km/h (1320mph)	Armament: 1 x General Electric M61A1 20mm
Range: 925km (525 miles)	(0.79in) multi-barrelled cannon, wingtip
Service ceiling: 15,240m (50,000ft)	missile stations; provision for up to 9276kg
Dimensions: span 9.45m (31ft);	(20,450lb) of stores

▼ **Fokker F-16A Fighting Falcon, 322 Squadron, Leeuwarden**

Fokker-built F-16A Block 15AC J-063 underwent the MLU upgrade, to become a Block 20-standard 'F-16AM'. J-063 was serving with 322 Squadron during Operation Allied Force in 1999, when it destroyed a Serbian MiG-29 using an AIM-120 missile. Since 2007 the aircraft has been flown by 306 Squadron.

Norway

ROYAL NORWEGIAN AIR FORCE

A valued NATO member, Norway's armed forces include the Luftforsvaret, or Royal Norwegian Air Force, responsible for all the country's military aviation, and divided into two commands.

THE TWO COMMANDS of the Royal Norwegian Air Force are Luftkommando Nord-Norge and Luftkommando Sør-Norge, with division of forces on a regional basis. Each air command is responsible for a number of squadrons (Skvadron).

Major combat type is the F-16, operated by three squadrons based at Bodø (two squadrons) and Ørland (one squadron). Smaller air stations comprise Andøya, Bardufoss, Sola, Rygge and Gardermoen. The air stations are provided with numbered Air Wings (Luftving), responsible for the various units at each base.

Maritime and transport assets

For maritime patrol, a single squadron of P-3C/Ns is based at Andøya, while Royal Norwegian Air Force transport capability is provided by a squadron of C-130Js based at Oslo. Two Falcon 20s are used in the electronic intelligence role from Rygge , where they serve alongside a single VIP-configured Falcon.

Bardufoss is the major helicopter base, with single squadrons of Lynx and Bell 412s. A total of 14 NH90s will eventually equip both these types, replacing the Lynx Mk86 as the Norwegian Navy's standard ship-based helicopter and superseding the

▲ **Bell 412SP**

Norway maintains a fleet of 15 Bell 412SP helicopters, some of which were assembled locally. These serve with 339 Skvadron at Bardufoss and with 720 Skvadron at Rygge, the latter with a special forces support role.

Bell 412 in the special forces role. Bell 412 and SAR-configured Sea King detachments are maintained at Bodø, Floro, Lakselv, Rygge and Ørland. The Sea Kings are home-based at Stavanger.

After initial flying training on the MFI-15 at Bardufoss, subsequent Royal Norwegian Air Force pilot training is conducted in the USA under the Euro-NATO Joint Jet Pilot Training Program.

Specifications

Crew: 1	length 15.09m (49ft 6in);
Powerplant: either 1 x 105.7kN (23,770lb)	height 5.09m (16ft 8in)
Pratt & Whitney F100-PW-200	Weight: 16,057kg (35,400lb) loaded
Maximum speed: 2142km/h (1320mph)	Armament: 1 x General Electric M61A1 20mm
Range: 925km (525 miles)	(0.79in) multi-barrelled cannon, wingtip
Service ceiling: 15,240m (50,000ft)	missile stations; provision for up to 9276kg
Dimensions: span 9.45m (31ft);	(20,450lb) of stores

▼ **Fokker F-16A Fighting Falcon, 331 Skvadron, Bodø**

This Fokker-built, MLU-upgraded F-16A was operated by 331 Skvadron until 2005, when changes within the Royal Norwegian Air Force saw it pooled within the NDLO (Norwegian Defence Logistics Organization), otherwise known as FLO (Forsvarets Logistikk Organisasjon).

672

Portugal
FORCA AEREA PORTUGUESA

The Portuguese Air Force (Força Aerea Portuguesa, FAP) is organized around numbered bases (Bases Aéreas, BA), each of which maintains operational, material and support groups.

THE ASSETS OF the FAP are divided among three major commands: Operational Command; Logistic and Administrative Command; and Personnel Command. The combat fleet is based on the F-16A/B, serving with two units at BA5 Monte Real. Overall air defence responsibility lies with the Portuguese Air Command and Control System.

The FAP transport fleet is centred at BA6 Montijo, with four squadrons under the command of Grupo Operativo 61. Three fixed-wing squadrons at BA6 operate the C-130H, C-212 and C-295, respectively. In addition to transport, the C-295 can also be configured for maritime patrol duties. The final units at BA6 are a SAR squadron with Pumas, and a squadron of Lynx Mk95 operated by the Navy (Marinha). Three Falcon 50s are permanently detached from Montijo to Lisbon for VIP duties.

FAP training fleet
Grupo Operativo 11 at BA11 Beja is home to the training effort, with three squadrons equipped with the Alouette III helicopter, Alpha Jet A advanced jet trainer and Epsilon basic trainer, respectively. Some pilots train in the USA under the Euro-NATO Joint Jet Pilot Training Program. Maritime patrol is the responsibility of the P-3P/C, which are also assigned to a single squadron at BA11.

Grupo Operativo 1 is at BA1 Sintra, and includes the Air Force Academy, equipped with gliders.

BA4 Lajes is home to Grupo Operativo 41, which maintains detachments of C-212s used for photo-survey and maritime patrol, and EH101s for SAR. A single SAR squadron with Pumas remains active at Lajes, until the EH101 attains full operational capability.

▲ **Aérospatiale SA330S1 Puma**
Although mainly replaced in the SAR role by the EH101, the FAP maintains a few Pumas. After being retired in 2006, five SA330s were reactivated in 2007 to provide island SAR cover for the Azores and Madeira.

Specifications
Crew: 1	length 15.09m (49ft 6in);
Powerplant: either 1 x 105.7kN (23,770lb)	height 5.09m (16ft 8in)
Pratt & Whitney F100-PW-200	Weight: 16,057kg (35,400lb) loaded
Maximum speed: 2142km/h (1320mph)	Armament: 1 x General Electric M61A1 20mm
Range: 925km (525 miles)	(0.79in) multi-barrelled cannon, wingtip
Service ceiling: 15,240m (50,000ft)	missile stations; provision for up to 9276kg
Dimensions: span 9.45m (31ft);	(20,450lb) of stores

▼ **General Dynamics F-16A Fighting Falcon, Esquadra 301 'Jaguares', BA5 Monte Real**
F-16A Block 15J 82-0918 has been upgraded to F-16A Block 20 MLU standard. Monte Real is home to two F-16 units: Esquadra 201 'Falcões' and Esquadra 201 'Jaguares'.

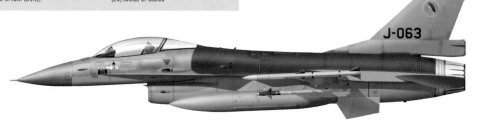

Spain

EJÉRCITO DEL AIRE, ARMADA AND ARMY AVIATION

The Spanish Air Force maintains a varied and powerful fleet, while the Armada possesses a carrier air wing and other ship-based assets, and Army Aviation has a large helicopter force.

SPAIN'S AIR ARM is organized on a regional basis, with three separate air commands: Mando Aéreo del Centro (MACEN, headquartered in Madrid); Mando Aéreo del Estrecho (MAEST, headquartered in Seville); and Mando Aéreo de Levante (MALEV, with its headquarters in Zaragoza).

Combat and transport assets of MACEN include and F/A-18A+/B+ wing at Torrejón and a transport wing with CN235s and C-295s at Getafe. A C-212 wing is based at Valladolid, while Cuatro Vientos has a mixed wing of AS332, AS532

C-212 and CN235 aircraft. Torrejón also supports a wing of CL-215T and CL-415 firefighters, a VIP squadron with A310 and Falcon 900 aircraft, a mixed group of Boeing 707, C-212 and Falcon 20 aircraft and a single squadron of C-212s and C-101 jet trainers.

MAEST combat types comprise an EF2000 fighter wing at Morón, and a Mirage F1M/BM fighter wing at Albacete. A wing of modernized F-5Ms operates from Badajoz. Also at Morón is a maritime patrol squadron with P-3A/B/M aircraft.

Specifications

Crew: 1	length 14.12m (46ft 4in);
Powerplant: 1 x 105.8kN (23,800lb) Rolls-Royce Pegasus vectored thrust turbofan	height 3.55m (11ft 7.75in)
	Weight: 14,061kg (31,000lb) loaded
Maximum speed: 1065km/h (661mph)	Armament: 1 x 25mm (1in) GAU-12U cannon,
Combat radius: 277km (172 miles)	six external hardpoints with provision for up
Service ceiling: more than 15,240m (50,000ft)	to 7711kg (17,000lb) (Short take-off) or
Dimensions: span 9.25m (30ft 4in);	3175kg (7000lb) (Vertical take-off) of stores

▼ Boeing (McDonnell Douglas) EAV-8B+ Harrier II, 9a Escuadrilla, Flotilla de Aeronaves de la Armada, *Príncipe de Asturias*

Known as the VA.1 Matador II in Armada service, Spain operates 12 single-seat AV-8B+ fighters and a single TAV-8B trainer. When not assigned to the carrier *Príncipe de Asturias*, the Harriers operate from Rota.

Specifications

Crew: 1	Dimensions: span 10.95m (35ft 11in);
Powerplant: 2 x 90kN (20,250lbf) Eurojet EJ200 afterburning turbofans	length 15.96m (52ft 5in);
	height 5.28m (17ft 4in)
Maximum speed: Mach 2 (2495km/h; 1550mph)	Weight: 16,000kg (35,300lb) loaded
	Armament: 1 x 27mm (1.06in) Mauser BK-27
Range: 2900km (1840 miles)	cannon; 13 hardpoints holding up to 7500kg
Service ceiling: 19,810m (65,000ft)	(16,500lb) of payload

▼ Eurofighter EF2000, 111 Escuadrón, Ala 11, Morón

Armed with AIM-120 AMRAAM and AIM-9L/M air-to-air missiles, this EF2000 is operated by the lead Spanish wing, Ala 11, based at Morón air base, near Seville. The fighter has the local designation C.16, while the two-seat version is the CE.16.

Combat units within MALEV consist of a Zaragoza-based wing with three squadrons of F/A-18A+/B+ Hornets, and a wing of KC/C-130H tanker/transport aircraft at the same base.

Mando Aéreo de Canarias (MACAN) provides airpower for the Canary Islands, and consists of a single squadron of F/A-18As together with a mixed squadron of F27 maritime patrol aircraft and AS332 SAR helicopters, based at Las Palmas.

Combat assets of the Armada comprise AB212 and SH-60B anti-submarine and utility helicopters, EAV-8B and EAV-8B+ carrier strike fighters, and SH-3s used for airborne early warning and transport.

The BO105 is the most numerous Army Aviation type, but a replacement is now required. A total of 45 NH90s are on order, while other current Army types include the AB212, AS332, AS532, CH-47D, EC135, Tiger HAD attack helicopter and the UH-1H.

▲ McDonnell Douglas F/A-18A+ Hornet

An Ala 12 Hornet armed with 228kg (500lb) laser-guided bombs and wingtip Sidewinders during Operation Allied Force. The Hornet fleet comprises 55 upgraded F/A-18A+ and 11 F/A-18B+ aircraft built for Spain under the manufacturer's EF-18 designation, together with 22 ex-U.S. Navy F/A-18As.

Specifications

Crew: 1

Powerplant: 2 x 79.2kN (17,750lb) thrust General Electric F404-GE-402 afterburning turbofan engines

Maximum speed: 1915km/h (1190mph)

Range: 3330km (2070 miles)

Service ceiling: 15,000m (50,000ft)

Dimensions: span 12.3m (40ft); length 17.1m (56ft); height 4.7m (15ft 4in)

Weight: 16,850kg (37,150lb) loaded

Armament: 1 x 20mm (0.787in) M61A1 Vulcan nose-mounted gatling gun; 9 external hardpoints for up to 6215kg (13,700lb) of stores

▼ McDonnell Douglas F/A-18A+ Hornet, 462 Escuadrón 'Halcones', Ala 66, Gran Canaria

In Spain, Hornets received the local designation C.15. This example is former U.S. Navy BuNo 161939, now in service at Gran Canaria to provide defence for the Canary Islands. The F/A-18A+/B+ upgrades brings the aircraft to near-F/A-18C/D standard.

Specifications

Crew: 2

Powerplant: 2 x 79.6kN (17900lb) thrust General Electric J79-GE-17 afterburning turbojet engines

Maximum speed: 2390km/h (1485mph)

Range: 800km (500 miles)

Service ceiling: 18,900m (62,000ft)

Dimensions: span 11.7m (38ft 5in); length 18m (59ft); height 4.96m (16ft 3in)

Weight: 24,766kg (54,600lb) loaded

▼ McDonnell Douglas RF-4C Phantom II, 123 Escuadrón, Ala 12, Torrejón

Spain's RF-4Cs received upgrades including AN/APQ-172 radar, updated avionics, digital radios, revised countermeasures, an Israeli refuelling probe and provision for AIM-9L Sidewinder missiles, allowing them to serve until 2002.

Sweden

FLYGVAPNET

Neutral, but with a strong tradition of military self-sufficiency, Sweden's Flygvapnet is a modern and well-equipped force, although in recent years a number of units have been deactivated.

THE VARIOUS UNITS of the Flygvapnet are part of the Försvarsmakten (Swedish Armed Forces). Previously organized on the basis of three independent regional Air Commands (South, Central and North), the Flygvapnet's units are now headed by a single unified command, the FlygTaktiska Kommando (FTK), with headquarters at Uppsala. Today, the military districts comprise the Northern Military District (HQ at Boden), Central Military District (HQ at Strängnäs), the Southern Military District (HQ at Gothenburg) and the Gotlands Military District (HQ at Visby).

The Flygvapnet's wings (Flygflottiljen) and helicopter battalions (Helikopterbataljonen) report to the four military districts. The fighter wings are equipped with the multi-role Gripen, with the original JAS 39A/B variants now undergoing upgrade to JAS 39C/D standard, which includes in-flight refuelling capability, large screen, full-colour cockpit displays, and a strengthened wing structure that allows new pylons to be fitted. Fighter pilots train on the Sk 60 jet trainer with the air combat school

(Luftstridsskolan), and these aircraft are assigned to each of the three fighter wings, alongside two Gripen units. A final operator of the Sk 60 is the Flygvapnet aerobatic display team, or TEAM 60.

Helicopter structure

The helicopter units have been integrated within a common structure as the Försvarsmaktens Helikopterflottilj Swedish Armed Forces Helicopter Wing, which is now equipped with four helicopter squadrons and a single independent direct-reporting unit. The Helikopterflottilj is in the process of modernization, for which it is receiving Hkp 15 (A109) and Hkp 14 (NH90) helicopters. The NH90 will be used for anti-submarine warfare and search and rescue (SAR), while the Hkp 15 will be used for utility and SAR and deploys on board Swedish Navy warships. Other helicopters currently in use are the Hkp 9 (B0105) for anti-armour and observation, and the Hkp 10 (Super Puma) for SAR.

Largest of the military districts are the Northern and Southern, each of which are provided with two fighter wings and five transport/communications

Specifications

Crew: 1	Weight: 12,473kg (27,500lb) loaded
Powerplant: 1 x 80.5kN (18,100lb. thrust) Volvo	Armament: 1 x 27mm (1.06in) Mauser BK27
Flygmotor RM12 turbofan	cannon; 6 external hardpoints with provision
Maximum speed: 2126km/h (1321mph)	for Rb71 Sky Flash and Rb24 Sidewinder
Range: 3250km (2020 miles)	air-to-air missiles, Maverick air-to-surface
Dimensions: span 8m (26ft 3in); length	missiles and other stores
14.10m (46ft 3in); height 4.70m (15ft 5in)	

▼ **SAAB JAS 39A Gripen, F7, Såtenäs**

The Gripen spearheads the Swedish Air Force and is equipped for air defence, attack, anti-shipping and reconnaissance missions. JAS 39A/Bs are being upgraded to C/D standard, with a refuelling probe, NATO-compatible avionics and other improvements.

FLYGVAPNET

F7 – Skaraborgs flygflottilj Såtenäs

1. Division	JAS 39A/B	Såtenäs
2. Division	JAS 39A/B	Såtenäs
Sambandsflygrupp	Sk 60	
TSFE Såtenäs	TP 84	Såtenäs
TSFE	S 100B, S 102B	Linköping
TSFE (Det) Bromma	OS 100, TP 102	Stockholm-Bromma

F17 – Blekinge flygflottilj Ronneby

1. Division	JAS 39C/D	Ronneby
2. Division	JAS 39C/D	Ronneby
Sambandsflygrupp	Sk 60	
TSFE (Det)	TP 100*	Ronneby
* TP 100 fleet is part of F7.		

F21 – Norbottens flygflottilj Luleå

1. Division	JAS 39C/D	Luleå
2. Division	JAS 39C/D	Luleå
Sambandsflygrupp	Sk 60	
TSFE (Det)	TP 100*	Kallax
* TP 100 fleet is part of F7.		

Hkpflj – Helicopterflottiljen

1.Hkpskv	Hkp 10	Luleå
2.Hkpskv	Hkp 9, Hkp 14, Hkp 15	Linköping
3.Hkpskv	Hkp 9, Hkp 10, Hkp 14, Hkp 15	Ronneby
3.Hkps Såtenäs	Hkp 10	Såtenäs

LSS – Luftstridsskolan

FlygS	Sk 60A/B/C	Linköping
TEAM 60	Sk 60A	Linköping

squadrons, the latter operating fixed-wing TP 84 Hercules, TP 100 Argus (Saab 340) and TP 102 (Gulfstream IV) VIP transports.

Other units include separate airborne early warning and signals intelligence units at Linköping, as part of the TSFE, with two S 102B (Gulfstream IV) aircraft equipped for SIGINT and six S 100 Argus (Saab 340) AEW platforms. A single OS 100 is equipped for Open Skies surveillance missions and serves at Stockholm-Bromma.

Miscellaneous units comprise a communications flight (Sambandsflygrupp), a basic flying training unit (Grundläggande Flygutbildning), a basic tactical training unit (Grundläggande Taktisk Utbildning) and a test centre (Försökscentralen).

▾ NH Industries NH90, 2.Hkpskv, Försvarsmaktens Helikopterflottilj, Linköping

Known as the Hkp 14 in local service, Sweden placed orders for 13 Tactical Troop Transport (TTT) versions of the NH90 that will also be used for SAR, plus five that will be dedicated to anti-submarine warfare. Sweden was launch customer for the High Cabin Version of the NH90.

Specifications

Crew: 2
Powerplant: 2 x 1599.5kW (2145hp) Rolls-Royce/Turbomeca/MTU RTM 322-01/9 turboshaft engines
Maximum speed: 295km/h (183mph)
Combat radius: 1110km (688 miles)
Hovering ceiling: 3500m (3500ft)
Dimensions: rotor diameter 16.3m (53ft 5in); length 16.81m (55ft 2in); height 5.42m (17ft 9in)
Weight: 9100kg (20,020lb) loaded

▼ Agusta-Bell AB412SP, Helicopterflottiljen, Linkoping

Receiving the local designation Hkp 11, five examples of the AB412 were operated in the SAR and medical evacuation roles from 1994, although the type was retired from service in the mid-2000s and has been superseded by the NH90.

Specifications

Crew: 3

Powerplant: 2 x 671 kW (900hp) Pratt &
   Whitney Canada PT6T-3D turboshafts

Maximum speed: 260km/h (160mph)

Range: 656km (405 miles)

Capacity: 10 troops or 6 stretchers

Dimensions: rotor diameter 14m (45ft 11in);
   length 17.1m (56ft 1in);
   height 4.6m (15ft 1in)

Weight: 5355kg (11,900lb)

Armament: 1 x 7.62mm (0.29in) C6 GPMG; 1 x
   7.62mm (0.29in) Dillon Aero M134D 'Minigun'

Switzerland

SCHWEIZER LUFTWAFFE

Highly trained and thoroughly equipped, the Swiss Air Force is tasked with preserving Swiss sovereignty, if threatened, and makes considerable use of reservists and reserve bases.

THE COMBAT EQUIPMENT of the Swiss Air Force is led by the multi-role F/A-18C/D, supplemented in the air defence role by the F-5E/F, for which a replacement is now sought. Helicopter transport is provided by the AS332 and AS532, supported by EC635 utility helicopters. Training is conducted on the PC-7 and the advanced PC-21, while PC-9s are in use for electronic warfare training and target towing. VIP transport is the primary role of single examples of the Cessna 560 Citation and Falcon 50. Light fixed-wing transport capacity is provided by the PC-6, also used for parachute training, and the PC-12. Mountain rescue and SAR are of particular importance to the Swiss Air Force, for which it relies on a large fleet of SA316 helicopters.

Restructuring had been pursued under the Armée XXI programme. The Überwachungsgeschwader 85, (surveillance wing) is now responsible for operational and training activities, via the Kommando Piloten Schule Luftwaffe 85, Kommando Lufttransporte and the Kommando Luftverteidigung 85, the latter commanding the Flieger Geschwader (air wings).

Specifications

Crew: 1

Powerplant: 2 x 79.2kN (17,750lb) thrust
   General Electric F404-GE-402 afterburning
   turbofan engines

Maximum speed: 1915km/h (1190mph)

Range: 3330km (2070 miles)

Service ceiling: 15,000m (50,000ft)

Dimensions: span 12.3m (40ft);
   length 17.1m (56ft); height 4.7m (15ft 4in)

Weight: 16,850kg (37,150lb) loaded

Armament: 1 x 20mm (0.78in) M61A1 Vulcan
   nose mounted gatling gun; 9 external
   hardpoints for up to 6215kg (13,700lb)
   of stores

▼ Boeing F/A-18C Hornet, Fliegerstaffel 11, Fliegergeschwader 13, Meiringen

J-5014 has been operated by Fliegerstaffel 11 since 1999. The Swiss Hornet has been upgraded locally by RUAG, adding a helmet-mounted sight, AIM-9X Sidewinder missiles and Link 16 datalink, among others.

Turkey

TÜRK HAVA KUVVETLERI

The Turkish Air Force (Türk Hava Kuvvetleri) is divided into two Air Force Commands (Hava Kuvvet Komutanligi): 1nci HKK in the west of the country, and 2nci HKK in the east.

THE LARGER OF the two commands, 1nci HKK is headquartered in Eskisehir and includes five air wings (or Ana Jet Üs, or AJÜ). In addition to its major operating bases, 1nci HKK also makes use of a number of secondary air bases (Hava Meydani), to which it regularly deploys its aircraft. With headquarters at Diyarbakir, the smaller 2nci HKK operates four air wings from a similar number of bases, and also from secondary air bases in the eastern part of the country.

The Turkish Air Force maintains an Air Logistics Command, responsible for military and VIP transport as well as maintenance. The final flying command is Air Training Command, with its headquarters in Izmir.

At the forefront of the Turkish Air Force is the F-16C/D, which is also assembled locally by Turkish Aerospace Industries (TAI). The upgraded F-4E remains an important fighter, while the RF-4E serves in the reconnaissance role. Surviving F-5s provide

Specifications

Crew: 2

Powerplant: 2 x 79.6kN (17,900lb) General Electric J79-GE-17C or 17E turbojets

Maximum speed: 2390km/h (1485mph)

Range: 817km (1750 miles)

Service ceiling: 19,685m (60,000ft)

Dimensions: span 11.7m (38ft 5in); length 17.76m (58ft 3in); height 4.96m (16ft 3in)

Weight: 25,558kg (56,346lb) loaded

Armament: 1 x 20mm (0.79in) M61A1 Vulcan cannon, capability to launch AGM-65D/G Maverick, AGM-88 HARM, GBU-8 HOBOS, GBU-10/12 Paveway II LGBs, general purpose and cluster bombs for air-to-ground missions

▼ **McDonnell Douglas F-4E Phantom II, 171 Filo, Malatya**

Turkey upgraded 54 of its Phantoms to F-4E-2020 Terminator standard with Israeli assistance, this consisting of structural and avionics improvements, including new strakes above the air intakes, multi-function cockpit displays, multi-mode fire-control radar and Litening II targeting pod for use with a range of precision weapons.

Specifications

Crew: 1

Powerplant: 1 x 126.7kN (28,500lb) thrust Pratt & Whitney F100-PW-229 afterburning turbofan

Maximum speed: 2177km/h (1353mph)

Range: 3862km (2400 miles)

Service ceiling: 15,240m (49,000ft)

Dimensions: span 9.45m (31ft); length 15.09m (49ft 6in); height 5.09m (16ft 8in)

Weight: 19,187kg (42,300lb) loaded

Armament: 1 x General Electric M61A1 20mm (0.79in) multi-barrelled cannon, wingtip missile stations; 7 external hardpoints with provision for up to 9276kg (20,450lb) of stores

▼ **General Dynamics F-16C Fighting Falcon, 162 Filo, Bandirma**

Turkey received 240 F-16C/D aircraft from the Block 30/40/50 production standards. 92-0003 is a Block 40L jet delivered in 1993, and it entered service with 162 Filo in 2001.

TURKISH AF COMBAT AND TRANSPORT UNITS

1nci HKK – 1st Air Force Command HQ Eskisehir

1nci AJÜ	Eskisehir	
111 Filo	F-4E	Eskisehir
112 Filo	F-4E	Eskisehir
113 Filo	RF-4E	Eskisehir
201 Filo	CN235, AS532	Eskisehir

3ncu AJÜ	Konya	
131 Filo	Boeing 737AEW&C	Konya
132 Filo	F-4E, F-16C/D	Konya
133 Filo	(N)F-5A/B	Konya
134 Filo Turkish Stars	NF-5A/B	Konya

4ncu AJÜ	Ankara/Akinci	
141 Filo	F-16C/D	
142 Filo	F-16C/D	
143 Filo	F-16C/D	

6nci AJÜ	Bandirma	
161 Filo	F-16C/D	Bandirma
162 Filo	F-16C/D	Bandirma

9nci AJÜ	Balikesir	
191 Filo	F-16C/D	Balikesir
192 Filo	F-16C/D	Balikesir

Hava Meydani (secondary air bases)
Izmir-Adnan Menderes
Çorlu
Afyon
Akhisar
Sivrihisar
Istanbul Atatürk International Airport

2nci HKK – 2nd Air Force Command HQ Diyarbakir

5nci AJÜ	Merzifon	
151 Filo	F-16C/D	Merzifon
152 Filo	F-16C/D	Merzifon

7nci AJÜ	Malatya	
171 Filo	F-4E	Malatya
173 Filo	F-4E, RF-4E	Malatya

8nci AJÜ	Diyarbakir	
181 Filo	F-16C/D	Diyarbakir
182 Filo	F-16C/D	Diyarbakir
202 Filo	CN235, AS532	

10nci TUK	Incirlik	
101 Filo	KC-135R	Incirlik

Hava Meydani (secondary air bases)
Batman
Erzurum
Mus
Sivas

Note: Most bases support a liaison and SAR flight (AJÜ A&KK) equipped with AS532 helicopters.

Hava Lojistik Komutanligi – Air Logistics Command HQ Etimesgut/Ankara

11nci HUAÜK	Etimesgut/Ankara	
211 Filo	CN235	Etimesgut/Ankara
212 Filo	CN235, Cessna 550/650, Gulfstream IV/550, UH-1H	Etimesgut/Ankara

12nci HUAU	Kayseri	
221 Filo	Transall	Kayseri
222 Filo	C-130B/E	Kayseri
223 Filo	CN235	Kayseri

lead-in fighter training and also equip the aerobatic demonstration team, the Turkish Stars. Training is also carried out on the T-37B/C and T-38A jet trainers, and the SF260 and T-41D primary trainer, although KT-1 Ungbis are on order to replace the latter types. Due to be delivered in 2010 were four Boeing 737 airborne early warning and control aircraft, together with additional Block 50 F-16C/Ds. The Turkish Army relies on a large fleet of helicopters to support its operations, the major front-line types being the AB204, AB205 and UH-H utility types, AH-1 attack helicopters, AS532s for combat search and rescue and S-70As for transport.

Front-line Naval Aviation aircraft are the AB212 and S-70B for anti-submarine warfare, with CN-235s used for maritime patrol. ATR-72s are on order.

United Kingdom
ROYAL AIR FORCE, FLEET AIR ARM AND ARMY AIR CORPS

In common with many Western European air arms, the RAF has undergone drastic cuts in recent years, while at the same time facing increasing operational demands.

A S A RESULT of cuts, the strength of the RAF has been reduced to 44,000 personnel, with front-line assets divided among nine Expeditionary Air Wings, which fall under the Air Command with its HQ at High Wycombe. Air Command is divided into Nos 1, 2 and 22 Groups, respectively responsible for fast jet, transport/refuelling and ISTAR, and training. Support helicopters are operated by Joint Helicopter Command (JHC), a tri-service organization. Another joint operation is the Harrier GR9 force, in which RAF Harriers operate alongside those of the Fleet Air Arm's Naval Strike Wing within Joint Force Harrier. The Harrier is ultimately to be replaced by the F-35 Joint Combat Aircraft. Eventually, the RAF hopes to field a 12-squadron front-line force, with seven Typhoon units, at least three F-35 units, and Unmanned Combat Aerial Vehicles (UCAVs).

Maritime patrol is handled by the Nimrod MR2, which is due to be replaced by the entirely rebuilt Nimrod MRA4. Three Nimrod R1s used for intelligence gathering will be replaced by RC-135V/W Rivet Joints. Battlefield ISTAR requirements are met by the Sentinel R1 ASTOR (Airborne STand-Off Radar), based on the Bombardier Global Express airframe. These latter serve alongside the Sentry AEW1 at Waddington.

Operational support

Transport and tanking capability is due to be overhauled by the A400M airlifter and A330 tanker transports. Currently the C-17 Globemaster III

RAF FLYING SQUADRONS		
Offensive Support		
No 1(F) Squadron	Harrier GR9/9A	Cottesmore
No 2(AC) Squadron	Tornado GR4/4A	Marham
No 4(AC) Squadron	Harrier GR9/9A	Cottesmore
No 9(B) Squadron	Tornado GR4	Marham
No 12(B) Squadron	Tornado GR4	Lossiemouth
No 13 Squadron	Tornado GR4/4A	Marham
No 14 Squadron	Tornado GR4	Lossiemouth
No 31 Squadron	Tornado GR4	Marham
No 617 Squadron	Tornado GR4	Lossiemouth

Specifications
Crew: 1

Powerplant: 2 x 88.9kW (20,000lbs) thrust
Eurojet EJ200 turbojets

Max speed: Mach 2 (2495km/h; 1550mph)

Range: 2900km (1840 miles)

Service ceiling: 19,812m (65,000ft)

Dimensions: span 11.09m (36ft 4.8in); length

15.96m (52ft 4in); height 5.28m (17ft 4in)

Weight: 16,000kg (35,300lb) loaded

Armament: 1 x 27mm (1.06in) Mauser BK-27 cannon; 13 hardpoints with provision for AMRAAM, ASRAAM air-to-air missiles; Storm shadow and Brimstone air-to-surface missiles, Enhanced Paveway laser-guided bombs

▼ **Eurofighter Typhoon F2, No 3(F) Squadron, Coningsby**
No 3(F) Squadron's Typhoons share the Quick Reaction Alert air defence mission with Tornado F3s based at Leuchars. No 3(F) Squadron stood up as the RAF's first operational front-line Typhoon squadron in 2006.

Specifications

Crew: 2

Powerplant: 1 x 23.1kN (5200lb) Rolls
  Royce/Turbomeca Adour Mk 151 turbofan

Maximum speed: 1038km/h (645mph)

Endurance: 4 hours

Service ceiling: 15,240m (50,000ft)

Dimensions: span 9.39m (30ft 9.75in);
  length 11.17m (36ft 7.75in);
  height 3.99m (13ft 1.75in)

Weight: 7750kg (17,085lb) loaded

▼ BAe Hawk T1, No 208(R) Squadron, Valley

Valley is home to RAF fast-jet training. Prospective fighter pilots complete Basic Fast Jet Training, beginning on the Tucano before moving to Valley and No 208(R) Squadron (conversion and advanced flying training) and No 19(R) Squadron (tactical weapons training).

Specifications

Crew: 2

Powerplant: 2 x 73.5kN (16,520lb) Turbo-Union
  RB.199-34R Mk 104 turbofans

Maximum speed: 2337km/h (1452mph)

Intercept radius: more than 1853km
  (1150 miles)

Service ceiling: 21,335m (70,000ft)

Dimensions: span 13.91m (45ft 7.75in) spread
  and 8.6m (28ft 2.5in) swept; length 18.68m
  (61ft 3in); height 5.95m (19ft 6.25in)

Weight: 27,987kg (61,700lb) loaded

Armament: 2 x 27mm (1.06in) IWKA-Mauser
  cannon, 6 external hardpoints with provision
  for up to 5806kg (12,800lb) of stores

▼ Panavia Tornado F3, No 111(F) Squadron, Leuchars

Based at Leuchars in Scotland, No 111(F) Squadron is the final RAF operator of the Tornado F3 interceptor. The RAF maintains two pairs of Quick Reaction Alert aircraft on round-the-clock alert at Leuchars (Northern QRA) and Coningsby (Southern QRA, with Typhoons).

Air Defence and Airborne Early Warning

No 3(F) Squadron	Typhoon F2	Coningsby
No 8 Squadron	Sentry AEW1	Waddington
No 11(F) Squadron	Typhoon FGR4	Coningsby
No 23 Squadron	Sentry AEW1	Waddington
No 43(F) Squadron	Tornado F3	Leuchars
No 111(F) Squadron	Tornado F3	Leuchars

Reconnaissance

No 5(AC) Squadron	Sentinel R1	Waddington
No 51 Squadron	Nimrod R1	Waddington

Flying Training

No 19(R) Squadron	Hawk T1A	Valley
No 45(R) Squadron	King Air 200	Cranwell
No 55(R) Squadron	Dominie T1	Cranwell
No 60(R) Squadron	Griffin HT1	Shawbury
No 72(R) Squadron	Tucano T1	Linton-on-Ouse
No 100 Squadron	Hawk T1A	Leeming
No 207(R) Squadron	Tucano T1	Linton-on-Ouse
No 208(R) Squadron	Hawk T1	Valley

Operational Conversion Units

No 15(R) Squadron	Tornado GR4	Lossiemouth
No 17(R) Squadron	Typhoon F2/FGR4	Coningsby
No 20(R) Squadron	Harrier GR9/T12	Wittering
No 29(R) Squadron	Typhoon T1/F2	Coningsby
No 41(R) Squadron	Harrier GR9, Tornado GR4	Coningsby
No 56(R) Squadron	Nimrod MR2/MRA4/R1, Sentinel R1, Sentry AEW1	
No 203(R) Squadron	Sea King HAR3	Valley

Air Transport and Air-to-Air Refuelling

No 24 Squadron	Hercules C4/5	Lyneham
No 30 Squadron	Hercules C4/5	Lyneham
No 32 (The Royal) Squadron	BAe 125 CC3, BAe 146 CC2, A109E	Northolt
No 47 Squadron	Hercules C1/C3/C3A	Lyneham
No 70 Squadron	Hercules C3	Lyneham
No 99 Squadron	C-17A	Brize Norton
No 101 Squadron	VC10 C1K/K3/K4	Brize Norton
No 216 Squadron	TriStar C2/C2A/K1/KC1	Brize Norton

Support Helicopter

No 7 Squadron	Chinook HC2/2A	Odiham
No 18 Squadron	Chinook HC2/2A	Odiham
No 27 Squadron	Chinook HC2/2A	Odiham
No 28(AC) Squadron	Merlin HC3	Benson
No 33 Squadron	Puma HC1	Benson
No 78 Squadron	Merlin HC3A	Benson
No 230 Squadron	Puma HC1	Benson

Maritime Patrol and Search and Rescue

No 22 Squadron	Sea King HAR3/3A	A Flight Chivenor, B Flight Wattisham, C Flight Valley
No 42(R) Squadron	Nimrod MR2	Kinloss
No 84 Squadron	Griffin HT1	Akrotiri
No 120 Squadron	Nimrod MR2	Kinloss
No 201 Squadron	Nimrod MR2	Kinloss
No 202 Squadron	Sea King HAR3/3A	A Flight Boulmer, D Flight Lossiemouth, E Flight Leconfield

Unmanned Aerial Vehicle

No 39 Squadron	MQ-9	Creech AFB

Specifications

Crew: 2

Powerplant: 2 x 76.8kN (17,270lbf) Turbo-Union RB199-34R Mk 103 afterburning turbofans

Maximum speed: Mach 2.34 (2417.6km/h; 1511mph)

Combat radius: 1390km (870 miles)

Service ceiling: 15,240m (50,000ft)

Dimensions: span 13.91m (45.6ft) unswept, 8.60m (28.2ft) swept; length 16.72m (54ft 10in); height 5.95m (19.5ft)

Weight: 28,000kg (61,700lb) loaded

Armament: 2 x 27mm (1.06in) Mauser BK-27 cannon, 4 x under-fuselage and 4 x swivelling underwing pylon stations holding up to 9000kg (19,800lb) of payload

▼ **Panavia Tornado GR4, No 12(B) Squadron, Lossiemouth**

The RAF has seven front-line Tornado GR4/4A strike/attack squadrons, divided between Lossiemouth in Scotland and Marham. Tornados have seen combat over Afghanistan and Iraq, and are now equipped with Litening III targeting pods for precision-weapons delivery and ISTAR.

provides the backbone of the RAF's airlift capability, together with the Hercules force. The older Hercules C1/3 models will be replaced by 25 A400Ms.

The Royal Navy's Fleet Air Arm is responsible for providing airpower to be deployed aboard its warships, and the primary aviation assets are the Lynx shipborne anti-submarine helicopter, due to be replaced by the new Lynx Wildcat from 2011. Other front-line helicopters are the Merlin for anti-

submarine warfare and the Sea King, used for airborne early warning, special operations and SAR.

The Army Air Corps inventory includes Apache attack helicopters, Lynx battlefield mobility helicopters (to be replaced by Lynx Wildcats from 2011), and Gazelle utility helicopters. 7 Regiment AAC is responsible for training. The AAC maintains a number of independent flights, including flights stationed in Belize, Brunei and Canada.

Specifications

Crew: 4	Dimensions: span 18.6m (61ft); length 22.8m
Powerplant: 3 x 1688kW (2263shp) Rolls-Royce	(74ft 8in); height 6.65m (21ft 10in)
Turbomeca RTM 322 turbines	Weight: 15,600kg (32,188lb) loaded
Maximum speed: 167 knots (309km/h;	Armament: 5 x general-purpose machine guns;
192mph)	960kg (2116lb) of anti-ship missiles, homing
Range: 1380km (863 miles)	torpedoes, depth charges and rockets
Service ceiling: 4572m (15,000ft)	

▼ **AgustaWestland Merlin HM1, 829 Naval Air Squadron, Culdrose**

Royal Navy Merlins operate within five squadrons, all based at Culdrose when disembarked. With a primary role of anti-submarine warfare, Merlins are flown from the flight decks of warships including aircraft carriers, Auxiliary Oilers (Replenishment), and Type 23 frigates.

FLEET AIR ARM FLYING SQUADRONS

Naval Strike Wing	Harrier GR7/7A/9/9A	Cottesmore	820 Naval Air Squadron	Merlin HM1	Culdrose
702 Naval Air Squadron	Lynx HAS3/HMA8	Yeovilton	824 Naval Air Squadron	Merlin HM1	Culdrose
703 Naval Air Squadron	Firefly T67/Tutor T1	RAF Barkston Heath	829 Naval Air Squadron	Merlin HM1	Culdrose
705 Naval Air Squadron	Squirrel HT1	RAF Shawbury	845 Naval Air Squadron	Sea King HC4/HC6CR	Yeovilton
727 Naval Air Squadron	Tutor T1	Yeovilton	846 Naval Air Squadron	Sea King HC4	Yeovilton
750 Naval Air Squadron	Jetstream T2/3, Super King Air	Culdrose	847 Naval Air Squadron	Lynx AH7	Yeovilton
771 Naval Air Squadron	Sea King HAS5/6	Culdrose	848 Naval Air Squadron	Sea King HC4	Yeovilton
792 Naval Air Squadron	Mirach 100/5	Culdrose	849 Naval Air Squadron	Sea King ASaC7	Culdrose
814 Naval Air Squadron	Merlin HM1	Culdrose	854 Naval Air Squadron	Sea King ASaC7	Culdrose
815 Naval Air Squadron	Lynx HAS3/HMA8	Yeovilton	857 Naval Air Squadron	Sea King ASaC7	Culdrose

RUSSIA

ESTONIA

LATVIA

LITHUANIA

RUSSIAN FED.

BELARUS

RUSSIA

POLAND

UKRAINE

CZECH REPUBLIC

SLOVAKIA

MOLDOVA

HUNGARY

SLOVENIA

CROATIA

ROMANIA

BOSNIA &
HERZEGOVINA

SERBIA

BLACK SEA

KOSOVO

BULGARIA

MONTENEGRO

MACEDONIA

ALBANIA

Chapter 13

Eastern Europe

The air forces of Eastern Europe have changed immeasurably since the fall of the Soviet Bloc. The former Warsaw Pact countries now increasingly look to the West, and a number have now joined NATO, or are hopeful of future membership in the alliance. The disintegration of the USSR also granted independence to former Soviet Republics in the European zone, and these have gone about establishing independent air forces, typically based on equipment inherited from the USSR. The traumatic break-up of the former Yugoslavia has left new entities in its wake, and these all now operate air arms, some of which are also within the NATO alliance. Russia, the dominant power in the region, has seen its air forces contract, and is proceeding to adapt from the previous Cold War structure to a leaner, more flexible air force of a significantly reduced size.

Albania

ALBANIAN AIR BRIGADE

NATO member Albania's air arm, or Forcat Ashtarake Ajore Shgipetare, operates a modest force of mainly helicopters now that its last Chinese-supplied jet types have been withdrawn.

OPERATING UNDER THE Albanian Joint Forces Command, it is organized as a single Air Brigade. In addition to a single A109, three AB205s, seven AB206s and six BO105 helicopters, Albania has four Y-5 transports. Orders have been placed for five AS532s. Major bases are at Kuçova and Tirana.

Specifications

Crew: 1–2

Powerplant: 1 x 820kW (1100shp) Lycoming
 T53-L-11A turboshaft

Maximum speed: 220km/h (135mph)

Range: 533km (331 miles)

Service ceiling: 5910m (19,390ft)

Dimensions: 14.63m (48ft); length 12.69m
 (41ft 8in); height 4.5m (14ft 7in)

Weight: 4310kg (9500lb) loaded

◀ **Agusta-Bell AB205, Helicopter Regiment 3340, Farke**
Albania received seven AB205s donated by the Italian Army in 2004.

Bosnia and Herzegovina

AIR FORCE AND ANTI-AIR DEFENCE BRIGADE

Headquartered in Sarajevo, the air arm of Bosnia and Herzegovina was created after the end of the Bosnian War in 1995, with the assistance of the U.S. 'Train and Equip' programme.

STRICTLY CONTROLLED BY the limits of the Dayton Peace Accords, the air component consists of 14 UH-1Hs, a similar number of Mi-8s, and eight Gazelle utility helicopters, plus a single VIP-configured Mi-17. Primary operating bases are Sarajevo, Banja Luka and Tuzla, with a helicopter squadron deployed at each.

Specifications

Crew: 1–4

Powerplant: 1 x 1044kW (1400hp) Avco
 Lycoming T53-L-13 turboshaft engine

Maximum speed: 204km/h (127mph)

Range: 511km (317 miles)

Service ceiling: 3840m (12,600ft)

Dimensions: rotor diameter 14.63m
 (48ft); length 12.77m (41ft 11in);
 height 4.41m (14ft 5in)

Weight: 4309kg (9500lb) loaded

◀ **Bell UH-1H, 1st Helicopter Squadron, Rajlovac/Sarajevo**
A total of 15 UH-1Hs were delivered as U.S. Army surplus in the mid-1990s.

Belarus

BELARUS AIR AND DEFENCE FORCE

The air force of Belarus was merged with the Air Defence Troops in 2001, creating a single Air and Air Defence Force. The structure of the air arm is organized around air bases.

BACKBONE OF THE Belarus Air and Air Defence Force, which has its headquarters in Minsk, is the fighter component, consisting of approximately 40 MiG-29s and 20 Su-27s, with a mixed fleet operated by the 61st Fighter Air Base (IAB) at Baranovichi, and a further MiG-29 regiment operating from the 927th IAB at Bereza. Su-24M frontal bombers and Su-24MR reconnaissance aircraft equip the 116th Bomber and Reconnaissance Base (BRAB) at Ross, while Su-25 attack aircraft serve with the 206th Attack Air Base (ShAB) at Lida. The transport force consists of the 50th Transport Aviation Base at

Minsk-Machulishche, with two squadrons of Il-76, An-26 and An-12 aircraft, as well as helicopters. It is likely that a single Tu-134 and a Mi-8S are retained by the presidential flight. An army aviation component is integrated within the Air and Air Defence Force, and this operates around 100 Mi-8, 40 Mi-24 and 10 Mi-26 helicopters. Helicopter units include the 181st Helicopter Air Bases (VAB) at Pruzhany and the aforementioned 50th TAB, as well as a training unit with Mi-2s at Minsk. The training fleet, with facilities at Bobruyk, Vitebsk and Vyaz'ma (in Russia) includes L-39s and Yak-52s.

Specifications

Crew: 5

Powerplant: 2 x 2103kW (2820ehp) Progress AI-24VT turboprops (plus 1 x 7.85kN (1795lb st) Tumansky Ru-19-A300 turbojet in right nacelle)

Maximum speed: 440km/h (273mph)

Range: 1100km (683 miles) with max payload

Service ceiling: 7500m (24,600ft)

Dimensions: span 29.2m (95ft 9.5in); length 23.80m (78ft 1in); height 8.58m (28ft 1.5in)

Weight: 24,000kg (52,911lb) loaded

▼ **Antonov An-26, Belarus Air and Air Defence Force**

This An-26 transport is operated by an unknown unit of the Belarus Air and Air Defence Force, but is likely home-based at Minsk-Machulishche, where the transport fleet is concentrated. As well as 'straight' An-26 transports, Belarus inherited former Soviet An-26RT 'Curl-B' electronic intelligence aircraft.

Specifications

Crew: 1

Powerplant: 2 x 122.5kN (27,557lb) Lyul'ka AL-31M turbofans

Maximum speed: 2150km/h (1335mph)

Range: 500km (930 miles)

Service ceiling: 17,500m (57,400ft)

Dimensions: span 14.7m (48ft 2.75in);

length 21.94m (71ft 11.5in); height 6.36m (20ft 10.25in)

Weight: 30,000kg (66,138lb) loaded

Armament: 1 x 30mm (1.18in) GSh-3101 cannon with 149 rounds; 10 external hardpoints with provision for 6000kg (13,228lb) of stores

▼ **Sukhoi Su-27UB, 2nd Squadron, 61st Fighter Air Base, Baranovichi**

Baranovichi is home to the Belarus Su-27 fleet, the 2nd Squadron operating alongside the 1st Squadron that is equipped with MiG-29s.

Bulgaria

BULGARIAN AIR FORCE AND NAVAL AVIATION

The Bulgarski Voenno Vzdushni Sili (BVVS) has suffered significant cutbacks since the end of the Cold War. Today, its units are controlled by the Air Defence Corps.

THE AIR DEFENCE Corps, or Korpus Protivovazdushna Otbrana is the controlling authority for the Bulgarian Air Force. In the 1990s the BVVS introduced a new organizational structure, using numbered air bases rather than regiments, all bases being commanded by the Korpus Takticheska Aviatsia. The five major bases of the BVVS respectively house air defence (3rd Fighter Base, at Graf Ignatievo, with MiG-21s and MiG-29s of the 1st Fighter Squadron, the MiG-21s due to remain in use until 2011-12), ground attack/reconnaissance (22nd Attack Base, Bezmer, Su-25), transport (16th Transport Base, Vrazhdebna, C-27J, An-24/26/30, L-410, PC-12), helicopter (24th Helicopter Base, Krumovo, AS532, Bell 206, Mi-17, Mi-24) and training (12th Training Air Base, Kamenets, PC-9 and L-39) elements. Bulgaria joined NATO in 2004 and recently received equipment includes AS532 helicopters and C-27J transports. Further new equipment on order includes AS565s for Aviatzia na Balgarski Voenno Morski Flot (Naval Aviation), these latter replacing the Mi-14s in use at Varna.

Specifications

Crew: 2–3

Powerplant: 2 x 1600kW (2200hp) Isotov TV3-117 turbines

Maximum speed: 335km/h (208mph)

Range: 450km (280 miles)

Service ceiling: 4500m (14,750ft)

Dimensions: span 6.5m (21ft 3in); length 17.5m (57ft 4in); height 6.5m (21ft 3in)

Weight: 12,000kg (26,500lb) loaded

Armament: 1 x 12.7mm (0.5in) Yakushev-Borzov gun, 4 x S-8 80mm (3.15in) rocket pods or up to 3460kg (7612lb) of rockets or missiles

▼ **Mil Mi-24, 1st Attack Helicopter Squadron, 24th Helicopter Base, Krumovo**

The 24th Vertoletna Avio Basa (4th Helicopter Base) hosts a squadron of Mi-24D/V assault helicopters, and a mixed squadron of transport helicopters, with AS532s, Bell 206s and Mi-17s.

Specifications

Crew: 1

Powerplant: 2 x 81.4kN (18,298lb) Sarkisov RD-33 turbofans

Maximum speed: 2443km/h (1518mph)

Range: 1500km (932 miles)

Service ceiling: 17,000m (55,775ft)

Dimensions: span 11.36m (37ft 3.75in); length (including probe) 17.32m (56ft 10in); height 7.78m (25ft 6.25in)

Weight: 18,500kg (40,785lb) loaded

Armament: 1 x 30mm (1.18in) GSh-30 cannon, provision for up to 4500kg (9921lb) of stores

▼ **Mikoyan MiG-29, 2nd Fighter Squadron, 3rd Fighter Base, Graf Ignatievo**

Bulgaria's 12 single-seat and four two-seat MiG-29s are flown by the 2nd Squadron at Graf Ignatievo, near Plovdiv. Resident MiG-21s and MiG-29s are both technically assigned to the base's line-maintenance unit.

Croatia

CROATIAN AIR FORCE AND AIR DEFENCE

Established as a fledgling air arm in the wake of Croatia's declaration of independence in 1991, the Croatian Air Force entered NATO structure in 2009, and activities now focus on two bases.

WHEN FIRST ESTABLISHED, the Croatian Air Force relied on mainly impressed civil types and light aircraft, with all combat aircraft from the former Socialist Federal Republic of Yugoslavia being evacuated from Croatia.

After the end of the Bosnian War in 1995, the lifting of the arms embargo allowed the Croatian Air Force to re-equip, acquiring Bell 206 helicopters and PC-9 trainers. In the meantime, MiG-21s had been obtained illicitly, and these, now upgraded, provide the main combat capability. Eight MiG-21bis and four two-seat MiG-21UM jets have been equipped to NATO standards in Romania. They serve at the 91st Air Force Base at Pleso, and are assigned to the 21st Fighter Squadron. The MiGs are also deployed to other bases around the country as required. Pleso is also responsible for the 27th Transport Aircraft Squadron with two An-32s. Pleso, home of the air arm's headquarters, also commands a rotary-wing unit, the 28th Transport Helicopter Squadron with Mi-171s.

Training and fire-fighting

Basic training is carried out on the Zlin 242s at the 93rd Air Force Base at Zadar, also home to PC-9 advanced trainers, Bell 206s (and a smaller number of Mi-8/17s) for training rotary-wing aircrew, and the 885th Firefighting Squadron with CL-215/415 and AT-802 aircraft. The latter unit also operates Mi-8/17s, from the Pleso-based 20th Transport Helicopter Squadron, and fire-fighting aircraft are detached around the country during fire season. Zadar is home to the military display team, Wings of Storm, flying PC-9s.

▲ **An-32s**

An An-32 releases flares. The Croatian Air Force includes two examples of this twin-turboprop transport, which are used for regular supply flight between bases. The aircraft can carry 40 passengers, or alternatively a typical cargo load of 6700 kg (14,700 lb) over 900 km (486 nm).

Specifications

Crew: 1	length (including probe) 15.76m (51ft 8.5in);
Powerplant: 1 x 73.5kN (16,535lb) Tumanskii	height 4.1m (13ft 5.5in)
R-25 turbojet	Weight: 10,400kg (22,925lb) loaded
Maximum speed: 2229km/h (1385mph)	Armament: 1 x 23mm (0.9in) GSh-23 twin-
Range: 1160km (721 miles)	barrel cannon in underbelly pack, provision
Service ceiling: 17,500m (57,400ft)	for about 1500kg (3307kg) of stores
Dimensions: span 7.15m (23ft 5.5in);	

▼ **Mikoyan-Gurevich MiG-21bisD, 21st Fighter Squadron, Pleso**

Based at Pleso, near Zagreb, the Croatian MiG-21 fleet is expected to be retained until 2013, by which time a new multi-role fighter ought to have been selected. This aircraft carries R-60 air-to-air missiles underwing.

Czech Republic
CZECH AIR FORCE

Renamed as the Vzdusné Síly Armády Ceské Republiky in 1998, the Czech Air Force is part of NATO and is now organized around four major air bases, with its headquarters in Olomouc.

THE FIVE MAJOR bases currently utilized by the Czech AF (Cáslav, Prague-Kbely, Námest nad Oslavou and Prerov) are responsible for the various flying squadrons. Current unit structure includes the 21st Tactical Air Force Base at Cáslav, responsible for the 211th Tactical Squadron that flies the JAS39 Gripen in the air defence role. Fourteen leased JAS39C/D fighters were delivered in the course of 2005. Cáslav is also home to a unit equipped with

around 24 L-159 Advanced Light Combat Aircraft (ALCA), the 212th Tactical Squadron.

The 22nd Air Force Base at Námest nad Oslavou operates the 221st Attack Helicopter Squadron with Mi-24/35s, and the 222nd Tactical Squadron with L-39 jet trainers. Further rotary-wing forces can be found with the 23rd Helicopter Base at Prerov, where the 231st Helicopter Squadron operates Mi-17s, Mi-171s and W-3s. Smaller helicopter detachments are maintained at Plzen and Prerov, with W-3s of the 243rd Helicopter Squadron outfitted for SAR.

Transport fleet
The 24th Air Transportation Base at Prague-Kbely includes the VIP fleet, in which the first of two A319s arrived in 2007 to begin to replace Tu-154s with the 241st Transport Squadron. Other duties of the 24th Air Transportation Base include movements of personnel and material, and the fleet also includes An-26, C-295 and L-410 tactical transport (242nd Transport and Special Squadron), CL-601 and Yak-40 short-range VIP transports (241st Transport Squadron) and Mi-8/17 and W-3 helicopters (243rd Helicopter Squadron).

Basic training is conducted at Pardubice, on civilian-owned Zlin 142s, fast-jet pilots then progressing to 222nd Tactical Squadron L-39s.

▲ **Aero L-159 Advanced Light Combat Aircraft**
Developed from the L-39 indigenous trainer, the L-159 ALCA provides the Czech Air Force with its air-to-ground capability. The aircraft are based alongside the Gripens at Cáslav, and are complemented by eight two-seat L-159T1 trainers.

Specifications

Crew: 1	Dimensions: span 8m (26ft 3in); length
Powerplant: 1 x 80.5kN (18,100lb) Volvo	14.1m (46ft 3in); height 4.7m (15ft 5in)
Flygmotor RM12 turbofan	Weight: 12,473kg (27,500lb) loaded
Maximum speed: more than Mach 2	Armament: 1 x 27mm (1.06in) Mauser BK27
Range: 3250km (2020 miles)	cannon, plus rockets, cluster bombs
Service ceiling: 15,240m (50,000ft)	and missiles

▼ **SAAB JAS 39C Gripen, 211th Tactical Squadron, 21st Tactical Air Force Base, Cáslav**
Selected by the Czech Republic as its new fighter in 2002, the Gripen is operated in JAS39C/D form, acquired under a 10-year lease arrangement.

Hungary
HUNGARIAN AIR FORCE

Hungary joined the NATO alliance in 1999 and its air arm, the Magyar Légierö, is now much depleted compared to its Warsaw Pact days, and is organized as a single air command.

FORCE REDUCTIONS MEAN that the Hungarian Air Force's fixed-wing aircraft now all operate from a single base, Kecskémet, or the 59th Air Wing. The air base supports one (reduced) squadron of five upgraded MiG-29s, and one of Gripens. The first of 14 leased JAS39s (including two twin-seaters) arrived at Kecskémet in March 2006. Transport assets comprise five An-26s of the wing's 3rd Squadron, but these are to be replaced after 2012. Pilot training begins on the Yak-52 at Szolnok's air academy. Fighter pilots finish their training under the NATO Flying Training in Canada (NFTC) programme.

Szolnok, the 86th Helicopter Regiment, is also home to the helicopter arm, with its 1st Squadron consisting of seven Mi-8s and seven Mi-17s, and the 2nd squadron being equipped with seven Mi-24s. Three R22s were purchased in 2010 in order to serve as training helicopters.

The Hungarian Pápa air base is also home to the three C-17A airlifters that are currenlty operated by NATO's Heavy Airlift Wing as part of the multi-national Strategic Airlift Capability initiative. The aircraft are operated in Hungarian Air Force markings.

Specifications

Crew: 2	Dimensions: span 9.46m (31ft 0.5in);
Powerplant: 1x 16.87kN (3792lbf) Ivchenko	length 12.13m (39ft 9.5in); height 4.77m
AI-25TL turbofan	(15ft 7.75in)
Maximum speed: 750km/h (466mph)	Weight: 3455kg (7617lb) loaded
Range: 1100km (683 miles)	Armament: External bomb load up to
Service ceiling: 11,000m (36,100ft)	1150kg (2250lb)

▼ Aero L-39ZO Albatros, 2nd Squadron 'Dongó', 59th Air Wing, Kecskémet

Hungary's ex-East German Air Force L-39s were operated by the 2nd Squadron of the 59th Air Wing alongside that unit's MiG-29s.

Specifications

Crew: 1	Dimensions: span 8m (26ft 3in); length 14.1m
Powerplant: 1 x 80.5kN (18,100lb) Volvo	(46ft 3in); height 4.7m (15ft 5in)
Flygmotor RM12 turbofan	Weight: 12,473kg (27,500lb) loaded
Maximum speed: more than Mach 2	Armament: 1 x 27mm (1.06in) Mauser BK27
Range: 3250km (2020 miles)	cannon, six external hardpoints, provision for
Service ceiling: 15,240m (50,000ft)	missiles, bombs, drop tanks and ECM pods

▼ SAAB JAS39EBS HU Gripen, 1st Squadron 'Puma', 59th Air Wing, Kecskémet

Hungary's Gripens are broadly similar to the JAS39C/D model. They are operated by the 1st Squadron of the 59th Air Wing, from Kecskémet.

Baltic States

ESTONIA, LATVIA AND LITHUANIA

The air arms of the three Baltic States are among the smallest in Europe, but all have been declared to NATO since 2004. Among them, only Lithuania operates its own jet equipment.

THE SMALLEST OF the Baltic States, Estonia's air arm (Eesti Õhuvägi) is equipped with two An-2 utility transports and two R22 light helicopters. These are based at Ämari.

The Latvijas Gaisa Spéki, or Latvian Air Force, maintains the 1 Aviacijas Eskadrila at Lielvarde. The unit is divided into transport and helicopter squadrons, equipped with An-2, L-410, Mi-2 and Mi-171 aircraft. The Mi-171s are also detached to Riga-Skulte for SAR duties.

Home of the Lithuanian Air Force is Siauliai, which also hosts rotating NATO air defence fighters from various air arms, these being charged with defending Baltic airspace. Lithuanian assets at Siauliai include two L-39s and seven Mi-8s, as well as a transport squadron with C-27J and L-410 aircraft. Mi-8 SAR detachments are maintained at Nemirseta and Kaunas. A single Yak-18T is in use for training.

Specifications

Crew: 3	Service ceiling: 9144m (30,000ft)
Powerplant: 2 x 3460kW (4640hp) Rolls-Royce AE2100-D2A turboprops	Dimensions: span 28.7m (94ft 2in); length 22.7m (74ft 6in); height 9.64m (31ft 8in)
Maximum speed: 602km/h (374mph)	Weight: 30,500kg (67,241lb) loaded
Range: 11852km (1151 miles) with 10,000kg (22,000lb) payload	

▼ **Alenia C-27J Spartan, Transporto Eskadrile, 1 Aviacijos Baze, Siauliai-Zokniai**
Lithuania ordered three C-27Js to replace its An-26 tactical transports.

Macedonia

MACEDONIAN AIR FORCE

Macedonia has emerged from the war against Kosovar extremists that broke out in 2001, and its air arm – with a single air brigade – is now hopeful of securing NATO membership.

ESTABLISHED IN JUNE 1991, the Macedonian Air Force's centre of operations is Pterovec air base. Initially, arms embargoes hindered the establishment of the air arm, but Mi-17s were inducted in 1994, and today three Mi-17s are complemented by two Mi-8s and four upgraded Mi-24s, the latter

representing the air force's most capable combat equipment. Units comprise 101 Squadron with a single An-2, 201 Squadron responsible for the Mi-24s, 301 Squadron (Mi-8/17) and 401 Squadron with Zlin 143 and 242 trainers together with a pair of UH-1Hs delivered during the 2001 conflict.

Specifications

Crew: 1

Powerplant: 2 x 44.1kN (9921lb) Tumanskii
R-195 turbojets

Maximum speed: 975km/h (606mph)

Range: 750km (466 miles)

Service ceiling: 7000m (22,965ft)

Dimensions: span 14.36m (47ft 1.5in); length
15.53m (50ft 11.5in); height 4.8m (15ft 9in)

Weight: 17,600kg (38,800lb) loaded

Armament: 1 x 30mm (1.18in) GSh-30-2
cannon; eight external pylons with provision
for up to 4400kg (9700lb) of stores

▼ **Sukhoi Su-25, 101 Squadron, Airborne Brigade, Petrovec**

This Su-25 was one of four (including one two-seater) acquired from Ukraine in the run-up to the fighting that broke out in 2001. Operated by 101 Squadron, the Su-25 fleet has now been placed in storage.

Moldova

MOLDOVAN AIR FORCE

The modestly sized Moldovan Air Force was created following Moldova's independence from the USSR in 1991. Current levels of strength are far below Conventional Forces in Europe limits.

ACCORDING TO THE legislation of the CFE Treaty, Moldova is permitted 50 armed helicopters and 50 armed aircraft, but the current fleet consists entirely of unarmed light transports and helicopters. Moldova inherited 34 MiG-29 fighters from the Soviet Navy, but these were sold off by the late 1990s.

The Moldovan Air Force maintains a personnel strength of just over 1000, and assets are organized into one helicopter squadron, and one missile battalion, the air arm being separated into separate air force and air defence organizations, along Soviet lines. Marculesti air base supports eight Mi-8 helicopters (including one in VIP configuration), two An-72 jet transports, two An-2 Colt utility transports, a single An-26 Curl tactical transport, and six PZL-104 Wilga utility transports.

Specifications

Crew: 3

Powerplant: 2 x 1454kW (1950shp) Klimov
TV3-117Mt turboshafts

Maximum speed: 260km/h (162mph)

Range: 450km (280 miles)

Service ceiling: 4500m (14,765ft)

Dimensions: rotor diameter 21.29m

(69ft 10in); length 18.17m (59ft 7in);
height 5.65m (18ft 6in)

Weight: 11,100kg (24,470lb) loaded

Armament: up to 1500kg (3300lb) of
disposable stores on six hardpoints, including
57mm (2.24in) S-5 rockets, bombs, or 9M17
Phalanga ATGMs

▼ **Mil Mi-8MTV-1, Helicopter Squadron, Marculesti**

Moldova's Mi-8 fleet is reported to include just four airworthy examples of the Mi-8MTV-1 and a single Mi-8PS VIP transport. This aircraft took part in the NATO Partnership for Peace exercise Cooperative Key in 1996.

Montenegro
MONTENEGRIN AIR FORCE

The Montenegrin Air Force, or Vazduhoplovstvo i protivvazdusna odbrana (ViPVO) was formed following the disintegration of Serbia and Montenegro in 2006, and operates around 40 aircraft.

AFTER MONTENEGRO BROKE away from Serbia, the new republic was left with a number of aircraft at Golubovci air base. These included 17 G-4 Super Galebs and three Utva 75 trainers, which will likely be returned to Serbia. Montenegro has meanwhile expressed its intention to operate only helicopters. Headquartered at Podgorica, the air arm operates 15 Gazelles in Gama and Hera configuration, and a single Mi-8T, although the latter was reportedly no longer airworthy as of 2010. These serve with a single helicopter squadron, headquartered at Golubovci, which maintains close air support, transport and utility flights. Three Air Tractor AT-802s have also been purchased for fire-fighting.

Specifications

Crew: 2

Powerplant: 1 x 17.8kN (4000lbf) licence-built Rolls-Royce Viper 632-46

Maximum speed: 910km/h (565mph)

Range: 2500km (1553 miles)

Service ceiling: 12,850m (42,160ft)

Dimensions: span 9.88m (32ft 5in); length 11.35m (37ft 27/8in); height 4.3m (14ft 1.25in)

Weight: 6300kg (13,889lb) loaded

Armament: 1 x 23mm (0.9in) GSh-23L cannon in ventral gun pod; 4 underwing pylons

▼ **SOKO G-4 Super Galeb, Montenegrin Air Force, Golubovci**
The only G-4 Super Galeb known to have received the markings of the new Montenegrin Air Force. Although still extant, the aircraft is apparently not in service, and the air force intends to operate Gazelle helicopters exclusively.

Poland
POLISH AIR FORCE, ARMY AVIATION AND NAVAL AVIATION

The Sily Powietrzne, or Polish Air Force, has undergone great changes as it has transitioned from its Cold War structure to join the NATO alliance, to which Poland was admitted in 1999.

OVERHAULING the Polish Air Force introduced the new F-16 Block 52+ fighter. Structural changes in 2009 saw the air brigades and subordinated units reorganized into air wings. Air Force Command is headquartered in Warsaw.

The 1st Tactical Aviation Wing is responsible for MiG-29 and Su-22 aircraft. The MiG-29 fighter is in use with 41.ELT (Tactical Aviation Squadron) at Malbork, the unit's aircraft comprising 14 ex-German Air Force machines from a total of 22 delivered from 2005. The second MiG-29 unit is 1.ELT at Minsk-Mazowiecki, and both squadrons provide aircraft for the national Quick Reaction Alert air defence mission. 1.ELT aircraft were acquired directly from the USSR and as part of an exchange deal with the Czech Air Force in the mid-1990s. The Su-22M4K attack aircraft (and its two-seat trainer derivative, the Su-22UM3K) is based at Miroslawiec

Specifications

Crew: 2

Powerplant: 1 x 126.7kN (28,500lb) thrust
Pratt & Whitney F100-PW-229 afterburning
turbofan

Maximum speed: 2177km/h (1353mph)

Range: 3862km (2400 miles)

Service ceiling: 15,240m (49,000ft)

Dimensions: span 9.45m (31ft); length 15.09m
(49ft 6in); height 5.09m (16ft 8in)

Weight: 19,187kg (42,300lb) loaded

Armament: 1 x GEc M61A1 20mm (0.79in)
multi-barrelled cannon, seven external
hardpoints with provision for up to 9276kg
(20,450lb) of stores

▼ **Lockheed Martin F-16D Fighting Falcon, 31.Baza Lotnictwa Taktycznego (31st Tactical Aviation Base), Poznan-Krzesiny**

The 31st Tactical Air Base supports two squadrons of F-16C/Ds, which were acquired under the Peace Sky programme as a replacement for ageing MiG-21 and Su-22 aircraft.

and Swidwin, home to a total of three squadrons. The 2nd Tactical Aviation Wing operates F-16s, and began to receive its 48 Block 52+ F-16C/Ds in 2006. The initial recipient was 3.ELT (3rd Tactical Aviation Squadron), and the type is also in service with 6.ELT and 10.ELT.

The 3rd Aviation Transport Wing operates a variety of transport aircraft, including the latest

SILY POWIETRZNE, POLISH AF COMBAT AND TRANSPORT UNITS

Unit	Base	Aircraft
36.Specialny Pulk Lotnictwa Transportowego	Warsaw-Okecie	Bell 412, M-28, Mi-8, Tu-154M, W-3, Yak-40
Lotniczej Grupy Poszukiwawczo-Ratowniczej	Bydgoszcz* *detachment at Kraków-Balice	W-3, Mi-8
1.Skrzydlo Lotnictwa Taktycznego – 1st Tactical Aviation Wing, HQ Swidwin		
1.Eskadra Lotnictwa Taktycznego	Minsk-Mazowiecki	MiG-29, MiG-29UB, TS-11, Mi-2
41.Eskadra Lotnictwa Taktycznego	Malbork	MiG-29, TS-11
7.Eskadra Lotnictwa Taktycznego	Swidwin	Su-22M4K, Su-22UM3K, TS-11
8.Eskadra Lotnictwa Taktycznego	Miroslawiec	Su-22M4K, Su-22UM3K, TS-11
40.Eskadra Lotnictwa Taktycznego	Swidwin	Su-22M4K, Su-22UM3K, TS-11

Unit	Base	Aircraft
2.Skrzydlo Lotnictwa Taktycznego – 2nd Tactical Aviation Wing, HQ Poznan-Krzesiny		
31.Baza Lotnictwa Taktycznego – 31st Tactical Aviation, Base Poznan-Krzesiny		
3.Eskadra Lotnictwa Tactycznego	Poznan-Krzesiny	F-16C/D
6.Eskadra Lotnictwa Taktycznego	Poznan-Krzesiny	F-16C/D
32.Baza Lotnictwa Taktycznego – 32nd Tactical Aviation, Base Lask		
10.Eskadra Lotnictwa Tactycznego	Lask	F-16C/D
3.Skrzydlo Lotnictwa Transportowego – 3rd Aviation Transport Wing, HQ Powidz		
2.Eskadra Lotnictwa Transportowo-Lacznikowego	Bydgoszcz	An-28, W-3
3.Eskadra Lotnictwa Transportowo-Lacznikowego	Wroclaw	Mi-2, TS-11, W-3
13.Eskadra Lotnictwa Transportowego	Kraków-Balice	M-28, C-295M
14.Eskadra Lotnictwa Transportowego	Powidz	C-130E, M-28

POLAND

Specifications

Crew: 1

Powerplant: 2 x 81.4kN (18,298lb) Sarkisov
RD-33 turbofans

Maximum speed: 2443km/h (1518mph)

Range: 1500km (932 miles)

Service ceiling: 17,000m (55,775ft)

Dimensions: span 11.36m (37ft 3.75in); length
(including probe) 17.32m (56ft 10in); height
7.78m (25ft 6.25in)

Weight: 18,500kg (40,785lb) loaded

Armament: 1 x 30mm (1.18in) GSh-30 cannon,
provision for up to 4500kg (9921lb) of stores

▼ Mikoyan MiG-29, 1.Eskadra Lotnictwa Taktycznego 'Warszawa', Minsk-Mazowiecki

MiG-29s of 1.ELT comprise aircraft that were received from the USSR in
between 1989-90 and 10 surplus Czech Air Force jets received in 1995-96.

Specifications

Crew: 5

Powerplant: 4 x 3021kW (4050hp) Allison T56-
A-7A turboprop engines

Maximum speed: 547km/h (340mph)

Range: 3896km (2420 miles)

Service ceiling: 7010m (23,000ft)

Dimensions: span 40.4m (132ft 7in);
length 29.8m (97ft 9in); height 11.7m
(38ft 6in)

Weight: 79,375kg (175,000lb) loaded

▼ Lockheed C-130E Hercules, 14.Eskadra Lotnictwa Transportowego, Powidz

Formerly operated by the USAF as 70-1262, this is
one of two C-130Es loaned to Poland pending
the five refurbished examples from the
U.S. The type made its combat debut in
2009 in Afghanistan.

addition, the C-130E, delivered to the 14th ELTR (Transport Aviation Squadron) in 2009. The 13.ELTR at Kraków employs C-295 and M-28 aircraft, while 2.ELTR at Bydgoszcz operates An-28s and W-3s. Wroclaw is home to 3.ELTR with Mi-2, TS-11 and W-3 aircraft.

The 4th Flight Training Wing is responsible for training pilots from the Polish Air Force Academy and operates TS-11 jet trainers, PZL-130 turboprop trainers, and SW-4s, from separate Air Training Centres at Deblin and Radom.

The 36th Special Assignment Regiment at Warsaw transports VIPs, and is equipped with Tu-154, Yak-40 Mi-2, Mi-8, W-3, SW-4 and Bell 412 aircraft.

The Lotnictwo Marynarki Wojennej, or Polish Naval Aviation, is headed by the 'City of Gdynia' Aviation Brigade, responsible for three Eskadra

Marinarki Wojennej (Naval Air Squadrons): 28.elMW at Gdynia-Babie Doly (with M-28s, Mi-8/17s, SH-2Gs and W-3s), 29.elMW at Darlowo (Mi-14 and W-3) and 30.elMW at Cewice-Siemerowice (M-28).

Polish Army Aviation

Polish Army Aviation (Lotnictwo Wojsk Ladowych) includes 49.PSB (Attack Helicopter Regiment) at Pruszcz Gdanski (equipped with two Mi-24 squadrons, and two squadrons of Mi-2s). 56.PSB at Inowroclaw has a single squadron of Mi-24s and three Mi-2 squadrons. Under the command of the 25th Air Cavalry Brigade are 37.DL (Air Wing) at Leznica-Wielka (two squadrons of Mi-8s) and 66.DL at Tomaszów-Mazowiecki with three squadrons of W-3s.

Romania
ROMANIAN AIR FORCE

Romania was the first East European signatory of NATO's Partnership for Peace, and joined the alliance in 2004, and the Fortele Aerienne Române is now evolving to meet new requirements.

THE ROMANIAN AIR arm is now looking forward to receiving F-16s to replace the upgraded MiG-21 Lancers that spearhead the fighter arm at present. Five air bases are in regular use, and the air arm uses a group structure. Lancers serve with 711 and 712 Squadrons at Câmpia Turzii, which is also home to the 713rd Helicopter Squadron with IAR-330s. The 714th Helicopter Squadron reports to Câmpia Turzii but is based at Timisoara. More Lancers are found with 861 and 862 Squadrons at Borcea-Fetesti, parent base to the 863rd Helicopter Squadron with

IAR-330s at Mihail Kogalniceanu. Final Lancer operator is the 951st Squadron at Bacau, co-located with the 205th Squadron, responsible for Lancer training, and the 952nd Squadron (IAR-330). The multi-mission IAR-330 SOCAT is assigned to the 904th and 905th Squadrons at Bucuresti-Otopeni. The latter base is also home to the transport fleet, with two squadrons of An-26/30s, C-27Js and C-130B/Hs, and the 903rd Squadron with IAR-330s. Training takes place at Boboc, where five squadrons fly Alouette III, An-2 IAK-52 and IAR-99 aircraft.

Specifications
Crew: 1

Powerplant: 1 x 60.8kN (14,550lb) thrust Tumanskii R-13-300 afterburning turbojet

Maximum speed: 2229km/h (1385mph)

Range: 1160km (721 miles)

Service ceiling: 17,500m (57,400ft)

Dimensions: span 7.15m (23ft 5.5in);

length (including probe) 15.76m(51ft 8.5in);

height 4.1m (13ft 5.5in)

Weight: 10,400kg (22,925lb) loaded

Armament: 1 x 23mm (0.90in) cannon, provision for about 1500kg (3307lb) of stores, including air-to-air missiles, rocket pods, napalm tanks, or drop tanks

▼ **Aerostar MiG-21MF Lancer A, 711 Squadron, Câmpia Turzii**

A total of 71 air-to-ground Lancer As, 25 air-defence Lancer Cs and 14 Lancer B trainers were produced via upgrade. 711 Squadron at Câmpia Turzii (Baza 71 Aerianâ) is equipped with a mix of Lancer A and B versions. Co-located 712 Squadron flies Lancer Bs and Cs.

Specifications
Crew: 1

Powerplant: 2 x 81.4kN (18,298lb) Sarkisov RD-33 turbofans

Maximum speed: 2443km/h (1518mph)

Range: 1500km (932 miles)

Service ceiling: 17,000m (55,775ft)

Dimensions: span 11.36m (37ft 3.75in);

length (including probe) 17.32m (56ft 10in);

height 7.78m (25ft 6.25in)

Weight: 18,500kg (40,785lb) loaded

Armament: 1 x 30mm (1.18in) GSh-30 cannon, provision for up to 4500kg (9921lb) of stores

▼ **Mikoyan MiG-29, 1st Squadron, Grupul 57 (57th Fighter Regiment), Mihail Kogalniceanu**

Formerly the pride of the Romanian Air Force, the 18 survivors of 20 MiG-29s (plus a single ex-Moldovan 'Fulcrum-C') were put into storage in 2003 after funding for their overhaul and upgrade was withheld.

Russia

RUSSIAN AIR FORCE AND NAVAL AVIATION

In terms of numbers, the Russian air arms are among the most powerful in the world, but after years of under-funding Russia is only now making strenuous efforts to restructure its air force.

AMONG THE KEY concerns of the Russian Air Force have been increasing flying hours and exercises, introduction of aircraft upgrades, and developing new combat aircraft. The last two objectives have been progressing only very slowly, although the Sukhoi T-50 new-generation fighter took to the air in 2010. Additionally, the strategic bomber force has significantly stepped up its tempo of activity.

Perhaps most significantly, the Russian Air Force is now on the verge of a major restructuring, replacing its Cold War-era organization with a new system centred around numbered air bases. The former Frontal Aviation is now designated as Tactical Aviation, and is responsible for all fighter, theatre bomber and attack types. In the future, the regiments indicated here (and many more besides them) will be organized around approximately 60 air bases. The previous structure was based on eight Air Armies, of which two were role-specific: the 37th Air Army with strategic bombers, and 61st Air Army with transport

Specifications

Crew: 1	length 21.94m (71ft 11.5in); height
Powerplant: 2 x 122.5kN (27,557lb) Lyul'ka	6.36m (20ft 10.25in)
AL-31M turbofans	Weight: 30,000kg (66,138lb) loaded
Maximum speed: 2150km/h (1335mph)	Armament: 1 x 30mm (1.18in) GSh-3101
Range: 500km (930 miles)	cannon with 149 rounds; 10 external
Service ceiling: 17,500m (57,400ft)	hardpoints with provision for 6000kg
Dimensions: span 14.7m (48ft 2.75in);	(13,228lb) of stores

▼ **Sukhoi Su-27UB, 206th Guards Fighter Aviation Regiment, Volzskiy**

This Su-27UB was operated by the 206th Guards Fighter Regiment (IAP) of the Astrakhan Military Region. The unit was disbanded in 2002, and its Su-27s were taken over by the 562nd IAP at Krymsk. That unit was in turn re-designated as the 3rd Guards IAP.

Specifications

Crew: 1	Dimensions: span 11.36m (37ft 3.75in);
Powerplant: 2 x 81.4kN (18,298lb) Sarkisov	length (including probe) 17.32m (56ft 10in);
RD-33 turbofans	height 7.78m (25ft 6.25in)
Maximum speed: 2443km/h (1518mph)	Weight: 18,500kg (40,785lb) loaded
Range: 1500km (932 miles)	Armament: 1 x 30mm (1.18in) GSh-30 cannon,
Service ceiling: 17,000m (55,775ft)	provision for up to 4500kg (9921lb) of stores

▼ **Mikoyan MiG-29, 120th Guards Fighter Aviation Regiment 'Brest', Domna**

This MiG-29 'Fulcrum-C' is operated by the 120th Guards IAP. Current plans call for the establishment of a new unit as Domna, the 6982nd Air Base, which will also receive a MiG-29 squadron transferred from the 28th Guards IAP at Andreapol.

Specifications

Crew: 2

Powerplant: 2 x 110.3kN (24,802lb) Lyul'ka
AL-21F-3A turbojets

Maximum speed: 2316km/h (1439mph)

Range: 1050km (650 miles)

Service ceiling: 17,500m (57,415ft)

Dimensions: span 17.63m (57ft 10in) spread,

10.36m (34ft) swept; length 24.53m

(80ft 5in); height 4.97m (16ft 0.75in)

Weight: 39,700kg (87,520lb) loaded

Armament: 1 x 23mm (0.9in) GSh-23-6

six-barrelled cannon; nine external pylons

with provision for up to 8000kg (17,635lb)

of stores

▼ **Sukhoi Su-24M, 455th Bomber Aviation Regiment, Baltimor**

This Su-24M is operated by the 455th BAP, part of the 105th BAD. Normally based at Baltimor, it was stationed at Mozdok for combat operations against Georgia in August 2008.

aircraft. The remaining six armies were arranged geographically, and tactical aircraft were provided to Military Districts. The basic unit was the regiment, these being subordinate to divisions, and divisions in turn to air armies or air corps. The 37th and 61st Air Armies are to be remodelled as commands, answering to Air Force High Command.

In future, Brigades of Air and Space Defence will be assigned to Air and Air Defence Forces Commands. Each brigade will consist of various air bases – as well as air defence missile units and radar sites – and will provide airpower for several Military Districts. In each Military District, a maximum of two air bases will be dedicated to air defence fighters. The new-look Tactical Aviation will be based around 15 squadrons of Su-27s, 14 of Su-25s, 14 of Su-24s, 12 of MiG-31s, and 10 of MiG-29s.

In 2008, it was estimated that the six tactical armies were responsible for 380 MiG-29, 370 Su-27 and 230 MiG-31 fighters, 300 Su-24 bombers, 260

LONG-RANGE AVIATION FRONT-LINE UNITS		
37th Strategic Air Army Moscow		
203rd Airborne Refuelling Aviation Regiment	Dyagilyevo	Il-78, Il-78M
22nd Heavy Bomber Aviation Division Engels		
121st Heavy Bomber Aviation Regiment	Engels	Tu-160
184th Heavy Bomber Aviation Regiment	Engels	Tu-95MS
52nd Heavy Bomber Aviation Regiment	Shaikovka	Tu-22M3
840th Heavy Bomber Aviation Regiment	Soltsy	Tu-22M3
326th Heavy Bomber Division Ukrainka		
79th Heavy Bomber Aviation Regiment	Ukrainka	Tu-95MS
182nd Heavy Bomber Aviation Regiment	Ukrainka	Tu-95MS
200th Heavy Bomber Aviation Regiment	Bobruisk	Tu-22M3, Tu-22MR
444th Heavy Bomber Aviation Regiment	Vozdvizhenka	Tu-22M3

◀ **Ilyushin Il-76**

The backbone of the Russian Air Force's transport fleet is the Il-76. Older Il-76Ms are to be removed from service, leaving the air arm with around 120 examples of the definitive Il-76MD version operating from six different transport air bases.

CENTRALLY SUBORDINATED UNITS		
4th Centre for Combat Training and Aircrew Conversion	Lipetsk	Su-27, Su-27SM, Su-34, Su-25, Su-25SM, Su-39, Su-24M, Su-24M2, MiG-29, MiG-29SMT
344th Centre for Army Aviation Combat Training and Aircrew Conversion	Torzhok	Mi-24, Mi-28, Mi-8, Mi-26, Ka-50
185th Centre for Combat Training and Aircrew Conversion	Astrakhan	MiG-29
2457th Aviation Base for Long-range Airborne Early Aircraft	Ivanovo	A-50, A-50M

Su-25 attack aircraft, plus 100 Su-24MR and 40 MiG-25RB reconnaissance aircraft. Today numbers have dropped, with the Su-24 numerically the most important type, with around 300 in service, followed by over 200 each of the MiG-29, Su-25 and Su-27. In addition, the Russian Air Force maintained in 2008 some 1000 Mi-8, Mi-24 and Mi-26 helicopters, 300 trainers and 250 support aircraft.

Long-Range Aviation Command will have a strength based around approximately 170 Tu-22M3, Tu-95MS and Tu-160 bombers, with front-line assets based at Engels, Shaikovka, Belaya and Ukrainka. Soltsy is due to close and a new base will be established at Belaya, with Tu-22M3/MRs. There are plans afoot to introduce a new strategic bomber, but in the meantime, low-rate production of the Tu-160 has resumed, and Tu-95MS and Tu-160 aircraft

Specifications

Crew: 3

Powerplant: 2 x 1454kW (1950shp) Klimov TV3-117Mt turboshafts

Maximum speed: 260km/h (162mph)

Range: 450km (280 miles)

Service ceiling: 4500m (14,765ft)

Dimensions: rotor diameter 21.29m

(69ft 10in); length 18.17m (59ft 7in); height 5.65m (18ft 6in)

Weight: 11,100kg (24,470lb) loaded

Armament: up to 1500kg (3300lb) of disposable stores on six hardpoints, including 57mm (2.24in) S-5 rockets, bombs, or 9M17 Phalanga ATGMs

▼ Mil Mi-8, Army Aviation

Operated by an unknown unit of Army Aviation, the Mi-8 remains the workhorse of the rotary-wing fleet. The type is still being built for Russian use, with the latest orders being for the Mi-8MTV-5 combat transport versions with a rear loading ramp.

Specifications

Crew: 2–3

Powerplant: 2 x 1600kW (2200hp) Isotov TV3-117 turbines

Maximum speed: 335km/h (208mph)

Range: 450km (280 miles)

Service ceiling: 4500m (14,750ft)

Dimensions: span 6.5m (21ft 3in); length 17.5m (57ft 4in); height 6.5m (21ft 3in)

Weight: 12,000kg (26,500lb) loaded

Armament: 1 x 12.7mm (0.5in) Yakushev-Borzov gun, 4 x S-8 80mm (3.15in) rocket pods or up to 3460kg (7612lb) of rockets or missiles

▼ Mil Mi-24, 27th Aviation Group, Army Aviation, Pristina

This Mi-24 was operated on behalf of KFOR (Kosovo Force), based at Pristina Airport, in 2000. Russian Air Force Mi-24s have also been deployed in a peacekeeping capacity to Freetown in Sierra Leone.

▼ Mikoyan MiG-31B, 174th Guards Fighter Aviation Regiment, Monchegorsk

The MiG-31 remains the most powerful long-range interceptor available to Russia. This example was operated by the 174th GvIAP in around 1998. Part of the Leningrad Military District, this unit was disbanded in 2001.

Specifications

Crew: 2

Powerplant: 2 x 91kN (lb) thrust D-30F6
Turbofan

Maximum speed at altitude 17,500m
(57,415ft): 2.83 Mach (3000km/h; 1864mph)

Range: 3300km (2050 miles)

Service ceiling: 20,600m (67,585ft)

Dimensions: span 13.464m (44ft 2in); length
22.69m (74ft 5in); height 6.15m (20ft 2in)

Weight: 46,200kg (101,854lb) loaded

Armament: 1 x 23mm (0.90in) GSh-6-23M six-
barrel gun, various anti-aircraft missiles

▲ Tupolev Tu-22M3

A highly capable asset (with no direct Western counterpart), older examples of the Tu-22M3 are already being withdrawn, and many have gone into storage. The type is also being transferred from Naval Aviation to Long-Range Aviation Command.

are being upgraded. By 2025-30, Russia hopes to double the fleet of front-line Tu-160s to 30 aircraft.

Military Transport Aviation Command will inherit the seven regiments of the 61st Air Army, (two will be disbanded). Fixed-wing transport strength will thereafter be focused at Ivanovo, Pskov, Seshtsha, Tver, Klin, Taganrog and Orenburg, with helicopters resident at Troitsk and Tshebenki.

Since 2002 Army Aviation has been part of the Air Force, with helicopter regiments incorporated as independent units within its structure. Russian Naval Aviation, headquartered in Moscow, divides

FIGHTER AVIATION REGIMENTS (IAP)		
9th IAP	Kilp-Yavr	Su-27
3rd IAP	Krymsk	Su-27
14th IAP	Khalino	MiG-29, MiG-29SMT
19th IAP	Millerovo	MiG-29
22nd IAP	Uglovaya	Su-27SM
23rd IAP	Dzemgi	Su-27SM
28th IAP	Andreapol	MiG-29
31st IAP	Zernograd	MiG-29
120th IAP	Domna	MiG-29
159th IAP	Besovets	Su-27
177th IAP	Lodeynoye Polye	Su-27
458th IAP	Savvatiya	MiG-31
530th IAP	Chuguyevka	MiG-31
712th IAP	Kansk	MiG-31
611th IAP	Dorokhovo	Su-27
764th IAP	Bolshoye Savino	MiG-31
790th IAP	Khotilovo	MiG-31

BOMBER AVIATION REGIMENTS (BAP)		
1st BAP	Lebyazhye	Su-24M
2nd BAP	Dzhida	Su-24M
67th BAP	Siverskii	Su-24M
277th BAP	Khurba	Su-24M
302nd BAP	Pereyaslavka	Su-24M, Su-24M2
455th BAP	Baltimor	Su-24M
523rd BAP	Vozhaevka	Su-24M, Su-24MR
559th BAP	Morozovsk	Su-24M
722nd BAP	Smuravyevo	Su-24M
959th BAP	Yeisk	Su-24M

Specifications

Crew: 1

Powerplant: 2 x 44.1kN (9921lb) Tumanskii
R-195 turbojets

Maximum speed: 975km/h (606mph)

Range: 750km (466 miles)

Service ceiling: 7000m (22,965ft)

Dimensions: span 14.36m (47ft 1.5in); length
15.53m (50ft 11.5in); height 4.8m (15ft 9in)

Weight: 17,600kg (38,800lb) loaded

Armament: 1 x 30mm (1.18in) GSh-30-2
cannon; eight external pylons with provision
for up to 4400kg (9700lb) of stores

▼ Sukhoi Su-25, 899th Assault Aviation Regiment, Mozdok

Deployed from its home base of Buturlinovka to Mozdok during the conflict in Georgia in August 2008, this Su-25 was hit and badly damaged by a man-portable surface-to-air missile during the conflict. The 899th ShAP is subordinate to the 105th Assault Aviation Division.

Specifications

Crew: 1

Powerplant: 2 x 175kN (39,360lb thrust)
unnamed NPO Saturn and FNPTS MMPP
Salyut engine

Maximum speed: Mach 2.45 (2600km/h;
1615mph) at 17,000m (45,000ft)

Range: 5500km (3417 miles)

Service ceiling: 20,000m (65,616ft)

Dimensions: span 14m (46.6ft); length 19.8m
(65.9ft); height 6.05m (19.8ft)

Weight: 26,000kg (57,320lb) loaded

Armament: No guns on prototype but provision
for a cannon and two internal hardpoint bays

▼ Sukhoi T-50, Prototype

Hopes for the future of the Russian Air Force's combat fleet rest with the T-50, which has been developed by Sukhoi under the Perspektivnyi Aviatsionnyi Kompleks Frontovoi Aviatsii, or Future Air Complex for Tactical Aviation initiative. Illustrated is the first prototype, which made its first flight in February 2010, before receiving this disruptive camouflage pattern.

its assets between the Northern, Pacific, Baltic, Caspian and Black Sea Fleets. It also includes a number of direct-reporting units, and a carrier-capable regiment, the 279th OKIAP, that deploys Su-33s and Su-25UTGs aboard the carrier *Admiral Kuznetsov*. The Ka-27 is the primary shipborne helicopter, while land-based aircraft include Su-24 bombers/reconnaissance aircraft, Tu-142 and Il-38 patrol aircraft, Be-12 amphibians and Mi-14 helicopters, plus transports and trainers.

RECONNAISSANCE AVIATION REGIMENTS (RAP)		
11th RAP	Marinovka	Su-24MR
47th RAP	Shatalovo	Su-24MR, MiG-25RB
98th RAP	Monchegorsk	Su-24MR, MiG-25RB
313th RAP	Bada	Su-24MR
799th RAP	Varfolomyeevka	Su-24MR

ASSAULT AVIATION REGIMENTS (SHAP)		
18th ShAP	Galenki	Su-25
187th ShAP	Chernigovka	Su-25
266th ShAP	Step	Su-25
368th ShAP	Budyonnovsk	Su-25
461st ShAP	Krasnodar	Su-25
899th ShAP	Buturlinovka	Su-25
960th ShAP	Primorsko-Akhtarsk	Su-25

Serbia

SERBIAN AIR FORCE

The Vazduhoplovstvo i protivvazdusna odbrana (ViPVO, or Serbian Air Force) emerged from the Yugoslavian civil war and the NATO bombing campaign of 1999 to be re-established in 2006.

Specifications

Crew: 1

Powerplant: 1 x 35.59kN (8000lb) Armstrong-
Siddeley Sapphire turbojet engine

Maximum speed: 144km/h (710mph)

Range: 689km (490 miles)

Service ceiling: 15,240m (50,000ft)

Dimensions: span 10.26m (33ft 8in); length
13.98m (45ft 10.5in); height 4.02m (13ft 2in)

Weight: 8501kg (18,742lb) loaded

Armament: 4 x 30mm (1.18in) Aden cannon;
up to 2722kg (6000lb) of bombs or rockets

▼ **Mikoyan MiG-29, 101st Fighter Squadron 'Knights', 204th Aviation Base, Batajnica**

One of only four survivors out of the original 16 aircraft, this overhauled MiG-29 is now in service alongside MiG-21s at Batajnica, near Belgrade.

THE EQUIPMENT OF the ViPVO is mainly inherited from the former Socialist Federal Republic of Yugoslavia's air arm, and is shared between two air bases: the 98th Aviation Base at Ladevci-Kraljevo and the 204th Aviation Base at Batajnica. The 98th Aviation Base incorporates the 241st Fighter-Bomber Squadron, 714th Combat Helicopter Squadron and the 2nd Reconnaissance Flight. The 119th Combat Helicopter Squadron operates from Nis under 98th Aviation Base command. Aircraft types comprise the J-22 Orao, G-4 Super Galeb, Utva 75, Gazelle, Mi-8 and An-2. At Batajnica are the 101st Fighter Squadron, 252nd Composite Squadron, 138th Composite Transport Squadron and the 2nd Reconnaissance Flight, equipped with the MiG-21, MiG-29, An-26, Mi-8, Yak-40, Utva 75, G-4 and Gazelle. Lasta 95 primary trainers are due to replace the Utva 75s in the same role.

◀ **Mikoyan-Gurevich MiG-21bis**

Serbian MiG-21bis fighters and two-seat MiG-21UM combat trainers are flown by the 204th Aviation Base's 101st Fighter Squadron, alongside MiG-29s. The MiG-21s are used for Quick Reaction Alert interception duty, for which they are armed with R-60 missiles and onboard cannon.

Slovakia

SLOVAK AIR FORCE AND AIR DEFENCE FORCE

The Velitelstvo Vzdusnych Sil was formed in 1993 after the division of Czechoslovakia, and received a proportion of the former Czechoslovakian Air Force inventory.

THE MAJOR BASES of the Slovak Air Force are Sliac, Malacky-Kuchyna and Presov. Headquarters, and the Air Operation Control Centre, are at Zvolen. The air arm has reported to NATO since Slovakia joined the alliance in 2004. Sliac is the Slovak fighter base, and is home to the Mixed Air Wing. This organization accommodates a squadron of 12 upgraded MiG-29s (including a pair of two-seaters) and a squadron of 15 L-39 jet trainers. At Malacky-

Kuchyna can be found the Air Transport Wing, responsible for a single squadron of two An-26s (due to be replaced by C-27Js), and one of L-410s in various configurations. Helicopter operations are centred at Presov, from where the Mixed Helicopter Wing hosts three squadrons equipped with the Mi-24, Mi-17 and Mi-2 respectively. A SAR unit with Mi-8/17s is also active at Presov. Air Force structure also includes an air defence missile brigade at Nitra.

Slovenia

SLOVENIAN AIR DEFENCE AND AVIATION BRIGADE

Part of NATO since 2004, Slovenia maintains a small but well-equipped air arm that was established following its declaration of independence from the Yugoslav Federation in 1991.

WITH NATO RESPONSIBLE for air defence of Slovenia, the air arm focuses on support of the ground forces, SAR and training. The three flying units comprise the 15th Helicopter Battalion, the Flight School, and the Air Transport Section. The Flight School at Cerklje ob Krki is responsible for basic and advanced training, with Zlin 143, Zlin

242, Bell 206 and PC-9 aircraft. The Air Transport Section, also at Cerklje ob Krki, uses two PC-6s and one L-410. Previously, the 15th Helicopter Battalion operated from Brnik, with a fleet of eight Bell 412 and four AS532 helicopters. With the exception of a single SAR Bell 412 at Brnik, all other helicopters have now moved to Cerklje ob Krki.

Specifications

Crew: 1–2

Powerplant: 1 x 857kW (1149hp) Pratt & Whitney Canada PT6A-62 turboprop

Maximum speed: 593km/h (368mph)

Range: 1593km (990 miles)

Service ceiling: 11,580m (37,992ft)

Dimensions: span 10.11m (33ft 2in); length 10.69m (35ft 1in); height 3.26m (10ft 8in)

Weight: 3200kg (7055lb) loaded

▼ **Pilatus PC-9M, Air Force Military School, Cerklje ob Krki**

Slovenia's PC-9 fleet includes three standard aircraft and nine PC-9M Hudournik (Swift) aircraft, upgraded by RADOM of Israel and featuring head-up displays, weapons systems and advanced communications.

Ukraine

UKRAINIAN AIR FORCE, ARMY AVIATION AND NAVY

Created through the amalgamation of the former Air Force and Air Defence Force, the Air Force of the Armed Forces of Ukraine is complemented by separate Army and Navy air components.

HEADQUARTERED AT VINNITSA, the Ukrainian Air Force is organized on the basis of three air commands: the Air Command South headquartered at Odessa; Air Command West (Lviv); and Air Command Centre (Vasilkiv); plus a tactical command in Crimea. Each command is responsible for bases and their attendant regiments. From its original strength of around 2800 aircraft and helicopters in 1992, the air arm has been considerable downsized, and in 2003 numbered just under 400 combat aircraft in 10 regiments. By 2015, a force of 190 aircraft of all types is projected.

Air defence is maintained by one fighter regiment with Su-27s (at Mirgorod, with another possibly at Ozerne) and four with MiG-29s (Belbek, Ivano-Frankivsk, Ozerne and Vasilkiv). A bomber regiment equipped with Su-24Ms is located at Starokostyantiniv, along with a squadron of Su-24MRs, while two attack regiments fly the Su-25 (Chortkiv and Kulbakino).

Transport is handled by the 7th Military Transport Aviation Division, which includes a single regiment equipped with the Il-76 at Melitopol. Other transport types are based at Borispol and Gavryshevka, and include An-12s, An-24/26/30s, a pair of Tu-134s, and Mi-8 helicopters.

Primary training is conducted by the Kharkiv Institute, with three aviation colleges, and a combat training centre. Tuition begins on the Yak-52, students later progressing to the L-39 at Chuguyiv. Air force Mi-2s train Army Aviation aircrews.

Army Aviation

Ukrainian Army Aviation consists of three brigades of two mixed helicopter squadrons each. Assets are divided geographically between two commands: Army Command West (HQ Lviv) and South (HQ Odessa). Army Command West incorporates the 3rd Brigade at Brody and the 7th Brigade at Novi Kaliniv. Army Command South is responsible for the 11th Brigade at Kherson and two independent squadrons. Types in service comprise various subtypes of Mi-8/9 and Mi-24, plus heavylift Mi-26s. Certain squadrons are assigned to a Rapid Reaction Force, and others have deployed on international peacekeeping assignments.

The Ukrainian Navy maintains a single major aviation base at Saki, from where it operates a mixed brigade consisting of Ka-25, Ka-27/29 and Mi-14 maritime helicopters, plus An-12s, An-26s and Mi-8s for transport. There is also a squadron of Be-12 maritime patrol amphibians in use.

Specifications

Crew: 1	Dimensions: span 11.36m (37ft 3.75in);
Powerplant: 2 x 81.4kN (18,298lb) Sarkisov	length (including probe) 17.32m (56ft 10in);
RD-33 turbofans	height 7.78m (25ft 6.25in)
Maximum speed: 2443km/h (1518mph)	Weight: 18,500kg (40,785lb) loaded
Range: 1500km (932 miles)	Armament: 1 x 30mm (1.18in) GSh-30 cannon,
Service ceiling: 17,000m (55,775ft)	provision for up to 4500kg (9921lb) of stores

▼ Mikoyan MiG-29, 9th Fighter Aviation Regiment, Ozerne

This MiG-29 of the 9th IAP is based at Ozerne, in the Zhitomyr region. The unit is part of Air Command Centre. Of a reported 80 MiG-29s of various subtypes in Ukrainian service, a handful have been locally upgraded to MiG-29MU1 standard, with improved weapons and avionics.

MONGOLIA

MONGOL

KAZAKHSTAN

UZBEKISTAN

KYRGYZSTAN

GEORGIA

ARMENIA

AZERBAIJAN

TURKMENISTAN

TAJIKISTAN

SYRIA

LEBANON

ISRAEL

IRAQ

IRAN

AFGHANISTAN

JORDAN

KUWAIT

BAHRAIN

SAUDI
ARABIA

QATAR

U.A.E.

OMAN

YEMEN

ARABIAN

SEA

INDIAN

OCEAN

Chapter 14

Central and Western Asia and the Middle East

Militarily, the region of central and western Asia is dominated by the Middle East, with its history of conflict and its position as the most profitable arms market in the world. This is reflected in its highly equipped air forces, although a very different situation is found among the former Soviet states further to the east, and Afghanistan, scene to successive conflicts over the last three decades. In addition to the continuing conflict in Iraq, and the ongoing Israel-Palestine confrontation, airpower has recently been deployed in combat by Lebanon, Saudi Arabia and Yemen, as well as in Georgia to the north of the region.

Afghanistan
AFGHAN NATIONAL ARMY AIR CORPS

Following the launch of Coalition military operations in Afghanistan in 2001 and the subsequent collapse of the Taliban, the Afghan National Army Air Corps has been established with U.S. help.

WITH A STRENGTH based around 36 Mi-17 and Mi-35 helicopters and eight An-26/32 and G222 fixed-wing transport aircraft, the ANAAC is divided into two wings – in Kabul in the north, and in Kandahar in the south. By 2009, the ANAAC had 3000 personnel en route to its goal of over 7000.

Specifications

Crew: 1

Powerplant: 1 x 73.5kN (16,535lb) Tumanskii R-25 turbojet

Maximum speed: 2229km/h (1385mph)

Range: 1160km (721 miles)

Service ceiling: 17,500m (57,400ft)

Dimensions: span 7.15m (23ft 5.5in);

length (including probe) 15.76m (51ft 8.5in); height 4.1m (13ft 5.5in)

Weight: 10,400kg (22,925lb) loaded

Armament: 1 x 23mm (0.9in) GSh-23 twin-barrel cannon in underbelly pack, provision for about 1500kg (3307kg) of stores

▼ **Mikoyan-Gurevich MiG-21bis, ANAAC**
The ANAAC operates a handful of MiG-21s for training purposes. Currently, the focus of ANAAC activities is on supply missions between military installations.

Armenia
ARMENIAN AIR FORCE

Economic problems have stifled the development of the Armenian air force, which during the 1990s saw combat against Azerbaijan over the disputed region of Nagorno-Karabakh.

AT THE END of the Cold War, Armenia officially possessed just three combat aircraft and 13 combat helicopters. Armenia's air arm now includes a handful of An-2, An-24/32 and Il-76 transports, MiG-25PD, Su-25 and L-39 jets, plus Mi-8 and Mi-24 helicopters, and Yak 18 and Yak-52 trainers.

Azerbaijan
AZERI AIR FORCE

The Azeri air force was left with only a handful of combat types following the collapse of the USSR, but has expanded to include fixed- and rotary-wing equipment from a variety of sources.

THE BACKBONE OF the Azeri air force is provided by a small number of MiG-29 fighters and Su-17M attack aircraft, supported by larger numbers of Su-24s, Su-25s and L-39s, the latter used for both light attack and training. The helicopter fleet is based around Mi-8s and Mi-24s.

Bahrain

ROYAL BAHRAINI AIR FORCE

Independent since 1971, the small kingdom of Bahrain is defended by a modern fleet of aircraft, with RBAF operations concentrated at air bases at Isa and Manama.

FIGHTER OPERATIONS FOR the RBAF (formerly known as the Bahrain Ameri Air Force – BAAF) are focused at the purpose-built Isa air base, home to No. 6 Squadron with F-5E/F jets, and two F-16C/D units (Nos 1 and 2 Squadrons). The most recent Bahraini F-16s are Block 40D aircraft procured under the Peace Crown II deal in 1998.

Flight training is conducted at Isa air base on six Hawk Mk129s ordered in 2003, from which students progress after time on Firefly primary trainers.

The RBAF helicopter fleet at Rifa'a comprises AH-1E attack helicopters, supported by AB212s, Bell 412s (on order) and BO105s. A total of three UH-60s provide a medium-lift helicopter capability, with another eight examples on order. Single examples of the BAe 146 and S-92 serve in the VIP transport role.

Manama air base (part of Bahrain International Airport), and located on Muharraq Island, was formerly the BAAF's main fighter base, but today supports the Bahrain Amiri Royal Flight.

▶ **Sikorsky S-92A**

The RBAF operates a single S-92 as a VIP transport, seen here landing on board the aircraft carrier USS *Dwight D. Eisenhower*. The helicopter was purchased new from the manufacturer in 2008 and now serves with No. 9 Squadron, part of the Helicopter Wing at Rifa'a air base.

Specifications

Crew: 1	length 15.09m (49ft 6in);
Powerplant: 1 x 126.7kN (28,500lb) thrust	height 5.09m (16ft 8in)
Pratt & Whitney F100-PW-229 afterburning	Weight: 19,187kg (42,300lb) loaded
turbofan	Armament: 1 x GE M61A1 20mm (0.79in)
Maximum speed: 2177km/h (1353mph)	multi-barrelled cannon, wingtip
Range: 3862km (2400 miles)	missile stations; 7 external hardpoints
Service ceiling: 15,240m (49,000ft)	with provision for up to 9276kg (20,450lb)
Dimensions: span 9.45m (31ft);	of stores

▼ **Lockheed Martin F-16C Fighting Falcon, No. 1 Fighter Squadron, Manama AB**

F-16C 90-0031 was delivered to the RBAF in July 1990, part of an initial order for eight F-16Cs and four F-16Ds placed in 1987. The two F-16 squadrons combine with the F-5E/F squadron to form the 1st Fighter Wing.

Georgia
GEORGIAN AIR FORCE

Following the August 2008 war fought against Russia over the disputed region of South Ossetia, the precise status of the Georgian Air Force must now be considered uncertain.

ESTABLISHED FOLLOWING THE demise of the USSR, the Georgian Air Force saw action in the 1990s after the breakaway republic of Abkhazia declared independence. Today, the air force includes around 3000 personnel, fixed- and rotary-wing aircraft and air defence missile units. Key air bases are located at Alekseyevka and Marneuli. The inventory includes Su-25 (including upgraded Su-25KM) attack aircraft, some of which were locally built in Tbilisi, L-39 jet trainers, Yak-52 piston-engined trainers, An-2, An-24 and Tu-134 transports, as well as Mi-2, Mi-8, Mi-14 Mi-24 and UH-1H helicopters, the latter provided as military aid by Turkey and the USA. A number of losses were sustained during the course of the brief South Ossetian War, both to Russian forces and through 'friendly fire', and reports suggest that the air force may be integrated within the structure of Georgia's land forces in the future.

Iraq
IRAQI AIR FORCE

In the wake of the U.S.-led invasion in 2003, the Iraqi Air Force is being rebuilt, with a focus on counter-insurgency and transport assets to support efforts against the insurgency campaign.

THE NEW-LOOK IRAQI air arm was re-established by the Coalition Provisional Authority (CPA), and now includes Mi-17V-5/171s used for special operations, King Air 350ER and Cessna 208 transports, some with ISR mission payloads, AT-6B COIN aircraft, and armed Bell 407 helicopters.

There are four active air bases (New Al Muthanna, Kirkuk, Basrah, and Taji), with five more bases under construction. Aircraft are operated by nine squadrons, with three more being established. The current squadrons comprise three for reconnaissance, one fixed-wing training, one helicopter training, one transport, one utility helicopter, one transport helicopter, and one special operations squadron.

Specifications

Crew: 5

Powerplant: 4 x 3021kW (4050hp) Allison T56-A-7A turboprop engines

Maximum speed: 547km/h (340mph)

Range: 3896km (2420 miles)

Service ceiling: 7010m (23,000ft)

Dimensions: span 40.4m (132ft 7in); length 29.8m (97ft 9in); height 11.7m (38ft 6in)

Weight: 79,375kg (175,000lb) loaded

▼ **Lockheed C-130E Hercules, No. 23 Transport Squadron, New Al Muthanna AB**
Three Iraqi Air Force C-130Es are due to be joined by six new C-130Js, with deliveries planned between 2012 and 2014.

YI-301

IRAQI AIR FORCE

Iran

ISLAMIC REPUBLIC OF IRAN AIR FORCE, NAVAL AND ARMY AVIATION

Once the most powerful air arm in the Middle East, today's IRIAF remains a potent and increasingly self-sufficient force, backed up by the Islamic Revolution Guards Corps Air Force.

THE PRIMARY ROLE of the IRIAF is to defend Iranian airspace, but the air arm can also undertake offensive operations and power projection beyond its own borders. The IRGCAF air arm, meanwhile, focuses on close support for the Islamic Revolution Guards Corps. Naval aviation is provided by the Islamic Republic of Iran Naval Aviation, while army airpower is operated by a separate organization.

The IRIAF strike force is headed by 32 Su-24MKs used by two squadrons. The F-4E is the most important fighter type, with at least six squadrons equipped with about 64 examples. Long-range missions by Su-24s and F-4s are supported by Boeing 707-3J9C tankers, which also have a designated airborne command post role.

Air defence force

In line with a new defensive posture, the IRIAF is fielding a larger number of dispersed air defence squadrons, with assets able to be stationed around some 60 airfields across the country. The premier interceptor remains the F-14A, 44 of which are available within four squadrons. Supporting the Tomcat in the air defence role are approximately 12 F-4Ds, some 20 MiG-29s, and 16 Mirage F1s, although the latter may be used mainly for training.

Additional combat assets comprise around 60 F-5E/Fs and some 35 Shenyang F-7Ns, which serve as advanced trainers, with a secondary interception role.

The IRGCAF is the organic air arm of the IRGC, and uses transport aircraft to deploy rapid-reaction forces, and combat types for close air support. IRGCAF equipment includes 10 Su-25 attack jets, four Il-76 and 11 An-74 transports, some 13 EMB-

▲ **Lockheed C-130H Hercules**

Iran maintains a fleet of around 20 C-130E/Hs, which are mainly based at TFB.1 Mehrabad, the centre of IRIAF tactical transport operations, with other examples observed at Shiraz. Reflecting the importance of the airlifter within the IRIAF is the fact that much of the fleet is being overhauled locally.

Specifications

Crew: 2

Powerplant: 2 x 92.9kN (20,900lb) Pratt & Whitney TF30-P-412A turbofan engines

Maximum speed: 2517km/h (1564mph)

Range: about 3220km (2000 miles)

Service ceiling: 17,070m (56,000ft)

Dimensions: span 19.55m (64ft 1.5in) unswept; 11.65m (38ft 2.5in) swept;

length 19.1m (62ft 8in); height 4.88m (16ft)

Weight: 33,724kg (74,349lb) loaded

Armament: 1 x 20mm (0.79in) M61A1 Vulcan rotary cannon; external pylons for a combination of AIM-7 Sparrow medium range air-to-air missiles, AIM-9 medium range air-to-air missiles, and AIM-54 Phoenix long range air-to-air missiles

▼ **Grumman F-14A Tomcat, TFB.8 Shahid Baba'ie**

Recently overhauled by Iranian Aircraft Industries at Mehrabad, F-14A 3-6073 is currently serving at TFB.8 Shahid Baba'ie AB, near Esfahan. The aircraft can now be armed with the AIM-23C Sejil air-to-air missile, a locally manufactured variant of the I-HAWK surface-to-air missile.

Specifications

Crew: 2

Powerplant: 2 x 79.6kN (17,900lb) General
Electric J79-GE-17 turbojets

Maximum speed: 2390km/h (1485mph)

Range: 817km (1750 miles)

Service ceiling: 19,685m (60,000ft)

Dimensions: span 11.7m (38ft 5in); length

17.76m (58ft 3in); height 4.96m (16ft 3in)

Weight: 26,308kg (58,000lb) loaded

Armament: 1 x 20mm (0.78in) M61A1 Vulcan
cannon and 4 x AIM-7 Sparrow recessed
under fuselage or other weapons up to
1370kg (3020lb) on centreline pylon; four
wing pylons for two AIM-7, or four AIM-9

▼ McDonnell Douglas F-4E Phantom II, 61st TFS, TFB.6 Bushehr

This F-4E is depicted carrying the indigenous Sattar-3 laser-guided missile together with an associated laser-marker. Phantoms serve alongside F-14s at Bushehr, in one of Iran's most strategically vital areas, and at least two examples of each fighter are kept on permanent alert at the base.

ISLAMIC REPUBLIC OF IRAN AIR FORCE COMBAT AND TRANSPORT UNITS

TFB.1 Tehran-Mehrabad

11th TFS	MiG-29, MiG-29UB
11th and 12th TS	C-130H
Unknown TS	Boeing 747-2J9F
Unknown TS	Boeing 707-3J9C

* a total of five Transport Squadrons operate from Mehrabad.

TFB.2 Tabriz

21st and 22nd TFS	F-5E/F
23rd TFS	MiG-29, MiG-29UB

* a total of four Tactical Fighter Squadrons operate from Tabriz.

TFB.3 Nojeh, Hamedan

31st, 32nd, 33rd TFS	F-4E, RF-4E
Unknown TFS	F-4E

TFB.4 Defzul-Vahdati

41st, 42nd, 43rd TFS	F-5E/F

TFB.5 Ardestani

51st, 52nd, 53rd TFS	F-7N/FT-7

TFB.6 Bushehr

61st and 62nd TFS	F-4E
Unknown TFS	F-14A

TFB.7 Dastghaib, Shiraz

71st and 72nd TFS	Su-24MK
Unknown squadron	P-3F

TFB.8 Shahid Baba'ie

81st, 82nd and 83rd TFS	F-14A

TFB.9 Bandar Abbas

91st or 92nd TFS	F-4E

TFB.10 Kangan (Chabahar)

101st TFS	F-4D
Unknown TFS	F-4D

TFB.12 Asyaee, Masjed-e Soleyman

No permanently assigned units

TFB.13 Gayem al-Mohammad

Unknown TFS	type unknown

TFB.14 Hashemi Nejad

Two fighter squadrons	Mirage F1EQ

Islamic Revolution Guards Corps Air Force Combat Units

Transport Wing	Il-76MD, An-74TK	Mehrabad
Helicopter Wing Fighter Wing	Su-25K/UBK, EMB-312	Shiraz and Zahedan
	Mi-171, AH-1	Mehrabad

312 Tucano turboprop trainers, approximately 30 Mi-171 assault helicopters, and AH-1 attack helicopters.

Although the exact nature of the IRIAF's order of battle remains unknown, organization is based around Tactical Fighter Bases (TFBs). Each TFB has a number of flying squadrons permanently attached. The TFB operates according to a wing structure, which may include up to six squadrons. Squadrons are assigned to TFBs as required, with TFBs therefore having a flexible, mixed-force structure.

Islamic Republic of Iran Naval Aviation maintains a force of fixed-wing types and helicopters, with AB205s, AB206s, AB212s, ASH-3Ds, Falcon 20s, F27s and Shrike Commanders likely operating from bases at Bushehr, Shiraz and Bandar Abbas.

Islamic Republic of Iran Army Aviation primarily operates helicopters, including AB205s, AB206s, AH-1s, Bell 214s and CH-47s, with fixed-wing assets including O-2s. Bases are believed to include Bakhtaran, Isfahan, Kerman and Tehran.

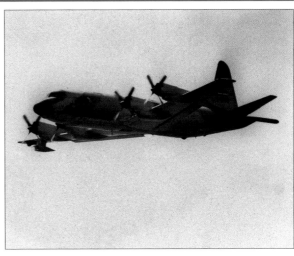

▲ **Lockheed P-3F Orion**

The P-3F variant was developed specifically for the then Imperial Iranian Air Force. Four examples are reported to remain in service in the maritime patrol role, and these have been outfitted with locally developed electro-optical sensors and are believed to have been equipped to launch Chinese-made anti-ship missiles.

Specifications

Crew: 1	length 14.45m (47ft 4.75in);
Powerplant: 2 x 22.2kN (5000lb) General	height 4.07m (13ft 4.25in)
Electric J85-GE-21B turbojets	Weight: 11,214kg (24,722lb) loaded
Maximum speed: 1741km/h (1082mph)	Armament: 2 x 20mm (0.78in) cannon; 2 x
Range: 306km (190 miles)	air-to-air missiles, five external pylons with
Service ceiling: 15,790m (51,800ft)	provision for 3175kg (7000lb) of stores,
Dimensions: span 8.13m (26ft 8in);	including missiles, bombs and ECM pods

▼ **IAMI (Northrop) F-5E Saeqeh, TFB.2 Tabriz**

The former first prototype for the Saeqeh programme, this jet is now in service at TFB.2. Iran has developed two indigenous upgrades of the F-5E/F, the Saeqeh and Azarakhsh, apparently with the eventual aim of launching local production of a reverse-engineered version.

Specifications

Crew: 2	10.36m (34ft) swept; length 24.53m
Powerplant: 2 x 110.3kN (24,802lb) Lyul'ka	(80ft 5in); height 4.97m (16ft 0.75in)
AL-21F-3A turbojets	Weight: 39,700kg (87,520lb) loaded
Maximum speed: 2316km/h (1439mph)	Armament: 1 x 23mm (0.9in) GSh-23-6
Combat radius: 1050km (650 miles)	six-barrelled cannon; nine external pylons
Service ceiling: 17,500m (57,415ft)	with provision for up to 8000kg (17,635lb)
Dimensions: span 17.63m (57ft 10in) spread,	of stores

▼ **Sukhoi Su-24MK, 71st TFS, TFB.7 Shiraz**

3-6853 is one of 24 ex-Iraqi Air Force Su-24s that were evacuated to Iran from Iraq in 1991. Another 12 Su-24s were purchased directly from the USSR in 1990. Armed with indigenous and Chinese-made weapons, the IRIAF Su-24s can be refuelled in flight by 707 and 747 tankers.

Israel

ISRAELI AIR AND SPACE FORCE

One of the world's most experienced air arms in terms of combat operations, the IASF occupies a unique position in the Middle East, operating some of the world's most advanced warplanes.

ONCE DESIGNATED the Israeli Defence Force/Air Force, the Israeli air arm was renamed in 2005 to reflect its dual air and space mission. Originally established in 1947, as the air component of the Jewish resistance movement, the antecedents of today's IASF fought with distinction in successive Middle East conflicts during which the very existence of Israel was under threat. The constant threat of terrorist action and insurgency in the Gaza Strip and Golan Heights, combined with geopolitical tensions within the region, ensure that the IASF remains at a high level of readiness.

The backbone of the IASF's combat units are numerous versions and subversions of the F-15 and

F-16, the total quantity of both types amounting to around 360 aircraft. They are responsible for air defence, long-range strike and interdiction duties. The acquisition of new types has added the F-15I and F-16I strike aircraft (both of which were developed to meet specific Israeli requirements), Beech 200, special missions Gulfstream 550s (comprising the Eitam airborne early warning and Shavit special electronic missions aircraft), AH-64D attack helicopter and Eitan UAV to the IASF fleet, while older aircraft are being upgraded locally. Most combat types are equipped with Israeli-produced electronic warfare equipment and weaponry. The 20 AH-64Ds join an

Specifications

Crew: 1

Powerplant: 2 x 77.62kN (17,450lbf) (dry thrust) Pratt & Whitney F100-PW-220 turbofans

Maximum speed: 2655km/h (1650mph)

Range: 5550km (3450 miles)

Service ceiling: 20,000m (65,000ft)

Dimensions: span 13.05m (42ft 9.75in); length 19.43in (63ft 9in); height 5.63m (18ft 5in)

Weight: 20,200kg (44,500lb) loaded

Armament: 1 x 20mm (0.79in) M61A1 cannon, provision for 7300kg (16,000lb) of stores

▼ McDonnell Douglas F-15C Eagle, 148 Squadron, Tel Nof

Israeli F-15C serial 640, nicknamed 'Commando', was active during 1982–85 before being re-serialled as 840. As originally coded, it was officially credited with 3.5 victories in the early 1980s (although six kill markings were originally applied, as seen here). It now serves with 106 Squadron.

Specifications

Crew: 1

Powerplant: 1 x 126.7kN (28,500lb) thrust Pratt & Whitney F100-PW-229 afterburning turbofan

Maximum speed: 2177km/h (1353mph)

Range: 3862km (2400 miles)

Service ceiling: 15,240m (49,000ft)

Dimensions: span 9.45m (31ft); length 15.09m (49ft 6in); height 5.09m (16ft 8in)

Weight: 19,187kg (42,300lb) loaded

Armament: 1 x GE M61A1 20mm (0.79in) cannon, wingtip missile stations; seven external hardpoints with provision for up to 9276kg (20,450lb) of stores

▼ General Dynamics F-16C Fighting Falcon, 110 Squadron 'The Knights of the North', Ramat David

This F-16C Block 30 wears one kill marking associated with the destruction of a Hezbollah Ababil UAV in August 2006. The jet carries a mixed air-to-air load of AIM-9 Sidewinder and (underwing) Python 4 missiles.

Kuwait IAP is the centre of KAF transport operations, with No. 41 Squadron's six L-100-30 Hercules, and a VIP Transport Flight equipped with A300s, A310s and Gulfstream IV and V types, as well as S-92A helicopters.

The training fleet is based around nine Hawk Mk64s and eight Tucano Mk52s of the Flight Training Centre at Ali al Salem, these types operated by Nos 12 and 19 Squadrons, respectively. The same

base is home to the helicopter fleet, comprising No. 32 Squadron with SA330Hs, No. 33 Squadron with SA342Ks, No. 62 Squadron with AS332B/Ms and AS532s, and the AH-64Ds of No. 88 Squadron.

Kuwait also maintains a Police Helicopter Wing with a fleet consisting of EC135 and AS365 types. The Police Helicopter Wing operated SA330 and SA342 helicopters in the past, but these are now likely withdrawn.

Lebanon
LEBANESE AIR FORCE

Plagued by civil war during the 1980s, and more recently the scene of Israel's anti-Hezbollah operations, the Lebanese Air Force maintains a small but active force of combat aircraft.

THE CURRENT CAPABILITIES of the Lebanese Air Force (LAF) are vested in a fleet of rotary-wing aircraft acquired from various sources, plus a token force of four Hunter jet fighters at Rayak, the first of which originally arrived in Lebanon in 1959.

Also still in use are around 10 ex-UAE SA342L anti-tank helicopters, flown by No. 8 Squadron at Beirut. The receipt of 16 UH-1H helicopters from U.S. Army surplus in 1995 allowed the formation of two more squadrons at Beirut. These aircraft are also used in an offensive role, fitted with locally with bomb racks, and can be found equipping Nos 10 and 11 Squadrons at Beirut, No. 12 Squadron at Rayak and No. 14 Squadron at Kleyate.

In 2005 a training unit, No. 15 Squadron, was

created at Rayak, co-located with the aviation school and equipped with four Robinson R44 helicopters.

The LAF has its headquarters in Beirut, while individual air bases are headed by an independent commander responsible for a Technical Wing and an Air Wing, the latter incorporating flying squadrons.

The LAF is hopeful of receiving Mi-24 attack helicopters, 10 of which were offered by Russia in 2010. If delivered, these will serve alongside around seven AB212 and SA330 helicopters, returned to service after they had been refurbished with financial assistance from Qatar. One AW139 is also in service for VIP transport, while the only other fixed-wing asset is a single armed Cessna 208 transport.

Specifications

Crew: 1

Powerplant: 1 x 45.13kN (10,145lb) thrust
Rolls-Royce Avon 207 turbojet engine

Maximum speed: 1144km/h (710mph)

Range: 689km (490 miles)

Service ceiling: 15,240m (50,000ft)

Dimensions: span 10.26m (33ft 8in); length
13.98m (45ft 10.5in); height 4.02m (13ft 2in)

Weight: 17,750kg (24,600lb) loaded

Armament: 4 x 30mm (1.18in) Aden Cannon;
up to 2722kg (6000lb) of bombs or rockets;
AIM-9 Sidewinder AAMs or AGM-65 ASMs

▼ **Hawker Hunter F70A, No. 2 Squadron, Rayak**

Lebanon's first Hunters were delivered in 1959 to equip the No. 1 Squadron at Khalde, and the type saw action in the Six-Day War of 1967. Grounded in 1994, the Hunter remained in storage for many years, but a handful of the jets were returned to operational service in 2008.

Kazakhstan

KAZAKHSTAN AIR FORCE

Based on equipment inherited from the USSR, the Kazakhstan air force is small but relatively well equipped, although a lack of funds has allowed only limited upgrade of the inventory.

MAJOR BASES ARE at Taldy Kurgan (MiG-27s) and Karaganda (MiG-31s, MiG-29s and Su-27s), and Almaty, which is home to the transport fleet, with An-12s and An-24/26s. Aktau houses Su-27s and Su-25s, while Shetygen supports Su-24s and MiG-29s, with the latter type also at Lugovoye. Utsharal and Taras are major helicopter bases, with Mi-8/17s, Mi-24s and Mi-26s. A reconnaissance regiment (MiG-25RBs and Su-24MRs) is at Balkash, while a border guard air fleet is at Almaty-Boralday.

Kyrgyzstan

KYRGYZSTAN AIR FORCE

With the break-up of the USSR, Kyrgyzstan was left with a former Soviet flight training school on its territory. Today, the Kyrgyzstan air force is reported to maintain two units.

THE CURRENT STRUCTURE of the Kyrgyzstan Air Force is likely based around a single transport unit and a training squadron, the latter a hangover from the previous Soviet training facility at Frunze. The current Kyrgyzstan Air Force training squadron is equipped with L-39s. The transport squadron is responsible for a mixed fleet of An-12s, An-26s and Mi-8s, plus VIP-configured Tu-154s and Yak-40s. Around nine Mi-24 assault helicopters are reportedly active, although 48 MiG-21 fighters are now stored.

Mongolia

MONGOLIAN PEOPLE'S AIR FORCE

Formerly organized along Soviet lines, the Mongolian air arm is controlled by the army, although economic problems mean that much of its fleet is now non-operational.

THE ASSETS OF the small Mongolian armed forces were divided into five branches in 1993, a year after Soviet forces left the country. These comprise the General Purpose Troops, Air Defence Forces, Construction Corps, Civil Defence and Mobilization Reserves. A separate body is responsible for internal security and border protection.

The last jet fighters to be received were MiG-21s that were delivered in the late 1970s, and the fleet must now be presumed to be grounded at Sainshand, although reports suggest there may have been efforts to return at least some of the aircraft to flying order. The most potent combat equipment is the Mi-24, although only four are reported to be in use at Nalayh, supported by around 25 Mi-8s.

A transport capability is provided by a small number of An-24/26 and Y-12 aircraft, together with around 10 An-2 utility aircraft. Around 80 airfields are available across the country, although the most important of these is at Ulan Bator – which is the centre of air force fixed-wing and helicopter transport operations – as well as at Altai and Choilbalsan.

Oman

ROYAL AIR FORCE OF OMAN

Originally formed as the Sultan of Oman's Air Force in 1959 with assistance from the UK, the RAFO adopted its current name in 1990 and is today undergoing re-equipment and upgrade.

THE CUTTING EDGE of RAFO airpower is provided by the fast-jet units at Thumrait. The three front-line units at the base are responsible for 16 Jaguars, first ordered in 1977 and since upgraded to Jaguar 97 standard. Meanwhile, 20 Squadron is equipped with eight single-seat multi-role F-16Cs and four two-seat F-16Ds that were ordered in 2002. Looking to the future, the RAFO hopes to replace its last Jaguars by 2010, with the Typhoon seen as a likely successor.

Transport arm

The RAFO transport fleet is headquartered at Seeb and consists of three C-130Hs (a single C-130J is also on order), one BAC 111 and a single Airbus A320, with another A320 due to arrive to allow the BAC 111 to be retired. Also at Seeb is a single Skyvan and three Seavans used for maritime patrol, and also due for replacement in the near term. A further three Skyvans are still in use at Salalah.

A new base is being built at Al Musana, and this installation has received the helicopters that were formerly based at Seeb. No. 14 Squadron is in the process of re-equipping with 20 NH90s, allowing the retirement of older helicopter models and the Skyvan. Helicopter training is conducted at Salalah using the Bell 206s of 3 Squadron.

Masirah Island is home to RAFO pilot training, supporting 12 PC-9(M) turboprop trainers and Super Mushshak primary trainers, divided into two flights. Advanced training and air defence are the roles of 6 Squadron's 11 single-seat Hawk Mk203s and four two-seat Hawk Mk103s. Masirah also supports a SAR detachment with Lynx Mk120s.

ROYAL AIR FORCE OF OMAN		
1 Squadron	Super Mushshak, PC-9	Masirah
2 Squadron	Skyvan/Seavan	Seeb
3 Squadron	Lynx Mk120, Bell 206	Salalah
4 Squadron	BAC 111, A320	Seeb
5 Squadron	Skyvan	Salalah
6 Squadron	Hawk Mk103/203	Masirah
8 Squadron	Jaguar	Thumrait
14 Squadron	AB205, SA330, AS332	Al Musanah*
* SAR detachment at Khasab.		
15 Squadron	Lynx Mk120	Al Musanah*
* SAR detachment at Masirah.		
16 Squadron	C-130H	Seeb
18 Squadron	F-16C/D	Thumrait
20 Squadron	Jaguar S/B	Thumrait

Specifications

Crew: 2

Powerplant: 1 x 131kN (29,400lbf)

F110-GE-129

Maximum speed: 2177km/h (1353mph)

Range: 3862km (2400 miles)

Service ceiling: 15,240m (49,000ft)

Dimensions: span 9.45m (31ft);

length 15.09m (49ft 6in);

height 5.09m (16ft 8in)

Weight: 19,187kg (42,300lb) loaded

Armament: 1 x 20mm (0.79in) GEc M61A1

multi-barrelled cannon, seven external

hardpoints with provision for up to 9276kg

(20,450lb) of stores

▼ **Lockheed Martin F-16D Fighting Falcon, 18 Squadron, Thumrait**

This two-seat F-16D Block 50 is one of four purchased by Oman, for use with 18 Squadron. The aircraft are multi-role, and can also be used for anti-shipping.

Specifications

Crew: 2 or 3

Powerplant: 2 x 835kW (1120shp) Rolls-Royce
  Gem turboshafts

Maximum speed: 324km/h (201mph)

Range: 528km (328 miles)

Dimensions: rotor diameter 12.80m (42ft);

length 15.241m (50ft);

height 3.734m (12.25ft)

Weight: 5330kg (11,750lb) loaded

Armament: 1 x 7.62mm (0.3in) heavy machine
  gun, 2 x 70mm (2.76in) rocket pods

▼ AgustaWestland Lynx Mk120, 15 Squadron, Al Musanah

Based at Al Musanah, 15 Squadron also maintains a permanent SAR detachment
at the RAFO training base at Masirah. The Lynx is also flown by 3 Squadron at
Salalah, the most southerly RAFO base, where the type is used for training
alongside the Bell 206.

Specifications

Crew: 1

Powerplant: 2 x 37.3kN (8400lb) Rolls-
  Royce/Turbomeca Adour Mk 811 turbofans

Maximum speed: 1699km/h (1056mph)

Range: 537km (334 miles)

Service ceiling: 14,000m (46,000ft)

Dimensions: span 8.69m (28ft 6in); length
  16.83m (55ft 2.5in); height 4.89m (16ft 0.5in)

Weight: 15,700kg (34,613lb) loaded

Armament: 2 x 30mm(1.18in) Aden Mk.4
  cannon; provision for 4763kg (10,500lb)
  of stores

▼ SEPECAT Jaguar S, 8 Squadron, Thumrait

This is an example from the first batch of Jaguar Internationals delivered to Oman
starting in 1977. Although the Omani fleet was upgraded to Jaguar 97 standard,
with expanded weapons options and improved navigation equipment, retirement
of the Jaguar is imminent.

Qatar

QATAR EMIRI AIR FORCE

The foundations of the modern-day QAEF were laid in 1974, when the Public Security Forces of the newly independent Qatar established an Air Wing, mainly equipped with helicopters.

IN ITS CURRENT guise, the QAEF relies primarily on equipment supplied by France and the UK, although Qatar now shows signs of turning increasingly to the USA for new aircraft. British-supplied equipment consists of nine Commando Mk2/3 helicopters. The Commandos equip two squadrons at Doha International Airport, Nos 8 and 9 Squadrons, tasked with anti-surface warfare and assault transport, respectively. The QAEF hoped to add 18 Hawk Mk100s to its inventory,

but limited budgets mean that this deal has been put on hold.

The French contribution to the QAEF comprises six Alpha Jets for light attack and training, and about a dozen SA342 close-support helicopters serving with No. 6 Squadron at Doha. The Alpha Jet fleet is the responsibility of No. 11 Squadron at Doha, which concentrates on close support. The arrival of nine single-seat Mirage 2000-5EDA and three two-seat Mirage 2000-5DDA multi-role fighters in 1997 allowed the

Specifications

Crew: 1

Powerplant: 2 x 97kN (21,834lb) SNECMA
M53-P2 turbofan

Maximum speed:2338km/h (1453mph)

Range: 1480km (920 miles)

Service ceiling: 18,000m (59,055ft)

Dimensions: span 9.13m (29ft 11.5in);

length 14.36m (47ft 1.25in);

height 5.2m (17ft 0.75in)

Weight: 17,000kg (37,480lb) loaded

Armament: 1 x DEFA 554 cannon; nine external

pylons with provision for up to 6300kg

(13,889lb) of stores

▼ **Dassault Mirage 2000-5EDA, No. 7 Squadron, Doha**

The QAEF operates three Mirage 2000 Mk5 DDA two-seaters and nine Mirage 2000 Mk5 EDA single-seat, multi-role fighters with No. 7 Air Superiority Squadron at Doha, where they form part of No. 1 Fighter Wing.

transfer of the QAEF's Mirage F1s to Spain. The Mirage fleet, also stationed at Doha, is operated by No. 7 Squadron, with air defence as a primary task. Latest helicopter to enter service is the AW139, with a total of 18 on order for use in the utility transport role.

New airlifters

Recently, the QAEF has set about establishing a strategic and intra-theatre airlift capability, with the purchase of four C-17A transports. Two C-17s were in service by 2010, and the QAEF is also to receive four C-130J-30 airlifters from 2011. These new aircraft will serve with a newly established transport squadron at Doha.

In addition to front-line assets, the government maintains a Qatar Amiri Flight responsible for a fleet of VIP aircraft based on the civilian side of Doha IAP. Qatar Emiri Flight aircraft include examples of the Airbus A310, A319, A320 and A340, Boeing 707, 727 and 747SP, and the Falcon 900.

▲ **Boeing C-17A Globemaster III**

The first Middle East nation to order the type, Qatar is assembling a fleet of four C-17A airlifters, after placing an order in 2008. The second example was delivered in Qatar Airways colours. 2008 also saw Qatar sign contracts for four C-130J airlifters and 18 AW139 medium helicopters.

305

Saudi Arabia

ROYAL SAUDI AIR FORCE, ARMY AVIATION COMMAND AND NAVAL AIR ARM

The largest country on the Arabian peninsula, Saudi Arabia entrusts its defence to the RSAF, one of the best-equipped air arms in the world, as well as separate Army and Navy air components.

THE UNITS OF the RSAF have long been engaged in a rolling series of capability upgrades, with major procurement programmes ensuring regular receipt of new and advanced warplanes. Numerically, the F-15 is the most important combat jet, with 57 single-seat F-15Cs and 25 two-seat F-15Ds serving in the air defence role (in which they are supported by five E-3A airborne early warning platforms) and 71 F-15S used for strike. The exact status of the 24 air defence-configured Tornado ADVs is uncertain, but

87 upgraded Tornado IDS interdictors remain in use. Despite its age, the F-5 remains in service in quantity, variants comprising the F-5A (83 examples) for air defence, and the F-5B (37) for training. New fighter equipment is arriving in the form of 72 Typhoons.

The RSAF transport fleet can call upon 30 C-130E/Hs, seven KC-130Hs and six Lockheed L-100-30s, with six A330 tanker/transports due to be delivered starting in 2011 to supersede seven KE-3As. The training component is based on the Hawk, the

Specifications

Crew: 2	Dimensions: span 10.5m (34ft 5.5in); length
Powerplant: 2 x 90kN (20,250lb) Eurojet	16.0m (52ft 6in); height 4m (13ft 1.5in)
EJ200 turbofans	Weight: 23,000kg (50,705lb) loaded
Maximum speed: 2125km/h (1321mph)	Armament: 1 x 27mm (1.06in) Mauser cannon;
Range: 2900km (1840 miles)	13 fuselage hardpoints for a wide
Service ceiling: 19,810m (65,000ft)	variety of stores

▼ **Eurofighter Typhoon, No. 10 Squadron, King Fahd AB, Taif**

Saudi Arabia ordered a total of 72 EF2000 Typhoons, including 48 Tranche 2 and 24 Tranche 3 jets, and the first of these are entering service with No. 10 Squadron. The eventual Typhoon order for the RSAF may reach 100 aircraft.

Specifications

Crew: 2	Service ceiling: 15,240m (50,000ft)
Powerplant: 2 x 40.5kN (9104lbf) dry thrust	Dimensions: span 13.91m (45.6ft) unswept,
Turbo-Union RB199-34R Augmented	8.6m (28.2ft) (swept); length 18.7m (61.3ft);
Turbofans	height 5.95m (19.5ft)
Maximum speed: Mach 2.27 (2338km/h;	Weight: 21,546kg (47,500lb) loaded
1452mph)	Armament: 1 x internal Mauser BK-27 and 10
Range: 1390km (869 miles)	hardpoints holding up to 9000kg (19,800 lb)

▼ **Panavia Tornado IDS, No. 75 Squadron, 11 Wing, King Abdullah Aziz AB, Dharan**

Alongside F-15S jets, RSAF Tornado IDS strike aircraft have seen action against Houthi insurgents in Yemen and along the Saudi-Yemen border. RSAF Tornado IDS have been upgraded to a standard similar to the RAF's Tornado GR4.

ROYAL SAUDI AIR FORCE

King Abdullah Aziz AB, Dharan

3 Wing

No. 13 Squadron	F-15C/D
No. 92 Squadron	F-15S
No. 44 Squadron	Bell 412

11 Wing

No. 7 Squadron	Tornado IDS
No. 35 Squadron	Jetstream 31
No. 75 Squadron	Tornado IDS
No. 83 Squadron	Tornado IDS

King Fahd AB, Taif

2 Wing

No. 3 Squadron	F-5E/F*
No. 5 Squadron	F-15C/D
No. 10 Squadron	Typhoon
No. 14 Squadron	AB212, Bell 412
No. 12 Squadron det	AB212
No. 17 Squadron	F-5E/F
No. 34 Squadron	F-15C/D

* may have been disbanded.

King Khalid AB, Riyadh

4 Wing

No. 1 Squadron (Royal Flight)	VC-130H, C-130H, L-100-30 Hercules, CN235, BAe 125, A340, AS61, Learjet 35, Boeing 707, Boeing 737, Boeing 747, MD-11, Gulfstream 1159, Cessna 550

King Faisal Air Academy

No. 8 Squadron	Cessna 172, Super Mushshak
No. 9 Squadron	PC-9
No. 22 Squadron	PC-9

King Khalid AB, Khamis Mushait

5 Wing

No. 6 Squadron	F-15S
No. 15 Squadron	F-5E/F*

* may have been disbanded.

No. 55 Squadron	F-15S
No. 99 Squadron	AS532
No. 14 Squadron det	AB212, Bell 412

▲ Lockheed C-130H Hercules

The RSAF maintains a large fleet of Hercules, including C-130E/H tactical transports,KC-130H air-to-air refuelling tankers, VIP-configured VC-130H personnel transports and civilian-standard L-100-30 cargo transports. Seen here moments before airdropping a cargo load, this C-130H serves with No. 16 Squadron at Jeddah.

Prince Sultan AB, Al Kharj	
6 Wing	
No. 18 Squadron	E-3A, KE-3A
No. 71 Squadron	RE-3A
No. 32 Squadron	KC-130H
King Faisal AB, Tabuk	
7 Wing	
No. 2 Squadron	F-15C/D
No. 21 Squadron	Hawk T65
No. 37 Squadron	Hawk T65
No. 79 Squadron	Hawk T65A
No. 88 Squadron	Hawk T65/65A
Prince Abdullah AB, Jeddah	
8 Wing	
No. 4 Squadron	C-130E/H
No. 16 Squadron	C-130E/H
No. 20 Squadron	C-130E/H
King Khalid Military City, Hafar Al Batin	
No. 12 Squadron	AB212

turboprop PC-9, the piston-engined Mushshak and Cessna 172, and the Jetstream crew trainer.

RSAF helicopter arm

RSAF helicopter forces are represented by around 30 AB212s used for search and rescue and utility, 12 AS532s for combat search and rescue, a handful of AS-61A VIP transports, 24 Bell 205 and 16 Bell 412 utility transports and 12 SA365s for medical evacuation. A total of 22 UH-60Ls are on order.

The Royal Saudi Land Forces began operating aircraft in 1986 and its inventory now comprises 12 AH-64A attack helicopters and 12 Bell 406 Combat Scouts, 12 S-70As and 18 VH-60L VIP transports.

The Royal Saudi Naval Forces are responsible for 20 AS332s and 12 SA365s, with AS565s on order for use on board Saudi warships.

Specifications
Crew: 1
Powerplant: 2 x 77.62kN (17,450lbf) (dry thrust) Pratt & Whitney F100-PW-220 turbofans
Maximum speed: 2655km/h (1650mph)
Range: 5550km (3450 miles)
Service ceiling: 20,000m (65,000ft)
Dimensions: span 13.05m (42ft 9.75in); length 19.43in (63ft 9in); height 5.63m (18ft 5in)
Weight: 20,200kg (44,500lb) loaded
Armament: 1 x 20mm (0.79in) M61A1 cannon, provision for up to 7300kg (16,000lb) of stores, including missiles, bombs, tanks, pods and rockets

▼ **McDonnell Douglas F-15C Eagle, No. 13 Squadron, 3 Wing, King Abdullah Aziz AB, Dharan**

This Eagle was flown by the RSAF's Captain Ayed Salah al-Shamrani when he used AIM-9P Sidewinder missiles to shoot down two Iraqi Mirage F1EQ fighters during the 1991 Gulf War.

Specifications
Crew: 2
Powerplant: 1 x 29kN (6500lbf) Rolls-Royce Adour Mk.861 turbofan with FADEC
Maximum speed: .84 Mach (1028km/h; 638mph)
Range: 2520km (1565 miles)
Service ceiling: 13,565m (44,500ft)
Dimensions: span 9.94m (32ft 7in); length 12.43m (40ft 9in); height 3.98m (13ft 1in)
Weight: 9100kg (20,000lb) loaded
Armament: 4 x 12.7mm (0.5in) M-3 MGs; up to 19,504kg (43,000lb) of bombs

▼ **BAe Hawk T65, No. 21 Squadron, 7 Wing, King Faisal AB, Tabuk**

Saudi Arabia's Hawk advanced trainers operate within four squadrons at Tabuk. A total of 50 aircraft are in service, including both Mk65 and Mk65A versions, and the type equips the Saudi Hawks aerobatic display team, part of No. 88 Squadron.

Chapter 15

South, East and Southeast Asia

Dominated by India in the west and China in the east, the regions of South, East and Southeast Asia are also home to the 'tiger' economies of the Far East, and many nations deploying thoroughly equipped and highly trained air arms. Key flashpoints include Korea, where a considerable U.S. military presence backs up the South Korean forces arranged against the communist North, and Taiwan, which maintains its stand-off against communist China, and which also receives significant U.S. military support. Finally, two nuclear powers, India and Pakistan, maintain a strained relationship, with sporadic outbreaks of warfare. Japan is also home to a major U.S. presence, while the air forces of Indonesia, Malaysia and Singapore have all been recently engaged in high-profile re-equipment programmes for their air forces, creating something of an arms race in the region.

Bangladesh
BANGLADESH AIR FORCE

Formed in 1973, the Bangladesh Biman Bahini (BBB) operates a mixture of mainly Chinese and Russian equipment from four major bases: Dhaka, Jessore, Chittagong and Bogra.

T HE BANGLADESH AIR Force is spearheaded by a squadron of MiG-29 fighters, two squadrons of Chengdu F-7 fighters of various subtypes, and one of Nanchang A-5 attack aircraft, all at Dhaka. Dhaka also houses two helicopter squadrons (with Bell 212s and Mi-17s) and a reduced-size squadron with four C-130B transports. An Air Academy is located at Jessore, with two squadrons flying the Air Academy's T-37s and Bell 206s respectively. Also at Jessore is the transport fleet. Further trainers are at Bogra, in the form of Nanchang FT-6 primary trainers operated by the Air Academy, the only types at this base. A squadron of L-39 jet trainers is stationed at Chittagong, together with further squadrons of An-32s and Mi-17s and a detachment of Bell 212s.

A small Bangladesh Army Aviation arm operates a Cessna 208, and several Mi-17 and Bell 206 helicopters. An aviation wing of the Bangladesh Navy was established in 2010 with an order placed for two AW109 helicopters.

Specifications

Crew: 1	Dimensions: span 11.36m (37ft 3.75in);
Powerplant: 2 x 81.4kN (18,298lb) Sarkisov	length (including probe) 17.32m (56ft 10in);
RD-33 turbofans	height 7.78m (25ft 6.25in)
Maximum speed: 2443km/h (1518mph)	Weight: 18,500kg (40,785lb) loaded
Range: 1500km (932 miles)	Armament: 1 x 30mm (1.18in) GSh-30 cannon,
Service ceiling: 17,000m (55,775ft)	provision for up to 4500kg (9921lb) of stores

▼ **Mikoyan MiG-29, No. 8 Squadron, Dhaka-Kurmitola (Bashar)**

A total of six MiG-29s (plus two twin-seat MiG-29UBs) are operated by No. 8 Squadron from Dhaka. Dhaka actually comprises two bases, Tejgaon (the former international airport) and Kurmitola (the new international airport).

Brunei
ROYAL BRUNEI AIR FORCE

The Royal Brunei Air Force, or Angkatan Tentera Udara Diraja Brunei, is the air arm of one of the smallest but wealthiest countries in the world.

A S A BRITISH protectorate, Brunei hosts a detachment of Royal Air Force Bell 212s at Brunei International Airport. The small local military includes the Royal Brunei Air Force, established in 1991. The Air Force comprises four squadrons, primarily equipped with helicopters based at Brunei International. The current Royal Brunei Air Force rotary-wing fleet consists of two Bell 206s, 10 Bell 212s, one Bell 214, five BO105s and six Sikorsky S-70s. Fixed-wing aircraft comprise four PC-7 trainers and a single CN235 turboprop transport, plus three maritime patrol CN235MPAs.

Specifications

Crew: 2

Powerplant: 2 x 1409kW (1890shp) General
  Electric T700-GE-701C turboshaft

Maximum speed: 361km/h (224mph)

Range: 463km (288 miles)

Service ceiling: 4021m (13,200ft)

Dimensions: rotor diameter: 16.36m
  (53ft 8in); length 19.76m (64ft 10in);
  height 5.33m (17ft 6in)

Weight: 9997kg (22,000lb) loaded

▼ **Sikorsky S-70A, 4 Squadron, Royal Brunei Air Force, Brunei International Airport**

Brunei operates six S-70s in the medium-lift transport and VIP transport roles. The aircraft comprise four S-70As and two Sikorsky S-70Ls.

Cambodia
ROYAL CAMBODIAN AIR FORCE

Aircraft of the Royal Cambodian Air Force, or Force Aérienne Royale Cambodge, are based at Phnom Penh and include a small component of jet fighters and jet trainers.

IN ADDITION TO the major operating base, Royal Cambodian Air Force aircraft may be periodically deployed to satellite bases including Battambang, Kampongchnang, Kohkong, Kompongsom and Siemreap. The modern air arm was re-established in 1993 and now includes a helicopter squadron with Mi-8/17s, and a transport element with two An-24s, two Harbin Y-12s and three Islanders. Six Tecnam Echo microlights serve with a reconnaissance squadron. Jet equipment returned to Cambodia in 1996, with six L-39 trainers. Two Mi-26 heavylift helicopters were acquired in 1998, and these serve in a helicopter squadron. Cambodia hoped to induct 12 Israeli-upgraded MiG-21s, but the deal has been hampered by sanctions and budget constraints. In 2000 a MiG-21bis and a two-seat a two-seat MiG-21UM were delivered from Israel after upgrade. A government-operated VIP transport squadron is also found at Phnom Penh, with a mixed fleet of helicopters, plus an An-24 and a Falcon 20 jet.

Specifications

Crew: 1

Powerplant: 1 x 73.5kN (16,535lb) Tumanskii
  R-25 turbojet

Maximum speed: 2229km/h (1385mph)

Range: 1160km (721 miles)

Service ceiling: 17,500m (57,400ft)

Dimensions: span 7.15m (23ft 5.5in);

length (including probe) 15.76m (51ft 8.5in);
  height 4.1m (13ft 5.5in)

Weight: 10,400kg (22,925lb) loaded

Armament: 1 x 23mm (0.90in) GSh-23 twin-
  barrel cannon, provision for about 1500kg
  (3307kg) of stores

▼ **Mikoyan-Gurevich MiG-21bis, 701st Regiment, Pochentong**

This is one of 24-28 MiG-21s that were operational with the 701st Regiment at Pochentong in the late 1980s. Attempts to overhaul the fleet in Israel in the early 1990s failed due to a lack of funding.

China

PLA Air Force, Navy Air Force and Army Aviation Corps

The airpower of the world's most populous country is vested in the People's Liberation Army Air Force and the PLA Navy Air Force, together with a PLA Army Aviation Corps.

ALL THREE CHINESE air arms are undergoing a rigorous programme of modernization that has seen older types removed from the inventory, new and upgraded aircraft introduced, and structure rationalized. At the same time, efforts are being made to improve training and increase logistics support.

As the largest of the air arms, the PLAAF and its structure is subordinated to the PLA, which has overall control of the armed forces via a unified command. The seven Air Force Districts are assigned to the seven PLA Military Regions: Beijing, Chengdu, Guangzhou, Jinan, Lanzhou, Nanjing and Shenyang. Every Air Force District consists of a number of divisions, each normally responsible for two or three regiments.

The PLAAF has embraced lessons of recent conflicts and embarked on a widespread re-equipment programme in the last decade, which embraces combined-arms and out-of-area operations, rapid reaction forces, precision-guided munitions and C4ISR. It is estimated that the PLAAF today operates around 1,300 fighters, and 600 bomber/attack aircraft, plus transport and support aircraft, allocated to approximately 32 regiments.

The PLAAF bomber arm continues to rely on the H-6, advanced versions of which remain in use with at least four PLAAF and three PLANAF front-line regiments and now carry cruise missile armament.

Ongoing modernization of the fighter arm is reflected by the fielding of the indigenous J-10. This now complements the J-11/Su-27SK in the air defence role. The 'light' J-10 is gradually replacing the Chengdu J-7, while Su-27 variants displace the Shenyang J-8. Both J-7 and J-8 have been upgraded, however, and continue to serve in large numbers.

Indigenous fighter

The J-10, revealed in 2006, is the PLAAF's latest multi-role fighter, with indigenous weapons and avionics. A two-seat, fully combat-capable J-10S is also available. Initial versions serve with four regiments, while improved J-10A and J-10AS models have been issued to three more regiments, with deliveries continuing. The latest development is the advanced J-10B, revealed in 2009.

First ordered in 1991, 20 Su-27SKs and six two-seat Su-27UBKs were followed by 16 additional Su-27SKs and 34 Su-27UBKs. Licence production of the Su-27 has yielded the J-11 as well as 'indigenous' developments: the improved J-11A and J-11B, the latter with Chinese multi-mode radar. A reported 11 PLAAF and PLANAF fighter regiments operate J-

Specifications

Crew: 2

Powerplant: 2 x 123kN (27,600lbf) Lyulka al-31f turbofans

Maximum speed: Mach 2.0 (2120km/h; 1320mph)

Range: 3000km (1864 miles)

Service ceiling: 17,300m (56,800ft)

Dimensions: span 14.7m (48ft 2.5in); length 21.94m (72in 11in); height 6.36m (20ft 9in)

Weight: 34,500kg (76,100lb) loaded

Armament: 1 x 30mm (1.18n) GSh-3-1 gun, plus air-to-air and air-to-surface missiles

▼ **Sukhoi Su-30MK2, 4th Fighter Division/10th Air Regiment, PLANAF, Feidong**

The PLANAF received 24 Su-30MK2s ordered in 2003 and delivered in 2004. This example is seen armed with R-77 and R-73 air-to-air missiles, although the type is optimized for naval strike, with the upgraded N001VEP radar used to guide Kh-31A and Kh-59MK anti-ship missiles.

▲ **Sukhoi Su-27UBK**

Chinese orders for Russian-built Su-27s included a significant proportion of two-seat Su-27UBK combat trainers, including this example, operated by the PLAAF's
1st Fighter Division/1st Air Regiment based at Anshan, Shenyang Military Region.

Specifications

Crew: 1

Powerplant: 1 x 122.5kN (27,557lbf) Saturn-
Lyulka AL-31FN or 129.4kN (29,101lbf)
WS-10A Taihang turbofan

Maximum speed: Mach 2.2 at altitude
(2696km/h; 1675mph)

Combat radius: 550km (341 miles)

Service ceiling: 18,000m (59,055ft)

Dimensions: span 9.7m (31ft 10in); length
15.5m (50ft 10in); height 4.78m (15.7ft)

Weight: 18,500kg (40,785lb) loaded

Armament: 1 x 23mm (0.90in) twin-barrel
cannon; 11 hardpoints with a capacity of
6000kg (13,228lb) external fuel and ordnance

▼ Chengdu J-10A, 44th Fighter Division/131st Air Regiment, PLAAF, Luliang

This J-10A is assigned to the Chengdu Military Region. The J-10A is a slightly
moderated version with a satellite communications/datalink antenna located
behind the canopy and a detachable refuelling probe.
The J-10AS is a two-seat version.

Specifications

Crew: 2

Powerplant: 1 x 122.5kN (27,557lbf) Saturn-
Lyulka AL-31FN or 129.4kN (29,101lbf)
WS-10A Taihang turbofan

Maximum speed: Mach 2.2 at altitude
(2696km/h; 1675mph)

Combat radius: 550km (341 miles)

*NB specifications are for J-10A.

Service ceiling: 18,000m (59,055ft)

Dimensions: span 9.7m (31ft 10in); length
15.5m (50ft 10in); height 4.78m (15.7ft)

Weight: 18,500kg (40,785lb) loaded

Armament: 1 x 23mm (0.90in) twin-barrel
cannon; 11 hardpoints with a capacity of
6000kg (13,228lb) external fuel and ordnance

▼ Chengdu J-10B

This aircraft was displayed at Zhuhai in 2009, and is likely the first prototype
J-10B. The J-10B features a new, fixed supersonic intake, an infra-red search and
track sensor, a new head-up display, underwing electronic warfare pods and a
modified tailfin. A re-profiled radome may contain a
new active electronically scanned array
(AESA) radar.

11s, or are in the process of conversion. Another Su-27 development, the J-15, is planned as China's first carrier-based fighter, for service on the former Soviet carrier *Varyag*, currently being refurbished at Dalian.

The J-7E equips seven front-line PLAAF and two PLANAF regiments, while the latest J-7G serves with three regiments. Some earlier J-8s have been adapted to become JZ-8 reconnaissance versions, while advanced developments of the J-8II continue in use as long-range interceptors. The upgraded J-8H and the further improved J-8F are used by five operational PLAAF units, and J-8s are also flown by two

▲ Chengdu J-10A

The first front-line PLAAF J-10 unit was established in 2004. Current estimates suggest that units will convert to the new fighter on the basis of one each year, with the J-10 initially replacing older J-7 versions.

PLANAF regiments. The J-8G is a defence-suppression version in limited PLAAF use.

The PLA is making efforts to introduce improved airborne early warning and electronic warfare capabilities, manifested in the KJ-2000 AEW platform, and EW versions of the Tu-154, Il-76 and Y-8. Increasing numbers of aircraft, including upgraded H-6s and J-8s, are equipped for aerial

Specifications

Crew: 2	length 13.68m (44ft 11in) (with rotors);
Powerplant: 2 x 632kW (847shp) Turbomeca	height 3.47m (11ft 4in)
Arriel-1C1 turboshafts	Weight: 4100kg (9038lb) loaded
Maximum speed: 315km/h (195mph)	Armament: 2 x 23mm (0.90in) fixed cannons;
Range: 1000km (621 miles)	pylon stores for rockets, gun pods, ET52
Service ceiling: 6000m (20,000ft)	torpedo, HJ-8 anti-tank missiles, or TY-90
Dimensions: rotor diameter 11.94m (39ft 2in);	air-to-air missiles

▼ Harbin Z-9, Hong Kong Garrison, PLA

A Chinese-built version of the Aérospatiale AS365N Dauphin 2, the Z-9 is in PLA service in army utility, maritime, and attack variants. The Z-9B version features a greater proportion of Chinese-built components, and around 150 are believed to be in PLA service.

refuelling, for which the PLAAF makes use of H-6 tankers, with Il-78 tankers on order.

The fleet of PLA fighter-bombers continues to employ the Nanchang Q-5 attack aircraft, which has also been updated, but the last few PLAAF regiments are now converting to advanced Su-30MKK and Xian JH-7 aircraft. China acquired 76 examples of the Su-30MKK, a two-seat multi-role development of the Su-27, followed by 24 of the maritime Su-30MK2 version for the PLANAF. The JH-7 was developed for the PLANAF as a maritime attack aircraft, but also serves with the PLAAF, equipping three regiments within each arm.

The backbone of the transport fleet is a large number of indigenous Y-5, Y-7 and Y-8 types, with Il-76s on order to provide a genuine strategic airlift capability. Most land-based helicopters are the responsibility of the Army Aviation Corps, where indigenous Z-8, Z-9 and Z-11 transport helicopters and WZ-9 attack helicopters are complemented by Mi-8/17s. Key types unique to the PLANAF include Ka-28 shipboard helicopters, plus Y-8s adapted for maritime patrol. Training is carried out on CJ-6 basic trainers, increasing numbers of JL-8 jet trainers (replacing JJ-5s), and JJ-7 advanced trainers, with the L-15 and JL-9 competing to replace the latter type.

Specifications

Crew: 1	Service ceiling: 18,800m (61,700ft)
Powerplant: 1 x 65.17kN (14,650lb) thrust	Dimensions: span 8.32m (27ft 4in); length
Liyang Wopen-13F (R-13-300) afterburning	14.89m (48ft 10in); height 4.1m (13ft 5in)
turbojet	Weight: 7540kg (16,620lb) loaded
Maximum speed: Mach 2.0 limited (2120km/h;	Armament: 2 x 30mm (1.18in) Type 30-1
1317mph)	cannon, plus five hardpoints for rockets,
Range: 2230km (1380 miles)	air-to-air missiles and bombs

▼ Chengdu J-7GB, 'August 1' Aerial Demonstration Team, PLAAF, Yangcun

An unarmed version of the J-7 fighter, the J-7GB until recently equipped the August 1 (Ba Yi) aerobatic team at Yangcun in the Beijing Military Region. The team has now re-equipped with modified versions of the J-10 designated J-10AY and J-10SY, the latter being a two-seater.

Specifications

Crew: 2	Dimensions: rotor diameter: 16.36m
Powerplant: 2 x 1409kW (1890shp) General	(53ft 8in); length 19.76m (64ft 10in);
Electric T700-GE-701C turboshaft	height 5.33m (17ft 6in)
Maximum speed: 361km/h (224mph)	Weight: 9997kg (22,000lb) loaded
Range: 463km (288 miles)	Armament: 2 x 7.62mm (0.3in) door guns, AGM-
Service ceiling: 4021m (13,200ft)	119 Penguin anti-ship missiles, MK46 torpedoes

▼ Sikorsky S-70C-2 Black Hawk, 2nd Army Aviation Regiment, 13th Group of Armies, Chengdu-Feng Huang Shan

Assigned to the Chengdu Military Region, this S-70 is one of 24 purchased for the PLA during the period of Sino-U.S. military cooperation in the mid-1980s. The S-70s are likely to be replaced in future by Mi-17s.

India

INDIAN AIR FORCE, NAVAL AVIATION AND ARMY AVIATION

Facing increasing obsolescence among its fleet of almost 1300 aircraft, the IAF is embarked on a process of modernization, introducing both foreign and indigenous equipment to its ranks.

MODERNIZATION HAS BEEN slowed by economic realities and difficulties encountered by major indigenous defence programmes, typified by the protracted development of the Tejas fighter, planned as a successor to the MiG-21, which once equipped some 20 squadrons. Today, the Su-30MKI is the most important combat aircraft, but large numbers of MiG-21s remain in IAF service, while Jaguars, Mirage 2000s and MiG-27s are all now beginning to show their age. The IAF plans to introduce a new fighter under its Medium Multi-Role Combat

Aircraft programme, with at least 126 new aircraft to be acquired. In the meantime, some MiG-21bis have been upgraded to Bison standard, and the MiG-27 is also subject to modernization, while avionics upgrades are being pursued for the Mirage and MiG-29. Licence production of the Su-30MKI is under way, and airborne early warning and aerial refuelling capabilities have been realized with the fielding of the A-50EI and the Il-78MKI, respectively, with six A330 tankers on order. Transport aviation will be overhauled through the induction of six C-130Js.

Specifications

Crew: 1	Dimensions: span 8.69m (28ft 6in);
Powerplant: 2 x 37.3kN (8400lb) Rolls-	length 16.83m (55ft 2.5in); height
Royce/Turbomeca Adour Mk 811 turbofans	4.89m (16ft 0.5in)
Maximum speed: 1699km/h (1056mph)	Weight: 15,700kg (34,613lb) loaded
Range: 537km (334 miles)	Armament: 2 x 30mm (1.18in) Aden Mk.4 cannon;
Service ceiling: Unavailable	provision for 4763kg (10,500lb) of stores

▼ SEPECAT Jaguar IT, 6 Squadron, Jamnagar

Known locally as the Shamsher, this is one of the 35 BAe-built Jaguars delivered to the IAF in the early 1980s. Built by HAL, Indian-made Jaguars wear serials in the 'JS' series. A total of 99 single-seat Jaguars were built by HAL, and these serve with six squadrons.

Specifications

Crew: 2	Service ceiling: 17,300m (56,800ft)
Powerplant: 2 x 131kN (27,557lbf) Lyulka	Dimensions: span 14.7m (48ft 2.5in); length
al-31FP turbofans	21.94m (72in 11in); height 6.36m (20ft 9in)
Maximum speed: Mach 2.35 (2500km/h;	Weight: 23,900kg (54,895lb) loaded
1533mph)	Armament: 1 x 30mm (1.18n) GSh-3-1 gun,
Range: 5000km (3106 miles)	plus air-to-air and air-to-surface missiles

▼ Sukhoi Su-30MKI, 30 Squadron, Pune

This is the last Su-30MKI Phase II from the fourth batch delivered to India, equipped with canards and thrust-vectoring Saturn AL-31FP engines. The aircraft is seen armed with a Kh-31P anti-radar missile.

BHARATIYA VAYU SENA – INDIAN AIR FORCE FIGHTER UNITS

Central Air Command HQ Allahabad

1 Squadron	Mirage 2000H/TH	Gwalior
7 Squadron	Mirage 2000H/TH	Gwalior
8 Squadron	Su-30MKI	Bareilly
9 Squadron	Mirage 2000H/TH	Gwalior
16 Squadron	Jaguar IS	Gorakhpur
24 Squadron	Su-30MKI	Bareilly
27 Squadron	Jaguar IS	Gorakhpur
35 Squadron	MiG-21M	Bakshi Ka Talab
TACDE	MiG-27	Gwalior

Eastern Air Command HQ Shillong

2 Squadron	Su-30MKI	Tezpur
18 Squadron	MiG-27	Kalaikunda
222 Squadron	MiG-27	Hashimara
MOFTU	MiG-21FL	Tezpur

Western Air Command HQ Palam

3 Squadron	MiG-21 Bison	Ambala
5 Squadron	Jaguar IS	Ambala
14 Squadron	Jaguar IS	Ambala
17 Squadron	MiG-21M	Bhisiana

21 Squadron	MiG-21 Bison	Sirsa
22 Squadron	MiG-27	Halwara
26 Squadron	MiG-21bis	Unknown
31 Squadron	Su-30MKI	Halwara?
37 Squadron	MiG-21M	Unknown
47 Squadron	MiG-29	Adampur
48 Squadron	An-32	Chandigarh
51 Squadron	MiG-21Bison	Srinagar
108 Squadron	MiG-21M	Pathankot
223 Squadron	MiG-29	Adampur

South Western Air Command HQ Gandhinagar

4 Squadron	MiG-21 Bison	Uttarlai
6 Squadron	Jaguar IM/IS	Jamnagar
10 Squadron	MiG-27	Jodhpur
15 Squadron	MiG-21bis	Bhuj
20 Squadron	Su-30MKI	Pune
23 Squadron	MiG-21 Bison	Suratgarh
28 Squadron	MiG-29	Jamnagar
29 Squadron	MiG-27	Jodhpur
30 Squadron	Su-30MKI	Pune
32 Squadron	MiG-21 Bison	Jodhpur
101 Squadron	MiG-21M	Naliya
224 Squadron	Jaguar IS	Jamnagar

◀ **HAL (SEPECAT) Jaguar IS**

This Jaguar IS is operated by the IAF's 14 Squadron at Amabala. Alongside the strike-optimized single-seater, the IAF also operates the two-seat Jaguar IB conversion trainer and the radar-equipped single-seat Jaguar IM, which is tailored for the maritime attack mission and equips a single squadron at Jamnagar.

INDIA

Specifications

Crew: 1

Powerplant: 1 x 73.5kN (16,535lb) Tumanskii
R-25 turbojet

Maximum speed: 2229km/h (1385mph)

Range: 1160km (721 miles)

Service ceiling: 17,500m (57,400ft)

Dimensions: span 7.15m (23ft 5.5in);

length (including probe) 15.76m (51ft 8.5in);

height 4.1m (13ft 5.5in)

Weight: 10,400kg (22,925lb) loaded

Armament: 1 x 23mm (0.9in) GSh-23 twin-
barrel cannon in underbelly pack, provision
for about 1500kg (3307kg) of stores

▼ Mikoyan MiG-29, 223 Squadron, Adampur

The IAF was the first export operator of the MiG-29, and the surviving fleet
of approximately 50 aircraft is now being modernized to extend the fighter's
service life by another 15 years, receiving multi-mode Zhuk-ME radar, Klimov
RD-33 engines, new avionics, cockpit displays and an in-flight refuelling
capability in the process.

▲ BAE Systems Hawk Mk132

India ordered 66 Hawk advanced trainers, and these entered service in 2008. BAE Systems built the first 24 aircraft, with the remaining 42 assembled locally by
Hindustan Aeronautics Limited. Induction of the Hawk is part of an overhaul of IAF training, which will also see introduction of the indigenous HAL HJT-36 jet trainer.
Between them, these are due to replace the ageing HJT-16 Kiran MkI and MkII.

The IAF Command is headquartered at Delhi and is led by the Chief of Air Staff. IAF Command is responsible for five operational commands, each headed by an Air Officer Commander-in-Chief. The operational commands are supplemented by Training Command and Maintenance Command.

Largest of the commands is Western Air Command, dominated by air defence and ground-attack squadrons, and responsible for the defence of Delhi, as well as Jammu and Kashmir. It is headquartered at Palam, which is also home to the Air Research Centre and Analysis Wing and the 'Pegasus' Squadron for VIP transport. South Western Air Command is primarily a defensive formation, although it maintains a strike mission. Central Air Command is responsible for most transport assets, and incorporates An-32, Do 228 and Il-76 squadrons, together with helicopter squadrons equipped with the Mi-8/17 and Mi-26. Eastern Air Command includes the areas bordering Bangladesh, Myanmar and Tibet. Headquartered in Kerala, Southern Air Command is the smallest of the operational commands, and lacks combat aircraft.

With headquarters at Yelahanka, Training Command's fleet is being revamped through the addition of 66 Hawk Mk132s acquired under the Advanced Jet Trainer programme, and also involving local production. Between them, the Hawk and the HJT-36 Sitara are planned to replace the HJT-16 Kiran, while the piston-engined HPT-32 Deepak will also require replacement in the near future. The indigenous Dhruv helicopter is also used for training, as well as being introduced by the IAF as a replacement for the ageing Cheetah and Chetak in the utility role. Other IAF helicopter types include the Mi-25/35, in use with two squadrons.

Naval Aviation

Indian Naval Aviation is responsible for land-based maritime aviation, and for providing shipborne detachments, including units that embark aboard the carrier INS *Viraat*. The MiG-29K carrier fighter has entered service in preparation for the commissioning of a new carrier, the INS *Vikramaditya*. *Viraat* embarks Sea Harrier fighters plus a Sea King anti-submarine helicopter, Ka-31 airborne early warning helicopters and Chetak utility helicopters, while smaller warships embark Ka-28s. Land-based patrol aircraft comprise Do 228s, Il-38s, Islanders, and Tu-142s, with eight P-8A Poseidons on order. The Dhruv is also entering Indian Navy service to supersede the Chetak. Naval Aviation training is conducted on the HPT-32 and HJT-16. Major naval aviation facilities are maintained at Arrakonam, Bombay, Cochin, Colaba and Goa-Dablomin.

Indian Army Aviation assets are dominated by the Cheetah and Chetak, although the Dhruv is now being fielded in increasing numbers.

Specifications

Crew: 3

Powerplant: 2 x 1454kW (1950shp) Klimov TV3-117Mt turboshafts

Maximum speed: 260km/h (162mph)

Range: 450km (280 miles)

Service ceiling: 4500m (14,765ft)

Dimensions: rotor diameter 21.29m (69ft 10in); length 18.17m (59ft 7in); height 5.65m (18ft 6in)

Weight: 11,100kg (24,470lb) loaded

Armament: up to 1500kg (3300lb) of disposable stores on six hardpoints

▼ **Mil Mi-8, 109 Helicopter Unit, Coimbatore**

One of 80 Mi-8s purchased by India in the 1970s and 1980s. In the medium utility role, the Mi-8 (known as Rana) is being replaced by Mi-17s, and in 2008 India and Russia finalized a deal covering the supply of 80 Mi-17V-5s.

Specifications

Crew: 1

Powerplant: 1 x 73.5kN (16,535lb) Tumanskii
R-25 turbojet

Maximum speed: 2229km/h (1385mph)

Range: 1160km (721 miles)

Service ceiling: 17,500m (57,400ft)

Dimensions: span 7.15m (23ft 5.5in);

length (including probe) 15.76m (51ft 8.5in);

height 4.1m (13ft 5.5in)

Weight: 10,400kg (22,925lb) loaded

Armament: 1 x 23mm(0.9in) GSh-23 twin-
barrel cannon in underbelly pack, provision
for about 1500kg (3307kg) of stores

▼ HAL (Mikoyan-Gurevich) MiG-21 Bison, 3 Squadron, Ambala

The upgraded Bison has been flown by 3 Squadron 'Cobras' since 2008. The Bison introduces a beyond-visual-range air-to-air capability through the use of the Kopyo multi-mode radar and the R-77 missile. Other advances include an Israeli head-up display, hands on throttle and stick (HOTAS) controls and multi-function cockpit display.

Indonesia

INDONESIAN AIR FORCE

The largest nation in Southeast Asia, Indonesia's air arm is the Tentara Nasional Indonesia Angkatan Udara, or TNI-AU, which includes two commands covering eastern and western zones.

THE PRIDE OF the TNI-AU is its fighter arm, which operates 10 F-16A/Bs and a few Su-27SK/Su-30MKs. The latter are arriving slowly, with two Su-27SKs in service (plus three on order), together with four multi-role Su-30MKs from a total of five ordered. The effects of international embargoes mean that the F-16 and F-5 fleets are suffering limited serviceability. Only four F-5Es are reported as active.

Transport is essential in order to cover Indonesia's countless islands, and the TNI-AU calls upon locally built CN235s and C-212s, as well as eight C-130Bs, two KC-130B tankers, and a handful of DHC-5s.

Primary training is conducted on SA 202s and SF260s, before students progress to the KT-1B Wong Bee turboprop trainer, which is replacing the T-34. The Hawk Mk53 advanced trainer is subject to limited availability, with much of the fleet grounded. The Hawk Mk109 trainer fares somewhat better, and the Hawk Mk209 remains in use for counter-insurgency and light attack. Helicopter pilot training relies on the EC120, which is replacing the Bell 47, and locally assembled transport helicopters in use include the Bell 412, BO105, Puma and Super Puma.

Specifications

Crew: 2

Powerplant: 2 x 131kN (27,557lbf) Lyulka
al-31FP turbofans

Maximum speed: Mach 2.35 (2500km/h;
1533mph)

Range: 5000km (3106 miles)

Service ceiling: 17,300m (56,800ft)

Dimensions: span 14.7m (48ft 2.5in); length
21.94m (72in 11in); height 6.36m (20ft 9in)

Weight: 23,900kg (54,895lb) loaded

Armament: 1 x 30mm (1.18in) GSh-3-1 gun,
plus air-to-air and air-to-surface missiles

▼ Sukhoi Su-30MK, Skadron Udara 11, Hasanuddin

TS-3002 is one of the first two Su-30MKs for Indonesia, delivered in December 2008 as replacements for the A-4 Skyhawk fleet, retired in 2004. SkU 11 is based at Hasanuddin, on the island of Sulawesi.

Japan

JAPAN AIR, MARITIME AND GROUND SELF-DEFENCE FORCES

Japan's three air arms are the Air Self-Defence Force, Maritime Self-Defence Force and Ground Self-Defence Force. All three are recipients of some of the most advanced aircraft available.

THE SHARP END of the JASDF is provided by 12 fighter squadrons, all under the command of the Air Defence Command (Koku Sotai). Nine of the 12 fighter squadrons are configured as fighter-interceptor units, and three as fighter support squadrons. However, the fighter support units, Dai 3, 6 and 8 Hiko-tai, also maintain air defence alert duties. The fighter squadrons are supported within the Koku Sotai by airborne early warning, reconnaissance and aggressor training units.

The Koku Sota defends Japan on the basis of four regional commands (Hometai), each of which is assigned two fighter wings, with a typical strength of two squadrons each. Being smaller, the Southwestern Air Command is designated as a Composite organization.

The Air Support Command (Koku Sien Shudan), with headquarters at Fuchu, is responsible for transport, SAR and flight-checking units, and maintains the Koku Kyunan-dan (Air Rescue Wing), together with four transport groups: Dai 1 Yuso Koku-tai (1st Tactical Airlift Group) at Komaki AB, Dai 2 Yuso Koku-tai at Iruma AB, Dai 3 Yuso Koku-tai at Miho AB, and the Tokubetu Koku Yuso-tai

Specifications

Crew: 2	17.76m (58ft 3in); height 4.96m (16ft 3in)
Powerplant: 2 x 79.6kN (17,900lb) General	Weight: 26,308kg (58,000lb) loaded
Electric J79-GE-17 turbojets	Armament: 1 x 20mm (.78in) M61A1 Vulcan
Maximum speed: 2390km/h (1485mph)	cannon and four AIM-7 Sparrow recessed under
Range: 2817km (1750 miles)	fuselage or other weapons up to 1370kg
Service ceiling: 19,685m (60,000ft)	(3020lb) on centreline pylon; four wing pylons
Dimensions: span 11.7m (38ft 5in); length	for stores up to 5888kg (12,980lb)

▼ McDonnell Douglas F-4EJ Phantom II, Dai 8 Hiko-tai, Dai 3 Koku-dan, Misawa AB

27-8306 was flown by Dai 8 Hiko-tai in 2004, although the unit has now re-equipped with the F-2, and this aircraft is now in storage at Misawa. The Kai upgrade outfitted the F-4EF with AN/APG-66J pulse-Doppler radar, for a look-down/shoot-down capability.

Specifications

Crew: 1	length 19.43in (63ft 9in); height 5.63m
Powerplant: 2 x 105.7kN (23,770lb) Pratt &	(18ft 5in)
Whitney F100-PW-220 turbofans	Weight: 30,844kg (68,000lb) loaded
Maximum speed: 2655km/h (1650mph)	Armament: 1 x 20mm (0.79in) M61A1 cannon,
Range: 5745km (3570 miles)	provision for up to 10,705kg (23,600lb) of
Service ceiling: 30,500m (100,000ft)	stores, including missiles, bombs, tanks,
Dimensions: span 13.05m (42ft 9.75in);	pods and rockets

▼ Mitsubishi (McDonnell Douglas) F-15J Eagle, Dai 305 Hiko-tai, Dai 7 Koku-dan, Hyakuri AB

F-15J 52-8849 is one of 213 F-15J/DJs purchased for the JASDF. The first two F-15Js and the first 14 two-seat F-15DJs were built in the USA, before Mitsubishi took over production.

KOKU SOTAI (AIR DEFENCE COMMAND) HQ FUCHU

Hokubu Koku Hometai (Northern Air Defence Force) HQ Misawa

Hokubu Sien Hiko-tai (Northern HQ Support Flight)	T-4	Misawa AB

Dai 2 Koku-dan (2nd Air Wing) Chitose AB

Dai 201 Hiko-tai (201st Squadron)	F-15J/DJ, T-4	Chitose AB
Dai 203 Hiko-tai (203rd Squadron)	F-15J/DJ, T-4	Chitose AB

Dai 3 Koku-dan (3rd Air Wing) Misawa AB

Dai 3 Hiko-tai (3rd Squadron)	F-2A/B, T-4	Misawa AB
Dai 8 Hiko-tai (8th Squadron)	F-2A/B, T-4	Misawa AB
Hokubu Sien Hiko-han (Northern Air Support Flight)	T-4	Misawa AB

Chubu Koku Hometai (Central Air Defence Force) HQ Iruma

Dai 6 Koku-dan (6th Air Wing) Komatsu AB

Dai 303 Hiko-tai (303rd Squadron)	F-15J/DJ, T-4	Komatsu AB
Dai 306 Hiko-tai (306th Squadron)	F-15J/DJ, T-4	Komatsu AB

Dai 7 Koku-dan (7th Air Wing) Hyakuri AB

Dai 302 Hiko-tai (302nd Squadron)	F-4EJ, T-4	Hyakuri AB
Dai 305 Hiko-tai (305th Squadron)	F-15J/DJ, T-4	Hyakuri AB

Seibu Koku Hometai (Western Air Defence Force) HQ Kasuga

Seiku Sien Hiko-tai (WADF HQ Support Flight)	T-4	Kasuga

Dai 5 Koku-dan (5th Air Wing) Nyutabaru AB

Dai 301 Hiko-tai (301st Squadron)	F-15J/DJ, T-4	Nyutabaru AB

Dai 8 Koku-dan (8th Air Wing) Tsuiki AB

Dai 6 Hiko-tai (6th Squadron)	F-2A/B, T-4	Tsuiki AB
Dai 304 Hiko-tai (304th Squadron)	F-15J/DJ, T-4	Tsuiki AB

Nansei Koku Konsei-Dan (Southwestern Composite Air Division) HQ Naha

Nansei Sien Hiko-han (SW Support Flight)	T-4	Naha AB

Dai 83 Koku-gun (83rd Air Group) Naha AB

Dai 204 Hiko-tai (204th Squadron)	F-15J/DJ, T-4	Naha AB

Chokkatu-butai (Direct Reporting Unit)

Sotai Sireibu Hiko-tai (ADC HQ Flight Group)	T-4, U-4	Iruma AB
Denshisen Sien-tai (ECM Support Unit)	EC-1, YS-11EA	Iruma AB
Denshi Hiko Hiko Sokutei-tai (ELINT Squadron)	YS-11EB	Iruma AB

Teisatu Koku-tai (Tactical Reconnaissance Group) Hyakuri AB

Dai 501 Hiko-tai (501st Squadron)	RF-4E/EJ, T-4	Hyakuri AB
Hiko Kyodi-tai (Tactical Fighter Training Group)	F-15DJ, T-4	Nyutarau AB

Koku Kyoiku Shudan

23 Hiko-tai	F-15D/DJ, T-4	Nyutarau AB

Keikai Koku-tai (Airborne Early Warning Group) Misawa AB

Hiko Keikai Kanshitai (Air Warning Surveillance Squadron)	E-2C	Misawa AB
Hiko Keikai Kanseita (Air Warning Control Squadron)	E-767	Hamamatsu AB

(Special Air Transport Group) at Chitose AB. Headquartered at Iruma AB, the Air Rescue Wing incorporates 11 Akita Kyunan-tai (Air Rescue Squadrons), all being equipped with UH-60J helicopters and fixed-wing U-125A aircraft.

The Air Support Command also includes four Iruma Herikoputa Kuyu-tai (Helicopter Airlift Squadrons), flying the CH-47J. The 1st Tactical Airlift Group) at Komaki AB has a squadron of C-130H transports and one of KC-767 tankers. The 2nd Tactical Airlift Group at Iruma AB has one squadron of C-1s and U-4s. The 3rd Tactical Airlift Group has a squadron of C-1, YS-11P and YS-11NT aircraft at Miho AB, a training squadron of T-400s at Miho AB, and a flight-check squadron with YS-11FC and U-125 aircraft at Iruma AB. Finally, the Special

Air Transport Group at Chitose AB operates a squadron of Boeing 747-47C VIP transports.

Other commands comprise Air Training Command (Koku Kyoiku Shudan) and Aviation Research and Development Command (Koku Kaihatsu Jikken Shudan). Training begins on the T-7 with 11 Hiko Kyoiku-dan or 12 Hiko Kyoiku-dan, while fighter pilots progress to the T-4 jet trainer (13 Hiko Kyoiku-dan and Dai 1 Koku-dan) and transport aircrew to the T-400 (41 Kyoiku Hikotai).

New equipment for the JASDF is to be procured in the form of a replacement for the F-4EJ, for which the F-X requirement has been formulated. A new transport aircraft will arrive in the form of the C-2, which will replace the C-1 and C-130.

Fleet Air Force

The structure of the JMSDF's Fleet Air Force (Koku Shudan), with headquarters at Atsugi AB, is based around Fleet Air Wings (Dai Koku-gun), each of which comprises a number of squadrons. Most operational units are equipped with the P-3C for land-based maritime patrol, or the SH-60J/K, the latter being deployed aboard Japanese Navy warships. P-3s will eventually be replaced by the indigenous P-1. Most Dai Koku-gun also include a base flight equipped with UH-60Js for SAR duties. There are seven Dai Koku-gun, four of which include fixed-wing (P-3C) squadrons at Kanoya AB, Hachinohe AB, Atsugi AB and Naha AB; two are helicopter wings (SH-60J/K, at Tateyama AB and Omura AB), while the remainder, Dai 31 Koku-gun, is a composite wing (with examples of the US-1 and US-2 flying-boat, P-3 of various subtypes, LC-90 King Air, U-36 Learjet, SH-60 and TH-135 training helicopter). There are three further squadrons that function as direct-reporting units. Dai 51 Koku-tai operates P-3s, SH-60s and OH-6s, Dai 61 Koku-tai is equipped with YS-11s and LC-90s, and Dai 111 Koku-tai is a specialist mine countermeasures unit, in the process of replacing its MH-53Es with MCH-101 and CH-101 helicopters.

Aviation units of the JGSDF are allocated according to five military districts. The Regional Army Aviation Groups comprise Northern, Northeastern, Eastern, Central and Western Groups. Each Regional Army Aviation Group (Homen Kokutai) normally includes an Army Air Group HQ Squadron (Homen Kokutai Honbu Zukitai) with fixed-wing LR-1 and LR-2s (Mitsubishi MU-2 and Beech 200s, respectively), an Army Helicopter Squadron (Homen Herikoputatai) with UH-1 and OH-6 helicopters, and an Anti-Tank Helicopter Squadron (Taisensha Herikoputatai) with AH-1S and OH-6D types. Liaison squadrons are in addition attached to each division (Shidan), these typically operating OH-6Ds. New attack helicopters are arriving in the shape of the AH-64DJP, to supplant the AH-1S, while the indigenous OH-1 scout helicopter is also in service as a complement to the OH-6, with deliveries continuing. Helicopter airlift is provided by CH-47Js and medium-lift UH-60Js, which are replacing the KV-107 and UH-1 fleets, respectively.

Specifications

Crew: 2

Powerplant: 2 x 105.4kN (23,700lb) Pratt & Whitney F100-PW-220 turbofans

Maximum speed: 2655km/h (1650mph)

Range: 4631km (2878 miles)

Service ceiling: 30,500m (100,000ft)

Dimensions: span 13.05m (42ft 9.75in); length 19.43in (63ft 9in); height 5.63m (18ft 5in)

Weight: 30,844kg (68,000lb) loaded

Armament: 1 x 20mm (.78in) M61A1 cannon with 960 rounds, external pylons with provision for up to 10,705kg (23,600lb) of stores

▼ **Mitsubishi (McDonnell Douglas) F-15DJ Eagle, Dai 304 Hiko-tai, Dai 8 Koku-dan, Tsuiki AB**

Japan's F-15D/DJ fleet has undergone a mid-life upgrade that adds licence-built F110-PW-220 engines, an upgraded ejection seat and a modernized radar, known as the AN/APG-63U. The Japanese Eagles can also employ indigenous weapons.

Laos

LAOS PEOPLE'S LIBERATION ARMY AIR FORCE

The Laos People's Liberation Army Air Force is based around a small force of transports and helicopters, with bases at Luang Prabang, Pakse, Savannakhet, Vientiane and Xiengkhouang.

WITH ITS JET fighters now retired from service, the LPLAAF is based around four military regions, with an HQ at Vientiane. Aircraft in use comprise An-2, An-24/26 and a single An-74 transport, plus Mi-8/17, Mi-26 and Z-9 helicopters, and a single Yak-40 for VIP transport duties.

Specifications

Crew: 1
Powerplant: 1 x 60.5kN (13,610lb) thrust
  Tumanskii R-11F2S-300 afterburning turbojet
Maximum speed: 2229km/h (1385mph)
Range:1670km (1037 miles)
Service ceiling: 19,000m (62,335ft)
Dimensions: span 7.15m (23ft 5.5in);
length (including pitot) 14.5m (47ft 7in);
height 4.1m (13ft 5.5in)
Weight: 7800kg (17,195lb) loaded
Armament: 1 x 23mm GSh-23 cannon,
  plus 2 x K-13A (R-3S) AAM or 2 x 500g
  (1102lb) of stores

▼ **Mikoyan-Gurevich MiG-21PFM, Interceptor Regiment, Vientiane**
Formerly operated by the LPLAAF, this was one of 15 MiG-21PFMs and two-seat MiG-21US trainers, as well as 15 improved MiG-21bis fighters, acquired from the USSR in the mid-1980s.

Malaysia

ROYAL MALAYSIAN AIR FORCE

Possessing a modern fleet of combat and support aircraft of varied origin, the RMAF (Tentera Udara Diraja Malaysia – TUDM) operates from bases on the Malayan Peninsula and Borneo.

THE COMBAT FLEET of the RMAF comprises 18 Su-30MKMs, 10 MiG-29s, eight F/A-18Ds, seven F-5E/Fs, 13 Hawk Mk208s for ground attack, and two RF-5Es for reconnaissance. MB339s and Hawk Mk108s provide advanced training, while a transport capability rests primarily with C-130s and CN235s. Most numerous helicopter is the S-61A Nuri.

Specifications

Crew: 2
Powerplant: 2 x 131kN (27,557lbf) Lyulka
  al-31FP turbofans
Maximum speed: Mach 2.35 (2500km/h;
  1533mph)
Range: 5000km (3106 miles)
Service ceiling: 17,300m (56,800ft)
Dimensions: span 14.7m (48ft 2.5in); length
  21.94m (72in 11in); height 6.36m (20ft 9in)
Weight: 23,900kg (54,895lb) loaded
Armament: 1 x 30mm (1.18n) GSh-3-1 gun,
  plus air-to-air and air-to-surface missiles

▼ **Sukhoi Su-30MKM, No. 11 Squadron, Gong Kedak**
One of 18 Su-30MKMs ordered for the RMAF in 2003 and delivered from 2007.
These multi-role fighters include equipment of French, Indian and Israeli origin.

Myanmar

MYANMAR AIR FORCE

The Tamdaw Lay, or Myanmar Air Force, operates a growing combat and support fleet, with equipment coming primarily from China and Russia, while Poland has provided helicopters.

THE MAJOR COMBAT types are Chinese-supplied, comprising A-5 attack jets, and J-6 and F-7 fighters. The fighters are being in the process of replacement by MiG-29s. G-4 Super Galebs and K-8s provide advanced training, while major helicopter types in use are the Mi-2, Mi-17, UH-1 and W-3.

Specifications

Crew: 1

Powerplant: 2 x 81.4kN (18,298lb) Sarkisov
   RD-33 turbofans

Maximum speed: 2443km/h (1518mph)

Range: 1500km (932 miles)

Service ceiling: 17,000m (55,775ft)

Dimensions: span 11.36m (37ft 3.75in);
   length (including probe) 17.32m (56ft 10in);
   height 7.78m (25ft 6.25in)

Weight: 18,500kg (40,785lb) loaded

Armament: 1 x 30mm (1.18in) GSh-30 cannon,
   provision for up to 4500kg (9921lb) of stores

▼ **Mikoyan MiG-29, Myanmar Air Force, Shante**

This is one of 10 MiG-29s from the original batch acquired, Myanmar since having ordered additional MiG-29SMTs. The MiG-29s are operated by an unknown unit based at Shante, near Meiktila.

Nepal

NEPAL ARMY AVIATION

Lacking an air force, the Himalayan kingdom of Nepal's army maintains an aviation element primarily equipped with helicopters. These are operated by the 11th Brigade (Army Air Wing).

THE ARMY AIR Wing bases its aircraft at Kathmandu-Tribhuvan, although as many as 36 satellite airfields are available. Types in use include AS350, Bell 206, Cheetah/Lancer, Chetak, Dhruv and Mi-17 helicopters, and small numbers of fixed-wing HS748, Islander, M-28 and Y-7 aircraft.

Specifications

Crew: 3

Powerplant: 2 x 1545kW (2225shp) Klimov
   TV3-117VM turboshafts

Maximum speed: 250km/h (156mph)

Range: 950km (594 miles)

Service ceiling: 6000m (19,690ft)

Dimensions: rotor diameter 21.35m

(69ft 10in); length 18.42m (60ft 5in);
   height 4.76m (15ft 7in)

Weight: 11,100kg (24,470lb) loaded

Armament: Capable of carrying up to 1500kg
   (3300lb) of bombs, rockets and gunpods on
   six hardpoints

▼ **Mil Mi-171MTV-5, 11th Brigade, Kathmandu**

Nepal purchased its first two Mi-171MTV-5s in January 2002. At total of four or six have since been acquired over the time, at least one of which was written off under unknown circumstances.

North Korea

DEMOCRATIC PEOPLE'S REPUBLIC OF KOREA AIR FORCE

One of the world's most secretive air arms, the DPRKAF is mainly equipped with Chinese, Soviet and Russian aircraft, and is headquartered at Pyongyang, with at least 25 operational airfields.

ALTHOUGH IT OPERATES a large number of aircraft, current levels of serviceability are unclear. Combat types delivered include the F-5, F-6, F-7 and MiG-21, MiG-23, MiG-29, Q-5, Su-7 and Su-25 jets, together with transport aircraft and trainers.

Specifications

Crew: 1

Powerplant: 2 x 81.4kN (18,298lb) Sarkisov RD-33 turbofans

Maximum speed: 2443km/h (1518mph)

Range: 1500km (932 miles)

Service ceiling: 17,000m (55,775ft)

Dimensions: span 11.36m (37ft 3.75in); length (including probe) 17.32m (56ft 10in); height 7.78m (25ft 6.25in)

Weight: 18,500kg (40,785lb) loaded

Armament: 1 x 30mm (1.18in) GSh-30 cannon, provision for up to 4500kg (9921lb) of stores

▼ **Mikoyan MiG-29, 55th Air Regiment, Sunchon**
The DPRKAF received an unknown number of MiG-29s. These are operated by a single squadron of the 55th Air Regiment, part of the 1st Air Combat Division.

Philippines

PHILIPPINE AIR FORCE

The combat potential of the Philippine Air Force has been reduced following the retirement of its F-5 combat jets. The current fleet is optimized for counter-insurgency, transport and training.

OPERATING WITH A USAF-style structure, the Philippine Air Force includes OV-10s and armed MD520 helicopters for COIN work, C-130, F27, Islander and Nomad transports and maritime patrol aircraft, and S-70, S-76 and UH-1H helicopters. Training is conducted on S211 jets, preceded by SF260s and T-41s. Also on order are W-3 helicopters.

Specifications

Crew: 1

Powerplant: 2 x 18.1kN (4080lb) General Electric J85-GE-13 turbojetsWhitney F100-PW-220 turbofans

Maximum speed: 1487km/h (924mph)

Range: 314km (195 miles)

Service ceiling: 15,390m (50,500ft)

Dimensions: span 7.7m (25ft 3in); length 7.7m (25ft 3in); height 4.01m (13ft 2in)

Weight: 9374kg (20,667lb) loaded

Armament: 2 x 20mm (0.79in) M39 cannon; provision for 1996kg (4400lb) of stores (missiles, bombs, cluster bombs, rocket launcher pods)

▼ **Northrop F-5A Freedom Fighter, 6th Tactical Fighter Squadron, 5th Fighter Wing, Basa**
This is one of 19 F-5As delivered to the Philippines in 1966 (together with three two-seat F-5Bs) that served until the mid-1990s. The type has meanwhile been withdrawn from service and the unit disbanded.

Pakistan

PAKISTAN AIR FORCE, ARMY AVIATION CORPS AND NAVAL AVIATION

The Pakistan Fiza'ya (Pakistan Air Force) is divided into Central, Northern and Southern Air Command, each of which contains two or three wings and their respective squadrons.

IN ADDITION TO the regional air commands, the PAF includes an Air Force Academy, headquartered at Risalpur, and a composite transport wing, 35 Wing, which reports directly to PAF headquarters. 35 Wing has three squadrons, all based at Chaklala. One operates the force of C-130/L-100 transports, one has the VIP fleet (F27, Falcon 20, Boeing 707 and Gulfstream IV and 350), and one comprises Cessna 172, Piper PA-34 and Y-12 liaison types. The Air Force Academy operates MFI-17 Mushshak primary trainers (Primary Flying Training Wing) and T-37 and K-8 jet trainers (Basic Flying Training Wing).

Central Air Command includes two wings. 34 Wing at Rafiqui has one squadron of F-7P/FT-7P fighters, two of Mirage III/5s, one of Mirage 5s, and a squadron of Alouette III helicopters. 38 Wing at Mushaf maintains two squadrons of F-16A/Bs, one of Falcon 20s outfitted for electronic warfare, and one squadron of Alouettes.

The largest of the three regional air commands, Northern Air Command, is equipped mainly with fighters and attack aircraft. 33 Wing at Kamra has a squadron each of F-7P/FT-7P and Mirage III/5 fighters, one squadron of Alouettes, and a test unit equipped with the new JF-17 Thunder fighter. 36 Wing, based at Peshawar, is optimized for attack and has one squadrons of A-5C attack aircraft, one of JF-17s and two of Alouettes. At Miawali, 37 (Combat Training) Wing operates two operational conversion

units of F-7P/FT-7P jets, one of FT-5 jet trainers, and one squadron of Alouettes.

Southern Air Command's 31 Wing is based at Quetta, but includes one squadron – with F-7P/FT-7P jets at Rafiqui. The two Quetta-based squadrons fly F-7P/FT-7Ps, and are joined by a squadron of Alouettes. 32 Wing is the largest PAF wing, with five squadrons. Three of these are equipped with Mirage III/5s, one with F-7P/FT-7Ps, and one with Alouettes and Mi-171s. All 32 Wing units are located at Masroor. Most bases maintain station flights equipped with MFI-17s.

Army and Navy

The Pakistan Army Aviation Corps operates AH-1F/S, Alouette II/III, AS350, Bell 206, Bell 412, Mi-17, Puma and UH-1H helicopters, MFI-17s, Y-12s and a handful of VIP types. Pakistan Naval Aviation includes Atlantic, Defender, F27 and P-3C maritime patrol aircraft, and Alouette III and Sea King Mk45 helicopters, all shore-based at Sharea Faisal, otherwise known as PNS *Mehran*, near Karachi.

Specifications

Crew: 1

Powerplant: either 1 x 105.7kN (23,770lb)
Pratt & Whitney F100-PW-200 or 1 x 128.9kN
(28,984lb) General Electric F110-GE-100
turbofan

Maximum speed: 2142km/h (1320mph)

Range: 925km (525 miles)

Service ceiling: 15,240m (50,000ft)

Dimensions: span 9.45m (31ft); length 15.09m
(49ft 6in); height 5.09m (16ft 8in)

Weight: 16,057kg (35,400lb) loaded

Armament: 1 x General Electric M61A1 20mm
(0.79in) multi-barrelled cannon, wingtip
missile stations; provision for up to 9276kg
(20,450lb) of stores

▼ **General Dynamics F-16A Fighting Falcon, 38 Wing, Sargodha**

F-16A 81-0921 was operated by 38 Wing until written off in June 1991. The fighter displayed two kill markings denoting victories scored against Afghan fighters in the 1980s. The PAF is in the process of receiving 24 advanced new Block 50/52 F-16C/Ds.

Singapore

REPUBLIC OF SINGAPORE AIR FORCE

One of the economic powerhouses of Southeast Asia, the island of Singapore's air arm is suitably equipped and proficiently trained, and also maintains permanent detachments overseas.

THE MOST IMPORTANT combat type flown by the RSAF is the F-16C/D, in its advanced Block 52 variant, and this is soon to be joined by 24 F-15SG strike aircraft. Remaining F-5 jets have been upgraded locally to F-5S/T and RF-5S standard, and both F-5s and F-16s are supported by KC-135R tankers and E-2C airborne early warning aircraft.

A number of RSAF assets are based overseas for training, including F-15s, F-16s, AH-64s and CH-47s in the US, S211 jet trainers and Puma helicopters

in Australia, and A-4SU/TA-4SU trainers in France.

Maritime patrol is the responsibility of Fokker 50MPAs, while ground forces are supported by a fleet of 20 AH-64D attack helicopters and CH-47SDs and S-70Bs for transport. Training is conducted using a fleet of EC120 and AS550 helicopters, with fixed-wing pilots provided with S211s and PC-21s. Transport assets comprise Cougar and Super Puma helicopters, C-130Hs, KC-130B/H tanker/transports and Fokker 50s.

Specifications

Crew: 2

Powerplant: 2 x 131kN (29,400lb) General Electric F110-GE-129 thrust engines

Maximum speed: 2655km/h (1650mph)

Range: 3900km (2400 miles)

Service ceiling: 18,200m (60,000ft)

Dimensions: span 13.05m (42ft 9.75in); length 19.43in (63ft 9in); height 5.63m (18ft 5in)

Weight: 36,700kg (81,000lb) loaded

Armament: 1 x 20mm (0.79in) M61A1 cannon, provision for up to 11,000kg (24,250lb) of external stores, including missiles, bombs, tanks, pods and rockets

▼ Boeing F-15SG Strike Eagle, 149 Squadron, Paya Lebar

06-0007 was introduced to service in 2010. The F-15SG features F110-129 engines, AN/APG-63 active electronically scanned array radar, helmet-mounted sight, sniper targeting and infra-red search and track pod and a range of precision-guided weapons.

Specifications

Crew: 1

Powerplant: 1 x 126.7kN (28,500lb) thrust Pratt & Whitney F100-PW-229 afterburning turbofan

Maximum speed: 2177km/h (1353mph)

Range: 3862km (2400 miles)

Service ceiling: 15,240m (49,000ft)

Dimensions: span 9.45m (31ft); length 15.09m (49ft 6in); height 5.09m (16ft 8in)

Weight: 19,187kg (42,300lb) loaded

Armament: 1 x GE M61A1 20mm (0.79in) multi-barrelled cannon, seven external hardpoints with provision for up to 9276kg (20,450lb) of stores

▼ Lockheed Martin F-16D Fighting Falcon, 143 Squadron 'Phoenix', Tengah

96-5030 is one of Singapore's two-seat Block 52 Fighting Falcons, these featuring an extended spine housing electronic warfare equipment.

South Korea
REPUBLIC OF KOREA AIR FORCE, NAVAL AVIATION

The RoKAF's raison d'être is to maintain a defensive posture against North Korea, and as a result the air arm pursues a constant programme of upgrades and acquisition of new equipment.

THE MOST SIGNIFICANT recent acquisition for the RoKAF is the F-15K strike aircraft, 60 of which are on order. These are joining a combat fleet dominated by the F-16C/D, the F-5E/F – both of which were produced under licence – and the F-4D/E. Other new equipment under contract includes 44 indigenous A-50 light attack aircraft and four Boeing 737 airborne early warning aircraft. RoKAF helicopters include HH-47Ds and UH-60Ps for combat SAR. The trainer fleet includes indigenous KT-1s, while Hawk jet trainers are being joined by locally built T-50s. Armed KO-1 versions of the KT-1 serve in the forward airborne controller role.

The primary equipment of RoK Naval Aviation are two squadrons of Lynx Mk99 anti-submarine helicopters, complemented by smaller numbers of Alouette IIIs, UH-1Hs and UH-60Ps. P-3Cs serve in the land-based maritime patrol role.

Army Aviation
The RoK Army's Aviation Operations Command includes two aviation brigades equipped with AH-1S and MD500 Defender attack helicopters, CH-47D and locally assembled UH-60P transport helicopters, and BO105 utility helicopters.

HANKOOK KONG GOON – REPUBLIC OF KOREA AF		
Air Force Operations Command		
5th Tactical Air Transport Wing		**Gimhae AB**
251st Tactical Air Support Squadron	C-130H	Gimhae AB
256th Tactical Air Transport Squadron	CN235	Gimhae AB
258th Tactical Air Transport Squadron	UH-60P	Gimhae AB
259th Tactical Air Support Squadron	C-130H	Gimhae AB
15th Composite Wing	**Seongnam AB**	
251st Tactical Control Squadron	KO-1	Seongnam AB
255th Special Operations Squadron	C-130H	Seongnam AB
257th Tactical Air Transport Squadron	C-130H	Seongnam AB
35th Combined Group*		
296th VIP Squadron	Boeing 737, VH-60P, CN235	Seongnam AB
* subordinate to 15th Composite Wing.		

Specifications
Crew: 1
Powerplant: 1 x 126.7kN (28,500lb) thrust Pratt & Whitney F100-PW-229 afterburning turbofan
Maximum speed: 2177km/h (1353mph)
Range: 3862km (2400 miles)
Service ceiling: 15,240m (49,000ft)
Dimensions: span 9.45m (31ft);
length 15.09m (49ft 6in); height 5.09m (16ft 8in)
Weight: 19,187kg (42,300lb) loaded
Armament: 1 x General Electric M61A1 20mm (0.79in) multi-barrelled cannon, wingtip missile stations; seven external hardpoints with provision for up to 9276kg (20,450lb) of stores

▼ **Lockheed Martin F-16C Fighting Falcon, 20th Fighter Wing, Sosan AB**
01-515 is a Block 52 F-16C, part of a total of 180 aircraft that were acquired. This particular aircraft was part of the Peace Bridge III programme, covering 20 aircraft delivered during 2003-4.

Air Force Northern Combat Command

8th Fighter Wing	Wongju AB	
103rd Fighter Squadron	F-5E/F	Wongju AB
203rd Fighter Squadron	F-5E/F	Wongju AB
207th Fighter Squadron	F-5E/F	Wongju AB
238th Fighter Squadron	A-37B	Wongju AB
239th Special Flying Squadron 'Black Eagles'	A-37B	Wongju AB

10th Fighter Wing	Suwon AB	
101st Fighter Squadron	F-5E/F	Suwon AB
201st Fighter Squadron	F-5E/F	Suwon AB

38th Fighter Group*		
111th Fighter Squadron	F-5E/F	Gunsan AB

* subordinate to 10th Fighter Wing.

39th Tactical Reconnaissance Group*		
125th Tactical Reconnaissance Squadron	Hawker 800	Seongnam AB
131st Tactical Reconnaissance Squadron	RF-4C	Suwon AB
132nd Tactical Reconnaissance Squadron	RF-5A, F-5A/B	Suwon AB

* subordinate to 15th Composite Wing.

17th Fighter Wing	Chongju AB	
152nd Fighter Squadron	F-4E	Chongju AB
153rd Fighter Squadron	F-4E	Chongju AB
156th Fighter Squadron	F-4E	Chongju AB

29th Tactical Development and Training Group *		
191st Tactical Development and Training Squadron	F-16C/D	Chongju AB
192nd Tactical Development and Training Squadron	F-16C/D	Chongju AB

* subordinate to 17th Fighter Wing.

6th Search and Rescue Group*		
233rd Combat Search and Rescue Squadron	HH-60P, AS332, Bell 412	Chongju AB
235th Search and Rescue Squadron	HH-47D, HH-32	Chongju

* subordinate to 17th Fighter Wing.

18th Fighter Wing	Gangneung AB	
105th Fighter Squadron	F-5E/F	Gangneung AB
112th Fighter Squadron	F-5E/F	Gangneung AB
205th FTS	F-5E/F	Gangneung AB

19th Fighter Wing	Yungwon AB	
161st Fighter Squadron	F-16C/D	Yungwon AB
162nd Fighter Squadron	F-16C/D	Yungwon AB
155th Fighter Squadron	F-16C/D	Yungwon AB
159th Fighter Squadron	F-16C/D	Yungwon AB

20th Fighter Wing	Sosan AB	
120th Fighter Squadron	F-16C/D	Sosan AB
121st Fighter Squadron	F-16C/D	Sosan AB
123rd Fighter Squadron	F-16C/D	Sosan AB
157th Fighter Squadron	F-16C/D	Sosan AB

Air Force Southern Combat Command

1st Fighter Wing	Kwangju AB	
102nd Fighter Squadron	F-15K	Daegu AB
122nd Fighter Squadron	F-15K	Daegu AB
206th Fighter Squadron	F-5E/F	Kwangju AB

11th Fighter Wing	Taegu AB	
110th Fighter Squadron	F-4D	Taegu AB
151st Fighter Squadron	F-4D	Taegu AB

16th Fighter Wing	Yechen AB	
115th FTS	T-38A, T-50	Yechen AB
189th FTS	T-38A, T-50	Yechen AB
202nd Fighter Squadron	F-5E/F	Yechen AB
216th FTS	Hawk Mk67	Yechen AB

Air Force Education and Training Command

Air Force Academy

208th FTS	CAP 10B	Seongmu AB
212th FTS	Il-103	Seongmu AB

3rd Training Wing		
213rd FTS	KT-1	Saechon AB
215th FTS	KT-1	Saechon AB
217th FTS	KT-1	Saechon AB
236th FTS	KT-1	Saechon AB

52nd Test Evaluation Group

281 Test Evaluation Squadron	KT-1, T-50	Saechon AB

Sri Lanka

SRI LANKAN AIR FORCE

In recent years the SLAF has been waging a campaign against the Tamil Tigers guerrilla movement, and its air arm has inducted increasingly potent combat types as a result.

AIR BASES USED by the SLAF include Katunayake, Ratmalana, Trincomalee, Minneriya and Vavuniya. The fighting in Sri Lanka included a guerrilla attack against Katunayake Airport in 2001 that claimed part of the SLAF destroyed.

Katunayake is home to three combat squadrons with Kfirs, F-7s of various subtype, and MiG-27s. It is expected that the air defence types will be replaced by MiG-29s, with reported orders for five examples. Two transport squadrons are stationed at Ratmalana, with An-32s, Cessna 421s, C-130s, MA60s and Y-12s. Four helicopter squadrons utilize a number of

bases around the country, operating Bell 206s, Bell 212s, Bell 412s, Mi-17s and Mi-24/35s.

The SLAF's basic training element is found at Trincomalee, where students fly the CJ-6 before moving on to the K-8 at Katunayake.

A small Sri Lankan Navy aviation component operates Chetak and Dauphin helicopters.

Specifications

Crew: 1	Service ceiling: 17,690m (58,038ft)
Powerplant: 1 x 79.41kN (17,860lb thrust)	Dimensions: span 8.22m (26.97ft); length
(with afterburner) IAI/General Electric	15.65m (51.35ft); height 4.55m (14.93ft)
licence-built J79-JIE turbojet engine	Weight: 16,500kg (36,376lbs) loaded
Maximum speed: 2440km/h (1516mph)	Armament: 2 x 30mm (1.18in) Rafael DEFA
Range: 548miles (882km)	533 cannons plus cluster bombs and missiles

▼ **IAI Kfir C7, No. 10 Fighter Squadron, Katunayake**

CF717 is one of the fleet of nine single-seat Kfirs operated from Katunayake, on the military side of Colombo-Bandaranaike international airport. A pair of two-seat Kfir TC2 trainers are also in service.

Specifications

Crew: 1	Dimensions: span 13.97m (45ft 10in
Powerplant: 1 x 103.4kN (23,353lb) Tumanskii	spread, 7.78m (25ft 6.25in) swept;
R-29B-300 turbojet	length 17.07m (56ft 0.75in);
Maximum speed: 1885km/h (1170mph)	height 5m (16ft 5in)
Combat radius on lo-lo-lo mission	Weight: 20,300kg (44,750lb) loaded
540km (335 miles)	Armament: 1 x 23mm (0.9in) GSh-6-30 cannon,
Service ceiling: 14,000m (45,900ft)	provision for up to 4000kg (8818lb) of stores

▲ **Mikoyan-Gurevich MiG-27M, No. 5 Jet Squadron, Katunayake**

Sri Lanka began purchasing MiG-27Ms from Ukraine in 2000. Over time the type became the most important strike asset for the SLAF, and played a dominant role during the final battle against the Tamil Tiger rebellion in northeast Sri Lanka in early 2009.

Taiwan

REPUBLIC OF CHINA AIR FORCE, NAVAL AVIATION AND ARMY AVIATION

The organization of the RoCAF is based aonlong USAF lines, with a Combat Air Command responsible for aircraft that are deployed within eight wings, plus training and support units.

OF THE EIGHT wings, five are designated as 'pure' Tactical Fighter Wings (TFW), one as a Composite TFW (TCW), one as a TFW/Tactical Training and Development Centre (TTDC) and one as a Transport and Early Warning Wing (T/EWW).

Three main types are integrated within the fighter force: the indigenous F-CK-1 Ching-Kuo; the Mirage 2000-5; and the F-16A/B. The F-16 has replaced most F-5E/Fs, although the latter continue with one wing in upgraded form, and with the TTDC, with which they also operate as aggressors. Adapted F-16s serve alongside RF-5Es converted locally for the reconnaissance role.

The relatively small transport arm is based around the C-130H, serving with two squadrons. The operating wing is also responsible for the E-2Ts that provide an airborne early warning and control capability, and a C-130H modified for the electronic warfare role. Beech 1900Cs operate in the navaid calibration role. Other transport aircraft are based at Sungshan as the Presidential Flight Section, equipped with Boeing 737 and Fokker F27s VIP transports.

The rescue Squadron conducts RoCAF search and rescue, flying S-70C Blue Hawk helicopters (similar to USAF HH-60A). The S-70Cs are also detached to other bases. Major training assets in use are the indigenous AT-3 jet trainer and the T-34C, with Beech 1900s available for training multi-engine aircrew.

RoC Naval Aviation maintains bases at Hualien and Pingtung South and operates both fixed- and rotary-wing equipment. The S-2Ts operated in the anti-submarine role are due to be replaced by 12 P-3Cs. Anti-submarine helicopters comprise the MD500 and S-70C Thunderhawk, both of which embark on warships of the RoC Navy.

Army helicopters

RoC Army Aviation includes two attack helicopter wings, as well as communications and training units, based at Longtang-Tao Yuan and Kuejien-Tainan. The offensive capability is provided by 62 AH-1W attack helicopters, with 30 AH-64Ds on order. Also operated are CH-47SD transports, OH-58D scout helicopters, UH-1Hs for utility and TH-67s for helicopter training.

Specifications

Crew: 1

Powerplant: either 1 x 105.7kN (23,770lb) Pratt & Whitney F100-PW-200 or 1 x 128.9kN (28,984lb) General Electric F110-GE-100 turbofan

Maximum speed: 2142km/h (1320mph)

Range: 925km (525 miles)

Service ceiling: 15,240m (50,000ft)

Dimensions: span 9.45m (31ft); length 15.09m (49ft 6in); height 5.09m (16ft 8in)

Weight: 16,057kg (35,400lb) loaded

Armament: 1 x General Electric M61A1 20mm (0.79in) multi-barrelled cannon, provision for up to 9276kg (20,450lb) of stores

▼ General Dynamics F-16A Fighting Falcon, 5th TFW, Hualien

Taiwan's Fighting Falcon fleet includes this F-16A Block 20, 93-0774, part of a total of 150 ordered under the Peace Fenghuang programme, with deliveries between 1997 and 2001. Taiwan has expressed interest in acquiring 66 more 66 F-16C/D Block 52 aircraft in the future.

◀ **Dassault Mirage 2000-5Ei**
Serving with the 2nd TFW at Hsinchu, Taiwan's fleet of Mirage 2000-5 fighters comprises 46 single-seat 2000-5Ei versions and 11 two-seat 5Di conversion trainers, survivors from an original order for 60 aircraft. These can be armed with Mica and Magic 2 air-to-air missiles, and have also been noted carrying indigenously developed air-to-ground weapons. AF was one of the last C-model aircraft in service.

TA CHUN KUO KUNG CHUANG — REPUBLIC OF CHINA AF

1st TFW (433rd TFW)*

1st TFG	F-CK-1A/B	Tainan
3rd TFG	F-CK-1A/B	Tainan
9th TFG	F-CK-1A/B	Tainan

* periodic F-CK-1A/B detachments to Makung.

2nd TFW (499th TFW)

41st TFG	Mirage 2000-5Ei/Di	Hsinchu
42nd TFG	Mirage 2000-5Ei/Di	Hsinchu
48th TFG	Mirage 2000-5Ei/Di	Hsinchu

3rd TFW (427th TFW)*

7th TFG	F-CK-1A/B	Ching Chuan Kang
28th TFG	F-CK-1A/B	Ching Chuan Kang

* periodic F-CK-1A/B detachments to Makung.

4th TFW, Hualien (455th TFW)

21st TFG	F-16A/B	Chia Yi
22nd TFG	F-16A/B	Chia Yi
23rd TFG	F-16A/B	Chia Yi
Rescue Squadron	S-70C	Chia Yi

5th TFW (401st TCW)

12th TRS	RF-5E, RF-16A	Hualien
17th TFG	F-16A/B	Hualien
26th TFG	F-16A/B	Hualien
27th TFG	F-16A/B	Hualien

6th T/EWW (439th CW)

10th TAG

101st TCS	C-130H	Pingtung North
102nd TCS	C-130H	Pingtung North

20th EWG

2nd Early Warning Squadron	E-2T	Pingtung North
6th Electronic Warfare Squadron	C-130H(EW)	Pingtung North

7th TFW (737th TFW)

44th TFS	F-5E/F	Taitung
45th TFS	F-5E/F	Taitung

Tactical Training and Development Centre

46th TFS	F-5E/F	Taitung

Sungshan Air Base Command

Special Transport Squadron	Beech 1900C, Fokker F27	Sunghsan
Presidential Flight Section	Boeing 737, Fokker F27	Sungshun

Air Force Academy

Basic Training Group	T-34C	Kangshan
Fighter Training Group Transport Training	AT-3	Kangshan
Group	Beech 1900C	Kangshan

Thailand

ROYAL THAI AIR FORCE, NAVY AIR DIVISION AND ARMY AIR DIVISION

The RTAF (Kongtap Agard Thai) is organized as four regional Air Divisions and a Flying Training School, and is backed up by a significant Royal Thai Navy Air Division.

THE FOUR AIR Divisions of the RTAF are responsible for the Bangkok area (1st AD), eastern Thailand (2nd AD), the central-northern provinces (3rd AD) and the south (4th AD). Each Air Division is responsible for two or three wings (for a total of 10), these being equipped with flying squadrons.

The RTAF's latest and most significant acquisitions are six JAS39C/D Gripen fighters. These will operate in conjunction with a SAAB 340 configured for airborne early warning and control. Fighters currently in service comprise the F-16A/B and F-5E/F. Transport aircraft in use are the A310, AU-23, C-130H, G222 and HS748. A significant VIP fleet includes Airbus A319, ATR-72, and Boeing 737 aircraft. Training is conducted on CT-4 Airtrainer and DA42 Twin Star primary trainers, and

Specifications	
Crew: 1	Service ceiling: 15,240m (50,000ft)
Powerplant: either 1 x 105.7kN (23,770lb) Pratt	Dimensions: span 9.45m (31ft); length 15.09m
& Whitney F100-PW-200 or 1 x 128.9kN	(49ft 6in); height 5.09m (16ft 8in)
(28,984lb) General Electric F110-GE-100	Weight: 16,057kg (35,400lb) loaded
turbofan	Armament: 1 x General Electric M61A1 20mm
Maximum speed: 2142km/h (1320mph)	(0.79in) multi-barrelled cannon, provision for
Range: 925km (525 miles)	up to 9276kg (20,450lb) of stores

▼ **General Dynamics F-16A Fighting Falcon, 102 Squadron 'Starfighters', Korat**

This ex-USAF F-16A Block 15G aircraft is one of a total of 54 F-16A/Bs ordered by Thailand. The RTAF received a further seven F-16A/B aircraft, donated by Singapore.

▲ **Northrop F-5 Tiger II**

The RTAF continues to maintain a significant fleet of F-5s. In addition to around two dozen single-seat F-5Es that serve in the air defence role, a handful of two-seat F-5Fs are used for operational conversion training. Three F-5E air defence squadrons are found at Bangkok-Don Muang, Ubon Ratchathani and Surat Thani.

PC-9 basic trainers, with Alpha Jets and L-39s employed on advanced training and secondary light attack duties. The rotary-wing inventory includes Bell 412s and UH-1s.

The Royal Thai Navy Air Division includes the air wing for the carrier HTMS *Chakri Naruebet*, although the AV-8S Harriers once operated are no longer active. Bell 212s, Lynx Mk300s and S-70Bs serve in the anti-submarine role, with MH-60S on order. Shore-based Do 228, F27, Nomad and P-3 aircraft conduct maritime patrol.

The Royal Thai Army Air Division maintains a large and varied fleet, including AH-1F attack helicopters, Beech 200/350s for transport and surveillance, Bell 206/212 and UH-1H utility helicopters, CH-47D and S-70/UH-60 transports (and Mi-17s on order), plus training and VIP assets.

Vietnam

VIETNAM PEOPLE'S AIR FORCE

Of almost entirely Soviet and Russian origin, aircraft of the VPAF are a blend of new and old, but recent procurement of new fighters suggests that a programme of overhaul is under way.

THE ORGANIZATIONAL STRUCTURE of the VPAF is based around three divisions, each of which has a specific role, and maintains squadrons at different bases. The 370th Division, headquartered at Da Nang, was formerly responsible for two squadrons of MiG-21bis fighters and one of Su-22M4 attack aircraft, and is now the recipient of the VPAF's latest fighter, the multi-role Su-30MK2V, which serves at Phan Rang, previously known as a Su-22M4 base. The 371st Division (HQ at Noi Bai) previously operated three squadrons of MiG-21bis, but may also have partly re-equipped with Su-27SK interceptors. The 372 Division operated three squadrons, flying the Su-22M and the MiG-21bis, and has headquarters at Tho Xuan.

VPAF transport arm

A Transport Brigade maintains at least three squadrons, operating Mi-8/17 and Mi-24 helicopters alongside An-2, An-24/26/30, An-38 and M-28 transports. Identified transport bases include Hoa Lac, Tan Son Nhut and Gia Lam. A quantity of UH-1H helicopters inherited from the former South Vietnamese Air Force are also believed to remain in use. The VPAF Air Force Academy operates L-39 advanced trainers from Hoa Lac (910 'Julius Fucik' Squadron) as well as MiG-21bis and MiG-21UMs for conversion training at Phu Cat. Operated on behalf of the Navy are Ka-25/27 anti-submarine helicopters, based at Kien An and Da Nang.

▲ **Sukhoi Su-30MK2V**

The most potent asset within the VPAF inventory is the handful of Su-30MK2V multi-role fighters delivered to date. The MK2 version is a further upgrade of the Su-30MKK developed for China, with improved avionics and expanded weaponry.

Specifications

Crew: 2	Dimensions: span 14.7m (48ft 2.5in);
Powerplant: 2 x 123kN (27,600lbf) Lyulka	length 21.94m (72in 11in);
al-31F turbofans	height 6.36m (20ft 9in)
Maximum speed: 2120km/h (1320mph)	Weight: 24,900kg (54,900lb) loaded
Range: 3000km (1900 miles)	Armament: 1 x 30mm (1.18in) GSh-3-1 gun,
Service ceiling: 17,300m (56,800ft)	plus air-to-air and air-to-surface missiles

▲ **Sukhoi Su-30MK2V, 370th Fighter Division, Phan Rang**

One of two Su-30MK2Vs delivered to Vietnam in 2006. Today, the VPAF operates four Su-30MK2Vs, with another eight on order. These will complement 12 earlier Su-27SKs and three two-seat Su-27UBKs.

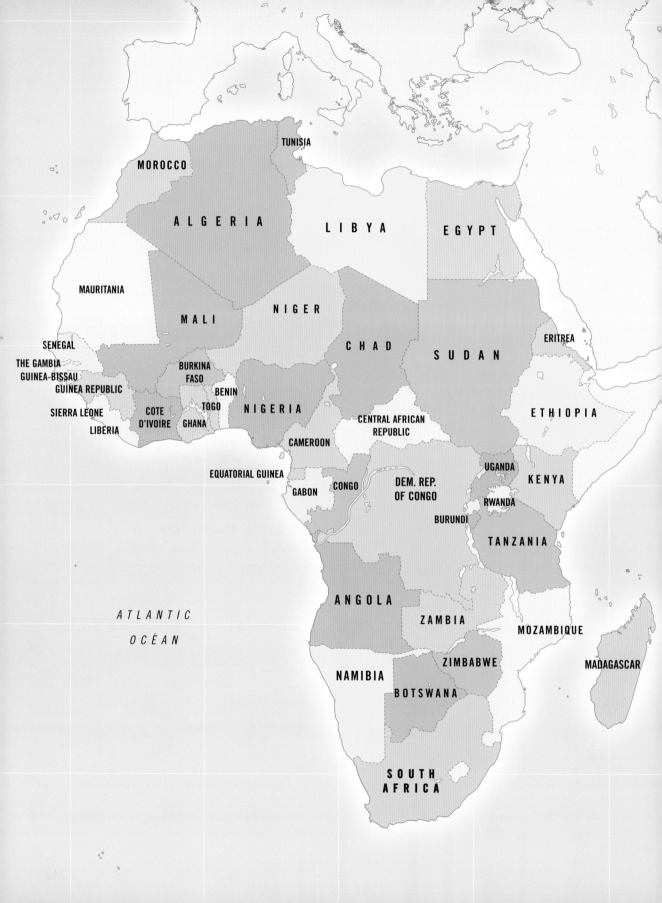

Chapter 16

Africa

Befitting a continent of its diversity, Africa is host to air forces that range greatly in terms of size and combat potential. In the north, air arms are typically larger and well equipped, and provide balanced capabilities. East Africa has seen its air arms take part in various conflicts in recent years, notably in Eritrea, Ethiopia and Sudan. West Africa's air forces are generally small and comparatively poorly equipped – armed trainers often form the backbone of the combat inventory – and a number suffer from the effects of low serviceability. In Central Africa, years of conflict have left their mark on the region's air arms, although most nations have at least token combat forces, in some cases supplementing combat helicopters with small fleets of jets. With the exception of South Africa and Zimbabwe, Southern Africa's air forces are generally small and have seen only limited combat since the end of the 'bush wars' that characterized much of the Cold War era.

Algeria
ALGERIAN AIR FORCE

Established in 1962 after Algeria won independence from France, the Algerian Air Force (al-Quwwat al-Jawwiya al-Jaza'eriya – QJJ) is an increasingly well-equipped air arm.

ORGANIZED ON THE basis of nine wings, each of which has a designated task, the QJJ also maintains a number of independent squadrons that report directly to air force headquarters. Wings have varying numbers of squadrons attached and occupy more than one air base. While squadrons have 'official' permanent bases, their aircraft can frequently be found operating from alternative locations.

QJJ wings comprise the 1st Combat Helicopter Regiment, 2nd Tactical Transport and Logistics Wing, 3rd Air Defence Wing, 4th Attack and Penetration Wing, 5th Reconnaissance Wing, 6th Transport Helicopter Regiment, 7th Transport and Refuelling Wing, 8th Training Wing and the 9th Helicopter Training Wing.

The Su-30MKA is now replacing the MiG-25 and supplementing three squadrons of Su-24MKs in the strike role. Other combat equipment includes three active MiG-29 air defence squadrons, MiG-25R, Su-24MR and Seeker UAV reconnaissance aircraft, and Il-76/78, C-130H and CN235 transports. Primary helicopters are the Mi-17/171 and Mi-24 MkIII.

Specifications

Crew: 2	Service ceiling: 17,300m (56,800ft)
Powerplant: 2 x 74.5kN (16,750lbf) AL-31FL low-bypass turbofans	Dimensions: span 14.7m (48ft 2.5in); length 21.94m (72in 11in); height 6.36m (20ft 9in)
Maximum speed: Mach 2.0 (2120km/h; 1320mph)	Weight: 24,900kg (54,900lb) loaded
Range: 3000km (1864 miles)	Armament: 1 x30mm (1.18n) GSh-3-1 gun, plus air-to-air and air-to-surface missiles

▼ **Sukhoi Su-30MKA, 120e Escadron de Chasse, Ain Beida**
The 120e Escadron de Chasse is receiving the multi-role Su-30MKA to replace the unit's remaining few MiG-25PDS interceptors. Another QJJ Su-30MKA squadron has been established at Oum el-Boughi.

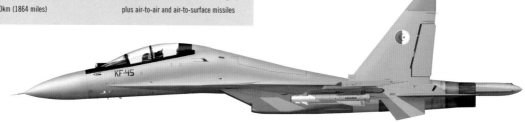

Egypt
ARAB REPUBLIC OF EGYPT AIR FORCE

Traditionally among most the powerful and best-equipped air arms on the continent, the Arab Republic of Egypt Air Force maintains a large inventory of both Western and Eastern equipment.

SUCCESSIVE ACQUISITION PROGRAMMES have provided Egypt with 220 F-16s, and the Fighting Falcon now spearheads the air arm, despite the continued use of older Soviet and Chinese aircraft.

Air Defence Command includes the 102nd Tactical Fighter Wing (TFW) with two squadrons of Shenyang F-7Bs at Mersa Matruh and the 103rd and 104th TFWs at Aswan and el-Mansourah, respectively, each wing operating two MiG-21MF squadrons. Two further F-7B squadrons are the responsibility of the 282nd TFW at Fayid, this expanded wing also having two F-16C/D squadrons.

Tactical Command comprises the 222nd TFW at Cairo West, with two squadrons of F-4Es co-located with an E-2C squadron. The F-16 is in use with the 232nd TFW at Inchas, the 242nd TFW at Bani Swayf and the 262nd TFW at Abu Suweir (two squadrons each), while the 272nd TFW at Giancalis maintains three F-16C/D squadrons. Mirage wings are the 236th TFW at Birma/el-Tanta (two Mirage 5 squadrons) and the 252nd TFW at Gabel al-Basur (a squadron each of Mirage 5s and Mirage 2000s).

Helicopter units include brigades at Hurghada (Mi-8/17), Qwaysina (Gazelle), Khutamiya (Gazelle and AH-64D) and Abu Hammad (AH-64D).

Arab Republic of Egypt Air Force Transport and Training Commands each operate at least two brigades together with constituent squadrons.

Specifications

Crew: 1

Powerplant: 1 x 126.7kN (28,500lb) thrust Pratt & Whitney F100-PW-229 afterburning turbofan

Maximum speed: 2177km/h (1353mph)

Range: 3862km (2400 miles)

Service ceiling: 15,240m (49,000ft)

Dimensions: span 9.45m (31ft); length 15.09m (49ft 6in); height 5.09m (16ft 8in)

Weight: 19,187kg (42,300lb) loaded

Armament: 1 x GE M61A1 20mm (0.79in) multi-barrelled cannon, seven external hardpoints with provision for up to 9276kg (20,450lb) of stores

▼ **Lockheed Martin F-16C Fighting Falcon, Arab Republic of Egypt Air Force**

Operated by an unknown unit, F-16C Block 40 96-0096 was delivered under the Peace Vector V programme, which was signed in 1996 and provided Egypt with 21 newly built F-16C/D aircraft. The Block 40 aircraft as flown by Egypt have provision for the AGM-88 HARM missile used for the defence-suppression mission.

Ethiopia
ETHIOPIAN AIR FORCE

Although not one of the biggest African air arms, the Ethiopian Air Force has been one of the most active in recent years, its aircraft having seen air-to-air combat against those of Eritrea.

WITH ALL REMAINING MiG-21s, MiG-23BNs and Su-25s now stored, Ethiopia relies on the Su-27s of No. 5 Squadron to provide the sharp end of its air force. In addition, there are at least two units flying helicopters and two more operating fixed-wing transport aircraft. Helicopters include Mi-35s, while transports include An-12s, An-26s and C-130s.

Specifications

Crew: 1

Powerplant: 1 x 73.5kN (16,535lb) Tumanskii R-25 turbojet

Maximum speed: 2229km/h (1385mph)

Range: 1160km (721 miles)

Service ceiling: 17,500m (57,400ft)

Dimensions: span 7.15m (23ft 5.5in); length (including probe) 15.76m (51ft 8.5in); height 4.1m (13ft 5.5in)

Weight: 10,400kg (22,925lb) loaded

Armament: 1 x 23mm (0.90in) GSh-23 twin-barrel cannon in underbelly pack, provision for about 1500kg (3307kg) of stores

▼ **Mikoyan-Gurevich MiG-21bis, Ethiopian Air Force, Debre Zebit**

One of more than 150 MiG-21s delivered to Ethiopia from 1977, these aircraft were mainly operated from Debre Zebit, and saw extensive service in the wars with Eritrea in the 1980s, and again between 1998–2001.

Libya

LIBYAN ARAB AIR FORCE

The LARAF has undergone significant change in the last decade, with older types being retired, and the government looking to acquire new types to replace generally ageing equipment.

A NUMBER OF older LARAF types have been withdrawn altogether, while others, such as the MiG-25, are now mainly in storage.

Most modern combat equipment is the Mirage F1, flown by two squadrons at Okba Ibn Nafa. The MiG-23 remains numerically the most important fighter, however, serving between five and seven squadrons. The MiG-21, in contrast, is now only operated by a single unit. Ground-attack assets comprise the Su-22M3 (two squadrons, one possibly non-operational), Su-22M4 (one unit) and Su-24MK (one unit, but with only a handful of aircraft operational). The MiG-23BN fleet is likely retired.

In terms of helicopter squadrons, these include units equipped with examples of the CH-47, Mi-2, Mi-8, Mi-14 and Mi-24. Transport equipment includes the An-26, C-130H, Falcon 20 and 50, Gulfstream (perhaps retired), Il-76 and L-410.

Specifications

Crew: 1	Dimensions: span 14.02m (45ft 11.75in);
Powerplant: 2 x 100kN (22,487lb) Tumanskii	length 23.82m (78ft 1.75in); height 6.1m
R-15B-300 turbojets	(20ft 0.5in)
Maximum speed: 2974km/h (1848mph)	Weight: 37,425kg (82,508lb) loaded
Combat radius: 1130km (702 miles)	Armament: 2 x R-40 and 4 x R-60 air-to-air
Service ceiling: over 24,385m (80,000ft)	missiles

▼ **Mikoyan-Gurevich MiG-25PD, 1015 Squadron, Sirte/Ghurdabiyah**

Libya purchased almost 80 MiG-25s of various subtypes in the late 1970s and the early 1980s, and the type formed the backbone of the LARAF interceptor fleet until its retirement from service in 2004. Despite this move, around 60 MiG-25s are retained in storage in an airworthy condition.

Morocco

ROYAL MOROCCAN AIR FORCE

The Royal Moroccan Air Force (Al-Quwwat al-Jawwiya al-Malakiya Marakishniya – QJMM) is a Western-influenced air arm with a balanced fleet of fighter, transport and training assets.

T HE STRUCTURE OF the QJMM divides assets among Fighter Aviation Command, Transport Aviation Command, Helicopter Command and Training Command, with squadrons distributed across numbered bases.

Fighter Aviation Command is responsible for air defence, with two squadrons of F-5E/Fs at Meknes and two of Mirage F1s at Sidi Slimane, the Mirage

units being allocated air defence and ground-attack roles respectively. A Fighter Pilot School is co-located at Meknes, this being equipped with Alpha Jets.

Workhorse of Transport Aviation Command is the C-130H, while other squadrons operate Boeing 707 tanker/transports and CN235s. Transport assets are based at Kénitra. Rabat-Sale is centre of rotary-wing operations, with types including the SA330, Bell 205,

CH-47C and SA342. A wide variety of trainers at Marrakech include AS 202s, T-34s and T-37s. Transport pilots are schooled on the Beech 200 and helicopter pilots on the Bell 205/206 and SA342. Gulfstreams and Falcons are available for VIP flights.

Specifications

Crew: 1

Powerplant: 2 x 22.2kN (5000lb) General Electric J85-GE-21B turbojets

Maximum speed: 1741km/h (1082mph)

Range: 306km (190 miles)

Service ceiling: 15,790m (51,800ft)

Dimensions: span 8.13m (26ft 8in);

length 14.45m (47ft 4.75in);

height 4.07m (13ft 4.25in)

Weight: 11,214kg (24,722lb) loaded

Armament: 2 x two 20mm (.78in) cannon; five external pylons with provision for 3175kg (7000lb) of stores

▼ **Northrop F-5E Tiger II, Escuadron de Chasse, Meknes-Bassatine (2nd Air Base)**

Morocco received a total of 24 F-5E/Fs over the years. At least two were lost in clashes with the Polisario Front in the 1980s. The survivors are operated by the Escadrones de Chasse 'Chahine' and 'Borak'. Morocco plans to replace its F-5s with 24 F-16C/Ds.

Sudan

SUDANESE AIR FORCE

Changing political allegiances have seen the Sudanese Air Force (Silakh al Jawwiya As'Sudaniya) receive aircraft from a variety of sources, and these have seen significant combat.

ALTHOUGH UNCONFIRMED, the probable order of battle of the Sudanese Air Force is based around three combat squadrons, three helicopter squadrons and a single fixed-wing transport squadron. In the last decade or so, oil revenues have allowed Sudan,

Africa's largest country, to begin acquiring new, and more modern military aircraft.

No. 1 Squadron flies Nanchang A-5C attack aircraft (and FT-6 trainers), No. 2 Squadron is equipped with MiG-29 fighters, and No. 3 Squadron is reported to have a mixed fleet of MiG-21s (12 of which may have been acquired from Ukraine) and MiG-23s (although these may have been retired). Sudan received 11 Su-25s from Belarus in 2008. Helicopters include around 24 Mi-25/35s, and a smaller number of Mi-17s. Training is conducted on Chinese-supplied CJ-6As and K-8s. The most modern fixed-wing transports are five An-74s.

Specifications

Crew: 1

Powerplant: 2 x 81.4kN (18,298lb) Sarkisov RD-33 turbofans

Maximum speed: 2443km/h (1518mph)

Range: 1500km (932 miles)

Service ceiling: 17,000m (55,775ft)

Dimensions: span 11.36m (37ft 3.75in);

length (including probe) 17.32m (56ft 10in);

height 7.78m (25ft 6.25in)

Weight: 20,000kg (44,090lb) loaded

Armament: 1 x 30mm (1.18in) GSh-30 cannon, provision for up to 4500kg (9921lb) of stores

▼ **Mikoyan MiG-29SE, No. 2 Fighter Squadron, Wadi Sayyidna**

This is one of between 12 and 24 MiG-29s delivered to Sudan to date. The type saw some combat service against JEM rebels, in Darfur, and one is known to have been lost during a rebel attack on Wadi Sayyidna, in May 2009.

Smaller North & East African states

ERITREA, KENYA, TANZANIA AND TUNISIA

While Tunisia has long been among the most stable African states, in East Africa, Eritrea has been plagued by conflict. Kenya and Tanzania both maintain modest air arms, albeit with jet equipment.

COMPARED TO OTHER North African air forces, that of Tunisia is small, and receives military aid from France and the USA. In East Africa, Eritrea has turned to Russia to provide combat aircraft, while Tanzania procures Chinese jets. Kenya's air arm traditionally maintains links with the UK.

Eritrean Air Force

With all operations based out of Asmara, the Eritrean Air Force consists of eight numbered squadrons. Equipment includes Westwinds and CL-601s for VIP transport, L-90 Redigo trainers,

Mi-8/17 and Mi-35 helicopters, MB339 jet trainers (although these may no longer be operational), a squadron each of MiG-29 and Su-27 fighters, Bell 412 helicopters and Y-12 transports.

Kenyan Air Force

Based around a fighter force of F-5E/Fs and Hawk Mk52 trainers, the Kenyan Air Force schools its pilots on Bulldog and Tucano trainers. Helicopters include armed MD500s and Z-9s, SA330s and Gazelles. DHC-5, DHC-8, Fokker 70 and Y-12 aircraft provide transport capacity.

Specifications

Crew: 1

Powerplant: 2 x 81.4kN (18,298lb) Sarkisov RD-33 turbofans

Maximum speed: 2443km/h (1518mph)

Range: 1500km (932 miles)

Service ceiling: 17,000m (55,775ft)

Dimensions: span 11.36m (37ft 3.75in); length (including probe) 17.32m (56ft 10in); height 7.78m (25ft 6.25in)

Weight: 18,500kg (40,785lb) loaded

Armament: 1 x 30mm (1.18in) GSh-30 cannon, provision for up to 4500kg (9921lb) of stores

▼ **Mikoyan MiG-29, No. 5 Squadron, Eritrean Air Force, Asmara**

This is an example from the first batch of four MiG-29s delivered to Eritrea from Ukraine in 1998. Two aircraft from this batch were lost during the subsequent war with Ethiopia.

Specifications

Crew: 1

Powerplant: 2 x 31.9kN (7165lb) Shenyang WP-6 turbojets

Maximum speed: 1540km/h (957mph)

Range: 1390km (864 miles)

Service ceiling: 17,900m (58,725ft)

Dimensions: span 9.2m (30ft 2.25in); length 14.9m (48ft 10.5in); height 3.88m (12ft 8.75in)

Weight: 10,000kg (22,046lb) loaded

Armament: 3 x 30mm (1.18in) NR-30 cannon; four external hardpoints with provision for up to 500kg (1102lb) of stores

▼ **Shenyang F-6C, Tanzanian Air Force**

One of only a handful of F-6Cs that remain operational with the Tanzanian AF, this aircraft was originally delivered in the early 1980s. The J-6s were stored for many years before being returned to service with Chinese assistance some time after 2005.

Tanzanian Air Force

This consists of one squadron of F-6C fighters, plus single helicopter and transport squadrons, the latter with Y-8s and Y-12s. A training squadron flies CJ-6s.

Tunisian Republic Air Force

Using a structure of squadrons and flights, most aircraft are based at Bizerte/Sidi Ahmed, Gafsa, Bizerte/La Karouba and Sfax. The sharp end of the Tunisian air arm is provided by a squadron of F-5E/Fs, supported by armed L-59s and MB326s. Basic and primary training is conducted on SF260s. Rotary-wing types include the AB205, AB412, Alouette II and III, Ecureuil, HH-3E and UH-1H. Transport assets include ex-USAF C-130Bs and newly built C-130Hs, as well as G222s and L-410s.

Specifications

Crew: 1	length 14.45m (47ft 4.75in); height
Powerplant: 2 x 22.2kN (5000lb) General	4.07m (13ft 4.25in)
Electric J85-GE-21B turbojets	Weight: 11,214kg (24,722lb) loaded
Maximum speed: 1741km/h (1082mph)	Armament: 2 x 20mm (.78in) cannon;
Range: 306km (190 miles)	two air-to-air missiles, five external pylons
Service ceiling: 15,790m (51,800ft)	with provision for 3175kg (7000lb) of stores
Dimensions: span 8.13m (26ft 8in);	

▼ **Northrop F-5E Tiger II, 15 Squadron, Tunisian Republic Air Force, Bizerte/Sidi Ahmed**

Tunisia began to receive 24 Tiger IIs in 1985. The surviving aircraft are now used for dual air defence and ground attack duties with 15 Squadron.

Angola
NATIONAL AIR FORCE OF ANGOLA

Angola's air arm emerged from the costly civil war of the 1980s and has now made some efforts to re-equip as well as reportedly adopting the new official title National Air Force of Angola.

ALTHOUGH DETAILS REMAIN scarce, the Angolan Air Force is understood to consist of a Transport Command (based in Luanda, together with a helicopter flight) a Military Air Training School (in Lobito), an Advanced Pilot Training Regiment (Catumbela), a Fighter Regiment (Lubango) and a Fighter-Bomber Regiment (Catumbela).

Specifications

Crew: 1	length 21.94m (71ft 11.5in); height 6.36m
Powerplant: 2 x 122.5kN (27,557lb)	(20ft 10.25in)
Lyul'ka AL-31M turbofans	Weight: 30,000kg (66,138lb) loaded
Maximum speed: 2150km/h (1335mph)	Armament: 1 x one 30mm (1.18in) GSh-3101
Range: 500km (930 miles)	cannon with 149 rounds; 10 external
Service ceiling: 17,500m (57,400ft)	hardpoints with provision for 6000kg
Dimensions: span 14.7m (48ft 2.75in);	(13,228lb) of stores

▼ **Sukhoi Su-27UB, Regimento de Caças (Fighter Regiment), Lubango**

Only one Su-27UB and one Su-27 entered Angolan service; the single-seater was later written off in a crash. The two-seat aircraft was last seen in 2009, and is reportedly still operational at Lubango.

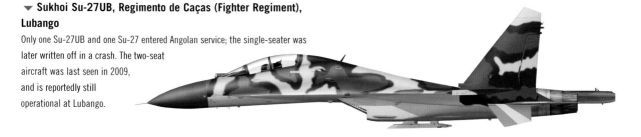

Smaller West African states
BURKINA FASO, CAMEROON, EQUATORIAL GUINEA, GABON, GHANA, GUINEA REPUBLIC, IVORY COAST, MALI, NIGERIA, SENEGAL AND TOGO

The smaller air arms of West Africa typically fly just a handful of armed trainers or combat helicopters, although most maintain assets to undertake transport, liaison and training duties.

THE FOLLOWING PROVIDES details of the most important of the smaller West African air arms. It should be noted that Benin, Cape Verde, Mauritania, Niger and Sierra Leone all maintain air arms, although most consist of little more than half a dozen helicopters and light transport types, and among them only Sierra Leone maintains credible combat equipment, in the form of a small number of Mi-24 assault helicopters. Gambia is another exception. It has obtained jet equipment, in the form of the Su-25 attack aircraft, though to date only a single example is in use with the Gambian National Army, and there is as yet no separate air arm branch. The air force of Guinea-Bissau retired almost its entire combat fleet in the early 1990s, and is likely now left with two Mi-24 assault helicopters and a small collection of transport. After years of civil war, Liberia's air arm has yet to be re-established.

Burkina Faso Air Force
Traditionally, the air force was based around two units, both based at Ouagadougou, and comprising the Escadron de Transport and the Escadron d'Helicopteres, followed by an Escadron de Chasse.

The Force Aérienne de Burkina Faso now divides its assets between two districts, each with one air base: Ouagadougou and Bobo Dioulasso. Aircraft are assigned to a single air brigade, which may have just one squadron. The most potent equipment is the SF260WP Warrior armed trainer, acquired from sources in Bolivia, Italy and Libya, with Libyan financial backing, but these are now stored. Also withdrawn are the MiG-21 fighters supplied by Libya. Otherwise, a range of transport and liaison types (including a single CN235) and helicopters (AS350, Mi-8/17, Mi-35 and SA365) are on strength.

Cameroon Air Force
The Armée de l'Air Cameroun operates from bases at Garoua, Koutaba, Yaoundé, Douala and Bamenda. Four Alpha Jets provide a light attack and advanced training capability, supported by four ex-South African Air Force Impala Mk2s (light attack) and a pair of Impala Mk1 jet trainers. Aravas, C-130Hs, DHC-4s, DHC-5s and Do 28s are the major transport types. Helicopters include examples of the Alouette II/III, Bell 206, Bell 412EP, SA330 and SA342. A single Do 128 is used for maritime patrol.

Specifications

Crew: 1	length 7.10m (23ft 4in); height 2.41m
Powerplant: 1 x Lycoming 194kW (260hp)	(7ft 11in)
IO540 D4A5	Weight: 1102kg (2430lb) loaded
Maximum speed: 441km/h (276mph)	Armament: 2 or 4 hardpoints for 7.62mm
Range: 2050km (1274 miles)	(0.3in) machine guns or general-purpose and
Service ceiling: 5790m (19,000ft)	practice bombs and one or two photo-
Dimensions: span 8.35m (27ft 5in);	reconnaissance pods or auxiliary drop tanks

▼ **SIAI-Marchetti SF260W Warrior, Force Aérienne de Burkina Faso, Bobo Dioulasso**
Burkina Faso received six ex-Philippine Air Force SF260s in mid-1986, before these were sold on to a Belgian dealer in 1993. The air force also received four more SF260s acquired as new from the manufacturer.

Specifications

Crew: 2

Powerplant: 2 x SNECMA/Turbomeca Larzac 04-
C6 each rated at 13.24kN (2976lb thrust)

Maximum speed: 1000km/h (621mph)

Range: 670km (415 miles)

Service ceiling: 14,630m (48,000ft)

Dimensions: span 9.11m (30ft); length 11.75m
(38ft); height 4.19m (14ft)

Weight: 8000kg (17,600lb) loaded

Armament: 1 x 30mm (1.18in) DEFA 553
cannon pod; up to 2500kg (5500lb) of bombs,
rockets or drop-tanks

▼ Dassault-Dornier Alpha Jet MS2, Armée de l'Air Cameroun, Garoua

One of seven Alpha Jets purchased by Cameroon, these aircraft are stationed at Garoua from where they are reportedly flown only sporadically. Two examples have been lost in accidents.

Equatorial Guinea National Guard

Previously equipped only with a handful of transport types, the Ala Aérea de Guardia Nacional (Air Wing of the National Guard) is developing a useful combat arm, benefiting from its status as third-biggest oil producer in sub-Saharan Africa. The air arm is based on between four and six Mi-24 assault helicopters and four single-seat Su-25 attack jets flown and is maintained by mainly Ukrainian mercenaries. Mercenaries also provide local pilots with instruction on two L-39 jet trainers and three or four two-seat Su-25UB combat trainers. A number of types also in use as VIP transports, comprise examples of the A109, Boeing 737, ERJ-145, Falcon 50, Mi-172 and S-92. Single examples of the An-32 and An-72 are used for military transport. The main operating base is Malabo, with a detachment of Mi-24s at Bata.

Gabonese Air Force

The Forces Aériennes Gabonaises structure has traditionally included No. 1 Transport Squadron, No. 2 Fighter Squadron (equipped with Mirages), No. 5 Advanced Training Squadron, No. 11 Transport-Reconnaissance Squadron (EMB-110 and EMB-111, the latter also used for maritime patrol) and No. 12 Heavy Transport Squadron (C-130H). Other types in use include ATR-42 and CN235 transports, Alouette II, Bell 412 and SA330 helicopters, and Magister and T-34C trainers. The Gabonese Army has a separate air arm, flying SA330 and SA342 helicopters.

Ghana Air Force

Ghana plans to upgrade its air arm – after past funding shortages – with four C-27J tactical transports and six Twin Star maritime patrol aircraft.

Specifications

Crew: 2

Powerplant: 1 x 16.87kN (3792lbf) Ivchenko
AI-25TL turbofan

Maximum speed: 750km/h (466mph)

Range: 1100km (683 miles)

Service ceiling: 11,000m (36,100ft)

Dimensions: span 9.46m (31ft 0.5in);
length 12.13m (39ft 9.5in);
height 4.77m (15ft 7.75in)

Weight: 4700kg (10,362lb) loaded

Armament: External bomb load up to
284kg (626lb)

▼ Aero L-39C Albatross, Ala Aérea de Guardia Nacional (Equatorial Guinea National Guard), Malabo

This is one of two L-39s delivered to Equatorial Guinea from the Ukraine between 2004 and 2006. Together with Su-25s, they are based at Malabo. All recent combat aircraft acquired by Equatorial Guinea (comprising L-39s, Mi-24s and Su-25s) were provided by Ukraine.

Specifications

Crew: 1

Powerplant: 1 x 100kN (15,873lb) SNECMA Atar
9K-50 turbojet

Maximum speed: 2350km/h (1460mph)

Range: 900km (560 miles)

Service ceiling: 20,000m (65,615ft)

Dimensions: span 8.4m (27ft 7in);

length 15m (49ft 2.25in); height 4.5m
(14ft 9in)

Weight: 15,200kg (33,510lb) loaded

Armament: 2 x internal DEFA 30mm
(1.18in) cannons, plus usually 6 x MK81
or MK82 bombs, 2 x Kentron Kukri V3b or
V3c missiles on wingtip rails

▼ **Dassault Mirage F1AZ, No. 2 Fighter Squadron, Forces Aériennes Gabonaises, Libreville**

This is one of the first two (of an eventual four) ex-South African Air Force Mirage F1ZAs, upgraded by Aerosud, and acquired by Gabon in 2006.

Current structure is reported to be based around No. 1 Squadron flying patrol aircraft, No. 2 Squadron (helicopters), No. 3 Squadron (transports) and No. 4 Squadron (with four MB339s and four K-8s used for advanced training). The latter unit likely also operates two armed L-39 jets. Other types include A109, Alouette III, Bell 412, Mi-2 and Mi-17 helicopters, plus Fokker 27, Fokker 28 and Islander transports.

Guinea Republic Air Force

The backbone of the Force Aérienne de Guinée (the air arm of Guinea Republic, otherwise known as Guinea-Conakry) was formerly a single fighter squadron with MiG-21s at Conakry. These fighters were delivered by the USSR and were operated with the assistance of Soviet advisors. Attrition replacements were also received from Ukraine. The

MiG-21 unit has apparently disbanded, leaving an inventory comprising three L-29 jet trainers, plus An-12, An-14 and An-24 transports, and a handful of AS350, MD500 Defender, Mi-8, SA330 and SA342 helicopters. A number of Yak-18s may remain in use for basic training.

Cote D'Ivoire Air Force

Successive military coups, in 1999 and 2001, followed by a civil war that began in September 2002, have left the air arm of the Ivory Coast in a parlous state. During the unrest, however, the government turned to Eastern Europe and assembled a relatively potent force of combat jets. Until 2004, the Force Aérienne de la Côte d'Ivoire kept a small combat element based around four Su-25s obtained from Belarus in 2002, plus two ex-Botswana

Specifications

Crew: 2

Powerplant: 1 x 16.01kN (3600lb) Garrett
TFE731-2A-2A turbofan

Maximum speed: Mach 0.75 (800km/h;
498mph)

Range: 2250km (1398 miles)

Service ceiling: 13,000m (42,651ft)

Dimensions: span 9.63m (31ft 7in); length
11.6m (38ft); height 4.21m (13ft 9in)

Weight: 4330kg (9546lb) loaded

Armament: 1 x 23mm (0.9in) cannon pod,
5 hard-points carrying up to 1000kg
(2205lb) external fuel and ordnance

▼ **Hongdu K-8, No. 4 Squadron, Ghana Air Force, Accra**

G913 is one of the aircraft from the second batch of K-8s delivered to Ghana in 2008. Four examples are currently in use for advanced training, with another two on order.

Strikemasters and a pair of former Bulgarian MiG-23MLD interceptors. The Su-25s (which included two two-seat Su-25UB models) were flown primarily by mercenaries until put out of action by French commandos in 2004, while the MiG-23s were impounded in Togo. At the same time, the Alpha Jet Cs were also abandoned, and most of the air force's helicopters were likewise rendered non-operational. Today, the air force mainly relies on leased and chartered aircraft in order to fulfil transport services.

Mali Air Force

The aircraft of the Force Aérienne de la République du Mali are stationed at two air bases (Bamako and Gao) that act as wings, and are responsible for one fighter and one helicopter squadron. Fighter equipment comprises MiG-17s and MiG-21MFs, plus L-29 jet trainers. For transport, the air force can

call upon a force of An-2, An-24/26 and BT-67 aircraft. AS350, Mi-8 and Mi-24 helicopters are also in service in small numbers. Mali has used its air force in successive combat operations against Burkina Faso over the disputed Agacher Strip, in order to put down Tuareg rebellion and, most recently, against rebels operating from bases in Niger. Known air bases of the FARMA include Base Aérienne 100 in Bamako (no longer in use), Base Aérienne 101 in Bamako-Senou and Base Aérienne 102 in Mopti-Sévaré.

Nigerian Air Force and Naval Air Arm

Dominating the region, Nigeria once possessed the most capable air arm in West Africa, although at the time of writing only a portion of its inventory remains serviceable. Formerly spearheaded by three combat wings (including Nos 1 and 2 Squadrons with MiG-21s and Alpha Jets at Kano, followed by

Specifications

Crew: 1	length (including probe) 15.76m (51ft 8.5in);
Powerplant: 1 x 73.5kN (16,535lb) Tumanskii	height 4.1m (13ft 5.5in)
R-25 turbojet	Weight: 10,400kg (22,925lb) loaded
Maximum speed: 2229km/h (1385mph)	Armament: 1 x 23mm (0.9in) GSh-23 twin-
Range: 1160km (721 miles)	barrel cannon in underbelly pack, provision
Service ceiling: 17,500m (57,400ft)	for about 1500kg (3307kg) of stores
Dimensions: span 7.15m (23ft 5.5in);	

▼ Mikoyan-Gurevich MiG-21, Guinea Republic Air Force, Conakry

Only three or four MiG-21s remain operational in Guinea Republic (Guinea Conakry). The survivors have been overhauled in Ukraine and are all based at the military side of Conakry international airport.

Specifications

Crew: 1	Dimensions: span 14.36m (47ft 1.5in); length
Powerplant: 2 x 44.1kN (9921lb) Tumanskii	15.53m (50ft 11.5in); height 4.8m (15ft 9in)
R-195 turbojets	Weight: 17,600kg (38,800lb) loaded
Maximum speed: 975km/h (606mph)	Armament: 1 x 30mm (1.18in) GSh-30-2
Range: 750km (466 miles)	cannon; eight external pylons with provision
Service ceiling: 7000m (22,965ft)	for up to 4400kg (9700lb) of stores

▼ Sukhoi Su-25, Escadrille de Chasse, Force Aérienne de la Côte d'Ivoire, Abidjan

One of two single-seat Su-25s received by the FACI's Escadrille de Chasse (Fighter Flight) in February 2003. The fleet has not been operational since November 2004, when most of the air arm was disabledby French troops.

Specifications

Crew: 1

Powerplant: 1 x 73.5kN (16,535lb) Tumanskii
R-25 turbojet

Maximum speed: 2229km/h (1385mph)

Range: 1160km (721 miles)

Service ceiling: 17,500m (57,400ft)

Dimensions: span 7.15m (23ft 5.5in);

length (including probe) 15.76m (51ft 8.5in);

height 4.1m (13ft 5.5in)

Weight: 10,400kg (22,925lb) loaded

Armament: 1 x 23mm (0.9in) GSh-23 twin-
barrel cannon in underbelly pack, provision
for about 1500kg (3307kg) of stores

▼ Mikoyan-Gurevich MiG-21bis, Force Aérienne de la République du Mali, Bamako

Mali received 12 MiG-21bis and four MiG-21UMs directly from the USSR in the mid-1970s. One MiG-21UM crashed in 1989 and the rest of the fleet was subsequently stored at Bamako, even though some were sporadically flown in the following years. The MiG-21bis have since been replaced by ex-Czech Air Force MiG-21MFs.

wings at Makurdi, Maiduguri and Kainji), all of these units' aircraft are now non-operational. However, in 2010 Nigeria had begun to induct the first of 15 new Chengdu F-7 fighters purchased from China. The F-7 fleet will eventually include 12 F-7NI single-seat interceptors and three FT-7NI two-seat trainers, and these are to be delivered together with PL-9 air-to-air missiles, rockets and bombs. The F-7s will be based at Makurdi. The only MiG-21 unit of the NAF to have been identified was No. 21 Operational Conversion Unit, part of the 64th Air Defence Group at Makurdi, and it is expected that the latter formation will be responsible for the F-7s.

An Air Transport Group consists of 221 Wing, with one Transport (C-130H-30 and G222), one Helicopter (AS332 and BO105), one Special Operations (Mi-24), and one VIP Squadron (BAe 125s and Falcon 900s). Training Command once had three squadrons (one flying PC-7s, one with L-39s and one with Mi-34s), but most of its assets are now likely not in service. Other types within the inventory include Alpha Jet trainers, ATR-42MP Surveyor maritime patrol aircraft, Fokker 27 transports, Air Beetle and Bulldog basic trainers, Do 27, 28 and Do 228 light transports, and MB339 jet trainers, though availability of these types remains questionable. The VIP transport fleet also includes civil-registered examples of the AW139, Boeing 727, Boeing 737, Cessna 550, Fokker 28 and Gulfstream IV/V. Other rotary-wing equipment includes the Mi-8 and Mi-24/35 assault helicopters.

A separate Nigerian Naval Air Arm operates Lynx Mk89s (obtained in order to serve on the Navy's single frigate) and A109s, although these are also reportedly mainly inactive.

Specifications

Crew: 2

Powerplant: 2 x SNECMA/Turbomeca Larzac 04-
C6 each rated at 13.24kN (2976lb thrust)

Maximum speed: 1000km/h (621mph)

Range: 670km (415 miles)

Service ceiling: 14,630m (48,000ft)

Dimensions: span 9.11m (30ft); length
11.75m (38ft); height 4.19m (14ft)

Weight: 8000kg (17,600lb) loaded

Armament: 1 x 30mm (1.18in) DEFA 553
cannon pod; up to 2500kg (5500lb) of bombs,
rockets or drop-tanks

▼ Dassault-Dornier Alpha Jet N, Nigerian Air Force

Nigeria purchased 25 Alpha Jets from Dornier (rather than from Dassault-Breguet, as was the norm), between 1981 and 1986. Four of these saw some combat in Sierra Leone in the 1990s. No fewer than nine have been lost in various mishaps.

Senegal Air Force

The Armée de l'Air du Senegal consists of a single air group (the 1st Senegalese Air Group) equipped with mainly transport types and helicopters. The most capable aircraft in the inventory are the F27 tactical transports, delivered in the mid-1970s, as well as two Mi-35 assault helicopters and two Mi-171 transport helicopters acquired more recently. Magister jet trainers have been retired, leaving training in the hands of a fleet of Epsilons, as well as Rallye 235s, the latter being outfitted as armed trainers. The air force operates from Dakar International Airport, although detachments are maintained elsewhere in the country. In 2008 Senegal received two UH-1Hs and two C-212s that were a donation from Spain. Other helicopter types in use include the AS355 and Mi-2.

Togo

The Force Aérienne Togolaise is split between two main air bases, Niamtougou and Lomé. Niamtougou has a fighter squadron with six Brazilian-supplied EMB-326GB Xavantes, and a training squadron flying Epsilons. The air force is reportedly interested in overhauling and returning to service the Alpha Jets once flown by the fighter squadron. Lomé supports a transport squadron, with DHC-5s and helicopters, and a presidential squadron, which includes a Boeing 707, a Fokker 28 and an SA365 Alpha Jets formerly flown by the fighter squadron. Lomé supports a transport squadron, with DHC-5s and helicopters, and a presidential squadron of a Boeing 707, a Fokker 28 and an SA365.

Specifications

Crew: 3	Dimensions: rotor diameter 21.35m
Powerplant: 2 x 1545kW (2225shp) Klimov	(69ft 10in); length 18.42m (60ft 5in);
TV3-117VM turboshafts	height 4.76m (15ft 7in)
Maximum speed: 250km/h (156mph)	Weight: 11,100kg (24,470lb) loaded
Range: 950km (594 miles)	Armament: Capable of carrying up to 1500kg
Service ceiling: 6000m (19,690ft)	(3300lb) of stores on six hardpoints

▼ **Mil Mi-171Sh, Armée de l'Air du Senegal, Ouakam**

Acquired as part of a recent modernization effort on the part of the Senegal Air Force, this Mi-171Sh is one of two examples operated from Ouakam (on the military side of the Léopold Sédar Senghhor international airport).

Specifications

Crew: 2	Dimensions: span 9.11m (30ft); length
Powerplant: 2 x SNECMA/Turbomeca Larzac	11.75m (38ft); height 4.19m (14ft)
04-C6 each rated at 13.24kN (2976lb thrust)	Weight: 8000kg (17,600lb) loaded
Maximum speed: 1000km/h (621mph)	Armament: 1 x 30mm (1.18in) DEFA 553
Range: 670km (415 miles)	cannon pod; up to 2500kg (5500lb) of bombs,
Service ceiling: 14,630m (48,000ft)	rockets or drop-tanks

▼ **Dassault/Dornier Alpha Jet E, Force Aérienne Togolaise, Niamtougou**

Togo was the first export customer for the Alpha Jet, ordering five in May 1977. Only three examples remained in service in 2000, when the fleet was put into storage at Niamtougou.

Smaller Central African states

BURUNDI, CHAD, CONGO BRAZZAVILLE, DR CONGO, MADAGASCAR, RWANDA AND UGANDA

The years of conflict that have afflicted Central Africa have left their mark on the region's air arms, and the armed forces of Rwanda and Uganda have both been drawn into the fighting in the Democratic Republic of Congo (as the former Zaïre was re-named in 1997).

IN ADDITION TO the air arms outlined, the region includes the Central African Republic, with its small Escadrille Centreafricaine. This has been in a parlous state since unrest in the country in the 1990s, but does include a single C-130, three helicopters, as well as a handful of AL-60 light transports.

Burundi

The Armée National de Burundi maintains a small air arm centred on a single helicopter squadron, equipped with two to four SA342s, at least two Mi-8MTV-5s and one or two Mi-24 assault helicopters.

Chad National Flight

Operating from N'Djamena international airport and Abéché, the Escadrille Nationale Tchadienne includes single fighter, helicopter and transport squadrons. By 2008 Chad had acquired three Su-25s from Ukraine (from six reportedly on order). An-26s and C-130Hs

▲ **Mil Mi-24, Armée National de Burundi, Bujumbura**

An unknown unit from Bujumbura international airport operates this Mi-24. The Mi-24 serves alongside SA342L Gazelles and Mi-8s and possibly a small number of surviving SA316B Alouette IIIs.

Specifications

Crew: 2–3	Dimensions: span 6.5m (21ft 3in); length
Powerplant: 2 x 1600kW (2200hp) Isotov TV3-	17.5m (57ft 4in); height 6.5m (21ft 3in)
117 turbines	Weight: 12,000kg (26,500lb) loaded
Maximum speed: 335km/h (208mph)	Armament: 1 x 12.7mm (0.5in) Yakushev-Borzov
Range: 450km (280 miles)	gun, 4 x S-8 80mm (3.15in) of rocket pods or
Service ceiling: 4500m (14,750ft)	up to 3460kg (7612lb) rockets or missiles

Specifications

Crew: 1	Dimensions: span 14.36m (47ft 1.5in); length
Powerplant: 2 x 44.1kN (9921lb) Tumanskii	15.53m (50ft 11.5in); height 4.8m (15ft 9in)
R-195 turbojets	Weight: 17,600kg (38,800lb) loaded
Maximum speed: 975km/h (606mph)	Armament: 1 x 30mm (1.18in) GSh-30-2
Range: 750km (466 miles)	cannon, eight external pylons with provision
Service ceiling: 7000m (22,965ft)	for up to 4400kg (9700lb) of stores

▼ **Sukhoi Su-25, Escadrille Nationale Tchadienne (Chad National Flight), N'Djamena**

TT-QAI is the only Chadian single-seat Su-25 identified so far (the air arm has also received a pair of two-seat Su-25UBs).

provide the mainstay of the transport squadron, while helicopters in use include the Alouette III, AS550, Mi-8/17/171 and Mi-35. A Beech 1900 and a DC-9 serve as VIP transports. Other types in use in small numbers comprise the Cessna 337, PC-6, PC-7, PC-9 and SF260W.

Congolese Air Force

No unit structure is known for the air force of Congo (also known as Congo-Brazzaville), although in the 1990s it was based on French-supplied helicopters, and Soviet-built fighters and transports. By 2001, most of the surviving aircraft had been grounded.

Specifications

Crew: 1

Powerplant: 1 x 73.5kN (16,535lb) Tumanskii R-25 turbojet

Maximum speed: 2229km/h (1385mph)

Range: 1160km (721 miles)

Service ceiling: 17,500m (57,400ft)

Dimensions: span 7.15m (23ft 5.5in);

length (including probe) 15.76m (51ft 8.5in); height 4.1m (13ft 5.5in)

Weight: 10,400kg (22,925lb) loaded

Armament: 1 x 23mm (0.9in) GSh-23 twin-barrel cannon in underbelly pack, provision for about 1500kg (3307kg) of stores

▼ **Mikoyan-Gurevich MiG-21bis, Congolese Air Force, Pointe Noire**

Wearing the markings of Congo Brazzaville, this MiG-21bis was one of the last two operational MiG-21s reported as such in September 1999, when they were stationed at Pointe Noire air base.

Specifications

Crew: 1

Powerplant: 2 x 44.1kN (9921lb) Tumanskii R-195 turbojets

Maximum speed: 975km/h (606mph)

Range: 750km (466 miles)

Service ceiling: 7000m (22,965ft)

Dimensions: span 14.36m (47ft 1.5in); length 15.53m (50ft 11.5in); height 4.8m (15ft 9in)

Weight: 17,600kg (38,800lb) loaded

Armament: 1 x 30mm (1.18in) GSh-30-2 cannon, eight external pylons with provision for up to 4400kg (9700lb) of stores

▼ **Sukhoi Su-25, Air Force of the DR Congo, N'Djili**

This Su-25 is one of four delivered in November 1999. Since then, two have crashed and the two survivors, both stationed at the military side of N'Djili international airport, are rarely flown.

Specifications

Crew: 1

Powerplant: 1 x 73.5kN (16,535lb) Tumanskii R-25 turbojet

Maximum speed: 2229km/h (1385mph)

Range: 1160km (721 miles)

Service ceiling: 17,500m (57,400ft)

Dimensions: span 7.15m (23ft 5.5in);

length (including probe) 15.76m (51ft 8.5in); height 4.1m (13ft 5.5in)

Weight: 10,400kg (22,925lb) loaded

Armament: 1 x 23mm (0.9in) GSh-23 twin-barrel cannon, provision for 1500kg (3307kg) of stores

▼ **Mikoyan-Gurevich MiG-21bis, Armée de l'Air Malgache (Malagasy Air Force), Ivato**

In common with the majority of the entire air force (with the exception of a few helicopters), all Malagasy MiG-21bis have been withdrawn from service and dumped at Ivato air base.

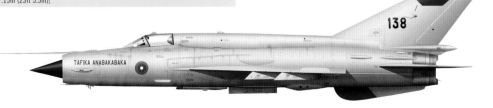

Air Force of the Democratic Republic of Congo

Since the late 1990s, the air arm of the Democratic Republic of Congo has been in a state of disarray. All combat aircraft (including MB326s and MiG-23s) are now believed to be stored, with only a few Mi-35s remaining operational. Congo acquired four Su-25s from Georgia in 1999, although only two now remain. Transport types reported include the An-26, C-47, C-130, DHC-5 and Islander. AS332, Mi-26, SA316 and SA330 helicopters have also been noted.

Madagascar – Malagasy Air Force

All combat aircraft (including MiG-17s and MiG-21s) and most transports formerly operated by the Armée de l'Air Malgache went into storage at Ivato during the mid-1990s, and were reportedly disposed of as scrap in 2008. Surviving types likely include Mi-8 helicopters and perhaps a number of light fixed-wing aircraft.

▼ **Mil Mi-24, Combat Squadron, Rwandan Air Force, Kigali**

Operated by the Combat Squadron (apparently this is an official designation; the unit is also sometimes cited as the Mi-24 Squadron), this aircraft is based on the military side of Kigali international airport.

Rwandan Air Force

After the country's years of civil war in the 1990s, the Force Aérienne Rwandaise is today believed to consist of two operational squadrons, one equipped with a pair of Mi-24 assault helicopters, the other with around eight Mi-8/17 transport helicopters. Single examples of the AS355 and SA365 utility helicopters may also remain in use.

Uganda People's Defence Force

The sharp end of the Ugandan air force is provided by a single fighter squadron, equipped with six MiG-21s, and a helicopter squadron (Mi-8/17s and a single Mi-24). Other assets comprise a small number of Bell 206s, three L-39s and an SF260 trainer, and a pair of Y-12 transports.

Specifications

Crew: 2–3	Dimensions: span 6.5m (21ft 3in); length
Powerplant: 2 x 1600kW (2200hp) Isotov	17.5m (57ft 4in); height 6.5m (21ft 3in)
TV3-117 turbines	Weight: 12,000kg (26,500lb) loaded
Maximum speed: 335km/h (208mph)	Armament: 1 x 12.7mm (0.5in) Yakushev-Borzov
Range: 450km (280 miles)	gun, 4 x S-8 80mm (3.15in) rocket pods or up
Service ceiling: 4500m (14,750ft)	to 3460kg (7612lb) of rockets or missiles

Specifications

Crew: 1	Dimensions: span 7.15m (23ft 5.5in);
Powerplant: 1 x 73.5kN (16,535lb) Tumanskii	length (including probe) 15.76m (51ft 8.5in);
R-25 turbojet	height 4.1m (13ft 5.5in)
Maximum speed: 2229km/h (1385mph)	Weight: 10,400kg (22,925lb) loaded
Range: 1160km (721 miles)	Armament: 1 x 23mm (0.9in) GSh-23 cannon,
Service ceiling: 17,500m (57,400ft)	provision for 1500kg (3307kg) of stores

▼ **Mikoyan-Gurevich MiG-21bis, Uganda People's Defence Force**

This aircraft is one of six MiG-21s purchased from Poland via Israel, and overhauled by IAI. Three have been lost in accidents to date, and additional examples have been acquired from Ukraine.

South Africa

SOUTH AFRICAN AIR FORCE

With capabilities unmatched in sub-Saharan Africa, the SAAF is combat proven and well equipped, and is in the process of introducing a number of advanced new types to its inventory.

ORIGINALLY ESTABLISHED IN 1920, today's SAAF operates on a much smaller budget than in previous years, but has nevertheless made efforts to maintain its edge in the region. It is now spearheaded by the first of 28 Gripen fighters. Other new equipment includes 24 Hawk Mk120s, four Super Lynx 300s, and 30 A109 utility helicopters, while older types have been withdrawn, and certain bases closed down in a process of rationalization.

The sole fighter unit now active is 2 Squadron at Makhado, flying the Gripen. Eleven Rooivalk attack helicopters are operated by 16 Squadron at Bloemspruit. Transport aircraft are centred at Waterkloof, with 28 Squadron's C-130BZs; C-212s, CN235s and Cessna 185s of 44 Squadron; Beech 200/300s, Cessna 208s and PC-12s of 41 Squadron, and the mixed VIP fleet of 21 Squadron. The turboprop-powered C-47TP survives in the maritime patrol role, with 35 Squadron at Ysterplaat.

Training syllabus

Before progressing to the Hawks of 85 Combat Flying School at Makhado, trainee pilots fly the PC-7 of the Central Flying School at Langebaanweg, also home to the Silver Falcons display team. Helicopter pilots are schooled by 87 Helicopter Flying School, flying A109s, BK117s and Oryx from Bloemspruit.

▲ **Denel AH-2 Rooivalk**
The Rooivalk project began in 1984 and led to a first flight in 1990. The attack helicopter suffers from limited operational capability and, to date, only 12 production examples have been completed for the SAAF.

Ysterplaat-based 22 Squadron is a mixed helicopter unit, with the maritime-configured Super Lynx and Oryx. With flights maintained at Durban and Port Elizabeth, 15 Squadron operates Oryx and BK117s. 17 and 19 Squadrons are both equipped with A109s and Oryx, and are based at Hoedspruit and Waterkloof. The SAAF also maintains a Test Flight and Development Centre, flying various types from the test ranges at Overberg.

▼ **SAAB JAS39C Gripen, 2 Squadron, Makhado**
The first of two single-seat Gripens delivered to the SAAF in November 2009. The type has replaced the Cheetah C/D as the SAAF's front-line fighter, with orders placed for 17 JAS39Cs and nine two-seat JAS39Ds.

Specifications

Crew: 1	Dimensions: span 8m (26ft 3in); length 14.1m
Powerplant: 1 x 80.5kN (18,100lb) Volvo	(46ft 3in); height 4.7m (15ft 5in)
Flygmotor RM12 turbofan	Weight: 12,473kg (27,500lb) loaded
Maximum speed: more than Mach 2	Armament: 1 x 27mm (1.06in) Mauser
Range: 3250km (2020 miles)	BK27 cannon, plus rockets, cluster
Service ceiling: 15,240m (50,000ft)	bombs and missiles

Smaller Southern African states

BOTSWANA, NAMIBIA, ZAMBIA AND ZIMBABWE

Although relatively peaceful today (the once powerful Mozambique air arm has effectively disbanded) the volatile situation in Zimbabwe ensures that neighbours remain on their guard.

THE SMALLER NATIONS in Southern Africa typically maintain proportionally sized air wings. However, while the air wings of Lesotho and Swaziland are equipped with small fleets for mainly paramilitary duties, those of their neighbours in the region include jet equipment of various types.

Botswana Defence Force Air Wing

The Botswana Defence Force Air Wing was created in 1977. The most important base is Molepolole, although Gaborone and Francistown are also used. Main combat equipment is Z28 Squadron's ex-Canadian CF-5A/Ds, 13 of which were ordered in 1996, followed by another five in 2000. Transport capacity is provided by C-212, CN235 and C-130B aircraft of Z10 Squadron and the Islanders of Z1 and Z12. Helicopters consist of the AS350 and Bell 412 (Z21 and Z23). Training is conducted on PC-7s of Z7, while O-2As (Z3) are used for anti-poaching operations. VIP transport at Molepolole consists of a Bell 412, a Beech 200 and a Gulfstream IV.

Namibia Defence Force

Namibia's Air Squadron includes a privately run basic flying school and a jet flying school that was established with Chinese assistance and operates K-8s. A fighter squadron equipped with 12 Chengdu F-7s is still in the process of establishment, although a helicopter squadron (Mi-8, Mi-35 and SA315/316) and a transport squadron (An-12, An-26 and Y-12) are active. A VIP flight is also operational.

Zambia Air Force and Air Defence

Zambia's single fighter squadron (once equipped with MiG-19s and MiG-21s) is now defunct, leaving a jet training squadron with K-8s, a transport squadron with two Y-12s, and a helicopter squadron equipped with AB205, AB212 and Mi-8 types, and reportedly a single Mi-24. The Zambian VIP flight is apparently no longer operational.

Air Force of Zimbabwe

The AFZ, which has been involved in the conflict in the Democratic Republic of Congo since the late 1990s, is primarily based at two locations: Gweru-Thornhill and Harare-Manyame. The most capable combat type is the Chengdu F-7, 20 of which are in service, including two twin-seat FT-7s, and these were deployed operationally during the fighting in the Congo. Training is conducted on around 30

Specifications

Crew: 1–2	Dimensions: span 7.87m (25ft 10in); length
Powerplant: 2 x 13.0kN (2925lbf) (dry thrust)	14.38m (47ft 2in); height 4.01m (13ft 2in)
Orenda-built GE J85-15 turbojet	Weight: 9249kg (20,390lb) loaded
Maximum speed: 1575km/h (978mph)	Armament: 2 x 20mm (0.787in) Pontiac M39A2
Range: 1400km (660 miles)	cannons in nose, 2 x AIM-9 Sidewinder Air-to-
Service ceiling: 12,000m (41,000ft)	air missiles and 3200kg (7000lb) payload

▼ **Canadair CF-5A Freedom Fighter, Z28 Squadron, Botswana Defence Force Air Wing, Molepolole**

Designated as CF-5s, Botswana's Freedom Fighters are actually ex-Canadian Forces CF-116s. Deliveries began in 1996, and the aircraft had been previously upgraded to serve as lead-in trainers for the Hornet.

SF260s and 11 K-8s, the latter replacing the now-grounded Hawks. The AFZ transport fleet is based at Harare and includes single examples of the An-12 and Il-76, plus C-47TPs, C-212s and Islanders. Around 15 FTB-337G Skymaster light transports

survive. A helicopter fleet relies on AB412s and Alouette IIIs, together with six Mi-24/35s, the latter having seen combat in the Congo. For VIP transport, the AFZ operates two AS532 helicopters, a BAe 146 and possibly a number of surviving Yak-40s.

Specifications

Crew: 2

Powerplant: 1 x 16.01kN (3600lb) Garrett TFE731-2A-2A turbofans

Maximum speed: Mach 0.75 (800km/h; 498mph)

Range: 2250 km (1398 miles)

Service ceiling: 13,000m (42,651ft)

Dimensions: span 9.63m (31ft 7in); length 11.6m (38ft); height 4.21m (13ft 9in)

Weight: 4330kg (9546lb) loaded

Armament: 1x 23mm (0.90in) cannon pod, 5 hardpoints with a capacity of 1000kg (2205lb)

▼ Hongdu K-8, Namibia Defence Force, Windhoek

It appears that Namibia received only four K-8 jet trainers, even though sources indicate deliveries of up to 12. The Chinese influence on the Namibia Defence Force is clear, with pilot graduates progressing from the K-8 to the Chengdu F-7 fighter.

Specifications

Crew: 2

Powerplant: 1 x 16.01kN (3600lb) Garrett TFE731-2A-2A turbofans

Maximum speed: Mach 0.75 (800km/h; 498mph)

Range: 2250 km (1398 miles)

Service ceiling: 13,000m (42,651ft)

Dimensions: span 9.63m (31ft 7in); length 11.6m (38ft); height 4.21m (13ft 9in)

Weight: 4330kg (9546lb) loaded

Armament: 1x 23mm (0.90in) cannon pod, 5 hardpoints with a capacity of 1000kg (2205lb)

▼ Hongdu K-8, Zambia Air Force and Air Defence, Ndola

Zambia purchased a total of eight K-8s, and this was the first example to enter service with an unknown training unit, based at Ndola in northern-central Zambia. Another former customer of Soviet equipment, Zambia's air arm is now turning increasingly to China.

Specifications

Crew: 1

Powerplant: 1 x 66.7kN (14,815lb) thrust Liyang Wopen-13F afterburning turbojet

Maximum speed: 2229km/h (1385mph)

Range: 1160km (721 miles)

Service ceiling: 17,500m (57,400ft)

Dimensions: span 7.15m (23ft 5.5in); length (including probe) 15.76m (51ft 8.5in); height 4.1m (13ft 5.5in)

Weight: 10,400kg (22,925lb) loaded

Armament: 1 x 23mm (0.9in) cannon, provision for about 1500kg (3307kg) of stores

▼ Chengdu F-7NI, 5 Squadron, Air Force of Zimbabwe, Gweru

This is one of only a few F-7NIs delivered to Zimbabwe, the majority of the AFZ's F-7Ns being of the NII sub-variant (differing in having four underwing hardpoints). Zimbabwe also purchased two FT-7BZs. All are operated by 5 Squadron 'Arrow' from Gweru air base.

Chapter 17

Australasia

Australia and New Zealand maintain the only significant air arms in their region, with aviation elements of the Australian Defence Force (ADF) providing a powerful bulwark against possible aggression from countries in Southeast Asia. Both countries are aligned with the USA under the ANZUS defence agreement, and support UN peacekeeping missions in the Pacific. The Royal New Zealand Air Force has been active in Timor-Leste in recent years, while major ADF operational commitments include support of Operation Enduring Freedom and Iraqi Freedom and the UN mission in East Timor, together with smaller assignments in Africa and Oceania.

Australia

ROYAL AUSTRALIAN AIR FORCE, NAVY FLEET AIR ARM AND ARMY AVIATION

Australia's island status and huge coastline demand a robust defence, and the three air arms of the Australian Defence Force (ADF) play a key role in preserving sovereignty.

AMONG SIGNIFICANT NEW equipment, the ADF is introducing six Wedgetail Airborne Early Warning and Control (AEW&C) platforms and the F/A-18F strike fighter as a replacement for the F-111. Both are almost certain to be joined by around 100 F-35s, which will replace 'legacy' F/A-18s from 2012.

New transport capacity is represented by four C-17As that provide a Responsive Global Airlift capability, and can be used to deploy ADF Chinook, MRH90 and Tiger helicopters. The five KC-30A tankers provide a refuelling capability, replacing 707s, and can also operate as strategic airlifters.

Rotary-wing modernization for the ADF is represented by 46 MRH90 transport helicopters, which will ultimately replace Army S-70As, UH-1Hs and, in navalized form, the Sea King. A new maritime helicopter to replace the S-70B will be selected from the MRH90 or MH-60R. The RAAF's first UAV is the Heron 1, acquired in conjunction with the Canadian Armed Forces and used in Afghanistan.

ROYAL AUSTRALIAN AIR FORCE

HQ Air Command, Glenbrook

Direct Reporting Unit

Aerospace Operational Support Group	F/A-18A/B, PC-9/A, P-3C	Edinburgh

Air Combat Group — Williamtown

78 Wing,	**Williamtown**	
76 Squadron	Hawk Mk127	Williamtown
79 Squadron	Hawk Mk127	Pearce
2 OCU	F/A-18A/B	Williamtown
81 Wing,	**Williamtown**	
3 Squadron	F/A-18A/B	Williamtown
75 Squadron	F/A-18A/B	Tindal
77 Squadron	F/A-18A/B	Williamtown
82 Wing	**Amberley**	
1 Squadron	RF/F-111C, F/A-18F	Amberley
6 Squadron	F-111C, F/A-18F	Amberley

Note: F/A-18F will replace F-111s with 1 and 6 Squadrons from 2010.

Forward Air Control Development Unit	PC-9/A	Williamtown

Surveillance and Response Group

42 Wing	**Williamtown**	
2 Squadron	Wedgetail	Williamtown

Air Lift Group Richmond

84 Wing	**Richmond**	
32 Squadron	Beech 350	East Sale
33 Squadron	KC-30A	Amberley
34 Squadron	Boeing 737-BBJ, CL-604	Canberra International Airport
86 Wing	**Richmond**	
36 Squadron	C-17A	Amberley
37 Squadron	C-130H/J	Richmond

Maritime Patrol Group

92 Wing	**Edinburgh**	
10 Squadron	AP-3C	Edinburgh
11 Squadron	AP-3C	Edinburgh
292 Squadron	AP-3C	Edinburgh

Training Command Williams

Central Flying School	PC-9/A	East Sale
2 FTS	PC-9/A	Pearce

Specifications

Crew: 2

Powerplant: 2 x 97.90kN (22,000lb) thrust
General Electric F414-GE-400
afterburning turbofan engines

Maximum speed: 1190 km/h (1190mph)

Range: 722km (449 miles)

Service ceiling: 15,000m (50,000ft)

Dimensions: span 13.62m (60ft 1in); length
13.62m (44ft 9in); height 4.88m (16ft)

Weight: 29,900kg (66,000lb) loaded

Armament: 1 x 20mm (.78in) M61A1 Vulcan
cannon; 11 external hardpoints for up to
8050kg (17,750lb) of stores

▼ **Boeing F/A-18F Super Hornet, 1 Squadron, RAAF Base Amberley**

The latest combat equipment for the RAAF is the two-seat F/A-18F. It has been procured as a successor to the F-111. Deliveries of the 24 aircraft began in 2010.

Order of battle

RAAF organization divides assets among the Air Combat Group (ACG), Surveillance and Response Group (SRG), Air Lift Group (ALG), together with training units, the latter including the Roulettes aerobatic team, equipped with PC-9/A trainers.

Australian Army Aviation Corps is spearheaded by the Tiger Armed Reconnaissance Helicopter (ARH), 22 of which are on order. Primary air mobility assets are six CH-47Ds and 35 S-70As, while the MRH90 is also now arriving in service, allowing retirement of the UH-H. The Army's 171 Squadron is used for anti-terrorist operations. AAAvn and RAN instructor training is handled by the School of Army Aviation.

The Royal Australian Navy's airborne activities are centred at Nowra (HMAS *Albatross*), the sole naval air station. S-70Bs operate from RAN frigates. The Sea King maritime support helicopter will be replaced by the MRH90. AS350s and A109s are used for lead-in pilot, observer and aircrew training, and occasional shipborne utility duties.

ROYAL AUSTRALIAN NAVY FLEET AIR ARM

723 Squadron	AS350, A109	Nowra
816 Squadron	S-70B	Nowra
817 Squadron	Sea King Mk50A/B	Nowra

AUSTRALIAN ARMY AVIATION CORPS

1st Aviation Regiment		
161(R) Squadron	Bell 206B/CA-32, Tiger ARH	Darwin
162(R) Squadron	Bell 206B/CA-32, Tiger ARH	Townsville
171(GS) Squadron	S-70A	Holsworthy
173(GS) Squadron	Beech 350, Beech 200	Oakey
5th Aviation Regiment		
A Squadron	MRH90	Townsville
B Squadron	S-70A	Townsville
C Squadron	CH-47D	Lavarack Barracks/ Townsville
School of Army Aviation		
Bell 206B/CA-32, Tiger ARH, S-70A		Oakey

▲ **Lockheed AP-3C Orion**

The parent unit of the AP-3C fleet is the Maritime Patrol Group, but the Orion is increasingly used by the RAAF for overland missions. The upgraded AP-3C has new mission equipment, including multi-mode radar and electro-optical sensors.

Specifications

Crew: 2

Powerplant: 2 x 1409kW (1890shp) General
Electric T700-GE-701C turboshaft

Maximum speed: 361km/h (224mph)

Range: 463km (288 miles)

Service ceiling: 4021m (13,200ft)

Dimensions: rotor diameter: 16.36m
(53ft 8in); length 19.76m (64ft 10in);
height 5.33m (17ft 6in)

Weight: 9997kg (22,000lb) loaded

Armament: 2 x 7.62mm door guns, AGM-119
Penguin anti-ship missiles, MK46 torpedoes

▼ Sikorsky S-70B-2 Seahawk, 816 Squadron, HMAS Anzac

Seen here armed with AGM-119 Penguin anti-ship missiles, this S-70B-2 is one of
16 examples shore-based at Nowra when not embarked on Royal Australian Navy
warships. Other weapons include 7.62mm (0.3in) door guns and Mk46 torpedoes.

Specifications

Crew: 2

Powerplant: 2 x 1160kW (1171hp) MTU/Rolls-
Royce/Turboneca MTR 390 turboshafts

Maximum speed: 280km/h (175mph)

Battle endurance: 2 hours 50 min

Initial climb rate: more than 600m/min
(1900fpm)

Dimensions: rotor diameter 13m (42ft 7in);
length 14m (46ft); height 4.32m (14ft 1in)

Weight: 6000kg (13,225lb) loaded

Armament: 4 wing stations for Hellfire II air-to-
ground missiles and 4 air-to-air missiles

▼ Eurocopter Tiger ARH, 161(R) Squadron, 1st Aviation Regiment, Roberts Barracks, Darwin

Armed with Hellfire II air-to-ground missiles, this is one of 22 Tigers acquired
under the ARH programme to equip 161(R) and 162(R) Squadrons, replacing the
Bell 206B/CA-32 as well as the UH-1H gunships, which are now retired.

▶ Lockheed C-130H Hercules

The RAAF's No. 37 Squadron, stationed at RAAF Base
Richmond, near Sydney, is equipped with the C-130H,
introduced in 1978, as well as the latest C-130J model,
which arrived in 1999. The C-130s are used for troop
transport, airdropping of paratroops and cargo, and
special forces insertion.

New Zealand

ROYAL NEW ZEALAND AIR FORCE

Tasked with, among others, defence of one of the world's largest Exclusive Economic Zones, the RNZAF fleet is based around maritime patrol, transport and helicopter elements.

THE THREE FORCE elements of the RNZAF are the Maritime Patrol Force, Fixed Wing Transport Force and the Rotary Wing Transport Force. The Maritime Patrol Force is comprised of No. 5 Squadron, with six P-3Ks, based at RNZAF Auckland. No. 40 Squadron, also at Auckland, provides the Fixed Wing Transport element, and is equipped with five C-130H and two 757-200 transports. The Rotary Wing Transport Force is at RNZAF Base Ohakea, and is assigned the UH-1H helicopters of No. 3 Squadron.

No. 42 Squadron, responsible for multi-engine pilot training, uses five King Air 200s. This unit is based at Ohakea alongside the Helicopter Conversion Flight (a branch of No. 3 Squadron). As well as using UH-1Hs as required, the Helicopter Conversion Flight has five of its own Sioux helicopters for conversion training. Also at Ohakea are the CT-4 Airtrainers of the Pilot Training Squadron and the Central Flying School. The PTS and CFS share the fleet of 13 Airtrainers, the CFS being responsible for the Flying Instructors Course, and also providing the Red Checkers aerobatic display team.

The RNZAF is acquiring eight NH90s to replace the UH-1H fleet, while the Sioux will be superseded by five A109 Light Utility Helicopters.

Five SH-2Gs are operated on behalf of the Navy as No. 6 Squadron, a joint RNZAF/RNZN-manned unit. Flying from RNZN vessels, the Seasprites are based at RNZAF Base Auckland in Whenuapai.

▲ **Kaman SH-2G Seasprite**

No. 6 Squadron's Seasprites are operated by Navy and Air Force personnel, but are flown by Navy pilots, trained by the RNZAF. The helicopters deploy onboard the frigates HMNZ *Te Mana* and *Te Kaha*.

Specifications

Crew: 11 + 4	length 35.61m (116ft 10in);
Powerplant: 4 x 4910 SHP Allison T56-A-14	height 10.29m (33ft 9in)
Maximum speed: 815km/h (508mph)	Weight: 57,834kg (127,500lb) loaded
Range: 7670km (4766 miles)	Armament: Bombload of 9000kg (20,000lb),
Service ceiling: 9296m (30,500ft)	missiles, torpedoes, mines and depth charges
Dimensions: span 30.38m (99ft 8in);	

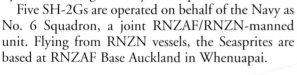

▲ **Lockheed P-3K Orion, No. 5 Squadron, RNZAF Auckland**

The RNZAF operates six P-3K Orions. The first five examples were acquired as P-3Bs in 1966, with a further P-3B transferred to the inventory from the RAAF in 1985. All six Orions received an avionics upgrade in the early 1980s, leading to the revised P-3K designation. P-3Ks have served operationally in the Persian Gulf, and a detachment supported Coalition forces during Operation Enduring Freedom between May 2003 and February 2004.

World Alliances
1950–1989

The ideological confrontation between the US and Soviet Union – and in turn, between their respective NATO and Warsaw Pact military alliances – formed the backdrop of the Cold War.

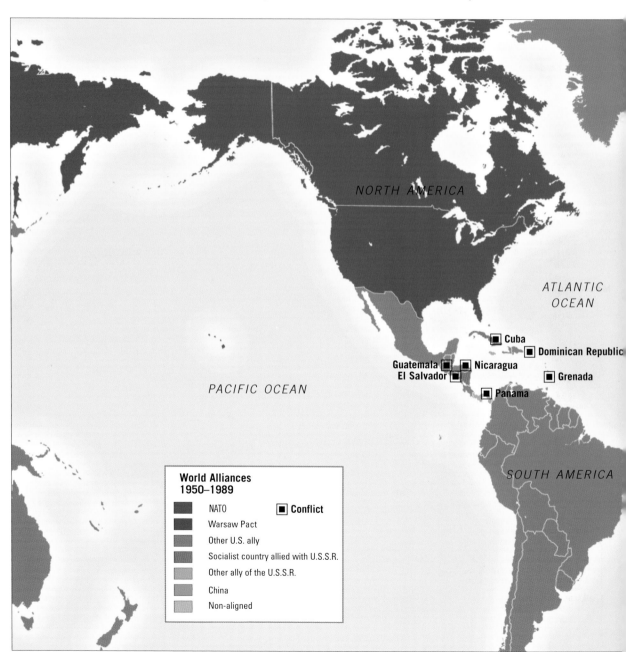

World Alliances 1950–1989

- NATO
- Warsaw Pact
- Other U.S. ally
- Socialist country allied with U.S.S.R.
- Other ally of the U.S.S.R.
- China
- Non-aligned
- ■ Conflict

Map labels: Cuba, Dominican Republic, Guatemala, Nicaragua, El Salvador, Grenada, Panama

NORTH AMERICA · SOUTH AMERICA · ATLANTIC OCEAN · PACIFIC OCEAN

However, the conflicts of the period were invariably fought by proxy, amid a complex political landscape of shifting allegiances, and with the superpowers typically becoming involved in actions that were initiated by local or civil strife, or by nationalist or anti-colonialist sentiment.

In Europe, the division created by the 'Iron Curtain' established the battle lines. The political situation in South America, seen as 'America's backyard', was closely controlled by the U.S. In Africa, as in the Middle East, the U.S. and U.S.S.R. time and again became involved in local conflicts in bids to undermine one another and to bolster their own divergent ideologies. A pattern of involvement in colonial struggles served as background to many of the conflicts fought in Southeast Asia.

Glossary

AAC	Army Air Corps	ASRAAM	Advanced Short-Range Air-to-Air Missile
AAF	Army Airfield	ASTOR	Airborne STand-Off Radar
AAM	Air-to-Air Missile	ASW	Anti-Submarine Warfare
AARGM	Advanced Anti-Radiation Guided Missile	ATGM	Anti-Tank Guided Missile
AASF	Army Aviation Support Facility	ATM	Anti-Tank Missile
AASM	Armament Air-Sol Modulair	AVN	Aviation
AB	Air Base	AVN CO	Aviation Company
ACC	Air Combat Command	AWACS	Airborne Warning And Control System
ACM	Advanced Cruise Missile		
ACS	Air Cavalry Squadron	BLU	Bomb Live Unit
ADV	Air Defence Variant (of the Tornado)	BROACH	Bomb Royal Ordnance Augmented Charge
AEF	Air & Space Expeditionary Force	BVR	Beyond Visual Range
AETC	Air Education and Training Command		
AEW	Airborne Early Warning	C2	Command and Control
AFB	Air Force Base	CAB	Command Aviation Battalion
AFGSC	Air Force Global Strike Command	CALCM	Conventional Air-Launched Cruise Missile
AFMC	Air Force Material Command	CAP	Combat Air Patrol
AFSOC	Air Force Special Operations Command	CAS	Close Air Support
AFSPC	Air Force Space Command	CAV	Cavalry Regiment or Cavalry Squadron
AGM	Air-to-Ground Missile	CBU	Cluster Bomb Unit
AHB	Assault Helicopter Battalion	CCD	Charge Coupled Device
ALARM	Air-Launched Anti-Radiation Missile	CEB	Combined Effects Bomblet
ALCM	Air-Launched Cruise Missile	CEM	Combined Effects Munition
AMC	Air Mobility Command	CNAF	Chinese Nationalist Air Force
AMRAAM	Advanced Medium-Range Air-to-Air Missile	COIN	Counter-Insurgency
AP	Airport	CSAR	Combat Search and Rescue
APKWS	Advanced Precision Kill Weapon System		
ARB	Air Reserve Base	Det	Detachment
ARM	Anti-Radiation Missile	DRAAF	Democratic Republic of Afghanistan Air Force
ARNG	Army National Guard		
ARS	Attack Reconnaissance Helicopter Squadron	ECCM	Electronic Counter-Countermeasures: measures taken to reduce the effectiveness of ECM by improving the resistance of radar equipment to jamming.
ASCC	Air Standardization Coordinating Committee		
ASF	Aviation Support Facility		
AShM	Anti-Ship Missile		
ASM	Air-to-Surface Missile	ECM	Electronic Countermeasures: systems designed to confuse and disrupt enemy radar equipment.
ASMP-A	Air-Sol Moyenne Portée Amélioré		

ECR	Electronic Combat Reconnaissance: a variant of the Panavia Tornado optimized for electronic warfare.
ELINT	Electronic Intelligence. Information gathered through monitoring enemy electronic transmissions by specially equipped aircraft, ships or satellites.
ERDL	Extended Range Data Link
EW	Electronic Warfare
FAA	Fleet Air Arm; or Federal Aviation Administration
FAC	Forward Air Controller. A battlefront observer who directs strike aircraft on to their targets near the front line.
FAE	Fuel/Air Explosive
FFAR	Forward-Firing Aircraft Rocket/Folding-Fin Aircraft Rocket
FLIR	Forward-Looking Infra-Red. Heat-sensing equipment fitted in an aircraft that scans the path ahead to detect heat from objects such as vehicle engines.
FRS	Fleet Readiness Squadron
GBU	Guided Bomb Unit
GCI	Ground Control Intercept
GP	General-Purpose (bomb)
GPS	Global Positioning System. A system of navigational satellites.
GSAB	General Support Aviation Battalion
HARM	High-speed Anti-Radiation Missile
HE	High Explosive
HM	Helicopter Mine Countermeasures Squadron
HOBOS	Homing Bomb System
HOT	Hautsubsonique Optiquement Téleguidé Tiré d'un Tube
HOTAS	Hands on Throttle and Stick. A system whereby the pilot exercises full control over his aircraft in combat without the need to remove his hands from the throttle and

	control column to operate weapons selection switches or other controls.
HS	Helicopter Anti-Submarine Squadron
HSC	Helicopter Sea Combat Squadron
HSL	Helicopter Anti-Submarine Light Squadron
HSM	Helicopter Maritime Strike Squadron
HUD	Head-Up Display. A system in which essential information is projected on to a cockpit windscreen so that the pilot has no need to look down at his instrument panel.
HVAR	High-Velocity Aircraft Rocket
IAF	Indian Air Force
IAP	International Airport
ICBM	Intercontinental Ballistic Missile
IDF/AF	Israeli Defence Force/Air Force
IFF	Identification Friend or Foe. An electronic pulse emitted by an aircraft to identify it as friendly on a radar screen.
IIR	Imaging Infra-Red
INS	Inertial Navigation System. An on-board guidance system that steers an aircraft or missile over a pre-determined course by measuring factors such as the distance travelled and reference to 'waypoints' (landmarks) en route.
IR	Infra-Red
IrAF	Iraqi Air Force
IRIAF	Imperial Iranian Air Force
IRST	Infra-Red Search and Track
ISTAR	Intelligence, Surveillance, Targeting and Reconnaissance
JASSM	Joint Air-to-Surface Standoff Missile
JDAM	Joint Direct Air Munition
JFTB	Joint Forces Training Base
JHC	Joint Helicopter Command
JNGS	Joint National Guard Station
JRB	Joint Reserve Base

JSF	Joint Strike Fighter		NSM	Naval Strike Missile
JSOW	Joint Standoff Weapon		NVG	Night Vision Goggles. Specially designed goggles that enhance a pilot's ability to see at night.
JSTARS	Joint Surveillance and Target Attack Radar System. An airborne command and control system that directs air and ground forces in battle.			
			OCU	Operational Conversion Unit
			OTH	Over The Horizon
kT	Kiloton			
			PACAF	Pacific Air Forces
LACM	Land-Attack Cruise Missile		PAF	Pakistan Air Force
LANTIRN	Low-Altitude, Navigation And Targeting by Infra-Red at Night		PGM	Precision-Guided Munitions
LGB	Laser-Guided Bomb		Phased-Array Radar	A warning radar system using many small aerials spread over a large flat area, rather than a rotating scanner. The advantage of this system is that it can track hundreds of targets simultaneously, electronically directing its beam from target to target in microseconds (millionths of a second).
LOAL	Lock On After Launch			
LOBL	Lock On Before Launch			
MAD	Magnetic Anomaly Detection. The passage of a large body of metal, such as a submarine, through the earth's magnetic field, causes disturbances that can be detected by special equipment, usually housed in an extended tail boom, in an anti-submarine warfare aircraft.		PLSS	Precision Location Strike System
			Pulse-Doppler Radar	A type of airborne interception radar that picks out fast-moving targets from background clutter by measuring the change in frequency of a series of pulses bounced off the targets. This is based on the well-known Doppler Effect, an apparent change in the frequency of waves when the source emitting them has a relative velocity towards or away from an observer.
MCAF	Marine Corps Air Facility			
MCAS	Marine Corps Air Station			
MCB	Marine Corps Base			
MFD	Multi-Function Display			
MICA	Missile d'Interception, de Combat et d'Autodéfense		RAM	Radar Absorbent Material
MMW	Millimetre-Wave		RAS	Regimental Aviation Squadron
MOAB	Massive Ordnance Air Blast		RHAWS	Radar Homing And Warning System
MOP	Massive Ordnance Penetrator		RSAF	Royal Saudi Air Force
MT	Megaton		RWR	Radar Warning Receiver. A device mounted on an aircraft that warns the pilot if he is being tracked by an enemy missile guidance or intercept radar.
MUPSOW	Multi-Purpose Standoff Weapon			
NAF	Naval Air Facility			
NAS	Naval Air Station		SAC	Strategic Air Command
NATO	North Atlantic Treaty Organization		SACLOS	Semi-Automatic Command Line-Of-Sight
NBC	Nuclear, Chemical and Biological (warfare)		SAM	Surface-to-Air Missile

SAR	Search And Rescue		TRIGAT	Third-Generation Anti-Tank
SARH	Semi-Active Radar Homing			
SATCOM	Satellite Communications		UARAF	United Arab Republic Air Force
SCALP EG	Système de Croisière conventionnel Autonome à Longue		UAV	Unmanned Aerial Vehicle
			UCAV	Unmanned Combat Aerial Vehicle
SDB	Small Diameter Bomb		USAF	United States Air Force
SEAD	Suppression of Enemy Air Defenses		USAFE	United States Air Force in Europe
SFW	Sensor Fused Munition		USARC	United States Army Reserve Command
SHAPE	Supreme Headquarters Allied Powers Europe		USMC	United States Marine Corps
SIGINT	Signals Intelligence. Information on enemy intentions gathered by monitoring electronic transmissions from his command, control communications network.		USN	United States Navy
			USNR	United States Naval Reserve
SLAM	Stand-off Land Attack Missile		VAQ	Electronic Attack Squadron
SLAM-ER	Stand-off Land Attack Missile-Extended Range		VAW	Carrier Airborne Early Warning Squadron
SLAR	Side-Looking Airborne Radar. A type of radar that provides a continuous radar map of the ground on either side of the aircraft carrying the equipment.		VFA	Strike Fighter Squadron
			VFC	Fighter Composite Squadron
			VHF	Very High Frequency
			VLF	Very Low Frequency
SOM	Stand-Off Munitions		VP	Patrol Squadron
SRAM	Short-Range Attack Missile		VQ	Fleet Air Reconnaissance Squadron
SSB	Security and Support Battalion		VR	Fleet Logistic Support Squadron
Stealth Technology	technology applied to aircraft to reduce their radar signatures		VRC	Fleet Logistic Support Squadron (Composite)
STOVL	Short Take-off, Vertical Landing		WAFAR	Wrap-Around Fin Aerial Rocket
SUU	Suspended Underwing Unit		WCMD	Wind-Corrected Munitions Dispenser
SyAAF	Syrian Arab Air Force			
TAB	Theater Aviation Battalion			
TAC	Tactical Air Command			
TALD	Tactical Air Launched Decoy			
TERCOM	Terrain Contour Matching			
TFR	Terrain-Following Radar			
TFW	Tactical Fighter Wing			
TIALD	Thermal Imaging Airborne Laser Designator			
TMD	Tactical Munitions Dispenser			
TOW	Tube-launched, Optically-tracked, Wire-guided			

Index